Lecture Notes in Computer Science 3024

Commenced Publication in 1973
Founding and Former Series Editors:
Gerhard Goos, Juris Hartmanis, and Jan van Leeuwen

T0189076

Springer
Berlin
Heidelberg
New York
Hong Kong
London
Milan
Paris
Tokyo

Tomáš Pajdla   Jiří Matas (Eds.)

Computer Vision – ECCV 2004

8th European Conference on Computer Vision
Prague, Czech Republic, May 11-14, 2004
Proceedings, Part IV

Springer

Volume Editors

Tomáš Pajdla
Jiří Matas
Czech Technical University in Prague, Department of Cybernetics
Center for Machine Perception
121-35 Prague 2, Czech Republic
E-mail: {pajdla,matas}@cmp.felk.cvut.cz

Library of Congress Control Number: 2004104846

CR Subject Classification (1998): I.4, I.3.5, I.5, I.2.9-10

ISSN 0302-9743
ISBN 3-540-21981-1 Springer-Verlag Berlin Heidelberg New York

Springer-Verlag is a part of Springer Science+Business Media

springeronline.com

© Springer-Verlag Berlin Heidelberg 2004
Printed in Germany

Typesetting: Camera-ready by author, data conversion by PTP-Berlin, Protago-TeX-Production GmbH
Printed on acid-free paper   SPIN: 11007777   06/3142   5 4 3 2 1 0

Preface

Welcome to the proceedings of the 8th European Conference on Computer Vision!

Following a very successful ECCV 2002, the response to our call for papers was almost equally strong – 555 papers were submitted. We accepted 41 papers for oral and 149 papers for poster presentation.

Several innovations were introduced into the review process. First, the number of program committee members was increased to reduce their review load. We managed to assign to program committee members no more than 12 papers. Second, we adopted a paper ranking system. Program committee members were asked to rank all the papers assigned to them, even those that were reviewed by additional reviewers. Third, we allowed authors to respond to the reviews consolidated in a discussion involving the area chair and the reviewers. Fourth, the reports, the reviews, and the responses were made available to the authors as well as to the program committee members. Our aim was to provide the authors with maximal feedback and to let the program committee members know how authors reacted to their reviews and how their reviews were or were not reflected in the final decision. Finally, we reduced the length of reviewed papers from 15 to 12 pages.

The preparation of ECCV 2004 went smoothly thanks to the efforts of the organizing committee, the area chairs, the program committee, and the reviewers. We are indebted to Anders Heyden, Mads Nielsen, and Henrik J. Nielsen for passing on ECCV traditions and to Dominique Asselineau from ENST/TSI who kindly provided his GestRFIA conference software. We thank Jan-Olof Eklundh and Andrew Zisserman for encouraging us to organize ECCV 2004 in Prague. Andrew Zisserman also contributed many useful ideas concerning the organization of the review process. Olivier Faugeras represented the ECCV Board and helped us with the selection of conference topics. Kyros Kutulakos provided helpful information about the CVPR 2003 organization. David Vernon helped to secure ECVision support.

This conference would never have happened without the support of the Centre for Machine Perception of the Czech Technical University in Prague. We would like to thank Radim Šára for his help with the review process and the proceedings organization. We thank Daniel Večerka and Martin Matoušek who made numerous improvements to the conference software. Petr Pohl helped to put the proceedings together. Martina Budošová helped with administrative tasks. Hynek Bakstein, Ondřej Chum, Jana Kostková, Branislav Mičušík, Štěpán Obdržálek, Jan Šochman, and Vít Zýka helped with the organization.

March 2004   Tomáš Pajdla and Jiří Matas

Organization

Conference Chair

Václav Hlaváč   CTU Prague, Czech Republic

Program Chairs

Tomáš Pajdla   CTU Prague, Czech Republic
Jiří Matas   CTU Prague, Czech Republic

Organization Committee

Tomáš Pajdla   CTU Prague, Czech Republic
Radim Šára   Workshops, Tutorials   CTU Prague, Czech Republic
Vladimír Smutný   Budget, Exhibition   CTU Prague, Czech Republic
Eva Matysková   Local Arrangements   CTU Prague, Czech Republic
Jiří Matas   CTU Prague, Czech Republic
Václav Hlaváč   CTU Prague, Czech Republic

Conference Board

Hans Burkhardt   University of Freiburg, Germany
Bernard Buxton   University College London, UK
Roberto Cipolla   University of Cambridge, UK
Jan-Olof Eklundh   Royal Institute of Technology, Sweden
Olivier Faugeras   INRIA, Sophia Antipolis, France
Anders Heyden   Lund University, Sweden
Bernd Neumann   University of Hamburg, Germany
Mads Nielsen   IT University of Copenhagen, Denmark
Giulio Sandini   University of Genoa, Italy
David Vernon   Trinity College, Ireland

Area Chairs

Dmitry Chetverikov   MTA SZTAKI, Hungary
Kostas Daniilidis   University of Pennsylvania, USA
Rachid Deriche   INRIA Sophia Antipolis, France
Jan-Olof Eklundh   KTH Stockholm, Sweden
Luc Van Gool   KU Leuven, Belgium & ETH Zürich, Switzerland
Richard Hartley   Australian National University, Australia

Michal Irani	Weizmann Institute of Science, Israel
Sing Bing Kang	Microsoft Research, USA
Aleš Leonardis	University of Ljubljana, Slovenia
Stan Li	Microsoft Research China, Beijing, China
David Lowe	University of British Columbia, Canada
Mads Nielsen	IT University of Copenhagen, Denmark
Long Quan	HKUST, Hong Kong, China
Jose Santos-Victor	Instituto Superior Tecnico, Portugal
Cordelia Schmid	INRIA Rhône-Alpes, France
Steven Seitz	University of Washington, USA
Amnon Shashua	Hebrew University of Jerusalem, Israel
Stefano Soatto	UCLA, Los Angeles, USA
Joachim Weickert	Saarland University, Germany
Andrew Zisserman	University of Oxford, UK

Program Committee

Jorgen Ahlberg	Joachim Buhmann	Alexei Efros
Narendra Ahuja	Hans Burkhardt	Irfan Essa
Yiannis Aloimonos	Aurelio Campilho	Michael Felsberg
Arnon Amir	Octavia Camps	Cornelia Fermueller
Elli Angelopoulou	Stefan Carlsson	Mario Figueiredo
Helder Araujo	Yaron Caspi	Bob Fisher
Tal Arbel	Tat-Jen Cham	Andrew Fitzgibbon
Karl Astrom	Mike Chantler	David Fleet
Shai Avidan	Francois Chaumette	Wolfgang Foerstner
Simon Baker	Santanu Choudhury	David Forsyth
Subhashis Banerjee	Laurent Cohen	Pascal Fua
Kobus Barnard	Michael Cohen	Dariu Gavrila
Ronen Basri	Bob Collins	Jan-Mark Geusebroek
Serge Belongie	Dorin Comaniciu	Christopher Geyer
Marie-Odile Berger	Tim Cootes	Georgy Gimelfarb
Horst Bischof	Joao Costeira	Frederic Guichard
Michael J. Black	Daniel Cremers	Gregory Hager
Andrew Blake	Antonio Criminisi	Allan Hanbury
Laure Blanc-Feraud	James Crowley	Edwin Hancock
Aaron Bobick	Kristin Dana	Horst Haussecker
Rein van den Boomgaard	Trevor Darrell	Eric Hayman
Terrance Boult	Larry Davis	Martial Hebert
Richard Bowden	Fernando De la Torre	Bernd Heisele
Edmond Boyer	Frank Dellaert	Anders Heyden
Mike Brooks	Joachim Denzler	Adrian Hilton
Michael Brown	Greg Dudek	David Hogg
Alfred Bruckstein	Chuck Dyer	Atsushi Imiya

Michael Isard
Yuri Ivanov
David Jacobs
Allan D. Jepson
Peter Johansen
Nebojsa Jojic
Frederic Jurie
Fredrik Kahl
Daniel Keren
Benjamin Kimia
Ron Kimmel
Nahum Kiryati
Georges Koepfler
Pierre Kornprobst
David Kriegman
Walter Kropatsch
Rakesh Kumar
David Liebowitz
Tony Lindeberg
Jim Little
Yanxi Liu
Yi Ma
Claus Madsen
Tom Malzbender
Jorge Marques
David Marshall
Bogdan Matei
Steve Maybank
Gerard Medioni
Etienne Memin
Rudolf Mester
Krystian Mikolajczyk
J.M.M. Montiel
Theo Moons
Pavel Mrazek
Joe Mundy
Vittorio Murino
David Murray
Hans-Hellmut Nagel
Vic Nalwa
P.J. Narayanan

Nassir Navab
Shree Nayar
Ko Nishino
David Nister
Ole Fogh Olsen
Theodore Papadopoulo
Nikos Paragios
Shmuel Peleg
Francisco Perales
Nicolas Perez
   de la Blanca
Pietro Perona
Matti Pietikainen
Filiberto Pla
Robert Pless
Marc Pollefeys
Jean Ponce
Ravi Ramamoorthi
James Rehg
Ian Reid
Tammy Riklin-Raviv
Ehud Rivlin
Nicolas Rougon
Yong Rui
Javier Sanchez
Guillermo Sapiro
Yoichi Sato
Eric Saund
Otmar Scherzer
Bernt Schiele
Mikhail Schlesinger
Christoph Schnoerr
Stan Sclaroff
Mubarak Shah
Eitan Sharon
Jianbo Shi
Kaleem Siddiqi
Cristian Sminchisescu
Nir Sochen
Gerald Sommer
Gunnar Sparr

Jon Sporring
Charles Stewart
Peter Sturm
Changming Sun
Tomas Svoboda
Rahul Swaminathan
Richard Szeliski
Tamas Sziranyi
Chi-keung Tang
Hai Tao
Sibel Tari
Chris Taylor
C.J. Taylor
Bart ter Haar Romeny
Phil Torr
Antonio Torralba
Panos Trahanias
Bill Triggs
Emanuele Trucco
Dimitris Tsakiris
Yanghai Tsin
Matthew Turk
Tinne Tuytelaars
Nuno Vasconcelos
Baba C. Vemuri
David Vernon
Alessandro Verri
Rene Vidal
Jordi Vitria
Yair Weiss
Tomas Werner
Carl-Fredrik Westin
Ross Whitaker
Lior Wolf
Ying Wu
Ming Xie
Ramin Zabih
Assaf Zomet
Steven Zucker

Additional Reviewers

Lourdes Agapito
Manoj Aggarwal
Parvez Ahammad
Fernando Alegre
Jonathan Alon
Hans Jorgen Andersen
Marco Andreetto
Anelia Angelova
Himanshu Arora
Thangali Ashwin
Vassilis Athitsos
Henry Baird
Harlyn Baker
Evgeniy Bart
Moshe Ben-Ezra
Manuele Bicego
Marten Björkman
Paul Blaer
Ilya Blayvas
Eran Borenstein
Lars Bretzner
Alexia Briassouli
Michael Bronstein
Rupert Brooks
Gabriel Brostow
Thomas Brox
Stephanie Brubaker
Andres Bruhn
Darius Burschka
Umberto Castellani
J.A. Castellanos
James Clark
Andrea Colombari
Marco Cristani
Xiangtian Dai
David Demirdjian
Maxime Descoteaux
Nick Diakopulous
Anthony Dicks
Carlotta Domeniconi
Roman Dovgard
R. Dugad
Ramani Duraiswami
Kerrien Erwan

Claudio Fanti
Michela Farenzena
Doron Feldman
Darya Frolova
Andrea Fusiello
Chunyu Gao
Kshitiz Garg
Yoram Gat
Dan Gelb
Ya'ara Goldschmidt
Michael E. Goss
Leo Grady
Sertan Grigin
Michael Grossberg
J.J. Guerrero
Guodong Guo
Yanlin Guo
Robert Hanek
Matthew Harrison
Tal Hassner
Horst Haussecker
Yakov Hel-Or
Anton van den Hengel
Tat Jen Cham
Peng Chang
John Isidoro
Vishal Jain
Marie-Pierre Jolly
Michael Kaess
Zia Khan
Kristian Kirk
Dan Kong
B. Kröse
Vivek Kwatra
Michael Langer
Catherine Laporte
Scott Larsen
Barbara Levienaise-
   Obadia
Frederic Leymarie
Fei-Fei Li
Rui Li
Kok-Lim Low
Le Lu

Jocelyn Marchadier
Scott McCloskey
Leonard McMillan
Marci Meingast
Anurag Mittal
Thomas B. Moeslund
Jose Montiel
Philippos Mordohai
Pierre Moreels
Hesam Najafi
P.J. Narayanan
Ara Nefian
Oscar Nestares
Michael Nielsen
Peter Nillius
Fredrik Nyberg
Tom O'Donnell
Eyal Ofek
Takahiro Okabe
Kazunori Okada
D. Ortin
Patrick Perez
Christian Perwass
Carlos Phillips
Srikumar Ramalingam
Alex Rav-Acha
Stefan Roth
Ueli Rutishauser
C. Sagues
Garbis Salgian
Ramin Samadani
Bernard Sarel
Frederik Schaffalitzky
Adam Seeger
Cheng Dong Seon
Ying Shan
Eli Shechtman
Grant Schindler
Nils T. Siebel
Leonid Sigal
Greg Slabaugh
Ben Southall
Eric Spellman
Narasimhan Srinivasa

Drew Steedly
Moritz Stoerring
David Suter
Yi Tan
Donald Tanguay
Matthew Toews
V. Javier Traver
Yaron Ukrainitz
F.E. Wang
Hongcheng Wang

Zhizhou Wang
Joost van de Weijer
Wolfgang Wein
Martin Welk
Michael Werman
Horst Wildenauer
Christopher R. Wren
Ning Xu
Hulya Yalcin
Jingyu Yan

Ruigang Yang
Yll Haxhimusa
Tianli Yu
Lihi Zelnik-Manor
Tao Zhao
Wenyi Zhao
Sean Zhou
Yue Zhou
Ying Zhu

Sponsors

BIG - Business Information Group a.s.
Camea spol. s r.o.
Casablanca INT s.r.o.
ECVision – European Research Network for Cognitive Computer Vision Systems
Microsoft Research
Miracle Network s.r.o.
Neovision s.r.o.
Toyota

Table of Contents – Part IV

Scale Space, Flow, Restoration

2D Shape Detection and Recognition

Posters IV

3D Shape Representation and Reconstruction

Table of Contents – Part I

Illumination, Reflectance, and Reflection

Table of Contents – Part II

Texture

Table of Contents – Part III

Learning and Recognition

Tracking II

Posters III

Information-Based Image Processing

A l^1-Unified Variational Framework for Image Restoration

Julien Bect[1], Laure Blanc-Féraud[1], Gilles Aubert[2], and Antonin Chambolle[3]

[1] Projet Ariana, I3S/INRIA 2004 route des Lucioles, BP93
06902 Sophia Antipolis Cedex, France
blancf@sophia.inria.fr
http://www-sop.inria.fr/ariana/

[2] Laboratoire J-A. Dieudonné, Parc Valrose Univertsité de Nice-Sophia Antipolis
06108 Nice Cedex 2, France
gaubert@math.unice.fr
http://math.unice.fr/~gaubert/

[3] Ceremade, Univertsité Paris-Dauphine 75775 Paris Cedex 16, France
antonin@ceremade.dauphine.fr

Abstract. Among image restoration literature, there are mainly two kinds of approach. One is based on a process over image wavelet coefficients, as wavelet shrinkage for denoising. The other one is based on a process over image gradient. In order to get an edge-preserving regularization, one usually assume that the image belongs to the space of functions of Bounded Variation (BV). An energy is minimized, composed of an observation term and the Total Variation (TV) of the image.

Recent contributions try to mix both types of method. In this spirit, the goal of this paper is to define a unified-framework including together wavelet methods and energy minimization as TV. In fact, for denoising purpose, it is already shown that wavelet soft-thresholding is equivalent to choose the regularization term as the norm of the Besov space $B_1^{1,1}$. In the present work, this equivalence result is extended to the case of deconvolution problem. We propose a general functional to minimize, which includes the TV minimization, wavelet coefficients regularization, mixed (TV+wavelet) regularization or more general terms. Moreover we give a projection-based algorithm to compute the solution. The convergence of the algorithm is also stated. We show that the decomposition of an image over a dictionary of elementary shapes (atoms) is also included in the proposed framework. So we give a new algorithm to solve this difficult problem, known as Basis Pursuit. We also show numerical results of image deconvolution using TV, wavelets, or TV+wavelets regularization terms.

1 Introduction

1.1 Image Restoration

Restoring images from blurred or/and noisy data is an important task of image processing. In the important literature developed since twenty years, most

T. Pajdla and J. Matas (Eds.): ECCV 2004, LNCS 3024, pp. 1–13, 2004.

approaches are based on an energy minimization. Such energy contains mainly two terms: the first term models how the observed data is derived from the original data one would like to reconstruct; the second term contains a priori information on the regularity of this original data. At this point, two important families of criteria emerge. In the first family the regularity criterion is a semi-norm that is expressed in a "simple" way in terms of the wavelet coefficients of the image (usually a Besov norm). This leads to a restoration process that is performed through some processing of the wavelet coefficients, such as a wavelet shrinkage (for example see [5] in denoising, [10] in deconvolution, [8] in Radon transform inversion).

In the second family, the regularity criterion is a functional of the gradient of the image, so that the resolution of the problem amounts to solving some more or less complex PDE. In order to get an edge-preserving regularization, one usually assumes that the image belongs to the space of functions of Bounded Variation (BV) and the criterion which is minimized is the Total Variation (TV) of the image (see [12] for example).

Recent contributions try to mix both types of method [9,14,6]. In this spirit, the goal of this paper is to define a unified-framework including together wavelet, TV, or a more general semi-norm. In fact, as it is shown in [2] for denoising and compression purposes, wavelet soft-thresholding is equivalent to choose the regularization term as the norm of the Besov space B_1^{11}. In the present work, this equivalence result is extended to the case of deconvolution problem. The proposed framework allows to include the TV minimization, mixed (TV+wavelet) regularization or more general terms. Moreover we give a projection-based algorithm to compute the solution in the more general case. The convergence of algorithm is also stated.

Image restoration can be considered as the minimization of a functional written as

$$\frac{1}{2\lambda} \|g - Au\|_{X_1}^2 + |u|_Y^s \tag{1}$$

A is a linear operator which can model the degradation during the observation of the object u:

$$\begin{aligned} X &\longrightarrow X_1 \\ u &\longmapsto g = Au + \eta \end{aligned} \tag{2}$$

X is the space describing the objects to be reconstructed and X_1 the space of observations. η is the acquisition noise. Typically $X = X_1 = L^2$ or $X = X_1$ a finite-dimensional space. As in [2], $|u|_Y$ is a norm or a semi-norm in a smoothness space Y. Standard example is $Y = L^2, s = 2$ defining quadratic regularization as proposed by Tikhonov [15]. Now, if Y is the BV space and $s = 1$, the solution is the one such that Au best approximates g (in the sense of the norm $\| \, \|_{X_1}$), with minimal Total Variation [12]. This general functional includes also wavelet shrinkage denoising/deconvolution methods by considering $A = I$ (where I is the identity operator) or A is the Point Spread Function of the transfert function of the optics and Y is the Besov space B_1^{11} and $s = 1$ [2]. Notice that if A defines a decomposition over a dictionary of possible atoms from which the signal u is built, (for example wavelet packets for textures, curvelets or bandlets for edges, and so on), then solving (1) corresponds exactly to the Basis Pursuit DeNoising algorithm (BPDN) by Chen, Donoho and Saunders [3].

1.2   Problem Statement

In this paper, we study the minimization of a functional of the form

$$\frac{1}{2\lambda} \|g - Au\|_{X_1}^2 + J(u) \tag{3}$$

where $J : X \to \mathbb{R}\cup\{\infty\}$ is a semi-norm on X. For sake of simplicity, we assume in the whole paper that u is a discrete image that is to say $X = X_1 = \mathbb{R}^{N \times N}$ and the symbol $\|.\|$ will denote any Hilbertian norm.

In order to minimize the functional (3), we describe a projection-based algorithm which extends the one proposed by Chambolle for the denoising case ($A = I$) with TV regularization [1].

The convergence of the algorithm is proved. This gives a new algorithm to solve several kinds of image processing: image deconvolution with TV regularization, with wavelet shrinkage, or with both kind of regularization; BPDN problem as decribed by Donoho in [3]. During the review process of the paper, our attention was drawn by S. Mallat to the independent works [7,4] which derive, by different approaches, essentially the same iterative algorithm as the one described in this paper. In [4], a strong convergence of the iterative algorithm is shown in infinite dimension. One difference is that our algorithm includes TV or mixed (TV+wavelet) regularization which seems not to be the case in [7,4].

In section 2, we recall some basic tools in convex analysis. The main contribution of this paper is detailed in section 3 where the minimization algorithm is given for the general functional (3). In section 4, we show that several standard methods in image restoration are special cases of the unified energy (3), and numerical results are given for deconvolution with TV plus wavelet regularization.

1.3   Notations

Let us fix some notations. A discrete image will be denoted by $u_{i,j}$, $i, j = 1 \dots N$. In order to define the TV of the discrete image u, we introduce the gradient $\nabla : X \to X \times X$ defined by:

$$(\nabla u)_{i,j}^1 = \begin{cases} u_{i+1,j} - u_{i,j} & \text{if } i < N \\ 0 & \text{if } i = N \end{cases} \quad \text{and} \quad (\nabla u)_{i,j}^2 = \begin{cases} u_{i,j+1} - u_{i,j} & \text{if } j < N \\ 0 & \text{if } j = N \end{cases}$$

We also introduce a discrete version of the divergence operator defined, by analogy with the continuous case, by $\text{div} = -\nabla^*$ where ∇^* is the adjoint of ∇.

We have

$$(\text{div}(p))_{i,j} = \begin{cases} p^1_{i,j} - p^1_{i-1,j} & \text{if } 1 < i < N \\ p^1_{i,j} & \text{if i=1} \\ -p^1_{i-1,j} & \text{if i=N} \end{cases} + \begin{cases} p^2_{i,j} - p^2_{i,j-1} & \text{if } 1 < j < N \\ p^2_{i,j} & \text{if j=1} \\ -p^2_{i,j-1} & \text{if j=N} \end{cases} \qquad (4)$$

The discrete TV denoted J_{TV} is defined as the l^1-norm of the vector ∇u by

$$J_{TV}(u) = \|\nabla u\|_1 = \sum_{i,j=1}^{N} \sqrt{\left\{(\nabla u)^1_{i,j}\right\}^2 + \left\{(\nabla u)^2_{i,j}\right\}^2}. \qquad (5)$$

2   Some Tools of Convex Analysis

We recall in this section some usual tools in convex analysis which are used to build our algorithm. We refer the reader to Rockafellar [11] for a more complete introduction of convex analysis.

Definition 1 (Legendre-Fenchel Conjugate). *Let ϕ be an application $X \to \mathbb{R} \cup \{+\infty\}$. We assume that $\phi \not\equiv +\infty$. The conjugate function of ϕ is defined as $\phi^* : X \to \mathbb{R} \cup \{+\infty\}$ by:*

$$\phi^*(s) = \sup_{x \in X} \left\{ \langle s, x \rangle - \phi(x) \right\} \qquad (6)$$

ϕ^* *is convex and lower semi-continuous (lsc).*

Definition 2 (Indicator function, support function).
Let $K \subset X$ be a non empty closed convex subset of X. The indicator function of K, called χ_K, is defined by:

$$\chi_K(x) = \begin{cases} 0 & \text{if } x \in K \\ +\infty & \text{otherwise} \end{cases} \qquad (7)$$

We call support function of K the function denoted δ_K, defined by:

$$\delta_K(s) = \sup_{x \in K} \langle s, x \rangle \qquad (8)$$

The link between χ_K and δ_K is given by the following results

Theorem 1. *Let $K \subset X$ a non empty convex closed subset of X. Then the functions χ_K and δ_K are convex, lsc and mutually conjugate.*

Theorem 2. *All support functions δ_K, associated to a non empty convex closed subset K, is convex and one-homogeneous (e.g. $\forall t > 0, \forall x \in X, \delta_K(tx) = t\delta_K(x)$) and lsc. Conversely, each function $\phi \not\equiv +\infty$ convex, one-homogeneous and lsc is the support function of a closed convex set K_ϕ defined by:*

$$K_\phi = \left\{ s \in X, \quad \forall x \in X, \langle s, x \rangle \leq \phi(x) \right\}. \qquad (9)$$

For example, in (3), we have supposed that $J(u)$ is a semi-norm. Therefore, it is a convex one-homogeneous and lsc function. So $J(u)$ is the support function of a closed convex set K_J defined by (9). If $J(u)$ is the discrete TV semi-norm given by (5), then

$$K_{TV} = \{ \operatorname{div}(p), \quad p \in X \times X, \ |p_{i,j}| \leq 1 \ \forall i,j \ \}. \tag{10}$$

We now introduce the notion of sub-differential of a function which generalizes the differential for convex functions.

Definition 3 (Sub-differential). *Let ϕ a convex function. We define the sub-differential $\partial\phi(x)$ of ϕ in $x \in X$ by:*

$$s \in \partial\phi(x) \qquad \Longleftrightarrow \qquad \forall x' \in X, \quad \phi(x') \geq \phi(x) + \langle s, x' - x \rangle \tag{11}$$

Note that if x is such that $\phi(x) < \infty$ and if ϕ is differentiable in x, then:

$$\partial\phi(x) = \{ \nabla\phi(x) \}. \tag{12}$$

3 Algorithm and Convergence Result

This section is devoted to the main contribution of this paper, namely the description and the convergence of our algorithm for numerically solving the minimization problem (3). Before doing that, in order to justify our algorithm, we need some preliminary results.

3.1 Preliminary Results

Theorem 3. *Let $B : X \to X$ be a linear self-adjoint and positive operator satisfying $\|B\| < 1$. Then*

$$\forall u \in X, \quad \langle Bu, u \rangle = \min_{w \in X} \left\{ \|u - w\|^2 + \langle Cw, w \rangle \right\} \tag{13}$$

where $C = B(I - B)^{-1}$. Moreover, the minimum is reached at a unique point w_u which verifies:

$$w_u = (I + C)^{-1}(u) = (I - B)(u). \tag{14}$$

Let us recall that the functional we want to minimize is given by

$$\frac{1}{2\lambda} \|g - Au\|^2 + J(u)$$

Let $\mu > 0$ be such that

$$\mu\|A^*A\| < 1 \tag{15}$$

and

$$B = \mu A^* A \tag{16}$$

B is a self-adjoint positive operator. From hypothesis(15), μ is such that $\|B\| <$ 1. Thanks to Theorem 3, we will be able to write the data term of (3), $(\frac{1}{2\lambda} \|g - Au\|^2)$, as the result of a new minimization problem, w.r.t an auxiliary variable w. We have

$$\|Au\|^2 = \langle A^* Au, u \rangle \tag{17}$$

$$= \frac{1}{\mu} \langle Bu, u \rangle \tag{18}$$

$$= \frac{1}{\mu} \min_{w \in X} \left\{ \|u - w\|^2 + \langle Cw, w \rangle \right\} \tag{19}$$

with $C = B(I - B)^{-1}$. Therefore

$$\frac{1}{2\lambda} \|g - Au\|^2 = \min_{w \in X} H(u, w) \tag{20}$$

where H is the convex differentiable function defined by:

$$H(u, w) = \frac{1}{2\lambda\mu} \left(\|u - w\|^2 + \langle Cw, w \rangle \right) + \frac{1}{2\lambda} \left(\|g\|^2 - 2 \langle Au, g \rangle \right). \tag{21}$$

Let us denote

$$\Psi_1 = I - B = I - \mu A^* A \tag{22}$$

From relation (14), w minimizes $H(u, .)$ if and only if $w = \Psi_1 u$. Let us now consider the function F defined by:

$$F(u, w) = H(u, w) + J(u) \tag{23}$$

F is a convex continuous function, and we deduce from the previous preliminary results, the following proposition:

Proposition 1. w *minimizes* $F(u, .)$ *defined in (21) and (23) if and only if* $w = \Psi_1 u$ *where* $\Psi_1 = I - \mu A^* A$ *and we have:*

$$\forall w \neq \Psi_1 u, \quad F(u, \Psi_1 u) < F(u, w) \tag{24}$$

Let us now show that computing the global minimizer of F reduces to minimize each of its partial functions $F(., w)$ and $F(u, .)$. This is a non trivial result even in the case of a strictly convex function (consider for instance $f(x, y) = (x^2 + y^2)/2 + |x - y|$ at $x = y = 1/2$).

Proposition 2. (u, w) *minimizes* F *if and only if:*

$$\begin{cases} u \text{ minimizes } F(., w) \\ w \text{ minimizes } F(u, .) \end{cases} \tag{25}$$

Proof. Since F is the sum of two convex continuous functions,

$$\partial F(u,w) \;=\; \partial H(u,w) \;+\; \partial J(u,w). \tag{26}$$

As H is differentiable and J does not depend on w, we deduce:

$$\partial F(u,w) \;=\; (\,\nabla_u H(u,w)\,,\, \nabla_w H(u,w)\,) \;+\; \partial J(u) \times \{0\} \tag{27}$$

So

$$0 \in \partial F(u,w) \quad \Leftrightarrow \quad \begin{cases} 0 \in \nabla_u H(u,w) + \partial J(u) \\ 0 = \nabla_w H(u,w) \end{cases} \tag{28}$$

which is exactly what we want to show.

The last result we need in order to derive our algorithm is the following:

Proposition 3. *Let us denote by $\Psi_2 : X \to X$ the application defined by:*

$$\Psi_2(w) \;=\; (I - \Pi_{\lambda\mu K_J})\,(w + \mu A^* g)\,. \tag{29}$$

Here $\Pi_{\lambda\mu K_J}(w)$ stands for the orthogonal projection of w on the convex set $\lambda\mu K_J$, where K_J is the convex set associated to $J(u)$ (see (9)). Then u minimizes $F(\,.\,,w)$ if and only if $u = \Psi_2(w)$.

The expression (29) is found by computing the dual problem of $\min_u F(u,w)$, for fixed w (see [1]).

3.2   The Algorithm for the Minimization of the Unified Functional

We are now able to describe the algorithm we propose to minimize the unified functional (3). Based on results given in Propositions 1, 2 and 3, we propose the following iterative algorithm to minimize (3)

$$w_n \;=\; (I - \mu A^* A)\,(u_n) \tag{30}$$
$$u_{n+1} \;=\; (I - \Pi_{\lambda\mu K_J})\,(w_n + \mu A^* g) \tag{31}$$

By a change of notation, using $v_n = w_n + \mu A^* g$, it results:

$$v_n \;=\; u_n + \mu\, A^* \,(g - A u_n) \tag{32}$$
$$u_{n+1} \;=\; (I - \Pi_{\lambda\mu K_J})\,(v_n) \tag{33}$$

In practice, we will use the algorithm (32)–(33) rather than the writting (30)–(31) and we use the numerical algorithm (35)–(36) described in section 3.3 to compute $\Pi_{\lambda\mu K_J}$.

The first equation of this algorithm is a fixed-step descent algorithm, considering only the minimization of the data term $\|g - Au\|^2$. The step is fixed by the parameter μ. The second equation corresponds to a denoising step over the current estimates v_n. Remark that the parameter considered in the denoising step is $\lambda\mu$ rather than λ as it should be suggested looking at the functional (3). We can also observe that in the case where A^*A is invertible then (32)–(33) correspond to a contraction with a ratio $1 - \mu\lambda_0$, where λ_0 is the smallest eigenvalue of A^*A. In the case where A^*A is not invertible, then the transformation (32)–(33) is 1–Lipschitz. In either situations the following theorem holds.

Theorem 4 (Convergence of the algorithm). *Let $\mu > 0$ and assume*

$$\mu \, \|A^*A\| \, < 1 \tag{34}$$

Then the algorithm (32)–(33) converges to a global minimizer of (3).

Before ending this section, let us remark that we always have the existence of a minimizer of the functional (3) in the discrete setting. However the difficult point for the convergence proof comes from the fact that the minimum is non necessarily unique.

3.3   Projection Algorithm of Chambolle

We give in this section the numerical algorithm to compute a projection $\Pi_{\lambda K_J}$, in the case of a regularizing term expressed as $J(u) = \|Qu\|_1 = \sum_\theta |(Qu)_\theta|$, where Q is a linear operator $Q : X \to \Theta$ and Θ is a product space (see section 4.3 for more details on the notations). The projection onto the convex closed set λK_J, where K_J is associated to $\|Qu\|_1$ can be numerically computed by a fixed point method, based on results in [1]. We build recursively a sequence in Θ of vectors $p_n = (p_{n,\theta})_\theta$ in the following way: we choose $p_0 \in B_\Theta = \{p \in \Theta : |p_\theta| \le 1 \; \forall\theta\}$ and for each $n \ge 0$ we let

$$q_n = Q(Q^*p_n - \frac{g}{\lambda}) \tag{35}$$

and for each θ

$$p_{n+1,\theta} = \frac{p_{n,\theta} - \tau(q_{n,\theta})}{1 + \tau|q_{n,\theta}|} \tag{36}$$

We have a sufficient condition ensuring the convergence of the algorithm:

Theorem 5. *Assume that the parameter τ in (36) verifies $\tau \le \frac{1}{\kappa^2}$ where $\kappa = \|Q^*\|$. Then for all initial condition $p_0 \in B_\Theta$, the algorithm (35)–(36) is such as:*

$$\lambda Q^*p_n \longrightarrow \lambda Q^*\hat{p} = \Pi_{\lambda K_J}(g) \tag{37}$$

4   Applications

For TV regularization, one just needs to apply the algorithm (32)–(33) with $K = K_{TV}$, so that the projection algorithm is given by (35)–(36) with $\Theta = X \times X$, $Q = \nabla$, $Q^* = -\text{div}$ (as described in [1]). Let us now look at regularization in the wavelet domain.

4.1   Wavelet Shrinkage

Let us consider the case where $J(u)$ is the norm in the Besov space B_1^{11}. In [2], it is shown that this norm is equivalent to the norm of the sequence of wavelet coefficients $c_{j,k,\psi}^u$:

$$\|u\|_{B_1^{11}} = \sum_{j,k,\psi} |c_{j,k,\psi}^u| \tag{38}$$

$\psi \in \{\psi^{(1)}, \psi^{(2)}\psi^{(3)}\} = \Psi$ defines bi-dimensional wavelets from a one-dimensional wavelet and a one-dimensional scaling function as usual. The set of functions $\{\psi_{j,k}(x) = 2^k\psi(2^kx - j)\}_{\psi \in \Psi, k \in Z, j \in Z^2}$ forms an orthogonal bases for $L^2(\mathbb{R}^2)$. Then, for $f \in L^2(\mathbb{R}^2)$, we have

$$f = \sum_{j,k,\psi} c_{j,k,\psi}^f \psi_{j,k} \tag{39}$$

For sake of simplicity, the range of the indexes is omitted: we work with discrete functions with bounded definition domain. Assume that our purpose is image deconvolution that is to say A is a convolution operator representing the transfert function of the optics. Then if we want to deconvolve the observed image g with a wavelet regularization term, we have to minimize an energy of the form

$$\frac{1}{2\lambda}\|g - Au\|^2 + \|u\|_{B_1^{11}}. \tag{40}$$

We know (see for example [2]), that if $A = I$, minimizing (40) is equivalent to a soft-thresholding algorithm. Let us now see what happens with algorithm (32)–(33) and a general operator A. The convex set K_1 associated to the norm in B_1^{11} is defined by (see (9))

$$K_1 = \left\{ s \in X \,/\, \forall x \in X, < s, x > \leq \|x\|_{B_1^{11}} \right\}. \tag{41}$$

We easily deduce that

$$K_1 = \left\{ s \in X \,/\, \forall j, k, \psi, |c_{j,k,\psi}^s| \leq 1 \right\}. \tag{42}$$

where c^s are the wavelet coefficients of s

Therefore equation (33) is a denoising step by soft-thresholding with threshold $\lambda\mu$. Then the algorithm iteratively computes a step of steepest gradient descent only for the deconvolution and then a denoising step by soft-thresholding. This algorithm is very easy to implement.

4.2   Basis Pursuit DeNoising (BPDN)

Representing a signal in terms of few high coefficients of a dictionary and a lot of vanishing coefficients allows representation of an image ensuring better performances of shrinkage methods or other restoration methods. The problem is to decompose a signal over a possibly large dictionary rather than one orthogonal basis. The dictionary should contain all possible atoms which can be used to represent any images. For example we can use in the dictionary DCT, DST, biorthogonal wavelets, wavelet packets, curvelets, and so on. Searching this representation is an ill-posed problem, since such a decomposition is non unique. In the Basis Pursuit DeNoising algorithm (BPDN) [3] the authors propose the following regularizing functional

$$\inf_{\alpha} \frac{1}{2\lambda} \|g - \Phi\alpha\|^2 + \|\alpha\|_1 \tag{43}$$

The function g is the signal to be decomposed, α the unknown coefficients and Φ the operator $\Phi : \alpha \longmapsto y = \sum_i \alpha_i \phi_i$ where ϕ_i are the elements of the dictionary.

The minimization (43) can be performed by using algorithm (32)–(33). Since the regularization is a l^1-norm, the step (33) is simply a soft-thresholding.

In [3], is proposed the algorithm IP (Interior Point) to solve (43). This algorithm is slow. A faster algorithm called BCR (Block Coordinate Relaxation) has been proposed in [13]. As algorithm (32)–(33), BCR is based on a soft-thresholding of the coefficients. In BCR, it is assumed that the dictionary is composed of a union of orthogonal bases. Our algorithm is more general since it can be applied by using any dictionary.

We have compared these three algorithms on some 1D-signals. The IP algorithm is available on the web (*http://www-stat.stanford.edu/atomizer*). We have chosen the same bases (wavelet transform, DCT and DST) for the three algorithms. On a 1D signal of 4096 samples, it appears that the convergence is much faster for algorithm (32)–(33) than the IP algorithm, and a little bit smaller than the BCR one. We may loose in time what we gain in generality. Of course these are very few results and much more experiments must be conducted for the comparison.

4.3 l^1-Regularization

In this section, we show that our algorithm can be applied to a general class of semi-norm $J(u)$ which is relevant in real problems. We will consider what we call l^1-regularization, which consists in the minimization of the following functional

$$\frac{1}{2\lambda} \|g - Au\|^2 + \|Qu\|_1. \tag{44}$$

Q is a linear application $Q : X \to \Theta$, where Θ is the product space defined as:

$$\Theta = \prod_{1 \leq \theta \leq r} \mathbb{R}^{n_\theta} \tag{45}$$

endowed with the norm

$$p \in \Theta \longmapsto \|p\|_1 = \sum_{1 \leq \theta \leq r} |p|_\theta \tag{46}$$

where $|\cdot|$ is the Euclidean norm on $\mathbb{R}^{n_\theta}$ and $p = (p_\theta)_{1 \leq \theta \leq r}$, $p_\theta \in \mathbb{R}^{n_\theta}$.

$\|Qu\|_1$ is a semi-norm over X and is a norm when Q is injective.
For example, if Q is a wavelet transform, $(Qu)_\theta$ are scalar coefficients and then

$$\|Qu\|_1 = \sum_\theta |(Qu)_\theta| \tag{47}$$

is a norm if the sum runs over all coefficients of the wavelet transform or a semi-norm otherwise.
In the TV case we have

$$\|Qu\|_1 = \|\nabla u\|_1 \tag{48}$$

This general framework also includes a regularization composed of a sum of a TV term and a wavelet term. For such a regularization, we will set $\Theta = X^2 \times X$, and $Q : X \to \Theta$ is defined as:

$$Q : \quad X \longrightarrow X^2 \times X \tag{49}$$

$$u \longmapsto \begin{pmatrix} \gamma \nabla u \\ (1-\gamma)\, Wu \end{pmatrix} \tag{50}$$

where W stands for an orthonormal wavelet transform. We use the norm $\|\cdot\|_1$ such that: $\forall\, (p^1, p^2) \in X^2$, $\forall\, w \in X$,

$$\|(p, w)\|_1 = \|p\|_1 + \|w\|_1 \tag{51}$$

$$= \sum_{1 \leq i,j \leq N} \sqrt{\left(p_{i,j}^1\right)^2 + \left(p_{i,j}^2\right)^2} + \sum_{1 \leq i,j \leq N} |w_{i,j}| \tag{52}$$

and the global regularization functional is

$$J_\gamma(u) = \gamma \|\nabla u\|_1 + (1-\gamma)\|Wu\|_1 = \|Qu\|_1 \tag{53}$$

Note that (53) defines a family of functional J_γ, which goes continuously from l^1-norm on the wavelet coefficient to the Total Varation as γ goes from 0 to 1. We show restoration results for deconvolution by using this functional for three values of γ. The Lena image has been blurred by a PSF (Point Spread Function) corresponding to a synthetic aperture optical system, with vanishing coefficients in the medium frequencies as well as in the high frequencies. A Gaussian white noise has been added with standard deviation $\sigma = 0.05$ (for u values in $[0, 1]$). This deconvolution problem is very difficult because of vanishing medium frequencies of the degradation, and a large amount of noise. We retrieve for $\gamma = 0$ and $\gamma = 1$ the specific drawbacks of wavelets and TV restoration respectively: blur and bad edges for the wavelets, loose of textures for TV. The value $\gamma = 0.2$ has been chosen by hand and gives a good compromise. The choice of this parameter is an open problem. The regularizing parameter λ is estimated following the ideas of [1].

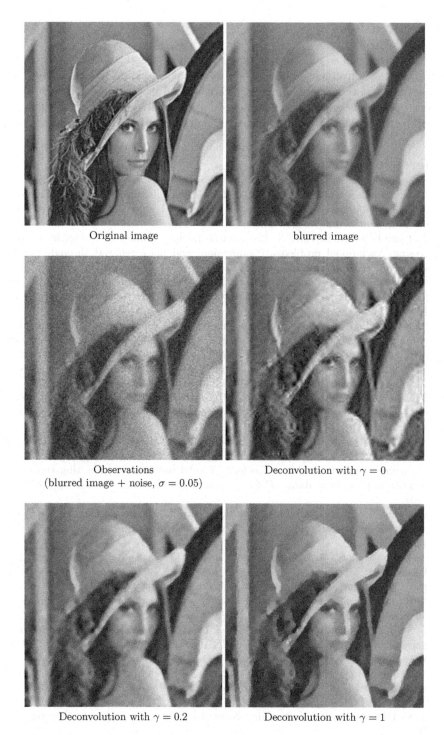

Original image

blurred image

Observations
(blurred image + noise, $\sigma = 0.05$)

Deconvolution with $\gamma = 0$

Deconvolution with $\gamma = 0.2$

Deconvolution with $\gamma = 1$

Fig. 1. Results of the algorithm on a deconvolution problem

5   Conclusion

We have presented a general functional unifying several approaches of image restoration. A convergent and easy to implement algorithm has been proposed for the minimization of this functional. For a good evaluation of our algorithm in terms of quality and rapidity for several applications, much more results will be conducted in each specific application as deconvolution or BPDN.

References

1. A. Chambolle. An algorithm for total variation minimization and applications. *Journal of Mathematical Imaging and Vision*, 20(1-2):89–97, 2004. Special Issue on Mathematics and Image Analysis.
2. A. Chambolle, R. DeVore, N. Lee, and B. Lucier. Nonlinear wavelet image processing: Variational problems, compression, and noise removal through wavelet shrinkage. *IEEE Trans. Image Proc.*, 7(3):319–333, 1998.
3. Scott Shaobing Chen, David L. Donoho, and Michael A. Saunders. Atomic decomposition by basis pursuit. *SIAM Journal on Scientific Computing*, 20(1):33–61, 1999.
4. Ingrid Daubechies, Michel Defrise, and Christine De Mol. An iterative algorithm for linear inverse problems with a sparsity constraint. Technical report, http://arxiv.org/abs/math.FA/0307152, 2003.
5. David L. Donoho and Iain M. Johnstone. Ideal spatial adaptation by wavelet shrinkage. *Biometrika*, 81(3):425–455, 1994.
6. Sylvain Durand and Jacques Froment. Reconstruction of wavelet coefficients using total variation minimization. *SIAM Journal of Scientific Computing*, 24(5):1754–1767, 2003.
7. Mario A.T. Figueiredo and Robert D. Nowak. An EM algorithm for wavelet-based image restoration. *IEEE Transactions on Image Processing*, 12(8), august 2003.
8. Namyong Lee and Bradley J. Lucier. Wavelet methods for inverting the radon transform with noisy data. *IEEE Transactions on Image Processing*, 10:79–94, 2001.
9. Fran cois Malgouyres. Minimizing the total variation under a general convex constraint for image restoration. *IEEE transactions on image processing*, 11(12):1450–1456, 2002.
10. Stéphane Mallat. *A Wavelet Tour of Signal Processing*. Academic Press, San Diego, 1998.
11. R.T. Rockafellar. *Convex Analysis*. Princeton University press, 1972.
12. L. Rudin, S. Osher, and E. Fatemi. Nonlinear total variation based noise removal algorithm. *Physica D*, 60:259–268, 1992.
13. S. Sardy, A. Bruce, and P. Tseng. Block coordinate relaxation methods for nonparametric signal denoising with wavelet dictionaries. Technical report, Seattle, WA, 1998.
14. Jean-Luc Starck, Fionn Murtagh, and Albert Bijaoui. Multiresolution support applied to image filtering and restoration. *Graphical Models and Image Processing*, 57(5):420–431, 1995.
15. A.N. Tikhonov and V.Y. Arsenin. *Solutions of ill-posed problems*. Winston and Wiley, 1977.

Support Blob Machines
The Sparsification of Linear Scale Space

Marco Loog

Image Group, IT University of Copenhagen
Copenhagen, Denmark
marco@itu.dk
Image Sciences Institute, University Medical Center Utrecht
Utrecht, The Netherlands
marco@isi.uu.nl

Abstract. A novel generalization of linear scale space is presented. The generalization allows for a sparse approximation of the function at a certain scale.

To start with, we first consider the Tikhonov regularization viewpoint on scale space theory [15]. The sparsification is then obtained using ideas from support vector machines [22] and based on the link between sparse approximation and support vector regression as described in [4] and [19]. In regularization theory, an ill-posed problem is solved by searching for a solution having a certain differentiability while in some precise sense the final solution is close to the initial signal. To obtain scale space, a quadratic loss function is used to measure the closeness of the initial function to its scale σ image.

We propose to alter this loss function thus obtaining our generalization of linear scale space. Comparable to the linear ϵ-insensitive loss function introduced in support vector regression [22], we use a quadratic ϵ-insensitive loss function instead of the original quadratic measure. The ϵ-insensitivity loss allows errors in the approximating function without actual increase in loss. It penalizes errors only when they become larger than the a priory specified constant ϵ. The quadratic form is mainly maintained for consistency with linear scale space.

Although the main concern of the article is the theoretical connection between the foregoing theories, the proposed approach is tested and exemplified in a small experiment on a single image.

1 Introduction

There are many extensions, variations, perturbations, and generalizations of linear scale space [10,24]. E.g. anisotropic, curvature, morphological, α, pseudo, Poisson, i, torsion, geometry driven and edge preserving scale spaces [1,2,3,7,9, 13,14,16,17,23]. All these approaches serve one or more purposes in image processing, general signal processing or computer vision, as a whole covering a large area of applications. This paper presents another interesting possibility for generalization of linear scale space that has not been explored up to now. I.e., those

T. Pajdla and J. Matas (Eds.): ECCV 2004, LNCS 3024, pp. 14–24, 2004.
© Springer-Verlag Berlin Heidelberg 2004

that allow for a sparse scale space representation of the function under consideration. Being sparse means that the approximation can be obtained using only a small collection of building block or basis functions. This sparseness is being enforced by setting certain constraints to the solution.

The proposed technique exploits links between scale space and support vector machines. The sparsified representation thus obtained is called the support blob machine (SBM), as blobs are the main building blocks used in the representation. The principal observation that leads to the notion of SBMs is that both support vector regression (SVR) [22,19] and scale space can be related to Tikhonov's regularization theory [21] (see [4], [15], and [20]). For more on the connection between scale spaces and regularization see [18].

Regularization is a technique typically used for solving ill-posed problems in a principled way. While scale space offers a solution to the problem of defining derivatives of a multidimensional (digital) signal in a well-posed way, the goal in regression is mainly to recover a function from a finite, possibly noisy, sampling of this function, which is also clearly ill-posed. Support vector regression (SVR) not only offers a well-posed solution to the regression problem but has the additional advantage that it can be used to give a sparse solution to the problem at hand. The sparse representation is acquired by allowing the regressed function to deviate from the initial data without directly penalizing such deviations. This sparseness behavior is accommodated for through the so-called ϵ-insensitive loss. The resulting behavior is clearly different from, for example, standard linear regression in which, using a quadratic loss function, only the slightest deviation from the given data is penalized immediately.

This article focuses on the relationships mentioned above, deriving the SBMs, providing a computational scheme to determine these scale spaces, and finally exemplifying the scale spaces obtained. However, before doing so, we mention several reasons why the kind of scale spaces proposed are of interest.

First of all, the approach may lead to improved image feature detectors. SVR, like support vector classifiers, has proven to be very successful in many applications which is partly due to the relation with robust statistics [8]. But not only may certain forms of sparsified scale space lead to more robust detection of edges, blobs and other visual cues, another advantage is that one could build on the structural risk minimization framework as proposed by Vapnik [22] and consequently one may be able to theoretically underpin the practical performance of these detectors in real-world applications.

Another useful application is in the area of feature-based image analysis and the related research into metamery classes and image reconstruction [6,11,12]. E.g., in [12], certain greedy methods are discussed for the selection of points of interest in an image, i.e., based on a certain form of reconstruction energy (that can be calculated for every point individually), the representing points are chosen starting with the one with the highest energy and going down gradually. These points, together with their associated receptive field weighting function are then taken as image representation. A greedy approach to the point selection problem was considered appropriate by the authors, because features must be detected and represented individually in early vision. However, they also note that this approach is not necessarily optimal for image representation purposes as the reconstruction information mutually conveyed by two or more points is not taken into account, leading to only a suboptimal solution for the image reconstruction task. The SBM does take the global information into account and can therefore obtain an improved selection of points of interest, which all in all could prove useful for, e.g., image compression.

Finally, a little more speculative, the data reduction that is achieved by the sparse representation of the data may facilitate the use of otherwise prohibitively computer intensive techniques in computer vision or image analysis. As an example one could think of the registration of two large 3D data volumes based on their sparse representation instead of all of the voxels.

The remainder of the paper is organized as follows. Subsection 2.1 gives the regularization formulation of scale space after which Subsection 2.2 discusses a more general formulation of regularized regularization taken from the SVR literature. Section 2.3 links the aforementioned techniques. The quadratic ϵ-insensitive loss functions is then introduced in Subsection 2.4 on which our principal generalizations is based. Section 3 describes some experiments to exemplify the novel scale space. Section 4 contains the discussions and concludes the article.

2   The Sparsification of Scale Space

2.1   Scale Space Regularization Formulation

This subsection recapitulates one of the principle contributions of [15] in which scale space is related to a specific instance of Tikhonov regularization. The authors consider the general regularization formulation given by Tikhonov [21]: The regularized function f associated to the function g on $\mathbb{R}^n$ minimizes the functional $\mathcal{E}$ defined as

$$\mathcal{E}[h] := \tfrac{1}{2} \int (h(x) - g(x))^2 + \sum_{j=1}^{\infty} \sum_{|J|=j} \lambda_J \left(\frac{\partial^{|J|} h(x)}{\partial x^J} \right)^2 dx. \tag{1}$$

All λ_J are nonnegative and J is an n-index used for denoting derivatives of order $|J|$. The first term of the right hand side penalizes any deviation of the function h from the given function (the data) g. The second part does not involve g and is the regularization term on h, which, in a certain way controls the smoothness.

It can be shown in this setting, that the solution to the problem, f, can be obtained by a linear convolution of g. Moreover, the authors prove that f equals $g * G_t$, where the latter is the Gaussian kernel

$$G_t(x) := \frac{1}{(2\sqrt{\pi t})^n} e^{-\frac{\|x\|^2}{4t}}, \tag{2}$$

if and only if

$$\lambda_J = \frac{t^{|J|}}{|J|!} = \frac{t^j}{j!} \tag{3}$$

for all J, thus relating scale space at scale $\sqrt{2t}$ to a specific form of Tikhonov regularization.

2.2   Regression and Regularization

The regression problem is generally formulated in terms of a discrete data set of ℓ (noisy) samples $\hat{g}(x_i)$ from the function g and the goal is to recover this underlying function g merely based on these ℓ samples [4,19,22]. To this end, an underlying functional form of g based on a set of linearly independent basis functions φ_i is assumed, i.e., g can be represented as

$$g(x) := \sum_{i=1}^{\infty} c_i \varphi_i(x) + c_0 \, . \tag{4}$$

The constant term c_0 and the parameters c_i have to be estimated from the data. This is clearly an ill-posed task since the problem as such has an infinite number of solutions. Again, regularization can be used to turn it into a well-posed problem by imposing smoothness constraints on the final solution. The regularized solution f minimizes the functional $\mathcal{R}$

$$\mathcal{R}[h] := C \sum_{i=1}^{\ell} L(\hat{g}(x_i) - h(x_i)) + \tfrac{1}{2}\Lambda[h] \, , \tag{5}$$

where L is the loss function penalizing deviation of f from the measurement data $\hat{g}$, Λ is a general constraint that enforces smoothness of the optimal solution f, and C is a positive constant that controls the tradeoff between the two previous data terms.

An important result is the following (see [4]). If the functional Λ has the form $\Lambda[h] = \sum_{i=1}^{\infty} \frac{c_i^2}{\lambda_i}$, where all λ_i are positive and $\{\lambda_i\}_{i=1}^{\infty}$ is a decreasing sequence, then the solution f to the regularization problem (5) takes on the form

$$f(x) = \sum_{i=1}^{\ell} a_i K(x, x_i) + c_0 \, , \tag{6}$$

with the kernel function K being defined as

$$K(x, x_i) = \sum_{i=1}^{\infty} \lambda_i \varphi_i(x) \varphi_i(x_i) \, . \tag{7}$$

A large class of regularizations can be defined based on the foregoing class of smoothing functionals and in the remainder of the article, only these kind of smoothness constraints are considered.

Note that if the cost function L is quadratic, the unknown parameters in Equation (6) can be determined by solving a linear system comparable to standard regression. When the cost function is not quadratic, the a_i can not be readily obtained by solving a linear system and one has to resort to different optimization methods. For particular loss functions, as the main one considered in this article, $\mathcal{R}[h]$ can be optimized using quadratic programming (QP), allowing the optimization to be done in a fairly straightforward way (see Subsection 2.4).

2.3   Kernel Formulation of Scale Space

Before formulating the sparsified version of scale space, first the regularizations in (1) and (5) are related to each other. That is, in the functional $\mathcal{R}$, the 'free parameters' are chosen such that a solution f that minimizes this functional is equal to the minimizing solution of $\mathcal{E}$ with the λ_J as given in Equation (3). In this case

$$\mathcal{E}[h] = \tfrac{1}{2} \int (h(x) - g(x))^2 + \sum_{j=1}^{\infty} \frac{t^j}{j!} \sum_{|J|=j} \left(\frac{\partial^{|J|} h(x)}{\partial x^J} \right)^2 dx. \qquad (8)$$

The fact that one formulation is continuous and the other uses discrete observations is disregarded. Doing so, it is of course immediately clear that in (5), the loss function L has to be the quadratic loss, i.e.,

$$L(\cdot) = (\cdot)^2. \qquad (9)$$

So now our main concern is the smoothing term in both functionals.

Starting with the smoothing term from (1)—with the λ_J as defined in Equation (3), based on induction and partial integration, and in addition properly rearranging terms, it can be shown that the following equivalence holds (cf. [15])

$$\sum_{|J|=j} \left(\frac{\partial^{|J|} h(x)}{\partial x^J} \right)^2 = \begin{cases} \left(\nabla \Delta^{\frac{j-1}{2}} h(x) \right)^2 & \text{if } j \text{ is odd} \\ \left(\Delta^{\frac{j}{2}} h(x) \right)^2 & \text{if } j \text{ is even} \end{cases} . \qquad (10)$$

Where Δ is the Laplacean and ∇ is the gradient operator.

Setting $2t = \sigma^2$ in Equation (8) and substituting the results from Equation (10), the expression obtained can be related to the result discussed in [20,19] (cf. [5]) in which Gaussian functions are shown to be the kernel functions associated to this specific form of regularization. That is, K in (7) should be defined as

$$K(x, x_i) := e^{\frac{-\|x - x_i\|^2}{2\sigma^2}} = e^{\frac{-\|x - x_i\|^2}{4t}}, \qquad (11)$$

for the regularized regression (5) to be equivalent to the Tikhonov regularization resulting in linear scale space of g.

Finally, with the constant C in (5) set to $\tfrac{1}{2}$, the regularization functionals $\mathcal{E}$ and $\mathcal{R}$ become completely equivalent.

2.4   Quadratic ϵ-Insensitive Loss and SBMs

Based on the foregoing equivalence, this subsection introduces to the generalization of linear scale space within the SVR framework via a quadratic ϵ-insensitive loss: The support blob machines (SBMs). The main idea behind using this quadratic ϵ-insensitive loss is that the generalization should possess a similar kind of ability to obtain sparse representations as the (linear) ϵ-insensitive loss function exhibits.

It is formulated for pixel-based discrete images and related to SVR based on the (linear) ϵ-insensitive loss. Subsequently, it is demonstrated how to obtain the minimizing solution under this loss function based on a quadratic programming (QP) formulation. This is similar to the optimization procedure used in standard ϵ-insensitive loss support vector machines [4,22,19].

The loss function originally proposed in the context of SVR [22] is the ϵ-insensitive loss $|\cdot|_\epsilon$. It allows for minimization of (5) using QP and is defined as

$$|x|_\epsilon := \begin{cases} 0 & \text{if } |x| \leq \epsilon \\ |x| - \epsilon & \text{otherwise} \end{cases} . \tag{12}$$

This loss function bears a resemblance to some loss functions used in statistics which provide robustness against outliers [8]. In addition to this important property, the loss has another distinctive feature: It assigns zero cost to deviations of h from $\hat{g}$ that are smaller than ϵ and therefore, every function h that comes closer than ϵ to the ℓ data points $\hat{g}(x_i)$ is considered to be a perfect approximation.

The similar quadratic ϵ-insensitive loss function, more closely related to the well-known quadratic loss in Equation (9), can be defined as follows

$$(x)_\epsilon^2 := \begin{cases} 0 & \text{if } |x| \leq \epsilon \\ (|x| - \epsilon)^2 & \text{otherwise} \end{cases} . \tag{13}$$

Using this loss, deviations form the underlying data are essentially quadratically penalized. However, the ϵ allows zero cost deviations from the data points $\hat{g}(x_i)$, which, for the minimizing solution f, leads to several a_i being zero in Equation (6). The number of a_i being equal to zero is dependent on the parameter ϵ. The larger ϵ is, the more a_i are zero. If $\epsilon = 0$, then $a_i \propto \hat{g}(x_i)$ (note that the Gaussian kernel in (11) is not normalized) and so in general a_i will be nonzero. Taking ϵ larger than zero, a sparse solution to the problem can be obtained (see [4] and [22] for the actual underlying mechanisms leading to sparseness).

Taking all of the foregoing into consideration, the regularization functional $\mathcal{E}_\epsilon$ for sparse scale space is now readily defined in its discrete form as

$$\mathcal{E}_\epsilon[h] := C \sum_{i=1}^{\ell} (h(x_i) - g(x_i))_\epsilon^2 + \sum_{i=1}^{\ell} \sum_{j=1}^{\infty} \frac{t^j}{j!} \sum_{|J|=j} \left(\frac{\partial^{|J|} h(x_i)}{\partial x^J} \right)^2 , \tag{14}$$

with, in general, C equal to $\frac{1}{2}$. Taking ϵ equal to zero, results in ordinary linear scale space.

Exploiting the link with SVR, a dual QP formulation that solves $\text{argmin}_h \mathcal{E}[h]_\epsilon$ can be stated (cf. [4,19]):

$$\underset{\alpha_i^-, \alpha_i^+}{\text{argmin}} \sum_{i=1}^{\ell} \left[\epsilon(\alpha_i^+ + \alpha_i^-) - \hat{g}(x_i)(\alpha_i^+ - \alpha_i^-) \right.$$
$$\left. + \frac{1}{2} \sum_{j=1}^{\ell} (\alpha_i^+ - \alpha_i^-)(\alpha_j^+ - \alpha_j^-)(K(x_i, x_j) + \frac{1}{C} + \delta_{ij}) \right] \tag{15}$$

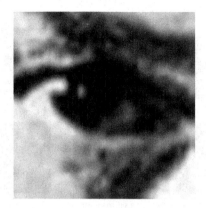

Fig. 1. On the right, the original image of Lenin. On the left is his right eye, the 50 by 50 sub-image used to exemplify the SBMs.

subject to $\sum_{j=1}^{\ell}(\alpha_i^+ - \alpha_i^-) = 0$ and $\alpha_i^-, \alpha_i^+ \geq 0$. After which the $\alpha_i^{-\star}$ and $\alpha_i^{+\star}$ that optimize (15) determine the optimal solution to the minimization of the functional $\mathcal{E}_\epsilon$, i.e., (cf. Equation (6))

$$f(x) = \sum_{i=1}^{\ell}(\alpha_i^{+\star} - \alpha_i^{-\star})K(x, x_i) + c_0^\star. \tag{16}$$

The optimal offset $c_0^\star$ can be determined by exploiting the Karush-Kuhn-Tucker condition, after the solution to the foregoing problem has been obtained. The condition basically states that at the optimal solution of QP (15), the product of the dual variables and their constraints should vanish (see [19,22]).

3   An Illustrative Experiment

The SBMs are exemplified on a single, small gray value image. The image is a 50 by 50 sub-image taken from a larger image of Lenin (see Figure 1). The sub-image is Lenin's right eye. The gray values of this image are scaled between 0 and 255 for this experiment. Note that it is important to know the range the gray values are in, because the function minimizing $\mathcal{E}_\epsilon$ with $\epsilon > 0$ is not invariant under (linear) intensity scalings, which is due to the ϵ-insensitivity.

For this image, for several settings of the parameters σ ($= \sqrt{2t}$) and ϵ, the support vectors are determined using the functional (14). Simultaneously, the optimal values for the parameters α_i^+ and α_i^- are obtained. These values, together with the Gaussian kernels, define the regularized image via Equation (16).

Figure 2 plots the values $\alpha_i^{+\star} - \alpha_i^{-\star}$ in the position of the blob it supports in the SBM for varying σ and ϵ. Figure 3 gives the regularized images, which are actually blurred versions (as is clear from Equation (16)) of the images in Figure 2. Put differently, the images in Figure 2 can be considered de-blurred images.

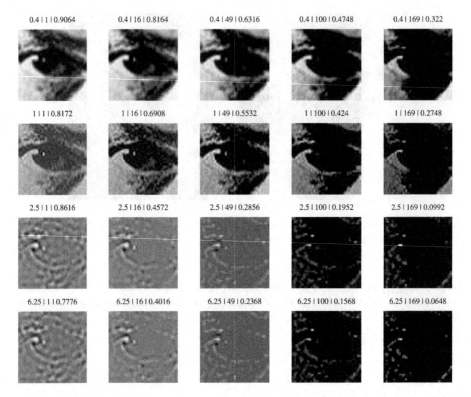

Fig. 2. Plots of the values $\alpha_i^{\cdot\ *} - \alpha_i^{\cdot\ *}$ given by the SBMs. On the top of every image the scale, the value of ϵ, and the relative number of support vectors is given.

Because it is not immediately clear from Figure 2 when there is actually a support vector present in a certain position, i.e., when $\alpha_i^{+\star} - \alpha_i^{-\star}$ is not equal to zero, Figure 4 indicates in black the positions that contain a support vector.

The additional text added at the top of every images in Figures 2 to 4 gives information on the scale σ, the ϵ, and the relative amount of support vectors (as $\cdot\,|\,\cdot\,|\,\cdot$). This last number is simply calculated by dividing the number of support vectors by $2500 = 50^2$.

4   Discussion and Conclusion

We introduced support blob machines (SBMs) based on a link between scale space theory and support vector regression, which are connected to each other via regularization theory. The SBMs give a sparsification of linear scale space by employing a quadratic ϵ-insensitive loss function in its regularization functional. Through the sparseness obtained, the regularized function can be represented using only a small collection of building block or basis functions.

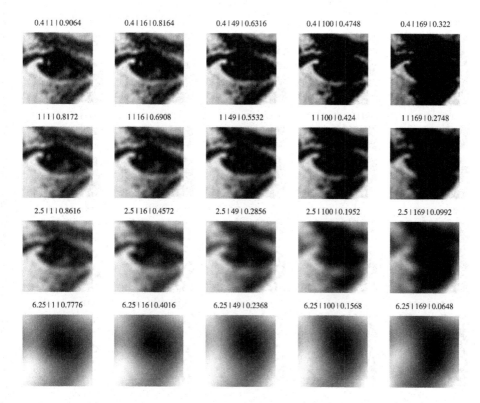

Fig. 3. The regularized images associated to a certain scale σ and value of ϵ. (The values are given on the top of every image. The relative number of support vectors is given here also as the last number.)

Some SBM instances were exemplified on a small 50 by 50 image, and it was shown that the technique indeed obtains sparse representations of images at a certain scale. However, in our tests, the reduction of information that was attained is certainly not overwhelming and further research should be conducted before a definite conclusion about the performance of SBMs can be stated. A simple suggestion, which could lead to improved sparseness performance is to increase the parameter C in the functional. In the tests this was set to $\frac{1}{2}$ to keep a close link with standard scale space. A larger value for C leads automatically to a sparser representation of the underlying signal.

The principal contribution of this article is, however, the formal link between two interesting techniques: scale space and support vector machines. This link could now be further exploited and more advanced regularization approaches may be considered.

Our future research will focus on developing a formulation that gives a sparse representation while taking all scales into account simultaneously and not merely one scale at a time. This may, in combination with different types of loss functions, lead to a robust form of scale selection in combination with blob detection

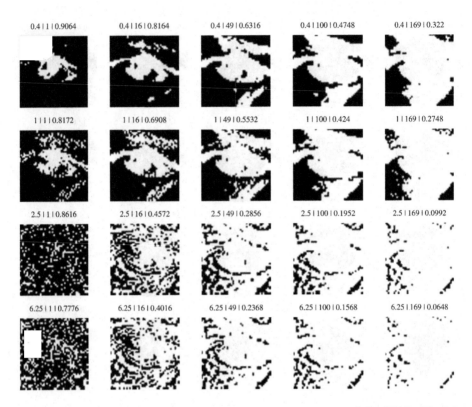

Fig. 4. In black are the positions that contain a support vector of the SBMs. The last number on top of every image gives the relative area of the image that is black, i.e., it gives the relative number of support vectors.

[13]. In addition to this, representations of higher order features may be incorporated, i.e., not only blobs, which makes a more closer connection to the work in, for example, [12] (see also Section 1) in which several receptive field weighting function are to be chosen in such a manner to represent the image in an optimal way. In this, also anisotropic forms of SBMs may be of interest.

References

1. R. van den Boomgaard and A. W. M. Smeulders. The morphological structure of images, the differential equations of morphological scale-space. *IEEE Transactions on Pattern Analysis and Machine Intelligence*, 16(11):1101–1113, 1994.
2. R. Duits, M. Felsberg, L. M. J. Florack, and B. Platel. α Scale spaces on a bounded domain. In *Scale Space Methods in Computer Vision, 4th International Conference, Scale-Space 2003*, pages 494–510, Isle of Skye, 2003.
3. L. M. J. Florack, R. Maas, and W. J. Niessen. Pseudo-linear scale-space theory. *International Journal of Computer Vision*, 31(2/3):247–259, April 1999.
4. F. Girosi. An equivalence between sparse approximation and support vector machines. *Neural Computation*, 10(6):1455–1480, 1998.

5. F. Girosi, M. Jones, and T. Poggio. Prior stabilizers and basis functions: From regularization to radial, tensor and additive splines. Technical Report AI Memo 1430, CBCL Paper 75, MIT, Cambridge, MA, 1993.

6. L. D. Griffin. Local image structure, metamerism, norms, and natural image statistics. *Perception*, 31(3), 2002.

7. B. M. ter Haar Romeny (ed.). *Geometry-Driven Diffusion*. Kluwer, Dordrecht, 1996.

8. P. J. Huber. *Robust Statistics*. John Wiley & Sons, New York, 1981.

9. P. R. Jackway. Morphological scale-space. In *11th IAPR International Conference on Pattern Recognition*, pages 252–255, The Hague, The Netherlands, 1992.

10. J. J. Koenderink. The structure of images. *Biological Cybernetics*, 50:363–370, 1984.

11. J. J. Koenderink and A. J. van Doorn. Metamerism in complete sets of image operators. In *Advances in Image Understanding '96*, pages 113–129, 1996.

12. M. Lillholm, M. Nielsen, and L. D. Griffin. Feature-based image analysis. *International Journal of Computer Vision*, 52:73–95, 2003.

13. T. Lindeberg. *Scale-Space Theory in Computer Vision*. Kluwer Academic Press, Boston, 1994.

14. M. Loog, M. Lillholm, M. Nielsen, and M. A. Viergever. Gaussian scale space from insufficient image information. In *Scale Space Methods in Computer Vision, 4th International Conference, Scale-Space 2003*, pages 757–769, Isle of Skye, 2003.

15. M. Nielsen, L. M. J. Florack, and R. Deriche. Regularization, scale-space, and edge detection filters. *Journal of Mathematical Imaging and Vision*, 7(4):291–307, 1997.

16. K.-R. Park and C.-N. Lee. Scale-space using mathematical morphology. *IEEE Transactions on Pattern Analysis and Machine Intelligence*, 18(11):1121–1126, 1996.

17. P. Perona and J. Malik. Scale space and edge detection using anisotropic diffusion. *IEEE Transactions on Pattern Analysis and Machine Intelligence*, 12:429–439, 1990.

18. O. Scherzer and J. Weickert. Relations between regularization and diffusion filtering. *Journal of Mathematical Imaging and Vision*, 12:43–63, 2000.

19. A. J. Smola and B. Schölkopf. A tutorial on support vector regression. Technical Report NC-TR-98-030, Royal Holloway College, University of London, UK, 1998.

20. A. J. Smola, B. Schölkopf, and K.-R. Müller. The connection between regularization operators and support vector kernels. *Neural Networks*, 11:637–650, 1998.

21. A. N. Tikhonov and V. Y. Arseninn. *Solution of Ill-Posed Problems*. W. H. Winston, Washington D.C., 1977.

22. V. Vapnik. *The Nature of Statistical Learning Theory*. Springer-Verlag, New York, 1995.

23. J. Weickert. *Anisotropic Diffusion in Image Processing*. B. G. Teubner, Stuttgart, 1998.

24. A. P. Witkin. Scale-space filtering. In *Proceedings of IJCAI*, Germany, 1983.

High Accuracy Optical Flow Estimation Based on a Theory for Warping*

Thomas Brox, Andrés Bruhn, Nils Papenberg, and Joachim Weickert

Mathematical Image Analysis Group
Faculty of Mathematics and Computer Science
Saarland University, Building 27, 66041 Saarbrücken, Germany
{brox,bruhn,papenberg,weickert}@mia.uni-saarland.de
http://www.mia.uni-saarland.de

Abstract. We study an energy functional for computing optical flow that combines three assumptions: a brightness constancy assumption, a gradient constancy assumption, and a discontinuity-preserving spatio-temporal smoothness constraint. In order to allow for large displacements, linearisations in the two data terms are strictly avoided. We present a consistent numerical scheme based on two nested fixed point iterations. By proving that this scheme implements a coarse-to-fine warping strategy, we give a theoretical foundation for warping which has been used on a mainly experimental basis so far. Our evaluation demonstrates that the novel method gives significantly smaller angular errors than previous techniques for optical flow estimation. We show that it is fairly insensitive to parameter variations, and we demonstrate its excellent robustness under noise.

1 Introduction

Optical flow estimation is still one of the key problems in computer vision. Estimating the displacement field between two images, it is applied as soon as correspondences between pixels are needed. Problems of this type are not only restricted to motion estimation, they are also present in a similar fashion in 3D reconstruction or image registration. In the last two decades the quality of optical flow estimation methods has increased dramatically. Starting from the original approaches of Horn and Schunck [11] as well as Lucas and Kanade [15], research developed many new concepts for dealing with shortcomings of previous models. In order to handle discontinuities in the flow field, the quadratic regulariser in the Horn and Schunck model was replaced by smoothness constraints that permit piecewise smooth results [1,9,19,21,25]. Some of these ideas are close in spirit to methods for joint motion estimation and motion segmentation [10,17], and to optical flow methods motivated from robust statistics where outliers are penalised less severely [6,7]. Coarse-to-fine strategies [3,7,16] as well as non-linearised models [19,2] have been used to tackle large displacements. Finally, spatio-temporal approaches have ameliorated the results simply by using the information of an additional dimension [18,6,26,10].

However, not only new ideas have improved the quality of optical flow estimation techniques. Also efforts to obtain a better understanding of what the methods do in detail,

---

* We gratefully acknowledge partial funding by the *Deutsche Forschungsgemeinschaft (DFG)*.

and which effects are caused by changing their parameters, gave an insight into how several models could work together. Furthermore, variational formulations of models gave access to the long experience of numerical mathematics in solving partly difficult optimisation problems. Finding the optimal solution to a certain model is often not trivial, and often the full potential of a model is not used because concessions to implementation aspects have to be made.

In this paper we propose a novel variational approach that integrates several of the before mentioned concepts and which can be minimised with a solid numerical method. It is further shown that a coarse-to-fine strategy using the so-called warping technique [7,16], implements the non-linearised optical flow constraint used in [19,2] and in image registration. This has two important effects: Firstly, it becomes possible to integrate the warping technique, which was so far only algorithmically motivated, into a variational framework. Secondly, it shows a theoretically sound way of how image correspondence problems can be solved with an efficient multi-resolution technique. It should be noted that – apart from a very nice paper by Lefébure and Cohen [14] – not many theoretical results on warping are available so far.

Finally, the grey value constancy assumption, which is the basic assumption in optical flow estimation, is extended by a gradient constancy assumption. This makes the method robust against grey value changes. While gradient constancy assumptions have also been proposed in [23,22] in order to deal with the aperture problem in the scope of a local approach, their use within variational methods is novel.

The experimental evaluation shows that our method yields excellent results. Compared to those in the literature, their accuracy is always significantly higher, sometimes even twice as high as the best value known so far. Moreover, the method proved also to be robust under a considerable amount of noise and computation times of only a few seconds per frame on contemporary hardware are possible.

Paper Organisation. In the next section, our variational model is introduced, first by discussing all model assumptions, and then in form of an energy based formulation. Section 3 derives a minimisation scheme for this energy. The theoretical foundation of warping methods as a numerical approximation step is given in Section 4. An experimental evaluation is presented in Section 5, followed by a brief summary in Section 6.

2   The Variational Model

Before deriving a variational formulation for our optical flow method, we give an intuitive idea of which constraints in our view should be included in such a model.

- **Grey Value Constancy Assumption**
  Since the beginning of optical flow estimation, it has been assumed that the grey value of a pixel is not changed by the displacement.

$$I(x, y, t) = I(x + u, y + v, t + 1) \qquad (1)$$

Here $I : \Omega \subset \mathbb{R}^3 \to \mathbb{R}$ denotes a rectangular image sequence, and $\mathbf{w} := (u, v, 1)^\top$ is the searched displacement vector between an image at time t and another image at time $t + 1$. The linearised version of the grey value constancy assumption yields the famous optical flow constraint [11]

$$I_x u + I_y v + I_t = 0 \tag{2}$$

where subscripts denote partial derivatives. However, this linearisation is only valid under the assumption that the image changes linearly along the displacement, which is in general not the case, especially for large displacements. Therefore, our model will use the original, non-linearised grey value constancy assumption (1).

– **Gradient Constancy Assumption**
The grey value constancy assumption has one decisive drawback: It is quite susceptible to slight changes in brightness, which often appear in natural scenes. Therefore, it is useful to allow some small variations in the grey value and help to determine the displacement vector by a criterion that is invariant under grey value changes. Such a criterion is the gradient of the image grey value, which can also be assumed not to vary due to the displacement [23]. This gives

$$\nabla I(x, y, t) = \nabla I(x + u, y + v, t + 1). \tag{3}$$

Here $\nabla = (\partial_x, \partial_y)^\top$ denotes the spatial gradient. Again it can be useful to refrain from a linearisation. The constraint (3) is particularly helpful for translatory motion, while constraint (2) can be better suited for more complicated motion patterns.

– **Smoothness Assumption**
So far, the model estimates the displacement of a pixel only locally without taking any interaction between neighbouring pixels into account. Therefore, it runs into problems as soon as the gradient vanishes somewhere, or if only the flow in normal direction to the gradient can be estimated (*aperture problem*). Furthermore, one would expect some outliers in the estimates. Hence, it is useful to introduce as a further assumption the smoothness of the flow field. This smoothness constraint can either be applied solely to the spatial domain, if there are only two frames available, or to the spatio-temporal domain, if the displacements in a sequence of images are wanted. As the optimal displacement field will have discontinuities at the boundaries of objects in the scene, it is sensible to generalise the smoothness assumption by demanding a *piecewise smooth* flow field.

– **Multiscale Approach**
In the case of displacements that are larger than one pixel per frame, the cost functional in a variational formulation must be expected to be multi-modal, i.e. a minimisation algorithm could easily be trapped in a local minimum. In order to find the global minimum, it can be useful to apply multiscale ideas: One starts with solving a coarse, smoothed version of the problem by working on the smoothed image sequence. The new problem may have a unique minimum, hopefully close to the global minimum of the original problem. The coarse solution is used as initialisation for solving a refined version of the problem until step by step the original problem is solved. Instead of smoothing the image sequence, it is more efficient to downsample the images respecting the sampling theorem, so the model ends up in a multiresolution strategy.

With this description, it is straightforward to derive an energy functional that penalises deviations from these model assumptions. Let $\mathbf{x} := (x, y, t)^\top$ and $\mathbf{w} :=$

$(u, v, 1)^\top$. Then the global deviations from the grey value constancy assumption and the gradient constancy assumption are measured by the energy

$$E_{Data}(u, v) = \int_\Omega \left(|I(\mathbf{x} + \mathbf{w}) - I(\mathbf{x})|^2 + \gamma |\nabla I(\mathbf{x} + \mathbf{w}) - \nabla I(\mathbf{x})|^2 \right) d\mathbf{x} \quad (4)$$

with γ being a weight between both assumptions. Since with quadratic penalisers, outliers get too much influence on the estimation, an increasing concave function $\Psi(s^2)$ is applied, leading to a robust energy [7,16]:

$$E_{Data}(u, v) = \int_\Omega \Psi \left(|I(\mathbf{x} + \mathbf{w}) - I(\mathbf{x})|^2 + \gamma |\nabla I(\mathbf{x} + \mathbf{w}) - \nabla I(\mathbf{x})|^2 \right) d\mathbf{x} \quad (5)$$

The function Ψ can also be applied separately to each of these two terms. We use the function $\Psi(s^2) = \sqrt{s^2 + \epsilon^2}$ which results in (modified) L^1 minimisation. Due to the small positive constant ϵ, $\Psi(s)$ is still convex which offers advantages in the minimisation process. Moreover, this choice of Ψ does not introduce any additional parameters, since ϵ is only for numerical reasons and can be set to a fixed value, which we choose to be 0.001.

Finally, a smoothness term has to describe the model assumption of a piecewise smooth flow field. This is achieved by penalising the total variation of the flow field [20,8], which can be expressed as

$$E_{Smooth}(u, v) = \int_\Omega \Psi \left(|\nabla_3 u|^2 + |\nabla_3 v|^2 \right) d\mathbf{x}. \quad (6)$$

with the same function for Ψ as above. The spatio-temporal gradient $\nabla_3 := (\partial_x, \partial_y, \partial_t)^\top$ indicates that a spatio-temporal smoothness assumption is involved. For applications with only two images available it is replaced by the spatial gradient.

The total energy is the weighted sum between the data term and the smoothness term

$$E(u, v) = E_{Data} + \alpha E_{Smooth} \quad (7)$$

with some regularisation parameter $\alpha > 0$. Now the goal is to find the functions u and v that minimise this energy.

3   Minimisation

3.1   Euler–Lagrange Equations

Since $E(u, v)$ is highly nonlinear, the minimisation is not trivial. For better readability we define the following abbreviations, where the use of z instead of t emphasises that the expression is *not* a temporal derivative but a difference that is sought to be minimised.

$$
\begin{aligned}
I_x &:= \partial_x I(\mathbf{x} + \mathbf{w}), \\
I_y &:= \partial_y I(\mathbf{x} + \mathbf{w}), \\
I_z &:= I(\mathbf{x} + \mathbf{w}) - I(\mathbf{x}), \\
I_{xx} &:= \partial_{xx} I(\mathbf{x} + \mathbf{w}), \\
I_{xy} &:= \partial_{xy} I(\mathbf{x} + \mathbf{w}), \\
I_{yy} &:= \partial_{yy} I(\mathbf{x} + \mathbf{w}), \\
I_{xz} &:= \partial_x I(\mathbf{x} + \mathbf{w}) - \partial_x I(\mathbf{x}), \\
I_{yz} &:= \partial_y I(\mathbf{x} + \mathbf{w}) - \partial_y I(\mathbf{x}).
\end{aligned}
\quad (8)
$$

According to the calculus of variations, a minimiser of (7) must fulfill the Euler-Lagrange equations

$$\Psi'(I_z^2 + \gamma(I_{xz}^2 + I_{yz}^2)) \cdot (I_x I_z + \gamma(I_{xx} I_{xz} + I_{xy} I_{yz}))$$
$$-\alpha \, \mathrm{div}\left(\Psi'(|\nabla_3 u|^2 + |\nabla_3 v|^2)\nabla_3 u\right) = 0,$$
$$\Psi'(I_z^2 + \gamma(I_{xz}^2 + I_{yz}^2)) \cdot (I_y I_z + \gamma(I_{yy} I_{yz} + I_{xy} I_{xz}))$$
$$-\alpha \, \mathrm{div}\left(\Psi'(|\nabla_3 u|^2 + |\nabla_3 v|^2)\nabla_3 v\right) = 0$$

with reflecting boundary conditions.

3.2   Numerical Approximation

The preceding Euler-Lagrange equations are nonlinear in their argument $\mathbf{w} = (u, v, 1)^\top$. A first step towards a linear system of equations, which can be solved with common numerical methods, is the use of fixed point iterations on $\mathbf{w}$. In order to implement a multiscale approach, necessary to better approximate the global optimum of the energy, these fixed point iterations are combined with a downsampling strategy. Instead of the standard downsampling factor of 0.5 on each level, it is proposed here to use an *arbitrary* factor $\eta \in (0, 1)$, what allows smoother transitions from one scale to the next[1]. Moreover, the full pyramid of images is used, starting with the smallest possible image at the coarsest grid. Let $\mathbf{w}^k = (u^k, v^k, 1)^\top$, $k = 0, 1, \ldots$, with the initialisation $\mathbf{w}^0 = (0, 0, 1)^\top$ at the coarsest grid. Further, let I_*^k be the abbreviations defined in (8) but with the iteration variable $\mathbf{w}^k$ instead of $\mathbf{w}$. Then $\mathbf{w}^{k+1}$ will be the solution of

$$\Psi'((I_z^{k+1})^2 + \gamma((I_{xz}^{k+1})^2 + (I_{yz}^{k+1})^2)) \cdot (I_x^k I_z^{k+1} + \gamma(I_{xx}^k I_{xz}^{k+1} + I_{xy}^k I_{yz}^{k+1}))$$
$$-\alpha \, \mathrm{div}\left(\Psi'(|\nabla_3 u^{k+1}|^2 + |\nabla_3 v^{k+1}|^2)\nabla_3 u^{k+1}\right) = 0 \qquad (9)$$
$$\Psi'((I_z^{k+1})^2 + \gamma((I_{xz}^{k+1})^2 + (I_{yz}^{k+1})^2)) \cdot (I_y^k I_z^{k+1} + \gamma(I_{yy}^k I_{yz}^{k+1} + I_{xy}^k I_{xz}^{k+1}))$$
$$-\alpha \, \mathrm{div}\left(\Psi'(|\nabla_3 u^{k+1}|^2 + |\nabla_3 v^{k+1}|^2)\nabla_3 v^{k+1}\right) = 0.$$

As soon as a fixed point in $\mathbf{w}^k$ is reached, we change to the next finer scale and use this solution as initialisation for the fixed point iteration on this scale.

Notice that we have a fully implicit scheme for the smoothness term and a semi-implicit scheme for the data term. Implicit schemes are used to yield higher stability and faster convergence. However, this new system is still nonlinear because of the nonlinear function Ψ' and the symbols I_*^{k+1}. In order to remove the nonlinearity in I_*^{k+1}, first order Taylor expansions are used:

$$I_z^{k+1} \approx I_z^k + I_x^k du^k + I_y^k dv^k,$$
$$I_{xz}^{k+1} \approx I_{xz}^k + I_{xx}^k du^k + I_{xy}^k dv^k,$$
$$I_{yz}^{k+1} \approx I_{yz}^k + I_{xy}^k du^k + I_{yy}^k dv^k,$$

where $u^{k+1} = u^k + du^k$ and $v^{k+1} = v^k + dv^k$. So we split the unknowns u^{k+1}, v^{k+1} in the solutions of the previous iteration step u^k, v^k and unknown increments du^k, dv^k.

---

[1] Since the grid size in both x- and y-direction is reduced by η, the image size in fact shrinks with a factor $\eta^\cdot$ at each scale.

For better readability let

$$
\begin{aligned}
(\varPsi')^k_{Data} \; &:= \varPsi'\Big((I^k_z + I^k_x du^k + I^k_y dv^k)^2 \\
&\quad + \gamma\big((I^k_{xz} + I^k_{xx} du^k + I^k_{xy} dv^k)^2 + (I^k_{yz} + I^k_{xy} du^k + I^k_{yy} dv^k)^2\big)\Big), \\
(\varPsi')^k_{Smooth} &:= \varPsi'(|\nabla_3(u^k + du^k)|^2 + |\nabla_3(v^k + dv^k)|^2),
\end{aligned}
\tag{10}
$$

where $(\varPsi')^k_{Data}$ can be interpreted as a robustness factor in the data term, and $(\varPsi')^k_{Smooth}$ as a diffusivity in the smoothness term. With this the first equation in system (9) can be written as

$$
\begin{aligned}
0 = (\varPsi')^k_{Data} \cdot \Big(I^k_x \big(I^k_z + I^k_x du^k + I^k_y dv^k\big)\Big) \\
+ \gamma\, (\varPsi')^k_{Data} \cdot \Big(I^k_{xx}(I^k_{xz} + I^k_{xx} du^k + I^k_{xy} dv^k) + I^k_{xy}(I^k_{yz} + I^k_{xy} du^k + I^k_{yy} dv^k)\Big) \\
- \alpha \operatorname{div}\big((\varPsi')^k_{Smooth}\nabla_3(u^k + du^k)\big),
\end{aligned}
\tag{11}
$$

and the second equation can be expressed in a similar way. This is still a nonlinear system of equations for a fixed k, but now in the unknown increments du^k, dv^k. As the only remaining nonlinearity is due to $\varPsi'$, and $\varPsi$ has been chosen to be a convex function, the remaining optimisation problem is a convex problem, i.e. there exists a unique minimum solution.

In order to remove the remaining nonlinearity in $\varPsi'$, a second, inner, fixed point iteration loop is applied. Let $du^{k,0} := 0$, $dv^{k,0} := 0$ be our initialisation and let $du^{k,l}, dv^{k,l}$ denote the iteration variables at some step l. Furthermore, let $(\varPsi')^{k,l}_{Data}$ and $(\varPsi')^{k,l}_{Smooth}$ denote the robustness factor and the diffusivity defined in (10) at iteration k, l. Then finally the *linear* system of equations in $du^{k,l+1}, dv^{k,l+1}$ reads

$$
\begin{aligned}
0 = (\varPsi')^{k,l}_{Data} \cdot \Big(I^k_x \big(I^k_z + I^k_x du^{k,l+1} + I^k_y dv^{k,l+1}\big) \\
+ \gamma I^k_{xx}(I^k_{xz} + I^k_{xx} du^{k,l+1} + I^k_{xy} dv^{k,l+1}) + \gamma I^k_{xy}(I^k_{yz} + I^k_{xy} du^{k,l+1} + I^k_{yy} dv^{k,l+1})\Big) \\
- \alpha \operatorname{div}\Big((\varPsi')^{k,l}_{Smooth}\nabla_3(u^k + du^{k,l+1})\Big)
\end{aligned}
\tag{12}
$$

for the first equation. Using standard discretisations for the derivatives, the resulting sparse linear system of equations can now be solved with common numerical methods, such as Gauss-Seidel or SOR iterations. Expressions of type $I(\mathbf{x} + \mathbf{w^k})$ are computed by means of bilinear interpolation.

4   Relation to Warping Methods

Coarse-to-fine warping techniques are a frequently used tool for improving the performance of optic flow methods [3,7,17]. While they are often introduced on a purely experimental basis, we show in this section that they can be theoretically justified as a numerical approximation.

In order to establish this relation, we restrict ourselves to the grey value constancy model by setting $\gamma = 0$. Let us also simplify the model by assuming solely spatial smoothness, as in [17]. Under these conditions, (11) can be written as

$$(\Psi')^k_{Data} \nabla I^k (\nabla I^k)^\top \begin{pmatrix} du^k \\ dv^k \end{pmatrix} - \alpha \begin{pmatrix} \text{div} \left((\Psi')^k_{Smooth} \nabla (u^k + du^k) \right) \\ \text{div} \left((\Psi')^k_{Smooth} \nabla (v^k + dv^k) \right) \end{pmatrix}$$
$$= -(\Psi')^k_{Data} I^k_z \nabla I^k \qquad (13)$$

For a fixed k, this system is equivalent to the Euler–Lagrange equations described in [17]. Also there, only the increments du and dv between the first image and the warped second image are estimated. The same increments appear in the outer fixed point iterations of our approach in order to resolve the nonlinearity of the grey value constancy assumption. *This shows that the warping technique implements the minimisation of a non-linearised constancy assumption by means of fixed point iterations on w.*

In earlier approaches, the main motivation for warping has been the coarse-to-fine strategy. Due to solutions u and v computed on coarser grids, only an increment du and dv had to be computed on the fine grid. Thus, the estimates used to have a magnitude of less than one pixel per frame, independent of the magnitude of the total displacement. This ability to deal with larger displacements proved to be a very important aspect in differential optical flow estimation.

A second strategy to deal with large displacements has been the usage of the non-linearised grey value constancy assumption [19,2]. Here, large displacements are allowed from the beginning. However, the nonlinearity results in a multi-modal functional. In such a setting, the coarse-to-fine strategy is not only wanted, but even necessary to better approximate the global minimum. At the end, both strategies not only lead to similar results. In fact, as we have seen above, they are completely equivalent. As a consequence, the coarse-to-fine warping technique can be formulated as a single minimisation problem, and image registration techniques relying on non-linearised constancy assumptions get access to an efficient multiresolution method for minimising their energy functionals.

5   Evaluation

For evaluation purposes experiments with both synthetic and real-world image data were performed. The presented angular errors were computed according to [5].

Let us start our evaluation with the two variants of a famous sequence: the *Yosemite* sequence with and without cloudy sky. The original version with cloudy sky was created by Lynn Quam and is available at ftp://ftp.csd.uwo.ca/pub/vision. It combines both divergent and translational motion. The version without clouds is available at http://www.cs.brown.edu/people/black/images.html.

Tab. 1 shows a comparison of our results for both sequences to the best results from the literature. As one can see, our variational approach outperforms all other methods. Regarding the sequence with clouds, we achieve results that are more than twice as accurate as all results from the literature. For the sequence without clouds, angular errors below 1 degree are reached for the first time with a method that offers full density. The corresponding flow fields presented in Fig. 1 give a qualitative impression of these raw numbers: They match the ground truth very well. Not only the discontinuity between the

Table 1. Comparison between the results from the literature with 100 % density and our results for the *Yosemite* sequence with and without cloudy sky. AAE = average angular error. STD = standard deviation. 2D = spatial smoothness assumption. 3D = spatio-temporal smoothness assumption.

Yosemite with clouds			Yosemite without clouds		
Technique	AAE	STD	Technique	AAE	STD
Nagel [5]	10.22°	16.51°	Ju *et al.* [12]	2.16°	2.00°
Horn–Schunck, mod. [5]	9.78°	16.19°	Bab-Hadiashar–Suter [4]	2.05°	2.92°
Uras *et al.* [5]	8.94°	15.61°	Lai–Vemuri [13]	1.99°	1.41°
Alvarez *et al.* [2]	5.53°	7.40°	**Our method (2D)**	**1.59°**	**1.39°**
Weickert *et al.* [24]	5.18°	8.68°	Mémin–Pérez [16]	1.58°	1.21°
Mémin–Pérez [16]	4.69°	6.89°	Weickert *et al.* [24]	1.46°	1.50°
Our method (2D)	**2.46°**	**7.31°**	Farnebäck [10]	1.14°	2.14°
Our method (3D)	**1.94°**	**6.02°**	**Our method (3D)**	**0.98°**	**1.17°**

Table 2. Results for the *Yosemite* sequence with and without cloudy sky. Gaussian noise with varying standard deviations σ_n was added, and the average angular errors and their standard deviations were computed. AAE = average angular error. STD = standard deviation.

Yosemite with clouds			Yosemite without clouds		
σ_n	AAE	STD	σ_n	AAE	STD
0	1.94°	6.02°	0	0.98°	1.17°
10	2.50°	5.96°	10	1.26°	1.29°
20	3.12°	6.24°	20	1.63°	1.39°
30	3.77°	6.54°	30	2.03°	1.53°
40	4.37°	7.12°	40	2.40°	1.71°

two types of motion is preserved, also the translational motion of the clouds is estimated accurately. The reason for this behaviour lies in our assumptions, that are clearly stated in the energy functional: While the choice of the smoothness term allows discontinuities, the gradient constancy assumption is able to handle brightness changes – like in the area of the clouds.

Because of the presence of second order image derivatives in the Euler-Lagrange equations, we tested the influence of noise on the performance of our method in the next experiment. We added Gaussian noise of mean zero and different standard deviations to both sequences. The obtained results are presented in Tab.2. They show that our approach even yields excellent flow estimates when severe noise is present: For the cloudy Yosemite sequence, our average angular error for noise with standard deviation 40 is better than all results from the literature for the sequence *without* noise.

In a third experiment we evaluated the robustness of the free parameters in our approach: the weight γ between the grey value and the gradient constancy assumption, and the smoothness parameter α. Often an image sequence is preprocessed by Gaussian convolution with standard deviation σ [5]. In this case, σ can be regarded as a third parameter. We computed results with parameter settings that deviated by a factor 2 in both directions from the optimum setting. The outcome listed in Tab. 3 shows that the method is also very robust under parameter variations.

Although our paper does not focus on fast computation but on high accuracy, the implicit minimisation scheme presented here is also reasonably fast, especially if the

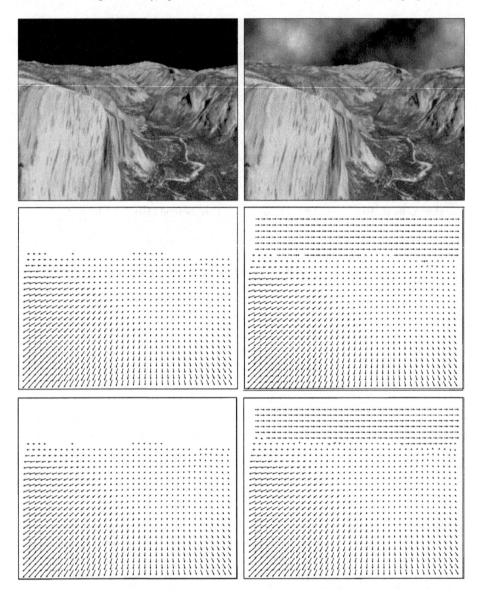

Fig. 1. *(a) Top left:* Frame 8 of the *Yosemite* sequence without clouds. *(b) Top right:* Corresponding frame of the sequence *with* clouds. *(c) Middle left:* Ground truth without clouds. *(d) Middle right:* Ground truth *with* clouds. *(e) Bottom left:* Computed flow field by our 3D method for the sequence without clouds. *(f) Bottom right:* Ditto for the sequence *with* clouds.

reduction factor η is lowered or if the iterations are stopped before full convergence. The convergence behaviour and computation times can be found in Tab. 4. Computations have been performed on a 3.06 GHz Intel Pentium 4 processor executing C/C++ code.

For evaluating the performance of our method for real-world image data, the *Ettlinger Tor* traffic sequence by Nagel was used. This sequence consists of 50 frames of size

Table 3. Parameter variation for our method with spatio-temporal smoothness assumption.

Yosemite with clouds			
σ	α	γ	AAE
0.8	80	100	1.94°
0.4	80	100	2.10°
1.6	80	100	2.04°
0.8	40	100	2.67°
0.8	160	100	2.21°
0.8	80	50	2.07°
0.8	80	200	2.03°

Table 4. Computation times and convergence for Yosemite sequence with clouds.

3D - spatio-temporal method					
reduction factor η	outer fixed point iter.	inner fixed point iter.	SOR iter.	computation time/frame	AAE
0.95	77	5	10	23.4s	1.94°
0.90	38	2	10	5.1s	2.09°
0.80	18	2	10	2.7s	2.56°
0.75	14	1	10	1.2s	3.44°

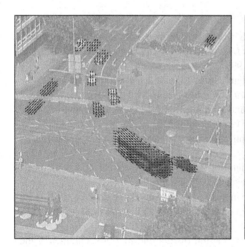 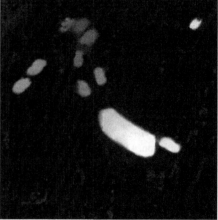

Fig. 2. *(a) Left:* Computed flow field between frame 5 and 6 of the *Ettlinger Tor* traffic sequence. *(b) Right:* Computed magnitude of the optical flow field.

512×512. It is available at http://i21www.ira.uka.de/image_sequences/. In Fig. 2 the computed flow field and its magnitude are shown. Our estimation gives very realistic results, and the algorithm hardly suffers from interlacing artifacts that are present in all frames. Moreover, the flow boundaries are rather sharp and can be used directly for segmentation purposes by applying a simple thresholding step.

6   Conclusion

In this paper we have investigated a continuous, rotationally invariant energy functional for optical flow computations based on two terms: a robust data term with a brightness constancy and a gradient constancy assumption, combined with a discontinuity-preserving spatio-temporal TV regulariser. While each of these concepts has proved its use before (see e.g. [22,26]), we have shown that their combination outperforms all methods from the literature so far. One of the main reasons for this performance is the use of an energy functional with *non-linearised* data term and our strategy to consequently postpone all linearisations to the *numerical* scheme: *While linearisations in the model immediately compromise the overall performance of the system, linearisations in the numerical scheme can help to improve convergence to the global minimum*. Another important result in our paper is the proof that *the widely-used warping can be theoretically justified as a numerical approximation strategy that does not influence the continuous model*. We hope that this strategy of transparent continuous modelling in conjunction with consistent numerical approximations shows that excellent performance and deeper theoretical understanding are not contradictive: They are nothing else but two sides of the same medal.

References

1. L. Alvarez, J. Esclarín, M. Lefébure, and J. Sánchez. A PDE model for computing the optical flow. In *Proc. XVI Congreso de Ecuaciones Diferenciales y Aplicaciones*, pages 1349–1356, Las Palmas de Gran Canaria, Spain, Sept. 1999.
2. L. Alvarez, J. Weickert, and J. Sánchez. Reliable estimation of dense optical flow fields with large displacements. *International Journal of Computer Vision*, 39(1):41–56, Aug. 2000.
3. P. Anandan. A computational framework and an algorithm for the measurement of visual motion. *International Journal of Computer Vision*, 2:283–310, 1989.
4. A. Bab-Hadiashar and D. Suter. Robust optic flow computation. *International Journal of Computer Vision*, 29(1):59–77, Aug. 1998.
5. J. L. Barron, D. J. Fleet, and S. S. Beauchemin. Performance of optical flow techniques. *International Journal of Computer Vision*, 12(1):43–77, Feb. 1994.
6. M. J. Black and P. Anandan. Robust dynamic motion estimation over time. In *Proc. 1991 IEEE Computer Society Conference on Computer Vision and Pattern Recognition*, pages 292–302, Maui, HI, June 1991. IEEE Computer Society Press.
7. M. J. Black and P. Anandan. The robust estimation of multiple motions: parametric and piecewise smooth flow fields. *Computer Vision and Image Understanding*, 63(1):75–104, Jan. 1996.
8. I. Cohen. Nonlinear variational method for optical flow computation. In *Proc. Eighth Scandinavian Conference on Image Analysis*, volume 1, pages 523–530, Tromsø, Norway, May 1993.
9. R. Deriche, P. Kornprobst, and G. Aubert. Optical-flow estimation while preserving its discontinuities: a variational approach. In *Proc. Second Asian Conference on Computer Vision*, volume 2, pages 290–295, Singapore, Dec. 1995.
10. G. Farnebäck. Very high accuracy velocity estimation using orientation tensors, parametric motion, and simultaneous segmentation of the motion field. In *Proc. Eighth International Conference on Computer Vision*, volume 1, pages 171–177, Vancouver, Canada, July 2001. IEEE Computer Society Press.

11. B. Horn and B. Schunck. Determining optical flow. *Artificial Intelligence*, 17:185–203, 1981.
12. S. Ju, M. Black, and A. Jepson. Skin and bones: multi-layer, locally affine, optical flow and regularization with transparency. In *Proc. 1996 IEEE Computer Society Conference on Computer Vision and Pattern Recognition*, pages 307–314, San Francisco, CA, June 1996. IEEE Computer Society Press.
13. S.-H. Lai and B. C. Vemuri. Reliable and efficient computation of optical flow. *International Journal of Computer Vision*, 29(2):87–105, Oct. 1998.
14. M. Lefébure and L. D. Cohen. Image registration, optical flow and local rigidity. *Journal of Mathematical Imaging and Vision*, 14(2):131–147, Mar. 2001.
15. B. Lucas and T. Kanade. An iterative image registration technique with an application to stereo vision. In *Proc. Seventh International Joint Conference on Artificial Intelligence*, pages 674–679, Vancouver, Canada, Aug. 1981.
16. E. Mémin and P. Pérez. A multigrid approach for hierarchical motion estimation. In *Proc. Sixth International Conference on Computer Vision*, pages 933–938, Bombay, India, Jan. 1998. Narosa Publishing House.
17. E. Mémin and P. Pérez. Hierarchical estimation and segmentation of dense motion fields. *International Journal of Computer Vision*, 46(2):129–155, 2002.
18. H.-H. Nagel. Extending the 'oriented smoothness constraint' into the temporal domain and the estimation of derivatives of optical flow. In O. Faugeras, editor, *Computer Vision – ECCV '90*, volume 427 of *Lecture Notes in Computer Science*, pages 139–148. Springer, Berlin, 1990.
19. H.-H. Nagel and W. Enkelmann. An investigation of smoothness constraints for the estimation of displacement vector fields from image sequences. *IEEE Transactions on Pattern Analysis and Machine Intelligence*, 8:565–593, 1986.
20. L. I. Rudin, S. Osher, and E. Fatemi. Nonlinear total variation based noise removal algorithms. *Physica D*, 60:259–268, 1992.
21. C. Schnörr. Segmentation of visual motion by minimizing convex non-quadratic functionals. In *Proc. Twelfth International Conference on Pattern Recognition*, volume A, pages 661–663, Jerusalem, Israel, Oct. 1994. IEEE Computer Society Press.
22. M. Tistarelli. Multiple constraints for optical flow. In J.-O. Eklundh, editor, *Computer Vision – ECCV '94*, volume 800 of *Lecture Notes in Computer Science*, pages 61–70. Springer, Berlin, 1994.
23. S. Uras, F. Girosi, A. Verri, and V. Torre. A computational approach to motion perception. *Biological Cybernetics*, 60:79–87, 1988.
24. J. Weickert, A. Bruhn, and C. Schnörr. Lucas/Kanade meets Horn/Schunck: Combining local and global optic flow methods. Technical Report 82, Dept. of Mathematics, Saarland University, Saarbrücken, Germany, Apr. 2003.
25. J. Weickert and C. Schnörr. A theoretical framework for convex regularizers in PDE-based computation of image motion. *International Journal of Computer Vision*, 45(3):245–264, Dec. 2001.
26. J. Weickert and C. Schnörr. Variational optic flow computation with a spatio-temporal smoothness constraint. *Journal of Mathematical Imaging and Vision*, 14(3):245–255, May 2001.

Model-Based Approach to Tomographic Reconstruction Including Projection Deblurring. Sensitivity of Parameter Model to Noise on Data

Jean Michel Lagrange[1] and Isabelle Abraham[1]

Commissariat à l'Energie Atomique, B.P. 12
91680 Bruyères le Chatel, France
{jean-michel.lagrange,isabelle.abraham}@cea.fr

Abstract. Classical techniques for the reconstruction of axisymmetrical objects are all creating artefacts (smooth or unstable solutions). Moreover, the extraction of *very* precise features related to big density transitions remains quite delicate. In this paper, we develop a new approach -in one dimension for the moment- that allows us both to reconstruct and to extract characteristics: an a priori is provided thanks to a density model. We show the interest of this method in regard to noise effects quantification ; we also explain how to take into account some physical perturbations occuring with real data acquisition.

Keywords: tomography, flexible models, regularization, deblurring.

1 Introduction

From the last ten years, teams of researchers have worked on tomographic reconstruction of objects from a very little number of views ; the final goal being to delimit very precisely big transitions of density between the various materials [15,8,20,19,23,9] (typically in angiography) and also to restitute good values of the density field when the objects are not binary.

The general context of our study is the reconstruction, from a single X-ray photograph, of an object with a symmetry of revolution ; here, we assume that X-rays are parallel (because the objects are sufficiently far from the emitter) and monoenergetic. This work is part of a hydrodynamic high yield test project where we study the dynamic behaviour of objects constrained by shock waves produced with explosives. Due to the very hostile experimental environment, there is only a single X-ray machine. So as to make out the signals received on detectors, we have to research, from the unique projection, the interfaces between the different areas of the object in order to labellize a posteriori the materials. Moreover, it is fundamental, for us, to estimate precisely their respective masses: this operation implies a very good knowlegde of the density field $\rho : I\!\!R^3 \longrightarrow I\!\!R$.

T. Pajdla and J. Matas (Eds.): ECCV 2004, LNCS 3024, pp. 37–49, 2004.

The data we get in our experiences are formed in the following way:

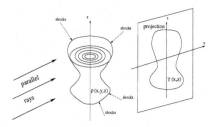

The attenuations of the X-ray beam are given by

$$att(x, z) = e^{-\int_l \frac{\mu}{\rho}(x,y,z)\rho(x,y,z)dl}$$

where $\frac{\mu}{\rho}(x, y, z)$ is the attenuation coefficient at the point (x, y, z). As source illumination is monoenergetic, we can define a reference attenuation coefficient $(\frac{\mu}{\rho})_{ref}$, constant everywhere in the spatial domain. This allows us to write:

$$att(x, z) = e^{-(\frac{\mu}{\rho})_{ref} \int_l \frac{\frac{\mu}{\rho}(x,y,z)}{(\frac{\mu}{\rho})_{ref}} \rho(x,y,z)dl} = e^{-(\frac{\mu}{\rho})_{ref} \int_l \rho_{ref}(x,y,z)dl}$$

where ρ_{ref} is the equivalent density of the reference material. The quantity

$$\mathcal{Y}(x, z) = \int_l \rho_{ref}(x, y, z)dl \tag{1}$$

is defined as the projection of the equivalent object.

Remark 1. *If ρ_{ref} is known at each point (x, y, z) and if the materials are labellized (very often thanks to expert analysis) then $\frac{\mu}{\rho}(x, y, z)$ is known and the whole density field can be obtained using the following conversion:*

$$\rho(x, y, z) = \rho_{ref}(x, y, z) \times \frac{(\frac{\mu}{\rho})_{ref}}{\frac{\mu}{\rho}(x, y, z)} \tag{2}$$

The datas $\mathcal{Y}$ of the reconstruction processes are biased by the systems of production and acquisition of X-ray photons. The two main perturbations are the **additive noise on the projections** and the presence of **blur** due to the X source and the detector (see [18] for more details).

Under these hypotheses, tomographic reconstruction of axisymmetrical objects from a single projection is technically achievable [1] (thanks to axisymmetry) but it remains very delicate: generally, this leads to an inverse problem which is well known to be ill-posed in the sense of Hadamard [13] because the solution sensitivity (to noise) is very high.

Historically, in this context, Abel proposed in 1826 [1] a method based on the inversion of his tranform [3]. This approach has been improved more recently [5] [14] [11] so as to decrease the artefacts generated by noise on projections. However, the results remain again too unstable.

Some authors [14] [10] [16] proposed also to adapt classical techniques used in "conventional" tomography (Fourier synthesis and filtered backprojection): the idea is to duplicate the unique projection to simulate acquisition from a large number of angles. All these reconstructions have in common to create loss of resolution while correlating noise leading to difficult segmentations.

Thanks to an optimal meshing technique described in [7], it is also possible to get, for each plane section of the object, a reconstruction by *Generalized Inversion* based on a natural sampling in torus:

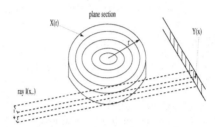

with $Y(x) = \mathcal{Y}(x,.)$ and $X(r) = X(\sqrt{x^2 + y^2}) = \rho_{ref}(x, y, .)$. On each section, we have a relation between Y and X given by $Y = HX$, where H is the projection matrix which is upper triangular and well conditionned. The solution is then simple and easy to compute as it consists in matrix inversion and multiplication, but it is very unstable: the noise is amplified, merely near the axis of symmetry [7].

The poor quality of the estimated density field lead to the introduction of regularization processes. The very easy Tikhonov-based approaches [24] are not efficient enough here because the solution is too smooth. Jean Marc Dinten [7] used Random Markov Fields (in the definition of a priori energy in a MAP criterium) allowing to decrease noise influence while preserving high density transitions. His method is indeed efficient but their remain a lot of parameters whose regulation is not straightforward.

The common characteristic of all the previous approaches is that they provide an equivalent density field ρ_{ref} which is not segmented in materials. So they necessit a supplementary process of labellization obtained after contour extraction and expert analysis in order to correct the density thanks to equation 2. The consequence is that additional uncertainties, inherent to the contour extractor, are added on the final field ρ.

Moreover, the blur present on attenuations (see section 4) is not taken into account (direct deblurring being not satisfactory) during the reconstruction process. The main effect, as shown in section 4, is to modify the estimated masses for all the materials.

In this paper, we propose a new approach where we introduce an a priori on the shape of the objects: an axisymmetrical density model. First, we treat a 1D technique where each plane section is processed in an independent way. In our experiences of high yield hydrodynamic, the shock wave propagation and multiple reflexion phenomena generate areas with approximatively linear varying

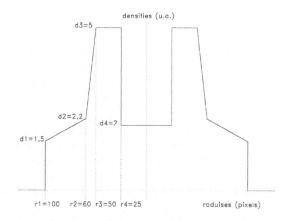

Fig. 1. Example of 1D density model

densities. (which is confirmed by physicists expert analysis), so a 1D realistic model, illustrated on figure 1, is built by juxtaposition of constant density areas and of linear varying density areas.

In section 2, we detail this approach by fitting of model. In section 3, we present a sensitivity study of the parameters of the deformable model in the case where the data are noisy. This is compared with the uncertainties obtained when we use the results of generalized inversion (that will be our reference method in this paper). In section 4, an original way to achieve deblurring/reconstruction from blurred data is exposed.

2   1D Reconstruction

We have presented, formerly, "classical techniques" for the reconstruction of a plane section of an object in equivalent densities. We also have mentionned the necessity to labellize the materials so as to correct their density.

We propose here a new approach that allows both to reconstruct and to extract the searched characteristics of the objects (radiuses of interfaces r_i and densities d_j as illustrated on figure 1) thanks to the introduction of an important a priori on the density. If we denote $\omega \in I\!R^n$ (where n is the number of parameters of the 1D model) the vector of radiuses r_i and of densities d_j, x the pixels' abscissa, $Y(x)$ the data (areal masses) and $proj_\omega(x)$ the projection model, the problem of reconstruction can be stated as follow:

$$(\mathcal{P}) \begin{cases} \widetilde{\omega} &= \arg\min_{\omega\in\Omega} \|proj_\omega - Y\|_2^2 = \arg\min_{\omega\in\Omega}(\varepsilon^2) \\ (\mathcal{C}) : & \theta(\omega) \geq 0, \\ \Omega &= \{\omega \in I\!R^n \ / \ \omega_l \leq \omega \leq \omega_u\} \end{cases} \tag{3}$$

where $\widetilde{\omega}$ is the solution $(\mathcal{P})$ that minimizes ε^2 ; The constraints $(\mathcal{C})$ are used to limit the domain and to ensure the existence of all the areas during the process (it's to say $r_i > r_{i+1}, \forall i$). We can notice here that the criteria ε^2 is defined continuously on Ω and performs a **sub-pixel reconstruction**.

The analysis of minimization methods (simulated annealing [12], I.C.M. [2] and gradient descents [4] [22] [21]), leads us to choose gradient descents under inequality contraints because they are faster and easier to compute with constraints (Lagrange multiplier theory) ; they also preserve the continuous aspect of the criteria.

The main problem is that $proj_\omega$, and consequently ε^2, are C^1 almost everywhere on Ω but on a finite number of points: we can show that ε^2 is infinitely differentiable with respect to the d_i and differentiable with respect to the r_i everywhere but on $r_i = |x|$, where x are the discrete positions of the data. So as to get C^1 class on Ω, we have proposed two kinds of regularizations.

Remark 2. *We will denote $A \underset{\omega}{\star} B$ the convolution of A and B in Ω and $A \underset{x}{\star} B$ the result of a spatial convolution.*

2.1   Regularization by Convolution

The main idea is to find a function $h : \mathbb{R}^n \longrightarrow \mathbb{R}^n$, C^1 class on Ω, such that $\left[proj_\omega \underset{\omega}{\star} h \right]$ is C^1 on Ω. So, the new criteria defined by

$$\varepsilon^2 = \left\| \left[proj_\omega \underset{\omega}{\star} h \right] - Y \right\|_2^2 \tag{4}$$

will have the desired property. An analysis of $\left[proj_\omega \underset{\omega}{\star} h \right]$ provides us a simple expression for h:

$$h(\omega) = \prod_{i=1}^{n_r} h_{1D}(r_i) \tag{5}$$

where n_r is the number of interface radiuses and h_{1D} a kernel defined on $\mathbb{R}$.

The kernel h_{1D} can then be expressed in the following way:

$$h_{1D}(r) = \frac{1}{\beta} \times f\left(\frac{r-x}{\beta} \right) \text{ if } x \in [r - \beta, r + \beta] \tag{6}$$

(β is the regularization parameter), where f is a gaussian like function whose support is $[-1, 1]$.

This technique proved to be efficient as we have obtained the convergence of the process of minimization of the energy given by equation 4 (for $\beta > 1$ numerically). But, as expected, the final solution depends sometimes severely on the choice of the regularization parameter β.

2.2   Regularization with a Weighting Function

In the previous subsection, we provide a way to solve our minimization problem. Unfortunately, we found that the final estimate of ω was unacceptably dependent on the regularization parameter β. Here, we propose a new manner to regularize that is simpler and quite "transparent" (i.e. independent of regularization parameters).

Let $u : \mathbb{R} \times \Omega \longrightarrow \mathbb{R}$ be a function of class $C^p, p \geq 1$, that equals zero in a neighbourhood of all the singular points r_i, then the criteria:

$$\varepsilon^2 = \sum_{x \in \mathcal{D}} \left\{ u(x,\omega) \left(proj_\omega(x) - Y(x) \right)^2 \right\}, \tag{7}$$

where $\mathcal{D}$ is the set of measure points, is C^p class on Ω.

The function u can be chosen as follow:

$$u(x,\omega) = \prod_{i=1}^{n_r} u(x, r_i) \tag{8}$$

where $u(x,0)$ is an even function, equaling 0 in $[0, \epsilon]$ and 1 in $[k\epsilon, +\infty[$. Its graph (and the one of its first and second derivative with respect to r) is given by:

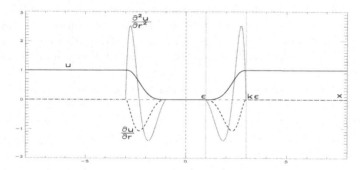

This approach, much more faster than the previous, allowed us to solve our minimization problem. Moreover, it appears that the final solution is quite independent of the choice of ϵ and k that we fix respectively at 1 and 3.

However, before reconstructing the object by 1D fitting, we must calculate the optimal number of linear varying density areas. If we denote $\widetilde{\sigma^2}$ an estimate of the noise variance, we demonstrated that this is number is correct if the optimal value of the criteria $\varepsilon^2(\widetilde{\omega})$ is close enough to $\widetilde{\sigma^2}$ and if the sensitivity (to noise present on the projections) of the parameter ω (whose expression is given in the next section) is small. For our objects, a model with eight parameters and two linear-varying areas (see figure 1) is always optimal.

3   Sensitivity to Noise

Getting a good precision on the position of the interfaces is very important in our context. If the function u defined in 2.2 is built to be C^2 class on $\mathbb{R} \times \mathbb{R}^n$, then the criteria given by equation 7 is C^2 on Ω. The zero-crossing condition of the gradient of ε^2 in an acceptable openset leads to an implicit system $F(\omega, Y) = 0$ where F is continuously differentiable and has an inversible jacobian matrix. Under these conditions, the implicit functions theorem [6] guaranties the existence of a function G (such that $\omega = G(Y)$) that is differentiable with respect to $Y(x)$ and whose derivative is:

$$G'(Y) = \left(\frac{\partial^2 \varepsilon^2}{\partial \omega_i \partial \omega_j} \right)^{-1}_{(i,j) \in I^2} \times \left(\frac{\partial^2 \varepsilon^2}{\partial \omega_i \partial Y_j} \right)_{(i,j) \in I \times J} \tag{9}$$

where I is the set $\{1...n\}$, J the set $\{1...N\}$, n the number of model parameters and N the number of data $Y(x)$.

In our case, we can assume that the additive noise on Y is gaussian, zero mean, spatially uncorrelated and stationary ($\sim N_N \left(0, \Sigma_b = \sigma^2 \times I_N \right)$) so, the differential expression $d\omega = G'(Y)dY$ allows us to compute the covariance matrix of ω:

$$\Sigma_\omega = G'(Y) \times \Sigma_b \times G'(Y)^t \tag{10}$$

So as to compare the precision on interfaces obtained with the present model-based approach and the classical approach (generalized inversion followed by contour extraction), we have also established the law of positions for this latter. This work is developped in an internal document whose main results are given here. To illustrate these results we generate our data by projection of the model given on figure 1.

So as to compare the two reconstructions (from model-based and classical approaches) when the projections are noisy, we add a realistic gaussian noise of standard deviation 8, as presented on figure 2. The comparison of the reconstructions with fitting and generalized inversion are then illustrated on figure 3.

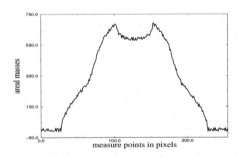

Fig. 2. noisy projection of the model

The strong unstability of the reconstruction obtained by generalized inversion (dotted lines) appears clearly whereas the model obtained by fitting (continuous line) is very similar to figure 1. For fitting, the parameter standard deviations (calculated with formula 10) are very low. We deduce absolute errors less than 2% for densities d_i, and the variation of the interfaces positions does not exceed

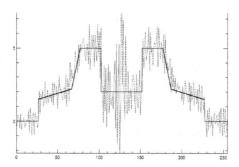

Fig. 3. comparison of the reconstructions (Generalized inversion in dotted and our approach in continuous line)

a half pixel. These results confirm the very good stability of reconstruction by fitting. For generalized inversion, error on density is between 10 and 90% and the standard deviation of interface position error is between 1 and 2 pixels.

We can conclude that *our approach* provides undoubtedly a *very important increase in precision* on the characteristic parameters that we are looking for.

4   1D Deblurring of 2D Blur

Blur is mainly due to the fact that the X-ray transmitter is not a pinpoint source of light; moreover, the detector acts as a low-pass filter. In the current section, we suppose that the blur kernel H^{2D} associated to those perturbations is circular symmetric with a known shape (from a specific experience). The origin of this perturbation is in the energy domain of X photons (i.e. attenuations of X photons going through the object). So, the blurred projection $\mathcal{Y}_{blur}$ is a function of the ideal projection $\mathcal{Y}$ of the object and is defined by:

$$\mathcal{Y}_{blur}(x, z) = -\left(\frac{\mu}{\rho}\right)^{-1} \ln\left[e^{-\frac{\mu}{\rho}\mathcal{Y}} \underset{x,z}{\star} H^{2D}\right](x, z) \tag{11}$$

This expression allows us to state a very important result: the total mass of the blurred object (M_{blur}) is different from its real mass (M). This is due to the fact that:

$$\left[M_{blur} = \int_{I\!R^2} \mathcal{Y}_{blur}\right] \neq \left[M = \int_{I\!R^2} \mathcal{Y}\right] \tag{12}$$

and therefore M can't be deduced directly from the data $\mathcal{Y}_{blur}$.

Mass retrieval of each materials constituting the object is one of the most important goal of our study. So the necessity to deblur the projections $\mathcal{Y}_{blur}$ is evident. Classical operations like Wiener, RIF filtering, ... [17] do not provide satisfactory results in our context because Y exhibits very high frequencies, additive noise is quite white and blur kernels are quite narrow.

In this section, we first deal with the general problem of the deblurring/ reconstruction in one dimension from a projection Y_{blur} blurred with a kernel H (formula 11 written in 1D). Afterwards, we develop the case of two kinds of 3D objects for which this process is achievable.

4.1   The Problem in One Dimension

So as to introduce a deblurring operation during reconstruction by fitting, we define the criteria in the following way:

$$\varepsilon^2 = \sum_{x \in \mathcal{D}} \left[\left(\frac{\mu}{\rho}\right)^{-1} \times \ln\left(e^{-\frac{\mu}{\rho}proj_\omega} \underset{x}{\star} H\left(x\right)\right) + Y\left(x\right) \right]^2 \tag{13}$$

In order to use a gradient descent to compute the solution of our problem, we first need to verify the differentiability of ε^2 with respect to ω, and so to analyse its partial derivatives with respect to ω_i:

$$\frac{\partial \varepsilon^2}{\partial \omega_i} =$$

$$2 \times \sum_{x \in \mathcal{D}} \left\{ \left[\left(\frac{\mu}{\rho}\right)^{-1} . \ln\left(e^{-\frac{\mu}{\rho}proj_\omega} \underset{x}{\star} H\left(x\right)\right) + Y\left(x\right) \right] \times \left[\frac{\left(\frac{\partial proj_\omega}{\partial \omega_i} . e^{-\frac{\mu}{\rho}proj_\omega}\right) \underset{x}{\star} H\left(x\right)}{e^{-\frac{\mu}{\rho}proj_\omega} \underset{x}{\star} H\left(x\right)} \right] \right\}$$

$$\tag{14}$$

If we denote att_{blur} the blurred attenuation of the object given by:

$$att_{blur}(x) = \int_{\mathbb{R}} \left(e^{-\frac{\mu}{\rho}proj_\omega(\tau)} \times H(x - \tau)d\tau \right) \tag{15}$$

then the only problematic term in the computation of the gradient is:

$$\left(\frac{\partial att_{blur}}{\partial \omega_i}\right)(x) = \left(\left(\frac{\partial proj_\omega}{\partial \omega_i}\right) e^{-\frac{\mu}{\rho}proj_\omega}\right) \underset{x}{\star} H(x) \tag{16}$$

because the derivatives of the projection do not exist for all the values of the parameter ω. We have shown that, in fact, the main difficulty is generically reduced to the case of a model with a constant density area whose parameters are called r and D, for which the expression of the previous equation turns out to be:

$$\frac{\partial att_{blur}}{\partial r}(x) = 2.D.r \int_{-r}^{r} \left(\frac{1}{\sqrt{r^2 - \tau^2}} \times e^{-\frac{\mu}{\rho}proj_\omega(\tau)} \times H(x - \tau)d\tau \right)$$

$$= \int_{-r}^{r} K(r, \tau, x)d\tau \tag{17}$$

The function $K(., \tau, .)$ can be integrated on $[-r, r]$ so this expression shows that ε^2 is differentiable if the convolution integral is performed on a continuous domain. In conclusion, the criteria is numerically not differentiable with respect to the r_i.

In the two following items, we demonstrate that, from the definition of a non differentiable criteria, we can supply very good approximations of its "true" gradient (i.e. calculated continuously as in 17) and so ensure the convergence of the minimization scheme to the exact solution.

Explicit Computation of the Gradient. If we denote τ_0 a positive integer lower than r and belonging to the set $\mathcal{D}$ (the set of points of measure x defined in 2.2), then a reformulation of equation 17 leads to:

$$\frac{1}{2.D.r} \cdot \frac{\partial att_{blur}}{\partial r}(x) = \underbrace{\int_{-\tau_0}^{\tau_0} K(r, \tau, x)d\tau}_{\substack{\text{computation by Discrete} \\ \text{Fourier Transform}}} + \underbrace{\int_{\tau_0}^{r} K(r, \tau, x)d\tau}_{\text{first rest } R.(x)} + \underbrace{\int_{-r}^{-\tau_0} K(r, \tau, x)d\tau}_{R.(x) = R.(-x)}$$

The first term is easily computable and the only difficult issue is the rest $R_1(x)$. Thanks to an integration of $R_1(x)$ by parts, we finally get a numerically convergent integral and then the searched approximation of the gradient.

The main drawback of this method is that we must have a formal expression of the blur kernel H, which is not the case in general.

Computation in the Fourier Domain. Let's recall the main problem in equation 16: the generic expression $\frac{\partial proj_\omega}{\partial r}(x)$ does not exist for all x. But, its Fourier Transform is defined everywhere and is given by its cosine transform:

$$\widehat{\frac{\partial proj_\omega}{\partial r}}(f) = \int_{-r}^{r} \frac{1}{\sqrt{r^2 - x^2}} \times \cos(2\pi x f)dx = \int_0^\pi \cos(2\pi r f \cos(\theta))d\theta = \pi \times J_0(2\pi r f)$$

We can now write the computation of blurred attenuation (eq. 17) if we adopt the following process:

$$\begin{cases} \frac{\partial att_{blur}}{\partial r}(x) = \left(\frac{\partial proj_\omega}{\partial r} \times e^{-\frac{\mu}{\rho}proj_\omega}\right) \star H(x) \\ \qquad FT \downarrow \qquad DFT \downarrow \qquad \downarrow DFT \\ \widehat{\frac{\partial att_{blur}}{\partial r}}(f) = \left(\widehat{\frac{\partial proj_\omega}{\partial r}} \star \widehat{e^{-\frac{\mu}{\rho}proj_\omega}}\right) \times \widehat{H}(f) \end{cases} \qquad (18)$$

where the convolution, in the Fourier domain, between $\widehat{e^{-\frac{\mu}{\rho}proj_\omega}}$ and $\widehat{\frac{\partial proj_\omega}{\partial r}}$ uses a sampling of $\widehat{\frac{\partial proj_\omega}{\partial r}}$; $\frac{\partial att_{blur}}{\partial r}$ is given by the inverse DFT of $\widehat{\frac{\partial att_{blur}}{\partial r}}$, which finally allows us to provide an approximation of the gradient of ε^2.

If we compare this technique with the one presented previously, we can notice that we don't have to know continuously the blur kernel H. The only constraints come from the sampling of the Fourier Transform of $\frac{\partial proj_\omega}{\partial r}$. It is indeed vanishing very slowly, so the cancellation of high frequencies generates small artefacts. However, these perturbations remain low enough not to disturb the minimization process. This approach is moreover the fastest one.

In the following two subsections, we deal with two kinds of 3D objects for which an extension of 1D deblurring/reconstruction by fitting is possible and moreover, once again, exact.

4.2   Application to "3D Cylindrical Objects"

For this kind of object, the projections $\mathcal{Y}$ are independent of z, so we can identify the 1D projection $Y(x)$ to $\mathcal{Y}(x, z)$, $\forall z$. So as to be able to use the previous results, we must search an expression relating the kernel H^{2D} applied to $\mathcal{Y}$ to a 1D kernel denoted H (that will be convolved with Y) that verifies:

$$\mathcal{Y}_{blur}(x, z) = \mathcal{Y} \underset{x,z}{\star} H^{2D}(x, z) = Y \underset{x}{\star} H(x), \forall z \tag{19}$$

This kernel H is known to be the Abel Transform [3] of H^{2D} and is given by:

$$H(x) = \int_x^\infty \left(\frac{2y \times \widetilde{H^{2D}}(y)}{\sqrt{y^2 - x^2}} \right) dy = AT\left[H^{2D}\right](x) \tag{20}$$

with $\widetilde{H^{2D}}(\sqrt{u^2 + v^2}) = H^{2D}(u, v)$, $\forall(u, v) \in \mathbb{R}^2$.

With this new definition of the criteria to be minimized:

$$\varepsilon^2 = \sum_{x \in \mathcal{D}} \left[\left(\frac{\mu}{\rho}\right)^{-1} \ln \left(e^{-\frac{\mu}{\rho} proj_\omega} \underset{x}{\star} \underbrace{AT\left[H^{2D}\right](x)}_{H} \right) + \mathcal{Y}_{blur}(x, .) \right]^2 \tag{21}$$

the problem is then well posed.

The results we have obtained with this technique are flagrant because, if the blur kernel is known, the reconstruction by model fitting is then exact, whereas classical techniques provide a very smooth reconstruction, often far from the object. An example is illustrated on next figure where our exact reconstruction is drawn in continuous lines and the reconstruction obtained by generalized inversion is in dotted.

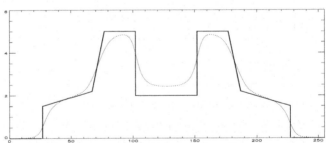

4.3   Application to 3D Spherical Objects

In this case, the 2D data $\mathcal{Y}$ are the projections of a spherical axisymmetrical object. They are then circular symmetrical, centered at the point (c, c) and Y can be defined by $\mathcal{Y}(x, c)$. If we use here a property of the Hankel Transform [3] (denoted HT), we get:

$$HT\left[\mathcal{Y}_{blur}(., c)\right](q) = HT\left[\mathcal{Y} \underset{x,z}{\star} H^{2D}(., c)\right](q) = HT[Y](q) \times HT\left[\widetilde{H^{2D}}\right](q) \tag{22}$$

where $\widetilde{H^{2D}}$ is given by formula 4.2. This expression allows us to identify H:

$$HT\,[H]\,(q) = HT\left[\widetilde{H^{2D}}\right](q) \tag{23}$$

The problem is then well posed if we formulate the criteria ε^2 as

$$\varepsilon^2 = \sum_{x\in\mathcal{D}}\left[-\left(\frac{\mu}{\rho}\right)^{-1}\ln\left\{HT^{-1}\!\left(HT\left[e^{-\frac{\mu}{\rho}proj_\omega}\right]\times HT\left[\widetilde{H^{2D}}\right]\right)(x)\right\}-\mathcal{Y}_{blur}(x,c)\right]^2$$

We demonstrate, thanks to relation 4.3, that the reconstruction is indeed achievable. But the processing of direct and inverse Hankel Transforms remains a delicate problem and extensively increases computation time.

5 Conclusion

In this paper, we have presented an original approach to the problem of tomographic reconstruction of an axisymmetrical object from one view. First, we have developped a 1D study where we deform a simple model of the object based on a description in density areas. We have described the formal aspects of the reconstruction and proposed two efficient regularizations allowing to minimize the derived energy by gradient descent under inequality constraints. We have also studied the bias generated by the noise on projections ; moreover, we have proposed a new formulation of the problem that enables us to deblur the projections during the reconstruction by fitting. In each case, we have compared our results to a reconstruction with generalized inversion ; we have obtained an important improvement in precision on the characteristic parameters we are looking for.

Our future works deal with the warping of a fully 3D axisymmetrical model of the objects. We are now working on the construction of smooth 3D density fields inserted between axisymmetrical surfaces under hypotheses of quasi linearity of the density.

References

1. N. H. Abel. Résolution d'un problème de mécanique. *J. Reine u. Angew. Math.*, 1:153–157, 1826.
2. J. Besag. On the statistical analysis of dirty pictures. *J.R. Static. Soc. Ser. B48*, 3:259–279, 1986.
3. R. Bracewell. *The fourier transform and its applications*. Mc Graw-Hill, , deuxième edition, 1978.
4. J. C. Culioli and P. Charpentier. *cours de l'école nationale des Mines de Paris*, volume II- optimisation libre en dimension finie. 1990.
5. M. Deutsch and I. Beniaminy. Derivative free inversion of abel's integral equation. *Applied Physics Letters*, 41(1), July 1982.
6. J. Dieudonne. *Eléments d'analyse*, volume 3. Gauthier-Villars, 1982.

7. J. M. Dinten. *Tomographie à partir d'un nombre limité de projections: régularisation par des champs markoviens*. PhD thesis, Université de Paris Sud, centre d'Orsay, 1990.

8. A. M. Djafari. Image reconstruction of a compact object from a few number of projections. *IASTED SIP 96, Floride*, November 1996.

9. A. M. Djafari. Slope reconstruction in X-ray tomography. *Processing of SPIE 1997, San Diego*, July 1997.

10. N. J. Dusaussoy. Image reconstruction from projections. *SPIE's international symposium on optics, imaging and instrumentation, San Diego*, July 1994.

11. E. Fugelso. Material density measurement from dynamic flash X-ray photographs using axisymmetric tomography. *Los Alamos Publication*, March 1981.

12. S. Geman and D. Geman. Stochastic relaxation, Gibbs distribution, and the bayesian restoration of images. *Transactions on pattern analysis and machine intelligence*, PAMI 6, n. 6:721–741, 1994.

13. J. Hadamard. Sur les problèmes aux dérivées partielles et leur signification physique. *Princetown University Bulletin*, 1902.

14. K. M. Hanson. Tomographic reconstruction of axially symmetric objects from a single radiograph. *Proceedings of the 16th International congress on high speed photography and photonics, Strasbourg*, Août 1984.

15. K. M. Hanson, G. S. Cunningham, G. R. Jennings, and D. R. Wolf. Tomographic reconstruction based on flexible geometric models. *Proceedings of the IEEE international conference on image processing, Austin , Texas*, November 1994.

16. Gabor T. Herman. *Image reconstruction from projections, the fundamentals of computerized tomography*. Academic Press, 1980.

17. A. J. Kain. *Fundamentals of digital signal processing*. Prentice Hall. International edition.

18. J. M. Lagrange. *Reconstruction tomographique à partir d'un petit nombre de vues*. PhD thesis, Ecole Normale Supérieure de Cachan, 1998.

19. H. Maître, C. Pellot, A. Herment, M. Sigelle, P. Horain, and P. Peronneau. A 3D reconstruction of vascular structures from two X-rays angiograms using an adapted simulated annealing algorithm. *IEEE transactions on medical imaging*, 13(1), March 1994.

20. C. Pellot, A. Herment, M. Sigelle, P. Horain, and P. Peronneau. Segmentation, modelling and reconstruction of arterial bifurcations in digital angiography. *Medical and biological engeeneering andcomputing*, November 1992.

21. M. J. D. Powell and Y. Yuan. A recursive quadratic programming algorithm that uses differentiable exact penalty functions. *Mathematical programming*, 35:265–278, 1986.

22. K. Schittkowski. Solving non linear problems with very many constraints. *Optimization*, 25:179–196, 1992.

23. M. Senasli, L. Garnero, A. Herment, and C. Pellot. Stochastic active contour model for 3D reconstruction from two X-ray projections. *1995 international meeting on fully 3D image reconstruction in radiology and nuclear medecine, Grenoble*, July 1995.

24. A. Tikhonov and V. Arsenin. *Solutions off il-posed problems*. Washington DC: Winston, 1977.

Unlevel-Sets: Geometry and Prior-Based Segmentation

Tammy Riklin-Raviv[1], Nahum Kiryati[1], and Nir Sochen[2]

. School of Electrical Engineering
. Dept. of Applied Mathematics
Tel Aviv University, Tel Aviv 69978, Israel

Abstract. We present a novel variational approach to top-down image segmentation, which accounts for significant projective transformations between a *single* prior image and the image to be segmented. The proposed segmentation process is coupled with reliable estimation of the transformation parameters, without using point correspondences. The prior shape is represented by a *generalized cone* that is based on the contour of the reference object. Its *unlevel* sections correspond to possible instances of the visible contour under perspective distortion and scaling. We extend the Chan-Vese energy functional by adding a shape term. This term measures the distance between the currently estimated section of the generalized cone and the region bounded by the zero-crossing of the evolving level set function. Promising segmentation results are obtained for images of rotated, translated, corrupted and partly occluded objects. The recovered transformation parameters are compatible with the ground truth.

1   Introduction

Classical methods for object segmentation and boundary determination rely on local image features such as gray level values or image gradients. However, when the image to segment is noisy or taken under poor illumination conditions, purely local algorithms are inadequate. Global features, such as contour length and piecewise smoothness [16], can be incorporated using a variational segmentation framework, see [1] and references therein. The handling of contours is facilitated by the level set approach [17]. In the presence of occlusion, shadows and low image contrast, prior knowledge on the shape of interest is necessary [20]. The recovered object boundary should then be compatible with the expected contour, in addition to being constrained by length, smoothness and fidelity to the observed image.

The main difficulty in the integration of prior information into the variational segmentation process is the need to account for possible pose transformations between the known contour of the given object instance and the boundary in the image to be segmented. Many algorithms [4,6,5,14,19,13] use a comprehensive training set to account for small deformations. These methods employ various statistical approaches to characterize the probability distribution of the shapes.

T. Pajdla and J. Matas (Eds.): ECCV 2004, LNCS 3024, pp. 50–61, 2004.

They then measure the similarity between the evolving object boundary (or level set function) and representatives of the training data. The performance of these methods depends on the size and coverage of the training set. Furthermore, none of the existing methods accommodates perspective transformations in measuring the distance between the known instance of the object and the currently segmented image.

We suggest a new method which employs a *single* prior image and accounts for significant *projective* transformations within a variational segmentation framework. This is made possible by two main novelties: the special form of the shape prior, and the integration of the projective transformations via *unleveled* sections. These allow concurrent segmentation and explicit recovery of projective transformation in a reliable way. Neither point correspondence nor direct methods [12] are used. The prior knowledge is represented by a *generalized cone*, which is constructed based on the known instance of the object contour. When the center of projection of a camera coincides with the vertex of the generalized cone, we are able to model the effects of the scene geometry.

We use an extension of the Chan-Vese functional [3] to integrate image data constraints with geometric shape knowledge. The level set function and the projective transformation parameters are estimated in alternation by minimization of the energy functional. The additional energy term that accounts for prior knowledge is a distance measure between a planar (not necessarily horizontal) section of the generalized cone and the zero-crossing of the evolving level set function. Correct segmentation of partly occluded and corrupted images is demonstrated based on a prior image taken with different perspective distortion. The transformation parameters are recovered as well and are in good agreement with the ground truth.

2   Unlevel-Sets

2.1   Previous Framework

Mumford and Shah [16] proposed to segment an input image $f: \Omega \to \mathbb{R}$ by minimizing the functional

$$E(u, C) = \frac{1}{2} \int_{\Omega} (f - u)^2 dxdy + \lambda \frac{1}{2} \int_{\Omega - C} |\nabla u|^2 dxdy + \nu |C| , \qquad (1)$$

simultaneously with respect to the segmenting boundary C and the piecewise smooth approximation u, of the input image f.

When the weight λ of the smoothness term tends to infinity, u becomes a piecewise constant approximation, $u = \{u_i\}$, of f. We proceed with

$$E(u, C) = \frac{1}{2} \sum_i \int_{\Omega_i} (f - u_i)^2 dxdy + \nu |C| \qquad \cup_i \Omega_i = \Omega, \quad \Omega_i \cap \Omega_j = \emptyset \quad (2)$$

In the two phase case, Chan and Vese [3] used a level-set function $\phi \in \mathbb{R}^3$ to embed the contour $C = \{x \in \Omega | \phi(x) = 0\}$, and introduced the Heaviside function $H(\phi)$ into the energy functional:

$$E_{CV}(\phi, u_+, u_-) = \int_{\Omega} \left[(f - u_+)^2 H(\phi) + (f - u_-)^2 (1 - H(\phi)) + \nu |\nabla H(\phi)| \right] dxdy \tag{3}$$

where

$$H(\phi) = \begin{cases} 1 & \phi \geq 0 \\ 0 & \text{otherwise} \end{cases} \tag{4}$$

Using Euler-Lagrange equations for the functional (3), the following gradient descent equation for the evolution of ϕ is obtained:

$$\frac{\partial \phi}{\partial t} = \delta(\phi) \left[\nu \; \text{div} \; (\frac{\nabla \phi}{|\nabla \phi|}) - (f - u_+)^2 + (f - u_-)^2 \right] . \tag{5}$$

A smooth approximation of $H(\phi)$ (and $\delta(\phi)$) must be used in practice [3]. The scalars u_+ and u_- are updated in alternation with the level set evolution to take the mean value of the input image f in the regions $\phi \geq 0$ and $\phi < 0$, respectively:

$$u_+ = \frac{\int f(x,y) H(\phi) dxdy}{\int H(\phi) dxdy} \qquad u_- = \frac{\int f(x,y)(1 - H(\phi)) dxdy}{\int (1 - H(\phi)) dxdy} \tag{6}$$

2.2   Shape Prior

The energetic formulation (3) can be extended by adding a prior shape term [7]:

$$E(\phi, u_+, u_-) = E_{CV}(\phi, u_+, u_-) + \mu E_{shape}(\phi), \qquad \mu \geq 0. \tag{7}$$

We present two novel contributions to this framework. One is a reformulation of the distance measure between the prior and the evolving level-set function, outlined, in a preliminary form, in the rest of this subsection and finalized in subsection 2.5. The other is our unique way of embedding the prior contour within the energy functional, motivated in subsections 2.3-2.4, and formulated in subsection 2.5.

Initially, the shape-term we incorporate in the energy functional measures the non-overlapping areas between the prior shape and the evolving shape. Let $\tilde{\phi}$ be the level set function embedding a prior shape contour. Then

$$E_{shape}(\phi) = \int_{\Omega} \left(H(\phi(x,y)) - H(\tilde{\phi}(x,y)) \right)^2 dxdy \tag{8}$$

Note that we do not enforce the evolving level set function ϕ to resemble $\tilde{\phi}$, instead we demand similarity of the regions within the respective contours. Minimizing this functional with respect to ϕ leads to the following evolution equation:

$$\frac{\partial \phi}{\partial t} = \delta(\phi) \left[\nu \; \text{div} \; (\frac{\nabla \phi}{|\nabla \phi|}) - (f - u_+)^2 + (f - u_-)^2 - 2\mu \left(H(\phi) - H(\tilde{\phi}) \right) \right] \tag{9}$$

This shape-term is adequate when the prior and segmented shapes are not subject to different perspective distortions. Otherwise, the shape-term should incorporate the projective transformation, as detailed in subsections 2.5-2.6. However, a few key concepts should be introduced first.

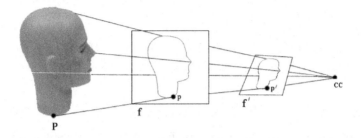

Fig. 1. The cone of rays with vertex at the camera center. An image is obtained by intersection of this cone with a plane. A ray between a $3D$ scene point P and the camera center CC pierces the plane in the image points $p \in f$ and $p^{\cdot} \in f$. All such image points are related by planar homography, $p^{\cdot} = H_p p$. See [11].

2.3 Plane to Plane Projectivity

An object in a $3D$ space and a camera center define a set of rays, and an image is obtained by intersecting these rays with a plane. Often this set is referred to as a *cone of rays*, even though it is not a cone in the classical sense. Now, suppose that this cone of rays is intersected by two planes, as shown in Fig. 1. Then, there exists a perspective transformation H mapping one image onto the other. This means that the images obtained by the same camera center may be mapped to one another by a plane projective transformation [8,11,9].

Let f and f' be the first and the second image planes, respectively. Let K denote a 3×3 internal calibration matrix. Consider two corresponding points, $p \in f$ and $p' \in f'$, expressed in homogeneous coordinates, which are two distinct images of the $3D$ object point $P = (X, Y, Z)$, taken with the same camera. Their relation can be described by $p' = KRK^{-1}p + \frac{1}{Z}K\mathbf{t}$. R is a 3×3 rotation matrix and $\mathbf{t} = [t_x, t_y, t_z]$ is a translation vector. Thus, for any given K, the homography matrix H_p, such that $p' = H_p p$, can be recovered simply by estimating the values of R and $\mathbf{t}$. Since only the plane transformation is important for the segmentation process, when the camera internal parameters are not known, K can be set to the identity matrix, implying that the optical axis is normal to the image plane f and the focal length is 1.

2.4 Generalized Cone

A generalized cone[1] or a conical surface, is a ruled surface generated by a moving line (the generator) that passes through a fixed point (the vertex) and continually intersects a fixed planar curve (the directrix). Let $P_v = (X_v, Y_v, Z_{vertex})$ denote the cone vertex, and let $p_v = (x_v, y_v)$ be the projection of the vertex on the directrix plane. We set, without loss of generality, $X_v = x_v$ and $Y_v = y_v$.

[.] The concept of generalized cone (or cylinder) in computer vision has been introduced to model $3D$ objects [2,15]. Its geometrical properties have been intensively investigated, see [10,18] and references therein.

Now, consider a directrix, $C = p(s) = (x(s), y(s))$ which is a closed contour, parameterized by arc-length s, of an object shape in the plane $Z = Z_{plane} = 0$. The generalized cone surface is the ruled surface defined by:

$$\Phi(r, s) = \Phi((1 - r)p(s) + rp_v) = (1 - r)Z_{plane} + rZ_{vertex} \qquad (10)$$

where r varies smoothly from 1, that corresponds to the vertex, via 0, the directrix, to some convenient negative value.

When the vertex of the generalized cone is located at the camera center, the definition of the generalized cone coincides with that of the cone of rays, presented in subsection 2.3. It follows that by planar slicing of the generalized cone, one can generate new image views as though they had been taken with a camera under the perspective model. There is, however, one exception to this analogy. The intersection of a cone and a plane is either a closed curve, an open curve or a point. In projective geometry terminology, the latter two correspond to projection of finite points in the first image plane to infinity. We do not consider ideal points and planes at infinity. Phrasing it explicitly, our only concern is the mapping of a given closed curve to another closed curve.

2.5   Reformulation of the Energy Functional

The shape-term in the energy functional (7) is now extended to account for projective transformations. The evolution of the level-set function, given the prior contour and an estimate of the pose parameters, is considered in this subsection. The recovery of the pose parameters, given the prior contour and the curve generated by the zero-crossing of the estimated level-set function, is described in subsection 2.6.

Following subsection 2.2, $\tilde{\phi}$ embeds the prior contour. For reasons that will soon be explained, it is referred to as the *unlevel-set function* and will take the form of a generalized cone. Let $\tilde{C} = \{x, y | \tilde{\phi}(x, y) = 0\}$ be the prior contour in f, and let T_p be a pose transformation applied to the unlevel-set function $\tilde{\phi}$:

$$(x', y', T_p(\tilde{\phi}))^T = R(x, y, \tilde{\phi})^T + \mathbf{t} . \qquad (11)$$

The evolving contour in the image to be segmented f' is iteratively compared with $\tilde{C}' = \{x', y' | T_p(\tilde{\phi}) = 0\}$ which is the zero-crossing of the transformed unlevel-set function. Note, that instead of changing the pose of the intersecting plane and maintaining the generalized cone fixed, we rotate the generalized cone around its vertex and translate it, while keeping the intersecting plane fixed. Next, we apply the Heaviside function to the transformed unlevel-set function. Thus, the shape-term of the energy functional (7) becomes

$$E_{shape}(\phi) = \int_{\Omega} \left(H(\phi) - H(T_p(\tilde{\phi})) \right)^2 dxdy \qquad (12)$$

and the gradient descent equation, derived similarly to (9), is

$$\frac{\partial \phi}{\partial t} = \delta(\phi) \left[\nu \operatorname{div} (\frac{\nabla \phi}{|\nabla \phi|}) - (f - u_+)^2 + (f - u_-)^2 - 2\mu \left(H(\phi) - H(T_p(\tilde{\phi})) \right) \right] \qquad (13)$$

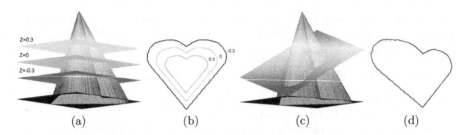

Fig. 2. (a) A generalized cone is sliced by three planes, at $Z = 0.3$, $Z = 0$ and $Z = -0.3$.(b) The resulting intersections. (c) A generalized cone is intersected by an inclined plane: $ax + by + cz + d = 0$. (d) The resulting contour.

2.6   Recovery of the Transformation Parameters

In order to solve (13), one has to evaluate ϕ simultaneously with the recovery of the transformation T_p of the unlevel-set function $\tilde{\phi}$. The transformation parameters are evaluated via the gradient descent equations obtained by minimizing the energy functional (12) with respect to each parameter. We demonstrate this for the special cases of pure translation and rotation.

Translation Translation of an image plane along the principal axis t_z results in scaling: As the planar section of the generalized cone is closer to the vertex, the cross-section shape is smaller, see Figs. 2a-b. Thus, a scale factor can be incorporated into the energy functional, in compatibility with the scene geometry, simply by translation. Equivalently, one can move the generalized cone along the principal axis, while the plane remains stationary at $Z = 0$. In the case of pure scaling, $T_p(\tilde{\phi})$ is reduced to $\tilde{\phi} + t_z$. Substituting this expression into the shape-term (12) of the energy functional, and minimizing with respect to t_z, gives the following equation:

$$\frac{\partial t_z}{\partial t} = 2\mu \int_\Omega \delta(\tilde{\phi} + t_z)(H(\phi) - H(\tilde{\phi} + t_z))dxdy \qquad (14)$$

To account for general translation $\mathbf{t} = (t_x, t_y, t_z)^T$, we can substitute the expression for $T_p(\tilde{\phi})$ (11) in (12), with $R = I$, where I is the identity matrix. The shape term takes the form

$$E_{shape}(\phi) = \int_\Omega (H(\phi)(x,y) - H(\tilde{\phi}(x + t_x, y + t_y) + t_z))^2 dxdy$$

and the translation parameters t_x and t_y can be recovered similarly to t_z.

Rotation Consider a tilted planar cut of the generalized cone, as shown in Figs. 2c,d. The resulting contour is perspectively deformed, as a function of the inclination of the intersecting plane and its proximity to the vertex of the cone. Equivalently, one may rotate the generalized cone around its vertex, and zero-cross to get the same perspective transformation.

Any rotation can be decomposed to rotations about the three axes (Euler's rotation theorem), and can be represented by a matrix $R = R_X(\alpha)R_Y(\beta)R_Z(\gamma)$ operating on a vector $(x, y, z)^T$:

$$
\begin{bmatrix} x' \\ y' \\ z' \end{bmatrix} = \begin{bmatrix} 1 & 0 & 0 \\ 0 & cos\alpha & sin\alpha \\ 0 & -sin\alpha & cos\alpha \end{bmatrix} \begin{bmatrix} cos\beta & 0 & -sin\beta \\ 0 & 1 & 0 \\ sin\beta & 0 & cos\beta \end{bmatrix} \begin{bmatrix} cos\gamma & sin\gamma & 0 \\ -sin\gamma & cos\gamma & 0 \\ 0 & 0 & 1 \end{bmatrix} \begin{bmatrix} x \\ y \\ z \end{bmatrix}
$$

Let η be some rotation angle corresponding to any of the angles α, β or γ. The general gradient descent equation for a rotation angle is of the form:

$$
\frac{\partial \eta}{\partial t} = 2\mu \int_\Omega \delta(T_p(\tilde{\phi})) \left(H(\phi) - H(T_p(\tilde{\phi})) \right) \left[\frac{\partial z'}{\partial x'} \frac{\partial x'}{\partial \eta} + \frac{\partial z'}{\partial y'} \frac{\partial y'}{\partial \eta} + \frac{\partial z'}{\partial \eta} \right] dxdy
$$

(15)

Note that $z = \tilde{\phi}(x, y)$ and $z' = T_p(\tilde{\phi})$. The partial derivatives for $\eta = \beta$, for example, are

$$
\frac{\partial x'}{\partial \beta} = -x \, cos\beta \, sin\gamma - y \, sin\beta \, sin\gamma - z \, cos\beta
$$

$$
\frac{\partial y'}{\partial \beta} = x \, sin\alpha \, cos\beta \, cos\gamma + y \, sin\alpha \, cos\beta \, sin\gamma - z \, sin\alpha
$$

(16)

$$
\frac{\partial z'}{\partial \beta} = x \, cos\alpha \, cos\beta \, cos\gamma + y \, cos\alpha \, cos\beta \, sin\gamma - z \, cos\alpha
$$

and similarly for $\eta = \alpha$ and $\eta = \gamma$. The values of $\partial z'/\partial x'$ and $\partial z'/\partial y'$ are derived numerically from the cone surface values.

2.7   The *Unlevel-Set* Algorithm

We summarize the proposed algorithm, for concurrent image segmentation given a prior contour, and recovery of the projective transformation between the current and prior object instances.

1. The inputs are two images f and f' of the same object, taken with the same camera, but under different viewing conditions. The boundary $\tilde{C}$ of the object in f is known. The image f' has to be segmented. The image plane of the first image f is assumed to be perpendicular to the principal axis, at distance 1 from the camera center. The second image plane, of f', is tilted and shifted relative to the first one.
2. Given the contour $\tilde{C}$, construct a generalized cone, using the expression in (10) with $Z_{vertex} = 1$.
3. Choose some initial level-set function ϕ, for example a standard right cone.
4. Set initial values (e.g. zero) for α, β , γ , t_x, t_y and t_z.
5. Compute the average gray level values of the object and background pixels, u_+ and u_-, using equation (6).

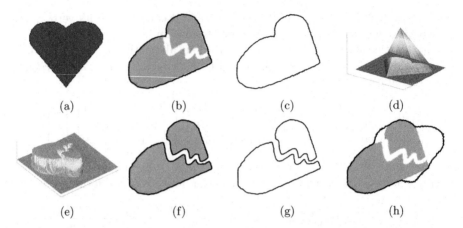

(a)   (b)   (c)   (d)

(e)   (f)   (g)   (h)

Fig. 3. Synthetic example. (a) Prior image. The contour is known (not shown). (b) Successful segmentation: the final contour is shown (black) on the transformed and corrupted image. (c) The final contour $\tilde{C}^{\cdot}$ obtained in (b). (d) Generalized cone $\tilde{\phi}$, based on the prior contour $\tilde{C}$. (e) Final level set function ϕ. (f) Wrong segmentation: prior knowledge was not used. (g) The final contour obtained in (f). (h) Wrong segmentation: the prior is used without incorporated the projective transformation.

6. Compute the values of $T_p(\tilde{\phi})$ according to equation (11), for the currently estimated transformation parameters.
7. Update ϕ according to the gradient descent equation (13).
8. Update $\mathbf{t}$, using (14) for t_z and similar equations for t_x and t_y, and (15) for α, β and γ, until convergence.
9. Repeat steps 5-8 until convergence.

3   Experimental Results

To demonstrate our model, we present segmentation results on various synthetic and real images. Relative scale and pose parameters between the image of the known contour and the image to be segmented have been estimated and compared to the ground-truth, where available. The strength of this algorithm is expressed by its weak sensitivity with respect to the parameters of the functional. We use $\nu = 50$, $\mu = 25$ unless otherwise stated. Exclusion of the shape prior knowledge from the functional means setting μ to zero.

Consider the synthetic images shown in Figs. 3a,b. Only the contour of the object in Fig. 3a (not drawn) was known in advance and used as prior. The object in Fig. 3b was generated from Fig. 3a by rotation and translation with the following parameters: $R_X(\alpha) = 0.3^0$, $R_Y(\beta) = -0.3^0$ and $R_Z(\gamma) = 60^0$ with scale factor of 0.9. It has also been broken and lightened. Note the significant perspective distortion despite the fairly small rotations around the X and Y axes. The black contour in Fig. 3b is the result of the segmentation process. For clarity, the final contour is presented by itself in Fig. 3c. The generalized cone

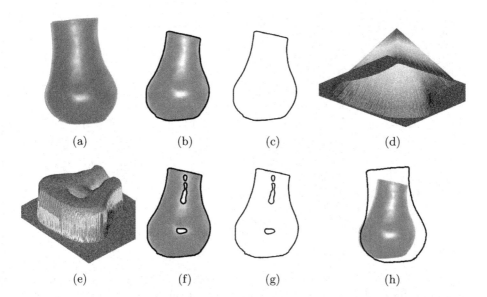

(a)   (b)   (c)   (d)

(e)   (f)   (g)   (h)

Fig. 4. Real image with synthetic transformation. (a) Prior image. The contour is known (not shown). (b) Successful segmentation: the final contour (black) on the transformed image. (c) The final contour $\tilde{C}^{\cdot}$ obtained in (b). (d) Generalized cone $\tilde{\phi}$, based on the prior contour $\tilde{C}$. (e) The final level set function ϕ. (f) Wrong segmentation: prior knowledge was not used. (g) The final contours obtained in (f). (h) Wrong segmentation: the prior is used without incorporating the projective transformation.

ϕ that was constructed, based on the known image contour, using Eq. (10), is shown in Fig. 3d. Fig. 3e shows the final evolving level-set function ϕ. It is worth emphasizing that ϕ and $T_p(\tilde{\phi})$ resemble in terms of their Heaviside functions - that is by their zero-crossings (the final contour), but not in their entire shapes. The estimated transformation parameters are: $\hat{R}_X(\alpha) = 0.38^0$, $\hat{R}_Y(\beta) = -0.4^0$, $\hat{R}_Z(\gamma) = 56.6^0$ and $\hat{t}_z = -0.107$ - which corresponds to scaling of 0.893. When no shape prior is used, each part of the broken heart is segmented separately (Figs. 3f-g). Segmentation fails when the prior is enforced without recovery of the transformation parameters, as shown in figure 3h.

We next consider real images, Figs. 4a-b, where the black contour around the object in figure 4b is again the segmentation result. The final contour itself is shown in Fig. 4c. The transformation between the images was synthetic, so that the calculated parameters could be compared with the ground-truth. The transformation parameters are: $R_X(\alpha) = -0.075^0$, $R_Y(\beta) = 0.075^0$ and $R_Z(\gamma) = 9^0$ with scaling factor of 0.8 . Compare with the recovered transformation parameters: $\hat{R}_X(\alpha) = -0.063^0$, $\hat{R}_Y(\beta) = 0.074^0$, $\hat{R}_Z(\gamma) = 7.9^0$ and scaling of 0.81. The generalized cone $\tilde{\phi}$, based on the given jar contour, and the final level set function ϕ are shown in Figs. 4d-e respectively. The jar shown is black with white background. Thus, without using the prior, the bright specular reflection spots spoil the segmentation, as shown in Figs. 4f-g. Again, when the prior is enforced,

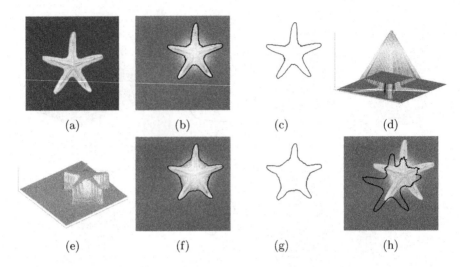

Fig. 5. Real image with synthetic noise. (a) Prior image. The contour is known (not shown). (b) Successful segmentation: the final contour (black) on the transformed image. (c) The final contour $\tilde{C}^*$ obtained in (b). (d) Generalized cone $\tilde{\phi}$, based on the prior contour $\tilde{C}$. (e) Final level set function ϕ. (f) Wrong segmentation: prior knowledge was not used. (g) The final contours obtained in (f). (h) Wrong segmentation: the prior is used without incorporating the projective transformation.

but the transformation parameters are not recovered, segmentation fails as seen in Fig. 4h.

To check simultaneous translations along the X, Y and Z axes we applied our algorithm to the images shown in Figs. 5a-b. The noisy Fig. 5b is segmented correctly (black contour) in spite of the significant translation with respect to the prior. No preprocessing alignment has been performed. The functional parameters in this case were $\mu = 13$ and $\nu = 40$. The recovered transformation parameters are: $t_x = 19.54$, $t_y = -18.8$, $t_z = 0.08$.

Finally, we demonstrate the method using a real object (mannequin head), which has actually been rotated, moved and occluded, as seen in Figs. 6a-c. The algorithm is able to segment the head precisely, in spite of the covering hat which has color similar to that of the mannequin. The segmenting contour accurately traces the profile of the mannequin, despite the significant transformation. Since the actual transformation was not measured, then in order to confirm the recovered transformation parameters, Fig. 6e shows the zero-crossing of the transformed generalized cone together with the final segmenting contour (Fig. 6d).

Translation and rotation of non-planar objects may reveal previously hidden points and hide others. Therefore, the visible contour in a new instance of the object might be significantly different from the reference. However, as seen in the jar and mannequin examples, for moderate transformations of these non-planar objects, promising segmentation results are obtained.

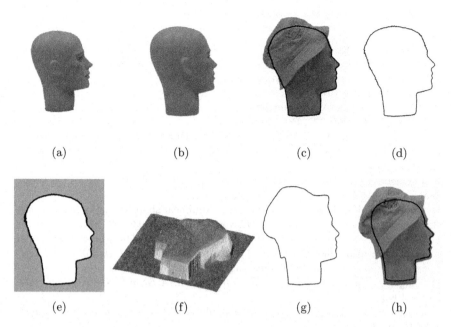

(a)   (b)   (c)   (d)

(e)   (f)   (g)   (h)

Fig. 6. Real example. (a) Reference image (mannequin head). The contour is known (not shown). (b) New instance of the mannequin head, rotated and translated. (c) Successful segmentation: the final contour (black) on the transformed mannequin head. The segmentation is precise despite the covering hat. (d) The final contour $\tilde{C}^*$ obtained in (b). (e) The final contour as in (d), drawn on the Heaviside function of the transformed generalized cone: $H(T_p(\tilde{\phi}))$. This shows the compatibility between the calculated and actual transformation parameters. (f) Final shape of the evolving level set function ϕ. (g) Final contour obtained without using a shape prior. (h) Final contour obtained using the prior but without recovery of the transformation parameters.

4   Discussion

Detection of an object in a corrupted image, based on a reference image taken with from a different view-point, is a classical challenge in computer vision. This paper presents a novel approach that makes substantial progress towards this goal. The key to this accomplishment is the unique integration of scene geometry with the variational approach to segmentation. The reference shape is the foundation of a generalized cone. In principle, the zero level set of an evolving function, related to the image features, is matched with *unlevel* sections of the generalized cone that correspond to projectively deformed views of the shape.

The suggested algorithm successfully accounts for scale and pose variations under the perspective model, including rotation outside the image plane, without using point correspondence. The algorithm converges empirically even for fairly large transformations and significantly corrupted images. Promising segmentation results and accurate numerical estimation of the transformation parameters, suggest this model as an efficient tool for segmentation and image alignment.

References

1. G. Aubert and P. Kornprobst. *Mathematical Problems in Image Processing: Partial Differential Equations and the Calculus of Variations.* Springer, 2002.
2. T.O. Binford. Visual perception by computer. In *Proc. IEEE Conf. Systems and Control,* December 1971.
3. T.F. Chan and L.A. Vese. Active contours without edges. *IEEE Trans. Image Processing,* 10(2):266–277, February 2001.
4. Y. Chen, S. Thiruvenkadam, H.D. Tagare, F. Huang, and D. Wilson. On the incorporation of shape priors into geometric active contours. In *VLSM01,* pages 145–152, 2001.
5. D. Cremers, T. Kohlberger, and C. Schnorr. Nonlinear shape statistics via kernel spaces. In *DAGM01,* pages 269–276, 2001.
6. D. Cremers, T. Kohlberger, and C. Schnorr. Nonlinear shape statistics in mumford-shah based segmentation. In *ECCV02,* volume II, pages 93–108, 2002.
7. D. Cremers, N. Sochen, and C. Schnorr. Towards recognition-based variational segmentation using shape priors and dynamic labeling. In *Intl. Conf. on Scale-Space Theories in Computer Vision,* pages 388–400, June 2003.
8. O. Faugeras. *Three-Dimensional Computer Vision: A Geometric Viewpoint.* MIT Press, 1993.
9. O. Faugeras, Q.T. Luong, and T. Papadopoulo. *The Geometry of Multiple Images.* MIT Press, 2001.
10. D.A. Forsyth and J. Ponce. *Computer Vision: A Modern Approach.* Prentice Hall, 2003.
11. R. I. Hartley and A. Zisserman. *Multiple View Geometry in Computer Vision.* Cambridge University Press, 2000.
12. M. Irani and P. Anandan. All about direct methods. In W. Triggs, A. Zisserman, and R. Szeliski, editors, *Vision Algorithms: Theory and Practice.* Springer-Verlag, 1999.
13. M. Leventon, O. Faugeraus, W. Grimson, and W. Wells III. Level set based segmentation with intensity and curvature priors. In *Workshop on Mathematical Methods in Biomedical Image Analysis Proceedings,* pages 4–11, June 2000.
14. M.E. Leventon, W.E.L. Grimson, and O. Faugeras. Statistical shape influence in geodesic active contours. In *CVPR00,* volume I, pages 316–323, 2000.
15. D. Marr. *Vision: A Computational Investigation into the Human Representation and Processing of Visual Information.* W.H. Freeman, 1982.
16. D. Mumford and J. Shah. Optimal approximations by piecewise smooth functions and associated variational problems. *Communications on Pure and Applied Mathematics,* 42:577–684, 1989.
17. S. Osher and J.A. Sethian. Fronts propagating with curvature-dependent speed: Algorithms based on Hamilton-Jacobi formulations. *Journal of Computational Physics,* 79:12–49, 1988.
18. K.G. Rao and G. Medioni. Generalized cones: Useful geometric properties. In *CVIP92,* pages 185–208, 1992.
19. A. Tsai, A. Yezzi, Jr., W.M. Wells, III, C. Tempany, D. Tucker, A. Fan, W.E.L. Grimson, and A.S. Willsky. Model-based curve evolution technique for image segmentation. In *CVPR01,* volume I, pages 463–468, 2001.
20. S. Ullman. *High-Level Vision: Object Recognition and Visual Cognition.* MIT Press, 1996.

Learning and Bayesian Shape Extraction for Object Recognition

Washington Mio, Anuj Srivastava, and Xiuwen Liu

Florida State University, Tallahassee FL 32306, USA

Abstract. We present a novel algorithm for extracting shapes of contours of (possibly partially occluded) objects from noisy or low-contrast images. The approach taken is Bayesian: we adopt a region-based model that incorporates prior knowledge of specific shapes of interest. To quantify this prior knowledge, we address the problem of learning probability models for collections of observed shapes. Our method is based on the geometric representation and algorithmic analysis of planar shapes introduced and developed in [15]. In contrast with the commonly used approach to active contours using partial differential equation methods [12,20,1], we model the dynamics of contours on vector fields on shape manifolds.

1 Introduction

The recognition and classification of objects present in images is an important and difficult problem in image analysis. Applications of shape extraction for object recognition include video surveillance, biometrics, military target recognition, and medical imaging. The problem is particularly challenging when objects of interest are partially obscured in low-contrast or noisy images. Imaged objects can be analyzed in many ways: according to their colors, textures, shapes, and other characteristics. The past decade has seen many advances in the investigation of models of pixel values, however, these methods have only found limited success in the recognition of imaged objects. Variational and level-set methods have been successfully applied to a variety of segmentation, denoising, and inpainting problems (see e.g. [1]), but significant advances are still needed to satisfactorily address recognition and classification problems, especially in applications that require real-time processing.

An emerging viewpoint among vision researchers is that global features such as shapes should be taken into account. The idea is that by incorporating some prior knowledge of shapes of objects of interest to image models, one should be able to devise more robust and efficient image analysis algorithms. Combined with clustering techniques for the hierarchical organization of large databases of shapes [22], this should lead to recognition and classification algorithms with enhanced speed and performance. In this paper, we construct probability models on shape spaces to model a given collection of observed shapes, and integrate these to a region-based image model for Bayesian extractions of shapes from images. Our primary goal is to capture just enough information about shapes

T. Pajdla and J. Matas (Eds.): ECCV 2004, LNCS 3024, pp. 62–73, 2004.

present in images to be able to identify them as belonging to certain categories of objects known *a priori*, not to extract fine details of the contours of imaged objects.

Shape analysis has been an important theme of investigation for many years. Following the seminal work of Kendall [13], large part of the research in quantitative shape analysis has been devoted to "landmark-based" studies, where shapes are represented by finite samplings of contours. One establishes equivalences of representations with respect to shape preserving transformations, and then compares shapes in the resulting quotient space [5,21]. Statistical shape models based on this representation have been developed and applied to image segmentation and shape learning in [7,6]; the literature on applications of this methodology to a variety of problems is quite extensive. A drawback of this approach is that the automatic selection of landmarks is not straightforward and the ensuing shape analysis is heavily dependent on the choices made. Grenander's deformable templates [8] avoids landmarks by treating shapes as points in an infinite-dimensional differentiable manifold, and modeling variations of planar shapes on an action of the diffeomorphism group of $\mathbb{R}^2$ [24,9,18]. However, computational costs associated with this approach are typically very high. A very active line of research in image analysis is based on active contours [12,20] governed by partial differential equations; we refer the reader to [1] for a recent survey on applications of level-set methods to image analysis. Efforts in the direction of studying shape statistics using partial differential equation methods have been undertaken in [17,3,2].

In [15], Klassen et al. introduced a new framework for the representation and algorithmic analysis of continuous planar shapes, without resorting to defining landmarks or diffeomorphisms of $\mathbb{R}^2$. To quantify shape dissimilarities and simulate optimal deformations of shapes, an algorithm was developed for computing geodesic paths in shape spaces. The registration of curves to be compared is automatic, and the treatment suggests a new technique for driving active contours [23]. In this paper, we investigate variants of this model for shape extraction from images. In our formulation, the dynamics of active contours is governed by vector fields on shape manifolds, which can be integrated with classical techniques and reduced computational costs. The basic idea is to create a manifold of shapes, define an appropriate Riemannian structure on it, and exploit its geometry to solve optimization and inference problems.

An important element in this stochastic geometry approach to shape extraction is a model for shape learning. Assuming that a given collection of observed shapes consists of random samples from a common probability model, we wish to learn the model. Examples illustrating the use of landmark-based shape analysis in problems of this nature are presented in [7,6,14,10]. The problem of model construction using the shape analysis methods of [15] presents two main difficulties: the shape manifold is *nonlinear* and *infinite-dimensional*. A most basic notion needed in the study of sample statistics is that of mean shape; Karcher means introduced in [11] are used. As in [5], other issues involving nonlinearity are handled by considering probability densities on the (linear) tangent space at the mean shape. To tackle the infinite dimensionality, we use approximate finite-dimensional representations of tangent vectors to shape manifolds. We consider multivariate normal models, so that learning reduces to estimations of the relevant parameters. (Other parametric models can be treated with similar techniques.) Implicit in this approach is that large collection of shapes have been pre-clustered and we are modeling clusters of fairly small diameters. Clustering algorithms and hierarchical organizations of large databases of shapes are discussed in [22].

This paper is organized as follows: in Section 2, we briefly review the material of [15], as it provides the foundations of our stochastic geometry approach to shape extraction. Section 3 is devoted to a discussion of shape learning. In Section 4, we present the image model used in the shape extraction algorithm, and applications of the algorithm to imagery involving partial occlusions of objects, low contrast, or noise.

2   Shape Spaces and Geodesic Metrics

In this section, we review the geometric representation of continuous planar shapes, the geodesic metric on shape space, and the algorithmic shape analysis methods introduced and developed in [15].

2.1   Geometric Representation of Shapes

Shapes of outer contours of imaged objects are viewed as closed, planar curves $\alpha \colon I \to \mathbb{R}^2$, where $I = [0, 2\pi]$. To make shape representations invariant to uniform scaling, the length is fixed to be 2π by requiring that curves be parameterized by arc length, i.e., $\|\alpha'(s)\| = 1$, for every $s \in I$. Then, the tangent vector can be written as $\alpha'(s) = e^{j\theta(s)}$, where $j = \sqrt{-1}$. We refer to $\theta \colon I \to \mathbb{R}$ as an *angle function* for α. Angle functions are invariant under translations of $\mathbb{R}^2$, and the effect of a rotation is to add a constant to θ. Thus, to make the representation invariant to rotations of $\mathbb{R}^2$, it suffices to fix the average of θ to be, say, π. In addition, to ensure that θ represents a closed curve, the condition $\int_0^{2\pi} \alpha'(s)\, ds = \int_0^{2\pi} e^{j\theta(s)}\, ds = 0$ is imposed. Thus, angle functions are restricted to the *pre-shape manifold*

$$
\mathcal{C} = \left\{ \theta \in \mathbb{L}^2 \,\middle|\, \frac{1}{2\pi} \int_0^{2\pi} \theta(s)\, ds = \pi \text{ and } \int_0^{2\pi} e^{i\theta(s)} ds = 0 \right\} . \tag{1}
$$

Here, $\mathbb{L}^2$ denotes the vector space of all square integrable functions on $[0, 2\pi]$, equipped with the standard inner product $\langle f, g \rangle = \int_0^{2\pi} f(s)g(s)\, ds$. For continuous direction functions, the only remaining variability in the representation is due to the action of the reparametrization group S^1 arising from different possible placements of the initial point $s = 0$ on the curve. Hence, the quotient space $\mathcal{S} \equiv \mathcal{C}/S^1$ is defined as the *space of continuous, planar shapes*.

2.2   Geodesic Paths between Shapes

At each point $\theta \in \mathcal{C}$, the tangent space $T_\theta \mathcal{C}$ to the pre-shape manifold $\mathcal{C} \subset \mathbb{L}^2$ naturally inherits an inner product from $\mathbb{L}^2$. Thus, $\mathcal{C}$ is a Riemannian manifold and the distance between points in $\mathcal{C}$ can be defined using minimal length geodesics. The distance between two points (i.e., shapes) θ_1 and θ_2 in $\mathcal{S}$ is defined as the infimum of all pairwise distances between pre-shapes representing θ_1 and θ_2, respectively. Thus, the distance $d(\theta_1, \theta_2)$ in $\mathcal{S}$ is realized by a shortest geodesic in $\mathcal{C}$ between pre-shapes associated with θ_1 and θ_2. We abuse terminology and use the same symbol θ to denote both a pre-shape and its associated shape in $\mathcal{S}$. We also refer to minimal geodesics in $\mathcal{C}$ realizing distances in $\mathcal{S}$ as geodesics in $\mathcal{S}$, and to tangent vectors to these geodesics as tangent vectors to $\mathcal{S}$.

One of the main results of [15] is the derivation of an algorithm to compute geodesics in $\mathcal{C}$ (and $\mathcal{S}$) connecting two given points. An easier problem is the calculation of geodesics satisfying prescribed initial conditions. Given $\theta \in \mathcal{C}$ and $f \in T_\theta \mathcal{C}$, let $\Psi(\theta, f, t)$ denote the geodesic starting at θ with velocity f, where t denotes the time parameter. The geodesic $\Psi(\theta, f, t)$ is constructed with a numerical integration of the differential equation satisfied by geodesics. The correspondence $f \mapsto \Psi(\theta, f, 1)$ defines a map $\exp_\theta \colon T_\theta \mathcal{C} \to \mathcal{C}$ known as the exponential map at θ. The exponential map simply evaluates the position of the geodesic Ψ at time $t = 1$. Consider the exponential map at θ_1. Finding the geodesic from θ_1 to θ_2 is equivalent to finding the direction f such that $\exp_{\theta_1}(f) = \theta_2$. For each $f \in T_{\theta_1} \mathcal{C}$, let $E(f) = \| \exp_{\theta_1}(f) - \theta_2 \|^2$ be the square of the $\mathbb{L}^2$ norm of the residual vector. The goal is to find the vector f that minimizes (i.e., annihilates) E. A gradient search is used in [15] to solve this energy minimization problem. This procedure can be refined to yield geodesics in $\mathcal{S}$ by incorporating the action of the re-parametrization group S^1 into the search.

Figure 1 shows an example of a geodesic path in $\mathcal{S}$ computed with this algorithm. In this paper, we have added the invariance of shapes to reflections in

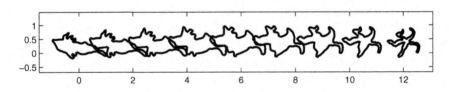

Fig. 1. A geodesic path in shape space

$\mathbb{R}^2$. Essentially, one computes geodesics for both a shape and a reflection, and selects the one with least length.

2.3   Karcher Mean Shapes

The use of *Karcher means* to define mean shapes in $\mathcal{S}$ is suggested in [15]. If $\theta_1, \ldots, \theta_n \in \mathcal{S}$ and $d(\theta, \theta_j)$ is the geodesic distance between θ and θ_j, a Karcher mean is defined as an element $\mu \in S$ that minimizes the quantity $\sum_{i=1}^{n} d^2(\theta, \theta_i)$. An iterative algorithm for computing Karcher means in Riemannian manifolds is presented in [16,11] and particularized to the spaces C and S in [15]. An example of a Karcher mean shape is shown in Figure 2.

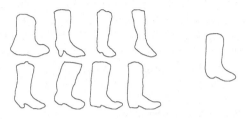

Fig. 2. The Karcher mean shape of eight boots.

2.4   Computational Speeds

To demonstrate the level of performance of the algorithm to compute geodesics between two shapes, Table 2.4 shows the average computation times achieved under several different settings, each estimated by averaging 1,225 calculations on a personal computer with dual Xeon CPUs (at 2.20 GHz) running Linux. Each shape is sampled using T points on the curve and tangent vectors are approximated using $2m$ Fourier terms. Consistent with our analysis, the algo-

Table 1. Average computation time (in seconds) per geodesic.

T	50	50	100	100	200	200	400	400
m	50	100	100	200	200	400	400	800
Time (secs.)	0.0068	0.0133	0.0268	0.0525	0.1044	0.2066	0.4172	0.8274

rithm for calculating geodesics is linear in T and m. Computational efficiency can be further improved with parallel processing, since the costliest step in the algorithm consists of $2m$ calculations that can be executed independently.

3   Shape Learning

An important problem in statistical shape analysis is to "learn" probability models for a collection of observed shapes. Assuming that the given shapes are random samples from the same probability model, we wish to learn the model. These models can then be used as shape priors in Bayesian inferences to recognize or classify newly observed shapes. Implicit in our considerations is the assumption that observed shapes have been pre-clustered, so that we are seeking probability models for clusters of fairly small diameters in S. Clustering techniques on the shape space S have been studied in [22].

Learning a probability model amounts to estimating a probability density function on shape space, a task that is rather difficult to perform precisely. In this paper, we assume a parametric form for the models so that learning is reduced to an estimation of the relevant parameters. To simplify the discussion of probability models on infinite-dimensional manifolds, the models will be presented in terms of their negative log-likelihood, i.e., the energy of the distribution.

The simplest model is a "uniform Gaussian" on S, whose energy is proportional to $d^2(\theta, \mu)/2$, where μ is the Karcher mean of the sample. The constant of proportionality is related to the variance, as usual. We wish to refine the model to a multivariate normal distribution. Two main difficulties encountered are the *nonlinearity* and the *infinite-dimensionality* of S, which are addressed as follows.

(i) **Nonlinearity.** Since S is a nonlinear space, we consider probability distributions on the tangent space $T_\mu \mathcal{C}$ at the mean pre-shape $\mu \in \mathcal{C}$, to avoid dealing with the nonlinearity of S directly. This is similar to the approach taken in [5].

(ii) **Dimensionality.** Our parametric models will require estimations of covariance operators of probability distributions on $T_\mu \mathcal{C} \subset \mathbb{L}^2$. We approximate covariances by an operators defined on finite dimensional subspaces of $T_\mu \mathcal{C}$.

Let $\Theta = \{\theta_1, \dots, \theta_r\}$ represent a finite collection of shapes. The estimation of the Karcher mean shape μ of Θ is described in [15]. Using μ and the shapes $\theta_j, 1 \le j \le r$, we find tangent vectors $g_j \in T_\mu S$ such that the geodesic from μ in the direction g_j reaches θ_j in unit time, that is, $\exp_\mu(v_j) = \theta_j$. This lifts the shape representatives to the tangent space at μ.

Let V be the subspace of $T_\mu S$ spanned by $\{v_1, \dots, v_r\}$, and $\{e_1, \dots, e_m\}$ an orthonormal basis of V. Given $v \in V$, write it as $v = x_1 e_1 + \dots + x_m e_m$. The correspondence $v \mapsto \mathbf{x} = (x_1, \dots, x_m)$ identifies V with $\mathbb{R}^m$, so we assume that $v_j \in \mathbb{R}^m$. We still have to decide what model to adopt for the probability distribution. We assume a multivariate Gaussian model for $\mathbf{x}$ with mean $\mathbf{0}$ and covariance matrix $K \in \mathbb{R}^{m \times m}$. The estimation of K using sample covariance follows the usual procedures. Depending on the number and the nature of the shape observations, the rank of K may be much smaller than m. Extracting the dominant eigenvectors and eigenvalues of the estimated covariance matrix, one captures the dominant modes of variation and the variances along these principal directions.

To allow small shape variations in directions orthogonal to those determined by the non-zero eigenvalues of K, choose $\varepsilon > 0$ somewhat smaller than the dominant eigenvalues of K. If $K_\varepsilon = K + \varepsilon^2 I_m$, where I_m is the $m \times m$ identity matrix, we adopt the multivariate normal distribution

$$\frac{1}{(2\pi)^{m/2} \det(K_\varepsilon)^{1/2}} \exp\left(-\frac{\mathbf{x}^T \cdot K_\varepsilon^{-1}(\mathbf{x})}{2}\right) \tag{2}$$

on the subspace V of $T_\mu S$. If $\theta \in S$, let $g \in T_\mu S$ satisfy $\Psi(\mu, g, 1) = \theta$, and let $g_V = \sum_{i=1}^m x_i e_i$ be the orthogonal projection of g onto V. We adopt a probability model on S whose energy is given up to an additive constant by

$$F(\theta; \mu, K) = \frac{\mathbf{x}^T \cdot K_\varepsilon^{-1}(\mathbf{x})}{2} + \frac{1}{\varepsilon^2} \|g^\perp\|^2, \qquad (3)$$

where $g^\perp \in T_\mu S$ is the component of g orthogonal to V. Strictly speaking, this definition is only well posed if the exponential map is globally one-to-one. However, for most practical purposes, one can assume that this condition is essentially satisfied because clusters are assumed to be concentrated near the mean and finite-dimensional approximations to θ are used.

The first row of Figure 3 shows eigenshapes associated with the first five eigenvalues (in decreasing order) of the multivariate normal model derived from the shapes in Figure 2. The solid lines show the mean shape, and the dotted lines represent variations about the mean along principal directions. Variations are uniformly sampled on an interval of size proportional to the eigenvalues.

Having obtained a probability model for observed shapes, an important task is to validate it. This can be done in a number of ways. As an illustration, we use the model for random sampling. The second and third rows of Figure 3 show examples of random shapes generated using the Gaussian model learned from the shapes in Figure 2.

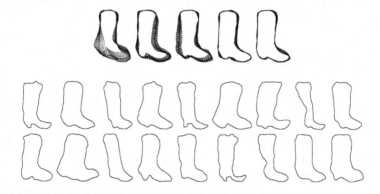

Fig. 3. The first row shows eigenboots in dotted lines, i.e., variations about the mean shape of Figure 2 (displayed in solid lines) along principal directions associated with the five dominant eigenvalues. The second and third rows display 18 random shapes sampled from the proposed multivariate normal model.

Another example is shown in Figure 4. A set of nineteen observed shapes of swimming ducks is analyzed for learning a probability model. We calculated the mean shape – shown on the lower right corner – and estimated the sample covariance matrix K. Figure 5 shows variations of the mean shape along the dominant principal directions and ten random shapes generated using the learned probability model.

Fig. 4. Nineteen shapes of swimming ducks and their mean shape displayed on the lower right corner.

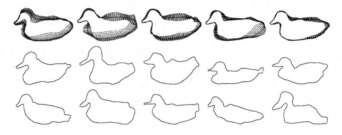

Fig. 5. Eigenducks (first row) and ten random shapes generated by sampling from a multivariate normal tangent-space model.

4   Bayesian Extraction of Shapes

The extraction of shapes of partially occluded objects from noisy or low-contrast images is a difficult problem. Lack of clear data in such problems may severely limit the performance of image segmentation algorithms. Thus, techniques for integrating some additional knowledge about shapes of interest into the inference process are sought. The framework developed in this paper is well suited to the formulation and solution of Bayesian shape inference problems involving this type of imagery. We assume that the shape to be extracted is known *a priori* to be related to a family modeled on a probability distribution of the type discussed in Section 3. The case of several competing models can be treated with a combination of our shape extraction method and hypothesis testing techniques. We emphasize that our goal is to extract just enough features of shapes present in images to be able to recognize objects as belonging to certain known categories, not to capture minute details of shapes. Such low-resolution approach is more robust to noise and allows for greater computational efficiency.

Our analysis thus far has focused on shape, a property that is independent of variables that account for rotations, translations, and scalings of objects. However, shapes appear in images at specific locations and scales, so the process of shape extraction and recognition should involve an estimation of these nuisance variables as well. Hence, in this context, the data likelihood term assumes knowledge of shape, location, and scale variables, while the prior term depends only on shape. Therefore, we first revisit our shape representation to incorporate these extra variables.

To account for translational effects, we introduce a variable $p \in \mathbb{R}^2$ that identifies the centroid of a constant-speed curve $\alpha \colon I \to \mathbb{R}^2$, which is given by $p = (1/2\pi) \int_0^{2\pi} \alpha(s)\, ds$. We adopt a logarithmic scale for the length by writing $L = e^\ell$, $\ell \in \mathbb{R}$. Lastly, to allow arbitrary rotations, we simply relax the constraints on θ used in the description of the pre-shape manifold $\mathcal{C}$ and only require that θ satisfy the closure conditions

$$\int_0^{2\pi} \cos\theta(s)\, ds = 0 \quad \text{and} \quad \int_0^{2\pi} \sin\theta(s)\, ds = 0. \tag{4}$$

Thus, pre-shapes that can change position and are free to shrink or stretch uniformly will be described by triples $(p, \ell, \theta) \in \mathbb{R}^2 \times \mathbb{R} \times \mathbf{L}^2$ satisfying (4). The collection of all such triples will be denoted $\mathcal{F}$. An element $(p, \ell, \theta) \in \mathcal{F}$ represents the curve

$$\alpha(s) = p + e^\ell \int_0^s e^{j\theta(x)}\, dx - \frac{e^\ell}{2\pi} \int_0^{2\pi} \int_0^s e^{j\theta(x)}\, dx\, ds. \tag{5}$$

For shape extraction, we do not need to further consider the quotient space under the action of the re-parameterization group $\mathbb{S}^1$ on $\mathcal{F}$. The data likelihood and shape prior terms will be invariant under the $\mathbb{S}^1$-action, so the posterior energy will be constant along $\mathbb{S}^1$ orbits. We now describe the posterior energy for our Bayesian inference.

(a) **Data Likelihood.** Let $D \subset \mathbb{R}^2$ be the image domain and $I \colon D \to \mathbb{R}^+$ be an image. A closed curve represented by (p, ℓ, θ) divides the image domain into a region $D_i(p, \ell, \theta)$ inside the curve, and a region $D_o(p, \ell, \theta)$ outside. Let p_i be a probability model for the pixel values inside the curve, and p_o be a model for pixels outside. For simplicity, we assume a binary image model choosing p_i and p_o to be Gaussian distributions with different means. (Alternatively, one can use variants of the Mumford-Shah image model [19]). For a given (p, ℓ, θ), the compatibility of an image I with (p, ℓ, θ) is proportional to

$$H(I|p, \ell, \theta) = - \iint_{D_i(p,\ell,\theta)} \log p_i(I(y))\, dy - \iint_{D_o(p,\ell,\theta)} \log p_o(I(y))\, dy. \tag{6}$$

(b) **Shape Prior.** Let μ_0 and K_0 represent the mean and the covariance matrix associated with the shape prior model. Set the prior energy to be $F([\theta]; \mu, K)$, as in Equation 3, where $[\theta]$ indicates that θ has been normalized to have average π.

Combining the two terms, up to an additive constant, the posterior energy is proportional to

$$P_\lambda(p, \ell, \theta|I) = \lambda H(I|p, \ell, \theta) + (1 - \lambda)F([\theta]; \mu, K),$$

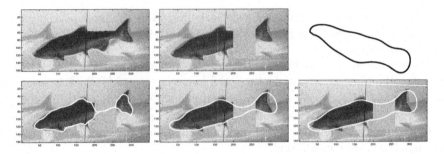

Fig. 6. An example of shape extraction. Top row from left to right: an image, the same image with a partial occlusion, and the prior mean. The bottom row shows MAP shape estimates with an increasing influence of the prior from left to right.

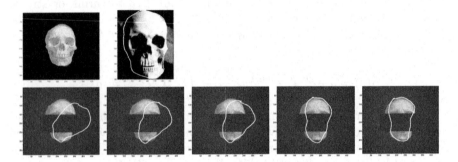

Fig. 7. A shape extraction experiment. The top row shows an image of a skull to be analyzed after being artificially obscured and a second skull whose contour is used as prior mean. The bottom row shows various stages of the curve evolution during the shape extraction.

where $0 < \lambda < 1$. As before, it is convenient to lift θ to the tangent space at the mean μ. Letting $\theta = \Psi(\mu, g, 1) = \exp_\mu(g)$, with g in the tangent space at μ, we rewrite the posterior energy as

$$E_\lambda(p, \ell, g | I) = P_\lambda\left(p, \ell, \exp_\mu(g) | I\right).$$

We use a gradient search for a MAP estimation of (p, ℓ, g), approximating g with a truncated Fourier series.

Shown in Figure 6 are illustrations of this Bayesian shape extraction using a uniform Gaussian prior. The top row shows an object embedded in an image, the same image with the object partially obscured, and the prior mean shape. The bottom row displays MAP estimates of the shape of the object under an increasing influence of the prior. The improvements in discovering hidden shapes despite partial occlusions emphasize the need and power of a Bayesian approach to such problems using shape priors.

Figure 7 depicts the results of another shape extraction experiment. On the top row, the first panel displays the image of a skull that is artificially obscured for shape extraction. The second panel shows the contour of a different skull used as prior mean. The second row shows various stages of the curve evolution during the gradient search of a MAP estimate of the shape.

5 Summary

We presented an algorithm for the extraction of shapes of partially obscured objects from noisy, low-contrast images for the recognition and classification of imaged objects. The image model adopted involves a data likelihood term based on pixel values and a shape prior term that makes the algorithm robust to image quality and partial occlusions. We discussed learning techniques in shape space in order to construct probability models for clusters of observed shapes using the framework for shape analysis developed in [15] A novel technique that models the dynamics of active contours on vector fields on shape manifolds was employed. Various shape extraction experiments were carried out to demonstrate the performance of the algorithm.

Acknowledgments. This work was partially supported by the National Science Foundation and the Intelligence Technology Innovation Center through the joint "Approaches to Combat Terrorism" Program Solicitation NSF 03-569 (DMS-0345242) and by the grants NSF (FRG) DMS-0101429 and NMA 201-01-2010.

References

1. Chan, T., Shen, J., Vese, L.: Variational PDE Models in Image Processing. Notices Amer. Math. Soc. **50** (2003) 14–26.
2. Cremers, D., Soatto, S.: A Pseudo Distance for Shape Priors in Level Set Segmentation. In: Proc. 2nd IEEE Workshop on Variational, Geometric, and Level-Set Methods in Computer Vision, Nice, France (2003).
3. Cremers, D., F. Tischhäuser, F., Weickert, J., Schnörr, C.: Diffusion Snakes: Introducing Statistical Shape Knowledge into the Mumford-Shah Functional. Internat. Journal Computer Vision, **50** (2002), 295–313.
4. Do Carmo, M.P.: Differential Geometry of Curves and Surfaces. Prentice-Hall (1976).
5. Dryden, I.L., Mardia, K.V.: Statistical Shape Analysis. John Wiley & Sons (1998).
6. Duta, N., Jain, A.K., Dubuisson-Jolly, M.P.: Automatic Construction of 2D Shape Models. IEEE Trans. Pattern Analysis and Machine Intelligence **23** (2001).
7. Duta, N., Sonka, M., Jain, A.K.: Learning Shape Models from Examples Using Automatic Shape Clustering and Procrustes Analysis. In: Proc. Information in Medical Image Processing, Lecture Notes in Computer Science, Vol. 1613. Springer-Verlag, Berlin Heidelberg New York (1999) 370–375.
8. Grenander, U.: General Pattern Theory. Oxford University Press (1993).
9. Grenander, U., Milller, M.I.: Computational Anatomy: an Emerging Discipline. Quarterly of Applied Mathematics, **LVI** (1998) 617–694.
10. Holbolth, A., Kent, J.T., Dryden, I.L.: On the Relation Between Edge and Vertex Modeling in Shape Analysis. Scandinavian Journal of Statistics **29** (2002) 355–374.

11. Karcher, H.: Riemann Center of Mass and Mollifier Smoothing. Comm. Pure Appl. Math. **30** (1977) 509–541.
12. Kass, M., Witkin, A., Terzopoulos, D.: Snakes: Active Contour Models. International Journal of Computer Vision **1** (1988) 321–331.
13. Kendall, D.G.: Shape Manifolds, Procrustean Metrics and Complex Projective Spaces. Bull. London Math. Society **16** (1984) 81–121.
14. Kent, J.T., Dryden, I.L., Anderson, C.R.: Using Circulant Symmetry to Model Featureless Objects. Biometrika **87** (2000) 527–544.
15. Klassen, E., Srivastava, A., Mio, W., Joshi, S.: Analysis of Planar Shapes Using Geodesic Paths on Shape Spaces. IEEE Trans. Pattern Analysis and Machine Intelligence **26** (2004).
16. Le, H.L., Kendall, D.G.: The Riemannian Structure of Euclidean Shape Spaces: a Novel Environment for Statistics. Annals of Statistics **21** (1993) 1225–1271.
17. Leventon, M., Grimson, W., Faugeras, O.: Statistical Shape Infuence in Geodesic Active Contours. In: Proc. IEEE Conference on Computer Vision and Pattern Recognition (2000).
18. Miller, M.I., Younes, L.: Group Actions, Homeomorphisms, and Matching: A General Framework. International Journal of Computer Vision **41** (2002) 61–84.
19. Mumford, D., Shah, J.: Optimal Approximations by Piecewise Smooth Functions and Associated Variational Problems. Comm. Pure Appl. Math. **42** (1989) 577–685.
20. Sethian, J.: Level Set Methods: Evolving Interfaces in Geometry, Fluid Mechanics, Computer Vision, and Material Science. Cambridge University Press (1996).
21. Small, C.G.: The Statistical Theory of Shape. Springer-Verlag (1996).
22. Joshi, S., Srivastava, A., Mio, W., Liu, X.: Hierarchical Organization of Shapes for Efficient Retrieval. In: Proc. 8th European Conference on Computer Vision. Prague, Czech Republic (2004).
23. Srivastava, A., Mio, W., Klassen, E., Liu, X.: Geometric Analysis of Constrained Curves for Image Understanding. In: Proc. 2nd Workshop on Variational, Geometric and Level-Set Methods in Computer Vision. Nice, France (2003).
24. Younes, L.: Computable Elastic Distance Between Shapes. SIAM Journal of Applied Mathematics **58** (1998) 565–586.

Multiphase Dynamic Labeling for Variational Recognition-Driven Image Segmentation

Daniel Cremers[1], Nir Sochen[2], and Christoph Schnörr[3]

. Department of Computer Science
University of California, Los Angeles, USA
. Department of Applied Mathematics
Tel Aviv University, Israel
. Department of Mathematics and Computer Science
University of Mannheim, Germany

Abstract. We propose a variational framework for the integration multiple competing shape priors into level set based segmentation schemes. By optimizing an appropriate cost functional with respect to both a level set function and a (vector-valued) labeling function, we jointly generate a segmentation (by the level set function) and a recognition-driven partition of the image domain (by the labeling function) which indicates where to enforce certain shape priors. Our framework fundamentally extends previous work on shape priors in level set segmentation by directly addressing the central question of *where* to apply *which* prior. It allows for the seamless integration of numerous shape priors such that – while segmenting both multiple known and unknown objects – the level set process may selectively use specific shape knowledge for simultaneously enhancing segmentation and recognizing shape.

1 Introduction

Image segmentation and object recognition in vision are driven both by low-level cues such as intensities, color or texture properties, and by prior knowledge about objects in our environment. Modeling the interaction between such data-driven and model-based processes has become the focus of current research on image segmentation in the field of computer vision. In this work, we consider prior knowledge given by the shapes associated with a set of familiar objects and focus on the problem of how to exploit such knowledge for images containing multiple objects, some of which may be familiar, while others may be unfamiliar.

Following their introduction as a means of front propagation [13], level set based contour representations have become a popular framework for image segmentation [1,10]. They permit to elegantly model topological changes of the implicitly represented boundary, which makes them well suited for segmenting images containing *multiple* objects. Level set segmentation schemes can be formulated to exploit various low level cues such as edge information [10,2,8], intensity homogeneity [3,18], texture [14] or motion information [6]. In recent years, there has been much effort in trying to integrate prior shape knowledge into level set based segmentation. This was shown to make the segmentation

T. Pajdla and J. Matas (Eds.): ECCV 2004, LNCS 3024, pp. 74–86, 2004.

process robust to misleading low-level information caused by noise, background clutter or partial occlusion of an object of interest (cf. [9,17,5,15]).

A key problem in this context is to ensure that prior knowledge is *selectively* applied at image locations only where image data indicate a familiar object. Conversely, lack of any evidence for the presence of some familiar object should result in a purely data-driven segmentation process. To this end, it was recently proposed to introduce a labeling function in order to restrict the effect of a given prior to a specific domain of the image plane [7] (for a use of a labeling field in a different context see [11]). During optimization, this labeling function evolves so as to select image regions where the given prior is applied. The resulting process segments corrupted versions of a known object in a way that does not affect the correct segmentation of other unfamiliar objects. A smoothness constraint on the labeling function induces the process to distinguish between occlusions (which are close to the familiar object) and separate independent objects (assumed to be sufficiently far from the object of interest).

All of the approaches mentioned above were designed to segment a *single* known object in a given image. But what if there are several known objects? Clearly, any use of shape priors consistent with the philosophy of the level set method should retain the capacity of the resulting segmentation scheme to deal with multiple independent objects, no matter whether they are familiar or not. One may instead suggest to iteratively apply the segmentation scheme with a different prior at each time and thereby successively segment the respective objects. We believe, however, that such a sequential processing mode will not scale up to large databases of objects and that – even more importantly – the parallel use of *competing priors* is essential for modeling the chicken-egg relationship between segmentation and recognition.

In this paper, we adopt the selective shape prior approach suggested in [7] and substantially generalize it along several directions:

- We extend the shape prior by pose parameters. The resulting segmentation process not only selects appropriate regions where to apply the prior, it also selects appropriate pose parameters associated with a given prior. This drastically increases the usefulness of this method for realistic segmentation problems, as one cannot expect to know the pose of the object beforehand.

- We extend the previous approach which allowed one known shape in a scene of otherwise unfamiliar shapes to one which allows two different known shapes. Rather than treating the second shape as background, the segmentation scheme is capable of reconstructing both known objects.

- Finally we treat the general case of an arbitrary number of known and unknown shapes by replacing the scalar-valued labeling by a vector-valued function. The latter permits to characterize up to 2^n regions with different priors, where n is the dimension of the labeling function. In particular, we demonstrate that – through a process of competing priors – the resulting segmentation scheme permits to simultaneously reconstruct three known objects while not affecting the segmentation of separate unknown objects.

In this work, the term *shape prior* refers to fixed templates with variable 2D pose. However, the proposed framework of selective shape priors is easily extended to statistical shape models which would additionally allow certain deformation modes of each template. For promising advances regarding level set based statistical shape representations, we refer to [4].

The outline of the paper is as follows: In Section 2, we briefly review the level set formulation of the piecewise constant Mumford-Shah functional proposed in [3]. In Section 3, we augment this variational framework by a labeling function which selectively imposes a given shape prior in a certain image region. In Section 4, we enhance this prior by explicit pose parameters and demonstrate the effect of simultaneous pose optimization. In Section 5, we extend the labeling approach from the case of one known object and background to that of two independent known objects. In Section 6, we come to the central contribution of this work, namely the generalization to an arbitrary number of known and unknown objects by means of a vector-valued labeling function. We demonstrate that the resulting segmentation scheme is capable of reconstructing corrupted versions of multiple known objects displayed in a scene containing other unknown objects.

2   Data-Driven Level Set Segmentation

Level set representations of moving interfaces, introduced by Osher and Sethian [13], have become a popular framework for image segmentation. A contour C is represented as the zero level set of an embedding function $\phi : \Omega \to \mathbb{R}$ on the image domain $\Omega \subset \mathbb{R}^2$:

$$C = \{x \in \Omega \mid \phi(x) = 0\}. \tag{1}$$

During the segmentation process, this contour is propagated implicitly by evolving the embedding function ϕ. In contrast to explicit parameterizations, one avoids the issues of control point regridding. Moreover, the implicitly represented contour can undergo topological changes such as splitting and merging during the evolution of the embedding function. This makes the level set formalism well suited for the segmentation of *multiple* objects. In this work, we will revert to a region-based level set scheme introduced by Chan and Vese [3]. However, other data-driven level set schemes could be employed.

In [3] Chan and Vese introduce a level set formulation of the piecewise constant Mumford-Shah functional [12]. In particular, they propose to generate a segmentation of an input image f with two gray values μ_1 and μ_2 by minimizing the functional

$$E_{CV}(\mu_1, \mu_2, \phi) = \int_\Omega (f - \mu_1)^2 H(\phi) + (f - \mu_2)^2 (1 - H(\phi))\, dx + \nu \int_\Omega |\nabla H(\phi)|,$$

$$\tag{2}$$

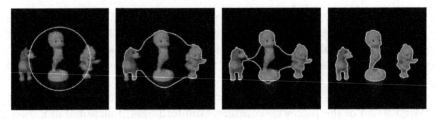

Fig. 1. Purely intensity-based segmentation. Contour evolution generated by minimizing the Chan-Vese model (2) [3]. The central figure is partially corrupted.

with respect to the scalar variables μ_1 and μ_2 and the embedding level set function ϕ. Here H denotes the Heaviside function

$$H(\phi) = \begin{cases} 1, & \phi \geq 0 \\ 0, & \text{else} \end{cases}.$$ (3)

The last term in (2) measures the length of the zero-crossing of ϕ.

The Euler-Lagrange equation for this functional is implemented by gradient descent:

$$\frac{\partial \phi}{\partial t} = \delta(\phi) \left[\nu \operatorname{div}\left(\frac{\nabla \phi}{|\nabla \phi|} \right) - (f - \mu_1)^2 + (f - \mu_2)^2 \right],$$ (4)

where μ_1 and μ_2 are updated in alternation with the level set evolution to take on the mean gray value of the input image f in the regions defined by $\phi > 0$ and $\phi < 0$, respectively:

$$\mu_1 = \frac{\int f(x) H(\phi) dx}{\int H(\phi) dx}, \quad \mu_2 = \frac{\int f(x)(1 - H(\phi)) dx}{\int (1 - H(\phi)) dx}.$$ (5)

Figure 1 shows a representative contour evolution obtained for an image containing three figures, the middle one being partially corrupted.

3 Selective Shape Priors by Dynamic Labeling

The evolution in Figure 1 demonstrates the well-known fact that the level set based segmentation process can cope with multiple objects in a given scene. However, if the low-level segmentation criterion is violated due to noise, background clutter or partial occlusion of the objects of interest, then the purely image-based segmentation scheme will fail to converge to the desired segmentation.

To cope with such degraded low-level information, it was proposed to introduce prior shape knowledge into the level set scheme (cf. [9,17,15]). The basic idea is to extend the image-based cost functional by a shape energy which favors certain contour formations:

$$E_{total}(\phi) = E_{CV}(\mu_1, \mu_2, \phi) + \alpha E_{shape}(\phi) \quad (\alpha > 0).$$ (6)

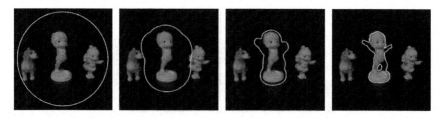

Fig. 2. Global shape prior. Contour evolution generated by minimizing the total energy (6) with a global shape prior of the form (7) encoding the figure in the center. Due to the global constraint on the embedding function, the familiar object is reconstructed while all unfamiliar structures are suppressed in the final segmentation. The resulting segmentation scheme lost its capacity to deal with multiple independent objects.

In general, the proposed shape constraints affect the embedding surface ϕ globally (i.e. on the entire domain Ω). In the simplest case, such a prior has the form:

$$E_{shape}(\phi) = \int_{\Omega} \left(\phi(x) - \phi_0(x)\right)^2 dx, \qquad (7)$$

where ϕ_0 is the level set function embedding a given training shape (or the mean of a set of training shapes). Uniqueness of the embedding function associated with a given shape is guaranteed by imposing ϕ_0 to be a signed distance function (cf. [9]). For consistency, we also project the segmenting level set function ϕ to the space of distance functions during the optimization [16].

Figure 2 shows several steps in the contour evolution with such a prior, where ϕ_0 is the level set function associated with the middle figure. The shape prior permits to reconstruct the object of interest, yet in the process, all unfamiliar objects are suppressed from the segmentation. The segmentation process with shape prior obviously lost its capacity to handle multiple (independent) objects.

In order to retain this favorable property of the level set method, it was proposed in [7] to introduce a labeling function $L : \Omega \to \mathbb{R}$, which indicates the regions of the image where a given prior is to be enforced. During optimization of an appropriate cost functional, the labeling evolves dynamically in order to select these regions in a recognition-driven way. The corresponding shape energy is given by:

$$E_{shape}(\phi, L) = \int (\phi - \phi_0)^2 (L+1)^2 dx + \int \lambda^2 (L-1)^2 dx + \gamma \int |\nabla H(L)| dx, \qquad (8)$$

with two parameters $\lambda, \gamma > 0$. The labeling L enforces the shape prior in those areas of the image where the level set function is similar to the prior (associated with labeling $L = 1$). In particular, for fixed ϕ, minimizing the first two terms in (8) induces the following qualitative behavior of the labeling:

$$L \to +1, \quad \text{if } |\phi - \phi_0| < \lambda$$
$$L \to -1, \quad \text{if } |\phi - \phi_0| > \lambda$$

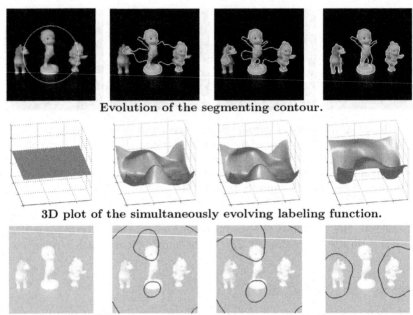

Evolution of the segmenting contour.

3D plot of the simultaneously evolving labeling function.

Zero-crossing of labeling function superimposed on the input image.

Fig. 3. Selective shape prior by dynamic labeling. Contour evolution generated by minimizing the total energy (6) with a selective shape prior of the form (8) encoding the figure in the center. Due to the simultaneous optimization of a labeling function $L(x)$ (middle and bottom row), the shape prior is restricted to act only in selected areas. The familiar shape is reconstructed, while the correct segmentation of separate (unfamiliar) objects remains unaffected. The resulting segmentation scheme thereby retains its capacity to deal with multiple independent objects. In this and all subsequent examples, labeling functions are initialized by $L \equiv 0$.

In addition, the last term in equation (8) imposes a regularizing constraint on the length of the zero crossing of the labeling, this induces topological "compactness" of both the regions with and without shape prior.

Figure 3 shows the contour evolution generated with the prior (8), where ϕ_0 encodes the middle figure as before. Again the shape prior permits to reconstruct the corrupted figure. In contrast to the global prior (7) in Figure 2, however, the process dynamically selects the region where to impose the prior. Consequently the correct segmentation of the two unknown objects is unaffected by the prior.

4   A Pose-Invariant Formulation

In the above formalism of dynamic labeling, the pose of the object of interest is assumed to be known. In a realistic segmentation problem, one generally does not know the pose of an object of interest. If the object of interest is no longer in the same location as the prior ϕ_0, the labeling approach will fail to generate the desired segmentation. This is demonstrated in Figure 4. While the labeling

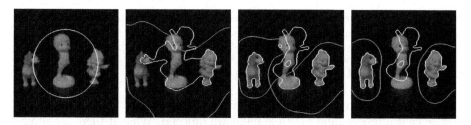

Fig. 4. Missing pose optimization. Evolution of contour (yellow) and labeling (blue) with selective shape prior (8) and a displaced template ϕ. . Without simultaneous pose optimization, the familiar shape is forced to appear in the displaced position.

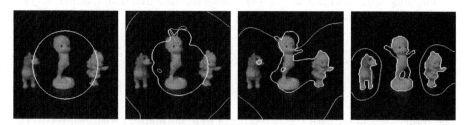

Fig. 5. Effect of pose optimization. By simultaneously optimizing a set of pose parameters in the shape energy (9), one jointly solves the problems of estimating the area where to impose a prior and the pose of the respective prior. Note that the pose estimate is gradually improved during the energy minimization.

still separates areas of known objects from areas of unknown objects, the known shape is not reconstructed correctly, since the pose of the prior and that of the object in the image differ.

A possible solution is to introduce a set of pose parameters associated with a given prior ϕ_0 (cf. [15,5]). The corresponding shape energy

$$E_{shape}(\phi, L, s, \theta, h) = \int \left(\phi(x) - \frac{1}{s}\phi_0(sR_\theta x + h) \right)^2 (L+1)^2 \, dx$$
$$+ \int \lambda^2 \, (L-1)^2 \, dx + \gamma \int |\nabla H(L)| \, dx \qquad (9)$$

is simultaneously optimized with respect to the segmenting level set function ϕ, the labeling function L and the pose parameters, which account for translation h, rotation by an angle θ and scaling s of the template. The normalization by s guarantees that the resulting shape remains a distance function.

Figure 5 shows the resulting segmentation: Again the labeling selects the regions where to apply the given prior, but now the simultaneous pose optimization also allows to estimate the pose of the object of interest.

The main focus of the present paper is to propose selective shape priors. For the sake of simplifying the exposition, we will therefore assume in the following, that the correct pose of familiar objects is known. Moreover, we will drop pose parameters associated with each shape template from the equations, so as to simplify the notation. We want to stress, however, that similar pose invariance can be demonstrated for all of the following generalizations.

5 Extension to Two Known Objects

A serious limitation of the labeling approach in (8) is that it only allows for a *single* known object (and multiple unknown objects). What if there are several familiar objects in the scene? How can one integrate prior knowledge about multiple shapes such as those given by a database of known objects? Before considering the general case, let us first study the case of *two* known objects.

The following modification of (8) allows for two different familiar objects associated with embedding functions ϕ_1 and ϕ_2:

$$E_{shape}(\phi, L) = \frac{1}{\sigma_1^2} \int (\phi - \phi_1)^2 (L+1)^2 \, dx + \frac{1}{\sigma_2^2} \int (\phi - \phi_2)^2 (L-1)^2 \, dx$$
$$+ \gamma \int |\nabla H(L)| \, dx. \tag{10}$$

The terms associated with the two objects were normalized with respect to the variance of the respective template: $\sigma_i^2 = \int \phi_i^2 dx - (\int \phi_i dx)^2$. The resulting shape prior has therefore merely one (instead of two) free parameters. The evolution of the labeling function is now driven by two competing shape priors: each image location will be ascribed to one or the other prior.

Figure 6 shows a comparison: The upper row indicates the contour evolution generated with the shape energy (8), where ϕ_0 encodes the figure on the left. The lower row shows the respective evolution obtained with the shape energy 10, with ϕ_1 and ϕ_2 encoding the left and right figures, respectively. Whereas the object on the right (occluded by a pen) is treated as unknown in the original formulation (upper row), both figures can be reconstructed by simultaneously imposing two competing priors in different domains (lower row).

6 The General Case: Multiphase Dynamic Labeling

The above example showed that the dynamic labeling approach can be transformed to allow for two shape priors rather than a single shape prior and possible background.

Let us now consider the general case of a larger number of known objects and possibly some further independent unknown objects (which should therefore be segmented based on their intensity only). To this end, we introduce a vector-valued labeling function

$$L : \Omega \to \mathbb{R}^n, \qquad L(x) = (L_1(x), \ldots, L_n(x)). \tag{11}$$

We employ the $m = 2^n$ vertices of the polytope $[-1, +1]^n$ to encode m different regions, $L_j \in \{+1, -1\}$, and denote by $\chi_i, i = 1, \ldots, m$ the indicator function for each of these regions. See [19] for a related concept in the context of multi-region

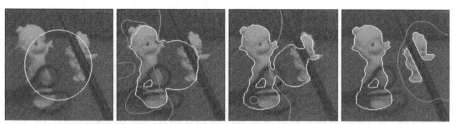

Dynamic Labeling with a single prior and background.

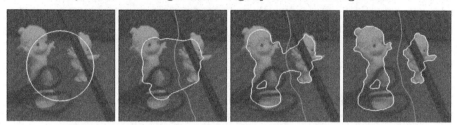

Dynamic Labeling allowing for two competing priors.

Fig. 6. Extension to two priors. Evolutions of contour (**yellow**) and labeling (**blue**) generated by minimizing energy (6) with a selective prior of the form (8) encoding the left figure (**top**) and with a selective prior of the form (10) encoding both figures (**bottom**). In both cases, the left figure is correctly reconstructed despite prominent occlusions by the scissors. However, while the structure on the right is treated as unfamiliar and thereby segmented based on intensities only (top row), the extension to two priors permits to simultaneously reconstruct both known objects (bottom row).

segmentation. For example, for $n = 2$, four regions are modeled by the indicator functions:

$$\chi_1(\boldsymbol{L}) = \tfrac{1}{16}(L_1 - 1)^2 (L_2 - 1)^2, \qquad \chi_2(\boldsymbol{L}) = \tfrac{1}{16}(L_1 + 1)^2 (L_2 - 1)^2,$$
$$\chi_3(\boldsymbol{L}) = \tfrac{1}{16}(L_1 - 1)^2 (L_2 + 1)^2, \qquad \chi_4(\boldsymbol{L}) = \tfrac{1}{16}(L_1 + 1)^2 (L_2 + 1)^2.$$

In the general case of an n-dimensional labeling function, each indicator function will be of the form

$$\chi_i(\boldsymbol{L}) \equiv \chi_{l_1 \dots l_n}(\boldsymbol{L}) = \frac{1}{4^n} \prod_{j=1}^{n} (L_j + l_j)^2, \quad \text{with} \ \ l_j \in \{+1, -1\}. \tag{12}$$

With this notation, the extension of the dynamic labeling approach to up to $m = 2^n$ regions can be cast into a cost functional of the form:

$$E_{total}(\phi, \boldsymbol{L}, \mu_1, \mu_2) = E_{CV}(\phi, \mu_1, \mu_2) + \alpha E_{shape}(\phi, \boldsymbol{L}), \tag{13}$$

$$E_{shape}(\phi, \boldsymbol{L}) = \sum_{i=1}^{m-1} \int \frac{(\phi - \phi_i)^2}{\sigma_i^2} \chi_i(\boldsymbol{L}) dx + \int \lambda^2 \chi_m(\boldsymbol{L}) dx + \gamma \sum_{i=1}^{m} \int |\nabla H(L_i)| dx.$$

Here, each ϕ_i corresponds to a particular known shape with its variance given by σ_i.

As mentioned before, we have – for better readability – neglected the pose parameters associated with each template. These can be incorporated by the replacements:

$$\phi_i \longrightarrow \frac{1}{s_i}\phi_i(s_i R_{\theta_i} x + h_i) \quad \text{and} \quad E_{shape}(\phi, \boldsymbol{L}) \longrightarrow E_{shape}(\phi, \boldsymbol{L}, \boldsymbol{p}),$$

where $\boldsymbol{p} = (p_1, \ldots, p_m)$ denotes the vector of pose parameters $p_i = (s_i, \theta_i, h_i)$ associated with each known shape.

7 Energy Minimization

In the previous sections, we have introduced variational formulations of increasing complexity to tackle the problem of multi-object segmentation with shape priors. The corresponding segmentation processes are generated by minimizing these functionals. In this section, we will detail the minimization scheme in order to illuminate how the different components of the proposed cost functionals affect the segmentation process. Let us focus on the case of multiple labels corresponding to the cost functional (13). Minimization of this functional is obtained by alternating the update of the mean intensities μ_1 and μ_2 according to (5) with a gradient descent evolution for the level set function ϕ, the labeling functions L_j and the associated pose parameters p_j. In the following, we will detail this for ϕ and L_j. Respective evolution equations for p_j are straight forward and not our central focus.

For fixed labeling, the evolution of the level set function ϕ is given by:

$$\frac{\partial \phi}{\partial t} = -\frac{\partial E_{total}}{\partial \phi} = -\frac{\partial E_{CV}}{\partial \phi} - 2\alpha \sum_{i=1}^{m-1} \frac{\phi - \phi_i}{\sigma_i^2} \chi_i(\boldsymbol{L}). \tag{14}$$

Apart from the image-driven first component given by the Chan-Vese evolution in equation (4), we additionally have a relaxation toward the template ϕ_i in all image locations where $\chi_i = 1$.

Minimization by gradient descent with respect to the labeling functions L_j corresponds to an evolution of the form:

$$\frac{1}{\alpha} \frac{\partial L_j}{\partial t} = -\sum_{i=1}^{m-1} \frac{(\phi - \phi_i)^2}{\sigma_i^2} \frac{\partial \chi_i(\boldsymbol{L})}{\partial L_j} - \lambda^2 \frac{\partial \chi_m(\boldsymbol{L})}{\partial L_j} - \gamma\delta(L_j)\nabla\left(\frac{\nabla L_j}{|\nabla L_j|}\right), \tag{15}$$

where the derivatives of the indicator functions χ_i are easily obtained from (12). The first two terms in (15) drive the labeling $\boldsymbol{L}$ to indicate the template ϕ_i which is most similar to the given function ϕ (or alternatively the background). The last term minimizes the length of the zero crossing of L_j. This has two effects: Firstly, it induces the labeling to decide for one of the possible templates (or the background), i.e. mixing of templates with label values between +1 and −1 are

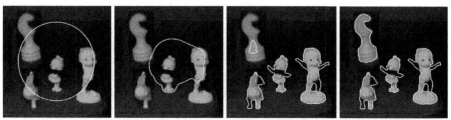

Evolution of the segmentation with multiphase dynamic labeling.

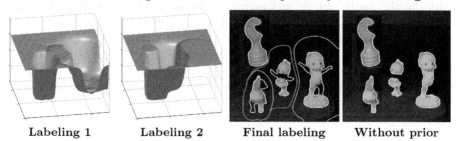

Labeling 1   Labeling 2   Final labeling   Without prior

Fig. 7. Coping with several objects by multiphase dynamic labeling. Contour
evolution generated by minimizing the total energy (6) with a multiphase selective
shape prior of the form (13) encoding the three figures on the left, center and right.
The appearance of all three objects is corrupted. Due to the simultaneous optimization
of a vector-valued labeling function, several regions associated with each shape prior
are selected, in which the given prior is enforced. All familiar shapes are segmented
and restored, while the correct segmentation of separate (unfamiliar) objects remains
unaffected. The images on the bottom show the final labeling and – for comparison –
the segmentation without prior (right).

suppressed. Secondly, it enforces the decision regions (regions of constant label)
to be "compact", because label flipping is energetically unfavorable.

Figure 7 shows a contour evolution obtained with the multiphase dynamic
labeling model (13) and $n = 2$ labeling functions. The image contains three corrupted objects which are assumed to be familiar and one unfamiliar object (in
the top left corner). The top row shows the evolution of the segmenting contour (yellow) superimposed on the input image. The segmentation process with
a vector-valued labeling function selects regions corresponding to the different
objects in an unsupervised manner and simultaneously applies three competing
shape priors which permit to reconstruct the familiar objects. Corresponding 3D
plots of the two labeling functions in the bottom rows of Figure 7 show which
areas of the image have been associated with which label configuration. For example, the object in the center has been identified by the labeling $L = (+1, -1)$.

8   Conclusion

We introduced the framework of multiphase dynamic labeling, which allows
to integrate multiple competing shape priors into level set based segmentation

schemes. The proposed cost functional is simultaneously optimized with respect to a level set function defining the segmentation, a vector-valued labeling function indicating regions where particular shape priors should be enforced, and a set of pose parameters associated with each prior. Each shape prior is given by a fixed template and respective pose parameters, yet the extension to statistical shape priors (which additionally allow deformation modes) is straight forward.

We argued that the proposed mechanism fundamentally generalizes previous approaches to shape priors in level set segmentation. Firstly, it is consistent with the philosophy of level sets because it retains the capacity of the resulting segmentation scheme to cope with multiple independent objects in a given image. Secondly, it addresses the central question of where to apply which shape prior.

The selection of appropriate regions associated with each prior is generated by the dynamic labeling in a recognition-driven manner. In this sense, our work demonstrates in a specific way how a recognition process can be modeled in a variational segmentation framework.

References

1. V. Caselles, F. Catté, T. Coll, and F. Dibos. A gemoetric model for active contours in image processing. *Numer. Math.*, 66:1–31, 1993.
2. V. Caselles, R. Kimmel, and G. Sapiro. Geodesic active contours. In *Proc. IEEE Intl. Conf. on Comp. Vis.*, pages 694–699, Boston, USA, 1995.
3. T. Chan and L. Vese. Active contours without edges. *IEEE Trans. Image Processing*, 10(2):266–277, 2001.
4. G. Charpiat, O. Faugeras, and R. Keriven. Approximations of shape metrics and application to shape warping and empirical shape statistics. Technical Report 4820, INRIA, Sophia Antipolis, May 2003.
5. Y. Chen, H. Tagare, S. Thiruvenkadam, F. Huang, D. Wilson, K. S. Gopinath, R. W. Briggs, and E. Geiser. Using shape priors in geometric active contours in a variational framework. *Int. J. of Computer Vision*, 50(3):315–328, 2002.
6. D. Cremers. A variational framework for image segmentation combining motion estimation and shape regularization. In C. Dyer and P. Perona, editors, *IEEE Conf. on Comp. Vis. and Patt. Recog.*, volume 1, pages 53–58, Madison, June 2003.
7. D. Cremers, N. Sochen, and C. Schnörr. Towards recognition-based variational segmentation using shape priors and dynamic labeling. In L. Griffith, editor, *Int. Conf. on Scale Space Theories in Computer Vision*, volume 2695 of *LNCS*, pages 388–400, Isle of Skye, 2003. Springer.
8. S. Kichenassamy, A. Kumar, P. J. Olver, A. Tannenbaum, and A. J. Yezzi. Gradient flows and geometric active contour models. In *Proc. IEEE Intl. Conf. on Comp. Vis.*, pages 810–815, Boston, USA, 1995.
9. M. E. Leventon, W. E. L. Grimson, and O. Faugeras. Statistical shape influence in geodesic active contours. In *Proc. Conf. Computer Vis. and Pattern Recog.*, volume 1, pages 316–323, Hilton Head Island, SC, June 13–15, 2000.
10. R. Malladi, J. A. Sethian, and B. C. Vemuri. Shape modeling with front propagation: A level set approach. *IEEE PAMI*, 17(2):158–175, 1995.
11. J. Marroquin, E.A. Santana, and S. Botello. Hidden markov measure field models for image segmentation. *IEEE PAMI*, 25(11):1380–1387, 2003.

12. D. Mumford and J. Shah. Optimal approximations by piecewise smooth functions and associated variational problems. *Comm. Pure Appl. Math.*, 42:577–685, 1989.

13. S. J. Osher and J. A. Sethian. Fronts propagation with curvature dependent speed: Algorithms based on Hamilton–Jacobi formulations. *J. of Comp. Phys.*, 79:12–49, 1988.

14. N. Paragios and R. Deriche. Geodesic active regions and level set methods for supervised texture segmentation. *Int. J. of Computer Vision*, 46(3):223–247, 2002.

15. M. Rousson and N. Paragios. Shape priors for level set representations. In A. Heyden et al., editors, *Proc. of the Europ. Conf. on Comp. Vis.*, volume 2351 of *LNCS*, pages 78–92, Copenhagen, May 2002. Springer, Berlin.

16. M. Sussman, Smereka P., and S. J. Osher. A level set approach for computing solutions to incompressible twophase flow. *J. of Comp. Phys.*, 94:146–159, 1994.

17. A. Tsai, A. Yezzi, W. Wells, C. Tempany, D. Tucker, A. Fan, E. Grimson, and A. Willsky. Model–based curve evolution technique for image segmentation. In *Comp. Vision Patt. Recog.*, pages 463–468, Kauai, Hawaii, 2001.

18. A. Tsai, A. J. Yezzi, and A. S. Willsky. Curve evolution implementation of the Mumford-Shah functional for image segmentation, denoising, interpolation, and magnification. *IEEE Trans. on Image Processing*, 10(8):1169–1186, 2001.

19. L. Vese and T. Chan. A multiphase level set framework for image processing using the Mumford–Shah functional. *Int. J. of Computer Vision*, 50(3):271–293, 2002.

Integral Invariant Signatures

Siddharth Manay[1], Byung-Woo Hong[2], Anthony J. Yezzi[3], and
Stefano Soatto[1,*]

[.] University of California at Los Angeles, Los Angeles CA 90024, USA,
[.] University of Oxford, Oxford OX1 3BW, UK
[.] Georgia Institute of Technology, Atlanta GA 30332, USA
{manay,hong,soatto}@cs.ucla.edu ayezzi@ece.gatech.edu

Abstract. For shapes represented as closed planar contours, we introduce a class of functionals that are invariant with respect to the Euclidean and similarity group, obtained by performing integral operations.
While such integral invariants enjoy some of the desirable properties
of their differential cousins, such as locality of computation (which allows matching under occlusions) and uniqueness of representation (in
the limit), they are not as sensitive to noise in the data. We exploit the
integral invariants to define a unique signature, from which the original
shape can be reconstructed uniquely up to the symmetry group, and a
notion of scale-space that allows analysis at multiple levels of resolution.
The invariant signature can be used as a basis to define various notions
of distance between shapes, and we illustrate the potential of the integral
invariant representation for shape matching on real and synthetic data.

1 Introduction

Geometric invariance is an important issue in computer vision that has received
considerable attention in the past. The idea that one could compute functions
of geometric primitives of the image that do not change under the various nuisances of image formation and viewing geometry was appealing; it held potential
for application to recognition, correspondence, 3-D reconstruction, and visualization. The discovery that there exist no generic viewpoint invariants was only
a minor roadblock, as image deformations can be approximated with homo-
graphies; hence the study of invariants to projective transformations and their
subgroups (affine, similarity, Euclidean) flourished. Toward the end of the last
millennium, the decrease in popularity of research on geometric invariance was
sanctioned mostly by two factors: the progress on multiple view geometry (one
way to achieve viewpoint invariance is to estimate the viewing geometry) and
noise. Ultimately, algorithms based on invariants did not meet expectations because most entailed computing various derivatives of measured functions of the
image (hence the name "differential invariants"). As soon as noise was present
and affected the geometric primitives computed from the images, the invariants
were dominated by the small scale perturbations. Various palliative measures

---

* Supported by NSF IIS-0208197, AFOSR F49620-03-1-0095, ONR N00014-03-1-0850

T. Pajdla and J. Matas (Eds.): ECCV 2004, LNCS 3024, pp. 87–99, 2004.

were taken, such as the introduction of scale-space smoothing, but a more principled approach has so far been elusive. Nowadays, the field is instead engaged in searching for invariant (or insensitive) measures of photometric (rather than geometric) nuisances in the image formation process. Nevertheless, the idea of computing functions that are invariant with respect to group transformations of the image domain remains important, because it holds the promise to extract compact, efficient representations for shape matching, indexing, and ultimately recognition.

In this paper, we introduce a general class of invariants that are *integral* functionals of the data, as opposed to differential ones. We argue that such functionals are far less sensitive to noise, while retaining the nice features of differential invariants such as locality, which allow for matching under occlusions. They can be exploited to define invariant signature curves that can be used as a representation to define various notions of distances between shapes. We restrict our analysis to Euclidean and similarity invariants, although extensions to the affine group are straightforward. The integration kernel allows us to define intrinsic scale-spaces of invariant signatures, so that we can represent shapes at different levels of resolution and under various levels of measurement noise. We also show that our invariants can be computed very efficiently without performing explicit sums (in the discretized domain). Finally, we show that in the limit where the kernel measure goes to zero, one class of integral invariant is in one-to-one correspondence with the prince of differential invariants, curvature. This allows the establishment of a completeness property of the representation, in the limit, in that a given shape can be reconstructed uniquely, up to the invariance group, from its invariant signature. This relationship allows us to tap into the rich literature on differential invariants for theoretical results, while in our experiments we can avoid computing higher-order derivatives. We illustrate our results with several experiments, showed as space allows.

2 Relation to Existing Work, and Our Contribution

The role of invariants in computer vision has been advocated for various applications ranging from shape representation [34,4] to shape matching [3,29], quality control [48,11], and general object recognition [39,1]. Consequently a number of features that are invariant under specific transformations have been investigated [14,25,15,21,33,46]. In particular, one can construct primitive invariants of algebraic entities such as lines, conics and polynomial curves, based on a global descriptor of shape [36,18]. In addition to invariants to transformation groups, considerable attention has been devoted to invariants with respect to the geometric relationship between 3D objects and their 2D views; while generic viewpoint invariants do not exist, invariant features can be computed from a collection of coplanar points or lines [40,41,20,6,17,52,1,45,26]. An invariant descriptor of a collection of points that relates to our approach is the shape context introduced by Belongie et al. [3], which consists in a radial histogram of the relative coordinates of the rest of the shape at each point.

Differential invariants to actions of various Lie groups have been addressed thoroughly [28,24,13,35]. An invariant is defined by an unchanged subset of the manifold which the group transformation is acting on. In particular, an invariant signature which pairs curvature and its first derivative avoids parameterization in terms of arc length [10,37]. Calabi and coworkers suggested numerical expressions for curvature and first derivative of curvature in terms of joint invariants. However, it is shown that the expression for the first derivative of curvature is not convergent and modified formulas are presented in [5].

In order to reduce noise-induced fluctuations of the signature, semi-differential invariants methods are introduced by using first derivatives and one reference point instead of curvature, thus avoiding the computation of high-order derivatives [38,19,27]. Another semi-invariant is given by transforming the given coordinate system to a canonical one [49].

A useful property of differential and (some) semi-differential invariants is that they can be applied to match shapes despite occlusions, due to the locality of the signature [8,7]. However, the fundamental problem of differential invariants is that high-order derivatives have to be computed, amplifying the effect of noise. There have been several approaches to decrease sensitivity to noise by employing scale-space via linear filtering [50]. The combination of invariant theory with geometric multiscale analysis is investigated by applying an invariant diffusion equation for curve evolution [42,43,12]. A scale-space can be determined by varying the size of the differencing interval used to approximate derivatives using finite differences [9]. In [32], a curvature scale-space was developed for a shape matching problem. A set of Gaussian kernels was applied to build a scale-space of curvature whose extrema were observed across scales.

To overcome the limitations of differential invariants, there have been attempts to derive invariants based on integral computations. A statistical approach to describe invariants was introduced using moments in [23]. Moment invariants under affine transformations were derived from the classical moment invariants in [16]. They have a limitation in that high-order moments are sensitive to noise which results in high variances. The error analysis and analytic characterization of moment descriptors were studied in [30]. The Fourier transform was also applied to obtain integral invariants [51,31,2]. A closed curve was represented by a set of Fourier coefficients and normalized Fourier descriptors were used to compute affine invariants. In this method, high-order Fourier coefficients are involved and they are not stable with respect to noise. Several techniques have been developed to restrict the computation to local neighborhoods: the Wavelet transform was used for affine invariants using the dyadic wavelet in [47] and potentials were also proposed to preserve locality [22]. Alternatively, semi-local integral invariants are presented by integrating object curves with respect to arc length [44].

In this manuscript, we introduce two general classes of integral invariants; for one of them, we show its relationship to differential invariants (in the limit), which allows us to conclude that the invariant signature curve obtained from the integral invariant is in one-to-one correspondence with the original shape, up to the action of the nuisance group. We use the invariant signature to define various notions of distance between shapes, and we illustrate the potential of our representation on several experiments with real and simulated images.

3   Integral Invariants

Throughout this section we indicate with $\gamma : \mathbb{S}^1 \to \mathbb{R}^2$ a closed planar contour with arclength ds, and G a group acting on $\mathbb{R}^2$, with dx the area form on $\mathbb{R}^2$. We also use the formal notation $\bar{\gamma}$ to indicate either the interior of the region bounded by γ (a two-dimensional object), or the curve γ itself (a one-dimensional object), and $d\mu(x)$ the corresponding measure, i.e. the area form dx or the arclength $ds(x)$ respectively. With this notation, we can define a fairly general notion of integral invariant.

Definition 1. *A function $I_\gamma(p) : \mathbb{R}^2 \to \mathbb{R}$ is an integral G-invariant if there exists a kernel $h : \mathbb{R}^2 \times \mathbb{R}^2 \to \mathbb{R}$ such that*

$$I_\gamma(p) = \int_{\bar{\gamma}} h(p, x) d\mu(x) \tag{1}$$

where $h(\cdot, \cdot)$ satisfies

$$\int_{\bar{\gamma}} h(p, x) d\mu(x) = \int_{g\bar{\gamma}} h(gp, x) d\mu(x) \; \forall \; g \in G. \tag{2}$$

where $g\gamma \doteq \{gx \mid g \in G, x \in \gamma\}$, and similarly for $g\bar{\gamma}$.

The definition can be extended to vector signatures, or to multiple integrals. Note that the point p does not necessarily lie *on* the contour γ, as long as there is an unequivocal way of associating $p \in \mathbb{R}^2$ to γ (e.g. the centroid of the curve).

Example 1 (Integral distance invariant). *Consider $G = SE(2)$ and the following function, computed at every point $p \in \gamma$:*

$$I_\gamma(p) \doteq \int_\gamma d(p, x) ds(x) \tag{3}$$

where $d(x, y) \doteq |y - x|$ is the Euclidean distance in $\mathbb{R}^2$. This is illustrated in Fig. 1-a.

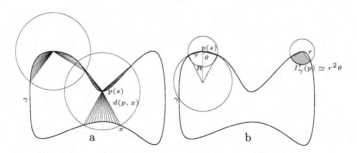

Fig. 1. (Left) Integral distance invariant defined in eq. (3), made local by means of a kernel as described in eq. (5). (Right) Integral area invariant defined by eq. (6).

It is immediate to show that this is an integral Euclidean invariant. The function I_γ associates to each point on the contour a number that is the average distance from that point to every other point on the contour. In particular, if the point $p \in \gamma$ is parameterized by arclength, the invariant can be interpreted as a function from $[0, L]$, where L is the length of the curve, to the positive reals:

$$\{\gamma : \mathbb{S}^1 \to \mathbb{R}^2\} \mapsto \{I_\gamma(p(s)) : [0, \ L] \to \mathbb{R}_+.\} \tag{4}$$

This invariant is computed for a few representative shapes in Fig. 2 and Fig. 3.

A more "local" version of the invariant signature I_γ can be obtained by weighting the integral in eq. (3) with a kernel $q(p, x)$, so that $I_\gamma(p) \doteq \int_\gamma h(p, x) ds(x)$ where

$$h(p, x) \doteq q(p, x) d(p, x). \tag{5}$$

The kernel $q(\cdot, \cdot)$ is free for the designer to choose depending on the final goal. This local integral invariant can be thought of as a continuous version of the "shape context," which was designed for a finite collection of points [3]. The difference is that the shape context signature is a local radial histogram of neighboring points, whereas in our case we only store the mean of their distance.

Example 2 (Integral area invariant). *Consider now the kernel $h(p, x) = \chi(B_r(p) \cap \bar{\gamma})(x)$, which represents the indicator function of the intersection of a small circle of radius r centered at the point p with the interior of the curve γ. For any given radius r, the corresponding integral invariant*

$$I_\gamma^r(p) \doteq \int_{B_r(p) \cap \bar{\gamma}} dx \tag{6}$$

can be thought of as a function from the interval $[0, \ L]$ to the positive reals, bounded above by the area of the region bounded by the curve γ. This is illustrated in Fig. 1-b and examples are shown in Fig. 2 and Fig. 3.

Naturally, if we plot the value of $I_\gamma^r(p(s))$ for all values of s and r ranging from zero to a maximum radius so that the local kernel encloses the entire curve $B_r(p) \supset \gamma$, we can generate a graph of a function that can be interpreted as a scale-space of integral invariants. Furthermore, $\chi(B_r(p))$ can be substituted by a more general kernel, for instance a Gaussian centered at p with $\sigma = r$.

Example 3 (Differential invariant). *Note that a regularized version of curvature, or in general a curvature scale space, can be interpreted as an integral invariant, since regularized curvature is an algebraic function of the first- and second-regularized derivatives [32]. Therefore, integral invariants are more general, but we will not exploit this added generality, since it contrary to the spirit of this manuscript, that is of avoiding the computation of derivatives of the image data, even if regularized.*

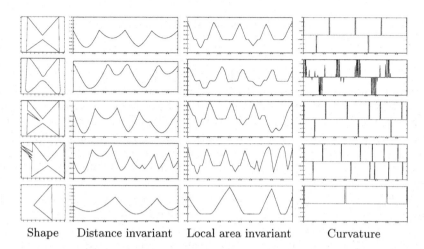

Fig. 2. For a set of representative shapes (left column), we compute the distance integral invariant of eq. (3) (middle left column), the local area invariant of eq. (6) with a kernel size $\sigma = 2$ (middle right column). Compare the results with curvature, shown in the rightmost column.

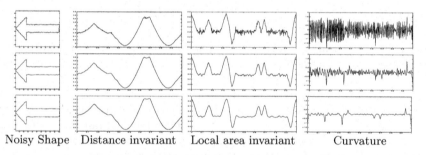

Fig. 3. For a noisy shape (left column), the distance invariant of eq. (3) with a kernel size of $\sigma = 30$ (middle left column), the local area invariant of eq. (6) with kernel size $r = 10$ (middle right column) and the differential invariant, curvature (right column). As one can see, noise is amplified in the computation of derivatives necessary to extract curvature.

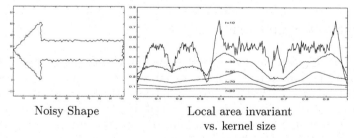

Fig. 4. For a noisy shape (left), the local area invariant of eq. (6) as a function of kernel size induces a scale-space of responses.

4   Relationship with Curvature and Local Differential Invariants

In this section we study the relationship between the local area invariant (6) and curvature. This is motivated by the fact that curvature is a *complete* invariant, in the sense that it allows the recovery of the original curve up to the action of the symmetry group. Furthermore, all differential invariants of any order on the plane are functions of curvature [49], and therefore linking our integral invariant to curvature would allow us to tap onto the rich body of results on differential invariants without suffering from the shortcomings of computing high-order derivatives of the data.

We first assume that γ is smooth, so that a notion of curvature is well-defined, and the curve can be approximated locally by the osculating circle[1] $B_R(p)$ (Fig. 1-b). The invariant $I_\gamma^r(p)$ denotes the area of the intersection of a circle $B_r(p)$ with the interior of γ, and it can be approximated to first-order by the area of the shaded sector in Fig. 1-b, i.e. $I_\gamma^r(p) \simeq r^2\theta(p)$. Now, the angle θ can be computed as a function of r and R using the cosine law: $\cos\theta = r/2R$, and since curvature κ is the inverse of R we have

$$I_\gamma^r(p) \simeq r^2 \arccos\left(\frac{1}{2}r\kappa(p)\right). \tag{7}$$

Now, since arc-cosine is an invertible function, to the extent in which the approximation above is valid (which depends on r), we can recover curvature from the integral invariant.

The approximation above is valid in the limit when $r \to 0$; as r increases, $B_r(p)$ encloses the entire curve γ (which is closed), and consequently I_γ^r becomes a constant beyond a certain radius $r = r_{max}$. Therefore, for values of r that range from 0 to r_{max} we obtain an *intrinsic scale-space* of invariants, in contrast to the extrinsic scale-space of curvature. We compare these two descriptors in Fig. 3 and Fig. 4.

Note also that the integral invariant can be normalized via $I_\gamma^r/\pi r^2$ so as to provide a *scale-invariant* description of the curve, which is therefore invariant with respect to the similarity group. The corresponding integral invariant is then bounded between 0 and 1.

5   Invariant Signature Curves

The invariant $I_\gamma^r(p(s))$ can be represented by a function of s for any fixed value of r. This means, however, that in order to register two shapes, an "initial point" $s = 0$ must be chosen. There is nothing intrinsic to the geometry of the curve in the choice of this initial point, and indeed it would be desirable to devise a description that, in addition to being invariant to the group, is invariant with respect to the choice of initial point.

---

[1] Notice that our invariant does *not* require that the shape be smooth, and this assumption is made only to relate our results to the literature on differential invariants.

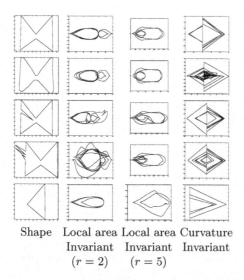

| Shape | Local area Invariant $(r=2)$ | Local area Invariant $(r=5)$ | Curvature Invariant |

Fig. 5. Example of signature curves for a set of representative shapes (left column); local area invariant with small kernel (middle left column) and large kernel (middle right column), differential invariant (right column).

In order to do so, we follow the classic literature on differential invariants (see [10] and references therein) and plot a *signature*, that is the graph of $\frac{\partial I_\gamma^r(p(s))}{\partial s}$ versus I_γ^r. We indicate such a signature concisely by

$$(\dot{I}_\gamma^r, I_\gamma^r) \tag{8}$$

which of course can be plotted for all values of $r \in [0, r_{max}]$, yielding a scale-space of signatures. Naturally, we want to avoid direct computation of the derivative of the invariant, so the signature can be computed more simply as follows: Consider the binary image $\chi(\bar{\gamma})$ and convolve it with the kernel $h(p, x) \doteq B_r(p - x)$, where $p \in \mathbb{R}^2$, not just the curve γ. Evaluating the result of this convolution on $p \in \gamma$ yields I_γ^r, without the need to parameterize the curve. For $\dot{I}_\gamma^r$, compute the gradient of the filter response and inner-multiply the result with the tangent vector field of the image $\chi(\bar{\gamma})$, formed by filtering again by a kernel *different* than $B_r(p - x)$ and rotating its normalized gradient by 90°. The result, when evaluated at $p \in \gamma$, yields $\dot{I}_\gamma^r$.

Notice that from the integral invariant signature we can reconstruct all differential invariants in the limit when $r \to 0$. In fact, from I_γ^r we can compute κ, and therefore from the signature we can compute $\dot{\kappa}$.

6   Distance between Shapes

In this section we outline methods for computing the distance between two shapes based on their invariants and invariant signatures curves.

▶	2	8	18	18	8	15	17	14	11	10	10	12	10	9	9	6	17	14	29	31	29	27	28
	40	78	78	77	70	359	466	428	322	337	*333*	378	369	373	386	383	361	393	541	526	557	484	484
▶	9	*1*	18	20	8	11	14	11	12	10	10	12	7	11	9	7	17	12	22	23	21	22	22
	67	*53*	77	80	72	377	482	441	330	349	386	386	389	383	400	399	373	406	548	535	567	489	496
▶	19	17	*2*	28	16	26	28	27	24	26	21	27	22	25	24	20	32	27	37	34	33	33	35
	70	84	*46*	84	72	378	487	443	333	356	401	393	388	389	401	406	382	413	557	540	580	498	500
▶	19	18	32	*2*	14	16	20	18	19	18	20	19	17	19	19	19	20	18	36	34	33	33	33
	75	89	90	*57*	80	381	511	468	356	371	417	409	402	408	420	419	400	429	567	546	589	503	513
◀	8	5	15	14	*1*	10	12	8	9	6	11	11	9	9	9	7	10	9	24	26	23	23	24
	56	69	67	71	*40*	332	439	*392*	279	311	346	*343*	343	341	358	*352*	328	360	*507*	*493*	*530*	*454*	458
↘	16	13	28	18	11	*0*	23	14	17	11	17	15	16	16	6	7	20	10	34	36	34	35	34
	197	212	226	224	197	*317*	668	596	493	508	556	535	546	541	540	363	521	572	763	732	789	689	681
↘	22	15	35	25	16	23	*1*	18	15	20	10	20	14	20	20	16	19	20	28	27	22	27	26
	244	247	246	264	240	567	*435*	663	522	548	613	588	579	588	578	579	595	622	815	775	826	751	732
↘	14	11	30	19	10	15	19	*0*	8	12	17	11	13	5	14	11	11	13	25	25	24	26	24
	208	223	231	240	210	539	678	*397*	486	521	557	534	547	358	564	558	547	551	769	749	801	708	721
↘	13	12	27	21	11	16	14	8	*0*	14	14	8	11	12	14	11	12	9	24	24	24	27	23
	197	216	215	217	186	519	662	570	*270*	474	545	526	543	523	542	544	521	559	748	736	785	685	701
↘	12	10	28	21	9	11	19	12	13	*1*	14	15	14	13	10	9	19	13	31	33	28	29	31
	221	231	236	237	212	507	686	601	469	*300*	557	566	560	547	567	560	498	577	771	750	794	717	716
↘	14	13	25	22	13	17	9	16	14	14	*1*	14	13	13	16	12	20	15	28	27	24	28	26
	205	229	251	248	218	546	688	608	513	535	*350*	557	544	566	593	545	549	595	789	774	803	727	713
↘	14	14	29	21	13	15	19	11	8	14	14	*1*	13	12	14	9	21	12	25	27	28	28	26
	224	240	240	251	226	555	683	643	520	529	575	*357*	563	571	582	568	558	599	794	762	800	729	725
↘	13	9	23	19	11	16	14	12	10	14	12	13	*1*	10	14	9	16	7	26	27	25	24	25
	222	239	232	244	225	559	680	631	501	510	581	557	*337*	536	570	576	541	374	773	740	798	720	698
↘	12	11	25	20	11	15	20	5	12	13	15	13	11	*0*	14	9	19	9	33	34	32	30	32
	194	208	214	223	180	520	646	394	456	496	526	536	532	*311*	553	548	519	542	738	710	765	663	675
←	13	11	25	19	11	6	19	14	13	10	16	15	14	13	*1*	10	16	10	36	37	34	33	35
	223	245	248	249	218	550	675	629	506	501	584	561	571	553	*328*	582	548	602	789	767	810	724	736
←	8	8	20	21	10	7	15	11	10	9	12	8	9	8	9	*1*	17	12	27	28	26	28	26
	213	224	231	232	207	345	676	613	471	514	541	544	556	545	564	*355*	532	573	783	743	807	712	708
↘	18	16	35	22	12	19	21	12	13	20	23	22	18	20	17	18	*0*	13	39	39	36	37	37
	191	198	211	218	184	529	659	607	467	492	536	526	540	528	538	519	*310*	538	751	723	775	688	689
↘	16	12	30	18	11	11	20	13	9	14	16	12	7	10	11	12	13	*0*	28	30	29	29	28
	180	200	210	216	178	515	642	598	470	502	542	528	344	480	539	518	506	*353*	740	707	765	668	675
♠	36	27	44	40	29	37	29	24	26	33	29	28	27	34	37	29	36	29	*1*	5	10	13	4
	314	332	338	334	325	696	831	811	666	689	726	727	734	715	693	722	699	751	*522*	910	972	864	868
♣	36	27	46	38	30	38	26	25	25	33	27	28	27	34	37	29	36	29	4	*1*	6	10	1
	248	262	259	262	258	607	753	703	569	607	662	634	640	644	642	619	628	646	824	*514*	843	767	*448*
♠	34	24	44	36	28	34	22	23	24	28	24	28	24	32	33	25	33	28	10	6	*1*	11	6
	290	310	311	319	303	682	798	796	631	675	737	677	707	708	714	720	687	719	902	873	*559*	802	825
♠	33	26	38	36	29	35	26	25	26	29	28	27	25	30	32	28	35	29	13	10	10	*1*	10
	296	298	308	304	303	671	789	751	622	635	697	698	677	660	700	689	650	705	861	847	910	*477*	836
♠	36	27	46	37	30	38	26	25	25	33	27	28	27	35	37	29	36	30	4	*1*	5	10	1
	246	259	259	262	259	596	773	713	586	593	650	653	643	644	661	619	612	637	830	*514*	852	765	448

Fig. 6. Noisy shape recognition from a database of 23 shapes. The upper number in each cell is the distance computed via the local-area integral invariant; the lower number is the distance computed via curvature invariant. The number in italics represents the best match for a noisy shape. See the text for more details

A straightforward distance between two shapes γ_1 and γ_2 is to compute a measure of the error between their invariants. One choice is the squared error.

$$D_E(\gamma_i, \gamma_j, r) = \int_0^1 (I_{\gamma_i}^r(p(s)) - I_{\gamma_j}^r(p(s)))^2 ds. \tag{9}$$

While this squared error can be computed for any invariant functional, we focus on invariants that preserve locality, such as the local area invariant, so that these distances will be valid for application to shape recognition despite occlusion.

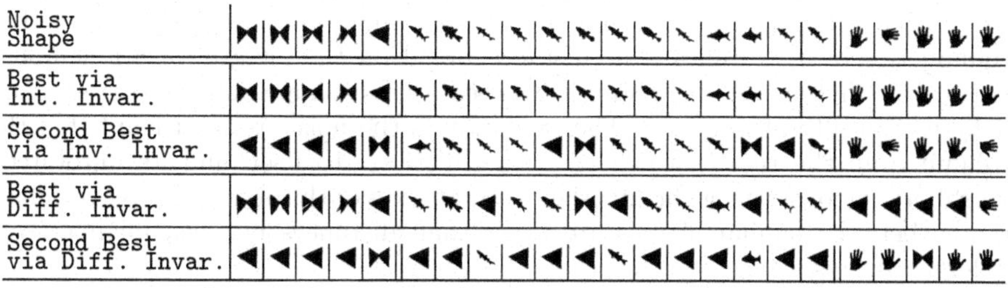

Fig. 7. Summary of noisy shape recognition from a database of 23 shapes.

However, as discussed in Sec. 5 this computation is sensitive to the parameterization of the shapes, specifically the assignment of the initial point. To avoid this dependence, the distance in eq. (9) must be optimized with respect to the choice of $s = 0$. We demonstrate the application of distance computed in this way in the Sec.(7), where we also define a distance based on curvature in the same way.

As an alternative to optimizing D_E, we can define a distance on a parameter-independent representation, such as the signature. The symmetric Hausdorff distance between signature curves (represented as point sets),

$$D_H(\gamma_i, \gamma_j, r) = H((I_{\gamma_i}^{\dot{r}}, I_{\gamma_i}^r), (I_{\gamma_j}^{\dot{r}}, I_{\gamma_j}^r)) \tag{10}$$

is one such distance. Hausdorff distance does not rely on correspondence between points, which is advantageous because it provides the parameter-independent distance we desire, but problematic when non-corresponding segments of the signatures are perturbed so that they overlap.

However, other measures that characterize the signature, such as winding number, can be integrated in into the distance measure to better discriminate these signatures. Additionally, a richer multiscale description of the curve can be created by computing the above distances for a set of kernel sizes. The integration of multiscale information, along with other measures such as winding number, is the subject of ongoing investigation.

7   Experiments

In this section we apply the invariant shape descriptions to the problem of Euclidean-invariant matching of shapes in noise. In Fig. 6, we demonstrate shape matching in a collection of 23 shapes, and summarize the results in Fig. 7. The collection contains several groups of shapes; shapes within a group are similar (i.e. different breeds of fish), but the groups are quite different (intuitively, hands are not like fish).

The figure shows the distance between the shapes (shown on the left side) and noisy versions of the shapes (shown across the top). Within each block are two distances; on top, the integral invariant distance D_E defined in the previous section, and on the bottom the differential invariant distance defined similarly.

In each column, the lowest distance for the shape shown at the top of the column is shown in italics. The distance based on the integral invariant finds the correct match (i.e. the distance between a noisy shape and the correct pair is lowest) in all but one case. The exception is the noisy, rotated hand (fourth column from the right), which has equal distance to itself and its unrotated neighbor, demonstrating the invariance to rotation of this model. Moreover, distances between similar shapes are lower than distances between members of different groups.

Matching results based on the differential invariant are not as consistent as those based on the integral invariant. There are eight mismatches among the 23 noisy images; most frequently, when a shape cannot be matched it is paired with the triangle (fifth from the right). This may be because the curvature of the triangle is zero almost everywhere, and best approximates the mean of many of the noisy curvature functions. More generally, and more problematically, for some groups distances between similar shapes are *higher* than distances between shapes belonging to other groups, violating the required properties of a distance. For instance, the average inter-group distance is 452.8, while the average intra-group distance is 316.6! Compare this to an inter-group distance of 11.0, which is *lower* than the intra-group distance of 17.4 for the integral invariant distance.

8   Conclusion

In this paper we have introduced a general class of integral Euclidean- and similarity-invariant functionals of shape data. We argue that these functionals are less sensitive to noise than differential ones, but can be exploited in similar ways, for instance, to define invariant signature curves that can be used as a representation to define various notions of shape distance. In addition, the integration kernel includes an *intrinsic* scale-space parameter. We presented efficient numerical implementations of these invariants, and, in the limit, established a completeness property for the representation by showing a one-to-one correspondence with curvature. We demonstrated our results with several experiments, including an application to shape matching using synthetic and real data.

References

1. R. Alferez and Y. F. Wang. Geometric and illumination invariants for object recognition. *PAMI*, 21(6):505–536, 1999.
2. K. Arbter, W. E. Snyder, H. Burkhardt, and G. Hirzinger. Applications of affine-invariant fourier descriptors to recognition of 3-d objects. *PAMI*, 12(7):640–646, 1990.
3. S. Belongie, J. Malik, and J. Puzicha. Shape matching and object recognition using shape contexts. *PAMI*, 24(4):509–522, 2002.
4. A. Bengtsson and J.-O. Eklundh. Shape representation by multiscale contour approximation. *PAMI*, 13(1):85–93, 1991.
5. M. Boutin. Numerically invariant signature curves. *IJCV*, 40(3):235–248, 2000.
6. R. D. Brandt and F. Lin. Representations that uniquely characterize images modulo translation, rotation and scaling. *PRL*, 17:1001–1015, 1996.

7. A. Bruckstein, N. Katzir, M. Lindenbaum, and M. Porat. Similarity invariant signatures for partially occluded planar shapes. *IJCV*, 7(3):271–285, 1992.

8. A. M. Bruckstein, R. J. Holt, A. N. Netravali, and T. J. Richardson. Invariant signatures for planar shape recognition under partial occlusion. *CVGIP:IU*, 58(1):49–65, 1993.

9. A. M. Bruckstein, E. Rivlin, and I. Weiss. Scale-space semi-local invariants. *IVC*, 15(5):335–344, 1997.

10. E. Calabi, P. Olver, C. Shakiban, A. Tannenbaum, and S. Haker. Differential and numerically invariant signature curves applied to object recognition. *IJCV*, 26:107–135, 1998.

11. D. Chetverikov and Y Khenokh. Matching for shape defect detection. *LNCS*, 1689(2):367–374, 1999.

12. T. Cohignac, C. Lopez, and J. M. Morel. Integral and local affine invariant parameter and applicatioin to shape recognition. *ICPR*, 1:164–168, 1994.

13. J. B. Cole, H. Murase, and S. Naito. A lie group theoretical approach to the invariance problem in feature extraction and object recognition. *PRL*, 12:519–523, 1991.

14. L. E. Dickson. *Algebraic Invariants*. John-Weiley & Sons, 1914.

15. J. Dieudonne and J. Carrell. *Invariant Theory: Old and New*. Academic Press, London, 1970.

16. J. Flusser and T. Suk. Pattern recognition by affine moment invariants. *Pat. Rec.*, 26(1):167–174, 1993.

17. D. A. Forsyth, J. L. Mundy, A. P. Zisserman, C. Coelho, A. Heller, and C. A. Othwell. Invariant descriptors for 3-d object recognition and pose. *PAMI*, 13(10):971–991, 1991.

18. D.A. Forsyth, J.L. Mundy, A. Zisserman, and C.M. Brown. Projectively invariant representations using implicit algebraic curves. *IVC*, 9(2):130–136, 1991.

19. L. Van Gool, T. Moons, E. Pauwels, and A. Oosterlinck. Semi-differential invariants. In J. Mundy and A Zisserman, editors, *Geometric Invariance in Computer Vision*, pages 193–214. MIT, Cambridge, 1992.

20. L. Van Gool, T. Moons, and D. Ungureanu. Affine/photometric invariants for planar intensity patterns. *ECCV*, 1:642–651, 1996.

21. J. H. Grace and A. Young. *The Algebra of Invariants*. Cambridge, 1903.

22. C. E. Hann and M. S. Hickman. Projective curvature and integral invariants. *IJCV*, 40(3):235–248, 2000.

23. M. K. Hu. Visual pattern recognition by moment invariants. *IRE Trans. on IT*, 8:179–187, 1961.

24. K. Kanatani. *Group Theoretical Methods in Image Understanding*. Springer, 1990.

25. E. P. Lane. *Projective Differential Geometry of Curves and Surfaces*. University of Chicago Press, 1932.

26. J. Lasenby, E. Bayro-Corrochano, A. N. Lasenby, and G. Sommer. A new framework for the formation of invariants and multiple-view constraints in computer vision. *ICIP*, 1996.

27. G. Lei. Recognition of planar objects in 3-d space from single perspective views using cross ratio. *Robot. and Automat.*, 6(4):432–437, 1990.

28. R. Lenz. *Group Theoretical Methods in Image Processing*, volume 413 of *LNCS*. Springer, 1990.

29. S. Z. Li. Shape matching based on invariants. In O. M. Omidvar (ed.), editor, *Progress in Neural Networks : Shape Recognition*, volume 6, pages 203–228. Intellect, 1999.

30. S. Liao and M. Pawlak. On image analysis by moments. *PAMI*, 18(3):254–266, 1996.

31. T. Miyatake, T Matsuyama, and M. Nagao. Affine transform invariant curve recognition using fourier descriptors. *Inform. Processing Soc. Japan*, 24(1):64–71, 1983.

32. F. Mokhtarian and A. K. Mackworth. A theory of multi-scale, curvature-based shape representation for planar curves. *PAMI*, 14(8):789–805, 1992.

33. D. Mumford, J. Fogarty, and F. C. Kirwan. *Geometric invariant theory*. Springer-Verlag, Berlin ; New York, 3rd edition, 1994.

34. D. Mumford, A. Latto, and J. Shah. The representation of shape. *IEEE Workshop on Comp. Vis.*, pages 183–191, 1984.

35. J. L. Mundy and A. Zisserman, editors. *Geometric Invariance in Computer Vision*. MIT, 1992.

36. L. Nielsen and G. Saprr. Projective area-invariants as an extension of the cross-ratio. *CVGIP*, 54(1):145–159, 1991.

37. P. J. Olver. *Equivalence, Invariants and Symmetry*. Cambridge, 1995.

38. T. Pajdla and L. Van Gool. Matching of 3-d curves using semi-differential invariants. *ICCV*, pages 390–395, 1995.

39. T. H. Reiss. Recognizing planar objects using invariant image features. In *LNCS*, volume 676. Springer, 1993.

40. C. Rothwell, A. Zisserman, D. Forsyth, and J. Mundy. Canonical frames for planar object recognition. *ECCV*, pages 757–772, 1992.

41. C. Rothwell, A. Zisserman, D. Forsyth, and J. Mundy. Planar object recognition using projective shape representation. *IJCV*, 16:57–99, 1995.

42. G. Sapiro and A. Tannenbaum. Affine invariant scale space. *IJCV*, 11(1):25–44, 1993.

43. G. Sapiro and A. Tannenbaum. Area and length preserving geometric invariant scale-spaces. *PAMI*, 17(1):67–72, 1995.

44. J. Sato and R. Cipolla. Affine integral invariants for extracting symmetry axes. *IVC*, 15(8):627–635, 1997.

45. A. Shashua and N. Navab. Relative affine structure: Canonical model for 3d from 2d geometry and applications. *PAMI*, 18(9):873–883, 1996.

46. C. E. Springer. *Geometry and Analysis of Projective Spaces*. Freeman, San Francisco, 1964.

47. Q. M. Tieng and W. W. Boles. Recognition of 2d object contours using the wavelet transform zero-crossing representation. *PAMI*, 19(8):910–916, 1997.

48. J. Verestoy and D. Chetverikov. Shape detect detection in ferrite cores. *Machine Graphics and Vision*, 6(2):225–236, 1997.

49. I. Weiss. Noise resistant invariants of curves. *PAMI*, 15(9):943–948, 1993.

50. A. P. Witkin. Scale-space filtering. *Int. Joint. Conf. AI*, pages 1019–1021, 1983.

51. C. T. Zahn and R. Z. Roskies. Fourier descriptors for plane closed curves. *Trans. Comp.*, 21:269–281, 1972.

52. A. Zisserman, D.A. Forsyth, J. L. Mundy, C. A. Rothwell, and J. S. Liu. 3D object recognition using invariance. *Art. Int.*, 78:239–288, 1995.

Detecting Keypoints with Stable Position, Orientation, and Scale under Illumination Changes[*]

Bill Triggs

GRAVIR-CNRS-INRIA, 655 avenue de l'Europe, 38330 Montbonnot, France
Bill.Triggs@inrialpes.fr
http://www.inrialpes.fr/lear/people/triggs

Abstract. Local feature approaches to vision geometry and object recognition are based on selecting and matching sparse sets of visually salient image points, known as 'keypoints' or 'points of interest'. Their performance depends critically on the accuracy and reliability with which corresponding keypoints can be found in subsequent images. Among the many existing keypoint selection criteria, the popular Förstner-Harris approach explicitly targets geometric stability, defining keypoints to be points that have locally maximal self-matching precision under translational least squares template matching. However, many applications require stability in orientation and scale as well as in position. Detecting translational keypoints and verifying orientation/scale behaviour post hoc is suboptimal, and can be misleading when different motion variables interact. We give a more principled formulation, based on extending the Förstner-Harris approach to general motion models and robust template matching. We also incorporate a simple local appearance model to ensure good resistance to the most common illumination variations. We illustrate the resulting methods and quantify their performance on test images.

Keywords: keypoint, point of interest, corner detection, feature based vision, Förstner-Harris detector, template matching, vision geometry, object recognition.

Local-feature-based approaches have proven successful in many vision problems, including scene reconstruction [16,5], image indexing and object recognition [20,21,32, 33,23,24,25]. The basic idea is that focusing attention on comparatively sparse sets of especially salient image points — usually called **keypoints** or **points of interest** — both saves computation (as most of the image is discarded) and improves robustness (as there are many simple, redundant local cues rather than a few powerful but complex and delicate global ones) [37]. However, local methods must be able to find 'the same' keypoints again in other images, and their performance depends critically on the reliability and accuracy with which exactly corresponding points can be found. Many approaches to keypoint detection exist, including 'corners' [2,17,38,28,4], parametric image models [3,31,1], local energy / phase congruency [27,29,30,18], and morphology [35,19]. One of the most popular is that developed by Förstner & Gülch [7,9] and Harris & Stephens [15] following earlier work by Hannah [14] and Moravec [26]. This approach brings the accuracy issue to the fore by *defining* keypoints to be points at which the predicted precision of local least squares image matching is locally maximal [14,22,6,10,12,11].

---

[*] This research was supported by the European Union FET-Open research project VIBES.

T. Pajdla and J. Matas (Eds.): ECCV 2004, LNCS 3024, pp. 100–113, 2004.
© Springer-Verlag Berlin Heidelberg 2004

Notionally, this is implemented by matching the local image patch against itself under small translations, using one of a range of criteria to decide when the 'sharpness' of the resulting correlation peak is locally optimal. Moravec did this by explicit single-pixel translations [26]; Hannah by autocorrelation [14]; and Förstner by implicit least squares matching, using Taylor expansion to re-express the accuracy in terms of the eigenvalues of the **scatter matrix** or **normal matrix** of the local image gradients, $\int \nabla I^{\top} \nabla I \, dx$ [7,9,8]. All of these methods use rectangular patches, usually with a scale significantly larger than that of the image gradients used. This is problematic for patches that contain just one strong feature, because the self-matching accuracy for these is the same wherever the feature is in the patch, *i.e.* the matching-based approach guarantees good self-matching accuracy, but not necessarily accurate *centring* of the patch on a visible feature. Working independently of Förstner, Harris & Stephens improved the localization performance by replacing the rectangular patches with Gaussian windows (convolutions) with a scale similar to that of the derivatives used [15]. With Gaussian-based derivative calculations and more careful attention to aliasing, the method has proven to be one of the most reliable keypoint detectors, especially in cases where there are substantial image rotations, scalings or perspective deformations [33,24].

One problem with the Förstner-Harris approach is that it optimizes keypoints only for good *translational* precision, whereas many applications need keypoints that are stable not only under translations, but also under rotations, changes of scale, perspective deformations, and changes of illumination (*c.f.* [34]). In particular, many local feature based object recognition / matching methods calculate a vector of local image descriptors at each keypoint, and later try to find keypoints with corresponding descriptors in other images [20,21,32,23,24,25]. This usually requires the extraction of a dominant orientation and scale at each keypoint, and keypoints that have poorly defined orientations or scales tend to produce descriptors that vary too much over re-detections to be useful. Hence, it seems useful to develop keypoint detectors that explicitly guarantee good orientation and scale stability, and also good stability under local illumination variations. This is the goal of the current paper, which generalizes the Förstner-Harris self-matching argument to include non-translational motions, and also provides improved resistance to illumination variations by replacing simple least squares matching with an illumination-compensated matching method related to Hager & Belhumeur's [13].

Much of the paper focuses on the low-level task of *characterizing the local stability of matching under geometric transformations and illumination variations*. The Förstner-Harris approach shows that such analysis is a fruitful route to practical keypoint detection in the translational case, and we argue that this continues to hold for more general transformations. Also note the relationship to invariance: if we use image descriptors based at the keypoints for matching, the more invariant the descriptors are to a given type of transformation, the less accurate the keypoint detection needs to be with respect to these transformations. But exactly for this reason, it is useful to develop detectors whose performance under different types of transformations is quantifiable and controllable, and our approach explicitly does this. We adopt the following basic philosophy:

(i) There is no such thing as generic keypoints. They should be selected specifically for the use to which they will be put, using a purpose-designed detector and parameters.

(ii) Keypoints are not just positions. Stability in orientation and scale and resistance to common types of appearance variations are also needed.

(iii) Each image (template) matching method defines a corresponding self-matching based keypoint detector. If the keypoints will be used as correspondence hypotheses that are later verified by inter-image template matching, the keypoint detector and parameters corresponding to the matching method should be used.

Contents: Section 1 describes our matching based framework for keypoint detection. Section 2 gives some specific examples and implementation details. Section 3 gives a few experimental results.

Notation: x stands for image coordinates, ∇ for x-derivatives, I, R for the images being matched (treated as functions of x), t for the image motion/warping model, c for the pixel comparison functional. Derivatives are always row vectors, *e.g.* $\delta I \approx \nabla I \, \delta x$. For most of the paper we assume continuous images and ignore sampling issues.

1 General Framework

This section develops a general framework for robust image (template) matching under analytical image deformation and appearance variation models, uses it to derive stability estimates for locally optimal matches, and applies this to characterize keypoint stability under self-matching.

Template Matching Model: We will use the following generalized error model for template matching, explained element-by-element below:

$$Q(\mu, \lambda) \equiv \int c\left(I(t(x, \mu), \lambda), R(x), x\right) \, dx \qquad (1)$$

I is the image patch being matched, R is the reference patch it is being matched against, x is a set of 2D image coordinates centred on R, and $c \geq 0$ (discussed further below) is a weighted image pixel comparison functional that is integrated over the patch to find the overall matching quality metric Q. $x' = t(x, \mu)$ is an image motion / warping model that maps R's coordinates x forwards into I's natural coordinate system, *i.e.*, I is effectively being pulled back (warped backwards) into R's frame before being compared. The motion model t is controlled by a vector of **motion parameters** μ (2D translation, perhaps rotation, scaling, affine deformation...). Before being compared, I may also undergo an optional appearance correction controlled by a vector of **appearance parameters** λ (*e.g.*, luminance or colour shifts/rescalings/normalizations, corrections for local illumination gradients...). Note that we think of the input patch I as an ad hoc function $I(x, \lambda)$ of both the position and appearance parameters, rather than as a fixed image $I(x)$ to which separate appearance corrections are applied. This allows the corrections to be image-content dependent and nonlocal within the patch (*e.g.* subtracting the mean in Zero Mean Cross Correlation). We assume that $\mu = 0$ represents a neutral position or reference transformation for the patch (*e.g.* no motion, $t(x, 0) = x$). Similarly, $\lambda = 0$ represents a default or reference appearance setting (*e.g.* the unchanged input, $I(x, 0) = I(x)$).

The patch comparison integral is over a spatial window centred on R, but for compactness we encode this in the pixel comparison metric c. So c usually has the form:

$$c(I(\boldsymbol{x}), R(\boldsymbol{x}), \boldsymbol{x}) \equiv w(\boldsymbol{x}) \cdot \rho(I(\boldsymbol{x}), R(\boldsymbol{x})) \tag{2}$$

where $w(\boldsymbol{x})$ is a spatial windowing function (rectangular, Gaussian...) that defines the extent of the relevant patch of R, and $\rho(I(\boldsymbol{x}), R(\boldsymbol{x}))$ is a spatially-invariant image pixel comparison metric, *e.g.*, the squared pixel difference $\|I(\boldsymbol{x}) - R(\boldsymbol{x})\|^2$ for traditional unweighted least squares matching. The "pixels" here may be greyscale, colour, multi-band, or even pre-extracted edge, feature or texture maps, so $\rho()$ can be quite complicated in general, *e.g.* involving nonlinear changes of luminance or colour space, perceptual or sensitivity-based comparison metrics, robust tailing-off at large pixel differences to reduce the influence of outliers, *etc.* Ideally, $\rho()$ should return the negative log likelihood for the pixels to correspond, so that (assuming independent noise in each pixel) Q becomes the total negative log likelihood for the patchwise match. For practical inter-image template matching, the reliability depends critically on the robustness (large difference behaviour) of $\rho()$. But for keypoint detection, we always start from the self-matching case $I = R$, so only the *local* behaviour of $\rho()$ near $I = R$ is relevant: keypoint detectors are oblivious to large-difference robustification of $\rho()$. We will assume that $\rho()$ has least-squares-like behaviour for small pixel differences, *i.e.* that it is locally differentiable with zero gradient and positive semi-definite Hessian at $I = R$, so that:

$$\left.\frac{\delta c}{\delta I(\boldsymbol{x})}\right|_{I=R} = \boldsymbol{0}, \qquad \left.\frac{\delta^{\cdot} c}{\delta I(\boldsymbol{x})^{\cdot}}\right|_{I=R} \geq \boldsymbol{0} \tag{3}$$

Our derivations will be based on 2nd order Taylor expansion at $I = R$, so they exclude both non-differentiable L_1 matching metrics like Sum of Absolute Differences (SAD) and discontinuous L_0 (on-off) style ones. Our overall approach probably extends to such metrics, at least when used within a suitable interpolation model, but their abrupt changes and weak resampling behaviour make general derivations difficult.

Finally, we allow c to be a *functional*, not just a function, of I, R. (*I.e.* a function of the local patches, not just their pointwise pixel values). In particular, c may run I, R through convolutional filters ('**prefilters**') before comparing them, *e.g.* to restrict attention to a given frequency band in scale-space matching, or simply to suppress high frequencies for reduced aliasing and/or low frequencies for better resistance to global illumination changes. In general, the resampling implied by $t()$ could significantly change I's spatial frequency content, so prefiltering only makes sense if we do it *after* warping. We will thus assume that prefilters run in $\boldsymbol{x}$-space, *i.e.* they are defined relative to the coordinates of the reference image R. For example, for affine-invariant keypoint detection [32, 24, 25], keypoint comparison should typically be done, and in particular prefiltering should be applied, in the characteristic affine-normalized frame of the reference keypoint, so $\boldsymbol{x}$ would typically be taken to be the affine-normalized coordinates for R. For any $t()$, derivatives of the unwarped input image I can always be converted to derivatives of its prefilter using integration by parts, so the effective scale of derivative masks always ends up being the $\boldsymbol{x}$-space scale of the prefilter.

Matching Precision: Now suppose that we have already found a locally optimal template match. Consider the behaviour of the matching quality metric Q under small perturbations

$I \rightarrow I + \delta I$. Under 2nd order Taylor expansion:

$$\delta Q \approx \int \left(\frac{\delta c}{\delta I} \delta I + \tfrac{1}{2} \delta I^\top \frac{\delta^{\cdot} c}{\delta I^{\cdot}} \delta I \right)_{x' = t(x)} dx \qquad (4)$$

For any perturbation of an exact match, $I(t(x)) = R(x)$, the first order (δI) term vanishes identically by (3). More generally, if we are already at a local optimum of Q under some class of perturbations δI, the integrated first order term vanishes for this class. Both hold for keypoints, so we will ignore the δI term from now on.

Using the parametric model $I(t(x, \mu), \lambda)$, the image I changes as follows under first order changes of the motion and appearance parameters μ, λ:

$$\delta I \approx L\, \delta\lambda + M\, \delta\mu, \quad \text{where} \quad L \equiv \frac{\partial I}{\partial \lambda}, \quad M \equiv \nabla I \cdot T, \quad T \equiv \frac{\partial t}{\partial \mu} \qquad (5)$$

Here, $\nabla I \equiv \frac{\partial I}{\partial t}(t(x))$ is the standard gradient of the original unwarped image I, evaluated in I's own frame at $t(x)$. The columns of the Jacobians L and M can be thought of as appearance and motion basis images, characterizing the linearized first-order changes in I as the parameters are varied. Putting (4, 5) together gives a quadratic local cost model for perturbations of the match around the optimum, based on a positive semidefinite **generalized scatter matrix S** :[1]

$$\delta Q(\delta\lambda, \delta\mu) \approx \tfrac{1}{2} \begin{pmatrix} \delta\lambda^{\cdot} & \delta\mu^{\cdot} \end{pmatrix} S \begin{pmatrix} \delta\lambda \\ \delta\mu \end{pmatrix} \qquad (6)$$

$$S \equiv \begin{pmatrix} A & B \\ B^{\cdot} & C \end{pmatrix} \equiv \int \begin{pmatrix} L^{\cdot} \\ M^{\cdot} \end{pmatrix} \frac{\delta^{\cdot} c}{\delta I^{\cdot}} \begin{pmatrix} L & M \end{pmatrix} dx \qquad (7)$$

S generalizes the matrix $\int \nabla I^\top \nabla I\, dx$ that appears in the Förstner-Harris keypoint detector (which assumes pure translation, $T = I, M = \nabla I$, quadratic pixel difference metric $\frac{\delta^{\cdot} c}{\delta I^{\cdot}} = I$, and empty illumination model L). To the extent that c gives the negative log likelihood for the match, S is the maximum likelihood saddle point approximation to the Fisher information matrix for estimating λ, μ from the match. *I.e.*, S^{-1} approximates the covariance with which the parameters λ, μ can be estimated from the given image data: the larger S, the stabler the match, in the sense that the matching error δQ increases more rapidly under given perturbations $\delta\lambda, \delta\mu$.

Now suppose that we want to ensure that the two patches match stably *irrespective of appearance changes*. For a given perturbation $\delta\mu$, the appearance change that gives the best match to the original patch — and hence that masks the effect of the motion as well as possible, thus creating the greatest matching uncertainty — can be found by minimizing $\delta Q(\delta\mu, \delta\lambda)$ w.r.t. $\delta\lambda$. By inspection from (6), this is $\delta\lambda(\delta\mu) = -A^{-1} B\, \delta\mu$. Back-substituting into (6) gives an effective quadratic **reduced penalty func-**

---

[1] Strictly, to be correct to $\mathcal{O}((\delta\mu, \delta\lambda)^{\cdot})$ we should also expand (5) to 2nd order, which introduces a 2nd order 'tensor' correction in the δI term of (4). But, as above by (3), the latter term vanishes identically for keypoint detection. Even for more general matching, the correction is usually negligible unless the match is poor *and* the motion / appearance models are very nonlinear. One can think of (7) as a Gauss-Newton approximation to the true S. It guarantees that S is at least positive semidefinite (as it must be at a locally optimal match). We will adopt it from now on.

tion $\delta Q_{red}(\delta\mu) \equiv \delta Q(\delta\mu, \delta\lambda(\delta\mu)) \approx \frac{1}{2}\delta\mu^\top C_{red}\,\delta\mu$ characterizing motion-with-best-appearance-adaptation, where the **reduced scatter matrix** is

$$C_{red} \equiv C - B^\top A^{-1}B \qquad (8)$$

with A, B, C as in (7). C_{red} and C quantify the precision of motion estimation respectively with and without appearance adaptation. Some precision is always lost by factoring out appearance, so C_{red} is always smaller than C. To the extent that the matching error metric c is a statistically valid log likelihood model for image noise, C^{-1} and C_{red}^{-1} estimate the covariances of the corresponding motion parameter estimates under trials with independent noise samples. More generally, if we also have prior information that appearance variations are not arbitrary, but have zero mean and covariance D^{-1}, the optimal $\delta\lambda(\delta\mu)$ becomes $-(A + D)^{-1}B\,\delta\mu$ and C_{red} is replaced by the less strongly reduced covariance $C'_{red} \equiv C - B^\top(A + D)^{-1}B$.

Keypoint Detection: Ideally, we want to find keypoints that can be *stably* and *reliably* re-detected under arbitrary motions from the given transformation family $t(x, \mu)$, despite arbitrary changes of appearance from the appearance family $I(x, \lambda)$. We focus on the 'stability' aspect[2], which we characterize in terms of the *precision of self-matching* under our robust template matching model. The idea is that the patch itself is its own best template — if it can not be matched stably even against itself, it is unlikely to be stably matchable against other patches. We are interested in stability despite appearance changes, so we use the reduced scatter matrix C_{red} (8) to quantify geometric precision.

The amount of precision that is needed depends on the task, and we adopt the design philosophy that visual routines should be explicitly parametrized in terms of objective performance criteria such as output accuracy. To achieve this we require keypoints to meet a lower bound on matching precision (equivalently, an upper bound on matching uncertainty). We quantify this by introducing a user-specified **criterion matrix** C_0 and requiring keypoints to have reduced precisions C_{red} greater than C_0 (*i.e.* $C_{red} - C_0$ must be positive semidefinite). Intuitively, this means that for a keypoint candidate to be accepted, its transformation-space motion-estimation uncertainty ellipse C_{red}^{-1} must be strictly contained within the criterion ellipse C_0^{-1}.

In textured images there may be whole regions where this precision criterion is met, so for isolated keypoint detection we must also specify a means of selecting 'the best' keypoint(s) within these regions. This requires some kind of 'saliency' or 'interest' metric, ideally an index of perceptual distinctiveness / reliable matchability modulo our appearance model. But here, following the Förstner-Harris philosophy, we simply use an index of overall matching precision as a crude substitute for this. In the translation-only case, Förstner [7,9] and Harris & Stephens [15] discuss several suitable precision indices, based on the determinant, trace and eigenvalues of the scatter matrix. In our case, there may be several (more than 2) motion parameters, and eigenvalue based criteria seem more appropriate than determinant based ones, owing to their clear links with

---

[2] We do not consider other matchability properties [7] such distinctiveness here, as this is more a matter for the descriptors calculated once the keypoint is found. Distinctiveness is usually characterized by probability of mismatch within a population of extracted keypoints (*e.g.* [33]). For a recent entropic approach to image-wide distinctiveness, see [36].

uncertainty analysis. Different motion parameters also have different units (translations in pixels, rotations in radians, dilations in log units), and we need to normalize for this. The criterion matrix C_0 provides a natural scaling, so as our final saliency criterion we will take the *minimum eigenvalue of the normalized reduced motion precision matrix* $C_0^{-1/2} C_{\text{red}} C_0^{-1/2}$. Intuitively, this requires the longest axis of the motion-estimation covariance ellipse, as measured in a frame in which C_0 becomes spherical, to be as small as possible. With this normalization, the keypoint-acceptability criterion $C_{\text{red}} > C_0$ simplifies to the requirement that the saliency (the minimum eigenvalue) must be greater than one. Typically, C_0 is diagonal, in which case the normalization matrix $C_0^{-1/2}$ is the diagonal matrix of maximum user-permissible standard errors in translation, rotation and scale.

As usual, pixel sampling effects introduce a small amount of aliasing or jitter in the image derivative estimates, which has the effect of spreading gradient energy across the various eigenvalues of **S** even when the underlying image signal is varies only in one dimension (*e.g.* a straight edge). As in the Förstner-Harris case, we compensate for this heuristically by subtracting a small user-specified multiple α of the maximum eigenvalue of $C_0^{-1/2} C_{\text{red}} C_0^{-1/2}$ (the 1-D 'straight edge' signal) before testing for threshold and saliency, so our final keypoint saliency measure is $\lambda_{\min} - \alpha \lambda_{\max}$.

In practice, the Schur complement in $C_{\text{red}} = C - B^\top A^{-1} B$ is calculated simply and efficiently by outer-product based partial Cholesky decomposition. A standard symmetric eigendecomposition method is then used to calculate the minimum eigenvalue, except that 2D eigenproblems are handled as a special case for speed.

2   Examples of Keypoint Detectors

Given the above framework, it is straightforward to derive keypoint detectors for specific pixel types and motion and appearance models. Here we only consider the simplest few motion and appearance models, and we assume greyscale images.

Comparison Function: As in the traditional Harris detector, we will use simple squared pixel difference to compare pixels, and a circular Gaussian spatial integration window. So modulo prefiltering, $\frac{\delta^\cdot c}{\delta I^\cdot}$ in (7) reduces to simple weighting by the window function.

Affine Deformations: For keypoints, only local deformations are relevant, so the most general motion model that is useful is probably the affine one. We will use various subsets of this, parametrizing affine motions linearly as $x' = x + T\mu$ where:

$$T\mu = \begin{pmatrix} 1 & 0 & -y & x & x & y \\ 0 & 1 & x & y & -y & x \end{pmatrix} \begin{pmatrix} u \\ v \\ r \\ s \\ a \\ b \end{pmatrix} = \begin{pmatrix} s+a & -r+b \\ r+b & s-a \end{pmatrix} \begin{pmatrix} x \\ y \end{pmatrix} + \begin{pmatrix} u \\ v \end{pmatrix} \quad (9)$$

Here, (x, y) are window-centred pixel coordinates, (u, v) is the translation, s the scale, and for small motions, r is the rotation and a, b are axis- and $45°$-aligned quadrupole deformations. The resulting M matrix is as follows, where $\nabla I = (I_x, I_y)$:

$$M = \begin{pmatrix} I_x & I_y & -yI_x+xI_y & xI_x+yI_y & xI_x-yI_y & yI_x+xI_y \end{pmatrix} \quad (10)$$

If the input image is being prefiltered (which, as discussed, must happen *after* warping, *i.e.* after (10)), we can integrate by parts to reduce the prefiltered M vector to the form:

$$M^p = \left(I^p_x,\ I^p_y,\ -(yI)^p_x + (xI)^p_y,\ (xI)^p_x + (yI)^p_y - 2I^p,\ (xI)^p_x - (yI)^p_y,\ (yI)^p_x + (xI)^p_y \right)$$
(11)

where $I^p \equiv p * I$, $(xI)^p_y \equiv p_y * (xI)$, etc., denote convolutions of I, xI, etc., against the prefilter p and its derivatives p_x, p_y. The $-2I^p$ term in the s entry corrects for the fact that prefiltering should happen after any infinitessimal scale change coded by M: without this, we would effectively be comparing patches taken at different derivative scales, and would thus overestimate the scale localization accuracy. If p is a Gaussian of width σ, we can use (10) or (11) and the corresponding identities $(xI)^p = xI^p + \sigma^2 I^p_x$ or $(xI)^p_x = x\,I^p_x + \sigma^2 I^p_{xx} + I^p$ (from $(x-x')g(x-x') = -\sigma^2 g_x(x-x')$, etc.) to move x, y outside the convolutions, reducing M^p to:

$$\left(I^p_x,\ I^p_y,\ -yI^p_x + xI^p_y,\ xI^p_x + yI^p_y + \sigma^2 I^p_{xx+yy},\ xI^p_x - yI^p_y + \sigma^2 I^p_{xx-yy},\ yI^p_x + xI^p_y + 2\sigma^2 I^p_{xy} \right)$$
(12)

Appearance model: Class-specific appearance models like [1, 13] can include elaborate models of appearance variation, but for generic keypoint detection we can only use simple generic models designed to improve resistance to common types of local illumination variations. Here, we allow for (at most) a scalar illumination shift, addition of a constant spatial illumination gradient, and illumination rescaling. So our linear appearance model is $I + L\,\lambda$ where $L(x)$ is a subset of:

$$L(x) = \begin{pmatrix} 1 & x & y & I(x) \end{pmatrix}$$
(13)

As with M, the elements of L must be prefiltered, but I is just smoothed to I^p and $1, x, y$ typically have trivial convolutions (*e.g.*, they are unchanged under Gaussian smoothing, and hence generate a constant diagonal block $\mathrm{diag}(1, \sigma^2_w, \sigma^2_w)$ in S).

Putting It All Together: The main stages of keypoint detection are: *(i)* prefilter the input image to produce the smoothed image and derivative estimates $I^p, I^p_x, I^p_y, I^p_{xx}, I^p_{xy}, I^p_{yy}$ needed for (12, 13); *(ii)* for each keypoint location x, form the outer product matrix of the (desired components of the) combined L/M vector at all pixels in its window, and sum over the window to produce the scatter matrix $S(x)$ (7) (use window-centred coordinates for x, y in (12Examples of Keypoint Detectorsequation.12, 13); *(iii)* at each x, reduce $S(x)$ to find $C_{\mathrm{red}}(x)$, normalize by C_0, and find the smallest eigenvalue (saliency). Keypoints are declared at points where the saliency has a dominant local maximum, *i.e.* is above threshold and larger than at all other points within a suitable non-maximum-suppression radius. For multiscale detection, processing is done within a pyramid and keypoints must be maxima in both position and scale. As usual, one can estimate subpixel keypoint location and scale by quadratic interpolation of the saliency field near its maximum. But note that, as in the standard Förstner-Harris approach, keypoints do not necessarily contain nameable features (corners, spots) that clearly mark their centres — they may just be unstructured patches with locally maximal matching stability[3].

---

[3] If well-localized centres are needed, specialized locators exist for specific image structures such as spots and corners (*e.g.* [8]), or more generally one could search for *sharp* (high-curvature)

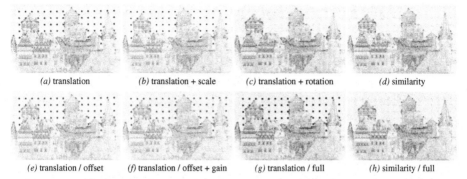

(a) translation   (b) translation + scale   (c) translation + rotation   (d) similarity

(e) translation / offset   (f) translation / offset + gain   (g) translation / full   (h) similarity / full

Fig. 1. Minimum-eigenvalue strength maps for a popular test image under various motion and illumination models. The saliency differences are much larger than they seem: the maps have been very strongly gamma compressed, normalized and inverted for better visibility. The prefilter and integration windows had $\sigma=1$ pixel, and $\alpha = 0$. Criterion standard deviations were 1 pixel in translation, 1 radian in rotation, $\sqrt{2}$ in scale, but these values are not critical.

When calculating **S**, instead of separate *ab initio* summation over each integration window, one can also use image-wide convolution of quadratic 'energies' as in the standard Förstner-Harris detector, but for the more complicated detectors there are many such maps to be calculated (76 for the full 10-entry L/M model). See the extended version of this paper for details.

In our current implementation, run times for the full 10-L/M-variable detector (which is more than one would normally use in practice) are a factor of about 10 larger than for the original two variable Förstner-Harris detector.

Relation to Zero Mean Matching: This common matching method compares two image patches by first subtracting each patches mean intensity, then summing the resulting squared pixel differences. We can relate this to the simplest nonempty illumination correction model, $\boldsymbol{L}= \begin{pmatrix} 1 \end{pmatrix}$, whose reduced scatter matrix over window $w(\boldsymbol{x})$ is:

$$C_{\mathrm{red}} = \int w\,\boldsymbol{M}^{\top}\boldsymbol{M}\,d\boldsymbol{x} - \overline{\boldsymbol{M}}^{\top}\overline{\boldsymbol{M}} = \int w\,(\boldsymbol{M}-\overline{\boldsymbol{M}})^{\top}(\boldsymbol{M}-\overline{\boldsymbol{M}})\,d\boldsymbol{x}$$

$$\overline{\boldsymbol{M}} \equiv \int w\,(\boldsymbol{M})\,d\boldsymbol{x} \,/\, \left(\int w\,d\boldsymbol{x}\right)^{1/2} \tag{14}$$

For the translation-only model, $\boldsymbol{T}$ is trivial, so the illumination correction simply has the effect of subtracting from each image gradient its patch mean (*c.f.* (10)). If w changes much more slowly than I, $\overline{\nabla I} \approx \nabla \overline{I}$ and hence $\nabla I - \overline{\nabla I} \approx \nabla(I - \overline{I})$, so this is approximately the same as using the gradient of the bandpassed image $I - \overline{I}$. The standard Förstner-Harris detector embodies least squares matching, not zero mean matching. It is invariant to constant illumination shifts, but it does not subtract the gradient of the mean $\nabla \overline{I}$ (or more correctly, the mean of the gradient $\overline{\nabla I}$) to discount the effects of smooth local illumination gradients superimposed on the pattern being matched. It thus

---

and preferably *isolated* maxima of the minimum eigenvalue field or local saliency measure, not just for *high* (but possibly broad) ones. For example, a minimum acceptable peak curvature could be specified via a second criterion matrix.

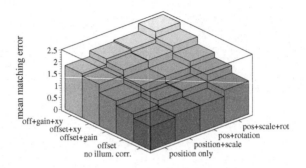

Fig. 2. Mean predicted standard error (inverse square root of saliency / minimum eigenvalue in normalized units) for template matching of keypoints under our motion and lighting models, for the model's top 100 keypoints on the Summer Palace image in Fig. 3.

systematically overestimates the geometric strength of keypoints in regions with strong illumination gradients, *e.g.* near the borders of smoothly shaded objects, or at the edges of shadows.

3 Experiments

Fig. 1 shows that the saliency (minimum eigenvalue) map emphasizes different kinds of image structures as the motion and illumination models are changed. Image (a) is the original Förstner-Harris detector. Images $(b), (c), (d)$ successively add scale, rotation and scale + rotation motions, while images $(e), (f), (g)$ adjust for illumination offset, offset + gain, and offset + gain + spatial gradients. Note the dramatic extent to which enforcing rotational stability in $(a) \rightarrow (c)$ and $(b) \rightarrow (d)$ eliminates the circular dots of the calibration pattern. In comparison, enforcing scale stability in $(a) \rightarrow (b)$ and $(c) \rightarrow (d)$ has more subtle effects, but note the general relative weakening of the points at the summits of the towers between (a) and (b): straight-edged 'corners' are scale invariant, and are therefore suppressed. Unfortunately, although ideal axis- and $45°$-aligned corners are strongly suppressed, it seems that aliasing and blurring effects destroy much of the notional scale invariance of most other rectilinear corners, both in real images and in non-axis-aligned ideal ones. We are currently working on this problem, which also reduces the cross-scale performance of the standard Förstner-Harris detector.

Adding illumination invariance seems to have a relatively small effect in this example, but note the general relative sharpening caused by including x and y illumination gradients in $(a), (e), (f) \rightarrow (g)$. Points on the borders of intensity edges have enhanced gradients owing to the slope alone, and this tends to make them fire preferentially despite the use of the minimum-eigenvalue (most uncertain direction) criterion. Subtracting the mean local intensity gradient reduces this and hence sharpens the results. However a negative side effect of including x, y gradients is that locally quadratic image patches — in particular small dots and ridge edges — become much less well localized, as adding a slope to a quadratic is equivalent to translating it.

(i) translation   *(j)* similarity   *(k)* affine

(a) translation   *(b)* translation + rotation   *(c)* translation + scale   *(d)* similarity

(e) translation / offset   *(f)* translation / offset + xy   *(g)* translation / full   *(h)* affine

Fig. 3. Examples of keypoints from the CMU and Summer Palace (Beijing) test images, under various motion and illumination models. The prefilter and integration windows had $\sigma=2$ pixels, $\alpha = 0$, and non-maximum suppression within 4 pixels radius and scale factor 1.8 was applied. Note that, *e.g.*, 'affine' means 'resistant to small affine deformations', not affine invariant in the sense of [32,24,25].

Allowing more general motions and/or quotienting out illumination variations always reduces the precision of template matching. Fig. 2 shows the extent of this effect by plotting the relative standard errors of template matching for our complete set of motion and lighting models, where the matching for each model is performed on the model's own keypoints. There is a gradual increase in uncertainty as parameters are added, the final uncertainty for a similarity transform modulo the full illumination model being about 2.5 times that of the original translation-only detector with no illumination correction.

Fig. 3 shows some examples of keypoints selected using the various different motion/lighting models. The main observation is that different models often select different keypoints, and more invariant models generate fewer of them, but beyond this it is difficult to find easily interpretable systematic trends. As in the Förstner-Harris case, keypoints are optimized for matching precision, not for easy interpretability in terms of idealized image events.

4 Summary and Conclusions

Summary: We have generalized the Förstner-Harris detector [7,9,15] to select keypoints that provide repeatable scale and orientation, as well as repeatable position, over re-detections, even in the face of simple local illumination changes. Keypoints are selected to maximize a minimum-eigenvalue-based local stability criterion obtained from a second order analysis of patch self-matching precision under affine image deformations, compensated for linear illumination changes.

Future Work: The approach given here ensures accurate re-localizability (by inter-image template matching) of keypoint image patches under various transformations, but it does not always provide accurate 'centres' for them. To improve this, we would like to characterize the stability and localization accuracy of the local maxima of the saliency measure (minimum eigenvalue) under the given transformations. In other words, just as we derived the local transformational-stability matrix $C_{red}(x)$ for *matching* from the scalar matching metric $Q(x)$, we need to derive a local transformational-stability matrix for *saliency* from the scalar saliency metric. Only here, the saliency measure is already based on matching stability, so a second level of analysis will be needed.

References

[1] S. Baker, S. Nayar, and H. Murase. Parametric feature detection. *Int. J. Computer Vision*, 27(1):27–50, 1998.

[2] P.R. Beaudet. Rotationally invariant image operators. In *Int. Conf. Pattern Recognition*, pages 579–583, 1978.

[3] R. Deriche and T. Blaszka. Recovering and characterizing image features using an efficient model based approach. In *Int. Conf. Computer Vision & Pattern Recognition*, pages 530–535, 1993.

[4] R. Deriche and G. Giraudon. A computational approach for corner and vertex detection. *Int. J. Computer Vision*, 10(2):101–124, 1993.

[5] O. Faugeras, Q-T. Luong, and T. Papadopoulo. *The Geometry of Multiple Images*. MIT Press, 2001.

[6] W. Förstner. On the geometric precision of digital correlation. *Int. Arch. Photogrammetry & Remote Sensing*, 24(3):176–189, 1982.

[7] W. Förstner. A feature-based correspondence algorithm for image matching. *Int. Arch. Photogrammetry & Remote Sensing*, 26 (3/3):150–166, 1986.

[8] W. Förstner. A framework for low-level feature extraction. In *European Conf. Computer Vision*, pages II 383–394, Stockholm, 1994.

[9] W. Förstner and E. Gülch. A fast operator for detection and precise location of distinct points, corners and centres of circular features. In *ISPRS Intercommission Workshop*, Interlaken, June 1987.

[10] A. Grün. Adaptive least squares correlation — concept and first results. Intermediate Research Report to Helava Associates, Ohio State University. 13 pages, March 1984.

[11] A. Grün. Least squares matching: A fundamental measurement algorithm. In *Close Range Photogrammetry and Machine Vision*, pages 217–255. Whittles Publishing, Caithness, Scotland, 1996.

[12] A. Grün and E.P. Baltsavias. Adaptive least squares correlation with geometrical constraints. In *SPIE Computer Vision for Robots*, volume 595, pages 72–82, Cannes, 1985.

[13] G. Hager and P. Belhumeur. Efficient region tracking with parametric models of geometry and illumination. *IEEE Trans. Pattern Analysis & Machine Intelligence*, 20(10):1025–1039, 1998.

[14] M.J. Hannah. *Computer Matching of Areas in Stereo Images*. Ph.D. Thesis, Stanford University, 1974. AIM Memo 219.

[15] C. Harris and M. Stephens. A combined corner and edge detector. In *Alvey Vision Conference*, pages 147–151, 1988.

[16] R. Hartley and A. Zisserman. *Multiple View Geometry in Computer Vision*. Cambridge University Press, 2000.

[17] L. Kitchen and A. Rosenfeld. Gray-level corner detection. *Patt. Rec. Lett.*, 1:95–102, 1982.

[18] P. Kovesi. Image features from phase congruency. *Videre: A Journal of Computer Vision Research*, 1(3), 1999.

[19] R. Laganière. Morphological corner detection. In *Int. Conf. Computer Vision*, pages 280–285, 1998.

[20] D. Lowe. Object recognition from local scale-invariant features. In *Int. Conf. Computer Vision*, pages 1150–1157, 1999.

[21] D. Lowe. Local feature view clustering for 3d object recognition. In *Int. Conf. Computer Vision & Pattern Recognition*, pages 682–688, 2001.

[22] B.D. Lucas and T. Kanade. An iterative image registration technique with an application to stereo vision. In *IJCAI*, 1981.

[23] K. Mikolajczyk and C. Schmid. Indexing based on scale invariant interest points. In *Int. Conf. Computer Vision*, pages 525–531, 2001.

[24] K. Mikolajczyk and C. Schmid. An affine invariant interest point detector. In *European Conf. Computer Vision*, pages I.128–142, 2002.

[25] K. Mikolajczyk and C. Schmid. A performance evaluation of local descriptors. In *Int. Conf. Computer Vision & Pattern Recognition*, 2003.

[26] H.P. Moravec. Towards automatic visual obstacle avoidance. In *IJCAI*, page 584, 1977.

[27] M. C. Morrone and R. A. Owens. Feature detection from local energy. *Patt. Rec. Lett.*, 6:303–313, 1987.

[28] J.A. Noble. Finding corners. *Image & Vision Computing*, 6(2):121–128, 1988.

[29] D. Reisfeld. The constrained phase congruency feature detector: Simultaneous localization, classification, and scale determination. *Patt. Rec. Lett.*, 17:1161–1169, 1996.

[30] B. Robbins and R. Owens. 2d feature detection via local energy. *Image & Vision Computing*, 15:353–368, 1997.

[31] K. Rohr. Localization properties of direct corner detectors. *J. Mathematical Imaging & Vision*, 4(2):139–150, 1994.

[32] F. Schaffalitzky and A. Zisserman. Viewpoint invariant texture matching and wide baseline stereo. In *Int. Conf. Computer Vision*, pages 636–643, Vancouver, 2001.

[33] C. Schmid, R. Mohr, and C. Bauckhage. Evaluation of interest point detectors. *Int. J. Computer Vision*, 37(2):151–172, 2000.

[34] J. Shi and C. Tomasi. Good features to track. In *Int. Conf. Computer Vision & Pattern Recognition*, pages 593–600, Seattle, 1994.

[35] S. M. Smith and J. M. Brady. SUSAN - a new approach to low level image processing. *Int. J. Computer Vision*, 23(1):45–78, 1997.

[36] M. Toews and T. Arbel. Entropy-of-likelihood feature selection for image correspondence. In *Int. Conf. Computer Vision*, pages 1041–1047, Nice, France, 2003.

[37] P. H. S. Torr and A. Zisserman. Feature based methods for structure and motion estimation. In B. Triggs, A. Zisserman, and R. Szeliski, editors, *Vision Algorithms: Theory and Practice*, pages 278–294, Corfu, Greece, 2000. Springer-Verlag LNCS.

[38] O. Zuniga and R. Haralick. Corner detection using the facet model. In *Int. Conf. Computer Vision & Pattern Recognition*, pages 30–37, 1983.

Spectral Simplification of Graphs

Huaijun Qiu and Edwin R. Hancock

Department of Computer Science,University of York
Heslington, York, YO10 5DD, UK

Abstract. Although inexact graph-matching is a problem of potentially exponential complexity, the problem may be simplified by decomposing the graphs to be matched into smaller subgraphs. If this is done, then the process may cast into a hierarchical framework and hence rendered suitable for parallel computation. In this paper we describe a spectral method which can be used to partition graphs into non-overlapping subgraphs. In particular, we demonstrate how the Fiedler-vector of the Laplacian matrix can be used to decompose graphs into non-overlapping neighbourhoods that can be used for the purposes of both matching and clustering.

1 Introduction

Graph partitioning is concerned with grouping the vertices of a connected graph into subsets so as to minimize the total cut weight [6]. The process is of central importance in electronic circuit design, map coloring and scheduling [19]. However, in this paper we are interested in the process since it provides a means by which the inexact graph-matching problem may be decomposed into a series of simpler subgraph matching problems. As demonstrated by Messmer and Bunke [9], error-tolerant graph matching can be simplified using decomposition methods and reduced to a problem of subgraph indexing. Our aim in this paper is to explore whether spectral methods can be used to partition graphs in a stable manner for the purposes of matching by decomposition.

Recently, there has been increased interest in the use of spectral graph theory for characterising the global structural properties of graphs. Spectral graph theory aims to summarise the structural properties of graphs using the eigenvectors of the adjacency matrix or the Laplacian matrix [2]. There are several examples of the application of spectral matching methods for grouping and matching in the computer vision literature. For instance, Umeyama has shown how graphs of the same size can be matched by performing singular value decomposition on the adjacency matrices [16]. Here the permutation matrix that brings the nodes of the graphs into correspondence is found by taking the outer product of the matrices of left eigenvectors for the two graphs. In related work Shapiro and Brady [13] have shown how to locate feature correspondences using the eigenvectors of a point-proximity weight matrix. These two methods fail when the graphs being matched contain different numbers of nodes. However, this problem can be overcomed by using the apparatus of the EM algorithm [8,18]. More recently, Shokoufandeh, Dickinson, Siddiqi and Zucker [15] have shown how graphs can

T. Pajdla and J. Matas (Eds.): ECCV 2004, LNCS 3024, pp. 114–126, 2004.
© Springer-Verlag Berlin Heidelberg 2004

be retrieved efficiently using an indexing mechanism that maps the topological structure of shock-trees into a low-dimensional vector space. Here the topological structure is encoded by exploiting the interleaving property of the eigenvalues.

One of the most important spectral attributes of a graph is the Fiedler vector, i.e. the eigenvector associated with the second smallest eigenvalue of the Laplacian matrix. In a useful review, Mohar [11] has summarized some important applications of Laplace eigenvalues such as the max-cut problem, semidefinite programming and steady state random walks on Markov chains. More recently, Haemers [5] has explored the use of interlacing properties for the eigenvalues and has shown how these relate to the chromatic number, the diameter and the bandwidth of graphs. In the computer vision literature, Shi and Malik [14] have used the Fiedler vector to develop a recursive partition scheme and have applied this to image grouping and segmentation. The Fiedler vector may also be used for the Minimum Linear Arrangement problem(MinLA) which involves placing the nodes of a graph in a serial order which is suitable for the purposes of visualisation [3].

An extension of the minimum linear arrangement problem is the seriation problem which involves finding a serial ordering of the nodes, which maximally preserves the edge connectivity. This is clearly a problem of exponential complexity. As a result approximate solution methods have been employed. These involve casting the problem in an optimization setting. Hence techniques such as simulated annealing and mean field annealing have been applied to the problem. It may also be formulated using semidefinite programming, which is a technique closely akin to spectral graph theory since it relies on eigenvector methods. However, recently a graph-spectral solution has been found to the problem. Atkins, Boman and Hendrikson [1] have shown how to use the Fiedler eigenvector of the Laplacian matrix to sequence relational data. The method has been successfully applied to the consecutive ones problem and a number of DNA sequencing tasks. There is an obvious parallel between this method and steady state random walks on graphs, which can be located using the leading eigenvector of the Markov chain transition probability matrix. However, in the case of a random walk the path is not guaranteed to encourage edge connectivity. The spectral seriation method, on the other hand, does impose edge connectivity constraints on the recovered path,

The aim in this paper is to consider whether the partitions delivered by the Fiedler vector can be used to simplify the graph-matching problem. We focus on two problems. The first of these is to use the Fiedler vector to decompose graphs by partitioning them into structural units. Our aim is to explore whether the partitions are stable under structural error, and in particular whether they can be used for the purposes of graph-matching. The second problem studied is whether the partitions can be used to simplify the graphs in a hierarchical manner. Here we construct a graph in which the nodes are the partitions and the edges indicate whether the partitions are connected by edges in the original graph. This spectral construction can be applied recursively to provide a hierarchy of simplified graphs. We show that the simplified graphs can be used for efficient and reliable clustering.

2   Laplacian Matrix and Fiedler Vector

Consider the unweighted graph $G = (V, E)$ where V is the set of nodes and E is the set of edges. The adjacency matrix of the graph is A, and has elements

$$A(i, j) = \begin{cases} 1 & \text{if } (i, j) \in E \\ 0 & \text{otherwise} \end{cases} \tag{1}$$

The weighted adjacency matrix is denoted by W.

The degree matrix of the graph is the diagonal matrix $D = diag(deg(i); i \in V)$ where the degree is the row-sum of the adjacency matrix $deg(i) = \sum_{j \in V} A(i, j)$. With these ingredients the Laplacian matrix $L = D - A$ has elements

$$L(i, j) = \begin{cases} \sum_{\langle i, k \rangle \in E} A(i, k) & \text{if } i = j \\ -A(i, j) & \text{if } i \neq j \text{ and } (i, j) \in E \\ 0 & \text{otherwise} \end{cases} \tag{2}$$

The Laplacian matrix has a number of important properties. It is symmetric and positive semidefinite. The eigenvector $(1, 1, \ldots, 1)^T$ corresponds to the trivial zero eigenvalue. If the graph is connected then all other eigenvalues are positive and the smallest eigenvalue is a simple one, which means the number of connected components of the graph is equal to the multiplicity of the smallest eigenvalue. If we arrange all the eigenvalues from the smallest to the largest i.e. $0 \leq \lambda_1 \leq \lambda_2 \ldots \leq \lambda_n$, the most important are the largest eigenvalue λ_{max} and the second smallest eigenvalue λ_2, whose corresponding eigenvector is referred to as the *Fiedler Vector* [4].

Our aim is to decompose the graph into non-overlapping neighbourhoods using a path-based seriation method. The aim is to find a path sequence for the nodes in the graph using a permutation π. The permutation gives the order of the nodes in the sequence. The sequence is such that the elements of the edge weight matrix W decrease as the path is traversed. Hence, if $\pi(i) < \pi(j) < \pi(k)$, then $W(i, j) > W(i, k)$ and $W(j, k) > W(i, k)$. This behaviour can be captured using the penalty function

$$g(\pi) = \sum_{i=1}^{|V|} \sum_{j=1}^{|V|} W(i, j)(\pi(i) - \pi(j))^2$$

By minimizing $g(\pi)$ it is possible to find the permutation that minimizes the difference in edge weight between adjacent nodes in the path, and this in turn sorts the edge weights into magnitude order. Unfortunately, minimizing $g(\pi)$ is potentially NP complete due to the combinatorial nature of the discrete permutation π. To overcome this problem, a relaxed solution is sought that approximates the structure of $g(\pi)$ using a vector $\boldsymbol{x} = (x_1, x_2, \ldots)$ of continuous variables x_i. Hence, the penalty function considered is

$$\hat{g}(\boldsymbol{x}) = \sum_{i=1}^{|V|} \sum_{j=1}^{|V|} W(i, j)(x_i - x_j)^2$$

The value of $\hat{g}(\boldsymbol{x})$ does not change if a constant amount is added to each of the components x_i. Hence, the minimization problem must be subject to constraints on the components of the vector $\boldsymbol{x}$. The constraints are that

$$\sum_{i=1}^{|V|} x_i^2 = 1 \quad \text{and} \quad \sum_{i=1}^{|V|} x_i = 0 \tag{3}$$

The solution to this relaxed problem may be obtained from the Laplacian matrix. If $\boldsymbol{e} = (1, 1, 1..., 1)^T$ is the all-ones vector, then the solution to the minimization problem is the vector

$$\boldsymbol{x} = \arg \min_{\boldsymbol{x}_*^T.e=0, \boldsymbol{x}_*^T \boldsymbol{x}_*=1} \boldsymbol{x}_*^T L \boldsymbol{x}_* = \arg \min_{\boldsymbol{x}_*^T.e=0, \boldsymbol{x}_*^T \boldsymbol{x}_*=1} \sum_{i>j} W(i,j)(x_{*_i} - x_{*_j})^2$$

When W is positive definite, then the solution is the Fiedler vector, i.e. the vector associated with the smallest non-zero eigenvalue of L. In fact, the associated eigenvalue minimizes the Rayleigh quotient

$$\lambda = \arg \min_{x_*} \frac{\boldsymbol{x}_*^T L \boldsymbol{x}_*}{\boldsymbol{x}_*^T \boldsymbol{x}_*}$$

3   Graph Partition

The aim in this paper is to use the Fiedler vector to partition graphs into non-overlapping structural units and to use the structural units generated by this decomposition for the purposes of graph-matching and graph-simplification.

3.1   Decomposition

The neighbourhood of the node i consists of its center node, together with its immediate neighbors connected by edges in the graph, i.e., $\hat{N}_i = \{i\} \cup \{u; (i,u) \in E\}$. An illustration is provided in Figure 1, which shows a graph with two of its neighbourhoods highlighted. Hence, each neighbourhood consists of a *center node* and *immediate neighbors* of the center node, i.e. $N_i = \hat{N}_i \setminus \{i\}$.

The problem addressed here is how to partition the graph into a set of non-overlapping neighbourhoods using the node order defined by the Fiedler vector. Our idea is to assign to each node a measure of significance as the centre of a neighbourhood. We then traverse the path defined by the Fielder vector selecting the centre-nodes on the basis of this measure.

We commence by assigning weights to the nodes on the basis of the rank-order of their component in the Fiedler vector. Let $\Gamma =< j_1, j_2, j_3, ... >$ be the rank-order of the nodes as defined by the Fiedler vector so that the permutation satisfies the condition $\pi(j_1) < \pi(j_2) < \pi(j_3).....$ and the components of the Fiedler vector follow the condition $x_{j_1} > x_{j_2} > .. > x_{j_{|V|}}$. We assign weights to the nodes based on their rank order in the permutation. The weight assigned to

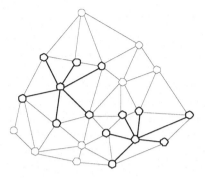

Fig. 1. Neighbourhoods.

the node $i \in V$ is $w_i = Rank\left(\pi_{(i)}\right)$. With this weighted graph in hand, we can gauge the significance of each node using the following score function:

$$\mathcal{F}_i = \alpha \left(deg(i) + |N_i \cap P|\right) + \frac{\beta}{w_i} \qquad (4)$$

where P is the set of nodes on the perimeter of the graph. The first term depends on the degree of the node and its proximity to the perimeter. Hence, it will sort nodes according to their distance from the perimeter. This will allow us to partition nodes from the outer layer first and then work inwards. The second term ensures that the first ranked nodes in the Fielder vector are visited first.

We use the score function to locate the non-overlapping neighbourhoods of the graph G. We traverse this list until we find a node k_1 which is neither in the perimeter, i.e. $k_1 \notin P$ nor whose score exceeds those of its neighbours, i.e. $\mathcal{F}_{k_1} = \arg\max_{i \in k_1 \cup N_{k_1}} \mathcal{F}_i$. When this condition is satisfied, then the node k_1 together with its neighbours N_{k_1} represent the first neighbourhood. The set of nodes $\hat{N}_{k_1} = k_1 \cup N_{k_1}$ are appended to a list T that tracks the set of nodes assigned to the neighbourhoods. This process is repeated for all the nodes which have not yet been assigned to a neighbourhood i.e. $R = \Gamma - T$. The procedure terminates when all the nodes of the graph have assigned to non-overlapping neighbourhood.

4   Matching

We match the graphs using the non-overlapping neighbourhoods detected using the Fiedler vector. Consider a data graph G_D which is to be matched onto a model graph G_M. The state of correspondence match can be represented by the function $f : V_D \mapsto V_M \cup \{\Phi\}$ from the node-set of the data graph onto the node-set of the model graph, where the node-set of the model graph is augmented by adding a NULL label, Φ, to allow for unmatchable nodes in the data graph. Our score function for the match is the average over the matching probabilities for the set of neighbourhoods of the graph

$$Q_{D,M}(f) = \frac{1}{|V_D|} \sum_{i \in V_D} P(F_i) \qquad (5)$$

where $F_i = (f(u_0), f(u_1), \ldots, f(u_{|N_i^D|}))$ denotes the relational image of the neighbourhood N_i^D in G_D under the matching function f.

We use the Bayes rule to compute the matching probability over a set of legal structure-preserving mappings between the data and model graphs. The set of mappings is compiled by considering the cyclic permutations of the peripheral nodes about the centre node of the neighbourhood. The set of feasible mappings generated in this way is denoted by $\Theta_i = \{S\}$ which consists of structure-preserving mapping of the form $S = (s_0, s_1, \ldots, s_u, \ldots, s_{|N_i^D|})$, where $s_u \in j \cup \{v; (j,v) \in N_j^M\} \cup \Phi$ is either one of the node-labels drawn from the model graph neighbourhood or the null-label Φ, and $u \in N_i^D$ is one of the node-labels drawn from the data graph neighbourhood N_i^D.

With the structure preserving mappings to hand we use the Bayes formula to compute the matching probability, $P(F_i)$. This is done by expanding over the set of structure preserving mappings Θ_i in the following manner

$$P(F_i) = \sum_{S \in \Theta_i} P(F_i|S) \cdot P(S) \qquad (6)$$

We assume a uniform distribution of probability over the structure preserving mappings and write $P(S) = \frac{1}{|\Theta_i|}$ The conditional matching probability $P(F_i|S)$ is determined by comparing every assigned match $f(u)$ in the configuration F_i with the corresponding item s_u in the structure preserving mapping S.

4.1 Edit Distance

To model the structural differences in the neighbourhoods, we use the Levenshtein or string edit distance [7,17,12]. This models structural error by considering insertions and deletions, in addition to relabelling. In what follows, the set of structure preserving mappings Θ_i^c which contains only cyclic permutations and whose size is therefore equal to $|N_i^D| - 1$.

Let X and Y be two strings of symbols drawn from an alphabet Σ. We wish to convert X to Y via an ordered sequence of operations such that the cost associated with the sequence is minimal. The original string to string correction algorithm defined *elementary edit operations*, $(a,b) \neq (\epsilon, \epsilon)$ where a and b are symbols from the two strings or the NULL symbol, ϵ. Thus, changing symbol x to y is denoted by (x,y), inserting y is denoted (ϵ, y), and deleting x is denoted (x, ϵ). A sequence of such operations which transforms X into Y is known as an *edit transformation* and denoted $\Delta = <\delta_1, \ldots, \delta_{|\Delta|}>$. Elementary costs are assigned by an elementary weighting function $\gamma : \Sigma \cup \{\epsilon\} \times \Sigma \cup \{\epsilon\} \mapsto \Re$; the cost of an edit transformation, $C(\Delta)$, is the sum of its elementary costs. The edit distance between X and Y is defined as

$$\mathbf{d}(X,Y) = \min\{C(\Delta)|\Delta \text{ transforms } X \text{ to } Y\} \qquad (7)$$

In [10], Marzal and Vidal introduced the notion of an *edit path* which is a sequence of ordered pairs of positions in X and Y such that the path monotonically traverses the edit matrix of x and y from $(0,0)$ to $(|X|, |Y|)$.

Essentially, the transition from one point in the path to the next is equivalent to an elementary edit operation:$(a, b) \rightarrow (a + 1, b)$ corresponds to deletion of the symbol in X at position a. Similarly, $(a, b) \rightarrow (a, b + 1)$ corresponds to insertion of the symbol at position b in Y. The transition $(a, b) \rightarrow (a + 1, b + 1)$ corresponds to a change from $X(a)$ to $Y(b)$. Thus, the cost of an edit path, $C(P)$, can be determined by summing the elementary weights of the edit operations implied by the path.

$$\mathbf{d}(X, Y) = \min \{C(P | P \text{ is an edit path from } X \text{ to } Y)\} \tag{8}$$

4.2   Matching Probabilities

If we replace X and Y by a structure preserving mapping, S_i, and the image of a data graph neighbourhood under the match, F_j, we can see that F_j could have arisen from S through the action of a memoryless error process, statistically independent of position (since the errors that "transformed" S to F_j could have occured in any order). So we can factorize (6) over the elementary operations implied by the edit path P^*

$$P(F_j | S_i) = \prod_{(f(u),v) \Leftarrow P^*_{F_j, S_i}} P(f(u) | v) \tag{9}$$

where $(f(u), v)$ is an insertion, a deletion, a change or an identity operation implied by the edit path $P^*_{F_j, S_i}$ between the neighbourhood F_j and the unpadded structure preserving mapping S_i. The role of the edit distance here is to obtain each operation instead of calculating the whole cost. We can trace every single operation by back tracking the edit matrix. For simplicity, we assume that different edit operations have identical cost, for example, 1. But this does not influence the probability because it is the probabilities of the transitions in the path which contribute to the matching prior not the edit weights themselves although they will determine the magnitude of the minimum cost.

$$\gamma(f(u), v) = \begin{cases} 0 \text{ if } (f(u), v) \text{ is an identity} \\ 1 \text{ otherwise} \end{cases} \tag{10}$$

So, the probability for the edit operation given to each pair is:

$$P(f(u) | v) = \begin{cases} (1 - P_e) \text{ if } (f(u), v) \text{ is an identity} \\ P_e \quad\quad\quad \text{ otherwise} \end{cases} \tag{11}$$

If we define the number of nonidentity transformations in the edit path to be $W\left(P^*_{F_j, S_i}\right)$, the matching probability of F_j can be given:

$$P(F_j) = \frac{K_{N_j^D}}{|\Theta|} \sum_{S_i \in \Theta} \exp\left[-K_w W\left(P^*_{F_j, S_i}\right)\right] \tag{12}$$

where $K_{N_j^D} = (1 - P_e)^{|N_j^D|}$ and $K_w = \ln \frac{(1 - P_e)}{P_e}$.

5   Hierarchical Simplification

The neighbourhoods extracted using the Fiedler vector may also be used to perform hierarchical graph simplification.

5.1   Partition Arrangements

Our simplification process proceeds as follows. We create a new graph in which each neighbourhood $\hat{N}_i = \{i\} \cup \{u; (i, u) \in E\}$ is represented by a node. In practice this is done by eliminating those nodes, which are not the center nodes of the neighbourhoods $N_i = \hat{N}_i \setminus \{i\}$. In other words, we select the center node of each neighbourhood to be node-set for the next level representation. The node set is given by $\hat{V} = \left\{ \hat{N}_1 \setminus N_1, \hat{N}_2 \setminus N_2, \ldots, \hat{N}_n \setminus N_n \right\}$. Our next step is to construct the edge-set for the simplified graph. We construct an edge between two nodes if there is a common edge contained within their associated neighbourhoods. The condition for the nodes $i \in \hat{V}$ and $j \in \hat{V}$ to form an edge in the simplified graph $\hat{G} = (\hat{V}, \hat{E})$ is $(i, j) \in \hat{E} \Rightarrow |\hat{N}_i \cap \hat{N}_j| \geq 2$.

5.2   Clustering

To provide an illustration of the usefulness of the simplifications provided by the Fiedler vector, we focus on the problem of graph clustering. The aim here is to investigate whether the simplified graphs preserve the pattern space distribution of the original graphs. There are a number of ways in which we could undertake this study. However, here we use a simple graph-spectral clustering method, which is in keeping with the overall philosophy of this paper.

Suppose that we aim to cluster the set of M graphs $\{G_1, ...G_k, ...G_M\}$ We commence by performing the spectral decomposition $L_k = \Phi_k \Lambda \Phi_T$ on the Laplacian matrix L_k for the graph indexed k, where $\Lambda_k = diag(\lambda_k^1, \lambda_k^2, ...)$ is the diagonal matrix of eigenvalues and Φ_k is a matrix with eigenvectors as columns. For the graph G_k, we construct a vector $B_k = \left(\lambda_k^1, \lambda_k^2, \ldots, \lambda_k^m\right)^T$ from the leading m eigenvalues. We can visualize the distribution of graphs by performing multidimensional scaling (MDS) on the matrix of distances $d_{k1,k2}$ between graphs. This distribution can be computed using either the edit distance technique used in the previous section where $d_{k1,k2} = -lnQ_{k1,k2}$ or by using the spectral features where $d_{k1,k2} = (B_{k1} - B_{k2})^T (B_{k1} - B_{k2})$.

6   Experiments

The aims in this section are twofold. First, we aim to illustrate that the neighbourhoods delivered by the Fiedler vector form useful structural units for computing edit distance. Second, we aim to illustrate that the simplification procedure results in a stable distribution of graphs in pattern-space.

6.1 Real-Word Data

The data used in our study is furnished by a sequence of views of a model-houses taken from different camera directions. In order to convert the images into abstract graphs for matching, we extract point features using a corner detector. Our graphs are the Delaunay triangulations of the corner-features.

We have matched the first image to each of the subsequent images in the sequence by using the edit distance method outlined earlier in this paper. The results are compared with those obtained using the method of Luo and Hancock [8] in Table 1. This table contains the number of detected corners to be matched, the number of correct correspondence, the number of missed corners and the number of miss-matched corners.

Figure 2 shows us the correct correspondence rate as a function of view difference for the two methods based on the data in the Table 1. From the results, it is clear that our new method degrades gradually and out performs [8]

Table 1. Correspondence allocation results and comparison with the EM method.

Method	House index	0	1	2	3	4	5	6	7	8	9
	Corners	30	32	32	30	30	32	30	30	30	31
EM[8]	Correct	-	29	26	24	17	13	11	5	3	0
	False	-	0	2	3	8	11	12	15	19	24
	Missed	-	1	2	3	5	6	7	10	8	6
Edit	Correct	-	26	24	20	19	17	14	11	13	11
Distance	False	-	3	5	8	11	12	16	15	17	19
	Missed	-	1	1	2	0	1	0	4	0	0

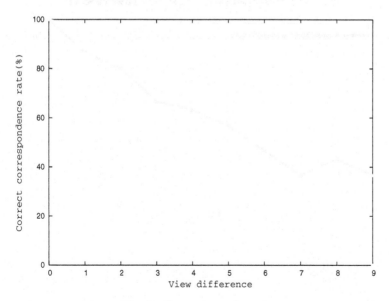

Fig. 2. Comparison of results

when the difference in viewing angle is large. Even in the worst case, our method has a correct correspondence rate of 36%.

6.2   Graph Clustering

Our graph clustering experiments are performed with three different sequences of model houses. In Figure 3 the two panels show the distances $d(k_1, k_2) = (B_{k_1} - D_{k_2})^T (B_{k_1} - B_{k_2})$ between the vectors of eigenvalues for the graphs indexed k_1 and k_2. The left panel is for the original graph and the right panel is for the simplified graph. It is clear that the simplification process has preserved much of the structure in the distance plot. For instance, the three sequences are clearly visible as blocks in the panels. Figure 4 shows a scatter plot of the distance between the simplified graphs (y-axis) as a function of the distance between the original graphs. Although there is considerable dispersion, there is an underlying linear trend.

Figure 5 and 6 repeat the distance matrices and the scatter plot using edit distance rather than the L2 norm for the spectral feature vectors. Again, there

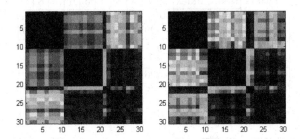

Fig. 3. Pairwise spectral graph distance; (left) original graph, (right) reduced graph

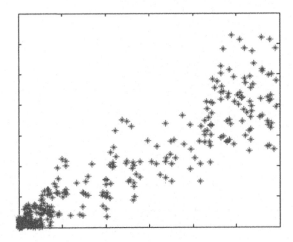

Fig. 4. Scatter plot for the original graph and reduced graph pairwise distance

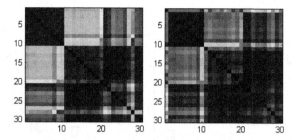

Fig. 5. Graph edit distance; (left) original graph, (right) reduced graph

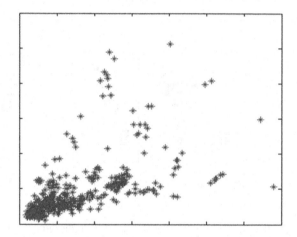

Fig. 6. Scatter plots for the original graph and reduced graph edit distance

is a clear block structure. However, the dispersion in the scatter plot is greater. To take this study one step further, in Figure 7 and 8 we show the result of performing MDS on the distances for both the edit distance and the spectral feature vector. In both cases the different views of the houses fall into distinct regions of the plot. Moreover, the reduction press does not destroy the cluster structure.

7   Conclusions

In this paper, we have used the Fiedler vector of the Laplacian matrix to partition the nodes of a graph into structural units for the purposes of matching. This allows us to decompose the problem of matching the graphs into that of matching structural subunits. We investigate the matching of the structural subunits using a edit distance method. The partitioning method is sufficiently stable under structural error that accuracy of match is not sacrificed. Our motivation in undertaking this study is to use the partitions to develop a hierarchical matching method. The aim is to construct a graph that represents the arrangement of

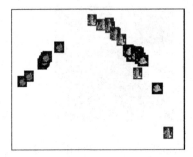 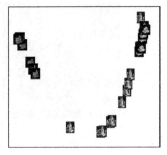

Fig. 7. MDS for the original graph (left) edit distance, (right)spectral feature vector

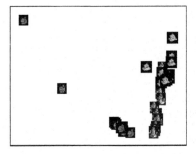 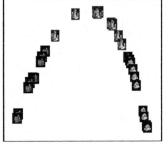

Fig. 8. MDS for the reduced graph (left) edit distance, (right)spectral feature vector

the partitions. By first matching the partition arrangement graphs, we provide constraints on the matching of the individual partitions.

References

1. J. E. Atkins, E. G. Boman, and B. Hendrickson. A spectral algorithm for seriation and the consecutive ones problem. *SIAM Journal on Computing*, 1998.
2. F.R.K. Chung. *Spectral Graph Theory.* CBMS series 92. American Mathmatical Society Ed., 1997.
3. J. Diaz, J. Petit, and M. Serna. A survey on graph layout problems. Technical report LSI-00-61-R, Universitat Polit'ecnica de Catalunya, 2000.
4. M. Fiedler. A property of eigenvectors of non-negative symmetric matrices and its application to graph theory. *Czechoslovak Mathematics Journal*, 25:619–633, 1975.
5. W.H. Haemers. Interlacing eigenvalues and graphs. *Linear Algebra and its Applications*, pages 593–616, 1995.
6. B.W. Kernighan and S. Lin. An efficient heuristic procedure for partitioning graphs. *The Bell System Technical Journal*, pages 291–307, 1970.
7. V. I. Levenshtein. Binary codes capable of correcting deletions insertions and reversals. *Soviet Physics-Doklandy*, 10(8):707–710, 1966.
8. B. Luo and E. R. Hancock. Structural graph matching using the em algorithm and singular value decomposition. *IEEE PAMI*, 23(10):1120–1136, 2001.
9. B.T. M. and H. Bunke. A new algorithm for error-tolerant subgraph isomorphism detection. *IEEE PAMI*, 20:493–504, 1998.

10. A. Marzal and E. Vidal. Computation of normalized edit distance and applications. *IEEE Trans. Systems, Man, and Cybernetics*, 25:202–206, 1995.

11. B. Mohar. Some applications of laplace eigenvalues of graphs. *Graph Symmetry: Algebraic Methods and Applications*, 497 NATO ASI Series C:227–275, 1997.

12. R. Myers, R. C. Wilson, and E. R. Hancock. Bayesian graph edit distance. *IEEE PAMI*, 22(6):628–635, 2000.

13. L. Shapiro and J. Brady. Feature-based correspondence: an eigenvector approach. *Image and Vision Computing*, 10(2):283–288, June 1992.

14. J. Shi and J. Malik. Normalized cuts and image segmentation. *IEEE PAMI*, 22(8):888–905, 2000.

15. A. Shokoufandeh, S.J. Dickinson, K. Siddiqi, and S.W. Zucker. Indexing using a spectral encoding of topological structure. *IEEE-ICPR*, pages 491–497, 1999.

16. S. Umeyama. An eigendecomposition approach to weighted graph matching problems. *IEEE PAMI*, 10:695–703, 1988.

17. R. A. Wagner and M. Fischer. The string-to-string correction problem. *J. ACM*, 21(1):168–173, 1974.

18. R. C. Wilson and E. R. Hancock. Structural matching by discrete relaxation. *IEEE PAMI*, 19(6):634–648, 1997.

19. R.J. Wilson and J. J. Watkins. *Graphs: an introductory approach: a first course in discrete mathematics*. Wiley international edition. New York, etc., Wiley, 1990.

Inferring White Matter Geometry from Diffusion Tensor MRI: Application to Connectivity Mapping

Christophe Lenglet, Rachid Deriche, and Olivier Faugeras

Odyssée Lab, INRIA Sophia-Antipolis, France
{clenglet,der,faugeras}@sophia.inria.fr

Abstract. We introduce a novel approach to the cerebral white matter connectivity mapping from diffusion tensor MRI. DT-MRI is the unique non-invasive technique capable of probing and quantifying the anisotropic diffusion of water molecules in biological tissues. We address the problem of consistent neural fibers reconstruction in areas of complex diffusion profiles with potentially multiple fibers orientations. Our method relies on a global modelization of the acquired MRI volume as a Riemannian manifold M and proceeds in 4 majors steps: First, we establish the link between Brownian motion and diffusion MRI by using the Laplace-Beltrami operator on M. We then expose how the sole knowledge of the diffusion properties of water molecules on M is sufficient to infer its geometry. There exists a direct mapping between the diffusion tensor and the metric of M. Next, having access to that metric, we propose a novel level set formulation scheme to approximate the distance function related to a radial Brownian motion on M. Finally, a rigorous numerical scheme using the exponential map is derived to estimate the geodesics of M, seen as the diffusion paths of water molecules. Numerical experimentations conducted on synthetic and real diffusion MRI datasets illustrate the potentialities of this global approach.

1 Introduction

Diffusion imaging is a magnetic resonance imaging technique introduced in the mid 1980s [1], [2] which provides a very sensitive probe of biological tissues architecture. Although this method suffered, in its very first years, from severe technical constraints such as acquisition time or motion sensitivity, it is now taking an increasingly important place with new acquisition modalities such as ultrafast echo-planar methods. In order to understand the neural fibers bundle architecture, anatomists used to perform cerebral dissection, strychnine or chemical markers neuronography [3]. As of today, diffusion MRI is the unique non-invasive technique capable of probing and quantifying the anisotropic diffusion of water molecules in tissues like brain or muscles. As we will see in the following, the diffusion phenomenon is a macroscopic physical process resulting from the permanent Brownian motion of molecules and shows how molecules tend to move from low to high concentration areas over distances of about 10 to 15 μm during

T. Pajdla and J. Matas (Eds.): ECCV 2004, LNCS 3024, pp. 127–140, 2004.

typical times of 50 to 100 ms. The key concept that is of primary importance for diffusion imaging is that diffusion in biological tissues reflects their structure and their architecture at a microscopic scale. For instance, Brownian motion is highly influenced in tissues such as cerebral white matter or the *annulus fibrosus* of inter-vertebral discs. Measuring, at each voxel, that very same motion along a number of sampling directions (at least 6, up to several hundreds) provides an exquisite insight into the local orientation of fibers and is known as diffusion-weighted imaging. In 1994, Basser et al. [4] proposed the model, now widely used, of the diffusion tensor featuring an analytic means to precisely describe the three-dimensional nature of anisotropy in tissues.

Numerous works have already addressed the problem of the estimation and regularization of these tensor fields. References can be found in [5], [6], [7], [8], [9]. Motivated by the potentially dramatic improvements that knowledge of anatomical connectivity would bring into the understanding of functional coupling between cortical regions [10], the study of neurodegenerative diseases, neurosurgery planning or tumor growth quantification, various methods have been proposed to tackle the issue of cerebral connectivity mapping. Local approaches based on line propagation techniques [11], [12] provide fast algorithms and have been augmented to incorporate some natural constraints such as regularity, stochastic behavior and even local non-Gaussianity ([13], [14], [15], [16], [17], [18], [19], [20]). All these efforts aim to overcome the intrinsic ambiguity of the diffusion tensor related to white matter partial volume effects. Bearing in mind this limitation, they enable us to generate relatively accurate models of the human brain macroscopic three-dimensional architectures. The tensor indeed encapsulates the averaged diffusion properties of water molecules inside a voxel whose typical extents vary from 1 to 3 mm. At this resolution, the contribution to the measured anisotropy of a voxel is very likely to come from different fibers bundles presenting different orientations. This voxel-wise homogeneous Gaussian model thus limits our capacity to resolve multiple fibers orientations since local tractography becomes unstable when crossing artificially isotropic regions characterized by a planar or spherical diffusion profile [8]. On the other side, new diffusion imaging methods have been recently introduced in an attempt to better describe the complexity of water motion but at the cost of increased acquisition times. This is a case of high angular diffusion weighted imaging [21], [22] where the variance of the signal could give important information on the multimodal aspect of diffusion. Diffusion Spectrum Imaging [23], [24] provides, at each voxel, an estimation of the probability density function of water molecules and has been shown to be a particularly accurate means to access the whole complexity of the diffusion process in biological tissues. In favor of these promising modalities, parallel MRI [25] will reduce the acquisition time in a near future and thus permit high resolution imaging.

More global algorithms such as [26] have been proposed to better handle the situations of false planar or spherical tensors (with fibers crossings) and to propose some sort of likelihood of connection. In [27], the authors make use of the major eigenvector field and in [28] the full diffusion tensor provides the metric of a Riemannian manifold but this was not exploited to propose intrinsic schemes.

We derive a novel approach to white matter analysis, through the use of stochastic processes and differential geometry which yield physically motivated distance maps in the brain, seen as a 3-manifold and thus the ability to compute intrinsic geodesics in the white matter. Our goal is to recast the challenging task of connectivity mapping into the natural framework of Riemannian differential geometry. Section 2 starts from the very definition of Brownian motion and show its link to the diffusion MRI signal for linear spaces in terms of its probability density function. Generalization to manifolds involves the introduction of the infinitesimal generator of the Brownian motion. We then solve, in Section 3, the problem of computing the intrinsic distance function from a starting point x_0 in the white matter understood as a manifold. The key idea is that the geometry of the manifold M has a deep impact on the behavior of Brownian motion. We claim that the diffusion tensor can be used to infer geodesic paths on M that coincide with neural tracts since its inverse defines the metric of M. Practically, this means that, being given any subset of voxels in the white matter, we will be able to compute paths most likely followed by water molecules to reach x_0. As opposed to many methods developed to perform tractography, we can now exhibit a bunch of fibers starting from a single point x_0 and reaching potentially large areas of the brain. Efficient numerical implementation is non-trivial and described in Section 4. Results, advantages and drawbacks of the method are presented and discussed in Section 5. We conclude and present potential extensions in Section 6.

2   From Molecular Diffusion to Anatomical Connectivity

2.1   The Diffusion MRI Signal

Diffusion MRI provides the only non-invasive means to characterize molecular displacements, hence its success in physics and chemistry. To measure diffusion in several directions, the Stejskal-Tanner imaging sequence is widely used. It basically relies on two strong gradient pulses positioned before and after the refocusing 180 degrees pulse of a classical spin echo sequence to control the diffusion weighting. For each slice, at least 6 independent gradient directions and 1 unweighted image are acquired to be able to estimate the diffusion tensor D and probe potential changes of location of water molecules due to Brownian motion. By performing one measurement without diffusion weighting S_0 and one (S) with a sensitizing gradient g, the diffusion coefficient D along g can be estimated through the relation:

$$S = S_0 \exp(-\gamma^2 \delta^2 \left(\Delta - \delta/3\right) |g|^2 D) \tag{1}$$

where δ is the duration of the gradient pulses, Δ the time between two gradient pulses and γ the gyromagnetic ratio of the hydrogen proton.

2.2   Brownian Motion and Anisotropic Molecular Diffusion

We recall the definition of a Brownian motion in Euclidean space, the simplest Markov process whose stochastic behavior is entirely determined by its initial distribution μ and its transition mechanism. Transitions are described by a probability density function p or an infinitesimal generator $\mathcal{L}$. In linear homogeneous spaces, p is easily derived as the minimal fundamental solution associated with $\mathcal{L}$ (solution of equation 2). On manifolds, constructing this solution is a tough task, but for our problem, we only need to characterize $\mathcal{L}$. Further details can be found in [29]. We denote by $\mathbf{V}^d = \mathcal{C}([0,\infty[\to \mathbb{R}^d)$ the set of d-dimensional continuous functions and by $\mathcal{B}(\mathbf{V}^d)$ the topological σ-algebra on $\mathbf{V}^d$. Then,

Definition 1. *A d-dimensional continuous process X is a $\mathbf{V}^d$-valued random variable on a probability space $(\Omega, \mathcal{F}, \mathbb{P})$*

By introducing the time $t \in [0,\infty[$ such that $\forall v \in \mathbf{V}^d$, $v(t) \in \mathbb{R}^d$, a time-indexed collection $\{X_t(\omega)\}$, $\forall \omega \in \Omega$ generates a d-dimensional continuous process if X_t is continuous with probability one. A Brownian motion is characterized by:

Definition 2. *With μ a probability on $(\mathbb{R}^d, \mathcal{B}(\mathbb{R}^d))$, $X_{t_0}, X_{t_1} - X_{t_0}, ..., X_{t_m} - X_{t_{m-1}}$ mutually independent with initial distribution specified by μ and Gaussian distribution for subsequent times (t_i are nonnegative and increasing), a process X_t is called a d-dimensional Brownian motion with initial distribution μ.*

X_t describing the position of water molecules, we now would like to understand how the diffusion behavior of these molecules is related to the underlying molecular hydrodynamics. Diffusion tensor, as thermal or electrical conductivity tensors, belongs to the broader class of general effective property tensors and is defined as the proportionality term between an averaged generalized intensity B and an averaged generalized flux F. In our particular case of interest B is the concentration gradient ∇C and F is the mass flux J such that Fick's law holds: $J = -\mathbf{D}\nabla C$. By considering the conservation of mass, the general diffusion equation is readily obtained:

$$\frac{\partial C}{\partial t} = \nabla.(\mathbf{D}\nabla C) = \mathcal{L}C \qquad (2)$$

In anisotropic cerebral tissues, water molecules motion varies in direction depending on obstacles such as axonal membranes. The positive definite order-2 tensor $\mathbf{D}$ has been related [30] to the root mean square of the diffusion distance by $\mathbf{D} = \frac{1}{6t}\langle(x-x_0)(x-x_0)^T\rangle$ ($\langle.\rangle$ denotes an ensemble average). This is directly related to the minimal fundamental solution of equation 2 for an unbounded anisotropic homogeneous medium and the regular Laplacian with initial distribution (obeying the same law as concentration) $\lim_{t\to 0} p(x|x_0,t) = \delta(x - x_0)$:

$$p(x|x_0,t) = \left(\frac{1}{4\pi|\mathbf{D}|t}\right)^{(d/2)} \exp\left(\frac{-(x-x_0)^T\mathbf{D}^{-1}(x-x_0)}{4t}\right)$$

Also known as the propagator, it describes the conditional probability to find a molecule, initially at position x_0, at x after a time interval t. All the above concepts find their counterparts when moving from linear spaces, such as $\mathbb{R}^d$, to Riemannian manifolds. Explicit derivation of p is non-trivial in that case and the Laplace-Beltrami operator, well known in image analysis [31], will be of particular importance to define $\mathcal{L}$.

3   White Matter as a Riemannian Manifold

3.1   Geometry of a Manifold from Diffusion Processes

We now want to characterize the anisotropic diffusion of water molecules in the white matter exclusively in term of an appropriate infinitesimal generator $\mathcal{L}$. Brownian motions are characterized by their Markovian property and the continuity of their trajectories. They have been, so far, generated from their initial distribution μ and their transition density function p, but they are characterized in terms of $\mathcal{L}$-diffusion processes. Without any further detail, we claim that under some technical hypothesis on $\mathcal{L}$ (with its domain of definition $D(\mathcal{L})$) and on the Brownian motion X_t, it is possible to define an $\mathcal{L}$-diffusion process on a Riemannian manifold M from the d-dimensional stochastic process X_t. We refer the interested reader to [29]. We focus, as in [32], on the case of a diffusion process with time-independent infinitesimal generator $\mathcal{L}$, assumed to be smooth and non-degenerate elliptic. We introduce Δ_M the Laplace-Beltrami differential operator such that, for a function f on a Riemannian manifold M, $\Delta_M f = \operatorname{div}(\operatorname{grad} f)$. In local coordinates $x_1, x_2, ..., x_d$, the Riemannian metric writes in the form $ds^2 = g_{ij} dx_i dx_j$ and the Laplace-Beltrami operator becomes

$$\Delta_M f(x) = \frac{1}{\sqrt{G}} \frac{\partial}{\partial x_j} \left(\sqrt{G} g^{ij} \frac{\partial f}{\partial x_i} \right) = g^{ij}(x) \frac{\partial^2 f}{\partial x_i \partial x_j}(x) + b^i(x) \frac{\partial f}{\partial x_i}(x)$$

where G is the determinant of the matrix $\{g_{ij}\}$ and $\{g^{ij}\}$ its inverse. Moreover,

$$b^i = \frac{1}{\sqrt{G}} \frac{\partial(\sqrt{G} g^{ij})}{\partial x_j} = g^{jk} \Gamma^i_{jk}$$

where Γ^i_{jk} are the Christoffel symbols of the metric $\{g_{ij}\}$. Δ_M is second order, strictly elliptic. At that point of our analysis, it turns out that constructing the infinitesimal generator $\mathcal{L}$ of our diffusion process boils down to (see [33]):

Definition 3. *The operator $\mathcal{L}$ is said to be an intrinsic Laplacian generating a Brownian motion on M if $\mathcal{L} = \frac{1}{2} \Delta_M$.*

Thus, for a smooth and non-degenerate elliptic differential operator on M of the form: $\mathcal{L} = \frac{1}{2} d^{ij}(x) \frac{\partial^2}{\partial x_i \partial x_j}$ we have the

Lemma 1. *If $(d_{ij}(x))_{i,j=1...d}$ denotes the inverse matrix of $(d^{ij}(x))_{i,j=1...d}$, then $g = d_{ij} dx_i dx_j$ defines a Riemannian metric g on M.*

Conclusion: In the context of diffusion tensor imaging, this is of great importance for the following since it means that the diffusion tensor $\mathbf{D}$ estimated at each voxel actually defines, after inversion, the metric of the manifold. We have made the link between the diffusion tensor data and the white matter manifold geometry through the properties of Brownian motion.

3.2   From Radial Processes to Neural Fibers Recovery

We can now measure in the intrinsic space of the white matter. The fundamental idea of what follows consists of the hypothesis that water molecules starting at a given point x_0 on M, under Brownian motion, will potentially reach any point on M through a unique geodesic. The sole knowledge of the metric g will enable us to actually compute those geodesics on the manifold inferred from the Laplace-Beltrami operator. Considering paths of Brownian motion (ie. fibers in the white matter) as the characteristics lines of the differential operator $\mathcal{L}$ we can easily extend the concept of radial process for that type of stochastic motion on a Riemannian manifold M [34]. Let us fix a reference point $x_0 \in M$ and let $r(x) = \phi(x_0, x)$ be the Riemannian distance between x and x_0. Then we define the radial process $r_t = r(X_t)$. The function $r : M \to \mathbb{R}^+$ has a well behaved singularity at the origin. We make the assumption that M is geodesically complete and recall the notion of exponential map which will be crucial for the numerical computation of neural fibers. We denote by c_e the geodesic with initial condition $c_e(0) = x$ and $c'_e(0) = e$ ($e \in T_x M$). We denote by $E \subset TM$ the set of vectors e such that $c_e(1)$ is defined. It is an open subset of the tangent bundle TM containing the null vectors $0_x \in T_x M$.

Definition 4. *The exponential map* $\exp : E \subset TM \to M$ *is defined by* $\exp(e) = c_e(1)$. *We denote by* $\exp_x$ *its restriction to one tangent space* $T_x M$.

Hence, in particular, for each unit vector $e \in T_{x_0} M$, there is a unique geodesic $c_e : [0, \infty[\to M$ such that $c'_e(x_0) = e$ and the exponential map gives $c_e(t) = \exp_{x_0}(te)$. For small time steps t, the geodesics $c_e[0, t[$ is the unique distance minimizing geodesic between its endpoints. We need one more notion to conclude this section: the cutlocus of x_0, $\mathbf{Cut}_{x_0}$, which will help us to characterize the distance function r. It is nothing but the locus of points where the geodesics starting orthonormally from x_0 stop being optimal for the distance. The radial function $r(x) = \phi(x_0, x)$ is smooth on $M/\mathbf{Cut}_{x_0}$ and we have $|\mathrm{grad}\phi(x)| = 1$

Conclusion: We have expressed the distance function on M. The objectives of the following section will be to propose accurate algorithms to compute this function ϕ everywhere on M and then to use it to estimate geodesics (Brownian paths) on this manifold (the brain white matter).

4   Intrinsic Distance Function, Geodesics

4.1   A Level Set Formulation for the Intrinsic Distance Function

We are now concerned with the effective computation of the distance function ϕ from a closed, non-empty subset K of the 3-dimensional, smooth, connected and complete Riemannian manifold (M, g). In the remaining, K will actually be restricted to the single point x_0, origin of a Brownian motion. We will nevertheless formulate everything in term of K since considering the distance to a larger subset of M will be of interest for future work. Let us now further discuss the notion of distance function on a Riemannian manifold. Given two points $x, y \in M$, we consider all the piecewise differentiable curves joining x to y. Since M is connected, by the Hopf-Rinow theorem, such curves do exist and

Definition 5. *The distance $\phi(x, y)$ is defined as the infimum of the lengths of the C^1 curves starting at x and ending at y.*

Corollary 1. *If $x_0 \in M$, the function $r : M \to \mathbb{R}$ given by $r(x) = \phi(x, x_0)$ is continuous on M but in general it is not everywhere differentiable.*

We consider a general Hamilton-Jacobi partial differential equation with Dirichlet boundary conditions

$$\begin{cases} H(x, D\phi(x)) = 0 \text{ in } M \setminus K \\ \phi(x) = \phi_0(x) \qquad \text{when } x \in K \end{cases}$$

where ϕ_0 is a continuous real function on K and the Hamiltonian $H : M \times T^\star M \to \mathbb{R}$ is a continuous real function on the cotangent bundle. We make the assumption that $H(x, .)$ is convex and we set $\phi_0(x) = 0 \ \forall x \in K$.

We denote by $|v|$ the magnitude of a vector v of TM, defined as $\sqrt{g(v, v)}$. In matrix notation, by forming $\mathbf{G} = \{g_{ij}\}$ the metric tensor, this writes $\sqrt{v^T \mathbf{G} v}$. Then, by setting $H(x, p) = |p| - 1$, we will work on the following theorem (for details on viscosity solutions on a Riemannian manifold, we refer to [35])

Theorem 1. *The distance function ϕ is the unique viscosity solution of the Hamilton-Jacobi problem*

$$\begin{cases} |grad\phi| = 1 \text{ in } M \setminus K \\ \phi(x) = 0 \quad \text{when } x \in K \end{cases} \tag{3}$$

in the class of bounded uniformly continuous functions.

This is the well-known eikonal equation on the Riemannian manifold (M, g). The viscosity solution ϕ at $x \in M$ is the minimum time $t \geq 0$ for any curve γ to reach a point $\gamma(t) \in K$ starting at x with the conditions $\gamma(0) = 0$ and $|\frac{d\gamma}{dt}| \leq 1$. ϕ is the value function of the minimum arrival time problem. This will enable us to solve equation 3 as a dynamic problem and thus to take advantage of the great flexibility of Level Set methods. On the basis of [36], [37], [38] and [39], we reformulate equation 3 by considering ϕ as the zero level set of a function ψ and requiring that the evolution of ψ generates ϕ so that

$$\psi(x, t) = 0 \Leftrightarrow t = \phi(x) \tag{4}$$

Osher ([36]) showed by using Theorem 5.2 from [39] that, under the hypothesis that the Hamiltonian H is independent of ϕ, the level set generated by 4 is a viscosity solution of 3 if ψ is the viscosity solution of

$$\begin{cases} \psi_t + F(t, x, D\psi(t, x)) = 0 \quad \forall t > 0 \\ \psi(x, 0) = \psi_0(x) \end{cases} \tag{5}$$

provided that $F > 0$ and does not change sign. This is typically the case for our anisotropic eikonal equation where the anisotropy directly arises from the manifold topology and not from the classical speed function of initial value problems (which equals 1 everywhere here). To find our solution, all we need to do is thus to evolve $\psi(x,t)$ while tracking, for all x, the time $\bar{t}$ when it changes sign. Now we have to solve 5 with

$$F(t, x, D\psi) = H(t, x, D\psi) + 1 = |\text{grad}\psi|$$

We first recall that for any function $f \in \mathbb{F}$, where $\mathbb{F}$ denotes the ring of smooth functions on M, the metric tensor $\mathbf{G}$ and its inverse define isomorphisms between vectors (in TM) and 1-forms (in T^*M). In particular, the gradient operator is defined as $\text{grad} f = \mathbf{G}^{-1} df$ where df denotes the first-order differential of f. It directly follows that

$$|\text{grad}\psi| = \sqrt{g(\text{grad}\psi, \text{grad}\psi)} = \left(g_{ij} \frac{\partial \psi}{\partial x_l} g^{li} \frac{\partial \psi}{\partial x_k} g^{kj} \right)^{1/2} = \left(\frac{\partial \psi}{\partial x_k} \frac{\partial \psi}{\partial x_l} g^{kl} \right)^{1/2}$$

and we now present the numerical schemes used to estimate geodesics as well as the viscosity solution of

$$\psi_t + |\text{grad}\psi| = 0 \tag{6}$$

4.2   Numerical Scheme for the Distance Function

Numerical approximation of the hyperbolic term in 6 is now carefully reviewed on the well-known basis of available schemes for hyperbolic conservative laws. We seek a three-dimensional numerical flux approximating the continuous flux $|\text{grad}\psi|^2$ and that is consistent and monotone so that it satisfies the usual jump and entropy conditions and converges towards the unique viscosity solution of interest. References can be found in [40]. On the basis of the Engquist-Osher flux [37] and the approach by Kimmel-Amir-Bruckstein for level set distance computation on 2D manifolds [41], we propose the following numerical flux for our quadratic Hamiltonian $d\psi^T \mathbf{G}^{-1} d\psi$:

$$|\text{grad}\psi|^2 = \sum_{i=1}^{3} g^{ii} (\max(D_{x_i}^- \psi, 0)^2 + \min(D_{x_i}^+ \psi, 0)^2) +$$

$$\sum_{\substack{i,j=1 \\ i \neq j}}^{3} g^{ij} \text{minmod}(D_{x_i}^+ \psi, D_{x_i}^- \psi) \text{minmod}(D_{x_j}^+ \psi, D_{x_j}^- \psi)$$

where the $D_{x_i}^\pm \psi$ are the forward/backward approximations of the gradient in x_i. Higher order implementation has also been done by using WENO schemes in order to increase the accuracy of the method. They consist of a convex combination of nth (we take $n = 5$) order polynomial approximation of derivatives [42]. A classical narrow band implementation is used to speed up the computations.

4.3   Numerical Scheme for the Geodesics Estimation

We finally derive an intrinsic method for geodesics computation in order to estimate paths of diffusion on M eventually corresponding to neural fibers tracts. Geodesics are indeed the integral curves of the intrinsic distance function and are classically obtained by back-propagating in its gradient directions from a given point x to the source x_0. Our problem of interest consists of starting from a given voxel of the white matter and of computing the optimal pathway in term of the distance ϕ until x_0 is reached. We propose to take into account the geometry of the manifold during this integration step by making use of the exponential map. If the geodesic $c(s)$ is the parameterized path $c(s) = (c_1(s), ..., c_d(s))$ which satisfies the differential equation

$$\frac{d^2 c_i}{ds^2} = -\Gamma^i_{jk}(c, \frac{dc}{ds})\frac{dc_j}{ds}\frac{dc_k}{ds} \tag{7}$$

where Γ^i_{jk} are the Christoffel symbols of the second kind defined as $\Gamma^i_{jk} = \frac{1}{2}g^{il}(\partial g_{kl}/\partial x_j + \partial g_{jl}/\partial x_k - \partial g_{jk}/\partial x_l)$. Equation 7 allows us to write $\exp$ in local coordinates around a point $x \in M$ as

$$c_i(\exp(X)) = X_i - \frac{1}{2}\Gamma^i_{jk}X_j X_k + \mathcal{O}(|X|^3) \quad \forall i = 1, ..., d$$

where X will be identified with the gradient of the distance function at x and derivatives of the metric are estimated by appropriate finite differences schemes. This leads to a much more consistent integration scheme on M.

5   Evaluation on Synthetic and Real Datasets

We have experimented with line propagation local methods which only produce macroscopically satisfying results. With trilinear interpolation of the tensor field and a 4th order Runge Kutta integration scheme, we used the advection-diffusion method [13] and obtained the results on Figure 1. Our global approach is actually more concerned to resolve local ambiguities due to isotropic tensors. We consider synthetic and real data[1] to quantify the quality of the estimated distance functions with upwind and WENO5 finite differences schemes. Our criterion is the a posteriori evaluated map $|\text{grad}\phi|$ which must be equal to 1 everywhere except at the origin x_0. As shown on Figure 2 [left], synthetic data corresponds to an anisotropic non-homogeneous medium for which the diffusion paths describe three (independently homogeneous) intersecting cylinders oriented along the x, y and z axis. It results perfectly isotropic tensors at the intersection of the three cylinders, surrounded by planar tensors in the area where only two cylinders cross each others. Though simple, it is a typical configuration where local methods become unreliable. x_0 denotes the origin of the distance function whose

---

[1] The authors would like to thank J.F. Mangin and J.B Poline, CEA-SHFJ/Orsay, France for providing us with the data

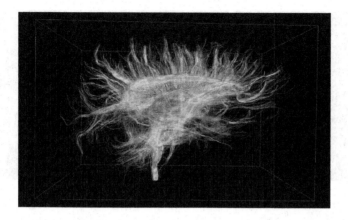

Fig. 1. Neural tracts estimated by the advection-diffusion based propagation method

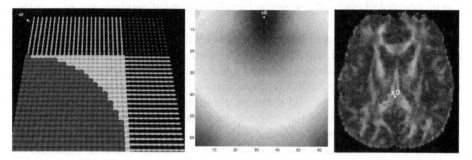

Fig. 2. [left]: Synthetic tensor field (partial), [center]: Associated distance function [right]: Real diffusion tensor MRI (RGB mapping of the major eigenvector)

Table 1. Statistics on $|\text{grad}\phi|$ for synthetic and real diffusion tensor MRI data

DataSet	Scheme	Mean	Std. Dev	Maximum
Synthetic	Upwind	0.9854	0.123657	4.50625
Synthetic	WENO5	0.977078	0.116855	2.0871
DT-MRI	Upwind	0.994332	0.116326	4.80079
DT-MRI	WENO5	0.973351	0.110364	3.72567

estimation with the level set scheme proposed in the previous section exhibits very good results in table 1 with a sensible improvement when using WENO5 schemes. The solution of equation 6 along the axis associated to the cylinder containing x_0 is presented on Figure 2 [center]. The recovery of the underlying pathways reaching x_0 by our intrinsic method turns out to be fast in practice and accurate. Figure 3 [left] shows the computed geodesics linking x_0 to anisotropic voxels located at the extremity of a different cylinder. This is basically what happens in the brain white matter when multiple fibers bundles pass through a single voxel. Our global approach seems particularly adequate to disambiguate

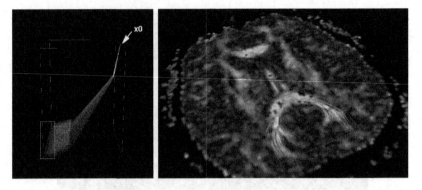

Fig. 3. Inferred geodesics by intrinsic integration - [left]: synthetic [right]: real data

the problem of fibers tracts crossings by minimizing the geodesic distance in the white matter.

Real diffusion data on Figure 2 [right] is used to focus on the posterior part of the corpus callosum. Estimation of the distance function with upwind and WENO5 schemes produces again very good results with evident advantage in term of robustness for WENO implementation. We must notice here that our numerical flux tends to be a bit diffusive, resulting in smooth distance functions. This may be a problem if the original data itself does not have a good contrast since this could yield geodesics with very low curvature. Exponential map based integration produces the result of Figure 3 [right] when starting from the extremities of the major forceps. We have noticed that our method is not influenced by locally spherical or planar tensors since the estimated fibers are not affected by the presence of lower anisotropy regions (in red) that coincide with crossings areas. This global approach thus brings coherence into diffusion tensor data and naturally handles the issues affecting local tractography methods like inconsistent tracking in locally isotropic areas.

6   Conclusion

Diffusion imaging is a truly quantitative method which gives direct insight into the physical properties of tissues through the observation of random molecular motion. However correct interpretation of diffusion data and inference of accurate information is a very challenging project. Our guideline has been to always bear in mind that the true and unique phenomenon that diffusion imaging records is Brownian motion. Taking that stochastic process as our starting point, we have proposed a novel global approach to white matter connectivity mapping. It relies on the fact that probing and measuring a diffusion process on a manifold M provides enough information to infer the geometry of M and compute its geodesics, corresponding to diffusion pathways. Clinical validation is obviously needed but already we can think of extensions of this method: intrinsic geodesics regularization under action of scalar curvature of M, geodesics classification to recover complete tracts. Estimation of geodesics deviation could be used to detect merging or fanning fiber bundles.

References

1. Bihan, D.L., Breton, E., Lallemand, D., Grenier, P., Cabanis, E., Laval-Jeantet, M.: MR imaging of intravoxel incoherent motions: Application to diffusion and perfusion in neurologic disorders. Radiology (1986) 401–407
2. Merboldt, K., Hanicke, W., Frahm, J.: Self-diffusion nmr imaging using stimulated echoes. J. Magn. Reson. **64** (1985) 479–486
3. Selden, N., Gitelman, D., Salamon-Murayama, N., Parrish, T., Mesulam, M.: Trajectories of cholinergic pathways within the cerebral hemispheres of the human brain. Brain **121** (1998) 2249–2257
4. Basser, P., Mattiello, J., LeBihan, D.: Estimation of the effective self-diffusion tensor from the NMR spin echo. Journal of Magnetic Resonance **B** (1994) 247–254
5. Tschumperlé, D., Deriche, R.: Variational frameworks for DT-MRI estimation, regularization and visualization. In: Proceedings of ICCV. (2003)
6. Chefd'hotel, C., Tschumperlé, D., Deriche, R., Faugeras, O.: Constrained flows on matrix-valued functions : application to diffusion tensor regularization. In: Proceedings of ECCV. (2002)
7. Coulon, O., Alexander, D., Arridge, S.: A regularization scheme for diffusion tensor magnetic resonance images. In: Proceedings of IPMI. (2001)
8. Westin, C., Maier, S., Mamata, H., Nabavi, A., Jolesz, F., Kikinis, R.: Processing and visualization for diffusion tensor MRI. In: Proceedings of Medical Image Analysis. Volume 6. (2002) 93–108
9. Wang, Z., Vemuri, B., Chen, Y., Mareci, T.: Simultaneous smoothing and estimation of the tensor field from diffusion tensor MRI. In: Proceedings of CVPR Volume I., (2003) 461–466
10. Guye, M., Parkera, G.J., Symms, M., Boulby, P., Wheeler-Kingshott, C., Salek-Haddadi, A., Barker, G., Duncana, J.: Combined functional MRI and tractography to demonstrate the connectivity of the human primary motor cortex in vivo. NeuroImage **19** (2003) 1349–1360
11. Mori, S., Crain, B., Chacko, V., Zijl, P.V.: Three-dimensional tracking of axonal projections in the brain by magnetic resonance imaging. Annals of Neurology **45** (1999) 265–269
12. Zhukov, L., Barr, A.: Oriented tensor reconstruction: Tracing neural pathways from diffusion tensor MRI. In: Proceedings of Visualization. (2002) 387–394
13. Lazar, M., Weinstein, D., Tsuruda, J., Hasan, K., Arfanakis, K., Meyerand, M., Badie, B., Rowley, H., V.Haughton, Field, A., Alexander, A.: White matter tractography using diffusion tensor deflection. In: Human Brain Mapping. Volume 18. (2003) 306–321
14. Basser, P., Pajevic, S., Pierpaoli, C., Duda, J., Aldroubi, A.: In vivo fiber tractography using DT-MRI data. Magn. Res. Med. **44** (2000) 625–632
15. Vemuri, B., Chen, Y., Rao, M., McGraw, T., Mareci, T., Wang, Z.: Fiber tract mapping from diffusion tensor MRI. In: Proceedings of VLSM. (2001)
16. Campbell, J., Siddiqi, K., Vemuri, B., Pike, G.: A geometric flow for white matter fibre tract reconstruction. In: Proceedings of ISBI. (2002) 505–508
17. Tuch, D.: Mapping cortical connectivity with diffusion MRI. In: Proceedings of ISBI. (2002) 392–394

18. Hagmann, P., Thiran, J., Jonasson, L., Vandergheynst, P., Clarke, S., Maeder, P., Meuli, R.: DTI mapping of human brain connectivity: Statistical fiber tracking and virtual dissection. NeuroImage **19** (2003) 545–554

19. Bjornemo, M., Brun, A., Kikinis, R., Westin, C.: Regularized stochastic white matter tractography using diffusion tensor MRI. In: Proceedings of MICCAI. (2002) 435–442

20. Parker, G., Alexander, D.: Probabilistic monte carlo based mapping of cerebral connections utilising whole-brain crossing fibre information. In: Proceedings of IPMI. (2003) 684–695

21. Tuch, D., Reese, T., Wiegell, M., Makris, N., Belliveau, J., Wedeen, V.: High angular resolution diffusion imaging reveals intravoxel white matter fiber heterogeneity. Magn. Res. Med. **48** (2002) 577–582

22. Frank, L.: Characterization of anisotropy in high angular resolution diffusion-weighted MRI. Magn. Res. Med **47** (2002) 1083–1099

23. Tuch, D., Wiegell, M., Reese, T., Belliveau, J., Weeden, V.: Measuring cortico-cortical connectivity matrices with diffusion spectrum imaging. In: Int. Soc. Magn. Reson. Med. Volume 9. (2001) 502

24. Lin, C., Weeden, V., Chen, J., Yao, C., Tseng, W.I.: Validation of diffusion spectrum magnetic resonance imaging with manganese-enhanced rat optic tracts and ex vivo phantoms. NeuroImage **19** (2003) 482–495

25. Bammer, R., Auer, M., Keeling, S., Augustin, M., Stables, L., Prokesch, R., Stollberger, R., Moseley, M., Fazekas, F.: Diffusion tensor imaging using single-shot sense-EPI. Magn. Res. Med. **48** (2002) 128–136

26. Mangin, J.F., Poupon, C., Cointepas, Y., Rivière, D., Papadopoulos-Orfanos, D., Clark, C.A., Régis, J., Bihan, D.L.: A framework based on spin glass models for the inference of anatomical connectivity from diffusion-weighted MR data. NMR in Biomedicine **15** (2002) 481–492

27. Parker, G., Wheeler-Kingshott, C., Barker, G.: Estimating distributed anatomical connectivity using fast marching methods and diffusion tensor imaging. Trans. Med. Imaging **21** (2002) 505–512

28. O'Donnell, L., Haker, S., Westin, C.: New approaches to estimation of white matter connectivity in diffusion tensor MRI: Elliptic PDEs and geodesics in a tensor-warped space. In: Proceedings of MICCAI. (2002) 459–466.

29. Ikeda, N., Watanabe, S.: Stochastic Differential Equations and Diffusion Processes. North-Holland Mathematical Library (1989)

30. Einstein, A.: Investigations on the Theory of the Brownian Movement. Dover Pubns (1956)

31. Sochen, N., Deriche, R., Lopez-Perez, L.: The beltrami flow over implicit manifolds. In: Proceedings of ICCV. (2003)

32. de Lara, M.: Geometric and symmetry properties of a nondegenerate diffusion process. An. of Probability **23** (1995) 1557–1604

33. Liao, M.: Symmetry groups of markov processes. Anal. of Prob. **20** (1992) 563–578

34. Hsu, E.: Stochastic Analysis on Manifolds. Volume 38 of Graduate Studies in Mathematics. AMS (2001)

35. Mantegazza, C., Mennucci, A.: Hamilton–jacobi equations and distance functions on Riemannian manifolds. App. Math. and Optim. **47** (2002) 1–25

36. Osher, S.: A level set formulation for the solution of the dirichlet problem for a hamilton-Jacobi equations. SIAM Journal on Mathematical Analysis **24** (1993) 1145–1152

37. Sethian, J.: Level Set Methods. Cambridge University Press (1996)

38. Tsai, Y.H., Giga, Y., Osher, S.: A level set approach for computing discontinuous solutions of Hamilton–Jacobi equations. Math. Comput. **72** (2003) 159–181
39. Chen, Y., Giga, Y., Goto, S.: Uniqueness and existence of viscosity solutions of generalized mean curvature flow equations. Journal on Differential Geometry **33** (1991) 749–786
40. LeVeque, R.: Numerical methods for conservation laws. Birkhäuser, Basel (1992)
41. Kimmel, R., Amir, A., Bruckstein, A.: Finding shortest paths on surfaces using level set propagation. Transactions on Pattern Analysis and Machine Intelligence **17** (1995) 635–640
42. Liu, X., Osher, S., Chan, T.: Weighted essentially non oscillatory schemes. J. Comput. Phys. **115** (1994) 200–212

Unifying Approaches and Removing Unrealistic Assumptions in Shape from Shading: Mathematics Can Help

Emmanuel Prados and Olivier Faugeras

Odyssée Lab., INRIA/ENS/ENPC, France
http://www-sop.inria.fr/odyssee/

Abstract. This article proposes a solution of the Lambertian Shape From Shading (SFS) problem by designing a *new mathematical framework* based on the notion of viscosity solutions. The power of our approach is twofolds: 1) it defines a notion of *weak* solutions (in the viscosity sense) which *does not necessarily require boundary data*. Note that, in the previous SFS work of Rouy et al. [23,15], Falcone et al. [8], Prados et al. [22,20], the characterization of a viscosity solution and its computation require the knowledge of its values on the boundary of the image. This was quite unrealistic because in practice such values are not known. 2) it *unifies* the work of Rouy et al. [23,15], Falcone et al. [8], Prados et al. [22,20], based on the notion of viscosity solutions and the work of Dupuis and Oliensis [6] dealing with classical (C^1) solutions. Also, we *generalize* their work to the "perspective SFS" problem recently introduced by Prados and Faugeras [20].

Moreover this article introduces a *"generic" formulation of the SFS problem*. This "generic" formulation summarizes various (classical) formulations of the Lambertian SFS problem. In particular it *unifies the orthographic and the perspective SFS problems*. This "generic" formulation significantly simplifies the formalism of the problem. Thanks to this generic formulation, a *single algorithm* can be used to compute numerical solutions of all these previous SFS formulations.

Finally we propose two algorithms which provide numerical approximations of the new weak solutions of the *"generic SFS" problem*. These provably convergent algorithms are quite *robust* and do not necessarily require boundary data.

1 Introduction

The application of the theory of Partial Differential Equations (PDEs) to the Shape from Shading (SFS) problem has been hampered by several types of difficulties. The first type arises from the kind of modelling that is used: orthographic cameras looking at Lambertian objects with a single point light source at infinity is the set of usual assumptions [29,10]. The second type is mathematical: characterizing the solution(s) of the corresponding PDE has turned out to be a very difficult problem; boundary conditions are assumed to be known, say at

T. Pajdla and J. Matas (Eds.): ECCV 2004, LNCS 3024, pp. 141–154, 2004.

image boundary, in contradiction with real practice [23,22,8]. The third type is algorithmic: assuming that existence has been proved, coming up with provably convergent numerical schemes has turned out to be quite involved [7].

Our approach is therefore based upon the interaction of the following three areas:

1. Mathematics: We use and "extend" the notion of viscosity solutions to solve such basic problems as the existence and uniqueness of a solution or the characterization of all solutions when uniqueness does not hold.
2. Algorithmic: In [2], Barles and Souganidis propose a large class of approximation schemes (called monotonous) of these solutions. Inspired by their work, we build such schemes for the SFS equations from which we obtain algorithms whose properties we can analyze in detail (stability, convergence, accuracy). This results in provably correct code within a set of well-defined assumptions.
3. Modeling: The classical theory of viscosity solutions (used until now for solving the SFS problem [23,15,22,20,8]) is not well-adapted to the natural constraints of the SFS problem. In particular it requires that boundary conditions be given, e.g. at the image boundary, and creates undesirable folds (see section 3). In order to be able to get rid of this constraint, we have adapted the notion of viscosity solutions.

Our contributions are first in the area of Mathematics: we adapt the notion of singular viscosity solutions (recently developed by Camilli and Siconolfi [3,4]) for obtaining a "new" class of viscosity solutions which is really more suitable to the SFS problem than the previous ones. This mathematical framework is very general and allows to improve and unify the work of [23,15,6,22,20,8]. Directly connected to the area of modeling, thanks to the introduction of this framework, we are able to relax the very constraining assumption that boundary conditions are known. Concerning the area of modeling, we extend the work of [20]: considering a pinhole camera, we allow the light source to be either at infinity or approximately at the optical center, as in the case of a flash. We also show that the orthographic and pinhole camera SFS equations are special cases of a general equation, thereby simplifying the formalization of the problem. Our contributions are also algorithmic: we propose two provably convergent approximation schemes for our "generic" SFS equation. Moreover, one of the algorithms we propose seems to be the most efficient iterative algorithms of the SFS literature. The article is written in a non mathematical style. The reader interested in the proofs is referred to [19,21].

2 A Unification of the "Perspective" and "Orthographic SFS"

We deal with Lambertian scenes and suppose that the albedo is constant and equal to 1. The scene is represented by a surface S. Let Ω, the image, be the rectangular domain $]0, X[\times]0, Y[$. S can be explicitly parameterized by using a function defined on the closure $\overline{\Omega}$. The particular type of parametrization is irrelevant here but may vary according to the camera type (orthographic versus pinhole) and the position of light source (finite or infinite distance). We note I the image intensity, a function from $\overline{\Omega}$ into the closed interval $[0, 1]$. The Lambertian hypothesis implies:

$$I(x) = \frac{\mathbf{n}(x) \cdot \mathbf{L}}{|\mathbf{n}(x)|}, \tag{1}$$

where $\mathbf{n}(x)$ is a normal vector to the surface S at the point $S(x)$ and $\mathbf{L}$ is the unit vector representing the light direction at this same point (the light source is assumed to be a point). Despite the notation, $\mathbf{L}$ can depend on $S(x)$, if the point source is at a finite distance from the scene.

2.1 "Orthographic SFS" with a Point Light Source at Infinity

This is the traditional setup for the SFS problem. We denote by $\mathbf{L} = (\alpha, \beta, \gamma)$ the unit vector representing the direction of the light source ($\gamma > 0$), $\mathbf{l} = (\alpha, \beta)$, and u the distance of the points in the scene to the camera. The SFS problem is then, given I and $\mathbf{L}$, to find a function $u : \overline{\Omega} \longrightarrow \mathbb{R}$ satisfying the brightness equation:

$$\forall x \in \Omega, \quad I(x) = (-\nabla u(x) \cdot \mathbf{l} + \gamma)/\sqrt{1 + |\nabla u(x)|^2},$$

In the SFS literature, this equation is rewritten in a variety of ways as $H(x, p) = 0$, where $p = \nabla u$:

1) In [23], Rouy and Tourin introduce $H_{R/T}(x, p) = I(x)\sqrt{1 + |p|^2} + p \cdot \mathbf{l} - \gamma$.
2) In [6], Dupuis and Oliensis consider
    $H_{D/O}(x, p) = I(x)\sqrt{1 + |p|^2 - 2p \cdot \mathbf{l}} + p \cdot \mathbf{l} - 1$.
(use the change of variables: $\Psi(x_1, x_2, z) = (x_1, x_2, x_1\alpha + x_2\beta + z\gamma)$)
3) In the case where $\mathbf{L} = (0, 0, 1)$, Lions et al. [15] deal with:

$$H_{Eiko}(x, p) = |p| - \sqrt{\frac{1}{I(x)^2} - 1}. \qquad \text{(called the Eikonal equation)}$$

The function H is called the *Hamiltonian*.

2.2 "Perspective SFS" with a Point Light Source at Infinity

Few SFS approaches deal with the perspective projection problem. To our knowledge, only eight authors [17,13,9,27,28,20,26,5] consider a pinhole camera model instead of an affine or orthographic model. Among these papers, only the work of Prados and Faugeras [20] proposes a formalism completely based on Partial Differential Equations (PDEs) and provides a rigourous mathematical study. The camera is characterized and represented by the retinal plane R and by the optical center as shown in figure 1. We note f the focal length. We assume that S can be explicitly parameterized by the depth modulation function u defined on $\overline{\Omega}$:

$$S = \{u(x).(x, -f); \quad x \in \overline{\Omega}\},$$

and that the surface is visible (in front of the retinal plane) hence $u \geq 1$. We also note $\mathbf{L} = (\alpha, \beta, \gamma)$ the unit vector representing the direction of the light source ($\gamma > 0$). Combining the expression of $\mathbf{n}(x)$ (easily obtained through differential calculus) and the change of variables $v = ln(u)$, Prados and Faugeras [18,20] obtain from the irradiance equation the following Hamiltonian:

$$H_{P/F}(x,p) = I(x)\sqrt{f^2|p|^2 + (x \cdot p + 1)^2} - (f\,\mathbf{1} + \gamma x) \cdot p - \gamma;$$

By using the change of variables $v(x) = \frac{\gamma}{f}[\gamma\,f - \mathbf{1} \cdot x]u(x)$, we obtain another Hamiltonian $H_{Pers}(x,p)$ which verifies more interesting properties (see [19]).

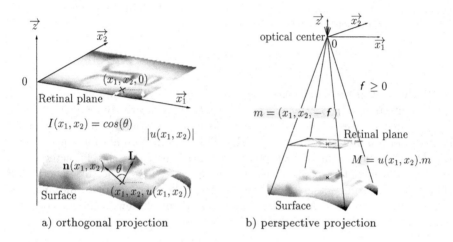

a) orthogonal projection   b) perspective projection

Fig. 1. Images arising from an orthogonal (versus perspective) projection.

2.3   "Perspective SFS" with a Single Point Light Source Located at the Optical Center

We present a new formulation of the "perspective SFS". This approximately models the situation encountered when we use a simple camera equiped with a flash and the scene is relatively far from the camera. In this case, we represent the scene by the surface S defined by $S = \left\{ \dfrac{f\ u(x)}{\sqrt{|x|^2 + f^2}}\,(x,\,f);\quad x \in \overline{\Omega} \right\}.$

Using the same trick as in the previous section ($v = ln(u)$), we readily obtain the Hamiltonian:

$$H_F(x,p) = I(x)\sqrt{f^2|p|^2 + (p \cdot x)^2 + Q(x)^2} - Q(x),$$

where $Q(x) = \sqrt{f^2/(|x|^2 + f^2)}$. See [19] for more details.

2.4   A Generic Hamiltonian

In [19], we prove that all the previous SFS Hamiltonians are special cases of the following "generic" Hamiltonian:

$$H_g(x,p) = \tilde{H}_g(x, A_x p + \overrightarrow{v_x}) + \overrightarrow{w_x} \cdot p + c_x,$$

with $\tilde{H}_g(x,q) = \kappa_x \sqrt{|q|^2 + K_x^2}$,
$\kappa_x, K_x \geq 0$, $A_x = D_x R_x$, $D_x = \begin{pmatrix} \mu_x & 0 \\ 0 & \nu_x \end{pmatrix}$, R_x is the rotation matrix $\frac{1}{|x|} \begin{pmatrix} x_2 & -x_1 \\ x_1 & x_2 \end{pmatrix}$
if $x \neq 0$, $R_x = Id_2$ if $x = 0$, $\mu_x, \nu_x \neq 0$ $(\mu_x, \nu_x \in \mathbb{R})$, $\overrightarrow{v_x}, \overrightarrow{w_x} \in \mathbb{R}^2$ and $c_x \in \mathbb{R}$.
By using the Legendre transform, we rewrite this Hamiltonian as a "generic" Hamilton-Jacobi-Bellman (HJB) Hamiltonian:

$$H_g(x,p) = \sup_{a \in B_2(0,1)} \{-f_g(x,a) \cdot p - l_g(x,a)\}.$$

In [19], we detail the exact expressions of f_g and l_g. The HJB formulations of the Hamiltonians H_{Eiko}, $H_{D/O}$, $H_{R/T}$ and $H_{P/F}$, respectively given in [23,6,22, 20], are special cases of the above generic formulation; thereby ours is a generalization and a unification of these works. This generic formulation considerably simplifies the formalism of the problem. All theorems about the characterization and the approximation of the solution are now proved by using this generic SFS Hamiltonian. In particular, this formulation unifies the orthographic and perspective SFS problems. Also, from a practical point of view, a unique code can be used to numerically solve these two problems.

3   Weaknesses of the Previous Theoretical Approaches

The notion of viscosity solutions was first used to solve SFS problems by Lions, Rouy and Tourin [23,15] in the 90s. Their work was based upon the notion of *continuous* viscosity solution. The viscosity solutions are PDE solutions in a weak sense. In particular, they are not necessarily differentiable and can have edges. This notion allows to define a solution of a PDE which does not have classical solutions. For example, the equation

$$|\nabla u(x)| = 1 \text{ for all } x \text{ in }]0,1[\tag{2}$$

with $u(0) = u(1) = 0$, does not have classical solutions (Rolles theorem) but has a continuous viscosity solution (see figure 2-a)). Let us emphasize that continuous viscosity solutions are continuous (on the closure of the set where it is defined) and that a solution in the classical sense is a viscosity solution. The weakness of this notion is due to the compatibility condition necessary to the existence of the solution (constraint on the variation of the boundary conditions [14]). Also, the same equation (2) with $u(0) = 0$, $u(1) = 1.5$ does not have continuous viscosity solutions. Now let us suppose that we make a large error on the boundary condition, when we compute a numerical solution of the SFS

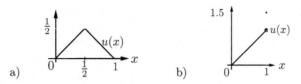

Fig. 2. a) Continuous viscosity solution of (2) with $u(0) = u(1) = 0$; b) discontinuous viscosity solution of (2) with $u(0) = 0$ and $u(1) = 1.5$.

problems. If this error is too large then there do not exist continuous viscosity solutions. In this case one may wonder what the numerical algorithm of [23,15] computes. In [22], Prados et al. answer this question by proposing to use the more general idea of *discontinuous* viscosity solutions. For example, equation (2) with $u(0) = 0$, $u(1) = 1.5$ has a discontinuous viscosity solution (see Figure 2-b)). Let us emphasize that a "discontinuous viscosity solution" *can* have discontinuities and that a continuous viscosity solution is a discontinuous viscosity solution.

The classical theory of viscosity solutions offers simple and general theorems of existence and uniqueness of solutions for exactly the type of PDEs that arise in the context of SFS. In particular the theory allows to characterize exactly all possible continuous viscosity solutions: given a particular Dirichlet condition on the image boundary (verifying the compatibility condition), if the set of *critical points* (points of maximal intensity, i.e. $I(x) = 1$) is empty, then there exists a unique continuous viscosity solution satisfying the boundary conditions; If the set of critical points is not empty there exists an infinity of continuous solutions which are characterized by their values at the critical points. Note that this result is general and applies equally to all the SFS models described in section 2 (see [19]). As a consequence, the SFS problem is ill-posed and to compute an approximation of a solution, Rouy et al. and Prados et al. [23,22,20] must assume that the values of the solutions are given at the image boundary and the critical points. This is quite unsatisfactory, even more so since small errors on these values create undesirable crests, see figure 3-b) or [22] for an example with a real image. Falcone [8] proposes not to specify anymore the values of the solution at the critical points (he still requires to specify the values at the image boundary though). In order to achieve this, he uses the notion of maximal viscosity solutions developed by Camilli and Siconolfi [3]. Despite its advantages, this approach is not really adapted to the SFS problem, see for

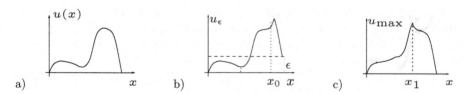

Fig. 3. a) original surface u; b) solution u_ϵ associated to corrupted boundary conditions and to the image obtained from the original surface a) with the Eikonal equation; c) maximal solution $u_{\max}$ (in Falcone's sense [8]) associated to the same image. u_ϵ and $u_{\max}$ present a kink at x_0 and x_1.

example figure 3-c). In this figure, the maximal solution $u_{\max}$ associated to the image obtained from the original surface u shows a highly visible crest where the surface should be smooth. Even with the correct boundary conditions, Falcone's method does not really provide a suitable solution.

To summarize, the work of Rouy et al. [23], Prados et al. [22,20] and Falcone et al. [8] suggests theories and numerical methods based on the concept of viscosity solutions and requiring data on the boundary of the image. At the opposite, Dupuis and Oliensis [6] consider C^1 solutions. They characterize a C^1 solution by specifying only its values at the critical points which are local minima. In particular, they do not specify the values of the solution on the boundary of the image. Also, they provide algorithms for approximating these smooth solutions. Nevertheless, in practice, because of noise, of incorrect modelization, errors on parameters or on the depth values enforced at the critical points, there do not exist C^1 solutions to the SFS equations [16]. Therefore, the theory of Dupuis and Oliensis does not apply.

Considering the drawbacks and the advantages of all these methods, it seems important to define a new class of weak solutions such that the characterization of Dupuis and Oliensis holds, and which provides a (theoretical and numerical) solution when there do not exist smooth solutions.

As we show in [21], the classical notion of viscosity solutions, like the notion of singular viscosity solutions (pioneered by Ishii and Ramaswamy [11] and recently upgraded by Camilli and Siconolfi [3]) does not provide a direct extension of the Dupuis and Oliensis work. For such an extension, we must modify these notions and we must consider a "new" type of boundary conditions (called "state constraints" [24]). It turns out that the correct notion of viscosity solution for the SFS problem is the "singular discontinuous viscosity solution with Dirichlet boundary conditions and state constraints". These solutions can be interpreted as maximal solutions and have the great advantage of not necessarily requiring boundary or critical points conditions. Moreover, this notion provides a mathematical framework unifying the work of Rouy et al. [15,23], Prados et al. [22, 20], Falcone et al. [8] and Dupuis and Oliensis [6].

4   Singular Discontinuous Viscosity Solutions for SFS

In this section we briefly describe the notion of "singular discontinuous viscosity solutions with Dirichlet boundary conditions and state constraints" (SDVS). We refer to [21] for more details. Also we do not recall the classical definition of viscosity solutions: see [1] for a recent overview.

Considering the generic SFS problem, we concentrate on the following HJB equation:

$$\sup_{a \in A}\{f(x,a) \cdot \nabla u(x) - l(x,a)\} = 0, \qquad \forall x \in \Omega \tag{3}$$

To simplify, we assume in this paper[1] that $l \geq 0$ and we denote $\mathcal{S} :=$ $\{x \mid l(x, a) = 0 \text{ for some } a \in A\}$. Also assume that $\mathcal{S}$ verifies $\mathcal{S} \cap \partial\Omega = \emptyset$. To equation (3), we add Dirichlet boundary conditions (DBC) on the boundary of the image and on $\mathcal{S}$:

$$u(x) = \varphi(x), \quad \forall x \in \partial\Omega \cup \mathcal{S}; \tag{4}$$

φ being continuous on $\partial\Omega \cup \mathcal{S}$ into $\mathbb{R} \cup \{+\infty\}$ (but $\varphi \neq +\infty$ everywhere). At the points x s.t. $\varphi(x) = +\infty$, we say that we impose a state constraint [24]. In the SFS context, $\mathcal{S}$ is the set of critical points $\{x \mid I(x) = 1\}$.

Definition: *u is a SDVS of (3)-(4), if u is a discontinuous viscosity solution of (3)-(4) on $\overline{\Omega} - \mathcal{S}$ and if $\forall x \in \mathcal{S}$, $[u^*(x) \leq \varphi(x)]$ and $[u_*(x) \geq \varphi(x)$ or u_* is a singular viscosity supersolution in Camilli's sense at the point $x]$.*

Definitions of u_* and u^* (not detailed here because of space) can be found in [1]. The notion of singular viscosity supersolution in Camilli's sense is completely described in [3,4].

In [21], we prove the *existence* and the *uniquess* of the SDVS of all SFS equations as soon as I is Lipschitz continuous and the Hamiltonian is coercive (e.g. $H_{D/O}$ and $H_{R/T}$ are coercive $\Leftrightarrow I(x) > |l|$). We also prove the *robustness* of this solution to *pixel noise* and to *errors on the light or focal length parameters*. Finally, note that, when we impose state contraints on the boundary of the images and some critical points, this solution can be interpreted as the *maximal* viscosity solution. See [21] for more details.

5   A General Framework for SFS

The main interest of this "new" class of solutions lies in the possibility to impose the heights of the solution at the critical points when we know them (this is impossible with discontinuous viscosity solutions; it is possible with continuous viscosity solutions but compatibility conditions are required) and in the possibility to "send at infinity" the boundary conditions when we do not know then (this possibility is not considered by Falcone et al. [8]). The relevance of this notion is amplified by its consistency with the work of Dupuis and Oliensis [6]. This is illustrated by the following proposition (see [21]):

Proposition 1. *Let u be a C^1 solution of equation (3). Let $\tilde{\mathcal{S}}$ be the subset of $\mathcal{S}$ corresponding to the local minima of u. If u verifies the assumption 2.1 of [6][2] then u is the SDVS of (3)-(4) for $\varphi(x) = u(x) \, \forall x \in \tilde{\mathcal{S}}$ and $\varphi(x) = +\infty$ elsewhere.*

---

[1] In [21], we do not assume that $l \geq 0$. Also, the definition of $\mathcal{S}$ and the developed tools are more sophisticated. Note that, except for $H_{R/T}$ and $H_{P/F}$, all the SFS Hamiltonians verify $l \geq 0$. This justifies our interest for the Hamiltonian $H_{D/O}$ and the original one H_{Pers}.

[2] Not stated here because of space.

Therefore, when there do not exist C^1 solutions, the SDVS consistently *extend* the work of Dupuis and Oliensis. Moreover, the SDVS *unify* the various theories used for solving the SFS problem. In effect, we can verify that [21]:

- In the case where the DBC are finite on $\partial\Omega \cup \mathcal{S}$ and the compatibility condition (see [14]) holds, then the SDVS of (3)-(4) is the continuous viscosity solution used by [23,15,22,20].
- When the DBC are finite on the boundary of the image and state constraints are imposed at the critical points, the SDVS of (3)-(4) corresponds to Camilli's singular viscosity solutions [3,4] used by Falcone [8].
- As seen above, the SDVS corresponds to the C^1 solution of (3), verifying the assumption 2.1 of Dupuis and Oliensis [6].

Consequently, the theoretical results of Falcone et al. [8] Rouy et al. [23,15], Prados et al. [22,20] and Dupuis et al. [6] are *automatically extended to the "perspective SFS"* (use H_F and H_{pers}). Finally, one can conjecture that by using the work of [12,25], the notion of SDVS can be extended to solve SFS problem with discontinuous images. This would be very difficult without the tool of viscosity solutions.

6   Numerical Approximation of the SDVS for Generic SFS

This section explains how to compute a numerical approximation of the SDVS of the generic SFS equation. This requires three steps. First we "regularize" the equation. Second, we approximate the "regularized" SFS equation by approximation schemes. Finally, from the approximation schemes, we design numerical algorithms.

Regularisation of the Generic SFS Equation:
For an intensity image I and $\epsilon > 0$, let us consider the truncated image I_ϵ defined by $I_\epsilon(x) = min(I(x), 1 - \epsilon)$. By using a stability result, we prove that for the generic SFS Hamiltonian, the SDVS associated with the image I_ϵ converges uniformly toward the SDVS associated with the image I, when $\epsilon \to 0$. Also, $\forall \epsilon > 0$, the generic SFS equation associated with I_ϵ is *no more degenerate*. Thus for approximating this equation, we can use the classical tools developed by Barles and Souganidis [2].

Approximation Schemes for the Nondegenerate SFS Equations:
Let us consider the "regularized" generic SFS equation. The theory of Barles and Souganidis [2] suggests to consider *monotonous* schemes. Therefore, we construct the following monotonous scheme (we call it "implicit") $S(\rho, x, u(x), u) = 0$ with

$$S(\rho, x, t, u) = \max_{s_1, s_2 = \pm 1} S_{s_1, s_2}(\rho, x, t, u),$$

where $\rho = (\Delta x_1, \Delta x_2)$ is the mesh size and where we choose:

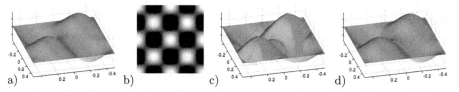

Fig. 4. a) original surface; b) image generated from a) by the Eikonal process [size 400×400]; c) reconstructed surface from b) after 15 iterations of Dupuis and Oliensis' algorithm (based on differential games) enforcing the exact Dirichlet condition on the boundary of the image and at all critical points: $\epsilon_1 = 0.015$, $\epsilon_2 = 5.7e - 05$, $\epsilon_* = 0.35$; d) reconstructed surface by the implicit algorithm with the same boundary data and after the same number (15) of iterations as c): $\epsilon_1 = 0.002$, $\epsilon_2 = 1.0e - 05$, $\epsilon_* = 0.014$.

$$S^{impl}_{s_1,s_2}(\rho,x,t,u) = \sup_{a \in A_{s_1,s_2}} \left\{ -f_g(x,a) \cdot \left(\begin{array}{c} \frac{t-u(x+s_1\Delta x_1 \vec{e_1})}{-s_1\Delta x_1} \\ \frac{t-u(x+s_2\Delta x_2 \vec{e_2})}{-s_2\Delta x_2} \end{array} \right) - l_g(x,a) \right\}.$$

$A_{s_1,s_2} = \{ a \in A \mid f_{g_1}(x,a)s_1 \geq 0 \text{ and } f_{g_2}(x,a)s_2 \geq 0 \}$.

By introducing a fictitious time $\Delta\tau$, we can transform the implicit scheme in a "semi-implicit" scheme (also monotonous):

$$S^{semi}_{s_1,s_2}(\rho,x,t,u) = t - \left(u(x) + \Delta\tau \, S^{impl}_{s_1,s_2}(\rho,x,u(x),u) \right),$$

where $\Delta\tau = (f_g(x,a_0) \cdot (1/\Delta x_1, 1/\Delta x_2))^{-1}$; a_0 being the optimal control.

Let us emphasize that these two schemes have exactly the same solutions.

Using Barles and Souganidis definitions [2], we prove in [19] that these schemes are always monotonous and *stable*. Also, they are *consistent* with the genereric SFS equation as soon as the intensity image is Lipschitz continuous. Finally, when the Hamiltonian is coercive, we prove that the solutions of these schemes *converge toward the unique SDVS* of the "regularized" generic SFS equation, when $\rho \to 0$.

Remark: These two schemes have also a control interpretation. It is easy to verify that the implicit scheme is an extension of the control-based schemes proposed by [23,15,22] and the semi-implicit scheme corresponds to the control-based scheme proposed by [6]. All these schemes have been designed for the "orthographic SFS" problem. Note that for a given Hamiltonian, they all have the same solutions. Therefore we have unified and generalized these various approaches.

Numerical Algorithms for the Generic SFS Problem:
In the previous section, we have proposed two schemes whose solutions u^ρ converge toward the unique SDVS of the "regularized" generic SFS equation. For each scheme, we now describe an algorithm that computes an approximation of u^ρ.

For a fixed mesh size $\rho = (\Delta x_1, \Delta x_2)$, let us denote $x_{ij} := (i\Delta x_1, j\Delta x_2)$ and $\mathcal{X} := \{ x_{ij} \in \Omega; \ i,j \in \mathbb{Z} \}$. The algorithms consist of the following computation of the sequence of values U^n_{ij}, $n \geq 0$ (U^n_{ij} being an approximation of $u^\rho(x_{ij})$).

Algorithm 1.   *1. Initialisation ($n = 0$): $U^0_{ij} = u_0(x_{ij})$.*

2. Choice of a pixel $x_{ij} \in X$ and modification of U^n_{ij}:   We choose U^{n+1} such that $\forall (k, l) \neq (i, j)$, $U^{n+1}_{kl} = U^n_{kl}$ and $S(\rho, x_{ij}, U^{n+1}_{ij}, U^n) = 0$.

3. Choose the next pixel $x_{ij} \in X$ in such a way that all pixels of X are regularly visited and go back to 2.

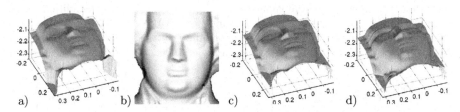

Fig. 5. a) original surface; b) image generated from a) [size $\simeq 200 \times 200$]; c) reconstructed surface from b) with the implicit algorithm (IA) after only 3 iterations, using the exact boundary data at all critical points and with state constraints on the boundary of the image: $\epsilon_1 \simeq 0.58$, $\epsilon_2 \simeq 0.0019$, $\epsilon_. \simeq 0.42$; d) reconstructed surface by the IA (after 3 iterations) with state constraints on the boundary of the image and at all the critical points except at that on the nose: $\epsilon_1 \simeq 0.60$, $\epsilon_2 \simeq 0.0020$, $\epsilon_. \simeq 0.42$.

We prove in [19] that if u_0 is a subsolution or a supersolution, then the computed numerical approximations converge toward u^ρ. In their work, Rouy, Prados et al. [23,15,22,20] use (some particular cases of) the implicit algorithm starting from a subsolution. When we start from a supersolution, we reduce the number of iterations by 3 orders of magnitude! In [20], Prados and Faugeras need around 4000 iterations for computing the surface of the classical Mozart's face [29]. Starting from a supersolution (in practice, a large constant function u_0 does the trick!), *only three iterations are sufficient* for obtaining a good result; see figure 5. As an example, we show in figure 4 a comparison of our results with those of what we consider to be the most efficient algorithm of the SFS literature [6]. Figures 4-c) and 4-d) show the results returned by our implementation of this algorithm and our algorithm, respectively, after 15 iterations. The results are visually different. This visual difference is confirmed by the computation of the errors with respect to the original surface (ϵ_1, ϵ_2 and $\epsilon_.$ are the errors of the computed surface measured according to the L_1, L_2 and $L_.$ norms, respectively). Nevertheless let us note that the cost of one update is slightly larger for our implicit algorithm than for the (semi-implicit) algorithm of Dupuis and Oliensis. This may also be because we have not optimized our code for this special case. Let us add that in this test, we have constrained the solution by the exact Dirichlet condition on the boundary of the image and at all the critical points. Let us recall that the SDVS method does not necessarily require boundary data. Figure 5 shows some reconstructions of the Mozart face when using the exact boundary data at all the critical points and state constraints on the boundary of the image (Fig.5-c), and with no boundary data, except for the tip of the nose (Fig.5-d). Moreover, let us emphasize that our implicit algorithm (as our semi-implicit one) allows to compute some numerical approximations of the *SDVS* of the *degenerate* (when the intensity reaches 1) and *generic* SFS problem. Thus, we only need to implement a *single* algorithm for all SFS modelizations. Finally, let us remark that, as the theory predicted, our algorithm shows an exceptional robustness to noise and errors on the parameters; This robustness is even bigger when we send the boundary to infinity (apply the state constraints). Figure 6 displays a reconstruction of Mozart's face from an image perturbed by additive uniformly distributed white noise (SNR $\simeq$ 5) by using the implicit algorithm with the wrong parameters $l_\epsilon = (0.2, -0.1)$ and $f_\epsilon = 10.5$ (focal length) and without any boundary data. The original image Fig.6-a) has been synthetized with $l = (0.1, -0.3)$ and $f = 3.5$. The angle between the initial light vector $\mathbf{L}$ and the corrupted light vector $\mathbf{L}_\epsilon$ is around $13°$. More details, experimental comparisons and stability tests can be found in [19,21]. These reports also contain the proofs of all our statements.

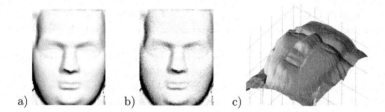

Fig. 6. a) Image generated from Mozart's face represented in Fig.5-a) with $l = (0.1, -0.3)$ and $f = 3.5$ [size $\simeq 200 \times 200$]; b) noisy image (SNR $\simeq$ 5); c) reconstructed surface from b) after 4 iterations of the implicit algorithm, using the incorrect parameters $l_\epsilon = (0.2, -0.1)$ and $f_\epsilon = 10.5$, and with state constraints on the boundary of the image and at all the critical points except at the critical point on the nose.

7   Conclusion

We have *unified various formulations* of the Lambertian SFS problem; in particular the orthographic and perspective problems. We have developed *a new mathematical framework* which *unifies* some SFS theories and *generalizes* them to all SFS Hamiltonians. Let us emphasize that we do not consider Mathematics as a goal in itself. Mathematics is simply a powerful tool allowing us to

- suggest some numerical methods and algorithms;
- certify algorithms, to guarantee their robustness and to describe their limitations;
- better understand what we compute. In particular, when the problem has several solutions, it allows to characterize all the solutions, a necessary preliminary step for deciding which solution we want to compute.

In effect, our theory ensures the stability and the convergence of our SFS method. Also it suggests a *robust* SFS algorithm which *seems to be the most efficient* iterative algorithm of the SFS literature. Moreover, our new class of weak solutions is really more adapted to the SFS specifications; in particular, it *does not necessarily require boundary data*. We are extending our approach to non Lambertian SFS and to SFS with discontinous images.

References

1. M. Bardi and I. Capuzzo-Dolcetta. *Optimal control and viscosity solutions of Hamilton-Jacobi-Bellman equations.* Birkhauser, 1997.
2. G. Barles and P. Souganidis. Convergence of approximation schemes for fully nonlinear second order equations. *Asymptotic Analysis*, 4:271–283, 1991.
3. F. Camilli and A. Siconolfi. Maximal subsolutions for a class of degenerate hamilton-jacobi problems. *Indiana Univ. Math. J.*, 48(3):1111–1132, 1999.
4. F. Camilli and A. Siconolfi. Nonconvex degenerate Hamilton-Jacobi equations. *Mathematische Zeitschrift*, 242:1–21, 2002.
5. F. Courteille, A. Crouzil, J.-D. Durou, and P. Gurdjos. Shape from Shading en conditions réalistes d'acquisition photographique. In *Proceedings of RFIA '04*, 2004.
6. P. Dupuis and J. Oliensis. An optimal control formulation and related numerical methods for a problem in shape reconstruction. *The Annals of Applied Probability*, 4(2):287–346, 1994.
7. J.-D. Durou and H. Maitre. On convergence in the methods of Strat and Smith for shape from shading. *IJCV*, 17(3):273–289, 1996.
8. M. Falcone, M. Sagona, and A. Seghini. A scheme for the shape-from-shading model with "black shadows". In *Proceedings of ENUMATH 2001*, 2001.
9. J. Hasegawa and C. Tozzi. Shape from shading with perspective projection and camera calibration. *Computers and Graphics*, 20(3):351–364, May 1996.
10. B. Horn and M. Brooks, editors. *Shape from Shading*. The MIT Press, 1989.
11. H. Ishii and M. Ramaswamy. Uniqueness results for a class of Hamilton-Jacobi equations with singular coefficients. *Comm. Par. Diff. Eq.*, 20:2187–2213, 1995.
12. J. Kain and D. Ostrov. Numerical shape-from-shading for discontinuous photographic images. *IJCV*, 44(3):163–173, 2001.
13. K. Lee and C. Kuo. Shape from shading with perspective projection. *CVGIP: Image Understanding*, 59(2):202–212, 1994.
14. P.-L. Lions. *Generalized Solutions of Hamilton–Jacobi Equations*. Number 69 in Research Notes in Mathematics. Pitman Advanced Publishing Program, 1982.
15. P.-L. Lions, E. Rouy, and A. Tourin. Shape-from-shading, viscosity solutions and edges. *Numer. Math.*, 64:323–353, 1993.
16. J. Oliensis. Uniqueness in shape from shading. *IJCV*, 2(6):75–104, 1991.
17. M. Penna. Local and semi-local shape from shading for a simple perspective image of a smooth object. *CVGIP*, 46:346–366, 1989.
18. E. Prados and O. Faugeras. Une approche du "Shape from Shading" par solutions de viscosité. Master's thesis, Université de Nice Sophia-Antipolis, France, 2001.
19. E. Prados and O. Faugeras. A mathematical and algorithmic study of the lambertian SFS problem for orthographic and pinhole cameras. Technical Report RR-5005, INRIA, Nov. 2003.
20. E. Prados and O. Faugeras. "Perspective Shape from Shading" and viscosity solutions. In *Proceedings of ICCV'03*, volume 2, pages 826–831, 2003.
21. E. Prados and O. Faugeras. A viscosity method for Shape from Shading without boudary data and some of its applications. Technical report, INRIA, To appear.
22. E. Prados, O. Faugeras, and E. Rouy. Shape from Shading and viscosity solutions. In *Proceedings of ECCV'02*, volume 2351, pages 790–804, May 2002.

23. E. Rouy and A. Tourin. A Viscosity Solutions Approach to Shape-from-Shading. *SIAM Journal of Numerical Analysis*, 29(3):867–884, June 1992.

24. H. M. Soner. Optimal control with state space constraints. *SIAM J. Contr. Optim*, 24:Part I: 552–562, Part II: 1110–1122, 1986.

25. P. Soravia. Optimal control with discontinuous running cost: eikonal equation and shape from shading. In *39th IEEE CDC*, pages 79–84, 2000.

26. A. Tankus, N. Sochen, and Y. Yeshurun. A new perspective [on] Shape-from-Shading. In *Proceedings of ICCV'03*, volume 2, pages 862–869, 2003.

27. I. Weiss. A perspective 3D formalism for shape from shading. In *Proceedings of DARPA Image Understanding Workshop*, volume 2, pages 1393–1402, May 1997.

28. S. Yuen, Y. Tsui, Y. Leung, and R. Chen. Fast marching method for sfs under perspective projection. In *Proceeding of VIIP'02*, pages 584–589, 2002.

29. R. Zhang, P.-S. Tsai, J.-E. Cryer, and M. Shah. Shape from Shading: A survey. *IEEE Trans. PAMI*, 21(8):690–706, Aug. 1999.

Morphological Operations on Matrix-Valued Images

Bernhard Burgeth, Martin Welk, Christian Feddern, and Joachim Weickert

Mathematical Image Analysis Group
Faculty of Mathematics and Computer Science, Bldg. 27
Saarland University, 66041 Saarbrücken, Germany
{burgeth,welk,feddern,weickert}@mia.uni-saarland.de
http://www.mia.uni-saarland.de

Abstract. The output of modern imaging techniques such as diffusion tensor MRI or the physical measurement of anisotropic behaviour in materials such as the stress-tensor consists of tensor-valued data. Hence adequate image processing methods for shape analysis, skeletonisation, denoising and segmentation are in demand. The goal of this paper is to extend the morphological operations of dilation, erosion, opening and closing to the matrix-valued setting. We show that naive approaches such as componentwise application of scalar morphological operations are unsatisfactory, since they violate elementary requirements such as invariance under rotation. This lead us to study an analytic and a geometric alternative which are rotation invariant. Both methods introduce novel non-component-wise definitions of a supremum and an infimum of a finite set of matrices. The resulting morphological operations incorporate information from all matrix channels simultaneously and preserve positive definiteness of the matrix field. Their properties and their performance are illustrated by experiments on diffusion tensor MRI data.

Keywords: mathematical morphology, dilation, erosion, matrix-valued imaging, DT-MRI

1 Introduction

Modern data and image processing encompasses more and more the analysis and processing of matrix-valued data. For instance, diffusion tensor magnetic resonance imaging (DT-MRI), a novel medical image acquisition technique, measures the diffusion properties of water molecules in tissue. It assigns a positive definite matrix to each voxel, and the resulting matrix field is a valuable source of information for the diagnosis of multiple sclerosis and strokes [13]. Matrix fields also make their natural appearance in civil engineering and solid mechanics. In these areas inertia, diffusion and permittivity tensors and stress-strain relationships are an important tool in describing anisotropic behaviour. In the form of the so-called structure tensor (also called Förstner interest operator, second moment matrix or scatter matrix) [7] the tensor concept turned out to be of great value in image analysis, segmentation and grouping [9].

T. Pajdla and J. Matas (Eds.): ECCV 2004, LNCS 3024, pp. 155–167, 2004.

So there is definitely a need to develop tools for the analysis of such data since anybody who attempts to do so, is confronted with the same basic tasks as in the scalar-valued case: How to remove noise, how to detect edges and shapes, for example.

Image processing of tensor fields is a very recent research area, and a number of methods consists of applying scalar- and vector-valued filters to the components, eigenvalues or eigenvectors of the matrix field. Genuine matrix-valued concepts with channel interaction are available for nonlinear regularisation methods and related diffusion filters [17,18], for level set methods [6], median filtering [19] and homomorphic filters [4]. To our knowledge, however, extensions of classical morphology to the matrix setting have not been considered so far.

Our paper aims at closing this gap by offering extensions of the fundamental morphological operations dilation and erosion to matrix-valued images. Mathematical morphology has been proven to be useful for the processing and analysis of binary and greyscale images: Morphological operators and filters perform noise suppression, edge detection, shape analysis, and skeletonisation in medical and geological imaging, for instance [15]. Even the extension of concepts of scalar-valued morphology to vector-valued data such as colour images, is by no means straightforward. The application of standard scalar-valued techniques to each channel of the image independently, that means component-wise performance of morphological operations, might lead to information corruption in the image, because, in general, these components are strongly correlated [1,8]. Numerous attempts have been made to develop satisfying concepts of operators for colour morphology. The difficulty lies in the fact that the morphological operators rely on the notion of infimum and supremum which in turn requires an appropriate ordering of the colours, i.e. vectors in the selected vector space. However, there is no generally accepted definition of such an ordering [2,16,12]. Different types of orderings such as marginal or reduced ordering [2] are reported to result in an unacceptable alteration of colour balance and object boundaries in the image [5], or in the existence of more than one supremum (infimum) creating ambiguities in the output image [12]. These are clear disadvantages for many applications. In connection with noise suppression morphological filters based on vector ranking concepts [2] have been developed [11,5]. In [3] known connections between median filters, inf-sup operations and geometrical partial differential equations [10] have been extended from the scalar to the vectorial case.

In any case, the lack of a generally suitable ordering on vector spaces is a very severe hindrance in the development of morphological operators for vector-valued images. Surprisingly the situation in the matrix-valued setting is more encouraging since we have additional analytic-algebraic or geometric properties of the image values at our disposal: (a) Unlike in the vectorial setting one can multiply matrices, define polynomials and even can take roots of matrices. (b) Real symmetric, positive definite matrices can be graphically represented by ellipses (2×2-matrices) or ellipsoids (3×3-matrices) in a unique way. However, there is also the burden of additional conditions that have to be fulfilled by the morphological operations to be defined: They have to be rotationally invariant and they must preserve the positive definiteness of the matrix field as well, since applications such as DT-MRI create such data sets. In this paper we will exploit the analytic-algebraic property (a) and the geometric property (b) by introducing novel notions for the supremum/infimum of a finite set of matrices. These notions are rotationally invariant and preserve positive definiteness.

Interestingly, already the requirement of rotational invariance rules out the straightforward component-wise approach: Consider for example

$$A_1 := \begin{pmatrix} 3 & 2 \\ 2 & 3 \end{pmatrix}, \quad A_2 := \begin{pmatrix} 2 & -1 \\ -1 & 2 \end{pmatrix}, \quad S := \begin{pmatrix} 3 & 2 \\ 2 & 3 \end{pmatrix}.$$

Here, S is the componentwise supremum of A_1, A_2. Rotating A_1 and A_2 by 90 degrees and taking again the componentwise supremum yields

$$A_1' = \begin{pmatrix} 3 & -2 \\ -2 & 3 \end{pmatrix}, \quad A_2' = \begin{pmatrix} 2 & 1 \\ 1 & 2 \end{pmatrix}, \quad S' = \begin{pmatrix} 3 & 1 \\ 1 & 3 \end{pmatrix}$$

where S' is clearly not obtained by rotating S. This counterexample shows that it is not obvious how to design reasonable extensions of morphological operations to the matrix-valued setting.

The structure of our paper is as follows: In the next section we give a very brief review of the basic greyscale morphological operations. Then we establish novel definitions of the crucial sup- and inf-operations in the vector valued case via the *analytic-algebraic* approach and investigate some of their properties in Section 3. Alternatively, in Section 4 we develop new definitions for the sup- and inf-operations starting from a *geometric* point of view. Section 5 is devoted to experiments where the two methodologies are applied to real DT-MRI images. Concluding remarks are presented in Section 6.

2   Mathematical Morphology in the Scalar Case

In greyscale morphology an image is represented by a scalar function $f(x, y)$ with $(x, y) \in \mathbb{R}^2$. The so-called *structuring element* is a set B in $\mathbb{R}^2$ that determines the neighbourhood relation of pixels with respect to a shape analysis task. Greyscale *dilation* $\oplus$ replaces the greyvalue of the image $f(x, y)$ by its supremum within a mask defined by B:

$$(f \oplus B)(x, y) := \sup \{f(x-x', y-y') \mid (x', y') \in B\},$$

while *erosion* $\ominus$ is determined by

$$(f \ominus B)(x, y) := \inf \{f(x+x', y+y') \mid (x', y') \in B\}.$$

The *opening* operation, denoted by $\circ$, as well as the closing operation, indicated by the symbol $\bullet$, are defined via concatenation of erosion and dilation:

$$f \circ B := (f \ominus B) \oplus B \quad \text{and} \quad f \bullet B := (f \oplus B) \ominus B.$$

These operations form the basis of many other processes in mathematical morphology [14,15].

3   Model 1: An Analytic Definition of Dilation and Erosion for Matrix-Valued Images

The decisive step in defining morphological dilation and erosion operations for matrix-valued data is to find a suitable notion of supremum and infimum of a finite set of positive definite matrices. For positive real numbers $a_1, \dots, a_k$, $k \in \mathbb{N}$, there is a well-known connection between their modified p-mean and their supremum:

$$\lim_{p \to +\infty} \left(\sum_{i=1}^{k} a_i^p \right)^{\frac{1}{p}} = \sup\{a_1, \dots, a_k\}. \tag{1}$$

A completely analogous relation holds also for the infimum with the difference that p now tends to $-\infty$:

$$\lim_{p \to -\infty} \left(\sum_{i=1}^{k} a_i^p \right)^{\frac{1}{p}} = \inf\{a_1, \dots, a_k\}. \tag{2}$$

That means, the p-means can serve as a substitute for the supremum (infimum) if p is large. The idea is now to replace the positive numbers in the above relation by their matrix generalisations, the positive definite matrices $A_1, \dots, A_k$. However, to this end we have to define the p-th root of a positive definite $(n \times n)$-matrix A. We know from linear algebra that there exists an orthogonal $(n \times n)$-matrix V (which means $V^\top V = VV^\top = I$, with unit matrix I) such that

$$A = V \cdot \mathrm{diag}(\alpha_1, \dots, \alpha_n) \cdot V^\top, \tag{3}$$

where the expression in the center on the right denotes the diagonal matrix with the positive eigenvalues $\alpha_1, \dots, \alpha_n$ of A as entries on the diagonal. Now taking the p-th root of a matrix is achieved by taking the p-th root of the eigenvalues in decomposition (3):

$$A^{\frac{1}{p}} := V \mathrm{diag}(\alpha_1^{\frac{1}{p}}, \dots, \alpha_n^{\frac{1}{p}}) V^\top.$$

Note that the p-th power A^p can be calculated in this manner as well. Hence we can give meaning to the expression $\left(\sum_{i=1}^{k} A_i^p \right)^{\frac{1}{p}}$ and can define new matrices $\sup\{A_1, \dots, A_k\}$ and $\inf\{A_1, \dots, A_k\}$ via the limits of their modified p-mean for $p \to \pm\infty$:

Definition 1. *The* supremum *and* infimum *of a set of positive definite matrices* $A_1, \dots, A_k$ *are defined as*

$$\sup\{A_1, \dots, A_k\} := \lim_{p \to +\infty} \left(\sum_{i=1}^{k} A_i^p \right)^{\frac{1}{p}}, \tag{4}$$

$$\inf\{A_1, \dots, A_k\} := \lim_{p \to -\infty} \left(\sum_{i=1}^{k} A_i^p \right)^{\frac{1}{p}}. \tag{5}$$

With this definition, taking the supremum is a rotationally invariant operation, i.e. $\sup\{UA_1U^\top,\ldots,UA_kU^\top\} = U \cdot \sup\{A_1,\ldots,A_k\} \cdot U^\top$ for any orthogonal $(n \times n)$-matrix U. This may be seen as follows. Since $\sum_{i=1}^{k} A_i^p$ is positive definite, there exist an orthogonal matrix V and a diagonal matrix D with $\sum_{i=1}^{k} A_i^p = VDV^\top$. As a consequence we obtain

$$\left(\sum_{i=1}^{k}(UA_iU^\top)^p\right)^{\frac{1}{p}} = \left(\sum_{i=1}^{k}UA_i^pU^\top\right)^{\frac{1}{p}} = \left(U\left(\sum_{i=1}^{k}A_i^p\right)U^\top\right)^{\frac{1}{p}}$$

$$= \left(UVDV^\top U^\top\right)^{\frac{1}{p}} = UVD^{\frac{1}{p}}V^\top U^\top = U\left(\sum_{i=1}^{k}A_i^p\right)^{\frac{1}{p}}U^\top,$$

where we have used the facts that $U^\top U = I$ and UV is also orthogonal. Therefore the p-th mean is rotationally invariant for all values of p, and hence also in the limits $p \to \pm\infty$.

Furthermore the p-th mean (and in the limit also supremum and infimum) inherits the positive definiteness of its arguments: Positive definiteness is a property stable under addition, and is also characterised by the positivity of the eigenvalues. By construction the p-th power A^p and the p-th root $A^{\frac{1}{p}}$ have positive eigenvalues whenever A has. Hence taking the p-th mean for any $p \in \mathbb{N}$ preserves positive definiteness.

For practical computations we will put p to a sufficiently large number, say 10 or 20, such that the resulting matrices can be considered as reasonable approximations to the supremum resp. infimum of $A_1,\ldots,A_k$.

Alternatively, the limiting matrix $M := \sup\{A_1,\ldots,A_k\}$ can also be obtained directly from the eigenvalues and eigenvectors of the given set of matrices $A_1,\ldots,A_k$. The largest eigenvalue and corresponding eigenvector are directly adopted for M. In the 2×2 case, the eigenvector system of M is already determined by this condition. The remaining eigenvalue of M is exactly the largest eigenvalue from the given set of matrices that corresponds to an eigenvector different from that of the largest eigenvalue – in general, the second largest eigenvalue from the given set. A similar statement holds in higher dimensions. Moreover, replacing largest by smallest eigenvalues, a characterisation of infima is obtained. We sketch the proof for suprema of 2×2 matrices. Note first that the sum $\sum A_i^p$ does not change if every matrix A_i is replaced by the two rank-one matrices $\lambda_1 v_1 v_1^\top$ and $\lambda_2 v_2 v_2^\top$ corresponding to the eigenvalue-eigenvector pairs (λ_1, v_1) and (λ_2, v_2) of A_i. Let now Λ be the largest eigenvalue from the given set of matrices, and λ the second-largest one in the sense described above. Without loss of generality, assume that the eigenvector of Λ is $(1,0)^\top$; the normalised eigenvector for λ is some $(c,s)^\top$, $c^2 + s^2 = 1$. Since the contributions of all smaller eigenvalues and corresponding eigenvectors vanish in the limit $p \to +\infty$, all we have to prove is that the p-mean

$$M_p := \left(\Lambda^p \begin{pmatrix} 1 \\ 0 \end{pmatrix}(1,0) + \lambda^p \begin{pmatrix} c \\ s \end{pmatrix}(c,s)\right)^{\frac{1}{p}} = \begin{pmatrix} \Lambda^p + \lambda^p s^2 & \lambda^p cs \\ \lambda^p cs & \lambda^p c^2 \end{pmatrix}^{\frac{1}{p}}$$

tends to $\mathrm{diag}(\Lambda, \lambda)$ for $p \to +\infty$. We introduce the abbreviations $D_p := \Lambda^{2p} - 2\Lambda^p \lambda^p (c^2 - s^2) + \lambda^{2p}$ and $E_p := \Lambda^p - \lambda^p (c^2 - s^2)$. Then we can express the eigenvalues of M_p by $\left(\frac{1}{2}\left(\Lambda^p + \lambda^p \pm \sqrt{D_p}\right)\right)^{1/p}$ which tend to Λ and λ for $p \to +\infty$. An eigenvector for the larger eigenvalue is given by $\left(\sqrt{\sqrt{D_p} + E_p}, \sqrt{\sqrt{D_p} - E_p}\right)^\top$, which encloses with $(1,0)^\top$ the angle φ_p that satisfies $\tan^2 \varphi_p = \frac{\sqrt{D_p} + E_p}{\sqrt{D_p} - E_p}$. Since the latter expression tends to 0 for $p \to +\infty$ if $\lambda < \Lambda$, we have that the limiting matrix is diagonal as claimed. In case $\lambda = \Lambda$ we have already that $\lim\limits_{p \to +\infty} M_p$ is diagonal because of the eigenvalues. This completes the proof.

With the supremum and infimum operations at our disposal we can apply the definitions of the basic morphological operations dilation, erosion, opening and closing to matrix-valued images essentially verbatim.

4   Model 2: A Geometric Definition of Dilation and Erosion for Matrix-Valued Images

We present now an alternative framework of dilation and erosion for positive definite symmetric matrices. To this end we remark that a positive definite symmetric $n \times n$ matrix A corresponds to a quadratic form $Q(x) = x^\top A^{-2} x$, $x \in \mathrm{I\!R}^n$. The ellipsoid $x^\top A^{-2} x = 1$ centered around 0 is an isohypersurface of Q. This ellipsoid has a natural interpretation in the context of diffusion tensors: Assuming that a particle is initially located in the origin and is subject to the diffusivity A, then the ellipsoid encloses the smallest volume within which this particle will be found with some required probability after a short time interval. The directions and lengths of the principal axes of the ellipsoid are given by the eigenvectors and corresponding eigenvalues of A, respectively. By including degenerate ellipsoids this description is easily extended to all positive definite symmetric matrices. Then each positive definite matrix A is represented by the image $A\mathcal{B}$ of the unit ball $\mathcal{B} \subseteq \mathrm{I\!R}^n$ under multiplication with A.

Geometric inclusion constitutes a natural semi-order for ellipsoids which leads directly to a semi-order for positive definite matrices.

Definition 2. *Let A, B be positive definite matrices. We define that $A \subseteq B$ if and only if $A\mathcal{B} \subseteq B\mathcal{B}$ where $\mathcal{B}$ is the unit ball in $\mathrm{I\!R}^n$.*

In the language of diffusion tensors $A \subseteq B$ means that for particles evolving under diffusivities A and B, the ellipsoid in which the first one is most probably found is completely contained in the corresponding ellipsoid for the second.

In the light of this semi-order, it makes sense to define the supremum of a set of positive definite matrices as a minimal element (in some sense) among all matrices that are greater or equal to all given matrices. Since, however, the $\subseteq$ semi-order itself is not sufficient to determine such a minimal element, we need an additional criterion. Therefore we introduce a second relation $\preccurlyeq$ which is compatible to the first one in the sense that $A \subseteq B$ always implies $A \preccurlyeq B$.

Definition 3. *Let A, B be as above. We define that $A \preccurlyeq B$ if the ordered sequence $\lambda_1(A) \geq \ldots \geq \lambda_n(A) \geq 0$ of the eigenvalues of A is lexicographically smaller or equal to the corresponding sequence $\lambda_1(B) \geq \ldots \geq \lambda_n(B) \geq 0$ of B, i.e. if there exists an index j, $1 \leq j \leq n+1$ such that $\lambda_i(A) = \lambda_i(B)$ for all $i < j$, and $\lambda_j(A) < \lambda_j(B)$ if $j \leq n$.*

Note that $\preccurlyeq$ is not a semi-order in strict sense because it does not allow to distinguish between a matrix and rotated versions of it. We can now define the supremum of a set of positive definite matrices.

Definition 4. *Let $A_1, \ldots, A_k$ be positive definite symmetric matrices. We define*

$$\sup\{A_1, \ldots, A_k\} := S$$

where S is chosen such that $A_i \subseteq S$ for $i = 1, \ldots, k$, and $S \preccurlyeq Y$ for each Y satisfying $A_i \subseteq Y$ for $i = 1, \ldots, k$.

By reverting all occurrences of $\subseteq$ and $\preccurlyeq$ we obtain an analog definition that introduces the infimum as a $\preccurlyeq$-maximal element in the set of all matrices which are inferior to all given matrices w.r.t. $\subseteq$. The positive definiteness of the so defined supremum and infimum is obvious from the definition, as is the rotational invariance. A closer look shows that if all A_i are positive definite, one has also that the supremum of the inverses A_i^{-1} is the inverse of the infimum of the A_i and vice versa. This is in analogy to the definitions based on the p-mean.

Since it is not obvious how to compute the supremum of a given set $\{A_1, \ldots, A_k\}$ of tensors, we shall now briefly derive the necessary formulae in the case of 2×2 matrices. Assume that Λ is the largest eigenvalue of all given matrices, and that $(1, 0)^\top$ is the corresponding eigenvector. Then this eigenvalue–eigenvector pair is also one for the desired supremum matrix S. We have therefore $S = \operatorname{diag}(\Lambda, \lambda)$ where $\lambda \leq \Lambda$ is still to be determined. The decisive constraint for λ is that for all given matrices A_i, the images of the unit disk under $S^{-1}A_i$ must be contained in the unit disk. For a single matrix $A_i = \left(\begin{smallmatrix} a & c \\ c & b \end{smallmatrix}\right)$ this condition comes down to

$$\sqrt{(a\Lambda^{-1} + b\lambda^{-1})^2 + (c\Lambda^{-1} - c\lambda^{-1})^2} + \sqrt{(a\Lambda^{-1} - b\lambda^{-1})^2 + (c\Lambda^{-1} + c\lambda^{-1})^2} \leq 2$$

(note that it is insufficient to consider only the largest eigenvalue of $S^{-1}A$ since this matrix is in general asymmetric!). From this inequality we obtain by squaring twice, re-arranging terms and finally taking the root again that

$$\lambda \geq \sqrt{\frac{(b^2 + c^2)\Lambda^2 - (ab - c^2)^2}{\Lambda^2 - a^2 - c^2}}. \tag{6}$$

Iterating over all A_i one finds the smallest λ which satisfies all the conditions simultaneously. Dismissing the condition that the eigenvector corresponding to Λ is $(1, 0)^\top$, the eigenvector system of S is still determined by this eigenvector. One only has to rotate all matrices A_i using this eigenvector system before computing the bounds for λ. This completes the algorithm in the 2×2 case.

Extension of the algorithm to 3×3 and larger matrices works by considering suitable sets of 2-dimensional sections to which the above formulae can be applied. That it is sufficient to consider sections is a consequence of the following observation: Given an ellipsoid centered at the origin and a point outside of it, then the smallest ellipsoid centered at 0 that encloses both is tangent to the first ellipsoid along an ellipse (or, in higher dimensions, an ellipsoid of next smaller dimension). Repeating the above reasoning for the case of erosions, it becomes clear that the smallest eigenvalue Λ of S and corresponding eigenvector are directly obtained as the smallest eigenvalue and corresponding eigenvector of one of the A_i. By analog considerations as above one derives upper bounds for the remaining eigenvalue λ (which is now the larger one). Surprisingly, the bounds are the same as in (6), only the relation sign is reverted to $\leq$.

Revisiting the p-mean approach from the viewpoint of the current section, one sees that the p-mean supremum M of a set $\{A_1, \ldots, A_k\}$ satisfies $A_i \subseteq M$ for all $i = 1, \ldots, k$, and has the same largest eigenvalue and corresponding eigenvector as the supremum S defined here. However, in generic cases $S \subseteq M$ and $S \neq M$ hold, and the eigenvalues of M except the largest one exceed the corresponding ones of S. Thus, M is in general not a minimal element in the set of all Y with $A_i \subseteq Y$ for all i. Analog considerations apply to the p-mean infimum.

5   Experimental Results

In order to illustrate the differences between model 1 and 2, we have computed their behaviour on two ellipses. This is depicted in Figure 1. We observe that model 1 tends to reduce the eccentricity of the ellipses, whereas the more complicated model 2 is constructed in such a way that it corresponds exactly with our geometric intuition.

As a real-world test image we use a DT-MRI data set of a human brain. We have extracted a 2-D section from the 3-D data. The 2-D image consists of four quadrants which show the four tensor channels of a 2×2 matrix. Each channel has a resolution of 128×128 pixels. The top right channel and bottom left channel are identical since the matrix is symmetric. Model 1 is always shown on the left side,

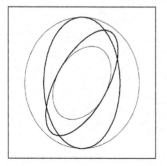 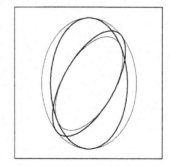

Fig. 1. *Left:* Ellipses representing two positive definite matrices (thick lines), their supremum and infimum (thin lines) according to model 1. *Right:* Same with model 2.

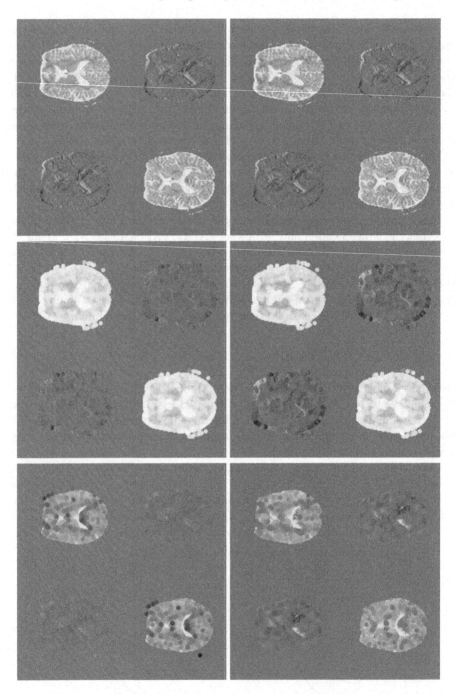

Fig. 2. Tensor-valued dilation and erosion. *Left column, from top to bottom:* Original tensor image of size 128×128 per channel, dilation model 1 with disk-shaped stencil of radius $\sqrt{5}$, erosion model 1 with disk-shaped stencil of radius $\sqrt{5}$. *Right column, from top to bottom:* Same with model 2.

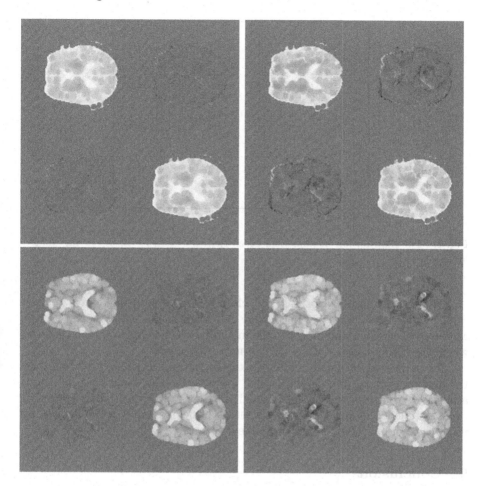

Fig. 3. Tensor-valued opening and closing. *Left column, from top to bottom:* Closing model 1 with disk-shaped stencil of radius $\sqrt{5}$, opening model 1 with disk-shaped stencil of radius $\sqrt{5}$ of the original tensor image depicted in Fig. 2. *Right column, from top to bottom:* Same with model 2.

model 2 always on the right side. All images are generated using a disk-shaped stencil of radius $\sqrt{5}$. As mentioned in section 2 the simplified algorithm has been used for model 1. Figure 2 shows the results of the erosion and dilation filter on tensor-valued data for both models. Corresponding filters give very similar results. The main difference, as mentioned before, is the tendency of model 1 to reduce direction information faster than model 2 does (see also Figure 4).

This results in a slightly higher contrast in the images in model 2. A number of dark spots that appear in the main diagonal parts of the eroded images indicate violations of the positive definiteness condition. Due to measurement errors, these are already present in the original data set but are widened by erosion.

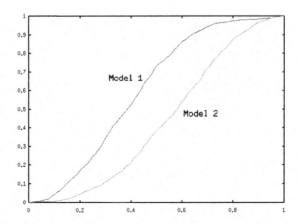

Fig. 4. The distribution of numerical eccentricities $e = \sqrt{1 - \lambda_2^* / \lambda_1^*}$ in the dilated images from Fig. 2.

The experiments for opening and closing can be seen in Figure 3. They confirm the previous impression: There is a high similarity between the test results from model 1 and model 2, the main difference being in the off diagonal where the higher contrast of model 2 is noticeable again.

The main goal, to create a filter for tensor valued erosion and dilation (and the derived opening and closing) which is similar to the scalar case, has been achieved by both models. Whereas model 2 shows somewhat better results in the experiments, model 1 has the advantage of being simpler to implement by using the method based on the two largest eigenvalues.

6   Conclusions

In this paper we have extended fundamental concepts of mathematical morphology to the case of matrix-valued data. Based on two alternative approaches, definitions for supremum and infimum of a set of positive definite symmetric matrices were given. One set of definitions relies on the property of scalar-valued p-means that they tend to the maximum and minimum of their argument sets for $p \rightarrow \pm\infty$; supremum and infimum of matrix sets are constructed by an analogous limiting procedure. The second approach combines geometrical and analytical tools to construct suprema and infima as minimal and maximal elements of sets of upper resp. lower bounds of the given matrix set. Each of the two approaches enables the generalisation of morphological dilation, erosion and the further operations composed from these, like opening and closing. In the experimental part, we have implemented the different concepts and evaluated them on diffusion tensor data. Our future investigation will include a more detailed study of the morphological framework built on these operations.

Acknowledgement. The authors would like to thank Anna Vilanova i Bartrolí and Carola van Pul from Eindhoven University for the DT-MRI data set and the discussion of data conversion issues as well as Susanne Biehl from Saarland Univesity for the conversion software.

References

1. J. Astola, P. Haavisto, and Y. Neuvo. Vector median filters. *Proceedings of the IEEE*, 78(4):678–689, 1990.
2. V. Barnett. The ordering of multivariate data. *Journal of the Royal Statistical Society A*, 139(3):318–355, 1976.
3. V. Caselles, G. Sapiro, and D. H. Chung. Vector median filters, inf-sup convolutions, and coupled PDE's: theoretical connections. *Journal of Mathematical Imaging and Vision*, 12(2):109–119, April 2000.
4. C. A. Castaño Moraga, C.-F. Westin, and J. Ruiz-Alzola. Homomorphic filtering of DT-MRI fields. In R. E. Ellis and T. M. Peters, editors, *Medical Image Computing and Computer-Assisted Intervention – MICCAI 2003*, Lecture Notes in Computer Science. Springer, Berlin, 2003.
5. M. L. Comer and E. J. Delp. Morphological operations for color image processing. *Journal of Electronic Imaging*, 8(3):279–289, 1999.
6. C. Feddern, J. Weickert, and B. Burgeth. Level-set methods for tensor-valued images. In O. Faugeras and N. Paragios, editors, *Proc. Second IEEE Workshop on Geometric and Level Set Methods in Computer Vision*, pages 65–72, Nice, France, October 2003. INRIA.
7. W. Förstner and E. Gülch. A fast operator for detection and precise location of distinct points, corners and centres of circular features. In *Proc. ISPRS Intercommission Conference on Fast Processing of Photogrammetric Data*, pages 281–305, Interlaken, Switzerland, June 1987.
8. J. Goutsias, H. J. A. M. Heijmans, and K. Sivakumar. Morphological operators for image sequences. *Computer Vision and Image Understanding*, 62:326–346, 1995.
9. G. H. Granlund and H. Knutsson. *Signal Processing for Computer Vision*. Kluwer, Dordrecht, 1995.
10. F. Guichard and J.-M. Morel. Partial differential equations and image iterative filtering. In I. S. Duff and G. A. Watson, editors, *The State of the Art in Numerical Analysis*, number 63 in IMA Conference Series (New Series), pages 525–562. Clarendon Press, Oxford, 1997.
11. R. Hardie and G. Arce. "Ranking in R^p" and its use in multivariate image estimation. *IEEE Transactions on Circuits, Systems and Video Technology*, 1(2):197–209, 1991.
12. G. Louverdis, M. I. Vardavoulia, I. Andreadis, and P. Tsalides. A new approach to morphological color image processing. *Pattern Recognition*, 35:1733–1741, 2002.
13. C. Pierpaoli, P. Jezzard, P. J. Basser, A. Barnett, and G. Di Chiro. Diffusion tensor MR imaging of the human brain. *Radiology*, 201(3):637–648, December 1996.
14. J. Serra. *Image Analysis and Mathematical Morphology*, volume 1. Academic Press, London, 1982.
15. P. Soille. *Morphological Image Analysis*. Springer, Berlin, 1999.
16. H. Talbot, C. Evans, and R. Jones. Complete ordering and multivariate mathematical morphology. In H. J. A. M. Heijmans and J. B. T. M. Roerdink, editors, *Mathematical Morphology and its Applications to Image and Signal Processing*, volume 12 of *Computational Imaging and Vision*. Kluwer, Dordrecht, 1998.

17. D. Tschumperlé and R. Deriche. Orthonormal vector sets regularization with PDE's and applications. *International Journal of Computer Vision*, 50(3):237–252, December 2002.
18. J. Weickert and T. Brox. Diffusion and regularization of vector- and matrix-valued images. In M. Z. Nashed and O. Scherzer, editors, *Inverse Problems, Image Analysis, and Medical Imaging*, volume 313 of *Contemporary Mathematics*, pages 251–268. AMS, Providence, 2002.
19. M. Welk, C. Feddern, B. Burgeth, and J. Weickert. Median filtering of tensor-valued images. In B. Michaelis and G. Krell, editors, *Pattern Recognition*, volume 2781 of *Lecture Notes in Computer Science*, pages 17–24, Berlin, 2003. Springer.

Constraints on Coplanar Moving Points

Sujit Kuthirummal*, C.V. Jawahar, and P.J. Narayanan

Centre for Visual Information Technology
International Institute of Information Technology
Hyderabad 50019 India
pjn@iiit.net

Abstract. Configurations of dynamic points viewed by one or more cameras have not been studied much. In this paper, we present several view and time-independent constraints on different configurations of points moving on a plane. We show that 4 points with constant independent velocities or accelerations under affine projection can be characterized in a view independent manner using 2 views. Under perspective projection, 5 coplanar points under uniform linear velocity observed for 3 time instants in a single view have a view-independent characterization. The best known constraint for this case involves 6 points observed for 35 frames. Under uniform acceleration, 5 points in 5 time instants have a view-independent characterization. We also present constraints on a point undergoing arbitrary planar motion under affine projections in the Fourier domain. The constraints introduced in this paper involve fewer points or views than similar results reported in the literature and are simpler to compute in most cases. The constraints developed can be applied to many aspects of computer vision. Recognition constraints for several planar point configurations of moving points can result from them. We also show how time-alignment of views captured independently can follow from the constraints on moving point configurations.

1 Introduction

The study of view-independent constraints on the projections of a configuration of points is important for recognition of such point configurations. A number of view-independent invariants have been identified for static point configurations [1,2]. They encapsulate information about the scene independent of the cameras being used and are opposite in philosophy to the scene-independent constraints like the Fundamental Matrix [1], the multilinear tensors [3,4,5], etc. Formulating view independent constraints on the projections of dynamic point configurations is more challenging and has been studied less. Many configurations of dynamic points are possible. Points could be in general positions or could lie on a plane or on a line. The motion could be arbitrary or constrained. An interesting case is linearly moving points with independent uniform velocities or accelerations. In this paper, we derive several simple constraints on the projections of moving points and their motion parameters.

---

* Currently with the Department of Computer Science, Columbia University

T. Pajdla and J. Matas (Eds.): ECCV 2004, LNCS 3024, pp. 168–179, 2004.
© Springer-Verlag Berlin Heidelberg 2004

As an example of view-independent constraints on point configurations, let us consider a set of 5 world points $\mathbf{P}[i] \in R^3$, $i = 1..5$ and their images $\mathbf{p}[i]$ in homogeneous and $(x[i], y[i])$ in Cartesian coordinates viewed by an affine camera $\mathbf{M}$. Let $\mathbf{m}_i$ be the vector of the first 3 elements in the ith row of $\mathbf{M}$ and let m_{i4} be the fourth element in the ith row. Therefore, $x[i] = \mathbf{m}_1.\mathbf{P}[i] + m_{14}$ and $y[i] = \mathbf{m}_2.\mathbf{P}[i] + m_{24}$. Alternatively, $\begin{bmatrix} P[i] & 1 & x[i] \end{bmatrix}^{\mathrm{T}} \begin{bmatrix} \mathbf{m}_1 & m_{14} & -1 \end{bmatrix} = \begin{bmatrix} P[i] & 1 & y[i] \end{bmatrix}^{\mathrm{T}} \begin{bmatrix} \mathbf{m}_2 & m_{24} & -1 \end{bmatrix} = 0$. If we have at least five points, then we can form a set of equations of the form $\mathbf{C}_1\theta_1 = \mathbf{C}_2\theta_2 = 0$, where $\theta_1 = \begin{bmatrix} \mathbf{m}_1 & m_{14} \end{bmatrix}^{\mathrm{T}}$, $\theta_2 = \begin{bmatrix} \mathbf{m}_2 & m_{24} \end{bmatrix}^{\mathrm{T}}$ and each row of the measurement matrix $\mathbf{C}_1$ (or $\mathbf{C}_2$) consists of the unknown world point $\mathbf{P}[i]$, unity and the $x[i]$ (or $y[i]$) coordinate. Note that the camera parameters are factored out into vectors θ_1 and θ_1. It is obvious that $\mathbf{C}_1$ and $\mathbf{C}_2$ are rank deficient and expanding their 5×5 determinant results in constraints of the form $\sum_{i=1}^{5} \alpha_i x[i] = 0$ and $\sum_{i=1}^{5} \alpha_i y[i] = 0$ where α_i are functions of the world position of the points $\mathbf{P}_i$ and hence is the same for all views, i.e the α_i are view-independent coefficients. Note that the coefficients of $x[i]$ and $y[i]$ in the above constraint are the same αs. Thus, the total number of unknowns is 4 (up to scale). Each view gives two equations in terms of α. Therefore, we need two views of the five points to compute all the view-independent coefficients.

When the points are not in general position, the rank of $\mathbf{C}$ would be less than 4 giving rise to simple algebraic constraints. A configuration of four points on a plane yields a view-independent constraint defined over two views. Three points on a line yield a view-independent constraint that can be computed from a single view itself. For linear motion, we can arrive at view-independent algebraic constraints by factoring out the camera parameters.

We derive several view-independent constraints on the projections of a dynamic scene in this paper. They are independent of the camera parameters. Some of these constraints are time-dependent while others are time-independent. The computational requirements of these constraints depend on the configuration and on its dependence on time. We also derive constraints on points with arbitrary planar motion under affine projection. These are computed from a Fourier domain representation of the trajectory. The constraints derived here find applications in recognition of dynamic point configurations in multiple views, time-alignment between views, etc.

2 Points with Linear Motion

We first consider the case of uniform linear motion. When a point moves in the world with uniform linear velocity or acceleration, its projections in various views move in a parameterizable manner. The view-independent relationships between projections of points moving with uniform velocity presented recently [6] fall under this category. The two view constraints on points moving with uniform velocity [7] is another contribution in this direction. In this section, we study the projection of points moving in a linear fashion imaged under affine and projective camera models. Let $\mathbf{P}$ be a 3D world point, moving with uniform linear polynomial motion. Its position at any time instant t is given by

$$\mathbf{P}_t = \begin{bmatrix} \mathbf{I} \\ 1 \end{bmatrix} + \begin{bmatrix} \mathbf{Q}_1 \\ 0 \end{bmatrix} t + \begin{bmatrix} \mathbf{Q}_2 \\ 0 \end{bmatrix} t^2 + \ldots + \begin{bmatrix} \mathbf{Q}_n \\ 0 \end{bmatrix} t^n \tag{1}$$

where $\mathbf{I}$ is the initial position and $\mathbf{Q}_i$ are 3-vectors. Let $\mathbf{p}_t^l = \begin{bmatrix} x_t^l \ y_t^l \ 1 \end{bmatrix}^{\mathrm{T}}$ be the projection of $\mathbf{P}$ in view l at time t due to a camera characterized by the camera matrix $\mathbf{M}^l$.

2.1   Uniform Linear Motion under Affine Projection

When the camera is affine, we can differentiate the projection $\mathbf{p}_t^l$ with respect to t to get the velocity

$$\tilde{\mathbf{v}}_t^l = \mathbf{M}^l \sum_{i=1}^{n} \begin{bmatrix} \mathbf{Q}_i \\ 0 \end{bmatrix} t^{(i-1)}. \tag{2}$$

If the point moves with uniform velocity $\mathbf{U}$ in the world, the image velocity can be written as $\tilde{\mathbf{v}}^l = \mathbf{M}^l[\mathbf{U} \ 0]^{\mathrm{T}}$. Thus, the projected point moves with uniform velocity that is the projection of the world velocity. If the point moves with uniform linear acceleration, its image velocity is given by $\tilde{\mathbf{v}}^l = \mathbf{M}^l([\mathbf{U} \ 0]^{\mathrm{T}} + [\mathbf{A} \ 0]^{\mathrm{T}} t)$ and its image acceleration is given by $\tilde{\mathbf{a}}^l = \mathbf{M}^l\mathbf{A}$, where $\mathbf{A}$ is the world acceleration of the point. This implies that the projection of a point moving with uniform linear acceleration in the world has uniform linear acceleration [8]. Such simple parameterization is not available for the general projective camera.

2.2   Uniform Linear Motion under Perspective Projection

We consider the image motion of points undergoing uniform linear motion in the world. Since the point $\mathbf{P}_t$ projects to $\mathbf{p}_t^l = \mathbf{M}^l\mathbf{P}_t$, we can write x_t and y_t as

$$x_t = \frac{\sum_{i=0}^{n} \psi_i t^i}{\sum_{i=0}^{n} \phi_i t^i} \quad \text{and} \quad y_t = \frac{\sum_{i=0}^{n} \chi_i t^i}{\sum_{i=0}^{n} \phi_i t^i} \tag{3}$$

where ψ_i, ϕ_i, and χ_i are functions of $\mathbf{I}$, $\mathbf{Q}_i$, and $\mathbf{M}^l$ and hence constant for a point in a particular view. We can parameterize the projection of the point at time t with $3n + 2$ unknowns up to scale. These parameters can be computed from $\lceil (1.5n + 1) \rceil$ time instants since each time instant provides two equations.

   We can parameterize the moving point as the intersection of the line of motion of the projection and lines perpendicular to it at various time instants. If $(b, -a, d)$ is the line of motion of the projection in the image over time, the line perpendicular to it can be written as $\mathbf{l}(t) = (a, b, c(t))$. Since a and b are constants, only $c(t)$ (a measure of the distance of the line from the origin) varies with time. Only two of the three parameters a, b, d are independent as a line is defined up to scale. Since $\mathbf{p}_t$ lies on $\mathbf{l}(t)$, we have $\mathbf{l}(t)^{\mathrm{T}}\mathbf{p}_t = 0$. Replacing $\mathbf{p}_t$ with $\mathbf{M}\mathbf{P}_t$ and expanding, we get

$$\sum_{i=0}^{n} \mu_i \, t^i + c(t) \, (\sum_{i=0}^{n} \eta_i \, t^i) = 0 \tag{4}$$

where μ_i and η_i are functions of $\mathbf{I}$, $\mathbf{Q}_i$, $\mathbf{M}^l$, a, and b, and are constant for a point in a view. The term $c(t)$ can be parameterized using $(2n + 1)$ unknowns up to scale. Since μ's and η's are functions of ϕ's, ψ's and χ's, no new information is gained by this parameterization. However, the time-dependent part of the motion can be parameterized using fewer parameters, by factoring the time-independent parts out. The point at time t can be obtained by taking the cross product of the lines $(b, -a, d)$ and $(a, b, c(t))$. This representation of the position of the projection has fewer *essential* unknowns than the parameterization of Equation 3.

Uniform Linear Velocity: If $n = 1$ Equation 4 becomes $\mu_0 + \mu_1 t + c(t)(\eta_0 + t) = 0$ with $\eta_1 = 1$. The parameterization will have 3 unknowns up to scale and needs 3 time instants to compute them. The parameters have been partitioned into time-dependent and time-independent parts. The line of motion $(b, -a, d)$ (2 unknowns up to scale) can be computed from projections at any two time instants. Together, the time-dependent and time-independent aspects make up the 5 degrees of freedom associated with the system.

Uniform Linear Acceleration: The simple parameterization gives x_t and y_t as ratios of two polynomials in t of degree 2, with 8 unknowns and needs measurements at 4 time instants to compute them. The new parameterization has only 5 unknowns and can be determined from 5 time instants. The polynomial constraint is given by $\mu_0 + \mu_1 t + \mu_2 t^2 + c(t)(\eta_0 + \eta_1 t + t^2) = 0$ with $\eta_2 = 1$.

2.3   General Linear Motion

Under general linear motion, the trajectories of the points will be straight lines and constraints on matching lines in multiple views are satisfied by each moving point independently. If a world line is imaged by projective cameras as l^1, l^2, and l^3, the projections are related by a trilinear constraint [3,4,9] as

$$l^1 = (l^2)^{\mathrm{T}} \mathcal{T} l^3 \qquad (5)$$

where $\mathcal{T}$ is a suitable tensor. This gives a constraint on the trajectories of points undergoing general linear motion. Nothing more can be said about them since no more information is available other than the linearity of their trajectories.

3   Motion Analysis in Fourier Domain

If we have a number of moving points, their collective properties can be exploited in addition to the motion constraints. Properties of collections can be captured in the Fourier domain. We consider a configuration of a large number of points moving with independent uniform linear velocities in this section. We also explore Fourier domain representation of a point undergoing arbitrary co-planar motion.

3.1   Multiple Linearly Moving Points

Recognition of deformable shapes has been studied and applied to tracking of non-rigid objects when the deformation between two consecutive frames is small [10,11], in the context of handwriting recognition [12,13], and for contour extraction and modeling [14]. Some approaches suggest learning a deformable model from examples, while some use deformable templates and ascertain a match by determining how much a template has to be deformed to get the test shape. These techniques do not assume any specific structure in the deformation. Our work on the other hand attempts to develop a sound theoretical model when the deformation has a particular structure.

Let $\mathbf{P}[i]$ be the sequence of N points moving with independent uniform linear velocities $\mathbf{V}[i]$ like points on the envelope of an evolving planar boundary. Let the projection of $\mathbf{P}[i]$ in view l at time t be $\mathbf{p}_t^l[i]$. A homography maps points in one view to points in the other [1]. If the homography is affine

$$\mathbf{p}_t^l[i] = \mathbf{A}^l \mathbf{p}_t^0[i] + \mathbf{b}^l, \quad 0 \le i < N \tag{6}$$

where $\mathbf{A}^l$ is the upper 2×2 minor of the homography and $\mathbf{b}^l$ is taken from its third column. An unknown shift λ_l aligns the points between views 0 and l. Taking the Fourier transform of Equation 6 and ignoring the frequency term corresponding to $k = 0$, we get

$$\bar{\mathbf{P}}_t^l[k] = \mathbf{A}^l \bar{\mathbf{P}}_t^0[k] e^{j2\pi\lambda_l k/N}, \quad 0 < k < N \tag{7}$$

where $\bar{\mathbf{P}}_t^l = \begin{bmatrix} \mathbf{X}_t^l & \mathbf{Y}_t^l \end{bmatrix}^T$; $\mathbf{X}_t^l$ and $\mathbf{Y}_t^l$ are the Fourier transforms of the sequences x_t^l and y_t^l respectively. A point moving with uniform velocity in the world moves with uniform velocity in an affine view (Section 2.1). The projection at any time t is given by $\mathbf{p}_t^l[i] = \mathbf{p}_0^l[i] + \mathbf{v}^l[i]t$, $0 \le i < N$ where $\mathbf{v}^l[i] = [v_x^l[i] \ v_y^l[i]]^T$ is the velocity vector in the image. Taking the Fourier Transform of both sides, we get

$$\bar{\mathbf{P}}_t^l[k] = \bar{\mathbf{P}}_0^l[k] + \bar{\mathbf{V}}^l[k] \ t \tag{8}$$

where $\bar{\mathbf{V}}^l$ is the Fourier Transform of the sequence $\mathbf{v}^l$. We define a sequence measure κ on $\bar{\mathbf{P}}_t^l$ as

$$\kappa_t^l[k] = \bar{\mathbf{P}}_t^l[k]^{*T} \begin{bmatrix} 0 & 1 \\ -1 & 0 \end{bmatrix} \bar{\mathbf{P}}_t^l[k], \quad 0 < k < N \tag{9}$$

Using Equations 7 and 8, it can be shown that

$$\kappa_t^l[k] = |\mathbf{A}^l| \ (\alpha_1[k] + \alpha_2[k] \ t + \alpha_3[k] \ t^2) \tag{10}$$

where α's are functions of measurements $\mathbf{p}^0$ and $\mathbf{v}^0$ (or their Fourier domain representation) made only in the reference view. The κ sequence and hence the α's are pure imaginary and can be computed by observing 2 frames in the reference view to determine position $(\mathbf{p}_0^0)$ values and velocity $(\mathbf{v}^0)$ values. No time synchronization or point correspondence is required between views as the shift term λ_l gets eliminated in κ. In the reference view, $\kappa_t^0[k] = \alpha_1[k] + \alpha_2[k] \ t + \alpha_3[k] \ t^2$. The sequence measure $\kappa_t^l[k]$ is thus view-independent but time-dependent.

3.2   Arbitrary Motion of a Point

Are there any view-independent constraints on a point undergoing arbitrary planar motion? The image of the point in any view will trace out a contour (closed or open) over time, which is the projection of its world trajectory. The problem reduces to the analysis of planar contours and view-independent constraints for planar contours will be applicable to the moving point. We now present the contour constraints presented in [15] to characterize arbitrary planar motion of a point under affine imaging conditions.

Let $\mathbf{P}[i]$ be the sequence of N points on the closed planar trajectory of a point and let $(x^l[i], y^l[i])$ be its images in view l. (The index i is a measure of time in this case as the point is at different locations at different times.) Assuming that the views are related by an affine homography, the points on the contour in view l are related to corresponding points on the contour in the reference view 0 as

$$\mathbf{p}^l[i] = \mathbf{A}^l \mathbf{p}^0[i] + \mathbf{b}^l, \ \ 0 \leq i < N \tag{11}$$

where $\mathbf{A}^l$ and b^l are as in Equation 6. The time alignment information across views is not typically available. Taking the Fourier transform of Equation 11 and discarding the DC term, we get $\bar{\mathbf{P}}^l[k] = \mathbf{A}^l \bar{\mathbf{P}}^0[k] e^{j2\pi\lambda_l k/N}$, $0 < k < N$ where λ_l is the time alignment parameter and $\bar{\mathbf{P}}^l$ the Fourier transform as in Equation 7. We can define a time-independent sequence measure κ^l similar to the one given in Equation 9. We can easily see

$$\kappa^l[k] = |A^l| \ \kappa^0[k]. \tag{12}$$

Thus, $\kappa[k]$ is a relative view-invariant sequence for the point having arbitrary motion. It can be computed in any view by tracking the point over time to construct the contour $\mathbf{p}[i]$.

4   Applications of View-Independent Constraints

We describe how the parameterizations and constraints developed in this paper can be applied to the problems of recognition and time-alignment.

4.1   Configuration of 4 Points under Affine Projection

In Section 2.1 we had parameterized the velocity and acceleration of the projection of a point moving with uniform linear polynomial motion. We now use those parameterizations to derive view independent constraints on configurations of 4 points moving with independent uniform linear motion parameters.

Equation 2 can be written as $v_x^l(t) = \mathbf{m}_1 \sum_i \mathbf{Q}_i \ t^{i-1}$ and $v_y^l(t) = \mathbf{m}_2 \sum_i \mathbf{Q}_i \ t^{i-1}$. Rearranging terms, we get

$$\left[(\sum_{j=1}^{n} \mathbf{Q}_j t^{j-1})^{\mathrm{T}} \ v_x^l(t) \right] [\mathbf{m}_1 \ -1]^{\mathrm{T}} = \left[(\sum_{j=1}^{n} \mathbf{Q}_j t^{j-1})^{\mathrm{T}} \ v_y^l(t) \right] [\mathbf{m}_2 \ -1]^{\mathrm{T}} = 0$$

where $[\mathbf{m}_i \; m_{i4}]$ is the i'th row of $\mathbf{M}^l$, and v^l_x and v^l_y are the x and y components of the point's velocity in view l. If we have at least four points, then we can form a set of equations of the form $\mathbf{C}\theta = 0$, where each row of the measurement matrix $\mathbf{C}$ consists of the unknown world point motion parameters $\mathbf{Q}_i$, and the velocities along the x or y coordinate. $\mathbf{C}$ is a rank deficient matrix with a maximum rank of 3. Equating its 4×4 determinant to 0 results in the following linear constraints.

$$\zeta_0 v^l_{1x} + \zeta_1 v^l_{2x} + \zeta_2 v^l_{3x} + \zeta_3 v^l_{4x} = \zeta_0 v^l_{1y} + \zeta_1 v^l_{2y} + \zeta_2 v^l_{3y} + \zeta_3 v^l_{4y} = 0 \qquad (13)$$

where ζ_i is a polynomial of order $3(n-1)$ in the time-parameter t. ζ_i's are view-independent as each has $3n - 2$ terms that are functions of the world motion parameters. The total number of view independent parameters is $4(3n-2)-1 = 12n - 9$ up to scale. Each time instant provides 2 equations in the unknowns; we need $(6n - 4)$ measurements of the velocities in one or more frames in one or more views to compute the ζ_i values.

Uniform Linear Velocity: When the points move with independent uniform linear velocities, $n = 1$ and we get linear view and time independent constraints on the velocities of the projections. These constraints have 3 view independent coefficients, computing which needs the measurement of the velocities of the four points in 2 views.

These results are better than the Recognition Polynomials and Shape Tensors presented earlier [7,6]. A view independent representation of a configuration of stationary points could be constructed from 2 views of 4 points under orthographic projections [16]. This was extended to recognize human gait using 2 views of 5 points under scaled-orthographic projections [7]. Time-dependent constraints involving a single view of 5 points with uniform velocity is presented in [6] for affine projection. Our results yield view and time independent constraints involving 4 points in 2 views under general affine projection – which is a significant improvement.

Uniform Linear Acceleration: When the points in the configuration move with independent uniform linear accelerations, $n = 2$, giving us linear, view-independent, time-dependent constraints on the velocities of the projections. These constraints have 15 view independent coefficients computing which needs measuring the velocities of the four points at a total of 8 time instants in one or more views.

Proceeding in a similar manner and factoring out the camera parameters as above, we can formulate linear time and view independent constraints on the accelerations of the projections, which have the same form and computational requirements as the constraints on the velocities of the projections of points moving with uniform linear velocities.

4.2   Configurations of 5 Points under Projective Cameras

Invariants provide us with the ability to come up with representations of the features in a scene that do not depend on the view, and can prove to be extremely handy when processing information from multiple views. For instance, to recognize a configuration of five coplanar points from any view of the same, we can compute the cross ratio of areas of the projections of the five points, which would be the same no matter which view we compute it in [2]. The cross-ratio of the areas of five points $\mathbf{x}[1]$, $\mathbf{x}[2]$, $\mathbf{x}[3]$, $\mathbf{x}[4]$, and $\mathbf{x}[5]$, no three of which are collinear, is defined as

$$cr(\mathbf{x}[1], \mathbf{x}[2], \mathbf{x}[3], \mathbf{x}[4], \mathbf{x}[5]) = \frac{\triangle_{\mathbf{x}[1]\mathbf{x}[2]\mathbf{x}[5]} \cdot \triangle_{\mathbf{x}[3]\mathbf{x}[4]\mathbf{x}[5]}}{\triangle_{\mathbf{x}[1]\mathbf{x}[3]\mathbf{x}[5]} \cdot \triangle_{\mathbf{x}[2]\mathbf{x}[4]\mathbf{x}[5]}} \tag{14}$$

where $\triangle_{\mathbf{x}[i]\mathbf{x}[j]\mathbf{x}[k]}$ is the area of the triangle formed by points $\mathbf{x}[i], \mathbf{x}[j], \mathbf{x}[k]$. This is for a static configuration of points or for snapshots of the scene taken at the same time. We now extend this to dynamic scenes where points move with uniform linear velocities or accelerations to arrive at time varying invariants for such configurations. Due to the novel parameterization for projective cameras described in the previous section, the number of unknowns needed to compute the time-varying invariants are fewer when compared to a naive parameterization approach.

Uniform Linear Velocity: If the points lie on a plane during the motion, the various views of the point configuration are related by a projective homography [1]. To express the configuration in a view-independent manner, we use an invariant to projective transformations of 2D [2]. Given the projections of a configuration of five coplanar points, which are in general position in the image, i.e., no three are collinear, we can define an invariant like the cross ratio of areas (Equation 14). The cross ratio of areas of the parametric representations of the projections of five points having independent uniform velocities is the ratio of two polynomials of degree 6 in the time parameter t.

$$I_v^l(t) = \frac{N_v^l(t)}{D_v^l(t)} = \frac{\sum_{i=0}^{6} \gamma^l t^i}{\sum_{i=0}^{6} \delta^l t^i}$$

where $I_v^l(t)$ is the invariant computed in view l at time t and γ^l and δ^l terms are functions of the parameters used to represent the points in view l. The number of essential unknowns in this expression is only 15 (3 for each point) and measurements made in only three time instants in each view are required to determine this time varying invariant. This is a significant theoretical advancement over the formulation presented in Levin et al. [6] that requires the projections of 6 points having coplanar independent uniform linear velocities, has 35 unknowns, computing which need 34 time instants.

To recognize a configuration, we need to determine whether the invariants computed in all the views are identical or not. This implies that

$$I_v^0(t) = I_v^l(t) \Rightarrow \frac{N_v^0(t)}{D_v^0(t)} = \frac{N_v^l(t)}{D_v^l(t)} \Rightarrow N_v^0(t) * D_v^l(t) = N_v^l(t) * D_v^0(t)$$

Therefore, for a configuration of 5 points moving with uniform linear velocities, the ratio of the coefficients of t^i in $N_v^0(t) * D_v^l(t)$ and $N_v^l(t) * D_v^0(t)$ should be 1 for $0 \le i \le 12$. This necessary constraint for recognition, however, holds only when time-alignment across views is known. For recognition, we can also make use of the additional necessary constraint that there should exist a unique homography that maps the lines of motion of the projection in the test and reference views.

Uniform Linear Acceleration: When all 5 points of a configuration moving with independent linear accelerations lie on the same plane always, we can define a time varying invariant for the configuration similar to the one above. The time varying invariant obtained on computing the cross ratio of the areas of the parametric projections of the configuration is the ratio of two polynomials of order 12 in the time parameter t and has only 25 unknowns (5 for each point) determining which need measurements made at 5 time instants.

$$I_a^l(t) = \frac{N_a^l(t)}{D_a^l(t)} = \frac{\sum_{i=0}^{12} \sigma^l t^i}{\sum_{i=0}^{12} \tau^l t^i}$$

where $I_a^l(t)$ is the invariant computed in view l at time t and the σ^l and τ^l terms are functions of the parameters used for representing the points in view l.

As in the case of uniform linear velocity, the value of the invariant computed in all the views have to be the same, which implies that the ratio of the coefficients of t^i in $N_a^0(t) * D_a^l(t)$ and $N_a^l(t) * D_a^0(t)$ should be 1 for $0 \le i \le 24$. Like in the case of uniform velocity, for recognition of the configuration, we can make use of the additional necessary constraint that there should exist a homography that relates the lines of motion in the two views.

4.3   Recognition Constraints in Fourier Domain

In Section 3.1 we had modeled configurations of many points having independent uniform linear velocities and their motion in the Fourier domain. In this subsection, we use those models to derive constraints for recognizing such configurations.

Configuration at the Same Time in Multiple Views: It has been shown in Equation 10 that

$$\kappa_t^l[k] = |\mathbf{A}^l|\kappa_t^0[k] \tag{15}$$

Equation 15 provides a recognition mechanism for such a case. Given M views, we can compute a $M \times (N-1)$ measurement matrix $\mathbf{C}_1$ constructed by stacking the κ_t^l measures for the various views, one row for each view. Since the various rows are scaled versions of each other, the rank of $\mathbf{C}_1$ would be 1. Therefore a necessary algebraic recognition constraint is $rank(\mathbf{C}_1) = 1$.

Configuration at Different Times in Multiple Views: The problem of recognizing the contour when we have its views at different time instants is a more challenging problem. Let us assume that in the reference view (0), we are able to track the points in two frames (identify points in a view across time) and hence able to identify all αs. Now given the configuration observed in any other view at any time t, we can recognize it to be the same as the one observed in the reference view. Observe that Equation 10 states that κ_t^l is a linear combination of the vectors α_i, the time t being a component of the linear combination coefficients. Given M views, we can construct a $(M+2) \times (N-1)$ measurement matrix $\mathbf{C}_2$ whose first three rows contain the vectors α_i, $i = 1, 2, 3$. The κ_t^l computed in the various views (except the reference view) then contribute one row each to $\mathbf{C}_2$. Note that the time instants at which κ is computed in a view need not be the same in all views. Since, every row constructed from κ_t^l can be expressed as a linear combination of the first 3 rows, a necessary algebraic recognition constraint is $rank(\mathbf{C}_2) = 3$. This technique does not need correspondence across views and assumes tracking only in the reference view.

Recognizing Arbitrary Point Motion: In Section 3.2, we modeled the motion of a point moving on a closed arbitrary planar trajectory in the world as a contour and mapped the problem of its analysis to contour analysis. We evaluate the κ measure for the Fourier domain representation of the contour in view l. It can be shown that [15]

$$\kappa^l[k] = |\mathbf{A}^l| \, \kappa^0[k], \quad 0 < k < N. \tag{16}$$

The κ values can be computed independently for each view from the Fourier domain. The κ sequence is invariant up to scale and can recognize the contour formed by the motion. Given M views of the motion, we can construct a $M \times (N - 1)$ matrix $\mathbf{C}_a$, the ith row of $\mathbf{C}_a$ consisting of the κ values computed in the ith view. It can be seen from Equation 16 that rank of $\mathbf{C}_a$ is 1. This constraint is view-independent as the κ can be computed independently in each view. There are no restrictions on the number of frames in which the motion is observed. In practice the Fourier transform will be reliable only if the curve has sufficient length. If a number of points can be tracked independently, each contour will yield a different constraint, all of which have to be satisfied simultaneously. The above result hints that there can exist a number of algebraic constraints on the trajectory traced out by the projections of a moving point in a view.

4.4   Time Alignment

The recognition constraints presented here do not need time alignment information across views. We can determine time alignment using these constraints as we show next. This time alignment can then be used to align frames of synchronized videos captured from multiple viewpoints. We consider the problem wherein we have to time align two image sequences $\mathbf{A}$ and $\mathbf{B}$ of the same world motion. To do this, we need to determine the shift λ that when applied to $\mathbf{B}$ would ensure that the kth image in each sequence is a snap shot of the world at the k time instant.

Point Configurations of 5 Points: We can use the invariants described in Section 4.2 to time align views $\mathbf{A}$ and $\mathbf{B}$ of a configuration of 5 points moving with independent uniform linear velocities or accelerations. Let time t in view $\mathbf{A}$ be the time instant with reference to which we want to align view $\mathbf{B}$. In view $\mathbf{A}$, we compute the value of the invariant for the point configuration at time t and in view $\mathbf{B}$, we compute the parameters of the time varying invariant (for uniform velocity or acceleration as the case may be). We then perform a search over the range of possible values of λ seeking that shift at which the invariants computed at times t in $\mathbf{A}$ and $(t + \lambda)$ in $\mathbf{B}$ are identical.

Point Configurations of Many Points: The techniques for recognizing a deforming contour presented in Section 4.3 do not depend on the time instant at which the κ values are computed in a view. In fact, they can be used to determine the time parameter. Let κ_τ^l be the κ sequence computed at time τ in view **B**. Normalizing $\kappa_\tau^l[k]$ (Equation 10) with respect to a fixed frequency (say p) gives

$$\frac{\kappa_\tau^l[k]}{\kappa_\tau^l[p]} = \frac{\alpha_1[k] + \alpha_2[k]t + \alpha_3[k]t^2}{\alpha_1[p] + \alpha_2[p]t + \alpha_3[p]t^2} \tag{17}$$

The αs can be computed in the reference view **A**, if we are able to track points in it for at least two frames. Equation 17 is a quadratic in time t, solving for which, we can find the time instant (frame number) in **A** corresponding to the time instant τ in **B**. The value of λ in this case is given by $(t - \tau)$.

Arbitrary Motion: In section 4.3 we have described how we can use the κ measure to recognize the projections of the closed planar trajectory of a point undergoing arbitrary motion. We can modify the definition of κ to define a new measure κ'

$$\kappa'^l[k] = \bar{\mathbf{P}}^l[k]^{*T} \begin{bmatrix} 0 & 1 \\ -1 & 0 \end{bmatrix} \bar{\mathbf{P}}^l[p] = \kappa'^0[k]e^{-j2\pi\lambda_l(k-p)/N}, \quad 0 < k < N \tag{18}$$

where p is a constant (typically 1 or 2). The ratio of $\frac{\kappa'^l}{\kappa'^0}$ will be a complex sinusoid. The inverse Fourier transform of this quotient series would show a peak at λ. Thus, by looking for a peak in the inverse Fourier transform spectrum of the quotient series, we can determine time alignment information.

Note that we have considered $\mathbf{p}[i]$ and $\mathbf{v}[i]$ to be independent. In an application, one would expect them to be correlated and consequently the signals representing the sequences of positions and velocities would be smooth. As a result, the higher frequencies in their Fourier representation would be negligible and hence we can work with fewer frequencies in these cases.

5   Discussion

In this paper, we presented several constraints on the projections of coplanar points in motion. Linear motion with uniform velocity or acceleration and arbi-

Table 1. Motion: Summary of the multiview constraints on moving points in general position (unless stated otherwise). (CC = Coplanar Configuration)

Type	Camera	Conditions	Time Invariant	Source
Uniform V	Affine	5 pts, 8 frames	No	Levin et al.
Uniform V	Affine	4 pts, 2 views	Yes	Authors
Uniform V	Projective	6 pts, 49 frames, 1 view	No	Levin et al.
Uniform V	Projective	6 pts, 35 frames, 1 view, (CC)	No	Levin et al.
Uniform V	Projective	5 pts, 3 frames, 1 view, (CC)	No	Authors
Uniform A	Affine	4 pts, 9 frames	No	Authors
Uniform A	Affine	4 pts, 2 views	Yes	Authors
Uniform A	Projective	5 pts, 5 frames, 1 view, (CC)	No	Authors
Uniform ω	Projective	6 pts	Yes	Levin et al.
Uniform V	Affine	Many pts (CC)	No	Authors
Arbitrary	Affine	1 pt, Planar closed trajectory	No	Authors

trary planar motion were considered. Table 1 summarizes the constraints available on moving points. Our constraints have fewer computational requirements than published results. We showed how these constraints translate into recognition constraints. We also presented methods to compute the time-alignment between views from image structure only. These can form the basis of recognition applications like human identification using motion characteristics, tracking moving points for ballistic applications, detecting inconsistent video sequences of a dynamic scene based on geometric inconsistency, etc.

References

1. Hartley, R., Zisserman, A.: Multiple View Geometry in Computer Vision. Cambridge University Press (2000)
2. Mundy, J., Zisserman, A.: Geometric Invariances in Computer Vision. MIT Press (1992)
3. Hartley, R.: Lines and points in three views and the trifocal tensor. International Journal of Computer Vision **22** (1997) 125–140
4. Shashua, A.: Trilinear tensor: The Fundamental Construct of Multiple-view Geometry and its applications. AFPAC (1997) 190–206
5. Triggs, B.: Matching Constraints and the Joint Image. International Conference on Computer Vision (1995) 338–343
6. Levin, A., Wolf, L., Shashua, A.: Time-varying Shape Tensors for Scenes with Multiple Moving Points. IEEE Conference on Computer Vision and Pattern Recognition (2001) I:623–630
7. Carlsson, S.: Recognizing walking people. European Conference on Computer Vision (June 2000) 472–486
8. Kuthirummal, S., Jawahar, C.V., Narayanan, P.J.: Algebraic constraints on moving points in multiple views. Indian Conference on Computer Vision, Graphics and Image Processing (2002)
9. Hartley, R.: Lines and points in three views: An integrated approach. Proc. ARPA Image Understanding Workshop (1994)
10. Cohen, I., Ayache, N., Sulger, P.: Tracking points on deformable objects using curvature information. European Conference on Computer Vision (1992) 458–466
11. Kass, M., Witkin, A., Terzopoulos, D.: Snakes:active contour models. International Journal on Computer Vision **1(4)** (1988) 321–331
12. Tsukumo, J.: Handprinted kanji character recognition based on flexible template matching. International Conference on Pattern Recognition (1992) 483–486
13. Basri, R., Costa, L., Geiger, D., Jacobs, D.: Determining the similarity of deformable shapes. IEEE Workshop on Physics-Based Modelling in Computer Vision (1995) 135–143
14. Lai, K., R, C.: Deformable contours:modeling and extraction. IEEE Conference on Computer Vision and Pattern Recognition (1994) 601–608
15. Kuthirummal, S., Jawahar, C.V., Narayanan, P.J.: Planar Shape Recognition across Multiple Views. International Conference on Pattern Recognition (2002) 456–459
16. Bennet, B.M., Hoffman, D.D., Prakash, C.: Recognition Polynomials. Journal of the Optical Society of America **10** (1993) 759–764

A PDE Solution of Brownian Warping

Mads Nielsen[1] and P. Johansen[2]

. IT U. of Copenhagen, Denmark
. DIKU, U. of Copenhagen, Denmark

Abstract. A Brownian motion model in the group of diffeomorphisms has been introduced as creating a least committed prior on warps. This prior is source destination symmetric, fulfills a natural semi-group property for warps, and with probability 1 create invertible warps. In this paper, we formulate a Partial Differential Equation for obtaining the maximum likelihood warp given matching constraints derived from the images. We solve for the free boundary conditions, and the bias toward smaller areas in the finite domain setting. Furthermore, we demonstrate the technique on 2D images, and show that the obtained warps are also in practice source-destination symmetric.

1 Introduction

In any non-rigid registration algorithm, one must weigh the data confidence against the complexity of the warp field mapping the source image geometrically into the destination image. This is typically done through spring terms in elastic registration [3,8,7], through the viscosity term in fluid registration [5] or by controlling the number of spline parameters in spline-based non-rigid registration [1,20].

If non-rigid registration algorithms, symmetric in source and destination, can be constructed, many problems in shape averaging and shape distribution estimation can be avoided. The regularizer is not symmetric with respect to source and destination in the methods mentioned above. While symmetric regularizers can be constructed in most cases simply by adding a term for the inverse registration [6], this solution is not theoretically satisfactory. In [17] we show that Brownian warps, described in detail below, are source-destination symmetric. They are constructed as a Brownian motion in the group of diffeomorphisms (Section 2 and 3).

This distribution on warps leads through a Maximum a Posteriori inference scheme to a functional minimization formulation. We derive a Partial Differential Equation as the gradient descend in this functional, and use a straightforward time explicit and spatial forward-backward scheme for discrete implementation (Section 4).

Finally, we give results on how source-destination symmetric the discrete implementation is in practice, and give comparisons to thin-plate spline warps in a randomized and bootstrapped experiment.

T. Pajdla and J. Matas (Eds.): ECCV 2004, LNCS 3024, pp. 180–191, 2004.

2   Definitions and Motivation

A non-rigid registration may be modeled by a warp field $W : \mathbb{R}^D \mapsto \mathbb{R}^D$ mapping points in one D-dimensional image into another D-dimensional image. We give the definition:

Definition 1 (Warp Field). *A warp field* $W(x) : \mathbb{R}^D \mapsto \mathbb{R}^D$ *maps all points in the source image* $I_S(x) : \mathbb{R}^D \mapsto \mathbb{R}$ *into points of the destination image* $I_D(x) : \mathbb{R}^D \mapsto \mathbb{R}$ *such that* $I_S(W(X))$ *is the registered source image. W is invertible and differentiable (i.e., a diffeomorphism) and has everywhere a positive Jacobian* $det(\partial_{x_i} W^j) > 0$

Here, we have made the assumption that warps are invertible and differentiable. This corresponds to, that we do not wish to warp in the case where structure change topology. Modeling shape changes, shape variability, this is the optimal setting. However, in computer vision problems like stereo and flow computation from projected images, occlusion boundaries is not modeled by our approach. In these cases, the ecological statistics of the local warps must modeled taking the projection into account.

A diffeomorphism will always have the same sign of the Jacobian everywhere. Our choice of positive Jacobian applies to those cases where the object is not geometrically reflected.

The identification of a warp field on the basis of images is a matter of inference. Below we will apply the Bayes inference machine [13], but a similar formulation should appear when using information theoretic approaches such as the minimum description length principle [18].

We wish to determine the warp field W that maximizes the posterior

$$p(W|I_S, I_D) = \frac{1}{Z} p(I_S, I_D|W) p(W)$$

where Z is a normalizing constant (sometimes denoted the partition function), $p(I_S, I_D|W)$ is the likelihood term, and $p(W)$ is the warp prior. The likelihood term is based on the similarity of the warped source and destination image and may, in this formulation, be based on landmark matches [4], feature matches [15, 19], object matches [2], image correlation [15], or mutual information [21]. The major topic of this paper is the the prior $p(W)$ that expresses our belief in the regularity of the warp field prior to identifying the images.

3   Brownian Warps

We seek that distribution of warps which is the analogue of Brownian motion. We wish this distribution to be independent of warps performed earlier (i.e., invariant with respect to warps). This property is of fundamental importance particularly when determining the statistics of empirical warps, creating mean warps etc. In such cases, it is required by consistency in order to avoid the use of a fiducial pre-defined standard warp. We may formulate this in the probabilistic setting as:

$$p(W = W_2 \circ W_1) = \int p(W_2) dW_1.$$

This corresponds to the semi-group property of Brownian motion: The distribution of positions after two moves corresponds to two independent moves and, through the central limit theorem, leads to a Gaussian distribution of positions. Since this also holds for a concatenation of many warps, we can construct a warp as

$$W_B = \lim_{N \to \infty} \prod_{i=0}^{N} \circ W_i,$$

where the W_i are independent infinitesimal warps. This corresponds exactly to the definition of a Brownian motion on the real axis if the concatenation product is replaced by an ordinary sum.

In order to find this limiting distribution when all W_i are independent, we investigate motion in the neighborhood of a single point following along all the warps and make the following lemma:

Lemma 1 (Local structure). *Let $J_W = \partial_{x_i} W^j$ be the local Jacobian of W. Then, the Jacobian of a Brownian warp*

$$J_{W_B} = \lim_{N \to \infty} \prod_{i=0}^{N} J_{W_i}$$

Proof. This is obviously true due to the chain rule of differentiation.   □

Assume that an infinitesimal warp acts as the infinitesimal independent motion of points. In this case, all entries in the local Jacobian are independent and identically distributed round the identity. Hence, we may now model

$$J_{W_B} = \lim_{N \to \infty} \prod_{i=0}^{N} I + \sigma \frac{1}{\sqrt{N}} H_i, \tag{1}$$

where H_i is a $D \times D$ matrix of independent identically distributed entries of unit spread. The denominator $\sqrt{N}$ is introduced to make the concatenation product finite, and σ is the spread or the "size" of the infinitesimal warps.

To summarize, the limiting distribution of Eq. 1 is the distribution of the Jacobian of a Brownian Warp. In turn, this defines the Brownian distribution on warps, as we have no reason to assume other structure in the distribution.

Unfortunately, the solution to Eq. 1 is not given in the literature on random matrices. Gill and Johansen [10] solve the problem for matrices with positive entries and Högnäs and Mukherjea [11] solve, among other cases, the situation when the matrices are symmetric. Recently, we have solved the case for two dimensions [12] and are presently considering the solution for three. Here, we present only the result.

Theorem 1 (2D Brownian Jacobian). *The limiting distribution of Eq.1 where H_i have independent entries of unit spread and $W : \mathbb{R}^2 \mapsto \mathbb{R}^2$, is given as*

$$p(J_{W_B}) = G(S/\sigma) \sum_{n=0}^{\infty} g_n(F/\sigma) \cos(n\theta), \qquad (2)$$

where G is the unit spread Gaussian, g_n are related to the Jacobi functions, and the parameters are given as follows:

$$Scaling \quad S = \log(det(J_{W_B}))$$

$$Skewness \; F = \frac{1}{2\,det(J_{W_B})} \|J_{W_B}\|_2^2$$

$$Rotation \quad \theta = \arctan(\tfrac{j_{12} - j_{21}}{j_{11} + j_{22}})$$

It is shown in [12] that the limiting distribution does not depend on features of the infinitesimal distribution other than its spread, σ. This limiting distribution is thus least committed in the sense that it arises from the sole assumption of invariance under warps. The parameter σ may be viewed as a measure of rigidity. The effects of the parameters are shown in Fig. 1.

Scaling Skew Rotation
$S \approx 0.8, \; F = 1, \; \theta = 0$ $S = 0, \; F \approx 2, \; \theta = 0$ $S = 0, \; F = 1, \; \theta \approx 0.5$

Fig. 1. The independent action of the parameters on a unit square.

It has been proved, that this distribution creates invertible warps (with probability 1), is invariant under inversion of the warp, and is Euclidean invariant[17]. Here we prove that the distribution is invariant under simultaneous and identical warping of source and destination.

Theorem 2 (Local diffeomorphic invariance). *The distribution of warps given as spatially independent Jacobians each distributed according to Eq. 2 is invariant with respect to a diffeomorphism simultaneously acting on source and destination.*

Proof. A source and destination are related by a local Jacobean J such that $n_2 = Jn_1$, where n_1, n_2 are local frames in the source and destination image respectively. An arbitrary diffeomorphism acts locally on the frames with its

Jacoben h. Acting on source and target simultaneously makes $n_2 h = J' n_1 h$. As all h, n_1, n_2 are invertible, obviously $J = J'$.   □

This theorem only hold as a local property, but is in general valid for a whole warp if an invariant measure is used for integration over the full warp field. Construction of such a measure is, however, not trivial in the general case. WE will do so for the pairwise image matching problem below.

For computational purposes it may be convenient to approximate the above distribution by a distribution which is also independent in F and θ. This can be done in many ways without loosing the symmetry and diffeomorphic invariance. However, the semi-group property of concatenation of warps will no longer hold exactly. We suggest the following approximation.

$$p(J) \approx G_\sigma(S) G_{\sigma/\sqrt{2}}(\theta) e^{-(F/\sigma)} \tag{3}$$

where G_σ is a Gaussian of spread σ. This approximation has a relative error at less than 3% for all reasonable values of S, θ, F when $\sigma > 0.4$.

Taken from local points to a global distribution of a full warp, we may assume spatial independence of the local Jacobean of the warp. This does not correspond to assuming local independent motion of points, but that the local spatial differences in motion are distributed independently, just like independent increments (gradient) of neighboring points of a function in turn leads to Tikhonov regularization for functions. Taking this Markov Random Field approach, we may say that we formulate a first order MRF on the point motion function. The above distribution may then be viewed as Gibbs distributions, and the energy or minus-log-likelihood of a full field then reads

$$E'_s(W) = -\log p(W) + c = \int_\Omega S^2 + 2\theta^2 + 2\sigma F dx,$$

However, the integration variable is not invariant under the warp, and the functional will not lead to warp invariance. This may be obtained by using a warp invariant integration measure $d\tilde{x}$:

$$E_s(W) = -\log p(W) + c = \int_\Omega S^2 + 2\theta^2 + 2\sigma F d\tilde{x},$$

where c is an arbitrary irrelevant constant and $\tilde{x} = x\sqrt{\det(J)}$ are integration variables invariant under the warp chosen to ensure global as well as local warp invariance. It may at first glace seem *ad hoc* to introduce this invariant measure. However it also follow directly from the probabilistic theory if one takes into account that after some (of the infinitely many) warps, it is more probable to see the areas that have increased in size. This is handled elegantly in the theory by Markussen in the Ito integral of the spatio-temporal warp [16] leading to the same result.

4   Implementation

In general the warp energy Eq. 3 is augmented by an image or landmark matching term, so that the full functional to minimize for a given warp inference task reads

$$E(W) = E_s(W) + \lambda E_I(W)$$

where E_I is an image matching functional such as cross-correlation, mutual information, or landmark distance. Unfortunately the energy functional Eq. 3 is very non-linear in the coordinate functions, and simple tricks such as eigenfunction expansions and derived linear splines are not possible. Therefore we will optimize this functional using a PDE as gradient descend. We only concentrate on E_s as E_I is thoroughly treated elsewhere [9].

We treat the energy minimization problem using a gradient descend scheme:

$$\partial_t W = -\frac{\delta E}{\delta W} = -\frac{\delta E_s}{\delta W} - \frac{\delta E_I}{\delta W}$$

Here we first concentrate on E_s' (not using the invariant integration variable $\tilde{x}$ but plainly dx):

$$\frac{\delta E_s'}{\delta W} = \frac{2 \log D - 2\sigma F}{D} \frac{\delta D}{\delta W} + \frac{1}{D} \frac{\delta \|J\|_2^2}{\delta W} + 2\theta \frac{\delta \theta}{\delta W}$$

where J is the Jacoby matrix of W and $D = \det(J)$. Using the invariant coordinates (substituting $dx \mapsto \sqrt{D} dx$) this yields

$$\frac{\delta E_s}{\delta W} = \frac{H_s/2 + 2 \log D - 2\sigma F}{\sqrt{D}} \frac{\delta D}{\delta W} + \frac{1}{\sqrt{D}} \frac{\delta \|J\|_2^2}{\delta W} + 2\sqrt{D}\theta \frac{\delta \theta}{\delta W}$$

where H_s is the local energy so that $E_s = \int H_s d\tilde{x}$. The variations left in these equations are very simple as all terms are co-linear or quadratic in coordinate functions of W.

Using E_s' directly serves the problem that the solution is no longer source-target symmetric as emphasis in the energy varies from point to point with respect to the local scaling. Using E_s in its full form using the invariant integration variable solves this problem.

On a bounded domain, this will lead to a simultaneous minimization on the size of the domain, to minimize the functional, and hence a bias toward shrinking warps. It will no longer give meaningful warps directly. This may be solved by fixing the size of the invariant domain directly using a Lagrange multiplier in the optimization problem. Now

$$E_{s-\text{bounded}} = \int_\Omega H_s d\tilde{x} + \lambda \int_\Omega d\tilde{x}$$

we directly solve for λ using the fact that the time evolution of $\int_\Omega d\tilde{x}$ vanishes if

$$\lambda = \frac{E_s'}{\int_\Omega d\tilde{x}}$$

By simple calculus of variation we obtain:

$$\frac{\delta E_{s-\text{bounded}}}{\delta W} = \frac{\lambda\sqrt{D} + H_s/2 + 2\log D - 2\sigma F}{\sqrt{D}}\frac{\delta D}{\delta W} + \frac{1}{\sqrt{D}}\frac{\delta\|J\|_2^2}{\delta W} + 2\sqrt{D}\theta\frac{\delta\theta}{\delta W}$$

where λ must be updated along the evolution. As λ is in integral measure, this actually is not a PDE but a partial integral-differential equation. So far, we have no proofs of stability of uniqueness of the solution. However, it works in the practical solution. It does not fall within the class for which uniqueness has been proved [9]. It also works on a totally different function space, since in previous work [9] the warps have been living in component-wise Sobolev spaces which has a non-empty intersection with the space of diffeomorphisms. However some diffeomorphisms are not in the Sobolev space, and some members of the component-wise Sobolev space does fold and are obviously not diffeomorphisms.

This algorithm guarantees that the resulting warp is a diffeomorphism. It corresponds to some degree to the large deformation diffeomorphisms by Joshi and Miller [14] in the sense that their formulation also seek a solution composed over many time steps. However, we have succeeded in integrating out the time, and found the closed form solution for the resulting functional. Hence, we find the solution directly by optimizing the warp, and not by optimizing the warp, and all the intermediate steps, from source to destination. An interesting theoretical link between the two approaches is found in Markussen [16], where a warp-time discretization is performed, but where a Brownian motion formulation is used.

Now turning toward discretization of the above algorithm: For time discretization we use a simple explicit scheme with alternating gradient descend step along the above variant and update of λ. For spatial discretization we approximate for every grid point the Jacoby as both forward and backward scheme in both coordinate giving the combinations of totally 12 discrete Jacobians in every grid point (see Fig. 2). Let us denote these $J_t, t \in [1; 12]$. The discretization

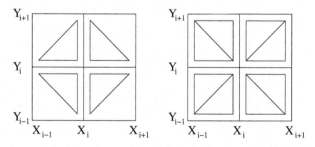

Fig. 2. In every point (x_i, y_i), the local Jacobean is estimated from the 12 local discrete frames including the point. To the left, the four frames, where the point contributes centrally, are illustrated, whereas the 8 frames where the point contributes to in extremal position are illustrated to the right.

of the variation is then performed as

$$\frac{\delta E_d}{\delta W} = \sum_t \frac{\lambda\sqrt{D_t} + H_{s,t}/2 + 2\log D_t - 2\sigma F_t}{\sqrt{D_t}} \frac{\delta D_t}{\delta W} + \frac{1}{\sqrt{D_t}}\frac{\delta\|J_t\|_2^2}{\delta W} + 2\sqrt{D_t}\theta\frac{\delta\theta_t}{\delta W}$$

The summation can not be performed by first summing over the variational parts as for example

$$\sum_t \frac{\delta D_t}{\delta W} = 0$$

At the boundary, the contributions from the discrete Jacobean leaving the domain are neglected, as the free boundary conditions are implemented in this way.

5 Results

We see from the energy formulation that the rigidity parameter determines the relative weight of the skewness term to the scaling and rotation terms. For illustration of the independent terms, see Fig. 3. For large deformations, the difference to spline-based methods, becomes obvious as for example thin plate splines can introduce folds in the warping (see Fig. 4).

For testing the source-target symmetry we conducted the following experiment. We kept the boundary fixed and moved two random points in the interior with a Brownian motion to new random positions (see Fig 5).

The figures clearly show that the warp generated by the above algorithm is statistically significant more symmetric than thin-plate spline warps. The motion

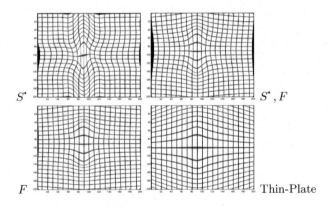

Fig. 3. Illustration of deformation of a regular grid. Two points in the center have been moved up and down respectively, while the corners are kept fixed. We see that the scaling term (top left) aims at keeping the area constant. The skewness term (bottom left) aims at keeping the stretch equally large in all directions. Top right is a combination of scaling and skewness ($\sigma = 1$). Bottom right is a thin plate spline for comparison.

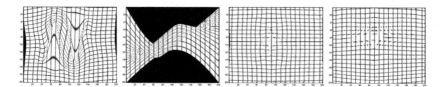

Fig. 4. Leftmost are two images of large deformations: Left is the maximum likelihood Brownian warp, right is a thin plate spline. Rightmost two images are two consecutive warps where landmark motions are inverse: Left is Brownian warps, right is thin plate spline. Brownian warps do not give the exact inverse due to numerical impression, but closer than the thin plate spline.

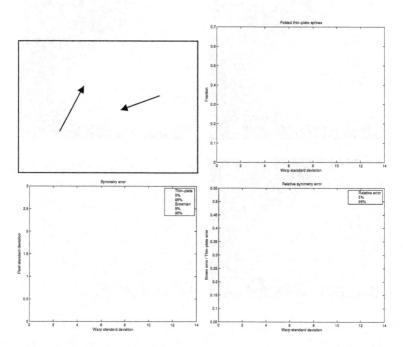

Fig. 5. Top-left the warp carried out at random is illustrated. Top-right is the fraction of thin-plate warps that contains a fold (is not invertible) as function of the spread of the random motion of the two interior point. Below is the absolute error in pixel position warping forward and concatenating with the backward warp. To the right is the same for the relative error of the Brownian warps and the thin-plate warps. 25 runs for each standard deviation on a 50 × 50 grid was performed. All error bounds are bootstrapped 90% confindence intervals.

of points after warping forward and back are less than a third than in the case of thin plate splines. Hence, not only is the theory symmetric, implementations show significant improvements. However, the warps are not totally symmetric, which to our opinion is due to the spatial discretization, as the error is smaller on a 50 × 50 grid than on a 10 × 10 grid.

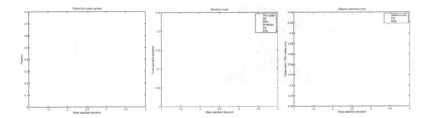

Fig. 6. As previous figure, but with 200 runs for each standard deviation on a 10×10 grid.

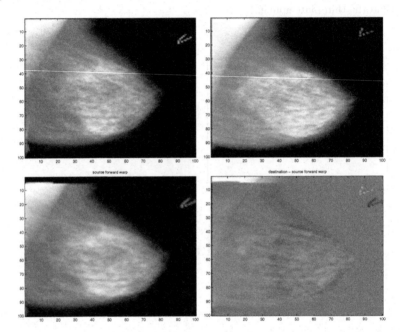

Fig. 7. Top-left a mammography taken in 1999. Top-right a mammography of the same breast taken in 2001 after hormonal treatment. Bottom-left 1999 breast warped to 2001. Bottom-right difference image. The correlaton of intensities are 0.72 without warping, 0.86 with thin plate warping, and 0.92 with Brownian warping.

6 Conclusion

We have exploited a prior for warps based on a simple invariance principle under warping. This distribution is the warp analogue of Brownian motion for additive actions. An estimation based on this prior guarantees an invertible, source–destination symmetric, and warp-invariant warp. When computational time is of concern, approximations can be made which violate the basic semi-group property while maintaining the invariances. For fast implementations, we recommend an approximation including only the skewness term, as this has nice regularizing properties.

We have developed a PDE scheme for implementing an algorithm computing the maximum-likelihood warp. We have tested this in the case of exact landmark matching, and shown that it does not fold (as theory predicts) as linear approaches will do, and shown that also in discrete approximation, the scheme yields solutions very close to being source-target symmetric.

Future work includes a joint optimization scheme with other image matching terms as used earlier [9]. As a final illustration we show an example of warping a mammogram in Figure 7, where the Brownian warping increases the intensity correlation compared to thin-plate warping.

References

1. A.A. Amini, R.W. Curwen, and J.C. Gore, *Snakes and splines for tracking non-rigid heart motion*, ECCV96, 1996, pp. II:251–261.
2. Per R. Andresen and Mads Nielsen, *Non-rigid registration by geometry-constrined diffusion*, Medical Image Analysis **6** (2000), 81–88.
3. R. Bajcsy and S. Kovacic, *Multiresolution elastic matching*, CVGIP **46** (1989), 1–21.
4. F.L. Bookstein, *Morphometric tools for landmark data: Geometry and biology*, Cambridge University Press, 1991.
5. M. Bro-Nielsen and C. Gramkow, *Fast fluid registration of medical images*, Proc. Visualization in Biomedical Imaging (VBC'96) (1996), 267–276.
6. P. Cachier and D. Rey, *Symmetrization of the Non-Rigid Registration Probem using Inversion-Invariant Energies: Application to Multiple Sclerosis*, Third International Conference on Medical Robotics, Imaging And Computer Assisted Surgery (MICCAI 2000) (Pittsburgh, Pennsylvanie USA) (A.M. DiGioia and S. Delp, eds.), Lectures Notes in Computer Science, vol. 1935, Springer, octobre 11-14 2000.
7. G.E. Christensen and J. He, *Consistent nonlinear elastic image registration*, MMBIA01, 2001, pp. xx–yy.
8. G.E. Christensen, M. I. Miller, and M. Vannier, *A 3d deformable magnetic resonance textbook based on elasticity*, AAAI Spring Symposion Series (1994), 153–156, Standford University.
9. Olivier Faugeras and Gerardo Hermosillo, *Well-posedness of eight problems of multi-modal statistical image-matching.*, Tech. report, INRIA, August 2001, Research Report 4235.
10. R. D. Gill and S. Johansen, *A survey of product-integration with a view toward application un survival analysis*, The annals of statistics **18** (1990), no. 4, 1501–1555.
11. G. Högnäs and A. Mukherjea, *Probability measures on semigroups*, Plenum Press, 1995.
12. A D Jackson, B Lautrup, P Johansen, and Mads Nielsen., *Products of random matrices*, Tech. report, Phys Rev E 66(6):5 article 66124, 2002.
13. E. T. Jaynes, *Probability theory: The logic of science*, http://omega.albany.edu:8008/JaynesBook.html, Fragmentary Edition of June 1994.
14. S. Joshi and M M Miller, *Landmark matching via large deformation diffeomorphisms*, IEEE IP **9** (2000), no. 8, 1357–1370.
15. J. Maintz and M. Viergever, *A survey of medical image registration*, 1998.

16. Bo Markussen, *Minimal variation filtration of flows of diffeomorphisms*, Theory of probability (2003).
17. Mads Nielsen, Peter Johansen, and A D Jacksonand B Lautrup, *Brownian warps*, Miccai 2002, LNCS 2489, Tokyo, 2002.
18. Jorma Rissanen, *Stochastic complexity in statistical enquiry*, World Scientific Publishing Company, Singapore, 1989.
19. K. Rohr, *Landmark-based image analysis: Using geometric and intensity models*, Kluwer, 2001.
20. D. Rueckert, L.I. Sonoda, C. Hayes, D.L.G. Hill, M.O. Leach, and D.J. Hawkes, *Nonrigid registration using free-form deformations: application to breast mr images*, MedImg **18** (1999), no. 8, 712–721.
21. P.A. Viola and W.M. Wells, III, *Alignment by maximization of mutual information*, Ph. D., 1995.

Stereovision-Based Head Tracking Using Color and Ellipse Fitting in a Particle Filter

Bogdan Kwolek

Rzeszów University of Technology, W. Pola 2, 35-959 Rzeszów, Poland
bkwolek@prz.rzeszow.pl

Abstract. This paper proposes the use of a particle filter combined with color, depth information, gradient and shape features as an efficient and effective way of dealing with tracking of a head on the basis of image stream coming from a mobile stereovision camera. The head is modeled in the 2D image domain by an ellipse. A weighting function is used to include spatial information in color histogram representing the interior of the ellipse. The lengths of the ellipse's minor axis are determined on the basis of depth information. The dissimilarity between the current model of the tracked object and target candidates is indicated by a metric based on Bhattacharyya coefficient. Variations of the color representation as a consequence of ellipse's size change are handled by taking advantage of the scale invariance of the similarity measure. The color histogram and parameters of the ellipse are dynamically updated over time to discriminate in the next iteration between the candidate and actual head representation. This makes possible to track not only a face profile which has been shot during initialization of the tracker but in addition different profiles of the face as well as the head can be tracked. Experimental results which were obtained on long image sequences in a typical office environment show the feasibility of our approach to perform tracking of a head undergoing complex changes of shape and appearance against a varying background. The resulting system runs in real-time on a standard laptop computer installed on a real mobile agent.

1 Introduction

Visual tracking of objects in video sequences is becoming an important task in a wide range of applications utilizing computer vision interfaces, including human action recognition, teleconferencing, robot teleoperation as well as human-computer interaction. Many different trackers for various tasks have been developed in recent years and particular interests and research activities have increased significantly in vision-based methods. One of the purposes of visual tracking is to estimate the states of objects of interest from an image sequence. However, cluttered backgrounds, unknown and changing lighting conditions and multiple moving objects make the vision-based tracking tasks challenging. Some vision-based systems allow a determination of a body position and real-time tracking of head and hands. Pfinder [1] uses a multi-class statistical model of color and shape to obtain a blob representation of the tracked silhouette in a

T. Pajdla and J. Matas (Eds.): ECCV 2004, LNCS 3024, pp. 192–204, 2004.
© Springer-Verlag Berlin Heidelberg 2004

wide spectrum of viewing conditions. In the techniques known as CamShift [2] and MeanShift [3] the current frame is searched for a region in a variable-size window, whose color content matches best a reference model. The searching process proceeds iteratively starting from the final location in the previous frame. The new object location is calculated based on the mean shift vector as an estimation of the gradient of the Bhattacharyya function. This method requires that the new target center lies within the kernel centered on the previous location of the target. The original application of the particle filter in computer vision was for object tracking in an image sequence [4]. Particle filtering is now a popular solution to problems relying on visual tracking. In the work of [5] a fixed ellipse is used to approximate the head outline during 2D tracking on the basis of the particle filter. A system developed recently by Chen *et al.* [6] uses a causal 1D contour model in dynamic programming to find the best contour with respect to a given initial one. A five dimensional ellipse is used to represent the head contour in multiple hypothesis framework. Nummiaro *et al.* [7] used an ellipse with fixed orientation to model a head and to extract the color distribution of the ellipse's interior. The likelihood is calculated on the basis of weighted histogram representing both color and shape of the head. Global color reference models and Bhattacharyya coefficient as a similarity measure between the color distribution of the model and target candidates have been used in a Monte Carlo tracker [8]. A histogram representation of the region of interest has been extracted in a rectangular window. Recently, the laser range fingers have been used to track people in populated environments for interactive robot applications [9].

In this paper, we focus our attention on tracking human head/face, one of the most important features in tasks consisting in people tracking and action recognition. The main objective of the research is to detect and track the head to perform person following with a real mobile agent which is equipped with an on-board camera. The initial position of the head to be tracked is determined by means of face detection. We consider scenarios where a stereo camera is mounted on a mobile agent and our aim is tracking the head which can undergo complex changes of shape and appearance. The appearance of the object of interest changes continuously due to non-rigid human motion and a change in viewpoints. There are many other difficulties in extracting features distinguishing the target and challenge lies in the fact that a background may not be static. We consider the problem of head tracking by taking advantage of gradient, color together with shape as well as depth information which are combined with the particle filter. One of the problems of tracking on the basis of color is that lighting conditions may have influence on perceived color of the target. Even in the case of constant lighting conditions, the seeming color of the target may change over a frame sequence, since the target can be shadowed by other objects. The color distributions representing the target in image sequences are therefore not stationary.

The main goal of the tracker is to find the most probable sample distribution. The particles representing the candidate ellipses are verified in respect of intensity gradient near the edge of the ellipse and matching score of the color histograms representing the interior of an ellipse surrounding the tracked object and currently analyzed one. During samples weighting stage in which candidate ellipses are considered one after another, the projected ellipse size into image is dependent on the depth information. The color histogram and parameters of the ellipse are dynamically updated over time to discriminate in the next iteration between the candidate and actual head representation.

The contribution of our work lies in the use of particle filters combined with mentioned above cues to robustly solve a difficult and a useful problem of head tracking in color images. The tracker has been evaluated in experiments consisting in face tracking with a stereovision camera mounted on a real mobile agent. A version of the tracker which utilizes gradient, color as well as shape information combined with particle filters has been evaluated using the PETS-ICVS 2003 video data set which is provided to conduct experiments relating to smart meeting room.

The rest of the paper is organized as follows. In the next section we briefly describe particle filtering. The usage of color cue, gradient, shape information and stereovision in a particle filter is explained in section 3. In sections 4 and 5 we report results which were obtained in experiments. Finally, some conclusions follow in the last section.

2   Particle Filtering

In this section we formulate the visual tracking problem in a probabilistic framework. Among the tracking methods, the ones based on particle filters have attracted much attention recently and have proved as robust solutions to reduce the computational cost by searching only those regions of the image where the object is predicted to be. The key idea underlying all particle filters is to approximate the probability distribution by a weighted sample collection.

The state of the tracked object at time t is denoted $\mathbf{x}_t$ and its history is $X_t = \{\mathbf{x}_1, ..., \mathbf{x}_t\}$. Similarly the set of image features at time t is $\mathbf{z}_t$ with history $Z_t = \{\mathbf{z}_1, ..., \mathbf{z}_t\}$. The evolution of the state forms a temporal Markov chain so that the new state is conditioned directly on the immediately preceding state and independent of the earlier state, $p(\mathbf{x}_t \mid X_{t-1}) = p(\mathbf{x}_t \mid \mathbf{x}_{t-1})$. Observations $\mathbf{z}_t$ are assumed to be independent, both mutually and with respect to the dynamical process, $p(Z_{t-1}, \mathbf{x}_t \mid X_{t-1}) = p(\mathbf{x}_t \mid X_{t-1}) \prod_{i=1}^{t-1} p(\mathbf{z}_i \mid \mathbf{x}_i)$. The observation process is defined by the conditional density $p(\mathbf{z}_t \mid \mathbf{x}_t)$. Given a continuous-valued Markov chain with independent observations, the conditional state density $p(\mathbf{x}_t \mid Z_t)$ represents all information about the state at time t that is deducible from the entire data-stream up to that time.

We can use Bayes' rule to determine the *a posteriori* density $p(\mathbf{x}_t \mid Z_t) = p(\mathbf{x}_t \mid \mathbf{z}_t, Z_{t-1})$ from the *a priori* density $p(\mathbf{x}_t \mid Z_{t-1})$ in the following manner

$$p(\mathbf{x}_t \mid Z_t) = \frac{p(\mathbf{z}_t \mid \mathbf{x}_t, Z_{t-1})p(\mathbf{x}_t \mid Z_{t-1})}{p(\mathbf{z}_t \mid Z_{t-1})} = k_t p(\mathbf{z}_t \mid \mathbf{x}_t)p(\mathbf{x}_t \mid Z_{t-1}) \qquad (1)$$

where k_t is a normalization factor that is independent of $\mathbf{x}$ and

$$p(\mathbf{x}_t \mid Z_{t-1}) = \int_{\mathbf{X}_{t-1}} p(\mathbf{x}_t \mid \mathbf{x}_{t-1})p(\mathbf{x}_{t-1} \mid Z_{t-1})dx_{t-1} \qquad (2)$$

This equation is used to propagate the probability distribution via the transition density $p(\mathbf{x}_t \mid \mathbf{x}_{t-1})$. The density function $p(\mathbf{x}_t \mid Z_{t-1})$ depends on the immediately preceding distribution $p(\mathbf{x}_{t-1} \mid Z_{t-1})$, but not on any function prior to $t-1$, so it describes a Markov process. Multiplication by the observation density $p(\mathbf{z}_t \mid \mathbf{x}_t)$ in the equation for *a priori* density $p(\mathbf{x}_t \mid Z_{t-1})$ applies the reactive effect expected from observations. The observation density $p(\mathbf{z}_t \mid \mathbf{x}_t)$ defines the likelihood that a state $\mathbf{x}_t$ causes the measurement $\mathbf{z}_t$. The complete tracking scheme, known as the recursive Bayesian filter first calculates the *a priori* density $p(\mathbf{x}_t \mid Z_{t-1})$ using the system model and then evaluates *a posteriori* density $p(\mathbf{x}_t \mid Z_t)$ given the new measurement, $p(\mathbf{x}_{t-1} \mid Z_{t-1}) \xrightarrow{dynamics} p(\mathbf{x}_t \mid Z_{t-1}) \xrightarrow{measurement} p(\mathbf{x}_t \mid Z_t)$.

The density $p(\mathbf{x}_t \mid Z_t)$ can be very complicated in form and can have multiple peaks. The need to track more than one of these peaks results from the fact that the largest peak for any given frame may not always correspond to the right peak. The random search which is known as particle filtering has proven useful in such considerable algorithmic difficulties and allows us to extract one or another expectation. One of the attractions of sampled representations of probability distributions is that some calculations can be easily realized.

Taking a sample representation of $p(\mathbf{x}_t \mid Z_t)$, we have at each step t a set $S_t = \left\{ (\mathbf{s}_t^{(n)}, \pi_t^{(n)}) \mid n = 1...N \right\}$ of N possibly distinct samples, each with associated weight. The sample weight represents the likelihood of a particular sample being the true location of the target and is calculated by determining on the basis of depth information the ellipse's minor axis and then by computing the gradient along ellipse's boundary as well as matching score of histograms representing the interior of ellipses which bound (i) the tracked object and (ii) currently considered one. Such a sample set composes a discrete approximation of the probability distribution. The prediction step of Bayesian filtering is realized by drawing with replacement N samples from the set computed in the previous iteration, using the weights $\pi_{t-1}^{(n)}$ as the probability of drawing a sample, and by propagating their state forward in time according to the prediction model $p(\mathbf{x}_t \mid \mathbf{x}_{t-1})$. This corresponds to sampling from the transition density [10]. The new set would predominantly consist of samples that appeared in previous iteration with large weights. In the correction step, a measurement density $p(\mathbf{z}_t \mid \mathbf{x}_t)$ is used to weight the samples obtained in the prediction step, $\pi_t^{(n)} = p(\mathbf{z}_t \mid \mathbf{x}_t = \mathbf{s}^{(n)})$. The complete scheme of the sampling procedure outlined above can be summarized in the following pseudo-code:

```
S_t = Ø
for n = 0 to N do
    select k with probability π_{t-1}^{(n)} / Σ_{i=1}^{N} π_{t-1}^{(i)}
    propagate s_t^{(n)} = As_{t-1}^{(k)} + w
    calculate non-normalized weight π_t^{(n)} = p(z_t | s_t^{(n)})
    add s_t^{(n)} to S_t
endfor
```

The component A in the propagation model is deterministic and w is a multivariate Gaussian random variable. As the number of samples increases, the precision with which the samples approximate the pdf increases. The mean state can be estimated at each time step as $E[S_t] = \sum_{n=1}^{N} \mathbf{s}_t^{(n)} \pi_t^{(n)}$, where $\pi_t^{(n)}$ are normalized to sum to 1.

3   Representation of the Target Appearance

The shape of the head is one of the most easily recognizable human parts and can be reasonably well approximated by an ellipse. In work [11] a vertically oriented ellipse has been used to model the projection of a head in the image plane. The intensity gradient near the edge of the ellipse and a color histogram representing the interior were used to handle the parameters of the ellipse over time. Additionally, this method assumes that all pixels in the search area are equally important. The discussed tracking method does not work when the object being tracked temporarily disappears from the camera view or changes shape significantly between frames. In the method proposed here, an ellipse-based head likelihood model, consisting of gradient along the head boundary as well as a matching score between color histograms as a representation of the interior of (i) an ellipse surrounding the tracked object and (ii) a currently considered ellipse, together with depth information is utilized to find the weights of particles during tracking. Particle locations where the weights have large values are then considered to be the most likely locations of the object of interest. The particle set improves consistency of tracking by handling multiple peaks representing hypotheses in the distribution.

Although the use of color discrimination is connected with some fundamental problems such as the lack of robustness in varying illumination conditions, color is perceived as a very useful discrimination cue because of its computational efficiency and robustness against changes in target orientations. The human skin color filtering has proven to be effective in several settings and has been successfully applied in most of the face trackers relying primarily on color [12],[13],[14],[15] or on color in conjunction with other relevant information [16]. Color information is particularly useful to support a detection of faces in image sequences because of robustness towards changes in orientation and scaling of an appearance of object being in movement. The efficiency of color segmentation techniques is especially worth to emphasize when a considered object is occluded during tracking or is in shadow.

In our approach we use color histogram matching techniques to obtain information about possible location of the tracked target. The main idea of such an approach is to compute a color distribution in form of the color histogram from the ellipse's interior and to compare it with the computed in the same manner histogram representing the tracked object in the previous iteration. The better a histogram representing the ellipse's interior at specific particle position matches the reference histogram from previous iteration, the higher the probability that the tracked target at considered candidate position is. The outcome of the histogram matching that is combined with gradient information is used to provide information about expected target location and is utilized during weighting particles.

In the context of head tracking on the basis of images from a mobile camera the features which are invariant under head orientations are particularly useful. In general, histograms are invariant to translation and rotation of the object and they vary slowly with the change of angle of view and with the change in scale. The histogram is constructed with a function $h : R^2 \rightarrow \{1...K\}$ which associates the color at location $\mathbf{y}$ to the corresponding bin. A histogram representation can be obtained in a simple way by quantizing the ellipse's interior colors into K bins and counting the number of times each discrete color occurs. Due to the statistical nature, a color histogram can only reflect the content of images in a limited way and thus the contents of the interior of the ellipses taken at small distances apart are strongly correlated. If the number of bins K is to high, the histogram is noisy. If K is too low, density structure of the image representing the ellipse's interior is smoothed. Histogram-based techniques are effective only when K can be kept relatively low and where sufficient data amounts are available. The reduction of bins makes a comparison between the histogram representing the tracked head and the histogram of candidate head faster. Additionally, such a compact representation is tolerant to noise that can result from imperfect ellipse-approximation of a highly deformable structure and curved surface of a face causing significant variations of the observed colors. The particle filter works well when the conditional densities $p(\mathbf{z}_t \mid \mathbf{s}_t)$ are reasonably flat.

It can be demonstrated that with a change of lighting conditions the major translation of skin color distribution is along the lightness axis of the RGB color space. Skin colors acquired from a static person tend to form tight clusters in several color spaces while color acquired from moving ones form widen clusters due to different reflecting surfaces. To make the histogram representation of the tracked head less sensitive to lighting conditions the HSV color space has been chosen and the V component has been represented by 4 bins while the HS components obtained the 8-bins representation.

The histogram intersection technique [17] is a popular measure between two distributions represented by a pair of histograms I and M, each containing L values. The intersection of the histograms is defined as follows: $H = \sum_{u=1}^{K} min(I^{(u)}, M^{(u)})$, where the terms $I^{(u)}$, $M^{(u)}$ represent the number of pixels inside the u-th bucket of the candidate histogram in the current frame and the histogram representing the tracked head in the previous frame, respectively, whereas K the total number of buckets. The result of the intersection of two histograms is the number of pixels that have the same color in both histograms. To obtain a match value between zero and one the intersection is normalized and the match value is determined as follows: $H_\cap = H / \sum_{u=1}^{K} I^{(u)}$. The work [3] demonstrated that the metric $\sqrt{1 - \rho(I, M)}$ derived from Bhattacharyya coefficient ρ is invariant to the scale of the target and therefore is superior to other measures such as histogram intersection or Kullback divergence. Considering discrete densities the considered coefficient is defined as follows

$$\rho(I, M) = \sum_{u=1}^{K} \sqrt{I^{(u)} M^{(u)}} \tag{3}$$

Given the center of the target, a feature distribution including spatial information in color histogram can be calculated using a 2-dimensional kernel centered on the target center [18]. The kernel is used to provide the weight for a particular feature according to its distance from the center of the kernel. In order to assign smaller weights to the pixels that are further away from the region center a nonnegative and monotonic decreasing function $k : [0, \infty) \to R$ can be used [18]. The probability of particular histogram bin u at location $\mathbf{y}$ is calculated as

$$d_{\mathbf{y}}^{(u)} = C_a \sum_{i=1}^{L} k \left(\left\| \frac{\mathbf{y} - \mathbf{y}_i}{a} \right\|^2 \right) \delta \left[h(\mathbf{y}_i) - u \right] \tag{4}$$

where $\mathbf{y}_i$ are pixel locations of the face candidate, L is the number of pixels in the region, δ is the Kronecker delta function and constant a is the radius of the kernel. The normalization factor

$$C_a = \frac{1}{\sum_{i=1}^{L} k \left(\left\| \frac{\mathbf{y} - \mathbf{y}_i}{a} \right\|^2 \right)}$$

ensures that $\sum_{u=1}^{K} d_{\mathbf{y}}^{(u)} = 1$. This normalization constant can be precalculated [3] for the utilized kernel and assumed values of a. The 2-dimensional kernels have been prepared offline and then stored in lookup tables for the future use.

The length of the minor axis of a considered ellipse is determined on the basis of depth information. Taking into account the length of the minor axis resulting from the depth information we also considered smaller and larger projection scale of the ellipse and therefore a larger as well as smaller minor axis about one pixel have been taken into account as well. The length of the minor axis has been maintained by performing the local search to maximize the goodness of the following match: $w^* = \arg\max_{w_i \in W} \{G(w_i) H_S(w_i)\}$, where G and H_S are normalized scores based on intensity gradients and color histogram similarity. In order to favor head candidates whose color distributions are similar to the target color distribution we utilized Gaussian weighting with σ variance [7]

$$H_S = \frac{1}{\sqrt{2\pi}\sigma} e^{-\frac{1-\rho}{2\sigma^2}} \tag{5}$$

where small Bhattacharyya distances correspond to large matching scores. The search space W comprises the ellipse's length obtained on the basis of depth information as well as smaller/larger minor axes about one pixel.

The samples are propagated on the basis of a dynamic model $\mathbf{s}_t = A\mathbf{s}_{t-1} + w_t$, where A denotes a deterministic component describing a constant velocity movement and w_t is a multivariate Gaussian random variable. The diffusion component represents uncertainty in prediction and therefore provides a way of performing a local search about a state. The weight of each hypothetical head region

$\pi_t^{(n)}$ is dependent on normalized intensity gradients and color histogram similarity which were obtained for the length of minor axis w^*.

The elliptical upright outlines with an assumed fixed aspect ratio equal to 1.4 have been prepared and stored for the future use in the construction phase. For each possible length of the minor axis we prepared off-line an elliptical outline to compute gradient and kernel lookup table to include spatial information in color histograms. Expanding the algorithm about non-upright ellipses is straightforward.

The histogram representing the tracked head has been adapted over time. This makes possible to track not only a face profile which has been shot during initialization of the tracker but in addition different profiles of the face as well as the head can be tracked. The actualization of the histogram has been realized on the basis of the equation $M_t^{(u)} = (1-\alpha)M_{t-1}^{(u)} + \alpha I_t^{(u)}$, where α is accommodation rate, I_t represents the histogram of the interior of the mean state ellipse, M_t the histogram of the target from previous frame, whereas $u = 1...K$.

4 Tracking on the Basis of Moving Camera

A kind of human-machine interaction which is useful in practice and can be very serviceable in testing a robustness of a tracking algorithm is person following with a mobile robot. In work [19] the condensation-based algorithm is utilized to keep track of multiple objects with a moving robot. The tracking experiments described in this section were carried out with a mobile robot Pioneer 2 DX [20] equipped with commercial binocular Megapixel Stereo Head. The dense stereo maps are extracted in that system thanks to small area correspondences between image pairs [21] and therefore poor results in regions of little texture are often provided. The depth map covering a face region is usually dense because a human face is rich in details and texture, see Fig. 1. Thanks to such a property this stereovision system provides a separate source of information and considerably supports the process of approximating the tracked head with an ellipse.

A typical laptop computer equipped with 2 GHz Pentium IV is utilized to run the prepared visual tracker operating at 320x240 images. The position of the tracked face in the image plane as well as person's distance to the camera are written asynchronously in block of common memory which can be easily

Fig. 1. Depth images (frame 1 and frame 600)

accessed by Saphira client. Saphira is an integrated sensing and control system architecture based on a client server-model whereby the robot supplies a set of basic functions that can be used to interact with it [20]. Every 100 milliseconds the robot server sends a message packet containing information on the velocity of the vehicle as well as sensor readings to the client. During tracking, the control module keeps the user face within the camera field of view by coordinating the rotation of the robot with the location of the tracked face in the image plane. The aim of the robot orientation controller is to keep the position of the tracked face at specific position in the image. The linear velocity has been dependent on person's distance to the camera. In experiments consisting in person following a distance 1.6 m has been assumed as the reference value that the linear velocity controller should maintain. To eliminate needless robot rotations as well as forward and backward movements we have applied a simple logic providing necessary insensitivity zone. The PD controllers have been implemented in the Saphira-interpreted Colbert language [20]. The tracking algorithm was implemented in C/C++ and runs at a frame rate about 10 Hz depending on image complexity.

We have undertaken experiments consisting in following a person facing the camera within walking distance without the tracked face loss. Experiments consisting in realization of only a rotation of mobile robot which can be seen as analogous to experiments with a pan-camera have also been conducted. In such experiments a user moved about a room, walked back and forth as well as around the mobile robot. The aim of such a scenario was to evaluate the quality of ellipse scaling in response of varying distance between the camera and the user during person following. Our experiment findings show that thanks to stereovision the ellipse is properly scaled and therefore because of appropriate head approximation, sudden changes of the minor axis length as well as ellipse's jumps are considerably eliminated. Figure 2 indicates selected frames from the discussed scenario, see also Fig. 1. The color of the door is very similar to that of human face and it can cause great difficulty to color-based tracking algorithms, see also image from frame 390 in Fig. 2. The region cue reflected by weighted color histogram varies slowly with slow translation of the target but does not express appropriately the content of the image with reduced scale, see image from frame 600 in Fig. 2. The likelihood model combining gradient information with a weighted histogram of the ellipse's interior demonstrated abilities to localize target correctly in case of reduced scale. The gradient modality complement the color modality when the object is moving because color information may become unreliable due to changes in the object pose and illumination, whereas strong localization cues may be obtained from the gradient information. The gradient information can therefore improve the accommodation of the color model over time. In particular, the depth information allows us to set accommodation rate α to zero when face is localized above an assumed distance to the camera.

The depth map covering the face region is usually dense and this together with skin-color and symmetry information as well as eyes-template assorted with the depth has allowed us to apply the eigenfaces method [22] and to detect the presence of the vertical and frontal-view faces in the scene very reliably and thus to initialize the tracker automatically. Thanks to the head position it is possible to recognize some static commands on the basis of geometrical relations of the face and hands and to interact with mobile robot during person following. Using the discussed system we have realized experiments in which the robot has followed a person at distances which beyond 100 m without the person loss. By dealing with multiple hypotheses this approach can track a head reliably in cases of temporal occlusions and varying illumination conditions.

Fig. 2. Face tracking relying only upon a rotation of the moving camera (frames 1,35,390,600)

5 Evaluation Using PETS-ICVS Data Sets

The experiments described in this section have been realized on the basis of PETS-ICVS data set which has been prepared in smart meeting room. The aim of the experiments was to track the meeting participants based on static color camera. The images of size 576x720 have been converted to size of 320x240 by subsampling (consisting in selecting odd pixels in only odd lines) and bicubic based image scaling. Initialization of the tracker has been performed by searching for an elliptical object in determined in advance head-entry and head-exit zones. A simple background subtraction procedure which was executed in mentioned above boxes has proven to be sufficient in person entry/exit detection. In this version of the tracker a sample in distribution represents an ellipse described by $s = \{\mathbf{y}, \dot{\mathbf{y}}, l, \dot{l}\}$, where $\mathbf{y}$ denotes the location in the xy-image plane, $\dot{\mathbf{y}}$ motion, l the length of the minor axis and $\dot{l}$ corresponding scale change.

Figure 3 depicts example frames from a typical experiment of Scenario C which was viewed from Camera 1. The frame 13667 demonstrates a behavior of the tracker in case of non-upright head orientation. Because of only vertical orientation of the ellipses which has been assumed in advance, the tracker fitted an ellipse in a search region in the proximity of the true location. Such a tug work of the tracker has been observed at 15 succeeded frames and after that the algorithm continued a smooth tracking of the head. In frames 13765, 13917, 14140 we can perceive a poor approximation of the head of the third person by an ellipse. But such undesirable effect has been observed occasionally during processing of PETS data sets. The number of poor misfits can be greatly reduced by utilizing the nearly constant distance of the tracked person to the camera and thus by operating with smaller range of lengths of the ellipse's minor axis. The experiments described in this section have been conducted using a relatively large range of the axis lengths which were needed during person following, namely from 6 to 30. A typical length of the ellipse's axis for the presented in the Fig. 3 frame range is about 11. Another method of improving the robustness of the tracker in situations where misfits have been observed is to combine it with fast and robust algorithm for detecting faces with out-of-plan rotation [23].

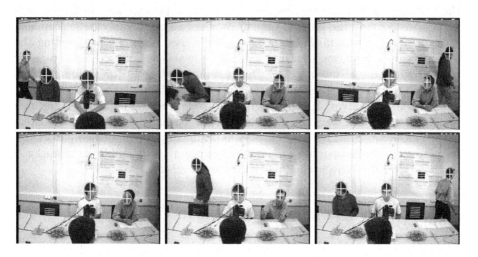

Fig. 3. Frames 11224, 13667, 13765, 13917, 14140, 14842 of Scenario C

Figure 4 illustrates example frames of tracking on the basis of the CamShift algorithm [2]. The tracker has been initialized in frame 10952, see the left frame in Fig. 4, with number of bins equals 30, Smin=40 and Vmin=60.

6   Conclusion

We have presented a vision module that robustly tracks and detects a human face. By employing shape, color, stereovision as well as elliptical shape features the proposed method can track a head in case of dynamic background. The combination of above-mentioned cues and particle filter seems to have a considerable

Fig. 4. Face tracking using CamShift

perspective of applications in robotics and surveillance. The algorithm is robust to sensor noise and uncertainty in localization. The resulting particle filter was able to track the head reliably, even during varying lighting conditions. Moreover, the particle filtering performs satisfactory even in the presence of partial occlusions. To show the correct work of the system, we have conducted several experiments in naturally occurring in laboratory circumstances. In particular, the tracking module enables the robot to follow a person. Thanks to the real-time robot control, the moving camera provides a considerably large searching area for a vision system. Face tracking can be used not only for directing the vision system's attention to a user/intruder but also as a prerequisite stage for face recognition and human action understanding. One of the future research directions of the presented approach is to explore the unscented particle filter [7],[24]. One difficulty of utilizing of gradient along the head boundary is the high nonlinearity of the observation likelihood and even small difference in parameters of the ellipse could involve large changes in likelihood. The unscented particle filter places the limited particles in an effective way in comparable computational overhead over the conventional particle filtering scheme.

Acknowledgment. This work has been supported by KBN within the project 4T11C01224

References

1. Wren, C., Azarbayejani, A., Darrell, T., Pentland, A.: Pfinder: Real-Time Tracking of the Human Body, IEEE Trans. on PAMI **19**(7) (1997) 780–785
2. Bradski, G.R.: Computer Vision Face Tracking as a Component of a Perceptual User Interface, In Proc. IEEE Workshop on Applications of Comp. Vision, Princeton (1998) 214–219
3. Recognition Comaniciu, D., Ramesh, V., Meer, P.: Real-Time Tracking of Non-Rigid Objects Using Mean Shift, In Proc. of IEEE Conf. on Comp. Vision and Pat. Rec. (2000) 142–149
4. Isard, M., Blake, A.: Contour Tracking by Stochastic Propagation of Conditional Density, European Conf. on Computer Vision, Cambridge (1996) 343–356
5. Rui, Y., Chen, Y.: Better Proposal Distributions: Object Tracking Using Unscented Particle Filter, In Proc. IEEE Conf. on Comp. Vision and Pat. Rec. (2001) 786–793

6. Chen, Y., Rui, Y., Huang, T.: Mode-based Multi-Hypothesis Head Tracking Using Parametric Contours, In Proc. IEEE Int. Conf. on Aut. Face and Gesture Rec. (2002) 112–117
7. Nummiaro, K., Koller-Meier, E., Van Gool, L.: An Adaptive Color-Based Particle Filter, Image and Vision Computing **21**(1) (2003) 99–110
8. Perez, P., Hue, C., Vermaak, J., Gangnet, M.: Color-Based Probabilistic Tracking, European Conf. on Computer Vision (2002) 661–675
9. Schulz, D., Burgard, W., Fox, D., Cremers A.B.: Tracking Multiple Moving Targets with a Mobile Robot using Particle Filters and Statistical Data Association, In Proc. of the IEEE Int. Conf. on Robotics and Automation (2001) 1665–1670
10. Isard, M., Blake, A.: A Mixed-State Condensation Tracker with Automatic Model-Switching, In Proc. of IEEE Int. Conf. on Comp. Vision, Mumbai (1998) 107–112
11. Recognition, Santa Birchfield, S.: Elliptical Head Tracking Using Intensity Gradients and Color Histograms, In Proc. of IEEE Conf. on Comp. Vision and Pat. Rec., Santa Barbara (1998) 232–237
12. Hunke, M., Waibel, A.: Face Locating and Tracking for Human-Computer Interaction, In Proc. of the 28th Asilomar Conf. on Signals, Systems and Computers (1994) 1277–1281
13. Fieguth, P., Terzopoulos, D.: Color-Based Tracking of Heads and Other Mobile Objects at Video Frame Rates, In Proc. of the IEEE Conf. on Comp. Vision Pat. Rec., Hilton Head Island (1997) 21–27
14. Schwerdt, K., Crowley, J.L.: Robust Face Tracking Using Color, In Proc. of the Int. Conf. on Automatic Face and Gesture Rec. (2000) 90–95
15. Sobottka, K., Pitas, I.: Segmentation and Tracking of Faces in Color Images, In Proc. of the Second Int. Conf. on Automatic Face and Gesture Rec. (1996) 236–241
16. Darrell, T., Gordon, G., Harville, M., Woodfill, J.: Integrated Person Tracking Using Stereo, Color, and Pattern Detection, Proc. of IEEE Conf. on Computer Vision and Pat. Rec., Santa Barbara (1998) 601–609
17. Swain, M.J., Ballard, D.H.: Color Indexing, Int. Journal of Computer Vision **7**(1) (1991) 11–32
18. Cheng, Y.: Mean Shift, Mode Seeking, and Clustering, IEEE Trans. on PAMI **17**(8) (1995) 790–799
19. Meier, E.B., Ade, F.: Using the Condensation Algorithm to Implement Tracking for Mobile Robots, In Proc. of the Third European Workshop on Advanced Mobile Robots (1999) 73–80
20. ActivMedia Robotics, Pioneer 2 mobile robots (2001)
21. Konolige, K.: Small Vision System: Hardware and Implementation, Proc. of Int. Symp. on Robotics Research, Hayama (1997) 111–116
22. Turk, M.A., Pentland, A.P.: Face Recognition Using eigenfaces, Proc. of IEEE Conf. on Comp. Vision and Pat. Rec. (1991) 586–591
23. Schneiderman, H., Kanade, T.: A Histogram-Based Method for Detection of Faces and Cars, In Proc. of the 2000 Int. Conf. on Image Processing (2000) 504–507
24. Merwe, R., Doucet, A., Freitas, N., Wan, E.: The Unscented Particle Filter, Advances in Neural Information Processing Systems (2000) 584–590

Parallel Variational Motion Estimation by Domain Decomposition and Cluster Computing

Timo Kohlberger[1], Christoph Schnörr[1], Andrés Bruhn[2], and Joachim Weickert[2]

. University of Mannheim, Dept. of Mathematics and Computer Science,
D-68131 Mannheim, Germany
{kohlberger,schnoerr}@uni-mannheim.de
http://www.cvgpr.uni-mannheim.de
. Saarland University, Dept. of Mathematics and Computer Science,
D-66041 Saarbrücken, Germany
{bruhn,weickert}@mia.uni-saarland.de
http://www.mia.uni-saarland.de

Abstract. We present an approach to parallel variational optical flow computation on standard hardware by domain decomposition. Using an arbitrary partition of the image plane into rectangular subdomains, the *global* solution to the variational approach is obtained by iteratively combining *local* solutions which can be efficiently computed in parallel by separate multi-grid iterations for each subdomain. The approach is particularly suited for implementations on PC-clusters because inter-process communication between subdomains (i.e. processors) is minimized by restricting the exchange of data to a *lower*-dimensional interface. By applying a dedicated interface preconditioner, the necessary number of iterations between subdomains to achieve a fixed error is bounded independently of the number of subdomains. Our approach provides a major step towards real-time 2D image processing using off-the-shelf PC-hardware and facilitates the efficient application of variational approaches to large-scale image processing problems.

1 Introduction

1.1 Overview and Motivation

Motion estimation in terms of optical flow [3,25] is an important prerequisite for many applications of computer vision including surveillance, robot navigation, and dynamic event recognition. Since real-time computation is required in many cases, much work has been done on parallel implementations of *local* motion estimation schemes (differential-, correlation-, or phase-based methods) [31,14]).

In contrast to local estimation schemes, less work has been done on the parallelization of *non-local variational* schemes for motion estimation, despite considerable progress during the last years related to robustness, non-linear regularization schemes, preservation of motion boundaries, and corresponding successful applications [27,26,13,1,1,21, 5,28,20,18,4,15,23,32,11,24]. It is precisely the *non-local* nature of these approaches which on the one hand allows to impose structural constraints on motion fields during estimation but, on the other hand, hampers a straightforward parallel implementation by simply partitioning the image domain into disjoint subdomains (see Figure 1).

T. Pajdla and J. Matas (Eds.): ECCV 2004, LNCS 3024, pp. 205–216, 2004.
© Springer-Verlag Berlin Heidelberg 2004

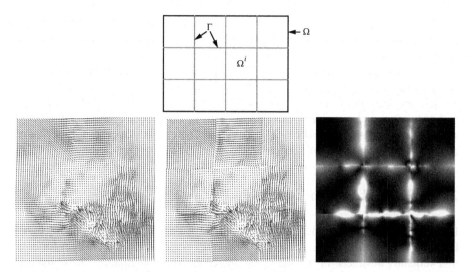

Fig. 1. Top: A partition of the image domain Ω into subdomains $\{\Omega^i\}$ and a lower-dimensional interface Γ. **Bottom, left:** Motion field estimated with a non-local variational approach. **Bottom, center:** Naive parallelization by estimating motion independently in each subdomain leads to boundary effects (a coarse 3×3 partition was used for better visibility). **Bottom, right:** The $l.$ -error caused by naive parallelization as grayvalue plot. The *global* relative error is 11.3%. The *local* error near boundaries of subdomains is much higher!

This motivates to investigate computational approaches for the parallelization of variational motion estimation by means of domain decompositions as shown in Figure 1, top. Ideally, any of the approaches cited above should be applicable independently in each subdomain. In addition to that, however, a mechanism is needed which fits together the subdomain solutions so as to yield the same global solution which is obtained when applying the respective approach in the usual non-parallel way to the entire image domain Ω. The investigation of such a scheme is the objective of this paper.

1.2   Contribution and Organization

We present an approach to the parallelization of *variational* optical flow computation which fulfils the following requirements:

(i) Suitability for the implementation on PC-clusters through the minimization of inter-process communication,
(ii) use of a mathematical framework which allows for applications to a large class of variational models.

In order to meet requirement (ii), our approach draws upon the general mathematical theory on domain decomposition in connection with the solution of partial differential equations [9,30,29]. Requirement (i) addresses a major source for degrading the performance of message-passing based parallel architectures. To this end, we focus on the subclass of *substructuring methods* because inter-process communication is minimized by restricting the exchange of data to a *lower*-dimensional interface between the subdomains.

After sketching a prototypical variational approach to motion estimation in section 2, we develop a corresponding domain decomposition framework in section 3. In section 4, we describe features of our parallel implementation, the crucial design of an interface-preconditioner, and report the influence of both preconditioning and the number of subdomains on the convergence rate. Finally, we report measurements for experiments on a PC-cluster with nodes in section 5.

2   Variational Motion Estimation

In this section, we sketch the prototypical variational approach of Horn and Schunck [19] and its discretization as a basis for domain decomposition. Note that our formulation suffiently abstracts for this particular approach. As a consequence, the framework developed in section 3 can be applied to more general variational approaches to motion estimation, as discussed in section 1.1.

2.1   Variational Problem

Throughout this section, $g(x) = g(x_1, x_2)$ is the grayvalue function, $\nabla = (\partial_{x_1}, \partial_{x_2})^\top$ denotes the gradient with respect to spatial variables, ∂_t the partial derivative with respect to time, and $u = (u_1, u_2)^\top, v = (v_1, v_2)^\top$ denote vector fields in the linear space $V = H^1(\Omega) \times H^1$.

With this notational convention, the variational problem to be solved reads [19]:

$$J(u) = \inf_{v \in V} \int_\Omega \left\{ (\nabla g \cdot v + \partial_t g)^2 + \lambda(|\nabla v_1|^2 + |\nabla v_2|^2) \right\} dx \tag{1}$$

Vanishing of the first variation of the functional J in (1) yields the variational equation:

$$a(u, v) = f(v), \quad \forall v \in V, \tag{2}$$

where

$$a(u, v) = \int_\Omega \left\{ (\nabla g \cdot u)(\nabla g \cdot v) + \lambda(\nabla u_1 \cdot \nabla v_1 + \nabla u_2 \cdot \nabla v_2) \right\} dx \tag{3}$$

$$f(v) = -\int_\Omega \partial_t g \nabla g \cdot v dx \tag{4}$$

Under weak conditions with respect to the image data g (i.e. $\partial_{x_1} g$ and $\partial_{x_2} g$ have to be independent in the L^2-sense), there exists a constant $c > 0$ such that:

$$a(v, v) \geq c \|v\|_V^2, \quad \forall v \in V \tag{5}$$

As a consequence, J in (1) is strictly convex and its global minimum u is the unique solution to the variational equation (2). Partially integrating in (2), we derive the *system of Euler-Lagrange equations*:

$$Lu = f \quad \text{in} \quad \Omega, \qquad \partial_n u = 0 \quad \text{on} \quad \partial\Omega, \qquad (6)$$

where

$$Lu = -\lambda\Delta u + (\nabla g \cdot u)\nabla g$$

2.2 Discretization

To approximate the vector field u numerically, equation (2) is discretized by piecewise linear finite elements over the triangulated section Ω of the image plane [10]. We arrange the vectors of nodal variables u_1, u_2 corresponding to the finite element discretizations of $u_1(x), u_2(x)$ as follows[1]: $u = (u_1^\top, u_2^\top)^\top$. Taking into consideration the symmetry of the bilinear form (3), this induces the following block structure of the discretized version $Au = f$ of (2):

$$\begin{pmatrix} A_{11} & A_{12} \\ A_{21} & A_{22} \end{pmatrix} \begin{pmatrix} u_1 \\ u_2 \end{pmatrix} = \begin{pmatrix} f_1 \\ f_2 \end{pmatrix}, \qquad (7)$$

where $\forall i, j = 1, \dots, N$:

$$(A_{11})_{ij} = a\big((\phi_i, 0)^\top, (\phi_j, 0)^\top\big)$$
$$(A_{12})_{ij} = a\big((\phi_i, 0)^\top, (0, \phi_j)^\top\big)$$
$$(A_{21})_{ij} = (A_{12})_{ji}$$
$$(A_{22})_{ij} = a\big((0, \phi_i)^\top, (0, \phi_j)^\top\big)$$
$$(f_1)_i = f\big((\phi_i, 0)^\top\big)$$
$$(f_2)_i = f\big((0, \phi_i)^\top\big)$$

Here, ϕ_k denotes the linear basis function corresponding to the nodal variable $(u_1)_k$ or $(u_2)_k$, respectively.

3   Domain Decomposition

3.1 Two Subdomains

Let $\Omega^1 \cup \Omega^2$ be a partition of Ω with a common boundary $\Gamma = \overline{\Omega^1} \cap \overline{\Omega^2}$. We denote the corresponding function spaces with V^1, V^2. In the following, superscripts refer to subdomains.

We wish to represent u from (6) by two functions $u^1 \in V^1, u^2 \in V^2$ which are computed by solving two related problems in Ω^1, Ω^2, respectively. The relation:

$$u(x) = \begin{cases} u^1(x) & x \in \Omega^1 \\ u^2(x) & x \in \Omega^2 \end{cases} \qquad (8)$$

---

[1] With slight abuse of notation, we use the same symbols $u_\cdot, u_\cdot$ for simplicity.

obviously holds iff the following is true:

$$Lu^1 = f^1 \quad \text{in } \Omega^1 \qquad\qquad \partial_{n^1} u^1 = 0 \quad \text{on } \partial\Omega^1 \cap \partial\Omega \qquad (9)$$

$$Lu^2 = f^2 \quad \text{in } \Omega^2 \qquad\qquad \partial_{n^2} u^2 = 0 \quad \text{on } \partial\Omega^2 \cap \partial\Omega \qquad (10)$$

$$u^1 = u^2 \quad \text{on } \Gamma \qquad\qquad\qquad\qquad\qquad\qquad\qquad (11)$$

$$\partial_{n^1} u^1 = -\partial_{n^2} u^2 \quad \text{on } \Gamma \qquad\qquad\qquad\qquad\qquad (12)$$

We observe that (6) cannot simply be solved by separately computing u^1 and u^2 in each domain Ω_1, Ω_2 (see also Fig. 1!) because the natural boundary conditions have to be changed on Γ, due to (11) and (12).

As a consequence, in order to solve the system of equations (9)-(12), we equate the restriction to the interface Γ of the two solutions u^1, u^2 to (9) and (10), due to equation (11), $u_\Gamma := u^1|_\Gamma = u^2|_\Gamma$, and substitute u_Γ into equation (12) (see Eqn. (19) below).

To this end, we solve

$$Lu = f \quad \text{in } \Omega, \quad \partial_n u = 0 \quad \text{on } \partial\Omega \setminus \Gamma, \quad u = u_\Gamma \quad \text{on } \Gamma \qquad (13)$$

and decompose u into two functions,

$$u = u_0 + u_f,$$

which are the unique solutions to the following problems:

$$Lu_0 = 0 \quad \text{in } \Omega, \quad \partial_n u_0 = 0 \quad \text{on } \partial\Omega \setminus \Gamma, \quad u_0 = u_\Gamma \quad \text{on } \Gamma \qquad (14)$$

$$Lu_f = f \quad \text{in } \Omega, \quad \partial_n u_f = 0 \quad \text{on } \partial\Omega \setminus \Gamma, \quad u_f = 0 \quad \text{on } \Gamma \qquad (15)$$

Clearly, the restriction of u_f to the interface Γ is zero, $u_f|_\Gamma = 0$, and:

$$u|_\Gamma = u_0|_\Gamma \qquad\qquad (16)$$

$$\partial_n u = \partial_n u_0 + \partial_n u_f \qquad\qquad (17)$$

The definition of the *Steklov-Poincaré operator* S is:

$$S : u_\Gamma \to \partial_n u_0|_\Gamma \qquad\qquad (18)$$

Applying this mapping to the solutions u^1, u^2 of equations (9) and (10) in the domains Ω^1 and Ω^2, respectively, equation (12) becomes with $u_\Gamma = u^1|_\Gamma = u^2|_\Gamma$ due to (11):

$$(S^1 + S^2)u_\Gamma + \partial_{n^1} u_f^1|_\Gamma + \partial_{n^2} u_f^2|_\Gamma = 0 \qquad\qquad (19)$$

It remains to discretize this equation in order to solve for u_Γ. This will be done in the following section.

3.2 Discretizing the Interface Equation

By virtue of definitions (14) and (15) and standard results [2], we obtain in each domain respective the linear systems:

$$\begin{pmatrix} A_{II}^i & A_{I\Gamma}^i \\ A_{\Gamma I}^i & A_{\Gamma\Gamma}^i \end{pmatrix} \begin{pmatrix} (u_0^i)_I \\ u_\Gamma^i \end{pmatrix} = \begin{pmatrix} 0 \\ \partial_n u_0^i|_\Gamma \end{pmatrix}, \quad i = 1, 2 \qquad (20)$$

and

$$\begin{pmatrix} A_{II}^i & A_{I\Gamma}^i \\ A_{\Gamma I}^i & A_{\Gamma\Gamma}^i \end{pmatrix} \begin{pmatrix} u_f^i \\ 0 \end{pmatrix} = \begin{pmatrix} f_I^i \\ f_\Gamma^i + \partial_{n^i} u_f^i |_\Gamma \end{pmatrix}, \quad i = 1, 2 \tag{21}$$

Due to the system (9)-(12), we have to solve simultaneously (20) and (21) in both domains. Since $u^i = u_0^i + u_f^i$, summation of (20) and (21) for each domain, respectively, gives:

$$\begin{pmatrix} A_{II}^i & A_{I\Gamma}^i \\ A_{\Gamma I}^i & A_{\Gamma\Gamma}^i \end{pmatrix} \begin{pmatrix} u_I^i \\ u_\Gamma^i \end{pmatrix} = \begin{pmatrix} f_I^i \\ f_\Gamma^i + \partial_{n^i} u^i |_\Gamma \end{pmatrix}, \quad i = 1, 2$$

We combine these equations into a single system:

$$\begin{pmatrix} A_{II}^1 & 0 & A_{I\Gamma}^1 \\ 0 & A_{II}^2 & A_{I\Gamma}^2 \\ A_{\Gamma I}^1 & A_{\Gamma I}^2 & A_{\Gamma\Gamma}^1 + A_{\Gamma\Gamma}^2 \end{pmatrix} \begin{pmatrix} u_I^1 \\ u_I^2 \\ u_\Gamma \end{pmatrix} = \begin{pmatrix} f_I^1 \\ f_I^2 \\ f_\Gamma + \partial_{n^1} u^1 |_\Gamma + \partial_{n^2} u^2 |_\Gamma \end{pmatrix}, \tag{22}$$

where

$$f_\Gamma = f_\Gamma^1 + f_\Gamma^2 .$$

By solving the first two equations for u_I^1, u_I^2 and substitution into the third equation of (22), we conclude that (12) holds iff:

$$A_{\Gamma I}^1 (A_{II}^1)^{-1} (f_I^1 - A_{I\Gamma}^1 u_\Gamma) + A_{\Gamma I}^2 (A_{II}^2)^{-1} (f_I^2 - A_{I\Gamma}^2 u_\Gamma) + (A_{\Gamma\Gamma}^1 + A_{\Gamma\Gamma}^2) u_\Gamma = f_\Gamma \tag{23}$$

This is just the discretized counterpart of (19):

$$(S^1 + S^2) u_\Gamma = f_\Gamma - A_{\Gamma I}^1 (A_{II}^1)^{-1} f_I^1 - A_{\Gamma I}^2 (A_{II}^2)^{-1} f_I^2 \tag{24}$$

$$S^i u_\Gamma = (A_{\Gamma\Gamma}^i - A_{\Gamma I}^i (A_{II}^i)^{-1} A_{I\Gamma}^i) u_\Gamma, \quad i = 1, 2 \tag{25}$$

Once u_Γ is computed by solving (24), u^1 and u^2 follow from (9), (10) with boundary values u_Γ on the common interface Γ.

3.3 Multiple Domains

Let R^i denote the restriction of the vector of nodal variables u_Γ on the interface Γ to those on $\overline{\Omega^i} \cap \Gamma$. Analogously to the case of two domains detailed above, the interface equation (19) in the case of multiple domains reads:

$$\left(\sum_i (R^i)^\top S^i R^i \right) u_\Gamma = f_\Gamma - \sum_i (R^i)^\top A_{\Gamma I}^i (A_{II}^i)^{-1} f_I^i, \quad \forall i \tag{26}$$

Note that all computations restricted to subdomains Ω^i can be done in parallel!

4   Preconditioning, Parallel Implementation, and Convergence Rates

4.1   Interface Preconditioner

While a fine partition of Ω into a large number of subdomains Ω^i leads to small-sized and "computationally cheap" local problems in each subdomain, the condition number of the Steklov-Poincaré operator S more and more deteriorates [29]. As a consequence, preconditioning of the interface equation becomes crucial for an efficient parallel implementation.

Among different but provably optimal ("spectrally equivalent") families of preconditioners (cf. [9,30]), we examined in particular the *Balancing-Neumann-Neumann-preconditioner (BNN)* [22,12]:

$$P_{BNN}^{-1} := (I - (R^0)^\top (S^0)^{-1} R^0 S) P_{NN}^{-1} (I - S(R^0)^\top (S^0)^{-1} R^0) + (R^0)^\top (S^0)^{-1} R^0 \,, \tag{27}$$

where

$$P_{NN}^{-1} := D \left(\sum_i (R^i)^\top (S^i)^{-1} R^i \right) D \tag{28}$$

This preconditioner applied in connection with conjugate gradient iteration [17] preserve the symmetry of S in (18) and naturally extends to more general problems related to three-dimensional image sequences or unstructured geometries and/or triangulations.

Preconditioner P_{BNN}^{-1} carries out a correction step (denoted as "balancing" in literature) before and after the application of the *Neumann-Neumann-preconditioner (NN)* (28) on a coarse grid given by the partition of the domain Ω into subdomains (see Figure 1).

The restriction operator R^0 sums up the weighted values on the boundary of each subdomain, where the weights are given by the inverse of the number of subdomains sharing each particular node, i.e.

$$(R^0)_{ji} := \begin{cases} \frac{1}{2} : \text{node } i \text{ is on an edge of } \Omega_j \\ \frac{1}{4} : \text{node } i \text{ is in a vertex of } \Omega_j \\ 0 : \text{else} \end{cases} \tag{29}$$

Then, S^0 is defined by

$$S^0 := R^0 S (R^0)^\top. \tag{30}$$

Note that S^0 is a dense matrix of small dimension (related to the number of subdomains) which can be efficiently inverted by a standard direct method.

4.2   Parallel Implementation

The preconditioned conjugate gradient iteration for solving the interface equations (19) and (26) provides several starting points for parallel computation. In the case of the NN-preconditioner (28) the calculation of $(S^i)^{-1}$, which is done indirectly by calculating

$(A^i)^{-1}$ on the whole subdomain, can be carried out in parallel. Then, the restriction matrices R^i and $(R^i)^\top$ amount to *scatter-operations* and *gather-operations* from the point of view of the central process. Furthermore, when calculating S during a conjugate gradient iteration, parallelization can be employed also. Since S is already written in decomposed form in (24) and (26) the procedure is done in an analogous manner as with P_{NN}^{-1} with the main difference (beneath leaving out the weighting by D) that here the Dirichlet system (25) has to be solved on each subdomain in order to calculate the action of S^i. Both parallelization procedures are combined in the calculation of the BNN-preconditioner (27) since both operators are involved here.

The inversion of the coarse operator S_0 does not provide any possibilities for parallelization since it has been shown to be most practical to calculate S_0 numerically in advance, by carrying out (30), and then computing S_0^{-1} in the central process by using again a conjugated gradient method. Since the coarse system is much smaller (the grid is equivalent to the subdomain partition) the computation time for this inversion has shown to be very small and can be neglected in practice. Furthermore, the initial computation of the right hand side in (19) or (26) can be parallelized in an analogous manner.

4.3 Multi-Grid Subdomain Solver

Evaluation of the right hand side in (26) as well as S^i and $(S^i)^{-1}$ (cf. (25)) needs in parallel for each domain (i.e. processor) the fast solution of the corresponding Dirichlet and Neumann boundary value problems, respectively. To this end, we implemented a multi-grid solver. Since domain decomposition methods depend strongly on the performance and accuracy of their internal solver, we considered the use of multi-grid methods [6, 16]. These methods are well-known to be among the fastest and most accurate numerical schemes for the solution of systems of linear equations.

In [7,8] such a multi-grid scheme has been proposed for the CLG approach. It allowed the computation of up to 40 flow fields for sequences of size 200×200 within a single second. Obviously, an integration of this strategy into our domain decomposition framework seems desirable. In fact, the only difference between the single and the multiple domain case is the possible cooccurrence of Neumann and Dirichlet boundary conditions in the same subdomain. Once this is taken into account, the implementation is straightforward.

Let us now sketch some technical details of our multi-grid solver. Our strategy is based on the pointwise coupled Gauß-Seidel method, which is hierarchically applied in form of a so called *full multi-grid* strategy. An example of such a full multi-grid scheme is given in Fig.2. It shows how a coarse version of the original problem is refined step by step and how correcting multi-grid methods, e.g. W-cycles, are used at each refinement level for solving. In this context, we chose W-cycles that perform two pointwise coupled Gauß-Seidel iterations in both its pre- and postsmoothing relaxation step. Besides the traversing strategy, operators have to be defined that handle the information transfer between the grids. For *restriction* (fine-to-coarse) simple averaging is used, while *prolongation* (coarse-to-fine) is performed by means of bilinear interpolation. Finally, coarser versions of the matrix operator have to be created. To this end we rediscretised the Euler-Lagrange equations. Such a proceeding is called *discretisation coarse grid approximation (DCA)*.

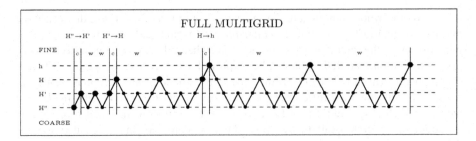

Fig. 2. Example of a full multi-grid implementation for four levels taken from [8]. Vertical solid lines separate alternating blocks of the two basic strategies : *Cascading* and *correcting* multi-grid. Blocks belonging to the cascading multi-grid strategy are marked with *c*. Starting from a coarse scale the original problem is refined step by step. This is visualised by the → symbol. Thereby the coarser solution serves as an initial approximation for the refined problem. At each refinement level, a correcting multi-grid solver is used in form of two W-cycles (marked with *w*). Performing iterations on the original equation is marked with large black dots, while iterations on residual equations are marked with smaller ones.

4.4   Convergence Rates

In this section, we examine the influence of both the number of subdomains and the coarse-grid correction step on the convergence rate of the preconditioned conjugate gradient iteration.

We first measured the number of outer iterations to reach a relative residual error $||u_\Gamma^k - \hat{u}_\Gamma||_S / ||\hat{u}_\Gamma||_S < 10^{-3}$ ($\hat{u}_\Gamma$: exact solution; k: iteration index) of equation (26) for different number of subdomains. The results are depicted in Figure 3 (1). They clearly show that the computational costs using the non-balancing preconditioner grow with the number of subdomains whereas they remain nearly constant for the preconditioner involving a coarse grid correction step (we neglected the time needed for solving the coarse small-sized system related to S^0). These results are confirmed by Figure 3 (2) where the residual error for a *fixed* number of outer PCG-iterations is shown. Thus, the BNN-preconditioner is much closer to an *optimal* preconditioner making the convergence rate independent w.r.t. both the pixel meshsize h and the coarse meshsize H by the number of subdomains. It also follows that the solver using this preconditioner scales much better with the number of subdomains since the reduced costs for the local problems associated with S^i by far compensate the additional costs for solving the coarse-grid system and process communication.

5   Cluster Computing

The algorithm, as described in sections 4.2 and 4.3, was implemented in C/C++ on a Linux operating system. An implementation of the *Message Passing Interface (MPI)* was used for parallelization. Benchmarking was conducted by the *MPE library* included in the MPI package. All experiments have been carried out on a dedicated PC-cluster "HELICS" at the University of Heidelberg, which comprises 256 Dual-Athlon MP

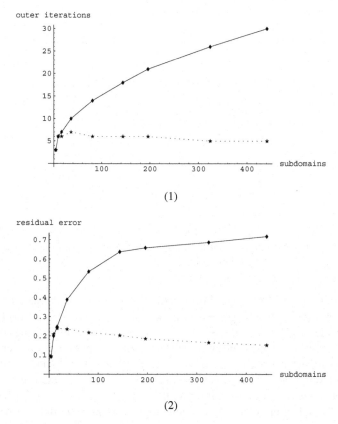

(1)

(2)

Fig. 3. Effect of coarse-grid correction. (1) Number of outer PCG-iterations until the residual error of system (26) is reduced to $||u_k - \hat{u}||_S/||u\cdot - \hat{u}||_S < 10^{\cdot\ \cdot}$ for coarse mesh sizes $H \in \{126, 84, 63, 42, 28, 21, 18, 14, 12\}$ on a 252×252 image using the NN-preconditioner (solid line) and the BNN-preconditioner (stippled line). The corresponding numbers of subdomains are $\{2^{\cdot}, 3^{\cdot}, 4^{\cdot}, 6^{\cdot}, 9^{\cdot}, 12^{\cdot}, 14^{\cdot}, 18^{\cdot}, 21^{\cdot}\}$. The *local systems* were solved in each subdomain to a residual error of $10^{\cdot\ \cdot}$. (2) Relative residual error after 10 outer PCG-iterations using the NN-preconditioner (solid line) and the BNN-preconditioner (stippled line) for the same set of coarse mesh sizes. The results clearly show the favourable influence of the coarse grid coupling leading to a nearly constant error and therefore to a nearly constant number of outer PCG-iterations when using the balancing preconditioner on 4×4 subdomains and above. Hence, the balancing preconditioner is much closer to an *optimal* preconditioner making the convergence rate nearly independent of h and H.

1.4 GHz nodes (i.e. 512 processors in total) connected by the interconnect network Myrinet2000.

As input data an image pair from a real air-flow sequence provided by the Onera Labs, Rennes, France, has been taken. The reference solution x_{ref} was calculated without parallelization by the use of the multi-grid solver (full multi-grid, 5 W-cycles, 3 pre- and post-relaxation-steps per level) and regularization parameter $\lambda = 0.05$ (the intensity values of the input images where normalized to $[0, 1]$). The objective was to compare the total computation time of the non-parallel solving (by multi-grid) on the whole image

Table 1. Computation times for different partitions. Compared to a dedicated one-processor multi-grid implementation, domain-decomposition accelerates the computation for 5×5 processors and above. The speed-up for 7×7 compared to the computation time on one processor is nearly 40 %.

Partition (h./v.) 512˙ pixels	Image size	Outer iter.	Run time	Comm. time
2×2	511˙	1	1550 ms	4 %
3×3	511˙	1	960 ms	5.6%
5×5	513˙	3	664 ms	10 %
6×6	511˙	4	593 ms	10 %
7×7	512˙	4	516 ms	11 %

plane on one machine to the total computation time of the parallel solving on $N \times N$ processors by using Neumann-Neumann preconditioning. Computation was stopped if an relative error of 1% had been reached, i.e. $||x^i - x_{ref}||_2/||x_{ref}||_2 < 0.01$, x^i : solution after i conjugate gradient-iterations.

Comparison to Single-Processor Multi-grid. The time for calculating the vector field without parallelization on one processor to the given accuracy was 721 ms (full-multi-grid, 2 W-cycles and 1 pre- and post-relaxations per level). In Table 1 the computation times of the parallel substructuring method for different partitions are depicted. The parameters of the local multi-grid solver where optimized by hand to minimize the total computation time. The results show that parallelization by the use of Neumann-Neumann preconditioning starts to improve the computation time from 5×5 processors and above. The speed-up for 7×7 compared to the computation time on one processor is nearly 40%.

Similar experiments for Balancing Neumann-Neumann preconditioning will be conducted in future.

References

1. P. Anandan. A computational framework and an algorithm for the measurement of visual motion. *Int. J. of Comp. Vision*, 2:283–310, 1989.
2. J.P. Aubin. *Approximation of Elliptic Boundary-Value Problems*. Wiley&Sons, New York, 1972.
3. J.L. Beauchemin, S.S. and Barron. The computation of optical flow. *ACM Computing Surveys*, 27:433–467, Sept. 1995.
4. M.J. Black and P. Anandan. The robust estimation of multiple motions: Parametric and piecewise–smooth flow fields. *Comp. Vis. Image Underst.: CVIU*, 63(1):75–104, 1996.
5. P. Bouthemy and E. Francois. Motion segmentation and qualitative dynamic scene analysis from an image sequence. *Int. J. of Comp. Vision*, 10(2):157–182, 1993.
6. A. Brandt. Multi-level adaptive solutions to boundary-value problems. *Mathematics of Computation*, 31(138):333–390, April 1977.
7. A. Bruhn, J. Weickert, C. Feddern, T. Kohlberger, and C. Schnörr. Real-time optic flow computation with variational methods. In N. Petkov and M. A. Westberg, editors, *Computer Analysis of Images and Patterns*, volume 2756 of *Lecture Notes in Computer Science*, pages 222–229. Springer, Berlin, 2003.

8. A. Bruhn, J. Weickert, C. Feddern, T. Kohlberger, and C. Schnörr. Variational optic flow computation in real-time. Technical Report 89/2003, Dpt. of Mathematics, Saarland University, Germany, June 2003.

9. T.F. Chan and T.P. Mathew. Domain decomposition algorithms. *Acta Numerica*, pages 61–143, 1994.

10. P.G. Ciarlet. *The Finite Element Method for Elliptic Problems*. North-Holland Publ. Comp., Amsterdam, 1978.

11. T. Corpetti, E. Mémin, and P. Pérez. Dense estimation of fluid flows. *IEEE Trans. Patt. Anal. Mach. Intell.*, 24(3):365–380, 2002.

12. M. Dryja and O.B. Widlund. Schwarz methods of neumann-neumann type for three-dimensional elliptic finite element problems. *Comm. Pure Appl. Math.*, 48:121–155, 1995.

13. W. Enkelmann. Investigation of multigrid algorithms for the estimation of optical flow fields in image sequences. *Comp. Vis. Graph. Imag. Proc.*, 43:150–177, 1987.

14. M. Fleury, A.F. Clark, and A.C. Downton. Evaluating optical-flow algorithms on a parallel machine. *Image and Vision Comp.*, 19(3):131–143, 2001.

15. S. Ghosal and P. Vaněk. A fast scalable algorithm for discontinuous optical flow estimation. *IEEE Trans. Patt. Anal. Mach. Intell.*, 18(2):181–194, 1996.

16. W. Hackbusch. *Multigrid Methods and Applications*. Springer, New York, 1985.

17. W. Hackbusch. *Iterative Solution of Large Sparse Systems of Equations*. Springer-Verlag, 1993.

18. F. Heitz, P. Perez, and P. Bouthemy. Multiscale minimization of global energy functions in some visual recovery problems. *Comp. Vis. Image Underst.: CVIU*, 59(1):125–134, 1994.

19. B.K.P. Horn and B.G. Schunck. Determining optical flow. *Artif. Intell.*, 17:185–203, 1981.

20. S.H. Hwang and S.U. Lee. A hierarchical optical flow estimation algorithm based on the interlevel motion smoothness constraint. *Patt. Recog.*, 26(6):939–952, 1993.

21. J. Konrad and E. Dubois. Bayesian estimation of motion vector fields. *IEEE Trans. Patt. Anal. Mach. Intell.*, 14(9):910–927, 1992.

22. J. Mandel. Balancing domain decomposition. *Comm. Numer. Meth. Eng.*, 9:233–241, 1993.

23. E. Mémin and P. Pérez. Optical flow estimation and object–based segmentation with robust techniques. *IEEE Trans. on Image Proc.*, 7(5):703–719, 1998.

24. E. Mémin and P. Pérez. Hierarchical estimation and segmentation of dense motion fields. *Int. J. of Comp. Vision*, 46(2):129–155, 2002.

25. A. Mitiche and P. Bouthemy. Computation and analysis of image motion: A synopsis of current problems and methods. *Int. J. of Comp. Vision*, 19(1):29–55, 1996.

26. H.H. Nagel. On the estimation of optical flow: Relations between different approaches and some new results. *Artif. Intell.*, 33:299–324, 1987.

27. H.H. Nagel and W. Enkelmann. An investigation of smoothness constraints for the estimation of displacement vector fields from image sequences. *IEEE Trans. Patt. Anal. Mach. Intell.*, 8(5):565–593, 1986.

28. P. Nesi. Variational approach to optical flow estimation managing discontinuities. *Image and Vis. Comp.*, 11(7):419–439, 1993.

29. A. Quarteroni and A. Valli. *Domain Decomposition Methods for Partial Differential Equations*. Oxford Univ. Press, 1999.

30. B. Smith, P. Bjorstad, and W. Gropp. *Domain Decomposition: Parallel Multilevel Methods for the Solution of Elliptic Partial Differential Equations*. Cambridge Univ. Press, 1996.

31. F. Valentinotti, G. Dicaro, and B. Crespi. Real-time parallel computation of disparity and optical flow using phase difference. *Machine Vision and Appl.*, 9(3):87–96, 1996.

32. J. Weickert and C. Schnörr. A theoretical framework for convex regularizers in pde–based computation of image motion. *Int. J. Computer Vision*, 45(3):245–264, 2001.

Whitening for Photometric Comparison of Smooth Surfaces under Varying Illumination

Margarita Osadchy[1], Michael Lindenbaum[2], and David Jacobs[3]

[1] NEC Laboratories America, Princeton NJ, USA
rita@nec-labs.com,
[2] Dept. of Computer Science, The Technion, Haifa, Israel
mic@cs.technion.ac.il
[3] Dept. of Computer Science,The University of Maryland, College Park, Maryland
djacobs@umiacs.umd.edu

Abstract. We consider the problem of image comparison in order to match smooth surfaces under varying illumination. In a smooth surface nearby surface normals are highly correlated. We model such surfaces as Gaussian processes and derive the resulting statistical characterization of the corresponding images. Supported by this model, we treat the difference between two images, associated with the same surface and different lighting, as colored Gaussian noise, and use the whitening tool from signal detection theory to construct a measure of difference between such images. This also improves comparisons by accentuating the differences between images of different surfaces. At the same time, we prove that no linear filter, including ours, can produce lighting insensitive image comparisons. While our Gaussian assumption is a simplification, the resulting measure functions well for both synthetic and real smooth objects. Thus we improve upon methods for matching images of smooth objects, while providing insight into the performance of such methods. Much prior work has focused on image comparison methods appropriate for highly curved surfaces. We combine our method with one of these, and demonstrate high performance on rough and smooth objects.

1   Introduction

Comparing images is a fundamental part of computer vision systems that perform recognition, alignment and tracking. Many approaches have tackled the critical problem of accounting for lighting variations [6,11,13,1,3] when making comparisons. These methods work well on rough objects containing discontinuities or places of rapid change in albedo or shape. However, comparing images of smooth surfaces with no edges or texture under varying illumination remains a challenging problem. This problem is important since most real surfaces contain rough and smooth regions. Handling smooth regions is important for improved recognition or dense registration or tracking of such objects. In this paper we propose a new measure for image comparison of smooth surfaces, and demonstrate its value on the problem of object identification under fixed pose but varying lighting.

T. Pajdla and J. Matas (Eds.): ECCV 2004, LNCS 3024, pp. 217–228, 2004.

There are three things that seems to be very important in constructing a representation for image comparison. First, finding a representation that captures similarities between images of the same object (eg., through quasi-invariance). Second, also capturing dissimilarity between images of different objects. Third, choosing an optimal measure for comparing the resulting representations. Most previous methods have focused on the first problem, by choosing representations of images that are invariant, or quasi-invariant to lighting. Edges are a classic example. [3] discuss the quasi-invariance to lighting changes of operators that use derivatives. Gabor jets are also widely used for image comparison, in part because they are also considered to be insensitive to lighting changes (eg., [13]). [6, 2,18] point out that the direction of the gradient is relatively insensitive to lighting changes. However, it is well-known that quasi-invariance to lighting changes is difficult to achieve for smooth objects.[1] Hence we will not focus on invariant representations, but tackle the other two problems: increasing dissimilarity between images of different objects while constructing an optimal comparison measure.

The primary problem presented by smooth objects is that nearby albedos and surface normals are highly correlated, which causes correlations in nearby intensities in their images. Consequently, comparisons that treat neighboring pixels as independent, such as sum-of-squared-differences (SSD) are not statistically valid. Moreover, correlations between image pixels improve the chances that images of two different objects will match well, since if they are similar at one point, they are likely to be similar at many. We approach this problem by constructing a statistical model of the dependencies between neighboring portions of smooth shapes. We then use this to model the effect that lighting changes have on the appearance of a smooth object. We can then design operators to decorrelate the pixels in images of these objects.

We use whitening to lessen dependencies in the difference between two images. Signal detection theory tells us that this is the optimal approach when the difference between images of the same object consists of colored (non-independent) Gaussian noise [19]. We show that for a simple model of smooth surfaces, this is a good characterization.

Whitening has often been used for decorrelation of images in image processing tasks such as watermarking [8,7], image restoration [20,4,5], and texture feature extraction [9,14]. Many methods have used some differential operators or the Laplacian [17] to approximate the whitening filter, though [14] used a 2D causal linear prediction model to derive whitening filters.

Whitening decorrelates image intensities, but it does not make them insensitive to lighting variation. In fact, we prove that no linear filter can produce an image representation that is more insensitive to lighting variation than the original image. One consequence of this is to prove that non-linear lighting in-

---

[1] This is made explicit in the analysis of [6], which shows that gradient direction is truly invariant to lighting direction for surfaces with discontinuities, and varies more rapidly with smoother objects.

sensitive methods for rough surfaces, such as the direction of gradient, are more lighting insensitive than any possible linear filter.

To summarize, whitening, like any linear filtering, does not make images of the same object more similar. However, it helps to increase dissimilarity between images of different objects and allows us to use SSD as the optimal measure for comparison. These make whitening a superior comparison method for smooth surfaces, which we confirm in our experiments on synthetic and real data. We combine whitening with the direction of gradient to produce a comparison method that performs very well on both smooth and rough objects.

2   The Whitening Approach

As mentioned above, discrimination between smooth objects is difficult due to the high correlation between nearby pixels in their images. One consequence of this is that pixel by pixel comparisons such as SSD are not optimal. In this section we show how to derive linear filters that remove correlations between neighboring pixels. These *whitened* images can then be optimally compared using SSD. We take a statistical approach, regarding the difference image, $I_d = I_1 - I_2$ as a random variable (I_1 and I_2 denote two images of the same surface). We analyze this considering a Lambertian surface illuminated by distant point sources. Neglecting shadows, we can model the images as: $I_1 = \rho \hat{N} s_1$ and $I_2 = \rho \hat{N} s_2$, where $\hat{N}$ are surface normals, ρ is albedo, and s_1, s_2 are light sources in two images. Then

$$I_d = \rho \hat{N} s_1 - \rho \hat{N} s_2 = \rho \hat{N}(s_1 - s_2) \qquad (1)$$

Dependencies that exist between nearby surface normals of an object lead to dependencies in I_d, which we treat by modeling I_d as *colored* Gaussian noise. (Colored Gaussian noise captures noise with dependencies, whereas white noise is independent.) While this model is not strictly true, it is a valuable approximation that opens the way to using a whitening filter, which is a standard tool in signal detection, to reduce dependency in the difference image.

2.1   Whitening in Signal Processing

First we describe whitening. Let $\mathbf{n}$ represent as a vector the pixels in the difference image. Assume that $\mathbf{n}$ is Gaussian colored noise. This implies that it is fully characterized by its first and second order statistics. In particular, the whitening filter may be designed using the covariance matrix. Let $C = E[\mathbf{n}\mathbf{n}^T]$ be the covariance matrix characterizing the distribution of $\mathbf{n}$ (E denotes expected value). Let W be a matrix composed of the scaled eigenvectors of C, $\frac{1}{\sqrt{\lambda_i}}\mathbf{e}_i$ as rows. Then, the components of $\mathbf{y} = W\mathbf{n}$ are independent, as implied from their Gaussianity and their covariance:

$$E[\mathbf{y}\mathbf{y}^T] = diag(\lambda_1, \lambda_2, \ldots \lambda_m)$$

That is, the multiplication by the matrix W "whitens" the vector $\mathbf{n}$.

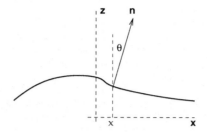

Fig. 1. The roughly planar (random) surface is specified (in 2D approximation) by the angle $\theta(x)$ that the normal makes with the z direction.

2.2   A Model for Natural Images – Rough Plane Covariance

To whiten a surface's images, we must understand their covariance structure. Consider a surface characterized by normal vectors that make small random perturbations about a common direction (without loss of generality the z axis). We refer to such a surface as *roughly planar* and assume that locally a smooth surface behaves like a roughly planar surface. This is a generalization of the common facet model [10]. Considering the simplified, 1D, variant, the "surface" is described by a function $z = f(x)$. The normals at every point x are random (but not independent!) and each of them is specified by a single parameter θ, which is its angle relative to the z axis (Figure 1). Quantitatively we characterize the function $\theta(x)$ as a wide sense (w.s.) stationary Gaussian random process [16]. That is, we assume that the expected value at every point is constant $\mu_\theta = 0$, that the variance $C_\theta(x, x) = \sigma_\theta^2$ is constant as well, and that the auto-correlation $C_\theta(x_1, x_2) = r(x_1, x_2)\sigma_\theta^2 = r(|x_1 - x_2|)\sigma_\theta^2$ depends only on the distance between two points. $r(|x_1 - x_2|)$ is a correlation coefficient. We also assume that the surface is Lambertian, and that its albedo ρ, is constant, at least locally. **Proposition 1:** Under the above assumptions and for a distant light source, illuminating the surface at angle ϕ (relative to the z axis), the reflected light function $I(x)$ is a random w.s. stationary process. Its expected value, variance and auto-correlation are:

$$E[I(x)] = \rho cos\phi e^{-\sigma_\theta^2/2}$$
$$\sigma_I^2 = \frac{1}{2}\rho^2(sin^2\phi(1 - e^{-2\sigma_\theta^2}) + cos^2\phi(1 - e^{-\sigma_\theta^2})^2) \tag{2}$$
$$C_I(x_1, x_2) = \frac{1}{2}\rho^2(sin^2\phi e^{-\sigma_\theta^2}(e^{r\sigma_\theta^2} - e^{-r\sigma_\theta^2}) + cos^2\phi(e^{-\sigma_\theta^2}(e^{r\sigma_\theta^2} + e^{-r\sigma_\theta^2}) - 2e^{-\sigma_\theta^2}))$$

where x_1, x_2 are the two points for which the correlation coefficient of the tangent direction is $r = r(|x_1 - x_2|)$.

Proof. (For details see [15]) The reflected light function $I(x)$ is a random process. Let x_1, x_2 be two points for which the correlation coefficient of the tangent direction is $r = r(\|x_1, x_2\|)$. Then, their autocorrelation is

$$
\begin{aligned}
C_I(x_1, x_2) &= E[(I(x_1) - E[I(x)])(I(x_2) - E[I(x)])] \\
&= \rho^2 E[(sin\phi sin\theta_1 + cos\phi cos\theta_1 - cos\phi E[cos\theta_1]) \cdot \\
&\qquad (sin\phi sin\theta_2 + cos\phi cos\theta_2 - cos\phi E[cos\theta_2])] \\
&= \rho^2 (sin^2\phi E[sin\theta_1 sin\theta_2] + cos^2\phi E[cos\theta_1 cos\theta_2] - cos^2\phi E[cos\theta]^2 \\
&= \frac{1}{2}\rho^2 (sin^2\phi e^{-\sigma_\theta^2}(e^{r\sigma_\theta^2} - e^{-r\sigma_\theta^2}) + cos^2\phi (e^{-\sigma_\theta^2}(e^{r\sigma_\theta^2} + e^{-r\sigma_\theta^2}) - 2e^{-\sigma_\theta^2}))
\end{aligned}
$$

Note that all $sin\theta_i cos\theta_j$ terms vanish due to symmetry. The rest of the derivation requires us to change variables, to the sum and difference of θ_1 and θ_2, which are independent. Simple trigonometric expressions and the Gaussian integral $\int_\infty cosx\, e^{-x^2/2a^2} dx = \sqrt{2\pi}|a|e^{-a^2/2}$ are used as well.

For rougher surfaces (larger σ_θ^2) correlation decreases while for the (impossible) white surface (independent normals, $r = 0$), the image is white as well.

The covariance in eq. 2 is non-stationary and it varies with ϕ. It can be shown however, that of the two additive terms in the covariance expression the first is dominant, provided the surface is smooth (σ_θ is small) and that the illumination angle ϕ is not very small. This readily implies that:

Covariance characterization for rough Lambertian plane: the second order statistical behavior of a rough Lambertian, planar surface, illuminated by a single source, is characterized by an autocorrelation function which, for nearly every illumination, is approximately invariant of the illumination direction up to a multiplicative factor.

See [15] for experimental validation of this result for real objects.

2.3   Whitening Using AR Models

Designing a whitening filter by estimating the covariance is problematic as the covariance (and the mean) are nonstationary. Fortunately, fitting a parametric Autoregressive (AR) model, allows us to get the whitening filter directly without explicitly estimating covariance [12].

A sequence $x(n)$ is called an AR process of order p if it can be generated as the output of the recursive causal linear system

$$
x(n) = \sum_{k=1}^{p} a(k)x(n - k) + \varepsilon(n), \forall n \tag{3}
$$

where $\varepsilon(n)$ is white noise, and the sum $\bar{x}(n) = \sum_{k=1}^{p} a(k)x(n - k)$, is the best linear mean squared (MS) predictor of $x(n)$ based on the previous p samples. Given a random sequence (with possible dependencies), an AR model can be fitted using SVD to estimate the overdetermined parameters $a(k)$ which minimize the empirical MS prediction error $\sum_n (x(n) - \bar{x}(n))^2$. For Gaussian signals the prediction error sequence: $\varepsilon(n) = x(n) - \bar{x}(n)$ is white, implying that the filter $W = (1, -a_1, \ldots, -a_p)$ is a whitening filter for $x(n)$. We have adopted a 2D "causal" model described in [12], where a gray level $x(n)$ is predicted from the previous gray levels in a $p \times p$ neighborhood in column by column scan. Using a non-causal neighborhood leads to a lower SSD, but the prediction error sequence is not white [12].

Note that scaling all the grey levels by the same factor would give a correlation function that is the same up to a multiplicative constant. This is essentially what happens when the angle between the average normal and the illumination direction changes. Fortunately, this does not change either the AR coefficients, or the resulting whitening filter, implying that it can be space invariant.

The whitening filter depends on the image statistics. Intuitively, for smoother images the correlation is larger and decorrelating it requires a wider filter. For images which are not so smooth the decorrelation is done over a small range, and the filter looks very much like the Laplacian, which is also known to have some whitening effect. Therefore, for rougher images, we do not expect to perform better than an alternative procedure using the Laplacian. As we shall see later, for smooth objects the performance difference is significant.

2.4   Whitening Images from Different Objects

Signal detection theory tells us that whitening is useful for image comparison because whitened images from the same object can be optimally compared using SSD. Whitening has another advantage, it makes images from different objects more distinctive.

To see this, let S denote a 3D surface. We will take two pictures of S in a fixed pose with two different point sources of light, s_1 and s_2. s_1, s_2 are each 3×1 vectors that encode lighting direction and magnitude. $p_{i,j}$ denotes a patch of the surface corresponding to an image pixel. We approximate $p_{i,j}$ as a planar patch, with surface normal $\hat{N}_{i,j}$, and albedo $\rho_{i,j}$. It will be convenient to denote the scaled surface normal $\rho_{i,j}\hat{N}_{i,j}$ by $N_{i,j}$. We denote the image pixels corresponding to $p_{i,j}$ by $I_{1,i,j}, I_{2,i,j}$ in the two images. So we may write, for example, $I_{1,i,j} = N_{i,j}^T s_1$, since we ignore the effects of shadows.

Let L denote a whitening filter, represented discretely as a matrix with elements $L_{k,l}$. Without loss of generality we suppose L is square and $-n \leq k, l \leq n$. If we apply this filter to the image I_1 we denote the output as $\mathcal{I}_1$. So:

$$\mathcal{I}_{1,i,j} = \sum_{k=-n}^{n} \sum_{l=-n}^{n} L_{k,l} I_{1,i+k,j+l}$$

We can define a new surface, $\mathcal{S}$, such that its scaled surface normals are:

$$\mathcal{N}_{i,j} = \sum_{k=-n}^{n} \sum_{l=-n}^{n} L_{k,l} N_{i+k,j+l}$$

Intuitively, $\mathcal{S}$ can be thought of as the surface filtered by L. According to our model, while the original normals are highly correlated, the whitened normals will be white noise, with randomized directions and scales. As high-dimensional, white noise, different whitened surfaces will also be uncorrelated with each other, with high probability. This is analogous to taking a smooth, white surface and splattering it with gray paint. Smooth surfaces are easily confused with each other, while highly textured ones are not. Of course, whitening does not add differences to signals, it makes explicit the differences that are already there.

More formally, communication theory tells us that discriminating between correlated models is difficult. Specifically, for two unit energy signals $z_1(x), z_j(x)$, the correlation coefficients is $\rho_{ij} = \int z_i(x)z_j(x)dx$. For best performance, the correlation coefficient between any pair of models should be as low as possible. For two signals the lowest correlation is -1, and choosing $z_2(x) = -z_1(x)$ is optimal. When the number of signals is large, such correlations between all signal are not possible, and the best we can get is $\rho \approx 0$ [19].

Whitening treats the signals and the noise equally and therefore leaves the signal to noise ratio (SNR) the same. However the whitened signals become uncorrelated and therefore with the same SNR we get better performance. The correlation between the original images associated with different objects is high initially and is almost zero afterwards, so the improvement is significant.

3   Invariance and Linear Filtering

While most prior work has focused on finding lighting insensitive image comparisons, we have not argued that whitening is lighting insensitive. We now prove a result that casts doubt on the ability of any linear filter to produce lighting insensitive representations.

Theorem 1. *Suppose that the lighting directions s_1 and s_2 are drawn from a uniform distribution, and that we neglect the effects of shadows in images. Then $I_{1,i,j}/I_{2,i,j}$ and $\mathcal{I}_{1,i,j}/\mathcal{I}_{2,i,j}$ are identically distributed. That is, the distribution of the ratio of intensities between one image of an object and another are unaffected by filtering with an arbitrary linear filter. In this sense, no linear filter can produce a lighting insensitive representation.*

Proof. This follows immediately once we consider that linearly filtering the images is equivalent to filtering the surface, as described above. Let $\mathcal{N}$ denote the filtered normals, as above, but now for an arbitrary linear filter. Let $\hat{\mathcal{N}}_{i,j}$ denote a unit vector in the direction of $\mathcal{N}_{i,j}$.

$$\frac{I_{1,i,j}}{I_{2,i,j}} = \frac{\hat{N}_{i,j}s_1^T}{\hat{N}_{i,j}s_2^T} \qquad \frac{\mathcal{I}_{1,i,j}}{\mathcal{I}_{2,i,j}} = \frac{\hat{\mathcal{N}}_{i,j}s_1^T}{\hat{\mathcal{N}}_{i,j}s_2^T}$$

Since s_1 and s_2 are uniformly distributed it is clear from symmetry that these two fractions are identically distributed, because $\hat{N}$ and $\hat{\mathcal{N}}$ are identical up to a rotation. In sum, we have created a filtered surface that is affected by lighting changes exactly as the original surface.

It is possible to extend this result to handle the case of attached shadows by restricting the distribution of light sources to appear in a hemisphere above the surface normal. However we omit details of this for lack of space.

4   Experiments

We tested our ideas by applying them to object recognition. A set of objects is represented in a library containing one image for every object. Let $I_{M_1}, I_{M_2}, \ldots$ be reference images in the library. Let I_Q be the query image of one of the objects from this set, taken with the same pose, but different illumination. The task is to decide which of the objects is the one in the query image. Since the reference image I_{M_j} was taken with a different illumination intensity than the test image, every scaled version of it is a valid model as well. Minimizing the SSD over all scaled versions is equivalent to taking the SSD between the normalized whitened images. which is monotonic in the projection as well. This normalization also compensates for the fact that some objects are rougher than others, which makes the difference between two differently illuminated images of them larger. Therefore we perform the following steps: 1) For every reference image, I_{M_j}, use the whitening operator W, to calculate the normalized L_2 norm $E_j = \|\frac{W(I_{M_j})}{\|W(I_{M_j})\|} - \frac{W(I_Q)}{\|W(I_Q)\|}\|$. 2) Choose the model associated with the smallest whitened error norm, E_j.

We tested the whitening approach on smooth textureless surfaces. We also integrated whitening with a comparison method designed for rough surfaces, and showed that this combined method could work on rough and smooth surfaces.

4.1   Synthetic Images

The first set of experiments was done using synthetic images. Every scene was created as a sum of random harmonic functions, with fixed amplitudes but random directions and phases. This provides an ensemble of images with similar statistical properties. These were rendered as Lambertian surfaces with point sources.

We trained a whitening filter using 1000-5000 images with a fixed illumination, deviating 67.5 degrees from the z direction. The training set was independent of the test set. A test was done as follows: two random scenes were illuminated by the same nearly vertical illumination to create two references images I_r, I'_r. The test image I_t was synthesized from the first scene, with a different illumination, making an angle ϕ with the z axis (see Figure 2).

For comparison we also tested other algorithms using the SSD of the gray level image, a Laplacian filtered image, and the direction of the gradient[2]. See Figure 2 for the results.

We came to several conclusions. First, whitening was the most successful method. Second, whitening worked best with a large filter, but it also worked

---

[*] We did not test Gabor Jets on the synthetic images, but later experiments show that they are not especially effective on smooth surfaces.

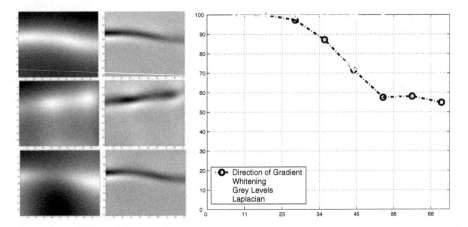

Fig. 2. The top and the center images in the left column correspond to different surfaces and one illumination. The bottom image is created from the same scene used for the top image, but with a different illumination. The center column shows the whitened images and illustrates that whitening reveals hidden differences. The plot on the right shows recognition performance of the tested methods on the synthetic images. The success rate is plotted against the average angle between the illumination source and the average surface normal.

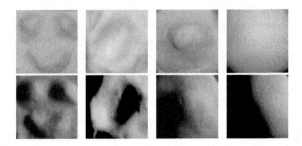

Fig. 3. Samples from the smooth real objects data set; top – frontal illumination, bottom – side illumination.

substantially better than other methods even with a 7×7 filter, except for extreme illumination angles. In particular whitening was always better than the Laplacian, even when a 3×3 filter was used, implying that both large distance correlations and causality are important.

4.2   Real Smooth Objects

Next, we describe experiments with real, smooth objects that produce images with substantial shadows (Figure 3). We created eighteen objects from clay and illuminated them by a single light source moving along a half circle, so that its distance from the object was roughly fixed. We used a camera placed vertically above the object, and took 14 images of every object with different lighting

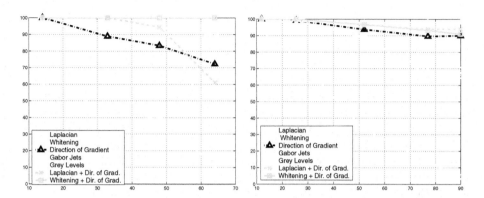

Fig. 4. Recognition performance of the tested methods on real smooth objects on the left and rough objects (Yale database) on the right. The success rate is plotted against the average angle (in degrees) between the illumination source and the average surface normal.

directions at angles in the range $[-70, 70]$ degrees to the vertical axis. One image of each object, associated with a nearly vertical illumination, were chosen as the reference images.

The whitening filter was trained on the difference images between reference images and corresponding images associated with the same object and six other illuminations. Only twelve images associated with 2 objects (out of 18) were used. We learned the whitening filter as a 2D causal filter with 25 coefficients inside 7×7 windows. All images of the 18 objects except the reference images were used as query images (234 images). We divided the query images into four groups according to their angular lighting direction:$10^\circ - 25^\circ$, $26^\circ - 40^\circ$, $41^\circ - 55^\circ$, and $56^\circ - 70^\circ$.

The plot in Figure 4 shows our results. Whitening again performed better than the other methods. We also observed that for a few of the roughest objects, the Laplacian, whitening and gradient angle performed equally well. For smoother 5objects, however, whitening worked considerably better. The Laplacian couldn't whiten the smooth surfaces, because its size was insufficient to handle the high correlations between the grey levels of the smooth surfaces.

4.3   The Combined Method

To handle objects that may be rough or smooth, we propose that whitening be combined with a measure that is geared towards handling rough objects, such as the direction of gradient. We have done a proof-of-concept implementation of a simple combined method. Direction of gradient is naturally normalized to the $[0, \pi]$ range. Whitening, however, requires normalization prior to combining. Let $s_1, s_2, ..., s_n$ denote the distances between the query image and n reference images after whitening. We normalize them to the $[0, 1]$ range by dividing all the distances by $\max |s_i|$. Different areas in the image can have different roughness levels. We compensate for this effect by choosing the normalization factor adaptively in 10×10 pixel areas instead of the whole image. Our experiments showed that adaptive normalization yields better results. We have also scaled the direction of gradient output to the $[0, 1]$ range. We have tested the combined method on both smooth (Figure 4 left) and rough data (Figure 4 right) sets. As a smooth set we took the clay objects described in the previous section. As a rough set we took the Yale database [6], which contains 20 objects with abrupt changes in albedo and shape. The database consists of 63 images of each object with lighting direction deviating up to 90 degrees from the frontal. Our experiments showed that the combination of whitening and direction of gradient (CWD) was better than either whitening or direction of gradient alone on both data sets; and CWD had the best (and perfect) performance on the smooth set. On the rough data the combined method performed very well, but not as well as Gabor Jets. In future work we plan to continue this approach and try to find a more clever combining technique that will integrate whitening with some variation of Gabor Jets. We also tested a combination of Laplacian and direction of gradient. This combination performed less well than CWD on smooth data and similar to CWD on the rough data. The Laplacian has some whitening effect, which explains its good performance on smooth data. On the other hand, decorrelation in the rough objects occurs over a small range, and the whitening filter looks very much like the Laplacian explaining the results on the rough set.

5   Conclusions

In this work we have proposed a measure for image comparison of smooth surfaces under varying illumination. The measure was motivated by a simple statistical model of smooth surfaces. This model showed that the error between two images associated with the same object under different lighting may be modelled as colored noise. We adapted well-known techniques of whitening to perform matching of images corrupted by such noise.

We found that whitening was more effective than other representations for comparing images of smooth surfaces taken under varying illumination conditions. Previous methods have commonly used the Laplacian or the magnitude of gradient, as whitening approximations. This seems to be adequate for rough images but leads to inferior results for smoother ones.

We believe that recognition (or image comparison in general) should use all the image information. Many current methods neglect photometric information and thus cannot handle smooth objects. Our preliminary results showed that a proper combining method, using both the information in edges and in smooth patches, would yield superior results, especially in hard tasks.

References

1. P.N. Belhumeur, J.P. Hespanha, and D.J. Kriegman. Eigenfaces vs. fisherfaces: Recognition using class-specific linear projection. *PAMI*, 19(7):711–720, July 1997.
2. M. Bichsel. *Strategies of Robust Object Recognition for the Identification of Human Faces*. ETH, Zurich, 1991.
3. R. Brunelli and T. Pggio. Face recognition: Features versus templates. *PAMI*, 15(10):1042–1062, 1993.
4. B. Bundschuh. A linear predictor as a regularization function in adaptive image restoration and reconstruction. In *5th Int, Conf. on Computer Analysis of Images and Patterns*, 1993.
5. H. Bundschuh, B. Schulz and D. Schneider. Adaptive least squares image restoration using whitening filters of short length. In *Second HST Image Restoration Workshop*, 1993.
6. H.F. Chen, P.N. Belhumeur, and D.W. Jacobs. In search of illumination invariants. In *CVPR00*, pages I: 254–261, 2000.
7. M. L. Cox, I. J. Miller and Bloom J. A. *Digital Watermarking*. Morgan Kaufmann, 2002.
8. T. Depovere, G. Kalker and J.P. Linnartz. Improved watermark detection using filtering before correlation. In *IEEE Int. Conf. on Image Processing*, pages I: 430–434, 1998.
9. O.D. Faugeras and W.K. Pratt. Decorrelation methods of texture feature extraction. *PAMI*, 2(4):323–332, July 1980.
10. R.M. Haralick and L.G. Shapiro. Computer and robot vision. In *Addison-Wesley*, 1992.
11. D.W. Jacobs, P.N. Belhumeur, and R. Basri. Comparing images under variable illumination. In *CVPR98*, pages 610–617, 1998.
12. A.K. Jain. Fundamentals of digital image processing. In *Prentice Hall*, 1989.
13. M. Lades, J.C. Vorbruggen, J. Buhmann, J. Lange, C. von der Malsburg, R.P. Wurtz, and W. Konen. Distortion invariant object recognition in the dynamic link architecture. *TC*, 42(3):300–311, March 1993.
14. Z. Lin and Y. Attikiouzel. Two-dimensional linear prediction model-based decorrelation method. *PAMI*, 11(6):661–665, June 1989.
15. M. Osadchy, M. Lindenbaum, and D.W. Jacobs. Whitening for photometric comparison of smooth surfaces under varying illumination. In *IEEE workshop on Statistical and Computational Theories of Vision*, October 2003.
16. A. Papoulis. *Probability, Random Variables, and Stochastic Processes*. McGraw Hill, 3rd edition, 1991.
17. W.K. Pratt. *Digital Image Processing (First Edition)*. Wiley, 1978.
18. S. Ravela and C. Luo. *Appearance-based global similarity retrieval of images*. edited by W. Bruce Croft, Kluwer Academic Publisher, 2000.
19. H.L. Van Trees. *Detection, Estimation, and Modulation Theory, Part I*. Wiley, New-York, 1965.
20. L.P. Yaroslavsky. *Digital Picture Processing. An Introduction*. Springer Verlag, Berlin, Heidelberg, 1985.

Structure from Motion of Parallel Lines

Patrick Baker and Yiannis Aloimonos

Center for Automation Research
AV Williams Bldg
University of Maryland
College Park, Maryland 20742
{pbaker,yiannis}@cfar.umd.edu

Abstract. We investigate the camera geometry of lines parallel in the world. In particular, we formalize the known rotational constraints and add new linear constraints on *camera position*. The constraints on camera position do not require the cameras to be viewing the same lines, thus providing applications for occluded scenes and calibration of cameras for which fields of view do not intersect. The constraints can also be viewed as constraints of camera geometry with planar patch coordinate systems, and provide a way to investigate texture in a deeper way than has been done to date.

1 Introduction

The geometry of parallel lines has been used extensively in computer vision, but to our knowledge only by way of the plane at infinity using the computation of vanishing points. The two main applications are calibration and shape from texture, and both are based on the principle that the vanishing point of a set of parallel lines is not affected by translation, as it lies on the plane at infinity. While these are important applications, there are geometric relations on sets of parallel lines embedded in a planar patch, which take into account distances between the lines rather than just their vanishing point.

Vanishing points have been used by many in computer vision, mostly for the determination of rotation and calibration for which they are particularly well suited, since they are unaffected by translation. There are numerous examples [1,3]. These methods have not looked further into the lines of which the vanishing points are composed, but it is helpful to look at the individual lines.

Lines have been used extensively in computer vision [5,7,4], but in general have not been as prominent as points, probably because they are difficult to work with. However, the use of of Plücker coordinates [6,2,8] can make many reconstruction and constraint derivations easier. In this paper we introduce an extension of the Plücker coordinates for lines in order to investigate lines embedded in a plane.

T. Pajdla and J. Matas (Eds.): ECCV 2004, LNCS 3024, pp. 229–240, 2004.

2   Notation and Reconstruction

Our use of parallelism restricts our world points to be represented by 3-vectors
P. We use homogeneous coordinates for image points **p**, so they are also 3-
vectors. Image lines are also represented by homogeneous 3-vectors $\boldsymbol{\ell}$. If a point
p is on a line ℓ, then their coordinates are perpendicular $\mathbf{p}^\mathrm{T}\boldsymbol{\ell} = 0$. We use the
general linear $B = KR$ to encapsulate a rotation followed by a calibration. For
a matrix B, we use $B^{-\mathrm{T}}$ to denote the inverse transpose of that matrix. Points
and lines that we actually measure in an image we denote by $\hat{\mathbf{p}}$ and $\hat{\boldsymbol{\ell}}$. Note
that if $\hat{\mathbf{p}} = B(\boldsymbol{\ell}_1 \times \boldsymbol{\ell}_2)$, then $\hat{\mathbf{p}} = (B^{-\mathrm{T}}\boldsymbol{\ell}_1) \times (B^{-\mathrm{T}}\boldsymbol{\ell}_2)$. For clarity, in equations
we often use **p** and $\boldsymbol{\ell}$, which denote the *calibrated and derotated* coordinates for
those points and lines.

2.1   Lines

We use the Plücker coordinate system for world lines, which is particularly well
suited for rigid motions of lines.

Definition 1. *A world line L is the set of all the points $P \in \mathbb{R}^3$ such that*
$\mathbf{P} = (1 - \lambda)\mathbf{Q}_1 + \lambda\mathbf{Q}_2$ *for two points* $\mathbf{Q}_i$, *and some scalar* λ. *The Plücker*
coordinates of this line are $\mathbf{L} = \left[\begin{smallmatrix} \mathbf{L}_d \\ \mathbf{L}_m \end{smallmatrix}\right]$, *where:*

$$\mathbf{L}_d = \mathbf{Q}_2 - \mathbf{Q}_1 \qquad\qquad direction\ of\ L \qquad\qquad (1)$$
$$\mathbf{L}_m = \mathbf{L}_d \times \mathbf{P} \qquad\qquad moment\ of\ L \qquad\qquad (2)$$

If we have a line L and a camera $(B, \mathbf{T})$, then the image line associated with
L is

$$\hat{\boldsymbol{\ell}} = B^{-\mathrm{T}}(\mathbf{L}_m - \mathbf{T} \times \mathbf{L}_d) \qquad\qquad (3)$$

where $\hat{\boldsymbol{\ell}}$ is perpendicular to the plane containing the line in the image. If B is the
rotation/calibration matrix for a point **P**, then $B^{-\mathrm{T}}$ is the rotation/calibration
matrix for a line **L**.

Lines are easier to reconstruct than points because the reconstruction always
exists. It is easily proved that:

Proposition 1. *If we have a line L in space which projects to two image lines*
$\hat{\boldsymbol{\ell}}_1$ *and* $\hat{\boldsymbol{\ell}}_2$ *in distinct cameras* $(B_1, \mathbf{T}_1)$, *and* $(B_2, \mathbf{T}_2)$, *then we can calculate the*
coordinates for **L** *if* $|\boldsymbol{\ell}_1 \times \boldsymbol{\ell}_2| \neq \mathbf{0}$, *if* $\ell_i = B_i^\mathrm{T}\hat{\ell}_i$:

$$\mathbf{L} = \begin{bmatrix} \boldsymbol{\ell}_1 \times \boldsymbol{\ell}_2 \\ \boldsymbol{\ell}_1\mathbf{T}_2^\mathrm{T}\boldsymbol{\ell}_2 - \boldsymbol{\ell}_2\mathbf{T}_1^\mathrm{T}\boldsymbol{\ell}_1 \end{bmatrix} \qquad\qquad (4)$$

It is possible that the cross product above will be zero. In this case the line exists
in the plane at infinity.

2.2   Singly Textured Planes

We introduce a new object to computer vision to encapsulate a set of parallel lines embedded in a plane. We motivate our definition as follows. Consider one line from the set of equally spaced lines in the plane, call it $\mathbf{L}_0$. We may represent this line using Plücker coordinates as $\mathbf{L}_0 = \left[\begin{smallmatrix} \mathbf{L}_d \\ \mathbf{L}_m \end{smallmatrix}\right]$. We take $\mathbf{Q}_0$ to be a point on $\mathbf{L}_0$, and the point $\mathbf{Q}_x = \mathbf{Q}_0 + x\mathbf{d}$ to be on the line at distance x in the texture for some direction $\mathbf{d}$. We can easily show that:

$$\mathbf{L}_d \times \mathbf{Q}_0 = \mathbf{L}_{m,0} \tag{5}$$

so that to get $\mathbf{L}_{m,n}$

$$\mathbf{L}_{m,n} = \mathbf{L}_d \times \mathbf{Q}_x \tag{6}$$
$$= \mathbf{L}_d \times \mathbf{Q}_0 + x\mathbf{L}_d \times \mathbf{d} \tag{7}$$
$$= \mathbf{L}_m + x\mathbf{L}_\lambda \tag{8}$$

where $\mathbf{L}_\lambda = \mathbf{L}_d \times \mathbf{d}$. Note that since both $\mathbf{L}_d$ and $\mathbf{d}$ are vectors which lie inside the plane, we must have that $\mathbf{L}_\lambda$ is normal to the textured plane. This leads us to the following definition, as shown in figure 1

Definition 2. *A **singly textured plane** H is a set of lines, equally spaced, embedded in a world plane. We give the textured plane coordinates*

$$\mathbf{H} = \begin{bmatrix} \mathbf{L}_d \\ \mathbf{L}_m \\ \mathbf{L}_\lambda \end{bmatrix} \tag{9}$$

with $\mathbf{L}_d^\mathsf{T}\mathbf{L}_m = 0$ and $\mathbf{L}_d^\mathsf{T}\mathbf{L}_\lambda = 0$. The coordinates of each line in the plane, indexed by n are:

$$\mathbf{L}_n = \begin{bmatrix} \mathbf{L}_d \\ \mathbf{L}_m + n\mathbf{L}_\lambda \end{bmatrix} \tag{10}$$

Our constraints are all based on intersection conditions between two textured planes.

Fact 1. *If we have two textured planes $\mathbf{H}_1$ and $\mathbf{H}_2$, then they lie on the same world plane if and only if:*

$$\mathbf{L}_{d,1}^\mathsf{T}\mathbf{L}_{m,2} + \mathbf{L}_{d,2}^\mathsf{T}\mathbf{L}_{m,1} = 0 \tag{11}$$

and

$$\mathbf{L}_{d,1}^\mathsf{T}\mathbf{L}_{\lambda,2} = 0 \qquad\qquad \mathbf{L}_{d,2}^\mathsf{T}\mathbf{L}_{\lambda,1} = 0 \tag{12}$$

We now turn to the reconstruction of a textured plane from image lines in four cameras. This reconstruction is non-intuitive in a sense because we do not require that the cameras be looking at the same lines. Each of the four cameras can look at a different line. We only require that we know which line has been imaged, that is, its index n. Given these four lines we can reconstruct a textured plane, as in figure 2, with the following *multilinear equation.*

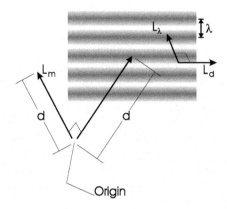

Fig. 1. The Parameters of a Textured Plane

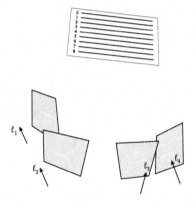

Fig. 2. Reconstructing a Textured Plane

Fact 2. *If we have a textured plane* $\mathbf{H}$ *which is imaged by four cameras into image lines* $\hat{\boldsymbol{\ell}}_i$, *and we know that our cameras have parameters* $(B_i, \mathbf{T}_i)$, *and further, we know that the image lines have indices* n_i, *then we may reconstruct the textured plane as:*

$$\mathbf{H} = \begin{bmatrix} \mathbf{L}_d \\ \mathbf{L}_m \\ \mathbf{L}_\lambda \end{bmatrix} = \sum_{[i_1\ i_2\ i_3\ i_4]\in\mathrm{perm}^+(1\ 2\ 3\ 4)} \begin{bmatrix} n_{i_1} n_{i_2} |\boldsymbol{\ell}_{i_3} \times \boldsymbol{\ell}_{i_4}| (\boldsymbol{\ell}_{i_1} \times \boldsymbol{\ell}_{i_2}) \\ 2 n_{i_1} n_{i_2} |\boldsymbol{\ell}_{i_1} \times \boldsymbol{\ell}_{i_2}| \boldsymbol{\ell}_{i_3} \mathbf{T}_{i_4}^{\mathrm{T}} \boldsymbol{\ell}_{i_4} \\ 2 n_{i_1} |\boldsymbol{\ell}_{i_2} \times \boldsymbol{\ell}_{i_3}| \boldsymbol{\ell}_{i_1} \mathbf{T}_{i_4}^{\mathrm{T}} \boldsymbol{\ell}_{i_4} \end{bmatrix} \quad (13)$$

Note that $|\cdot|$ *is the* signed *magnitude, and since the coordinates are homogeneous, it does not matter which sign is chosen. The same result could be obtained by defining*

$$|\boldsymbol{\ell}_i \times \boldsymbol{\ell}_j| = |\boldsymbol{\ell}_j \ \mathbf{v} \ \boldsymbol{\ell}_i| \quad (14)$$

where $\mathbf{v}$ *is any arbitrary vector not in the plane of* $\boldsymbol{\ell}_i \times \boldsymbol{\ell}_j$.

The proof of this is in the supplement.

3   Rotational Constraints

If we have three image lines $\hat{\ell}_i$, each of which are images of one of a set of parallel world lines, then using two of the cameras we may reconstruct the direction $\mathbf{L}_d$ of the world lines. From the construction of the Plücker lines, we know that any line with direction $\mathbf{L}_d$ must have moment vector perpendicular to $\mathbf{L}_d$. Putting these two facts together, we obtain

Proposition 2. *If we have one, two, or three parallel world lines, and three cameras with rotation/calibration matrices B_i, then if these three cameras view images of one of our world lines as $\hat{\ell}_i$, with the lines not necessarily the same in all cameras, then we obtain* **the prismatic line constraint.**

$$\hat{\ell}_2^{\mathsf{T}} B_2 (B_1^{\mathsf{T}} \hat{\ell}_1 \times B_3^{\mathsf{T}} \hat{\ell}_3) = 0 \qquad (15)$$

If we identify cameras 2 and 1 by setting $B_2 = B_1$, which corresponds to the case where both ℓ_1 and ℓ_2 are taken from the same camera. If these are different parallel lines, then we obtain the *vanishing point constraint*, noted by many, for example [9]

Proposition 3. *We have two or three parallel world lines, and two cameras with rotation/calibration matrices B_i. If camera 1 views image lines $\hat{\ell}_1$ and $\hat{\ell}_3$ and camera 2 views image line $\hat{\ell}_2$ we obtain* **the vanishing point constraint.**

$$\hat{\ell}_2^{\mathsf{T}} B_2 B_1^{-1} (\hat{\ell}_1 \times \hat{\ell}_3) = 0 \qquad (16)$$

$$\hat{\ell}_2^{\mathsf{T}} B_2 B_1^{-1} \hat{\mathbf{p}} = 0 \qquad (17)$$

The quantity $\hat{\mathbf{p}} = \hat{\ell}_1 \times \hat{\ell}_3$ is called a vanishing point, and it is the point through which all images of world lines of direction $\mathbf{L}_d$ will pass. The constraint says that if we have a vanishing point in one image and a line in another image which we know is parallel to the lines in the first camera, then we have a constraint on the B_i.

If we further identify cameras 2 and 1, then given an image of a set of parallel lines in one camera, we know that we must still have a zero triple product.

Proposition 4. *We have three parallel world lines, and a camera with rotation/calibration nonlinear function $B : \mathbb{R}^3 \to \mathbb{R}^3$. Given images of these three world lines $\hat{\ell}_i$, $i \in [1, \ldots, 3]$. We obtain the* **the vanishing point existence constraint.**

$$|B^{\mathsf{T}} \hat{\ell}_1 \ B^{\mathsf{T}} \hat{\ell}_2 \ B^{\mathsf{T}} \hat{\ell}_3| = 0 \qquad (18)$$

This last constraint means nothing if B is a linear function, since the constraint would be trivially satisfied. However, in the case where there is some nonlinear distortion in the projection equation, there will be a constraint on B, so we may say that the prismatic line constraint operates on 1, 2, or 3 cameras. We next go over the standard multilinear constraints to show how the prismatic line constraint relates to them.

4   Translational Constraints

It is as simple to form the texture constraints as it was to form the previous constraint. There is a line texture constraint a point texture constraint, and a mixed constraint. Keep in mind that all these constraints can be applied to fewer cameras by identifying the camera positions associated with various subsets of lines.

The first is the five camera constraint, which we call the harmonic trifocal, as shown in figure 3

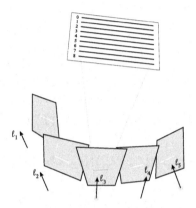

Fig. 3. The Harmonic Trifocal Constraint operates on five image lines

Fact 3. *If we have five cameras* $(B_i, \mathbf{T}_i)$, *and measure five lines* $\hat{\boldsymbol{\ell}}_i$, *which have indices* n_i *from a textured plane* **H**. *We may form the* $\boldsymbol{\ell}_i$ *using the* $\hat{\boldsymbol{\ell}}_i$ *and the* B_i *and have the following constraint:*

$$0 = \sum_{[i_1..i_5]\in\mathrm{P}^+[1..5]} n_{i_1} n_{i_2} (\boldsymbol{\ell}_{i_1} \times \boldsymbol{\ell}_{i_2})^{\mathrm{T}} (\boldsymbol{\ell}_{i_3} \times \boldsymbol{\ell}_{i_4}) \mathbf{T}_{i_5}^{\mathrm{T}} \boldsymbol{\ell}_{i_5} \tag{19}$$

Where perm$^+$ denote the even permutations.

Proof. Using fact 2, we may reconstruct the textured plane to obtain the parameters of the textured plane **H** using the lines one through four. Using this reconstruction, we can find the fifth image line as:

$$\boldsymbol{\ell}_5 = \mathbf{L}_m + n_5 \mathbf{L}_\lambda - \mathbf{T}_5 \times \mathbf{L}_d \tag{20}$$

If $\mathbf{p}_5$ is a point on $\boldsymbol{\ell}_5$, we know that $\mathbf{p}_5$ is perpendicular to $\boldsymbol{\ell}_5$, so that $\mathbf{p}_5^{\mathrm{T}}\boldsymbol{\ell}_5 = 0$. We can use this with the above equation to formulate the constraint. Note that since $\mathbf{L}_d$ is perpendicular to $\boldsymbol{\ell}_5$ that $\mathbf{L}_d$ is a point on the line $\boldsymbol{\ell}_5$, but if we set $\mathbf{p} = \mathbf{L}_d$, all of the right hand side terms disappear and we have no constraint.

Therefore we know that there is only one equation in our constraint, and we use $\mathbf{p}_5 = \mathbf{L}_d \times \boldsymbol{\ell}_5$. We can derive

$$0 = (\mathbf{L}_d \times \boldsymbol{\ell}_5)^\mathrm{T} (\mathbf{L}_m + n_5 \mathbf{L}_\lambda - \mathbf{T}_5 \times \mathbf{L}_d) \tag{21}$$

$$= |\mathbf{L}_d \; \boldsymbol{\ell}_5 \; \mathbf{L}_m| + n_5 |\mathbf{L}_d \; \boldsymbol{\ell}_5 \; \mathbf{L}_\lambda| - (\mathbf{L}_d \times \boldsymbol{\ell}_5)^\mathrm{T} (\mathbf{T}_5 \times \mathbf{L}_d) \tag{22}$$

we use vector algebra and the fact that $\mathbf{L}_d^\mathrm{T} \boldsymbol{\ell}_5 = 0$ to obtain $-\mathbf{L}_d^\mathrm{T} \mathbf{L}_d \mathbf{T}^\mathrm{T} \boldsymbol{\ell}_5$ for the last term

$$= \sum_{[j_1..j_4] \in \mathrm{P}^+[1..4]} [2 n_{j_1} n_{j_2} (\boldsymbol{\ell}_{j_1} \times \boldsymbol{\ell}_{j_2})^\mathrm{T} (\boldsymbol{\ell}_5 \times \boldsymbol{\ell}_{j_3}) \mathbf{T}_{j_4}^\mathrm{T} \boldsymbol{\ell}_{j_4} \tag{23}$$

$$+ 2 n_{j_1} n_5 (\boldsymbol{\ell}_{j_2} \times \boldsymbol{\ell}_{j_3})^\mathrm{T} (\boldsymbol{\ell}_5 \times \boldsymbol{\ell}_{j_1}) \mathbf{T}_{j_4}^\mathrm{T} \boldsymbol{\ell}_{j_4} \tag{24}$$

$$+ n_{j_1} n_{j_2} (\boldsymbol{\ell}_{j_3} \times \boldsymbol{\ell}_{j_4})^\mathrm{T} (\boldsymbol{\ell}_{j_1} \times \boldsymbol{\ell}_{j_2}) \mathbf{T}_5^\mathrm{T} \boldsymbol{\ell}_5 \tag{25}$$

which we can expand to

$$= \sum_{[j_1..j_4] \in \mathrm{P}^+[1..4]} [n_{j_1} n_{j_2} (\boldsymbol{\ell}_{j_1} \times \boldsymbol{\ell}_{j_2})^\mathrm{T} (\boldsymbol{\ell}_5 \times \boldsymbol{\ell}_{j_3}) \mathbf{T}_{j_4}^\mathrm{T} \boldsymbol{\ell}_{j_4} \tag{26}$$

$$+ n_{j_2} n_{j_1} (\boldsymbol{\ell}_{j_2} \times \boldsymbol{\ell}_{j_1})^\mathrm{T} (\boldsymbol{\ell}_{j_3} \times \boldsymbol{\ell}_5) \mathbf{T}_{j_4}^\mathrm{T} \boldsymbol{\ell}_{j_4} \tag{27}$$

$$+ n_5 n_{j_1} (\boldsymbol{\ell}_5 \times \boldsymbol{\ell}_{j_1})^\mathrm{T} (\boldsymbol{\ell}_{j_2} \times \boldsymbol{\ell}_{j_3}) \mathbf{T}_{j_4}^\mathrm{T} \boldsymbol{\ell}_{j_4} \tag{28}$$

$$+ n_{j_1} n_5 (\boldsymbol{\ell}_{j_1} \times \boldsymbol{\ell}_5)^\mathrm{T} (\boldsymbol{\ell}_{j_3} \times \boldsymbol{\ell}_{j_2}) \mathbf{T}_{j_4}^\mathrm{T} \boldsymbol{\ell}_{j_4} \tag{29}$$

$$+ n_{j_1} n_{j_2} (\boldsymbol{\ell}_{j_1} \times \boldsymbol{\ell}_{j_2})^\mathrm{T} (\boldsymbol{\ell}_{j_3} \times \boldsymbol{\ell}_{j_4}) \mathbf{T}_5^\mathrm{T} \boldsymbol{\ell}_5] \tag{30}$$

and this is equal to the desiderata.

Next is the mixed constraint, which operates on six cameras, as in figure 4.

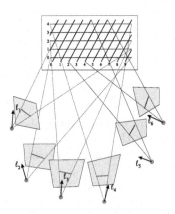

Fig. 4. The Hexalinear Constraint operates on six image lines

Fact 4. *If we have six cameras* $(B_i, \mathbf{T}_i)$ *which measure six lines* $\hat{\boldsymbol{\ell}}_i$ *on a doubly textured plane, and the first four lines measure one texture with indices* n_i *and the last four lines measure the other texture with unknown indices, then we may form the following constraint:*

$$0 = \sum_{[i_1..i_4]\in\mathrm{P}^+[1..4]} n_{i_1} |\boldsymbol{\ell}_5 \, \boldsymbol{\ell}_6 \, \boldsymbol{\ell}_{i_1}| |\boldsymbol{\ell}_{i_2} \times \boldsymbol{\ell}_{i_3}| \mathbf{T}_{i_4} \boldsymbol{\ell}_{i_4} \tag{31}$$

Proof. We may reconstruct the $\mathbf{L}_{\lambda,1}$ of the singly textured plane from the first four cameras. We may reconstruct the $\mathbf{L}_{d,2}$ of the world line using the last two cameras. Using fact 1 and 2 we may easily obtain the equation.

Last is the harmonic epipolar constraint, which operates on eight cameras, as in figure 5

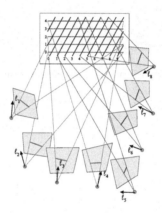

Fig. 5. The Harmonic Epipolar Constraint operates on eight image lines

Fact 5. *If we have eight cameras* $(B_i, \mathbf{T}_i)$ *which measure eight lines* $\hat{\boldsymbol{\ell}}_i$ *on a doubly textured plane, and the first four lines measure one texture with indices* $n_i \; i \in [1..4]$ *and the last four lines measure the other texture with indices* $n_i \; i \in [5..8]$, *then we may form the following constraint:*

$$0 = \sum_{[i_1..i_8]\in\mathrm{sP}^+} n_{i_1} n_{i_2} n_{i_5} n_{i_6} |\boldsymbol{\ell}_{i_3} \times \boldsymbol{\ell}_{i_4}| \cdot |\boldsymbol{\ell}_{i_5} \times \boldsymbol{\ell}_{i_6}| \cdot |\boldsymbol{\ell}_{i_1} \, \boldsymbol{\ell}_{i_2} \, \boldsymbol{\ell}_{i_7}| \boldsymbol{\ell}_{i_8}^{\mathrm{T}} \mathbf{T}_{i_8} \tag{32}$$

where sP^+ *indicates the even permutations among the first four and the last four indices, plus switching the first and last four sets of indices wholesale.*

5 Applications

While these constraints seem strange, they are also useful and can solve problems in computer vision not accesible with current methods. We present a few examples here.

5.1   Rotation from Oriented Textures

If we have three cameras, the rotational constraints can be used even if we can't find vanishing points, or even lines. If we use a simple autocorrelation metric on projected textures of wood as in figure 6, we can get a line direction, which is enough to input into our prismatic line constraint if we have three cameras.

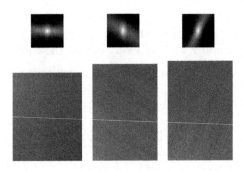

Fig. 6. A simple autocorrelation can measure orientation for use with the harmonic directionality constraint

5.2   Calibration

With the advent of the use of many cameras, the problem of calibrating them has come to the fore. More and more camera system whose cameras do not necessarily share fields of view are being created. For cameras which do not share fields of view, it is certainly possible to calibrate them rotationally together using bundles of parallel lines, and using the prismatic line constraint. This has been known.

However, the new constraints, particularly the harmonic epipolar constraint, allow us to calibrate *translationally* by showing a grid of boxes, with a couple of boxes singled out by a different appearance. This allows us to input the known line indices into our harmonic epipolar equation which then results in the computation of translation for sufficiently numerous and different views of the boxes in the plane.

5.3   Textures and Correspondence

One of the more interesting applications for these equations lies in the analysis of the correspondence problem together with our camera geometry. In order obtain a deeper insight into the correspondence problem, we need to relax our idea of correspondence. For if we have corresponding points as input there is clearly no reason to develop constraints on textures. Often obtaining these correspondences is difficult, so we break up the problem.

If we have two images, we say that two image regions are in **patch correspondence** if they are images of the same planar patch with some uniform texture property. For instance, in figure 7, the amorphous patches of the two buildings are in patch correspondence, even though we have not corresponded individual points. We show how to use this idea as a basis for hard geometry constraints.

 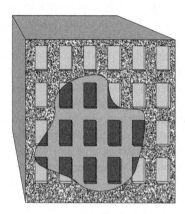

Fig. 7. The amorphous regions are in **patch correspondence**

Somehow, the intuitive notion of the wavelength in some signal has to enter the consideration. If you have a collection of textured planes, and these planes do not contain any wavelength greater than λ, then it is clear that if our camera positions are not known to accuracy at least less than λ, then it is impossible to compute any sort of correspondence. On the other hand, if we know our camera positions to within $\alpha << \lambda$, and we have many textures with wavelengths greater than λ, then it should somehow be possible to match with a high degree of probability. The smaller α is, the higher the probability that we find a match.

The above intuitive notions strongly suggest that the next step in making 3D models is to formulate a feedback mechanism. Bundle adjustment is some form of feedback, but it doesn't utilize any new measurements. Somehow, the feedback mechanism should work in a way that better measurements are introduced in the process.

We can use our new constraints in the following way, with some admittedly broad assumptions. We assume that we have obtained a reasonable estimate of the camera calibration and rotation. We also assume that we have knowledge of our cameras positions to within α. If we know that our cameras are looking at a regular texture, then we can measure the positions of some equally spaced lines with distance $\lambda >> \alpha$. Since we know these lines are equally spaced, then we know that our line indices $n = m\lambda$, for some integer m. So we can use our approximate camera positions the knowledge that m is an integer to form a search over the set of integers for the m that give us the least error. These will probably be the correct m. We can then use these m to obtain more accurate translational positions. This feedback loop can continue from larger to smaller wavelengths.

In order to use these constraints we need to be able to demonstrate that we can find lines within textures. While in this paper we cannot lay out an entire theory on finding lines (or peaks in the Fourier domain), we will show a few examples where we can address textures using geometric constraints where the standard multilinear constraints would have difficulty.

Obviously there are some textures which actually contain lines, such as in figure 8. However, there are other textures for which the lines are not readily apparent but in which we may find "virtual lines" corresponding to strong frequency components, such as in figure 9. We posit that a singly textured plane corresponds to a particular peak in frequency space, if such a peak exists. A real texture may have many peaks in frequency space, some of which are more prominent than others. If we have a few prominent peaks, this means that there is a strong regular repetition in the texture. This is just the situations where standard correspondence methods would have trouble. In this way our method complements the standard structure from motion methods.

Fig. 8. Lines are easy to find in this texture

Fig. 9. We can still find the same lines in affinely transformed textures

We showed above two textures for which it is relatively easy to find lines. We may apply our multilinear constraints to the lines in these textures.

Many textures are not as regular as the above textures. In this case, we need the entire patch to be visible in all cameras for the peaks to correspond to each other. But if the entire patch is visible from various cameras, we may find corresponding peaks.

But what if we have textures for which lines are not at all apparent, such as the beans in figure 10? This picture still has some frequency peaks, which generate the lines shown in that picture. Indeed, even if we affinely transform the image of the beans we may still find the same set of lines, as in figure 10. This allows us to use our constraints on the position of plane containing the beans and the position of the cameras.

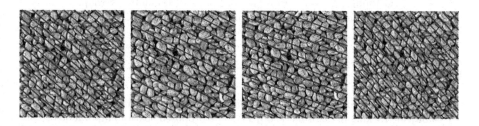

Fig. 10. Even with random textures the lines still exist if we have the whole patch

References

1. Stephen T. Barnard. Methods for interpreting perspective images. *Artificial Intelligence*, pages 435–462, 1983.
2. O. Bottema and B. Roth. *Theoretical Kinematics.* Dover, 1990.
3. Konstantinos Daniilidis and Joerg Ernst. Active intrinsic calibration using vanishing points. In *Proc. IEEE Conference on Computer Vision and Pattern Recognition*, pages 708–713, 1996.
4. R.I. Hartley. Camera calibration using line correspondences. In *DARPA93*, pages 361–366, 1993.
5. Y. Liu and T. S. Huang. Estimation of rigid body motion using straight line correspondences. *Computer Vision, Graphics, and Image Processing*, 43:37–52, 1988.
6. J. Plücker. On a new geometry of space. *Philisophical Transactions of the Royal Society of London*, 155:725–791, 1865.
7. A. Shashua. Algebraic functions for recognition. *IEEE Transactions on Pattern Analysis and Machine Intelligence*, 17(8):779–789, 1995.
8. F. Shevlin. Analysis of orientation problems using plucker lines. In *ICPR98*, page CVP1, 1998.
9. L. Shigang, S. Tsuji, and M. Imai. Determining of camera rotation from vanishing points of lines on horizontal planes. *International Journal of Computer Vision*, pages 499–502, 1990.

A Bayesian Framework for Multi-cue 3D Object Tracking

J. Giebel[1], D.M. Gavrila[1], and C. Schnörr[2]

. Machine Perception, DaimlerChrysler Research and Technology,
Wilhelm Runge Str. 11, 89089 Ulm, Germany
{jan.giebel,dariu.gavrila}@daimlerchrysler.com
. Computer Vision, Graphics and Pattern Recognition Group,
Department of Mathematics and Computer Science, University of Mannheim,
68131 Mannheim, Germany
schnoerr@uni-mannheim.de

Abstract. This paper presents a Bayesian framework for multi-cue 3D object tracking of deformable objects. The proposed spatio-temporal object representation involves a set of distinct linear subspace models or Dynamic Point Distribution Models (DPDMs), which can deal with both continuous and discontinuous appearance changes; the representation is learned fully automatically from training data. The representation is enriched with texture information by means of intensity histograms, which are compared using the Bhattacharyya coefficient. Direct 3D measurement is furthermore provided by a stereo system.
State propagation is achieved by a particle filter which combines the three cues shape, texture and depth, in its observation density function. The tracking framework integrates an independently operating object detection system by means of importance sampling. We illustrate the benefit of our integrated multi-cue tracking approach on pedestrian tracking from a moving vehicle.

1 Introduction

Object tracking is a central theme in computer vision with applications ranging from surveillance to intelligent vehicles. We are interested in tracking complex, deformable objects through cluttered environments, for those cases when simple segmentation techniques, such as background subtraction, are not applicable.

This paper presents a probabilistic framework for integrated detection and tracking of non-rigid objects. Detections from an independent source of information are modeled as "mixture" of Gaussians and are integrated by two means: They control initialization and termination by a set of rules and serve as additional source of information for the active tracks.

To increase robustness three independent visual cues are considered. Object shape is used, since it is (quite) independent of the complex illumination conditions found in real world applications and efficient matching techniques exist to compare shape templates with images [6]. Texture distributions are modeled

T. Pajdla and J. Matas (Eds.): ECCV 2004, LNCS 3024, pp. 241–252, 2004.

as histograms [14,15], which are particularly suitable for tracking since they are independent of object shape, invariant to rotation, scale, and translation, and easy to compute. Finally stereo measurements are integrated into the system.

In this work, tracking proceeds directly in 3D-space, which allows a more natural incorporation of real-world knowledge (e.g. kinematical properties of objects) and simplifies reasoning about occlusion and data association.

The outline of the paper is as follows: Section 2 reviews previous work. Our proposed multi-cue object representation is described in Section 3. It consists of two parts; the first deals with the spatio-temporal shape representation and the second relates to the texture model. The proposed particle filtering approach for multi-cue 3D object tracking is presented in Section 4. It integrates an independently operating external detection system. We illustrate our approach in Section 5 on the challenging topic of pedestrian tracking from a moving vehicle. Finally, we conclude Section 6.

2   Previous Work

Bayesian techniques are frequently used for visual tracking. They provide a sound mathematical foundation for the derivation of (posterior) probability density functions (pdf) in dynamical systems. The evolution of the pdf can in principle be calculated recursively by optimal Bayesian filtering. Each iteration involves a prediction step based on a dynamical model and a correction step based on a measurement model. Analytical solutions for the optimal Bayesian filtering problem are known only for certain special cases (e.g. Kalman filtering). For others, approximate techniques have been developed, such as extended Kalman [1], particle [2,4], and "unscented" filters [13]. In particular particle filters have become widespread, because of their great ease and flexibility in approximating complex pdfs, and dealing with a wide range of dynamical and measurement models Their multi-modal nature makes them particularly suited for object tracking in cluttered environments, where uni-modal techniques might get stuck and loose track.

Several extensions have been proposed to the early particle filter techniques, e.g. dealing with discrete/continuous state spaces [9,11], multiple target tracking [12,15,21], or multiple sources of information [10,17]. The latter has involved techniques such as importance sampling [10] or democratic integration [17,19], and have been used to combine visual cues such as edge and texture in a particle filter framework. Particle filters have furthermore been applied in combination with low-level [14,15], high-level [9], exemplar-based [18], or mixed-level [11] object representations.

In terms of representation, compact low-dimensional object parameterizations can be obtained by linear subspace techniques, e.g. using shape (PDMs) [3,9], or texture [20]. However, these methods have some limitations concerning the global linearity assumption: nonlinear object deformations have to be approximated by linear combinations of the modes of variation. They are not the most compact representations for objects undergoing complex (non-linear) deformations, nor do they tend to be very specific, since implausible shapes can be generated, when invalid combinations of the global modes are used.

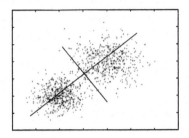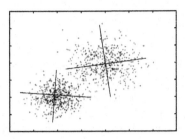

Fig. 1. Feature spaces: Linear and locally-linear feature spaces

Our approach, discussed in the next sections, builds upon the locally linear shape representation of [9] (see Figure 1). We extend this by a spatio-temporal shape representation, which does not utilize a common object parameterization for all possible shapes. Instead, a set of unconnected local parameterizations is used, which correspond to clusters of similar shapes. This allows our spatio-temporal shape representation to be fully automatically learned from training sequences of closed contours, without requiring prior feature correspondence.

We model texture by means of histograms similar to [14,15]. However, we do not rely on circular/rectangular region primitives, but take advantage of the detailed shape information to derive appropriate object masks for texture extraction. Furthermore, unlike previous work, we derive a 3D tracking framework also incorporating stereo measurements for added robustness.

Finally, our tracking framework integrates an independently operating object detection system by means of importance sampling.

3   Multi-cue Object Representation

3.1   Spatio-temporal Shape Representation

Dynamic point distribution models capture object appearance by a set of linear subspace models with temporal transition probabilities between them. This spatio-temporal shape representation can be learned automatically from example sequences of closed contours. See Figure 2. Three successive steps are involved.

Integrated registration and clustering: At first an integrated registration and clustering approach [8] is performed. The idea of integration is motivated by the fact, that general automatic registration methods are not able to find the physically correct point correspondences, if the variance in object appearance is too high. This is in particular the case for self occluding objects, when not all object parts are visible for all time. Our proposed approach therefore does not try to register all shapes into a common feature space prior to

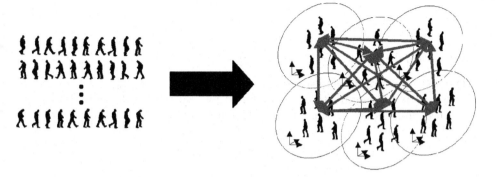

Fig. 2. Learning Dynamic Point Distribution Models

clustering. Instead the clustering is based on a similarity measure derived from the registration procedure. To be specific, the average distance between corresponding points after alignment. Only if this distance is lower than a user defined threshold, the shapes fall into the same cluster and the registration is assumed valid. For details, the reader is referred to [8].

Linear subspace decomposition: A principal component analysis is applied in each cluster of registered shapes to obtain compact shape parameterizations known as "Point Distribution Models" (PDMs) [3]. From the N^c shape vectors of cluster c given by their u- and v-coordinates

$$\mathbf{s}_i^c = (u_{i,1}^c, v_{i,1}^c, u_{i,2}^c v_{i,2}^c, ..., u_{i,n^c}^c, v_{i,n^c}^c), i \in \{1, 2, ..., N^c\} \tag{1}$$

the mean shape $\bar{\mathbf{s}}^c$ and covariance matrix K^c is derived. Solving the eigensystem $K^c \mathbf{e}^c_j = \lambda_j^c \mathbf{e}^c_j$ one obtains the $2n^c$ orthonormal eigenvectors, corresponding to the "modes of variation". The k^c most significant "variation vectors" $E^c = (\mathbf{e}_1^c, \mathbf{e}_2^c, ..., \mathbf{e}_{k^c}^c)$, the ones with the highest eigenvalues λ_j^c, are chosen to cover a user specified proportion of total variance contained in the cluster. Shapes can then be generated from the mean shape plus a weighted combination of the variation vectors

$$\mathbf{s}^c = \bar{\mathbf{s}}^c + E^c \mathbf{b}. \tag{2}$$

To ensure that the generated shapes remain similar to the training set, the weight vector $\mathbf{b}$ is constrained to lie in a hyperellipsoid about the subspace origin. Therefore $\mathbf{b}$ is scaled so that the weighted distance from the origin is less than a user-supplied threshold M_{max}

$$\sum_{l=1}^{k^c} \frac{b_l^{c2}}{\lambda_l^c} \leq M_{max}^2 \tag{3}$$

Markov transition matrix: To capture the temporal sequence of PDMs a discrete Markov model stores the transition probabilities $T_{i,j}$ from cluster i to j. They are automatically derived from the transition frequencies found in the training sequences. An extension for covering more complex temporal events (e.g. [5]) is conceivable and straightforward.

3.2   Modeling Texture Distributions

The texture distribution over a region $\mathbf{R} = (u_1, v_1, u_2, v_2, ..., u_{n_R}, v_{n_R})$, given by its n_R u- and v-coordinates, is represented by a histogram $\theta_{\mathbf{R}} = \{\theta^r\}_{r=1,...,m}$, which is divided into m bins. It is calculated as follows

$$\theta_{\mathbf{R}}^r = \frac{1}{n_R} \sum_{i=1}^{n_R} \delta(h(u_i, v_i) - r), \tag{4}$$

whereas $h(u_i, v_i)$ assigns one of the m bins for the grey value at location u_i, v_i and δ is the Kronecker delta function.

To measure the similarity of two distributions $\theta_1 = \{\theta_1^r\}_{r=1,...,m}$ and $\theta_2 = \{\theta_2^r\}_{r=1,...,m}$ we selected (among various possibilities [16]) the Bhattacharyya coefficient, which proved to be of value in combination with tracking [14,15]

$$\rho(\theta_1, \theta_2) = \sum_{r=1}^{m} \sqrt{\theta_1^r \theta_2^r}. \tag{5}$$

$\rho(\theta_1, \theta_2)$ ranges from 0 to 1, with 1 indicating a perfect match. The Bhattacharyya distance $d(\theta_1, \theta_2) = \sqrt{1 - \rho(\theta_1, \theta_2)}$ can easily be calculated from the coefficient.

For tracking, a reference distribution θ is calculated at track initialization, which is updated over time to compensate for small texture changes. As in [14] the update is done with the mean histogram $\bar{\theta}$ observed under the shape of all particles

$$\theta_{t+1}^r = \alpha \bar{\theta}_t^r + (1 - \alpha) \theta_t^r. \tag{6}$$

The user specified parameter α controls the contribution of the previous reference and the observed mean histograms.

4   Bayesian Tracking

In this work particle filtering is applied to approximate optimal Bayesian tracking [2,4] for a single target. The state vector $\boldsymbol{x} = (\Pi, \Sigma)$ of a particle comprises the position and velocity $\Pi = (x, y, z, v_x, v_y, v_z)$ in three dimensional space (a fixed object size is assumed), and the shape parameters $\Sigma = (c, \mathbf{b})$ introduced in Section 3.1. For tracking, the dynamics $p(\boldsymbol{x_{k+1}}|\boldsymbol{x_k} = s_k^i)$ and the conditional density $p(\boldsymbol{z_k}|\boldsymbol{x_k} = s_k^i)$ have to be specified, whereas s_k^i is the ith sample at time k.

4.1   Dynamics

Object dynamics is assumed independent for the two components Π and Σ of our state vector and is defined separately as follows.

During each sampling period T_k the position and velocity vector Π is assumed to evolve according to the following dynamic equation

$$\Pi_{k+1} = \begin{pmatrix} 1 & 0 & 0 & T_k & 0 & 0 \\ 0 & 1 & 0 & 0 & T_k & 0 \\ 0 & 0 & 1 & 0 & 0 & T_k \\ 0 & 0 & 0 & 1 & 0 & 0 \\ 0 & 0 & 0 & 0 & 1 & 0 \\ 0 & 0 & 0 & 0 & 0 & 1 \end{pmatrix} \Pi_k + \Gamma_k \nu_k, \tag{7}$$

whereas ν_k is the user defined process noise, which has to be chosen to account for velocity changes during each sampling interval T_k, and Γ_k is the time dependent noise gain [1,2].

The shape component $\Sigma = (c, \mathbf{b})$ is composed of a discrete parameter c_k modeling the cluster membership and the continuous valued weight vector $\mathbf{b}$. To deal with this "mixed" state the dynamics is decomposed as follows

$$p(\Sigma_{k+1}|\Sigma_k) = p(\mathbf{b}_{k+1}|c_{k+1}, \Sigma_k)p(c_{k+1}|\Sigma_k). \tag{8}$$

Assuming that the transition probabilities $T_{i,j}$ of our discrete Markov model are independent of the previous weight vector $\mathbf{b}_k$, the second part of Equation 8 reduces to

$$p(c_{k+1} = j|c_k = i, \mathbf{b}_k) = T_{i,j}(\mathbf{b}_k) = T_{i,j}. \tag{9}$$

For the continuous parameters we now have to consider two cases: In case of $i = j$, when no PDM transition occurs, we assume

$$p(\mathbf{b}_{k+1}|c_{k+1} = j, c_k = i, \mathbf{b}_k) = p_{i,j}(\mathbf{b}_{k+1}|\mathbf{b}_k) \tag{10}$$

to be a Gaussian random walk. For $i \neq j$ the cluster is switched from i to j and the parameters $\mathbf{b}$ are assumed to be normally distributed about the mean shape of PDM j.

4.2   Multi-cue Observation

Three cues are integrated in this work, which contribute to the particle weights: shape, texture, and stereo. Their distributions are assumed conditionally independent so that

$$p(\mathbf{z}_k|\mathbf{x}_k = s_k^i) = p_{shape}(\mathbf{z}_k|\mathbf{x}_k = s_k^i)\, p_{texture}(\mathbf{z}_k|\mathbf{x}_k = s_k^i)\, p_{stereo}(\mathbf{z}_k|\mathbf{x}_k = s_k^i). \tag{11}$$

Since the shape and texture similarity measures between the prediction and observation are defined in the image plane, the shape of each particle is generated using Equation 2. Its centroid coordinates u, v and the scale factor s are derived using a simple pinhole camera model with known (intrinsic/extrinsic) parameters from the 3D-coordinates x, y, z and the specified 3D object dimensions.

Shape: A method based on multi-feature distance transforms [6] is applied to measure the similarity between the predicted shapes and the observed image edges. It takes into account the position and direction of edge elements. Formally, if the image I is observed at time k and S is the shape of particle s_k^i we define

$$p_{shape}(z_k|x_k = s_k^i) \propto \exp(-\alpha_{shape}(\frac{1}{|S|}\sum_{s\in S}D_I(s))^2), \tag{12}$$

whereas $|S|$ denotes the number of features s in S, $D_I(s)$ is the distance of the closest feature in I to s, and α_{shape} is a user specified weight.

Texture: For texture, $p_{texture}(z_k|x_k = s_k^i)$ is defined as

$$p_{texture}(z_k|x_k = s_k^i) \propto \exp(-\alpha_{texture}d^2(\omega, \theta)), \tag{13}$$

whereas $d(\omega, \theta)$ is the Bhattacharyya distance described in Section 3.2 between the reference distribution θ and the observed texture distribution ω under the shape of particle s_k^i. Like above, $\alpha_{texture}$ is a user defined weighting factor.

Stereo: A stereo vision module generates a depth image I_{depth}, which contains the distance to certain feature points. To measure the depth d_{stereo} of particle s_k^i the distance of the feature points under its shape are averaged. Given the predicted distance z of s_k^i and the measurement d_{stereo}, we define

$$p_{stereo}(z_k|x_k = s_k^i) \propto \exp(-\alpha_{stereo}(d_{stereo} - z)^2), \tag{14}$$

whereas α_{stereo} is a weighting factor.

4.3   Integrated Detection and Tracking

A set of particle filters is used to track multiple objects in this work. Each is in one of the states *active* or *inactive*. An *active* track is either *visible* or *hidden*.

A detection system provides possible object locations, which are modeled as "mixture" of Gaussians, whereas one component corresponds to one detection. The mixture is exploited in two ways: As importance function for the particle filters and for the initialization and termination of tracks.

The following rules, which depend on the actual detections, observations, and geometric constraints control the evolution of tracks.

A track is initialized, if no mean state of an *active* track is in the 3σ-bound of a detection. To suppress spurious measurements it starts *hidden*. Initialization involves drawing the 3D position and velocity of the particles according to the Gaussian of the detection. Since no shape information is provided by the detection system, the cluster membership and the continuous parameters are randomly assigned. After the first particle weighting the reference texture distribution is initialized with the mean histogram observed under the shape of all particles.

A track is *visible*, if it has at least t_1 associated detections, if the last associated detection is at most t_2 time steps old, and if the actual match values were better than user defined thresholds for the last t_3 times. Otherwise the track is *hidden*.

A track becomes *inactive*, if the prediction falls outside the detection area or image, if the actual match values were worse than user specified thresholds for t_4 successive times, or if a second track is tracking the same object.

4.4   Sampling

For particle filtering an algorithm based on *icondensation* [10] is applied. It integrates the standard factored sampling technique of *condensation* [2], importance sampling, and sampling from a "reinitialization" prior probability density.

This allows us to integrate the mixture of Gaussians from the detection system as an importance function into the tracking framework. Like in [10], it is also used as a reinitialization prior, which gives us the possibility to draw samples independently of the past history using the Gaussian of the nearest detection.

Like in [9,11] a two step sampling approach is followed for the decomposed dynamics of the mixed discrete/continuous shape space. At first the cluster of our shape model is determined using the transition probabilities $T_{i,j}$ and afterwards the weight vector **b** is predicted according to the Gaussian assumptions described in Section 4.1.

5   Experiments

To evaluate our framework we performed experiments on pedestrian tracking from a moving vehicle. The dynamic shape model, outlined in Section 3.1, was trained from approximately 2500 pedestrian shapes of our training set. The resulting cluster prototypes and the temporal transition probabilities between the associated PDMs are illustrated in Figure 3. As expected (and desired), the

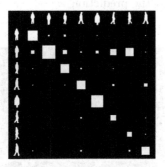

Fig. 3. Cluster transition matrix: The squares represent the transition probabilities from a PDM of column j to row i.

diagonal elements of the transition matrix contain high values, so that there is always a high probability of staying in the same cluster during tracking. Figure 4 shows three random trajectories generated with the proposed dynamic shape model assuming that a camera is moving at 5m/s towards the object in 3D-space, which is moving laterally at 1m/s. Each greyscale change corresponds to a PDM transition.

Pedestrian detection is performed by the ChamferSystem in the experiments. It localizes objects according to their shape in a coarse to fine approach over a

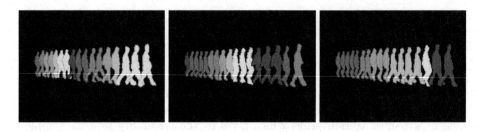

Fig. 4. Predicting shape changes using Dynamic Point Distribution Models: Three random trajectories assuming that the camera is moving at 5m/s towards the object, which is moving laterally at 1m/s. Each greyscale change corresponds to a PDM transition.

template hierarchy by correlating with distance transformed images. For details the reader is referred to [7]. The 3D position is derived by backprojecting the 2D shape with our camera model, assuming that the object is standing on the ground.

The tracking system was tested on a 2.4GHz standard workstation and needs about 300ms/frame for an active track and an image resolution of 256 × 196. The number of particles is set to 500 in the experiments.

During tracking, the a-priori and a-posteriori probability of each PDM can be observed online, as shown in Figure 5. The size of the dark and light grey boxes indicate the a-priori and a-posteriori probability respectively. The more similar they are, the better the prediction.

Fig. 5. Tracking results: The dark box indicates the a-priori and the light the a-posteriori confidence of each cluster. The larger the box the higher the probability.

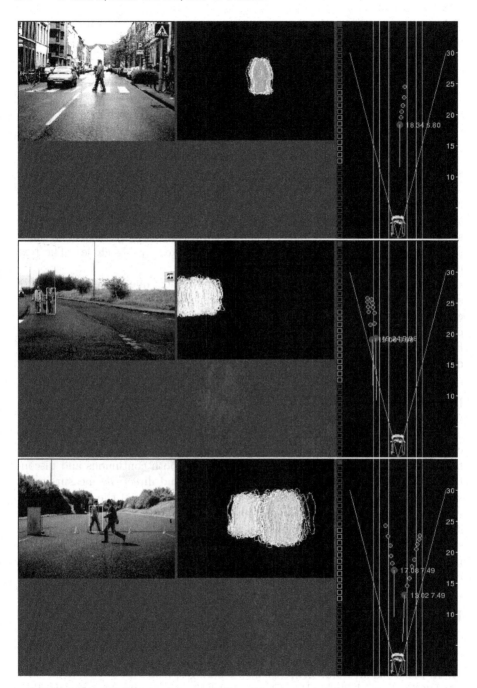

Fig. 6. Tracking results: In the left images the best sample is shown for each track. In addition the detections are illustrated as boxes. The shapes of all particles, which approximate the posterior pdf, are drawn in the middle. Finally a top view of the scene can be viewed on the right.

Table 1. Average distances of the true and estimated pedestrian locations for a sequence of 34 images.

cues	distance	lateral error	error in depth
edge	1.37m	0.085m	1.34m
edge + texture	1.28m	0.14m	1.25m
edge + texture + stereo	1.05m	0.11m	1.03m

Results of the overall system are given in Figure 6 for urban, rural, and synthetic environments. In the original images (left column) the best sample of each active track is shown. Whenever detections are observed, they are also represented there as grey boxes. The shapes of all particles, which approximate the posterior pdf, are drawn in the middle column. Finally, a top view of the scene can be viewed on the right. The past trajectories are represented by small circles while the current position estimate is marked by big circles. The text contains the actual distance and velocity estimates.

To substantiate the visually observable improvement due to the integration of shape, texture, and stereo information, the position estimates of the system were compared against ground truth. Table 1 shows the results for the first sequence of Figure 6, which consists of 34 images. As expected, the average error in depth is higher than the lateral and an improved performance due to the integration of multiple cues can be observed.

6   Conclusions

This paper presented a general Bayesian framework for multi-cue 3D deformable object tracking. A method for learning spatio-temporal shape representations from examples was outlined, which can deal with both continuous and discontinuous appearance changes. Texture histograms and direct 3D measurements were integrated, to improve the robustness and versatility of the framework. It was presented how measurements from an independently operating detection system can be integrated into the tracking approach by means of importance sampling. Experiments show, that the proposed framework is suitable for tracking pedestrians from a moving vehicle and that the integration of multiple cues can improve the tracking performance.

References

1. Y. Bar-Shalom, X.R. Li, and T. Kirubarajan, editors. *Estimation with applications to tracking and navigation*. Wiley, 2001.
2. A. Blake and M. Isard. *Active Contours*. Springer, 1998.
3. T.F. Cootes, C.J. Taylor, D.C. Cooper, and J. Graham. Active shape models - their training and application. *Computer Vision and Image Understanding*, 61(1):38–59, January 1995.
4. A. Doucet, N. de Freitas, and N. Gordon, editors. *Sequential Monte Carlo Methods in Practice*. Springer, 2001.

5. R.J. Elliot, L. Aggoun, and J.B. Moore. *Hidden Markov Models*. Springer, 2nd edition, 1997.
6. D. M. Gavrila. Multi-feature hierarchical template matching using distance transforms. In *Proc. of the ICPR*, pages 439–444, Brisbane, 1998.
7. D. M. Gavrila. Pedestrian detection from a moving vehicle. In *Proc. of the ECCV*, pages 37–49, 2000.
8. D.M. Gavrila and J. Giebel. Virtual sample generation for template-based shape matching. In *Proc. of the IEEE CVPR Conf.*, pages I:676–681, 2001.
9. T. Heap and D. Hogg. Wormholes in shape space: Tracking through discontinuous changes in shape. In *Proc. of the ICCV*, pages 344–349, 1998.
10. M. Isard and A. Blake. Icondensation: Unifying low-level and high-level tracking in a stochastic framework. In *Proc. of the ECCV*, pages 893–908, 1998.
11. M. Isard and A. Blake. A mixed-state condensation tracker with automatic model-switching. In *Proc. of the ICCV*, pages 107–112, 1998.
12. M. Isard and J. MacCormick. Bramble: A bayesian multiple-blob tracker. In *Proc. of the ICCV*, pages 34–41, 2001.
13. S. Julier and J. Uhlmann. A new extension of the kalman filter to nonlinear systems. In *Int. Symp. Aerospace/Defense Sensing, Simul. and Controls*, 1997.
14. K. Nummiaro, E. Koller-Meier, and L. Van Gool. Object tracking with an adaptive color-based particle filter. In *Proc. of the Deutsche Arbeitsgemeinschaft für Mustererkennung*, Zurich, Switzerland, 2002.
15. P. Perez, C. Hue, J. Vermaak, and M. Gangnet. Color-based probabilistic tracking. In *Proc. of the ECCV*, pages 661–675, 2002.
16. Y. Rubner, J. Puzicha, C. Tomasi, and J.M. Buhmann. Empirical evaluation of dissimilarity measures for color and texture. *CVIU*, 84(1):25–43, 2001.
17. M. Spengler and B. Schiele. Towards robust multi-cue integration for visual tracking. *Machine, Vision and Applications*, 14:50–58, 2003.
18. K. Toyama and A. Blake. Probabilistic tracking with exemplars in a metric space. *Int. J. of Computer Vision*, 48(1):9–19, 2002.
19. J. Triesch and C. von der Malsburg. Self-organized integration of adaptive visual cues for face tracking. In *Proc. of the IEEE Int. Conf. on Automatic Face and Gesture Recognition*, Los Alamitos, 2000.
20. M. Turk and A. Pentland. Eigenfaces for recognition. *Journal of Cognitive Neuro Science*, 3(1):71–86, 1991.
21. J. Vermaak, A. Doucet, and P. Perez. Maintaining multi-modality through mixture tracking. In *Proc. of the ICCV*, 2003.

On the Significance of Real-World Conditions for Material Classification

Eric Hayman, Barbara Caputo, Mario Fritz, and Jan-Olof Eklundh

Computational Vision and Active Perception Laboratory
Dept. of Numerical Analysis and Computer Science
Royal Institute of Technology (KTH), SE-100 44 Stockholm, Sweden
{hayman,caputo,mjfritz,joe}@nada.kth.se

Abstract. Classifying materials from their appearance is a challenging problem, especially if illumination and pose conditions are permitted to change: highlights and shadows caused by 3D structure can radically alter a sample's visual texture. Despite these difficulties, researchers have demonstrated impressive results on the CUReT database which contains many images of 61 materials under different conditions. A first contribution of this paper is to further advance the state-of-the-art by applying Support Vector Machines to this problem. To our knowledge, we record the best results to date on the CUReT database.

In our work we additionally investigate the effect of *scale* since robustness to viewing distance and zoom settings is crucial in many real-world situations. Indeed, a material's appearance can vary considerably as fine-level detail becomes visible or disappears as the camera moves towards or away from the subject. We handle scale-variations using a pure-learning approach, incorporating samples imaged at different distances into the training set. An empirical investigation is conducted to show how the classification accuracy decreases as less scale information is made available during training.

Since the CUReT database contains little scale variation, we introduce a new database which images ten CUReT materials at different distances, while also maintaining some change in pose and illumination. The first aim of the database is thus to provide scale variations, but a second and equally important objective is to attempt to recognise *different samples* of the CUReT materials. For instance, does training on the CUReT database enable recognition of *another* piece of sandpaper? The results clearly demonstrate that it is *not* possible to do so with any acceptable degree of accuracy. Thus we conclude that impressive results even on a well-designed database such as CUReT, does not imply that material classification is close to being a solved problem under real-world conditions.

1 Introduction

The recognition of materials from their visual texture has many applications, for instance it facilitates image retrieval and object recognition. As a step towards the use of such techniques in the real world, recent developments have concentrated on being able to recognise materials from a variety of poses and with different illumination conditions [16,9,31]. This is a particularly challenging task when the material has considerable 3-dimensional structure. With such 3D textures, cast shadows and highlights can cause the

T. Pajdla and J. Matas (Eds.): ECCV 2004, LNCS 3024, pp. 253–266, 2004.
© Springer-Verlag Berlin Heidelberg 2004

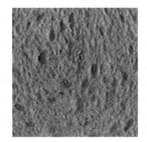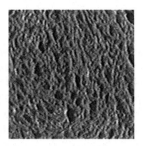

Fig. 1. Three images of white bread taken from the CUReT database demonstrating the variation of appearance of a 3D texture as the pose and illumination conditions change.

appearance to change radically with different viewing angles and illumination conditions. An example from the CUReT database [10] (white bread) is given in Fig. 1.

The overall goal of our work is to bring material recognition algorithms closer still to the stage where they will be useful in real-world applications. Thus a major objective is providing robustness to variations in *scale*. Experiments will show that failure in this regard rapidly leads to a deterioration in classification accuracy. Our solution is a pure-learning approach which accommodates variations in scale in the training samples, similar to how differing illumination and pose are modelled.

A further contribution concerns demonstrating the suitability of Support Vector Machines (SVMs) [8,29] as classifiers in this recognition problem. Experiments show that the SVM classifier systematically outperforms the nearest-neighbour classification scheme adopted by Varma and Zisserman [31] with which we compare our results, and we also demonstrate that we achieve an improvement on their Markov Random Field (MRF) approach [32] which, to our knowledge, previously yielded the best overall classification rate on the CUReT database.

As already alluded to, experiments are conducted on the CUReT image database [10] which captures variations in illumination and pose for 61 different materials, many of which contain significant 3D structure. This database does not, however, contain many scaling effects. Some indication of the performance under varying scale can be achieved by artificially scaling the images by modifying the scales of the filters in the filter bank. However, we also investigate classification results on pictures of materials present in the CUReT database, imaged in our laboratory. The objectives of these experiments are two-fold. First, it permits a systematic study of scale effects while still providing some variations in pose and illumination. Second, we investigate whether it is possible to recognise materials in this new database given models trained on the CUReT database. This indeed proves a stern test, since both the sample of material, the camera and lighting conditions are different to those used during training.

Thus the final contribution of this paper is the construction of a new database, designed to complement the CUReT database with scale variations. This database, called KTH-TIPS (Textures under varying Illumination Pose and Scale) is freely available to other researchers via the web [12].

The remainder of the paper is organised as follows. Section 2 reviews previous literature in the field. Particular emphasis is placed on the algorithm of Varma and

Zisserman [31] on which we ourselves to a large extent build. Section 3 discusses the application of Support Vector Machines to this problem, and also presents experiments which demonstrate their superior performance relative to the original approach of [31]. Further experiments in the paper also make use of SVMs. Then, Section 4 discusses issues with scale, presents a pure learning approach for tackling the problem, and conducts experiments on the CUReT database. Section 5 introduces the new database designed to supplement the CUReT database for experiments with scale. Conclusions are drawn and potential avenues for future research outlined in Section 6.

2   Previous Work

Most work on texture recognition [21,23,14] has dealt with planar image patches sampled, for instance, from the Brodatz collection [4]. The training and test sets typically consist of non-overlapping patches taken from the same images. More recently, however, researchers have started to combat the problems associated with recognising materials in spite of varying pose and illumination. Leung and Malik [16] modelled 3D materials in terms of *texton histograms*. The notion of textons is familiar from the work of Julesz [13], but it was only recently defined for greyscale images as a cluster centre in a feature space formed by the output of a filter bank. Given a vocabulary of textons, the filter output of each pixel is assigned to its nearest texton, and a histogram of textons is formed over an extended image patch. This procedure was described for 2D textures in [20] and for 3D textures in [16] by stacking geometrically registered images from the training set. Recognition is achieved by gathering multiple images of the material from the same viewpoints and illuminations, performing the geometric registration, computing the texton histogram and classifying it using a nearest-neighbour scheme based on the χ^2 distance between model and query histograms.

Cula and Dana [9] adapted the method of Leung and Malik to form a faster, simpler and more accurate classifier. They realised that the 3D registration was not necessary, and instead described a material by multiple histograms of 2D textons, where each histogram is obtained from a single image in the training set. This also implies that recognition is possible from a single query image.

Varma and Zisserman [31] argued strongly for a rotationally invariant filter bank. First, two images of the same material differing only by an image-plane rotation should be equivalent. Second, removing the orientation information in the filter bank considerably reduced the size of the feature vector. Third, it led to a more compact texton vocabulary since it was no longer necessary for one texton to be a rotated version of another. Rotational invariance was achieved by storing only the maximum response over orientation of a given type of filter at a given scale. As Fig. 2 indicates, the filter bank contains 38 filters, but only 8 responses are stored, yielding the so-called MR8 (Maximum Response 8) descriptor. Not only did the use of this descriptor reduce storage requirements and computation times, an improvement in recognition rate was also achieved. In their experiments [31] they use 92 of the 205 images in the CUReT database, removing samples at severely slanted poses. Splitting these 92 images of each material equally into 46 images for training and 46 images for the test set, they obtain an impressive classification accuracy of up to 97.43% [32]. This is the system that we will be using as a reference in our own experiments.

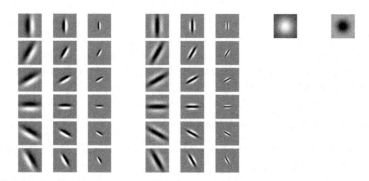

Fig. 2. Following [31] we use a filter bank consisting of edge and bar filters (first and second Gaussian derivatives) at 3 scales and 6 orientations, and also a Gaussian and Laplacian. Only the maximum response is stored for each orientation, yielding the 8-dimensional MR8 descriptor.

Many different descriptors have been proposed for texture discrimination. Filter banks are indeed very popular [21,16,9,31,24], and there is evidence that biological systems process visual stimuli using filters resembling those in Fig. 2. However, non-filter descriptors have recently been regaining popularity [11,32,19,15]. [32] presents state-of-the-art results on the CUReT database using a Markov Random Field (MRF) model. Määenpää and Pietikäinen [19] extend the Local Binary Pattern approach [23] to multiple image resolutions and obtain near-perfect results on a test set from the Outex database. However, this database does not contain any variations in pose or illumination, and the variation in scale is rather small (100dpi images in the training set and 120dpi images in the test set). Recent, impressive work by Lazebnik *et al.* [15] considers simultaneous segmentation and classification of textures under varying scale. Interest points are detected, normalised for scale [18], skew and orientation, and intensity domain spin images computed as descriptors. Each interest point is assigned to a texture class before a relaxation scheme is used to smooth the response. It remains to be seen, however, whether this scheme can handle large variations in illumination, and the number of classes in their experiments is rather small. Scale-invariant recognition using Gabor filters on Brodatz textures was considered by Manthalkar *et al.* [22].

3   Using Support Vector Machines for Texture Classification

The first contribution of this paper is to demonstrate that recent advances in machine learning prove fruitful in material classification. Support Vector Machines are state--of-the-art large margin classifiers which have gained popularity within visual pattern recognition, particularly for object recognition. Pontil and Verri [26] demonstrated the robustness of SVMs to noise, bias in the registration and moderate amounts of occlusion while Roobaert *et al.* [27] examined their generalisation capabilities when trained on only a few views per object. Barla *et al.* [2] proposed a new class of kernel inspired by similarity measures successful in vision applications. Other notable work includes [17,5,1]. Although SVMs have previously been used on planar textures [14], they have not, to our knowledge, been applied to 3D material classification under varying imaging conditions.

Before demonstrating in experiments the improvements that can be achieved with SVMs, we provide a brief review of the theory behind this type of algorithm. For a more detailed treatment, we refer to [8,29].

3.1 Support Vector Machines: A Review

Consider the problem of separating a set of training data $(x_1, y_1), (x_2, y_2)...(x_m, y_m)$, where $x_i \in \Re^N$ is a feature vector and $y_i \in \{-1, +1\}$ its class label. If we assume that the two classes can be separated by a hyperplane $w \cdot x + b = 0$, and that we have no prior knowledge about the data distribution, then the optimal hyperplane (the one with the lowest bound on the expected generalisation error) is that which has maximum distance to the closest points in the training set. The optimal values for w and b can be found by solving the following constrained minimisation problem:

$$\underset{w,b}{\text{minimise}} \frac{1}{2}\|w\|^2 \quad \text{subject to} \quad y_i(w \cdot x_i + b) \geq 1, \forall i = 1, \ldots m \qquad (1)$$

Introducing Lagrange multipliers $\alpha_i (i = 1, \ldots m)$ results in a classification function

$$f(x) = \text{sign}\left(\sum_{i=1}^{m} \alpha_i y_i w \cdot x + b\right). \qquad (2)$$

where α_i and b are found by Sequential Minimal Optimisation (SMO, [8,29]). Most of the α_i's take the value of zero; those x_i with nonzero α_i are the "support vectors". In cases where the two classes are non-separable, Lagrange multipliers are introduced, $0 \leq \alpha_i \leq C, i = 1, \ldots m$, where C determines the trade-off between margin maximisation and training error minimisation. To obtain a nonlinear classifier, one maps the data from the input space $\Re^N$ to a high dimensional feature space $\mathcal{H}$ by $x \rightarrow \Phi(x) \in \mathcal{H}$, such that the mapped data points of the two classes are linearly separable in the feature space. Assuming there exists a kernel function K such that $K(x, y) = \Phi(x) \cdot \Phi(y)$, a nonlinear SVM can be constructed by replacing the inner product $w \cdot x$ by the kernel function $K(x, y)$ in eqn. (2). This corresponds to constructing an optimal separating hyperplane in the feature space. Kernels commonly used include polynomials $K(x, y) = (x \cdot y)^d$, and the Gaussian Radial Basis Function (RBF) kernel $K(x, y) = \exp\{-\gamma\|x - y\|^2\}$. The Gaussian RBF has been found to perform better for histogram-like features [7,5], thus unless specified otherwise, this is the kernel we will use in the present paper.

The extension of SVM from 2-class to M-class problems can be achieved following two basic strategies: In a *one-vs-others* approach, M SVMs are trained, each separating a single class from all remaining classes. Although the most popular scheme for extending to multi-class problems (see for instance [8,5,7]), there is no bound on its generalisation error, and the training time of the standard method scales linearly with M [8]. In the second strategy, the *pairwise approach*, $M(M - 1)/2$ two-class machines are trained. The pairwise classifiers are arranged in trees, where each tree node represents an SVM. Decisions can be made using a bottom-up tree similar to the elimination tree used in tennis tournaments [8], or a Directed Acyclic Graph (DAG, [25]).

3.2 Results

Platt and others [25] presented an analysis of the generalisation error for DAG, indicating that building large margin DAGs in a high dimensional feature space can yield good generalisation performance. On the basis of this result and of several empirical studies, we used a pairwise approach with DAG in this paper, using the *LibSVM* library [6]. C was fixed at 100 whereas γ in the RBF was obtained automatically by cross-validation. The histograms were treated as feature vectors and normalised to unit length.

We compared the SVM classifier with our own implementation of the algorithm of Varma and Zisserman [31], which from now on will be denoted the VZ algorithm, and we use the same 200×200 pixels greyscale image patches as they do. The patches are selected such that only foreground is present.

A first experiment ascertains the maximum performance that can be achieved on the CUReT database by using a very large texton vocabulary. 40 textons were found from each of the 61 materials, giving a total dictionary of $40 \times 61 = 2440$ textons. The 92 images per sample were split equally into training and test sets. Varma and Zisserman [32] previously reported a 97.43% success rate, while our own implementation of their algorithm gave an average of 97.66% with a standard deviation of 0.11% over 10 runs[1]. In contrast, the SVM classifier gave $98.36 \pm 0.10\%$ using an RBF kernel and $98.46 \pm 0.09\%$ using the χ^2-kernel $K = \exp\{-\gamma\chi^2\}$. We implemented this Mercer kernel [3] within *LibSVM*. This performs better even than the very best result obtained in [32] using an MRF model (98.03%) which, to our knowledge, previously represented the best overall classification rate on the CUReT database.

Another natural extension to the Varma and Zisserman algorithm is to replace the Nearest Neighbour classifier with a k-Nearest Neighbour scheme. Several variants of k-NN were tried with different strategies to resolve conflicts [28]. Of these, Method 2 from [28] proved best in our scenario, but no variant yielded an improved recognition rate for any choice of $k > 1$. This is probably due to a relatively sparse sampling of the pose and illumination conditions in the training set.

Further experiments examine the dependency on the size of the training set (Fig. 3a) and the texton vocabulary (Fig. 3b). Both plots clearly demonstrate that the SVM classifier reduces the error rate by $30 - 50\%$ in comparison with the method of [31]. In both experiments, textons were found from the 20 materials specified in [16] rather than all 61 materials. In Fig. 3a, 10 textons per material are used, giving a dictionary of $20 \times 10 = 200$ textons. In Fig. 3b, the training set consists of 23 images per material, and the remaining 69 images per material are placed in the test set.

---

[1] The variability within experiments is due to slightly different texton vocabularies; images are selected at random when generating the dictionary with K-means clustering. The difference of 0.23% between our results and the figure of 97.43% reported in [32] is caused by our use of more truncated filter kernels (41×41 compared to 49×49 [30]) although the scales used to compute the kernels were identical. For a texton to be assigned to a pixel, the entire support region of the filter kernel is required to lie inside the 200×200 image patch. Thus the texton histograms contain more entries when a smaller filter kernel is used. It may be noted that the MRF algorithm of [32] computes descriptors from significantly smaller regions, for instance 7×7.

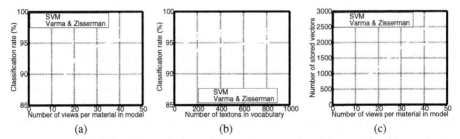

Fig. 3. Experiments comparing our SVM scheme with the VZ [31] approach. (a) plots the reliance on the number of views in the training set, (b) the dependency on the size of the texton vocabulary, and (c) the size of the stored model. In (c) the model reduction schemes of [31,32] were not implemented.

Training times for SVM vary from about 20 seconds (with a vocabulary of 100 textons, 12 views per material in the training set) up to roughly 50 minutes (for 2440 textons, 46 views per material). Finding γ by cross-validation, if required, typically incurs a further cost of 3–7 times the figures reported above.

The size of the resulting model is illustrated in Fig. 3c. Recalling that only the support vectors need be stored, and noting that storing the coefficients α_i incurs little overhead, SVM reduces the size of the model by 10 – 20%. This is significantly less than the reduction by almost 80% obtained using the greedy algorithms described in [31] and [32]. However, the scheme in [31] used the test set for validating the model, which is unreasonable in a recognition task, while the method in [32] was extremely expensive in training, in fact by a few orders of magnitude [30] in comparison with the more expensive times listed for SVM above. Moreover, their procedure for selecting a validation set from the training set is largely heuristic and at a high risk of over-fitting, in which case the performance on the test set would drop very significantly [30].

4 Material Classification under Variations in Scale

The results presented so far on the CUReT database were obtained without significant scale variation in the images [2]. In the real world, scale undoubtedly plays an important role, and it seems unlikely that the classifiers described so far will perform well. First, the individual filters are tuned to certain frequencies, and zooming in or out on a texture changes the characteristic frequencies of its visual appearance. Second, zooming in on a texture can make visible fine-level details which could not be recorded at coarser scales due to the finite resolution of the imaging device. Examples are given in Fig. 4. With cotton, for instance, at a coarse scale a vertical line structure is just about visible, whereas at a fine scale the woven grid can be seen clearly, including horizontal fibres.

---

[2] Four samples are zoomed in images of other materials. In the experiments reported in this paper, classifying one material as the zoomed in version of that same material is labelled an incorrect match. In practise such confusions are fairly common for those four materials, but this does not have a very large effect on classification rates when averaged over all materials.

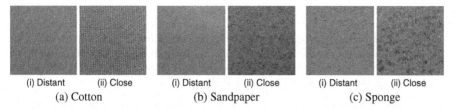

(i) Distant   (ii) Close   (i) Distant   (ii) Close   (i) Distant   (ii) Close
        (a) Cotton   (b) Sandpaper   (c) Sponge

Fig. 4. The appearance of materials can change dramatically with distance to the camera.

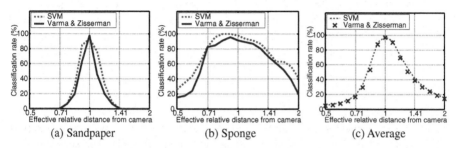

        (a) Sandpaper   (b) Sponge   (c) Average

Fig. 5. Variations in scale can have a disastrous effect. In this experiment the training set contains images only at the default scale whereas the test set contains images rescaled by amounts up to a factor of two both up and down. For sandpaper (a) the recognition rate drops dramatically, whereas for sponge (b) they are more stable, probably since the salient features are repeated over a wide range of scales. Results averaged over the entire CUReT database are shown in (c).

4.1   A Motivational Experiment

Experimental confirmation of the scale-dependence of the texton-histogram based schemes was obtained by supplementing the CUReT database with artificially scaled versions of its images. Rather than rescaling the images, which raises various issues with respect to smoothing and aliasing, the *filters* were rescaled. For instance, reducing the size of the image (zooming out) by a factor of two is equivalent to doubling the standard deviations in the filters. This procedure was repeated at eight logarithmically spaced intervals per octave, scaling both up and down one octave. This resulted in $2 \times 8 = 16$ scaled images in addition to the unscaled original, giving a total of 17 images. Only the unscaled images were placed in the training set, whereas recognition was attempted at all 17 scales [3]. The 92 images per sample were split evenly into training and test sets, and a texton vocabulary of 400 textons was used.

Fig. 5 illustrates this dependency on scale for two materials. Sandpaper (Fig. 5a), shows almost no robustness to changes in scale, whereas sponge (Fig. 5b) is much more resilient. These effects can be attributed to two main factors. The first concerns *intra-class* properties: materials with a highly regular pattern have a clear characteristic scale, whereas others, such as sponge, exhibit similar features over a range of scales. The

---

[3] We acknowledge that this method is no true replacement for real images since (i) it is not possible to increase the resolution while artificially zooming in, and (ii) the information content is reduced somewhat when artificially zooming out since the size of the 200×200 pixels patch is effectively reduced.

Table 1. The recognition rate (in %) on the artificially rescaled CUReT database as the richness of the model is varied both with respect to the sampling density in the scale direction and in how many of the original 92 images are incorporated in the training set (per scale). With 3 scales present, the training set includes the original image and also samples at scales one octave up and one octave down. With five scales, half-octave positions are made available during training, and with 9 scales, quarter-octave positions are also used.

		No. of original images per sample					No. of original images per sample		
		46	23	12			46	23	12
No. of scales	9	97.58	94.59	91.60	No. of scales	9	92.14	89.23	83.65
	5	95.89	92.67	89.89		5	81.19	77.91	71.95
	3	81.75	78.04	76.80		3	58.00	55.69	51.57
	1	36.85	36.12	34.08		1	34.47	33.16	30.90

(a) SVM	(b) Varma and Zisserman [31]

feature vector for the former material could be severely mutated, whereas we expect the descriptor of the latter to be more robust to changes in scale. The second factor depends on the *inter-class* variation in the database: the recognition rate depends on the degree of distraction caused by other materials. It is feasible that a material imaged at a certain scale closely resembles another material at the default scale. Fig. 5c shows corresponding plots for an average over all 61 materials in the CUReT database.

4.2 Robustness to Scale Variations: A Pure Learning Approach

The experiment described above indicated that providing robustness to changes in image scale can be crucial if material recognition is to function in the real world. A natural strategy for providing such robustness is to extend the training set to cover not just variations in *pose* and *illumination* conditions, but also *scale*. An alternative, left unexplored here, would be to include only images at one scale during training, but then artificially rescale the query image to a number of candidate scales by rescaling the filter bank.

An open question is how densely it is necessary to sample in the scale direction, particularly since the size of the training set has obvious implications for algorithm speed and memory requirements. Clearly there will be some dependence on the bandwidth of the filters, but the amount of inter-class variation will also be of consequence.

This dependence on sampling in the scale dimension was ascertained empirically on the rescaled CUReT database, and our findings are summarised in Tables 1a and b for the SVM and VZ classifiers respectively with a vocabulary of 400 textons. The most noteworthy aspect of these results is that impoverishing the model in the *scale* dimension appears to have a more severe effect than reducing the size of the training set with respect to the proportion of the original 92 images which were placed in the training set. Both SVM and the VZ schemes exhibit such behaviour. A further point worth emphasising is that SVM systematically outperforms the VZ classifier, as was also seen in Section 3. Again, we attempted replacing the Nearest Neighbour classifier in the Varma and Zisserman approach with k-Nearest Neighbour schemes, but without observing any improvement for $k > 1$.

(a) The variation with respect to scale in the KTH-TIPS database.

(b) The variation of pose and illumination present in the KTH-TIPS database.

Fig. 6. The variations contained in the new KTH-TIPS (Textures under varying Illumination Pose and Scale) database. In (a) the middle image, depicting the central scale, was selected to correspond roughly to the scale used in the CUReT database. The left and right images are captured with the sample at half and twice that distance, respectively. 3 further images per octave (not shown) are present in the database. (b) shows 3 out of 9 images per scale, showing the variation of pose and illumination. Prior to use, images were cropped so only foreground was present.

5   The KTH-TIPS Database of Materials under Varying Scale

Although the results presented above gave some indication as to the deterioration in performance under changes in scale, the artificial rescaling is no perfect replacement for real images. Therefore we created a new database to supplement CUReT by providing variations in *scale* in addition to pose and illumination. Thus we named it the KTH-TIPS (Textures under varying Illumination Pose and Scale) database. A second objective with the database was to evaluate whether models trained on the CUReT database could be used to recognise materials from pictures taken in other settings. This could indeed prove challenging since not only the camera, poses and illuminant differ, but also the actual samples: can *another* sponge be recognised using the CUReT sponge?

To date, our database contains ten materials also present in the CUReT database. These are sandpaper, crumpled aluminium foil, styrofoam, sponge, corduroy, linen, cotton, brown bread, orange peel and cracker B. These are imaged at nine distances from the camera to give equidistant log-scales over two octaves, as illustrated in Fig. 6a for the cracker. The central scale was selected, by visual inspection, to correspond roughly to the scale used in the CUReT database. At each distance images were captured using three different directions of illumination (front, side and top) and three different poses (central, $22.5°$ turned left, $22.5°$ turned right) giving a total of $3 \times 3 = 9$ images per scale, and $9 \times 9 = 81$ images per material. A subset of these is shown in Fig. 6b. For each image we selected a 200×200 pixels region to remove the background.

The database is freely available on the web [12].

We now present three sets of experiments on the KTH-TIPS database, differing in how the model was obtained. The first uses the CUReT database for training, the second a combination of both databases, and the third only KTH-TIPS.

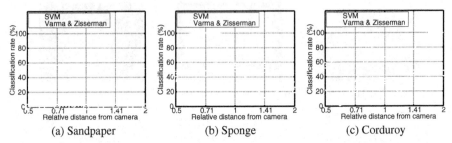

Fig. 7. Experiments attempting to recognise images from the new KTH-TIPS database using a model trained on all 61 materials of the CUReT database. The recognition rate is plotted against scale for three materials.

Using the CUReT database for training. We attempted to recognise the materials in KTH-TIPS using a model obtained by training on the 61 materials of the CUReT database. 46 out of 92 images per material were placed in the training set. To cope with variations in scale, the procedure described in Section 4.2 is used: the model is acquired by rescaling each training sample from the CUReT database by adapting the Gaussian derivative filters. For this experiment the training set contained data from 9 scales, equidistantly spaced along the log-scale dimension over two octaves.

Results for sandpaper, sponge and corduroy can be seen in Fig. 7a, b and c respectively. Performance on sandpaper is very poor. This failure could be due to differences between our sample of sandpaper and the CUReT sample of sandpaper, despite our efforts to provide similar samples. We did, however, note that sandpaper was a very difficult material to recognise also in experiments using the CUReT database as the test set. This indicates that many of the other materials can be confused with sandpaper.

Results were much improved for sponge and corduroy where recognition results of around 50% were achieved. It is interesting to note that the VZ classifier outperformed SVM in these experiments. The success rate of the VZ approach varies considerably with scale. It would seem that there is not perfect overlap between the two octaves in scale in the two datasets. Another explanation for a drop-off in performance at fine scales is that the rescaling of the CUReT database cannot improve the resolution: rescaling the filters does not permit sub-pixel structure to appear. A third reason is that the images closest to the camera were poorly focused in some cases. The SVM classifier provided much more consistent results over varying scales, as could perhaps be expected from the experiment reported in Table 1. However, the recognition rate was consistently fairly low over *all* scales. By supplying a test set too different to the samples provided during training, we are asking the SVM to perform a task for which it was not optimised; SVMs are designed for *discrimination* rather than *generalisation*.

The recognition rates for all 10 materials, averaged over all scales, is provided in Table 2a. Results are, on the whole, well below 50%, clearly demonstrating that material recognition cannot be performed reliably in the real world merely using the CUReT database to form the model. We have, however, confirmed that many of the confusions are reasonable. For instance, cotton was frequently confused with linen.

Table 2. Attempting to recognise samples from the KTH-TIPS database. Results are averaged over all scales.

Material	Recognition rate (%)	
	SVM	VZ
sandpaper	0.00	1.23
aluminium foil	11.35	12.35
styrofoam	34.72	38.27
sponge	50.62	54.32
corduroy	46.91	59.26
linen	30.41	25.93
cotton	11.11	20.99
brown bread	5.11	7.41
orange peel	11.11	11.11
cracker B	3.70	7.41
AVERAGE	**20.50**	**23.83**

Material	Recognition rate (%)	
	SVM	VZ
sandpaper	77.78	66.67
aluminium foil	91.67	88.89
styrofoam	100.00	91.67
sponge	100.00	100.00
corduroy	80.56	80.56
linen	61.11	41.67
cotton	61.11	47.22
brown bread	77.78	80.56
orange peel	100.00	63.89
cracker B	91.67	80.56
AVERAGE	**84.17**	**74.17**

(a) Training only on CUReT   (b) Training on *both* CUReT and KTH-TIPS

Using a combination of databases for training. In a second experiment we combined the CUReT and KTH-TIPS databases for training. Thus we no longer needed to worry about training and tests being performed on different samples, but now some classes in the model contained a wider variety, thus increasing the risk of classes overlapping in the feature space. We report experimental results for training with 5 equidistant scales in the log-scale dimension, spanning two octaves. For KTH-TIPS materials, at each scale 3 out of 9 images in the KTH-TIPS database were used for training, as were 43 images from the CUReT database. This same total number of 46 training images per scale was also used for the 51 materials only found in CUReT; these were included as distractors in the experiment. Results are summarised in Table 2b. As expected, including the KTH-TIPS samples in the training set yielded much better results; the average over all materials increased to 84.17% for SVM and 79.17% for VZ .

Training on KTH-TIPS. We also performed similar experiments using only the KTH-TIPS database for training, implying that the model contained only 10 classes rather than 61. Thus there are fewer distractions, and the overall recognition rate increased to 90.56% for SVM and 84.44% for VZ with 5 scales. Using only the central scale resulted in classification rates of 64.03% and 59.70% for SVM and VZ respectively. We will not report results from these experiments further.

6   Discussion and Conclusions

This paper attempted to bring material classification a step closer to real-world applications by extending work on 3D textures under varying *pose* and *illumination* to also accommodate changes in *scale*. We showed in experiments that it is crucial to model scale in some manner, and we demonstrated a scale-robust classifier which incorporates the variations in scale directly into the training set. Experiments were conducted both on an artificially rescaled version of the CUReT database, and on a new database designed to supplement the CUReT database by imaging a subset (currently 10 out of 61) of the materials at a range of distances, while still maintaining some variation in pose and illumination. This database represents the second contribution of this paper, and is available to other researchers via the web [12].

A third contribution was to demonstrate the superiority of Support Vector Machines (SVMs) in this application. We obtained a recognition rate of 98.46% on the CUReT database at constant scale which, to our knowledge, represents the highest rate to date.

However, a more sobering conclusion, and perhaps the most important message from this paper, is that such success on the CUReT database does *not* necessarily imply that it is possible to recognise those materials in the real world, even when scale is modelled. The main reason is probably that the samples imaged in our laboratory were not identical to those in CUReT. Naturally it is possible to include multiple samples of the same material in a database, but with increased intra-class variability, the risk of inter-class confusion increases. As this risk depends on the number of classes in the database, keeping this number low (e.g. in production line applications) should make it feasible to separate the classes, but with a large number it might only be possible to classify into broader *groups* of materials. The performance will again depend on scale since most materials appear more homogeneous with increased imaging distance.

In other work we are currently investigating mechanisms for scale selection as a pre-processing step [18]. Although it might still be necessary to store models at multiple characteristic scales, this number should still be smaller than with the pure-learning approach. This would reduce storage requirements, and also the recognition time.

A possible reason for sandpaper proving so hard to recognise in the experiments reported in Fig. 5a, is that the representation in terms of filters blurs the information too much with this kind of salt-and-pepper structure. Indeed, the role of filter banks has recently been questioned, and other representations have proved effective [11,32,19]. Thus we intend to explore such descriptors in our future work.

Acknowledgements. The authors are very grateful to Manik Varma and Andrew Zisserman for discussions regarding their algorithms, and for providing appropriately cropped images from the CUReT database.

This work was funded by the EU-IST projects IST-2000-29688 *Insight2+* (EH,MF) and IST-2000-29375 *Cogvis* (BC), and the *VISCOS* project funded by the Swedish Foundation for Strategic Research (EH).

References

1. S. Avidan. Support vector tracking. In *Proc. CVPR, Kauai, Hawaii*, pages I:184–191, 2001.
2. A. Barla, F. Odone, and A. Verri. Hausdorff kernel for 3D object acquisition and detection. In *Proc. ECCV, Copenhagen*, page IV: 20 ff., 2002.
3. S. Belongie, C. Fowlkes, F. Chung, and J. Malik. Spectral partitioning with indefinite kernels using the Nyström extension. In *Proc. ECCV, Copenhagen*, page III: 531 ff., 2002.
4. P. Brodatz. *Textures.* Dover, 1966.
5. B. Caputo and Gy Dorko. How to combine color and shape information for 3D object recognition: kernels do the trick. In *Proc. NIPS, Vancouver*, 2002.
6. Chih-Chung Chang and Chih-Jen Lin. *LIBSVM: a library for support vector machines*, 2001. Software available at http://www.csie.ntu.edu.tw/~cjlin/libsvm.

7. O. Chapelle, P. Haffner, and V. Vapnik. SVMs for histogram-based image classification. IEEE Trans. on Neural Networks, 10(5), 1999.

8. N. Cristianini and J. S. Taylor. *An introduction to support vector machines and other kernel-based learning methods.* Cambridge University Press, 2000.

9. O.G. Cula and K.J. Dana. Compact representation of bidirectional texture functions. In *Proc. CVPR, Kauai, Hawaii*, pages I:1041–1047, 2001.

10. K.J. Dana, B. van Ginneken, S.K. Nayar, and J.J. Koenderink. Reflectance and texture of real-world surfaces. *ACM Transactions on Graphics*, 18(1):1–34, January 1999.

11. A. Efros and T. Leung. Texture synthesis by non-parametric sampling. In *Proc. ICCV, Kerkyra, Greece*, pages 1033–1038, 1999.

12. M. Fritz, E. Hayman, B. Caputo, and J.-O. Eklundh. The KTH-TIPS database. Available at http://www.nada.kth.se/cvap/databases/kth-tips.

13. B. Julesz and R. Bergen. Textons, the elements of texture perception, and their interactions. *Nature*, 290:91–97, 1981.

14. K.I. Kim, K. Jung, S.H. Park, and H.J. Kim. Support vector machines for texture classification. *PAMI*, 24(11):1542–1550, November 2002.

15. S. Lazebnik, C. Schmid, and J. Ponce. Affine-invariant local descriptors and neighbourhood statistics for texture recognition. In *Proc. ICCV, Nice*, pages 649–655, 2003.

16. T. Leung and J. Malik. Representing and recognizing the visual appearance of materials using three-dimensional textons. *IJCV*, 43(1):29–44, June 2001.

17. S.Z. Li, Q.D. Fu, L. Gu, B. Scholkopf, Y. Cheng, and H.J. Zhang. Kernel machine based learning for multi-view face detection and pose estimation. In *Proc. ICCV, Vancouver*, pages II: 674–679, 2001.

18. T. Lindeberg. Feature detection with automatic scale selection. *IJCV*, 30(2):79–116, 1998.

19. T. Mäenpää and M. Pietikäinen. Multi-scale binary patterns for texture analysis. In *Proc. SCIA, Gothenberg, Sweden*, pages 885–892, 2003.

20. J. Malik, S. Belongie, J. Shi, and T. Leung. Textons, contours and regions: Cue integration in image segmentation. In *Proc. ICCV, Kerkyra, Greece*, pages 918–925, 1999.

21. B.S. Manjunath and W.Y. Ma. Texture features for browsing and retrieval of image data. *PAMI*, 18(8):837–842, Aug 1996.

22. R. Manthalkar, P.K. Biswas, and B.N. Chatterji. Rotation and scale invariant texture classification using gabor wavelets. In *Texture Workshop*, pages 87–90, 2002.

23. T. Ojala, M. Pietikäinen, and D. Harwood. A comparative study of texture measures with classification based on feature distributions. *PR*, 29(1):51–59, Jan 1996.

24. A. Penirschke, M.J. Chantler, and M. Petrou. Illuminant rotation invariant classification of 3D surface textures using Lissajous's ellipses. In *Texture Workshop*, pages 103–108, 2002.

25. J. C. Platt, N. Cristianini, and J. Shawe-Taylor. Large margin DAGs for multiclass classification. In *Proc. NIPS 2000, Denver, Colorado*, 2000.

26. M. Pontil and A. Verri. Support vector machines for 3D object recognition. *PAMI*, 20(6):637–646, June 1998.

27. D. Roobaert, M. Zillich, and J.O. Eklundh. A pure learning approach to background-invariant object recognition using pedagogical support vector learning. In *Proc. CVPR, Kauai, Hawaii*, pages II:351–357, 2001.

28. S. Singh, J. Haddon, and M. Markou. Nearest-neighbour classifiers in natural scene analysis. *PR*, 34(8):1601–1612, August 2001.

29. V. Vapnik. *Statistical learning theory.* Wiley and Son, New York, 1998.

30. M. Varma. Private communication, 2003.

31. M. Varma and A. Zisserman. Classifying images of materials: Achieving viewpoint and illumination independence. In *Proc. ECCV, Copenhagen*, page III: 255 ff., 2002.

32. M. Varma and A. Zisserman. Texture classification: are filter banks necessary? In *Proc. CVPR, Madison, Wisconsin*, pages II: 691–698, 2003.

Toward Accurate Segmentation of the LV Myocardium and Chamber for Volumes Estimation in Gated SPECT Sequences

Diane Lingrand[1], Arnaud Charnoz[1], Pierre Malick Koulibaly[2],
Jacques Darcourt[2], and Johan Montagnat[3]

[1] I3S, UNSA/CNRS UMR 6070, B.P. 121, F06903 Sophia Antipolis, France
lingrand@i3s.unice.fr
http://www.i3s.unice.fr/~lingrand/
[2] Centre Antoine Lacassagne, Nice, France
[3] CREATIS, CNRS/INSA Lyon, F69621 Villeurbanne Cédex, France
johan@creatis.insa-lyon.fr

Abstract. The left ventricle myocardium and chamber segmentation in gated SPECT images is a challenging problem. Segmentation is however the first step to geometry reconstruction and quantitative measurements needed for clinical parameters extraction from the images. New algorithms for segmenting the heart left ventricle myocardium and chamber are proposed. The accuracy of the volumes measured from the geometrical models used for segmentation is evaluated using simulated images. The error on the computed ejection fraction is low enough for diagnosis assistance. Experiments on real images are shown.

1 Introduction

The Left Ventricle (LV) myocardium accurate segmentation in gated SPECT (Single Photon Emission Computed Tomography) images is a challenging problem due to the high level of noise and the signal drops resulting of insufficiently perfused regions. The LV chamber automated segmentation is even more difficult as the upper bound of the ventricle does not appear in the images. However, the accurate segmentation of the LV myocardium and chamber is very important for the estimation of the heart wall thickness and the chamber volume variation during the heart cycle. These parameters are needed to estimate clinically well established diagnosis indicators such as the ejection fraction.

In this paper, we propose an implicit model-based segmentation algorithm of the LV myocardium and chamber. Our model is guided by the need of accuracy for volumes quantitative estimation. Indeed, the coarse spatial and temporal resolution of gated SPECT images causes large partial volume effects that can significantly alter the volume estimation results. This paper follows an earlier study on levelset-based segmentation of gated SPECT image [4].

To model objects and segment images, both explicit [20] and implicit [16,2] deformable models have been proposed in the literature [15]. The levelset has

T. Pajdla and J. Matas (Eds.): ECCV 2004, LNCS 3024, pp. 267–278, 2004.
© Springer-Verlag Berlin Heidelberg 2004

been widely used in segmentation [17,3,5], medical images segmentation [13,18, 8,11,14], heart segmentation [9] and SPECT images segmentation [7]. Some are taken into account shape priors [6]. Contrarily to many earlier approaches, our algorithm is taking into account a complete heart cycle sequence rather than processing volume frames independently. It is therefore better able to filter the image noise and to take into account temporal partial volume effects.

2   Segmentation Model

2.1   LV Myocardium Model

The LV myocardium is modeled using a levelset-based method. The levelset provides a geometrical representation of the LV as well as a deformation process needed for extracting the myocardium shape from the image. In the levelset framework, a surface model S is implicitly represented as the 0 isosurface of a higher dimension function u. S deforms when u evolves according to an evolutive equation. Most evolution criteria found in the literature are spatial [12]. In the case of dynamic sequences, we prefer the Debreuve et al criterion [7]:

$$\frac{\partial u_n}{\partial t} = \left(\lambda_{in}(I_n - \mu_{in_n})^2 - \lambda_{out}(B - I_n)^2 + \lambda_c \kappa_n\right) \|\nabla u_n\| \tag{1}$$

where I_n represents the image at instant n. The whole sequence is used in order to filter noise and determine the mean background intensity B, reestimated at each iteration. κ_n is the curvature at instant n and μ_{in_n} the mean of image n internal part, also reestimated at each iteration from the zero level of u_n. λ_{in}, λ_{out}, and λ_c are weight parameters. This criterion makes the hypothesis that the image is composed of a uniform intensity region (the object to segment) and a background B. This approximation is only roughly valid for SPECT images due to the image noise, the inhomogeneity of the heart and the perfusion defaults causing signal drops. A forward Euler based on finite differences is used for PDE resolution. We note that there is no relation between iteration time (t) and physical time (n).

2.2   LV Chamber Model

The LV chamber surface is delimited by the myocardium inner boundaries and the valves plane on top. However, the LV myocardium has a U shape opened on top in gated SPECT images and the valves are not visible. A method to enclose the chamber volume is therefore needed.

User Guided Methods. Some manual or semi-manual methods have been proposed in the literature. In [7], the authors manually set the two planes location. The result of this method is very user dependent. Faber, Cooke et al [10] approximate the LV valves by two fixed planes (see left of figure 1). The location and orientation of the two planes were empirically fixed on a dataset and is merely valid for a given acquisition protocol. Moreover, it is difficult to ensure that the chamber volume is always closed by the two planes: the myocardium upper part is irregular and holes are likely to appear between the myocardium boundaries and the planes.

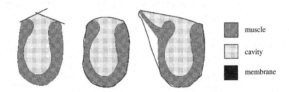

Fig. 1. Left: manual LV chamber closure. Center: membrane algorithm. Right: segmentation error inducing a volume estimation error.

Membrane Algorithm To face the difficulty to accurately close the ventricle using planes, a new convex envelope algorithm was developed. This membrane method, depicted in center of figure 1, is completely automatic. The membrane is a deformable surface initialized from the result of the myocardium segmentation and deformed using the following evolution equation:

$$\frac{\partial u}{\partial t} = (\lambda_1 I^2 + \lambda_2 \kappa)\|\nabla u\| \tag{2}$$

where I is a binary image resulting from the myocardium segmentation. The drawback of the membrane method is its sensitivity to the correct LV segmentation: for example when the visible bright region shape is not a U-shape. The membrane encloses the outliers and the inside volume is poorly estimated as illustrated in right of figure 1.

Once the membrane has been deformed, the LV chamber is obtained by binary image processing: a binary myocardium image is produced from the myocardium segmentation and the chamber is filled up to the membrane boundary. An isosurface of the resulting inner volume is computed as illustrated in figure 9. From the LV chamber volume, we can estimate the heart ejection fraction (EF). The EF is computed as the ratio between the volume of blood ejected at each heart beat (the difference of volumes between the chamber at end of dilation phase, or *diastole*, and contraction phase, or *systole*) over the chamber maximal volume: $EF = (V_d - V_s)/V_d \times 100\%$ where V_d and V_s are the end of diastole and end of systole volumes, respectively.

2.3   Challenging the Homogeneous Intensity Region Hypothesis

The criterion 1 used in this study is based on the hypothesis that the image is composed of an homogeneous object on an homogeneous background. This is only roughly true in real images due to two partial volume effects and temporal blurring.

Partial Volume Effects. The partial volume effect is responsible for myocardium intensity variations during the cardiac cycle: the myocardium appears brighter at end of systole and darker at end of diastole. When the thickness of the myocardium is only a few voxels wide (at the end of diastole), many voxels do not contain only myocardium but also part of the outside region, lowering their intensity. Conversely, at end of systole, the thickening of the muscle leads to brighter muscle voxels. This artefact is used as an index of wall thickenning [1]. We can observe this phenomena on figure 2.

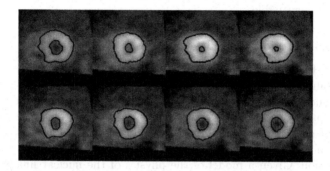

Fig. 2. Time frames 0 to 7, from left to right and top to bottom, showing one short axis slice. The intensity is higher in frames 2 and 3 (end of systole) than in the others.

Temporal Blurring. Due to the images reconstruction process, a blurring appears in the image sequences. This temporal blurring is mostly visible at the base (top) of the myocardium while the more static apex part is unaffected. The visual consequences are that (i) during diastole, extremities of the ventricle muscle are darker than the apex and (ii) during systole, borders of the muscle near the apex are darker.

Consequences of Segmentation Errors on Volume Estimation. Partial volume effects and temporal blurring combine their effects, leading to different segmentation errors during the systole and diastole phases. At end of diastole, the myocardium extremities are darker and tend to be truncated. The temporal blurring, will also cause the myocardium to appear slightly thicker than it is in reality. This leads to underestimating the chamber volume. Conversely at end of systole, the myocardium extremities are overestimated while the myocardium appears slightly thinner than it should be. This leads to overestimating the chamber volume. The EF estimation is significantly affected by the combination of these segmentation errors. Figure 4 shows the erroneous estimated volumes using the segmentation algorithm for different weights of the internal force term λ_{in}. Although they appear visually insignificant, these segmentation errors have a drastic impact on the volume estimations. Due to the coarse resolution of gated SPECT images and the small size of the LV, even an error of only one voxel all along the LV chamber surface leads to an error of about 50% of the chamber volume, making the computed EF absolutely meaningless.

3   Segmentation and Quantification Experiments

To validate the algorithm accuracy, experiments on simulated images were first performed. With simulated images, a ground truth (the actual volumes of the virtual objects used for simulation) is known and the algorithm can be quantitatively evaluated. Experiments were then lead on real images for which no ground truth is available.

3.1   Experiments on Simulated Images

Simulating Images Using the NCAT Phantom. W.P. Segars [19] has developed a four-dimensional NURBS-based CArdiac-Torso (NCAT) phantom for simulating nuclear medicine images. The organ models are based on non-uniform rational B-splines which define continuous surfaces. The phantom can thus be used at any spatial resolution. An important innovation is the extension of NURBS to a fourth dimension, time, to model the cardiac beat and the respiratory motion. Given a model of the physics of the nuclear imaging process, simulated images of the numerical phantom can be computed by the NCAT simulator. The main advantage of using computerized organ models in medical studies is that the exact anatomy and physiological functions of the phantom are known, thus providing a gold standard against which the image processing and reconstruction algorithms can be evaluated quantitatively.

Volume Estimation. Figure 3 shows an example of volume estimation after segmentation of an image produced by the NCAT simulator and extraction of the chamber by the membrane algorithm. The volume estimation error is small compared to the spatial resolution of the simulated images (less than 6% in the worst case) and the error on the computed EF is lower than 2%. The membrane algorithm therefore estimates a realistic closure of the LV boundary.

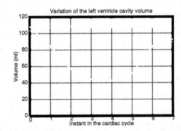

Fig. 3. Comparison of the LV chamber volume estimation on simulated NCAT images against the ground truth.

Realistic Images. Raw images produced by the NCAT simulator are not realistic since they are not noisy and they do not introduce temporal blurring as described in section 2.3. For further evaluating our algorithm, an artificial temporal blurring was introduced by convolving the longitudinal sequences with a Gaussian kernel in the time direction ($\sigma = 6$), and a spatial Gaussian noise ($\sigma = 4$) was added in each image. Straight segmentation of blurred and noisy images is not satisfying. A high level of noise requires increasing the internal force weight. However, this also causes less precise location of the myocardium boundaries.

Different internal weight values have been tested in the criterion 1. Fixing $\lambda_{out} = 1$ and $\lambda_c = 1$, figure 5 shows the segmentation results for different values of λ_{in}. For low values of the internal force weight ($\lambda_{in} = 1$ and $\lambda_{in} = 2$), the region near the apex is poorly segmented: the myocardium surface is too thick. For a higher value ($\lambda_{in} = 3$), the thickness is correct but a significant part of the extremities is truncated. A small part of the extremities is also truncated for $\lambda_{in} = 1$, due to the temporal blurring (for better visualization, we superimposed the segmentation results on the original NCAT images but the segmentation is computed on blurred and noisy images). Figure 4 shows that the estimated volume of the LV chamber is indeed under-evaluated except at the end of systole. Both myocardium extremities troncature (for high values of λ_{in}) and myocardium thickness overestimates (for low values of λ_{in}) lead to underestimating the chamber volume.

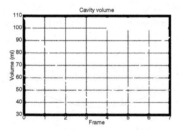

Fig. 4. LV chamber volume after segmentation of NCAT simulated data for different values of λ_{in} and ground truth.

3.2   A New Adaptive Algorithm

Since the accurate segmentation of the different parts of the myocardium requires different tunings of the relative weights of the internal and external objects and no satisfying trade-off can be found for the complete image, we propose an adaptive algorithm described by the following steps:

- **Normal segmentation of the end of systole volume.** The temporal blurring is minimum and the myocardium intensity is maximum at end of systole.

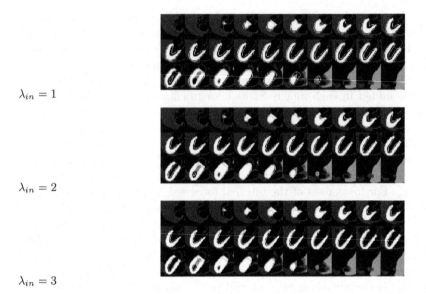

$\lambda_{in} = 1$

$\lambda_{in} = 2$

$\lambda_{in} = 3$

Fig. 5. Segmentation results for $\lambda_{\text{in}} = 1$ (top), $\lambda_{\text{in}} = 2$ (center), and $\lambda_{\text{in}} = 3$ (bottom).

- **LV barycenter and principal axis estimation.** The principal axis computed from the segmented image roughly corresponds to the heart long axis.
- **Image volume splitting.** The volume space is split by several short axis planes. Different parameters can be attributed to each space region.

Locating the Heart Long Axis. The end of systole volume presents the lowest temporal blurring and the highest myocardium contrast. It is therefore the easiest frame to segment. Moreover, this stage is not very sensitive to small segmentation errors. The myocardium is first extracted in this frame. The resulting model is used to produce a binary image. Only the largest connex component is kept from this image to remove outliers. The LV barycenter $(\bar{x}, \bar{y})$ and the principal axis are estimated. The principal axis is the eigenvector corresponding to the highest eigenvalue of the inertia matrix:

$$M = \begin{bmatrix} m_{20} & m_{11} \\ m_{11} & m_{02} \end{bmatrix} \text{ with } m_{ij} = \sum (x - \bar{x})^i (y - \bar{y})^j \delta(x, y) \tag{3}$$

Estimation of the Different Planes. The image volume is split by planes normal to the heart long axis estimated in the previous step. The first volume region contains the heart apex. This region is delimited by a plane orthogonal to the principal axis and close enough to the LV barycenter to cut the myocardium extremities segmented at the end of systole with $\lambda_{in} = 1$ (see figure 6). The last region will fall outside the ventricle, beyond the myocardium extremities. It is determined by a plane parallel to the first one, and outside the segmentation obtained at the end of diastole with $\lambda_{in} = 3$. Two other planes, equally spaced

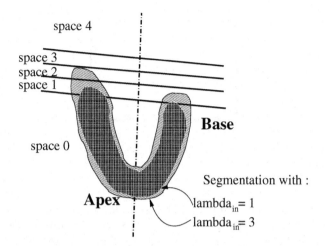

Fig. 6. Splitting the image volume by planes normal to the heart long axis.

between the two previous ones, finish to split the image volume in 5 regions (see figure 6).

Deformation with Variable Weights. Once the splitting planes have been located, all frames of the cardiac sequence are segmented. Different values are set for the λ_{in} weight in each frame and each volume region. The criterion equation 1 is modified for a new criterion with varying weights λ_{in}:

$$\frac{\partial u_n}{\partial t} = (\lambda_{S_i,n}(I_n - \mu_{in_{S_i,n}}) - \lambda_{out}(B - I_n) - \lambda_c \kappa_n) \|\nabla u_n\| \tag{4}$$

where S_i is a 3D region delimited by planes (see figure 6): S_0 corresponds to the region containing the apex, S_4 to the region beyond the base.

The different weights were determined empirically on an image dataset. Following the observations made in paragraph 3.1, we choose the λ_{in} weights growing from S_0 to S_4 near the diastole, and growing from S_4 to S_0 near the systole. The weights used for NCAT simulated sequences are shown in left of figure 7.

	0	1	2	3	4	5	6	7		0	1	2	3	4	5	6	7
S.	5	5	0.5	0.2	0.2	0.2	5	5	S.	3	2.5	1.5	1.5	2.5	3	3	3
S.	4	4	3	8	8	3	4	4	S.	2	2	4	4	2	2	2	2
S.	2.5	2.5	3	8	8	3	2.5	2.5	S.	1	1.5	4	4	1.5	1.5	1	1
S.	1.2	1	2.5	8	8	2	1	1.2	S.	0.1	0.5	4	4	0.5	0.12	0.2	0.1
S.	0.4	0.6	2	8	8	2	0.6	0.4	S.	0.05	0.3	4	4	0.2	0.1	0.1	0.05

Fig. 7. Adaptive weights. On the left, values for NCAT sequences. On the rigth, values used for the real gated SPECT data.

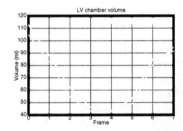

Fig. 8. LV chamber volume variations along the cardiac cycle using NCAT data: real values and computed values.

For other sequences, a different weights tuning might be needed. This parameterization is constant for a given image acquisition protocol. Manual tuning is only needed when changing the acquisition device or protocol.

Segmentation Results with the Adaptive Algorithm. The adaptive algorithm segmentation, leads to a good profile for the LV chamber volume variations during the cardiac cycle as shown in figure 8. The values are close to the real ones with an error of about 15 ml (about 13%). This is sufficient to compute accurate EF values (with an error of 8%).

3.3 Experiments on Real Images from Healthy Patients

Segmentation experiments were made on real images provided by the Centre Antoine Lacassagne nuclear medicine department in Nice. The images were acquired and filtered by a Butterworth low-pass filter before 3D reconstruction. The voxels dimension is $3.46 \times 3.46 \times 7.12$ mm.

Figure 9 shows a segmentation example. The myocardium segmentation (left), the convex envelope extracted by the membrane algorithm (center), and the LV chamber surface (right) are shown for 4 out of the 8 images of a complete sequence.

The weights used for λ_{in} are shown in right of figure 7. Figure 10 compares the evolution of the LV chamber volume obtained using basic segmentation and the adaptive algorithm. With the later method, the profile of the curve is improved and the EF value (75.5% instead of 56.5%) is more realistic.

4   Conclusion

The accurate estimation of the LV myocardium and chamber volumes is very sensitive to segmentation errors in gated SPECT images. In this paper, we proposed a novel adaptive algorithm taking into account the temporal nature of the image sequences to more precisely locate the heart wall boundaries. Our algorithm uses the whole image sequence to estimate the background intensity in the deformation criterion 1. Furthermore, the temporal blurring of the sequences

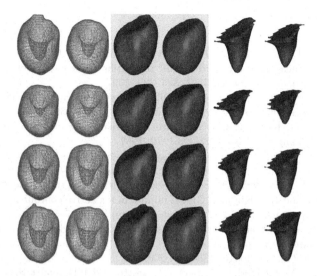

Fig. 9. LV chamber estimation: meshes (computed using Marching Cubes algorithm) of the myocardium segmentation (left), membrane with Gouraud shading (center), and chamber estimation with Gouraud shading (right).

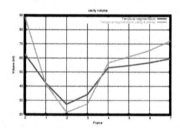

Fig. 10. Comparison of LV chamber volume variations during the cardiac cycle, on real SPECT data, from a healthy patient.

is compensated through the spatial and temporal adaptation of the algorithm parameters. A membrane algorithm was developed to automatically extract the LV chamber from the myocardium segmentation.

We could validate the accuracy of the method on simulated images. The error in the LV chamber volume computation do not exceed 15 ml. The resulting variability of the EF is about 8% which is low enough for a practical use. First results on real images are encouraging although a clinical study is needed to compare the results to established gold standards. Setting the adaptive parameters automatically is highly desirable from the user point of view. Some work also need to be done in the case of pathological images showing severe signal drops due to myocardium perfusion defaults: holes then appear in the myocardium wall that need to be taken into account for volumes estimation.

References

1. I. Buvat, M.L. Bartlett, A.N. Kitsiou, V. Dilsizian, and S.L. Bacharach. A hybrid method for measuring myocardial wall thickening from gated pet/spect images. *Journal of Nuclear Medicine*, 38(2):324–329, 1997.
2. V. Caselles, F. Catte, T. Coll, and F. Dibos. A geometric model for active contours in image processing. In *Numerische Mathematik*, volume 66, pages 1–33, 1993.
3. V. Caselles, R. Kimmel, and G. Sapiro. Geodesic active contours. *International Journal of Computer Vision*, 22(1):61–79, 1997.
4. A. Charnoz, D. Lingrand, and J. Montagnat. A levelset based method for segmenting the heart in 3d+t gated spect images. In *Functional Imaging and Modeling of the Heart (FIMH) 2003*, LNCS, pages 52–61. Springer-Verlag, June 2003.
5. L.D. Cohen and Ron Kimmel. Global minimum for active contour models: A minimal path approach. *Int. J. of Computer Vision*, 24(1):57–78, 1997.
6. D. Cremers and S. Soatto. A pseudo distance for shape priors in level set segmentation. In *2nd IEEE International Workshop on Variational, Geometric and Level Set Methods (VLSM)*, pages 169–176, 2003.
7. E. Debreuve, M. Barlaud, G. Aubert, I. Laurette, and J. Darcourt. Space-Time Segmentation Using Level Set Active Contours Applied to Myocardial Gated SPECT. *IEEE Transactions on Medical Imaging*, 20(7):643–659, 2001.
8. M. Droske, B. Meyer, M. Rumpf, and C. Schaller. An adaptive level set method for medical image segmentation. In R. Leahy and M. Insana, editors, *Proc. of the Annual Symposium on Information Processing in Medical Imaging*. Springer, Lecture Notes Computer Science, 2001.
9. Stegmann etal. Fame – a flexible appearance modeling environment. *IEEE Trans. on Medical Imaging*, 22(10), 2003.
10. T.L. Faber, C.D. Cooke, R.D. Folks, J.P. Vansant, K.J. Nichos, E.G. DePuey, R.I. Pettigrew, and E.V. Garcia. Left ventricular function and perfusion from gated spect perfusion images: An intergrated method. *Journal of Nuclear Medicine*, 40:650–659, 1999.
11. J. Gomes and O. Faugeras. Segmentation of the inner and outer surfaces of the cortex in man and monkey: an approach based on Partial Differential Equations. In *Proc. of the 5th Int. Conf. on Functional Mapping of the Human Brain*, 1999.
12. S. Jehan-Besson, M. Barlaud, and G. Aubert. A 3-step algorithm using regionbased active contours for video objects detection. *EURASIP Journal of Applied Signal Processing*, 2002(6):572–581, 2002.
13. R. Malladi, J. A. Sethian, and B.C. Vemuri. Shape modeling with front propagation: A level set approach. *IEEE Transactions on Pattern Analysis and Machine Intelligence*, 17(2):158–175, February 1995.
14. R. Malladi and J.A. Sethian. A Real-Time Algorithm for Medical Shape Recovery. In *International Conference on Computer Vision (ICCV'98)*, pages 304–310, Bombay, India, January 1998.
15. J. Montagnat and H. Delingette. A review of deformable surfaces: topology, geometry and deformation. *Image and Vision Comput.*, 19(14):1023–1040, Dec. 2001.
16. S. Osher and J. Sethian. Fronts propagating with curvature dependent speed: algorithms based on the Hamilton-Jacobi formulation. *Journal of Computational Physics*, 79:12–49, 1988.
17. Nikos Paragios and Rachid Deriche. Geodesic active contours and level sets for the detection and tracking of moving objects. *IEEE Transactions on Pattern Analysis and Machine Intelligence*, 22(3):266–280, March 2000.

18. Nikos Paragios, Mikael Rousson, and Visvanathan Ramesh. Knowledge-based registration and segmentation of the left ventricle: A level set approach. In *IEEE Workshop on Applications in Computer Vision,* Orlando, Florida, December 2002.
19. P.H. Pretorius, W. Xia, M. A. King, B. M. W. Tsui, T.-S. Pan, and B.J. Villegas. Determination of left and right ventricular volume and ejection fraction using a mathematical cardiac torso phantom for gated blood pool spect. *Journal of Nuclear Medicine,* 37:97, 1996.
20. D. Terzopoulos, A. Witkin, and M. Kass. Constraints on deformable models: Recovering 3d shape and non rigid motion. *Artificial Intelligence,* 36(1):91–123, 1988.

An MCMC-Based Particle Filter for Tracking Multiple Interacting Targets

Zia Khan, Tucker Balch, and Frank Dellaert

College of Computing
Georgia Institute of Technology
Atlanta, GA
USA
{zkhan,tucker,frank}@cc.gatech.edu

Abstract. We describe a Markov chain Monte Carlo based particle filter that effectively deals with *interacting* targets, i.e., targets that are influenced by the proximity and/or behavior of other targets. Such interactions cause problems for traditional approaches to the data association problem. In response, we developed a joint tracker that includes a more sophisticated motion model to maintain the identity of targets throughout an interaction, drastically reducing tracker failures. The paper presents two main contributions: (1) we show how a Markov random field (MRF) motion prior, built on the fly at each time step, can substantially improve tracking when targets interact, and (2) we show how this can be done efficiently using Markov chain Monte Carlo (MCMC) sampling. We prove that incorporating an MRF to model interactions is equivalent to adding an additional *interaction factor* to the importance weights in a joint particle filter. Since a joint particle filter suffers from exponential complexity in the number of tracked targets, we replace the traditional importance sampling step in the particle filter with an MCMC sampling step. The resulting filter deals efficiently and effectively with complicated interactions when targets approach each other. We present both qualitative and quantitative results to substantiate the claims made in the paper, including a large scale experiment on a video-sequence of over 10,000 frames in length.

1 Introduction

This work is concerned with the problem of tracking multiple interacting targets. Our objective is to obtain a record of the trajectories of targets over time, and to maintain correct, unique identification of each target throughout. Tracking multiple identical targets becomes challenging when the targets pass close to one another or merge.

The classical multi-target tracking literature approaches this problem by performing a data-association step after a detection step. Most notably, the multiple hypothesis tracker [1] and the joint probabilistic data association filter (JPDAF) [2] are influential algorithms in this class. These multi-target tracking algorithms have been used extensively in the context of computer vision. Some examples

T. Pajdla and J. Matas (Eds.): ECCV 2004, LNCS 3024, pp. 279–290, 2004.
© Springer-Verlag Berlin Heidelberg 2004

are the use of nearest neighbor tracking in [3], the multiple hypothesis tracker in [4], and the JPDAF in [5]. Recently, a particle filtering version of the JPDAF has been proposed in [6].

In this paper we address the problem of *interacting* targets, which causes problems for traditional approaches. Dealing appropriately with this problem has important implications for vision-based tracking of animals, and is generally applicable to any situation where many interacting targets need to be tracked over time. Visual animal tracking is not an artificial task: it has countless applications in biology and medicine. In addition, our long term research goals involve the analysis of multi-agent system behavior in general, with social insects as a model [7]. The domain offers many challenges that are quite different from the typical radar tracking domain in which most multi-target tracking algorithms are evaluated.

In contrast to traditional methods, our approach relies on the use of a more capable motion model, one that is able to adequately describe target behavior throughout an interaction event. The basic assumption on which all established data-association methods rely is that targets maintain their behavior before and after the targets visually merge. However, consider the example in Figure 1, which shows 20 ants being tracked in a small arena. In this case, the targets do *not* behave independently: whenever one ant encounters another, some amount of interaction takes place, and the behavior of a given ant before and after an interaction can be quite different. The approach we propose is to have the motion model reflect this additional complexity of the target behavior.

The first contribution of this paper is to show how a Markov random field motion prior, built on the fly at each time step, can adequately model these interactions and defeat these failure modes. Our approach is based on the well known particle filter [8,9], a multi-hypothesis tracker that uses a set of weighted particles to approximate a density function corresponding to the probability of the location of the target given observations over time. The standard particle

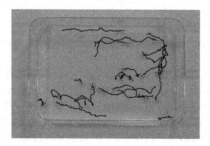

Fig. 1. 20 ants are being tracked by an MCMC-based particle filter. Targets do *not* behave independently: whenever one ant encounters another, some amount of interaction takes place, and the behavior of a given ant before and after an interaction can be quite different. This observation is generally applicable to any situation where many interacting targets need to be tracked over time.

(a) frame 9043   (b) frame 9080   (c)frame 9083

Fig. 2. (a) Three interacting ants are being tracked using independent particle filters. (b) The target with the best likelihood score typically "hijacks" the filters of nearby targets. (c) Resulting tracker failure. We address this problem using an Markov random field motion prior, built on the fly at each time step, that can adequately model these interactions and defeat these failure modes.

filter weights particles based on a likelihood score, and then propagates these weighted particles according to a motion model. Simply running multiple particle filters, however, is not a viable option: whenever targets pass close to one another, the target with the best likelihood score typically "hijacks" the filters of nearby targets, as is illustrated in Figure 2. In these cases, identity could be maintained during tracking by providing a more complex motion model that approximates the interaction between targets. We show below that incorporating an MRF to model interactions is equivalent to adding an additional *interaction factor* to the importance weights in a joint particle filter.

The second contribution is to show how this can be done efficiently using Markov chain Monte Carlo (MCMC) sampling. The joint particle filter suffers from exponential complexity in the number of tracked targets, n. Computational requirements render the joint filter unusable for more than than three or four targets [10]. As a solution, we replace the traditional importance sampling step in the particle filter with an MCMC sampling step. This approach has the appealing property that *the filter behaves as a set of individual particle filters when the targets are not interacting, but efficiently deals with complicated interactions when targets approach each other.* The idea of using MCMC in the sequential importance resampling (SIR) particle filter scheme has been explored before, in [11]. Our approach can be consider a specialization of this work with an MRF-based joint posterior and an efficient proposal step to achieve reasonable performance.

In other related work, MCMC has been used in different ways in a particle filter setting. [12,13] introduce periodic MCMC steps to diversify particles in a fixed-lag smoothing scheme. Similarly, Marthi et. al. [14] developed "Decayed MCMC" sequential Monte Carlo, in which they focus the sampling activity of the MCMC sampler to state variables in the recent past.

Finally, several other particle-filter based approaches exist to tracking multiple identical targets. [15] "binds" particles to specific targets. [16] uses partitioned sampling and a probabilistic exclusion principle, which adds a term to the measurement model that assures that every feature measured belongs to only one target. BraMBLe [17] addresses tracking and initializing multiple targets in a variable-dimension framework. However, all of these are joint particle filter approaches and are less suitable to tracking a large number of targets.

2   Bayesian Multi-target Tracking

The multiple target tracking problem can be expressed as a Bayes filter. We recursively update the posterior distribution $P(X_t|Z^t)$ over the joint state of the *all* n targets $\{X_{it}|i \in 1..n\}$ given all observations $Z^t = \{Z_1..Z_t\}$ up to and including time t, according to:

$$P(X_t|Z^t) = kP(Z_t|X_t) \int_{X_{t-1}} P(X_t|X_{t-1})P(X_{t-1}|Z^{t-1}) \tag{1}$$

The likelihood $P(Z_t|X_t)$ expresses the *measurement model,* the probability we observed the measurement Z_t given the state X_t at time t. The *motion model* $P(X_t|X_{t-1})$ predicts the state X_t at time t given the previous state X_{t-1}. In all that follows we will assume that the likelihood $P(Z_t|X_t)$ factors as across targets as $P(Z_t|X_t) = \prod_{i=1}^n P(Z_{it}|X_{it})$ and that the appearances of targets are conditionally independent.

2.1   Independent Particle Filters

When identical targets do *not* interact, we can approximate the exact Bayes filter by running multiple single-target *particle filters*. Mathematically, this is equivalent to factoring the motion model $P(X_t|X_{t-1})$ as $\prod_i P(X_{it}|X_{i,t-1})$.

For each of the n independent filters, we need to approximate the posterior $P(X_{it}|Z^t)$ over each target's state X_{it}. A particle filter can be viewed as an importance sampler for this posterior $P(X_{it}|Z^t)$, using the predictive density on the state X_{it} as the proposal distribution. Briefly, one inductively assumes that the posterior at the previous time step is approximated by a set of weighted particles

$$P(X_{it}|Z^{t-1}) \approx \{X_{,it-1}^{(r)}, \pi_{i,t-1}^{(r)}\}_{r=1}^N$$

Then, for the current time-step, we draw N samples $X_{it}^{(s)}$ from a proposal distribution

$$X_{it}^{(s)} \sim q(X_{it}) = \sum_r \pi_{i,t-1}^{(r)} P(X_{it}|X_{i,t-1}^{(r)})$$

which is a mixture of motion models $P(X_{it}|X_{i,t-1}^{(r)})$. Then we weight each sample so obtained by its likelihood given the measurement Z_{it}, i.e.

$$\pi_{i,t}^{(s)} = P(Z_{it}|X_{it}^{(s)})$$

This results in a weighted particle approximation $\{X_{it}^{(s)}, \pi_{it}^{(s)}\}_{s=1}^N$ for the posterior $P(X_{it}|Z^t)$ over the target's state X_{it} at time t. There are other ways to explain the particle filter (see e.g. [18]) that more easily accommodate other variants, but the mixture proposal view above is particularly suited for our application.

While using independent filters is computationally tractable, the result is prone to frequent failures. Each particle filter samples in a small space, and the resulting "joint" filter's complexity is linear in the number of targets, n. However, in cases where targets *do* interact, as in an insect tracking scenario, single particle filters are susceptible to failures exactly when interactions occur. In a typical failure mode, illustrated in Figure 2, several trackers will start tracking the single target with the highest likelihood score.

3   MRF Motion Model

Our approach to addressing tracker failures resulting from interactions is to introduce a more capable motion model, based on Markov random fields (MRFs). We model the interaction between targets using a graph-based MRF constructed on the fly for each individual time-step. An MRF is a graph (V, E) with undirected edges between nodes where the joint probability is factored as a product of local potential functions at each node, and interactions are defined on neighborhood cliques. See [19] for a thorough exposition. The most commonly used form is a pairwise MRF, where the cliques are pairs of nodes that are connected in the undirected graph. We assume the following pairwise MRF form, where the $\psi(X_{it}, X_{jt})$ are pairwise interaction potentials:

$$P(X_t|X_{t-1}) \propto \prod_i P(X_{it}|X_{i(t-1)}) \prod_{ij \in E} \psi(X_{it}, X_{jt}) \tag{2}$$

The interaction potentials of the MRF afford us the possibility of easily specifying domain knowledge governing the joint behavior of interacting targets. At the same time, the absence of an edge in the MRF encodes the domain knowledge that targets do not influence each other's behavior. As a concrete example, in the insect tracking application we present in the Section 6, we know that two insects rarely occupy the same space. Taking advantage of this assumption can help greatly in tracking two targets that pass close to one another. An example MRF for our test domain is illustrated in Figure 3; in this case, targets within 64 pixels (about 2 cm) of one another are linked by MRF edges. The absence of edges between two ants provides mathematical rigor to the intuition that ants far away will not influence each other's motion.

Since it is easier to specify the interaction potential in the log domain, we express $\psi(X_{it}, X_{jt})$ by means of the Gibbs distribution:

$$\psi(X_{it}, X_{jt}) \propto \exp\left(-g(X_{it}, X_{jt})\right) \tag{3}$$

where $g(X_{it}, X_{jt})$ is a penalty function. For example, in the ant tracking application the penalty function $g(X_{it}, X_{jt})$ we use depends only on the number of pixels overlap between the target boxes of two targets. It is maximal when two targets coincide and gradually falls off as targets move apart.

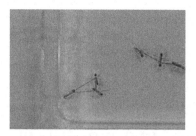

Fig. 3. To model interactions, we dynamically construct a Markov random field at each time step, with edges for targets that are close to one another. An example is shown here for 6 ants. Targets that are far from one another are not linked by an edge, reflecting that there is no interaction.

4   The Joint MRF Particle Filter

The MRF terms that model interactions can be incorporated into the Bayes filter in a straightforward manner, but now we are forced to consider the full *joint* state of all n targets. In particular, analogous to the single target filter explained in Section 2.1, we recursively approximate the posterior on the joint state X_t as a set of N weighted samples, obtaining the following Monte Carlo approximation to the Bayes filter (1):

$$P(X_t|Z^t) \approx kP(Z_t|X_t) \sum_r \pi_{t-1}^{(r)} P(X_t|X_{t-1}^{(r)}) \qquad (4)$$

We can easily plug in the MRF motion model (2) into the joint particle filter equation (4). Note that the interaction potential (3) does not depend on the previous target state X_{t-1}, and hence the target distribution (4) for the joint MRF filter factors as

$$P(X_t|Z^t) \approx kP(Z_t|X_t) \prod_{ij \in E} \psi(X_{it}, X_{jt}) \sum_r \pi_{t-1}^{(r)} \prod_i P(X_{it}|X_{i(t-1)}^{(r)}) \qquad (5)$$

In other words, the interaction term moves out of the mixture distribution. This means that *we can simply treat the interaction term as an additional factor in the importance weight*. In other words, we sample from the joint proposal distribution function

$$X_t^{(s)} \sim q(X_t) = \sum_r \pi_{t-1}^{(r)} \prod_i P(X_{it}|X_{i(t-1)}^{(r)})$$

and weight the samples according to the following factored likelihood expression:

$$\pi_t^{(s)} = \prod_{i=1}^{n} P(Z_{it}|X_{it}^{(s)}) \prod_{ij \in E} \psi(X_{it}^{(s)}, X_{jt}^{(s)})$$

However, the joint particle filter approximation is not well suited for multi-target tracking. Each particle contains the joint position of all n targets, $X_t^{(s)} =$

$\{X_{1t}^{(s)}, ..., X_{nt}^{(s)}\}$, and the filter suffers from exponential complexity in the number of tracked targets, n. If too few particles are used, all but a few importance weights will be near-zero. In other words, the Monte Carlo approximation (4), while asymptotically unbiased, will have high variance. These considerations render the joint filter unusable in practice for more than than three or four targets [10].

5   The MCMC-Based MRF Particle Filter

The second contribution of this paper is to show how that we can efficiently sample from the factored target posterior distribution (5) using Markov chain Monte Carlo (MCMC) sampling [20,21,22]. In effect, we are replacing the inefficient importance sampling step with an efficient MCMC sampling step.

All MCMC methods work by generating a sequence of *states*, in our case joint target configurations X_t at time t, with the property that the collection of generated states approximates a sample from the target distribution (5). To accomplish this, a Markov chain is defined over the space of configurations X_t such that the stationary distribution of the chain is exactly the target distribution. The Metropolis-Hastings (MH) algorithm [23] is a way to simulate from such a chain. We use it to generate a sequence of samples from $P(X_t|Z^t)$.

5.1   Proposal Density

The key to the efficiency of this sampler rests in the specific proposal density we use. In particular, *we only change the state of one target at a time* by sampling directly from the factored motion model of the selected target $Q(X_t'|X_t) = \frac{1}{N}Q(X_t'|X_t, i) = \frac{1}{N}\sum_r P(X_{it}'|X_{i(t-1)}^{(r)})\prod_{j \neq i}\delta(X_{jt}' = X_i)$. Each target is equally likely to be selected. The acceptance ratio for this proposal can be calculated very efficiently, as only the likelihood and MRF interaction potential for the chosen target need to be evaluated:

$$a_{\mathbf{S}} = \min\left(1, \frac{P(Z_t|X_{it}')\prod_{j \in E_i} \psi(X_{it}', X_{jt}')}{P(Z_t|X_{it})\prod_{j \in E_i} \psi(X_{it}, X_{jt})}\right)$$

This also has the desirable consequence that, if targets do *not* interact, the MCMC-based filter above is just as efficient as multiple, independent particle filters.

5.2   Algorithm Summary

In summary, the detailed steps of the MCMC-based tracking algorithm we propose are:

1. At time $t - 1$ the state of the targets is represented by an set of samples $\{X_{t-1}^{(r)}\}_{r=1}^N$ each containing the joint state $X_{t-1}^{(r)} = \{X_{1(t-1)}^{(r)}, \dots, X_{n(t-1)}^{(r)}\}$.

2. Initialize the MCMC sampler for time t by drawing X_t from the interaction-free predictive density $\sum_r \prod_i P(X_{it}|X_{i(t-1)}^{(r)})$.

1. Perform Metropolis-Hastings iterations to obtain M samples from the factored posterior (5). Discard the first B samples to account for sampler burn-in. In detail:

   a) Proposal step:
      i. Randomly select a joint sample $X_{t-1}^{(r)}$ from the set of unweighted samples from the previous time step.
      ii. Randomly select a target i from n targets. This will be the target that we propose to move.
      iii. Using the previous state of this i^{th} target $X_{i(t-1)}^{(r)}$, sample from the conditionally dependent motion model $P(X'_{it}|X_{i(t-1)}^{(r)})$ to obtain X'_{it}

   b) Compute the acceptance ratio:

$$a_{\mathbf{S}} = \min\left(1, \frac{P(Z_{it}|X'_{it})\prod_{j\in E_i}\psi(X'_{it}, X'_{jt})}{P(Z_{it}|X_{it})\prod_{j\in E_i}\psi(X_{it}, X_{jt})}\right)$$

   c) If $a_{\mathbf{S}} \geq 1$ then accept X'_{it}, set the the ith target in X_t to X'_{it}. Otherwise, we accept it with probability $a_{\mathbf{S}}$. If rejected, we leave the ith target in X_t unchanged. Add a copy of the current X_t to the new sample set.

2. The sample set $\{X_t^{(s)}\}_{s=1}^M$ at time t represents an estimated joint state of the targets.

6   Experimental Validation

We evaluated our approach by tracking through a very long video-sequence of roaming ants, and present both quantitative results as well as a graphical comparison of the different tracker methodologies. The test sequence consists of 10,400 720 by 480 24-bit RGB frames at 30 Hz of 20 ants, roaming about an arena. The ants themselves are about 1 cm long and move about the arena as quickly as 3 cm per second. Interactions occur frequently and can involve 5 or more ants in close proximity. In these cases, the motion of the animals is difficult to predict. After pausing and touching one another, they often walk rapidly sideways or even backward. This experimental domain provides a substantial challenge to any multi-target tracker.

6.1   Experimental Details and Results

We evaluated a number of different trackers with respect to a baseline "pseudo ground truth" sequence. As no ground truth was available we obtained the baseline sequence by running a slow but accurate tracker and correcting any mistakes it made by hand. In particular, we ran our MCMC tracker with 2000 samples, which lost track only 15 times in the entire sequence. When we observed a tracker failure, we reinitialized by hand the positions of the targets and resumed tracking.

Below are the specific implementation choices we made to specialize the general algorithm of Section 5.2 to the ant tracking application:

- The *state* X_{it} of the ith ant i is its position (x_{it}, y_{it}) and orientation θ_{it}.
- For the *likelihood model* we used an appearance template approach with a robust error norm. In particular, we use a 10 by 32 pixel rectangular template containing a mean appearance image μ_F and a standard deviation image σ_F, both estimated from 149 manually selected ant images. We also learned a background mean image μ_B and standard deviation image σ_B from 10,000 randomly selected pixels. The log-likelihood is then calculated as $\log P(X_{it}|Z_t) = -\frac{1}{2}\frac{|F(X_{it})-\mu_F|}{4\sigma_F} + \frac{1}{2}\frac{|F(X_{it})-\mu_B|}{4\sigma_B}$. Here $F(X_{it})$ is the vector of pixels from a target with state X_{it} after translation and rotation to the template coordinate frame.
- For the *motion model* we used a normal density centered on the previous pose X_{t-1} $X_t|X_{t-1} = R(\theta_{t-1}+\Delta\theta)[\,\Delta x\ \Delta y\ 0\,]^{\top}+X_{t-1}$ where $[\Delta x, \Delta y, \Delta\theta] \sim [N(0,\sigma_x^2), N(0,\sigma_y^2), N(0,\sigma_\theta^2)]$ with $(\sigma_x,\sigma_y,\sigma_\theta) = (3.0, 5.0, 0.4)$.
- For the *MRF interaction terms* we used a simple linear interaction function γp where p is the area of overlap between two targets and $\gamma = 5000$.
- *MCMC parameters*: we discard 25% of the samples to let the sampler burn in, regardless of the total number of samples.

Table 1 shows the number of tracking failures for all the tracker/sample size combinations we evaluated. We automatically identified failures of these trackers when the reported position of a target deviated 50 pixels from the pseudo ground truth position. This allowed us to detect switched and lost targets without manual intervention.

Figure 4 shows the result graphically, comparing 3 different samplers, each with an equivalent sample size of 1000. For each of the trackers, we show exactly where failures occur throughout the sequences by tick-marks. To obtain a measure of trajectory quality, we also recorded for each frame the average distance

Table 1. Tracker failures observed in the 10,400 frame test sequence

Tracker	Number of Samples	Number of Failures
MCMC	50	123
MCMC	100	49
MCMC	200	28
MCMC	1000	16
single particle filter	10 per target	148
single particle filter	50 per target	125
single particle filter	100 per target	119
joint particle filter	50	544
joint particle filter	100	519
joint particle filter	200	479
joint particle filter	1000	392

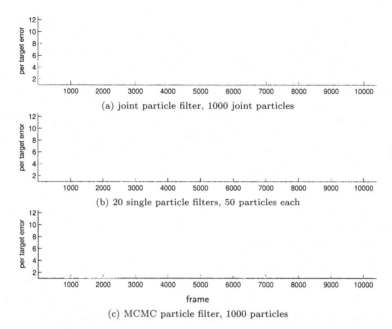

(a) joint particle filter, 1000 joint particles

(b) 20 single particle filters, 50 particles each

(c) MCMC particle filter, 1000 particles

Fig. 4. (a-c): Qualitative comparison of 3 trackers, each tracking 20 ants using an equivalent sample size of 1000. Tick marks show when tracking failures occur throughout the sequence. The time series plot shows average distance from ground truth (averaged per target and per second)

of the targets to their ground truth trajectories. This is shown in the figure as a time series, for each tracker, averaged per second time unit.

6.2   Discussion

From the quantitative results in Table 1 and the qualitative comparison in Figure 4 we draw the following conclusions:

1. The joint filter is clearly unusable for tracking this many targets. The track quality is very low and number of errors reported is very high.
2. The MCMC-based trackers perform significantly better than independent particle filters with a comparable number of samples, both in track quality and failures reported. For example, both MCMC trackers with 1000 samples had only 16 failures, as compared to 125 for 20 independent particle filters with 50 particles each.
3. To our surprise, an MCMC-based tracker with only 50 samples *total* performed as well as or better than 20 independent particle filters with 50 samples *each* (1000 samples total).
4. The MCMC-based trackers rapidly improve their performance as we increase the number of samples. The number of failures falls from 123 to 16 as the number of samples is increased from 50 to 1000. Such an effect is not seen for

(a) frame 3054   (b) frame 3054   (c) frame 3072

Fig. 5. Typical failure modes of MCMC-based MRF particle filter occur when the assumption that targets do not overlap is violated. (a) Two targets undergoing extensive overlap. (b) The tracker reports the incorrect position for the overlapped ant. (c) The resulting tracker failure.

an equivalent increase in computation for the single particle filters, because in that case increasing the number of samples does not improve the ability to deal with ant interactions.

7   Conclusions

In conclusion, the MCMC-MRF approach proposed in the paper has significantly improved the tracking of multiple interacting targets. Figure 5 shows that for the insect tracking case, the few remaining tracking failures that remain for the MCMC-based tracker occur when our assumption that targets do not overlap is violated. In these cases, it is unclear that any data-association method offers a solution. A more complicated joint likelihood model might be helpful in these cases.

In future work, we intend to validate the approach proposed here by tracking hundreds of interacting targets. Our long term research goals involve the analysis of multi-agent system behavior in general, with social insects as a model [7]. In particular, we are looking at honey bees in an active bee hive as a challenging test for multi-target tracking. Finally, it is our hope that the MRF-based motion model and its efficient sequential implementation using MCMC will benefit other application domains besides vision-based animal tracking, for which it has clearly been shown to be useful.

Acknowledgments. This work was funded under NSF Award IIS-0219850.

References

1. Reid, D.: An algorithm for tracking multiple targets. IEEE Trans. on Automation and Control **AC-24** (1979) 84–90
2. Bar-Shalom, Y., Fortmann, T., Scheffe, M.: Joint probabilistic data association for multiple targets in clutter. In: Proc. Conf. on Information Sciences and Systems. (1980)
3. Deriche, R., Faugeras, O.: Tracking line segments. Image and Vision Computing **8** (1990) 261–270

4. Cox, I., Leonard, J.: Modeling a dynamic environment using a Bayesian multiple hypothesis approach. Artificial Intelligence **66** (1994) 311–344
5. Rasmussen, C., Hager, G.: Probabilistic data association methods for tracking complex visual objects. PAMI **23** (2001) 560–576
6. Schulz, D., Burgard, W., Fox, D., Cremers., A.B.: Tracking multiple moving targets with a mobile robot using particle filters and statistical data association. In: IEEE Intl. Conf. on Robotics and Automation (ICRA). (2001)
7. Balch, T., Khan, Z., Veloso, M.: Automatically tracking and analyzing the behavior of live insect colonies. In: Proc. Autonomous Agents 2001, Montreal (2001)
8. Gordon, N., Salmond, D., Smith, A.: Novel approach to nonlinear/non-Gaussian Bayesian state estimation. IEE Procedings F **140** (1993) 107–113
9. Isard, M., Blake, A.: Contour tracking by stochastic propagation of conditional density. In: Eur. Conf. on Computer Vision (ECCV). (1996) 343–356
10. Khan, Z., Balch, T., Dellaert, F.: Efficient particle filter-based tracking of multiple interacting targets using an MRF-based motion model. In: IEEE/RSJ Intl. Conf. on Intelligent Robots and Systems (IROS), Las Vegas (2003)
11. Berzuini, C., Best, N.G., Gilks, W., Larizza, C.: Dynamic conditional independence models and Markov chain Monte Carlo methods. Journal of the American Statistical Association **92** (1996) 1403–1412
12. Gilks, W., Berzuini, C.: Following a moving target–Bayesian inference for dynamic Bayesian models. Journal of the Royal Statistical Society, Series B **63** (2001) 127–146
13. Doucet, A., Gordon, N.J., Krishnamurthy, V.: Particle filters for state estimation of jump Markov linear systems. IEEE Transactions on Signal Processing **49** (2001)
14. Marthi, B., Pasula, H., Russel, S., Peres, Y.: Decayed MCMC filtering. In: Proceedings of the 18th Annual Conference on Uncertainty in AI (UAI). (2002)
15. Tweed, D., Calway., A.: Tracking many objects using subordinate Condensation. In: British Machine Vision Conference (BMVC). (2002)
16. MacCormick, J., Blake, A.: A probabilistic exclusion principle for tracking multiple objects. In: Intl. Conf. on Computer Vision (ICCV). (1999) 572–578
17. Isard, M., MacCormick, J.: BraMBLe: A Bayesian multiple-blob tracker. In: Intl. Conf. on Computer Vision (ICCV). (2001) 34–41
18. Arulampalam, S., Maskell, S., Gordon, N., Clapp, T.: A tutorial on particle filters for on-line non-linear/non-Gaussian Bayesian tracking. IEEE Transactions on Signal Processing **50** (2002) 174–188
19. Li, S.: Markov Random Field Modeling in Computer Vision. Springer (1995)
20. Neal, R.: Probabilistic inference using Markov chain Monte Carlo methods. Technical Report CRG-TR-93-1, Dept. of Computer Science, University of Toronto (1993)
21. Gilks, W., Richardson, S., Spiegelhalter, D., eds.: Markov chain Monte Carlo in practice. Chapman and Hall (1996)
22. Doucet, A., de Freitas, N., Gordon, N., eds.: Sequential Monte Carlo Methods In Practice. Springer-Verlag, New York (2001)
23. Hastings, W.: Monte Carlo sampling methods using Markov chains and their applications. Biometrika **57** (1970) 97–109

Human Pose Estimation Using Learnt Probabilistic Region Similarities and Partial Configurations

Timothy J. Roberts, Stephen J. McKenna, and Ian W. Ricketts

Division of Applied Computing
University of Dundee
Dundee DD1 4HN, Scotland
{troberts,stephen,ricketts}@computing.dundee.ac.uk
http://www.computing.dundee.ac.uk

Abstract. A model of human appearance is presented for efficient pose estimation from real-world images. In common with related approaches, a high-level model defines a space of configurations which can be associated with image measurements and thus scored. A search is performed to identify good configuration(s). Such an approach is challenging because the configuration space is high dimensional, the search is global, and the appearance of humans in images is complex due to background clutter, shape uncertainty and texture.

The system presented here is novel in several respects. The formulation allows differing numbers of parts to be parameterised and allows poses of differing dimensionality to be compared in a principled manner based upon learnt likelihood ratios. In contrast with current approaches, this allows a part based search in the presence of self occlusion. Furthermore, it provides a principled automatic approach to other object occlusion. View based probabilistic models of body part shapes are learnt that represent intra and inter person variability (in contrast to rigid geometric primitives). The probabilistic region for each part is transformed into the image using the configuration hypothesis and used to collect two appearance distributions for the part's foreground and adjacent background. Likelihood ratios for single parts are learnt from the dissimilarity of the foreground and adjacent background appearance distributions. It is important to note the distinction between this technique and restrictive foreground/background specific modelling. It is demonstrated that this likelihood allows better discrimination of body parts in real world images than contour to edge matching techniques. Furthermore, the likelihood is less sparse and noisy, making coarse sampling and local search more effective. A likelihood ratio for body part pairs with similar appearances is also learnt. Together with a model of inter-part distances this better describes correct higher dimensional configurations. Results from applying an optimization scheme to the likelihood model for challenging real world images are presented.

T. Pajdla and J. Matas (Eds.): ECCV 2004, LNCS 3024, pp. 291–303, 2004.
© Springer-Verlag Berlin Heidelberg 2004

1   Introduction

It is popular in the literature to match a high-level shape model to an image in order to recover human pose (see the review papers [1,2]). Samples are drawn from the shape configuration space to search for a good match. The success of this approach, in terms of its accuracy and efficiency, depends critically on the choice of likelihood formulation and its implicit assumptions. This paper presents a strong likelihood model and a flexible, effectively low dimensional formulation that allows efficient inference of detailed pose from real-world images. Pose estimation is performed here from single colour images so no motion information is available. This method could however form an important component in an automatically (re)initialising human tracker.

1.1   Assumptions

Estimation of human body pose from poorly constrained scenes is made difficult by the large variation in human appearance. The system presented here aims to recover the variation due to body pose automatically and efficiently in the presence of other variations due to:

- *unknown* subject identity, clothing colour and texture
- *unknown*, significantly cluttered, indoor or outdoor scenes
- uncontrolled illumination
- general, other object occlusion

It is assumed that perspective effects are weak and that the scale is such that distributions of pixel values or local features can be estimated and used to characterise body parts. It is further assumed that the class of view point is known, in this case a side on view. These assumptions apply to a large proportion of real world photographs of people.

1.2   Formulation

There are two main approaches to human pose estimation. The 'top-down' approach makes samples in a high dimensional space and fully models self-occlusion (e.g. [3,4,5,6]). It does not incorporate bottom-up part identification and is inappropriate without a strong pose prior (and is therefore mostly used in trackers). The 'bottom-up' approach identifies the body parts and then assembles them into the best configuration. Whilst it does sample globally it does not model self-occlusion. Both approaches tend to rely on a fixed number of parts being parameterised (a notable exception being the recent work of Ramanan and Forsyth [7]). However, occlusion by other objects or weak evidence may make some parts unidentifiable. The approach of *partial configurations* presented here bridges these two approaches by allowing configurations of different dimensionalities to be compared. This is done by combining learnt likelihood ratios computed only from the parameterised, visible parts. The method has several advantages.

Firstly, it allows general occlusion conditions to be handled. Secondly, it makes use of the fact that some parts might be found more easily than others. For example, it is often easier to locate parts that do not overlap. Thirdly, it makes use of the fact that configurations with small numbers of parts contain much of the overall pose information because of inter-part linking. For example, knowing the position of just the head and outer limbs greatly constrains the overall pose. The approach of partial configurations, along with a global stochastic optimization scheme, is more flexible than pictorial structures [8] since it allows a large range of occlusion conditions. When employed in a time-constrained optimization scheme, it allows the system to report lower dimensional solution(s) should a higher dimensional one not be found in time. A consequence of the formulation is that parts must be parameterised in their own co-ordinate system rather than hierarchically as is often the case in tracking systems, e.g. [3]. Whilst this might appear to increase the dimensionality of the pose parameter space, in practice an offset term is often required to model complex joints like the shoulder [6] making the difference one of mathematical convenience.

1.3 Outline

The remainder of the paper details the three components that make up the likelihood ratio used to find humans in real images. For ease of exposition, Section 2 begins by describing the likelihood ratio used to find single body parts. A probabilistic region template is transformed into image space and used to estimate foreground and adjacent background appearances. The hypothesised foreground and background appearances are compared and a likelihood ratio is computed, based upon learnt PDFs of the similarity for on-part responses and off-part responses. The performance of this technique is then demonstrated and compared to a competing method. Section 3.2 presents a method for comparing hypothesised pose configurations incorporating inter-part joint constraints in which subsets of the body parts are instantiated. Section 3.3 then introduces a constraint based on the *a priori* expectation that pairs of parts will have similar appearance. Finally, pose estimation results are presented and conclusions drawn.

2 Finding Single Parts Using Probabilistic Regions

The model of body parts proposed here provides an efficient mechanism for the evaluation of hypothesised body parts in everyday scenes due to a highly discriminatory response and characteristics that support efficient sampling and search. This Section describes the method used for modelling body part shape and the use of image measurements to score part hypotheses. It concludes with an investigation of the resulting response.

2.1 Modelling Shape

Current systems often use 2D or 3D geometric primitives such as ellipses, rectangles, cylinders and tapered superquadrics to represent body parts (e.g. [3,4,5]).

These are convenient but rather *ad hoc* approximations. Instead, *probabilistic region templates* are used here as body part primitives. Due to the limited presence of perspective effects and 3D shape variation, a 2D model with depth ordering is used to represent the body. A variation of the scaled prismatic model [9] is used to parameterise the transformed appearance. This reduces the dimensionality compared to a 3D model and removes kinematic singularities [10].

A body part, labelled here by $i (i \in 1...N)$, is represented using a single probabilistic region template, M_i, which represents the uncertainty in the part's shape without attempting to enable shape instances to be accurately reconstructed [1]. This is particulary important for efficient sampling when the subject wears lose fitting clothing. The probability that an image pixel at position (x, y) belongs to a hypothesised part i is then given by $M_i(T_i(x, y))$ where T_i is a linear transformation from image coordinates to template coordinates determined by the part's centre, (x_c, y_c), image plane rotation, θ, elongation, e, and scale, s. The elongation parameter alters the aspect ratio of the template and is used to approximate rotation in depth about one of the part's axes. The probabilities in the template are estimated from example shapes in the form of binary masks obtained by manual segmentation of training images in which the elongation is maximal (i.e. in which the major axis of the part is parallel to the image plane). These training examples are aligned by specifying their centres, orientations and scales. Un-parameterised pose variations are marginalised over, allowing a reduction in the size of the state space. Specifically, rotation about each limb's major axis is marginalised since these rotations are difficult to observe. The templates are also constrained to be symmetric about this axis. It has been found, due to the insensitivity of the likelihood model described below to precise contour location, that upper and lower arm and leg parts can reasonably be represented using a single template. This greatly improves the sampling efficiency. Some learnt probabilistic region templates are shown in Fig. 1. The uncertain regions in these templates arise because of (i) 3D shape variation due to change of clothing and identity, (ii) rotation in depth about the major axis, and (iii) inaccuracies in the alignment and manual segmentation of the training images.

2.2   Single Part Likelihood

Several methods for body part detection have been proposed although in the opinion of the authors much work remains to be done. Matching geometric primitives to an edge field is popular, e.g. [11]. Wachter and Nagel [3] used only the edges that did not overlap with other parts. Sidenbladh *et al.* [12] emphasised learning the distribution of foreground and background filter responses (edge, ridge and motion) rather than forming *ad hoc* models. Ronfard *et al.* [8] learned part detectors from Gaussian derivative filters. Another popular method is modelling the background, but this has the obvious limitation of requiring knowledge of the empty scene. Matching model boundaries to local image gradients often

---

[*] Note that while it would be possible to represent the body parts using a set of basis regions, the mean was found to be sufficient here.

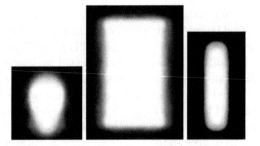

Fig. 1. Head, torso and limb probabilistic region templates. The upper and lower arm and legs are represented using a single mask (increasing sampling efficiency). Notice the masks' symmetries.

results in poor discrimination. Furthermore, edge responses provide a relatively sparse cue which necessitates dense sampling. In order to achieve accurate results in real world scenes the authors believe that a description that takes account of colour or texture is necessary. To accomplish this the high-level shape model can be used earlier in the inference process. One might envisage learning a model that described the wide variation in the foreground appearance of body parts present in a population of differently clothed people. Such a model would seek to capture regularities due to the patterns typically used in clothing. However, such an approach would require a high dimensional model and prohibitively large amounts of training data. Furthermore, it would not be strongly discriminatory because most clothing and image regions are uniformly textured.

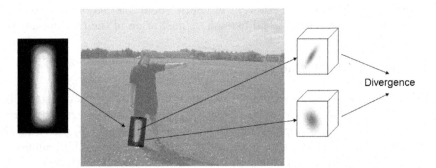

Fig. 2. The flow of data: A lower leg body part probabilistic region template is transformed into the image. The spatial extent of the template is such that the areas (in the probabilistic sense) of the foreground and background regions are approximately equal. The probabilistic region is used to estimate the foreground appearance and adjacent background appearance histograms. A likelihood is learnt based upon the divergence of the two histograms.

The approach taken here is to use the dissimilarity between the appearance of the foreground and background of a transformed probabilistic region as illustrated in Fig. 2. These appearances will be dissimilar as long as a part is not completely camouflaged. The appearances are represented here as PDFs of intensity and chromaticity image features, resulting in 3D distributions. In general, local filter responses could also be used to represent the appearance (c.f. [13]). Since texture can often result in multi-modal distributions, each PDF is encoded as a histogram (marginalised over position). For scenes in which the body parts appear small, semi-parametric density estimation methods such as Gaussian mixture models would be more appropriate. The foreground appearance histogram for part i, denoted here by F_i, is formed by adding image features from the part's supporting region proportional to $M_i(T_i(x, y))$. Similarly, the adjacent background appearance distribution, B_i, is estimated by adding features proportional to $1 - M_i(T_i(x, y))$.

It is expected that the foreground appearance will be less similar to the background appearance for configurations that are correct (denoted by on) than incorrect (denoted by $\overline{on}$). Therefore, a PDF of the Bhattacharya measure given by Equation (1) is learnt for on and $\overline{on}$ configurations [14]. The on distribution was estimated from data obtained by manually specifying the transformation parameters to align the probabilistic region template to be on parts that are neither occluded nor overlapping. The $\overline{on}$ distribution was estimated by generating random alignments elsewhere in 100 images of outdoor and indoor scenes. The on PDF can be adequately represented by a Gaussian (although in fact the distribution is skewed). Equation (2) defines $SINGLE_i$ as the ratio of these two distributions. This is the response used to score a single body part configuration and is plotted in Fig. 3.

$$I(F_i, B_i) = \sum_{\mathbf{f}} \sqrt{F_i(\mathbf{f}) \times B_i(\mathbf{f})} \tag{1}$$

$$SINGLE_i = \frac{p(I(F_i, B_i)|on)}{p(I(F_i, B_i)|\overline{on})} \tag{2}$$

2.3   Enhancing Discrimination Using Adjoining Regions

When detecting single body parts, the performance can be improved by distinguishing positions where the background appearance is most likely to differ from the foreground appearance. For example, due to the structure of clothing, when detecting an upper arm, *adjoining* background areas around the shoulder joint are often similar to the foreground appearance (as determined by the *structural* model used here to gather appearance data). The histogram model proposed thus far, which marginalises appearance over position, does not use this information optimally. To enhance discrimination, two separate adjacent background histograms are constructed, one for adjoining regions and another for non-adjoining regions. It is expected that the non-adjoining region appearance will be less similar to the foreground appearance than the adjoining region

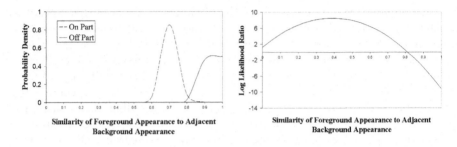

Fig. 3. Left: A plot of the learnt PDFs of foreground to background appearance similarity for the *on* and $\overline{on}$ part configurations of a head template. Right: The log of the resulting likelihood ratio. It can be seen that the distributions are well separated.

appearance. Currently, the adjoining and non-adjoining regions are specified manually during training by a hard threshold. A probabilistic approach, where the regions are estimated by marginalising over the relative pose between adjoining parts (to get a low dimensional model), would be better, but requires large amounts of training data. It is important to note that this is only important, and thus used for, better bottom-up identification of body parts. When the adjoining part is specified using a multiple part configuration, the formulation presented later in Section 3.1 is used.

2.4 Single Part Response Investigation

The middle column of Fig. 4 shows the projection of the likelihood ratio computed using Equation (2) onto typical images containing significant clutter. The top image shows the response for a head while the other two images show the response of a vertically-oriented limb filter. It can be seen that the technique is highly discriminatory, producing relatively few false maxima. Note the false response in between the legs in the second image: the space between the legs is itself shaped like a leg. Although images were acquired using various cameras, some with noisy colour signals, system parameters were fixed for all test images.

In order to provide a comparison with an alternative method, the responses obtained by comparing the hypothesised part boundaries with edge responses were computed in a similar manner to Sidenbladh and Black [12]. These are shown in the rightmost column of Fig. 4. Orientations of significant edge responses for foreground and background configurations were learned (using derivatives of the probabilistic region template), treated as independent and normalised for scale. Contrast normalisation was not used. Other formulations (e.g. averaging) proved to be weaker on the scenes under consideration. The responses using this method are clearly less discriminatory.

Fig. 5 illustrates the typical spatial variations of both the body part likelihood response proposed here and the edge-based likelihood. The edge response, whilst indicative of the correct position, has significant false positive likelihood ratios. The proposed part likelihood is more expensive to compute than the

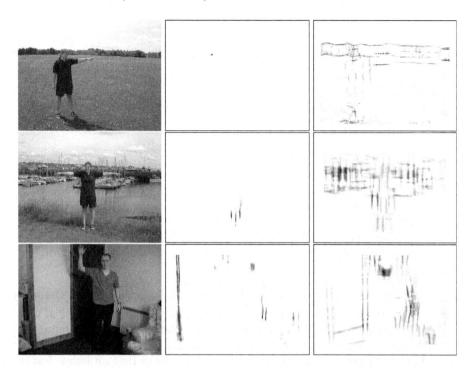

Fig. 4. First column: Typical input images from both outdoor and indoor environments. Second column: projection of the log likelihood (positive only, re-scaled) from the part filters. Third column: projection of the log likelihood ratio (positive only, rescaled) for an edge-based model. First row: head model. Second and third rows: limb model (vertical orientation).

edge-based filter (approximately an order of magnitude slower in our implementation). However, it is far more discriminatory and as a result, fewer samples are needed when performing pose search, leading to an overall performance benefit. Furthermore, the collected foreground histograms are useful for other likelihood measurements as discussed below.

3   Body Pose Estimation with Partial Configurations

Since any single body part likelihood will result in false positives it is important to encode higher order relationships between body parts to improve discrimination. In this system this is accomplished by encoding an expectation of structure in the foreground appearance and the spatial relationship of body parts.

3.1   Extending Probabilistic Regions to Multi-part Configurations

Configurations containing more than one body part can be represented using a straightforward extension of the probabilistic region approach described

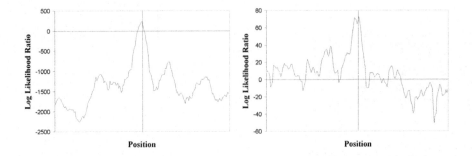

Fig. 5. Comparison of the spatial variation (plotted for a horizontal change of 200 pixels) of the learnt log likelihood ratios for the model presented here (left) and the edge-based model (right) of the head in the first image in Fig. 4. The correct position is centered and indicated by the vertical bar. Anything above the horizontal bar, corresponding to a likelihood ratio of 1, is more likely to be a head than not.

above. In order to account for self-occlusion, the pose space is represented by a depth ordered set, V, of probabilistic regions with parts sharing a common scale parameter, s. When taken together, the templates determine the probability that a particular image feature belongs to a particular parts foreground or background. More specifically, the probability that an image feature at position (x, y) belongs to the foreground appearance of part i is given by $M_i(T_i(x, y)) \times \prod_j (1 - M_j(T_j(x, y))$ where j labels closer, instantiated parts. Forming the background appearance is more subtle since some parts often have a similar appearance. Therefore, a list of paired body parts is specified manually and the background appearance histogram is constructed from features weighted by $\prod_k (1 - M_k(T_k(x, y))$ where k labels all instantiated parts other than i and those paired with i. Thus, a single image feature can contribute to the foreground and adjacent background appearance of several parts. When insufficient data is available to estimate either the foreground or the adjacent background histogram (as determined using an area threshold) the corresponding likelihood ratio is set to one.

3.2 Inter-part Joint Constraints

A link is introduced between parts i and j if and only if they are physically connected neighbours. Each part has a set of control points that link it to its neighbours. A link has an associated value $LINK_{i,j}$ given by:

$$LINK_{i,j} = \begin{cases} 1 & \text{if } \delta_{i,j}/s < \Delta_{i,j} \\ e^{(\delta_{i,j}/s - \Delta_{i,j})/\sigma} & \text{otherwise} \end{cases} \qquad (3)$$

where $\delta_{i,j}$ is the image distance between the control points of the pair, $\Delta_{i,j}$ is the maximum un-penalised distance and σ relates to the strength of penalisation. If the neighbouring parts do not link directly, because intervening parts are not instantiated, the un-penalised distance is found by summing the un-penalised

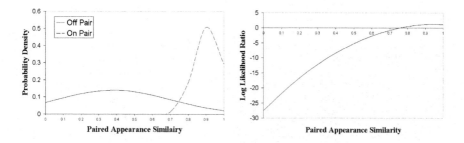

Fig. 6. Left: A plot of the learnt PDFs of foreground appearance similarity for paired and non-paired configurations. Right: The log of the resulting likelihood ratio. It can be seen, as would be expected, that more similar regions are more likely to be a pair.

distances over the complete chain. This can be interpreted as a force between parts equivalent to a telescopic rod with a spring on each end.

3.3   Learnt Paired Part Similarity

Certain pairs of body parts can be expected to have a similar foreground appearance to one another. For example, a person's upper left arm will nearly always have a similar colour and texture to the upper right arm. In the current system, the limbs are paired with their opposing parts. To encode this knowledge, a PDF of the divergence measure (computed using Equation (1)) between the foreground appearance histograms of paired parts and non-paired parts is learnt. Equation (4) shows the resulting likelihood ratio and Fig. 6 graphs this ratio. Fig. 7 shows a typical image projection of this ratio and shows the technique to be highly discriminatory. It limits possible configurations if one limb can be found reliably and helps reduce the likelihood of incorrect large assemblies.

$$PAIR_{i,j} = \frac{p(I(F_i, F_j)|on_i, on_j)}{p(I(F_i, F_j)|\overline{on_i, on_j})} \tag{4}$$

3.4   Combining the Likelihoods

Learning the likelihood ratios allows a principled comparison of the various cues. The individual likelihood ratios are combined by assuming independence and the overall likelihood ratio is given by Equation(5). This rewards correct higher dimensional configurations over correct lower dimensional ones.

$$R = \prod_{i \in V} SINGLE_i \times \prod_{i,j \in V} PAIR_{i,j} \times \prod_{i,j \in V} LINK_{i,j} \tag{5}$$

Fig. 7. Investigation of a paired part response. Left: an image for which significant limb candidates are found in the background. Right: the projection of the likelihood ratio for the paired response to the person's lower right leg in the image.

3.5 Pose Estimation Results

The sampling scheme is described only briefly here as the emphasis of this paper is on a new formulation and likelihood. The search techniques will be more fully developed in future work. It is emphasised that the aim of the sampler is treated as one of maximisation rather than density estimation. The system begins by making a coarse regular scan of the image for the head and limbs. These results are then locally optimised. Part configurations are sampled from the resulting distribution and combined to form larger configurations and then optimised (in the full dimensional pose space, including the body part label) for a fixed period of time. It is envisaged that, due to the flexibility of the parametrisation, a set of optimization methods such as genetic style combination, prediction, local search, re-ordering and re-labelling can be combined using a scheduling algorithm and a shared sample population to achieve rapid, robust, global, high dimensional pose estimation. The system was implemented using an efficient, in-house C++ framework. Histograms with $8 \times 8 \times 8$ bins were used to represent a part's foreground and adjacent background appearance. The system samples single part configurations at the scale shown in Fig. 2 at approximately $3KHz$ from an image with resolution 640×480 on a 2GHz PC. Fig. 8 shows results of searching for partial pose configurations. It should be emphasised that although inter-part links are not visualised here, these results represent estimates of *pose configurations* with inter-part connectivity as opposed to independently detected parts. The scale of the model was fixed and the elongation parameter was constrained to be above 0.7.

4 Summary

A system was presented that allows detailed, efficient estimation of human pose from real-world images. The focus of the paper was the investigation of a novel likelihood model. The two key contributions were (i) a formulation that allowed

Fig. 8. Results from a search for partial pose configurations. The images are of both indoor and outdoor scenes and contain a significant amount of background clutter and in one case a door which partially occludes the subject. The samples with maximum score after searching for 2 minutes are shown.

the representation and comparison of partial (lower dimensional) solutions and modelled other object occlusion and (ii) a highly discriminatory learnt likelihood based upon probabilistic regions that allowed efficient body part detection. It should be stressed that this likelihood depends only on there being differences between a hypothesised part's foreground appearance and adjacent background appearance. It does not make use of scene-specific background models and is, as such, general and applicable to unconstrained scenes. The results presented confirm that it is possible to use partial configurations and a strong likelihood model to localise the body in real-world images. To improve the results, future work will need to address the following issues. A limited model of appearance was employed based on colour values. Texture orientation features should be employed to disambiguate overlapping parts (e.g. the arm lying over the torso). The model should be extended through closer consideration of the distinction between structural (kinematic) and visual segmentation of the body. The assumptions of independence between the individual likelihoods, particularly for the link and paired appearance likelihoods, needs investigation. Lastly, and perhaps most importantly, future work needs to improve the sampler to allow high dimensional configurations that contain self occlusion and visually similar neighbouring parts to be localised.

Acknowledgments. This work was funded by the UK EPSRC.

References

1. D. M. Gavrila. The visual analysis of human movement: A survey. *Computer Vision and Image Understanding*, 73(1):82–98, January 1999.
2. T. B. Moeslund and E. Granum. A survey of computer vision-based human motion capture. *Computer Vision and Image Understanding*, 81(3):231–268, March 2001.
3. S. Wachter and H. H. Nagel. Tracking persons in monocular image sequences. *Computer Vision and Image Understanding*, 74(3):174–192, June 1999.
4. J. Deutscher, A. Davison, and I. Reid. Automatic partitioning of high dimensional search spaces associated with articulated body motion capture. In *IEEE Conference on Computer Vision and Pattern Recognition*, volume 2, pages 669–676, Hawaii, 2001.
5. T. J. Roberts, S. J. McKenna, and I. W. Ricketts. Adaptive learning of statistical appearance models for 3D human tracking. In *British Machine Vision Conference*, pages 333–342, Cardiff, 2002.
6. C. Sminchisescu and B. Triggs. Covariance scaled sampling for monocular 3D body tracking. In *IEEE Conference on Computer Vision and Pattern Recognition*, volume 1, pages 447–454, Hawaii, 2001.
7. D. Ramanan and D. A. Forsyth. Finding and tracking people from the bottom up. In *IEEE Conference on Computer Vision and Pattern Recognition*, Madison, Wisconsin, June 2003.
8. R. Ronfard, C. Schud, and B. Triggs. Learning to parse pictures of people. In *European Conference on Computer Vision*, pages 700–714, Copenhagen, 2002.
9. T. J. Cham and J. M. Rehg. A multiple hypothesis approach to figure tracking. In *IEEE Conference on Computer Vision and Pattern Recognition*, volume 2, pages 239–245, Fort Collins, Colorado, USA, 1999.
10. J. Deutscher, B. North, B. Bascle, and A. Blake. Tracking through singularities and discontinuities by random sampling. In *IEEE International Conference on Computer Vision*, pages 1144–1149, September 1999.
11. J. Deutscher, A. Blake, and I. Reid. Articulated body motion capture by annealed particle filtering. In *IEEE Conference on Computer Vision and Pattern Recognition*, volume 2, pages 126–133, South Carolina, USA, 2000.
12. H. Sidenbladh and M. J. Black. Learning image statistics for Bayesian tracking. In *IEEE International Conference on Computer Vision*, volume 2, pages 709–716, Vancouver, 2001.
13. B. Schiele and J. L. Crowley. Recognition without correspondence using multidimensional receptive field histograms. *International Journal of Computer Vision*, 36(1):31–50, 2000.
14. J. Puzicha, Y. Rubner, C. Tomasi, and J. M. Buhmann. Empirical evaluation of dissimilarity measures for color and texture. *IEEE International Conference on Computer Vision*, pages 1165–1173, 1999.

Tensor Field Segmentation Using Region Based Active Contour Model*

Zhizhou Wang and Baba C. Vemuri

Department of CISE, University of Florida
Gainesville, Fl. 32611
{zwang,vemuri}@cise.ufl.edu

Abstract. Tensor fields (matrix valued data sets) have recently attracted increased attention in the fields of image processing, computer vision, visualization and medical imaging. Tensor field segmentation is an important problem in tensor field analysis and has not been addressed adequately in the past. In this paper, we present an effective region-based active contour model for tensor field segmentation and show its application to diffusion tensor magnetic resonance images (MRI) as well as for the texture segmentation problem in computer vision. Specifically, we present a variational principle for an active contour using the Euclidean difference of tensors as a discriminant. The variational formulation is valid for piecewise smooth regions, however, for the sake of simplicity of exposition, we present the piecewise constant region model in detail. This variational principle is a generalization of the region-based active contour to matrix valued functions. It naturally leads to a curve evolution equation for tensor field segmentation, which is subsequently expressed in a level set framework and solved numerically. Synthetic and real data experiments involving the segmentation of diffusion tensor MRI as well as structure tensors obtained from real texture data are shown to depict the performance of the proposed model.

1 Introduction

Tensor fields are the essential components in many applications like DT-MRI processing, texture image segmentation, solid and fluid mechanics etc. Several interesting problems constitute tensor field analysis in the context of imaging applications, for example : tensor field data acquisition, restoration, segmentation and visualization. Though, much effort has been expended on tensor field data acquisition, restoration and visualization, tensor field segmentation has not been adequately addressed in the past. In this paper, we will address the general problem of tensor field segmentation and then depict examples of application of the algorithm to medical image analysis, specifically to diffusion tensor MRI segmentation and additionally to texture image segmentation. In the following, we will present a brief overview of various techniques currently invogue in using tensor-based information for segmenting motion fields, textures and DT-MRI.

---

* This research was in part funded by the NIH grant RO1-NS42075

T. Pajdla and J. Matas (Eds.): ECCV 2004, LNCS 3024, pp. 304–315, 2004.
© Springer-Verlag Berlin Heidelberg 2004

There are many algorithms in literature for motion segmentation, however, not many of them use the structure tensor. Kühne et.al [11] proposed an interesting tensor-driven active contour model for moving object segmentation, a 3D structure tensor is computed in the spatio-temporal domain of a video sequence and is used to create the stopping function in a geometric active contour model. The results they shown are quite promising for motion segmentation. Some other examples of published research on the use of the structure tensor in the context of optical flow computation are [4,9].

Recently, Rousson et.al, in [12] developed a technique for segmenting textures where in they first construct texture features based on the image and its structure tensor, then use an active and adaptive contour model to segment this feature vector field. The texture segmentation results are very impressive in their work.

In the context of DT-MRI segmentation, recently, Zhukov et.al., [18] proposed a level set segmentation method which is in fact a segmentation of a scalar anisotropic measure of the diffusion tensor. The fact that Zukhov et.al., [18] use a scalar field computed from the diffusion tensor field implies they have ignored the direction information contained in the tensor field. Thus, this method will fail if two homogeneous regions of tensor field have the same anisotropy property but are oriented in a totally different direction! Moreover, any of the numerous (well tested and well understood) scalar image segmentation techniques could have been employed for achieving the goal of segmenting the scalar field of anisotropy measures. In contrast, we present an algorithm to segment tensor field using all the information contained in a tensor, not only scalar anisotropy properties, but also its orientation.

To the best of our knowledge, there is no published work in literature which aims to segment tensor fields. In this paper, we tackle the tensor field segmentation problem using an effective region based active contour model. Geometric active contour model has long been used in scalar and vector images segmentation [5,6,13,14,10,17]. Our work can be viewed as an *extension* of the work on the region-based active contours ([7],[8], [17]), *to matrix valued images*. These region-based active contours are curve evolution implementation of the Mumford-Shah functional [15]. *Our key contribution is the incorporation of a discriminant of tensors into the region based active contour model and to show its effectiveness in tensor field segmentation.* The specific discriminant we use is the Forbenius norm of the difference of two tensors. Although this norm has been used in the past for tensor field restoration, to the best of our knowledge, it has never been used for tensor field segmentation.

Rest of the paper is organized as follows: in section 2, the piecewise smooth and piecewise constant region-based active contour models for tensor field segmentation are described. The Euler-Lagrange equation and the curve evolution equation are given for the piecewise constant model for simplicity of exposition. Section 3 contains a detailed description of the level set formulation and the implementation using an explicit scheme. In section 4, we present experiments on application of our model to synthetic as well as real data. Finally in section 5, we discuss the pros and cons of our approach and some future directions.

2   Model Description

Our model for tensor field segmentation in R^2 is posed as minimization of the following variational principle based on the Mumford-Shah functional ([15]):

$$E(\mathbf{T}, \mathbf{C}) = \int_\Omega dist(\mathbf{T}(\mathbf{x}, \mathbf{T_0}(\mathbf{x}))^2 d\mathbf{x} + \alpha \int_{\Omega/\mathbf{C}} \|\nabla \mathbf{T}(\mathbf{x})\|^2 d\mathbf{x} + \beta|\mathbf{C}| \qquad (1)$$

Where the curve $\mathbf{C}$ is the boundary of the desired unknown segmentation, Ω is the image domain, $\mathbf{T_0}$ is the original noisy tensor field, $\mathbf{T}$ is a piecewise smooth approximation of $\mathbf{T_0}$ with discontinuities only along $\mathbf{C}$, $\nabla \mathbf{T}$ is a component wise gradient of each element of the tensor, $|\mathbf{C}|$ is the arclength of the curve $\mathbf{C}$, α and β are control parameters, $dist(.,.)$ is a measure of the distance between two tensors.

The above variational principle will capture piecewise smooth regions while maintaining a smooth boundary. A simplified form which aims to capture two types of piecewise constant regions is given by:

$$E(C, \mathbf{T_1}, \mathbf{T_2}) = \int_R dist^2(\mathbf{T}(\mathbf{x}), \mathbf{T_1})d\mathbf{x} + \int_{R^c} dist^2(\mathbf{T}(\mathbf{x}), \mathbf{T_2})d\mathbf{x} + \beta|C| \qquad (2)$$

where R is the region enclosed by C and R^c is the region outside C.

The above model in equation (2) can be viewed as a modification of the active contour model without edges for scalar valued images in [7]. The difference measures in [7] for the scalar values are simple, be it intensity or curvature. In the proposed model, a key issue will be the right choice of a tensor difference measure. Any other segmentation models that are generalizations of the one proposed here for tensor fields, will unavoidably encounter this fundamental problem. Alexander et.al., [1] discussed different similarity measures for matching of diffusion tensor images and indicated that the Euclidean difference measure of tensors is the best in the context of image registration. The Euclidean difference metric is defined as follows:

$$dist(A, B) = \sqrt{trace[(A - B)^2]} = \|A - B\|_F \qquad (3)$$

where A and B are two rank 2 tensor of the same size, or simply two matrices of the same size, $\|.\|_F$ is the matrix Frobenius Norm.

In the context of tensor field segmentation, we also found that the Euclidean difference measure of tensors is a good choice. We define the mean value of tensors in a region R as:

$$\mu(\mathbf{T}; R) = min_\mu \int_R [dist(\mu, \mathbf{T}(\mathbf{x})]^2 d\mathbf{x} \qquad (4)$$

When we choose $dist(.,.)$ to be the Euclidean difference measure, it is not hard to verify that $\mu(\mathbf{T}) = \int_R \mathbf{T}(\mathbf{x})d\mathbf{x}/|R|$.

We followed the two phases implementation of ([7]). First fixed $\mathbf{C}$, then $\mathbf{T_1} = \mu(\mathbf{T}; R)$ and $\mathbf{T_2} = \mu(\mathbf{T}; R^c)$. Then fixed $\mathbf{T_1}$ and $\mathbf{T_2}$, the Euler Lagrange equation for the variational principle (2) is:

$$\left[\beta k - dist^2(\mathbf{T}, \mathbf{T_1}) + dist^2(\mathbf{T}, \mathbf{T_2})\right] \mathbf{N} = 0$$

where $\mathbf{N}$ is the outer normal of the curve C. We then have the corresponding gradient flow or the curve evolution form for the above equation as:

$$\frac{\partial C}{\partial t} = -\left[\beta k - dist^2(\mathbf{T}, \mathbf{T_1}(t)) + dist^2(\mathbf{T}, \mathbf{T_2}(t))\right]\mathbf{N}$$

$$\mathbf{T_1} = \frac{\int_R \mathbf{T}(\mathbf{x})d\mathbf{x}}{|R|}, \quad \mathbf{T_2} = \frac{\int_{R^c} \mathbf{T}(\mathbf{x})d\mathbf{x}}{|R^c|} \tag{5}$$

This can be easily solved numerically as described subsequently. In a similar fashion, one can write down the curve evolution equation for equation (1).

3 Level Set Implementation and Numerical Methods

The curve evolution equation (5) can be easily implemented in a level set framework. The corresponding level set formulation is given by:

$$\frac{\partial \phi}{\partial t} = \left[\beta div(\frac{\nabla\phi}{|\nabla\phi|}) - dist^2(T, T_1) + dist^2(T, T_2)\right]|\nabla\phi|$$

$$T_1 = \frac{\int_\Omega (1 - H(\phi))T(\mathbf{x})d\mathbf{x}}{\int_\Omega (1 - H(\phi))d\mathbf{x}}, \quad T_2 = \frac{\int_\Omega H(\phi)T(\mathbf{x})d\mathbf{x}}{\int_\Omega H(\phi)d\mathbf{x}} \tag{6}$$

where $H(.)$ is the Heaviside function, $H(\phi(\mathbf{x})) = 0$ for $x \in R$ and $H(\phi(\mathbf{x})) = 1$ otherwise. Equation (6) can be easily discretized using an explicit Euler scheme. We can assume the spatial grid size to be 1, then the finite differences of the partial derivatives are:

$$\Delta^i \phi_{i,j} = \frac{1}{2}(\phi_{i+1,j} - \phi_{i-1,j}), \quad \Delta^j \phi_{i,j} = \frac{1}{2}(\phi_{i,j+1} - \phi_{i,j-1})$$

$$\Delta^i_- \phi_{i,j} = \phi_{i,j} - \phi_{i-1,j}, \quad \Delta^j_- \phi_{i,j} = \phi_{i,j} - \phi_{i,j-1}$$

$$\Delta^i_+ \phi_{i,j} = \phi_{i+1,j} - \phi_{i,j}, \quad \Delta^j_+ \phi_{i,j} = \phi_{i,j+1} - \phi_{i,j}$$

$$\Delta^{ii} \phi_{i,j} = \phi_{i+1,j} - 2\phi_{i,j} + \phi_{i-1,j}$$

$$\Delta^{ij} \phi_{i,j} = \frac{1}{4}(\phi_{i+1,j+1} - \phi_{i+1,j-1} - \phi_{i-1,j+1} + \phi_{i-1,j-1})$$

$$\Delta^{jj} \phi_{i,j} = \phi_{i,j+1} - 2\phi_{i,j} + \phi_{i,j-1}$$

In this case, we have the following update equation:

$$\frac{\phi_{i,j}^{n+1} - \phi_{i,j}^n}{\Delta t} = \left[\beta k_{i,j}^n - dist^2(T_{i,j}, T_1^n) + dist^2(T_{i,j}, T_2^n)\right]\sqrt{(\Delta^i \phi_{i,j})^2 + (\Delta^j \phi_{i,j})^2}$$

$$T_1^n = \frac{\sum_{i,j}(1 - H(\phi_{i,j}^n))T_{i,j}}{\sum_{i,j}(1 - H(\phi_{i,j}^n))}, \quad T_2^n = \frac{\sum_{i,j} H(\phi_{i,j}^n)T_{i,j}}{\sum_{i,j} H(\phi_{i,j}^n)} \tag{7}$$

where the curvature $k_{i,j}^n$ of ϕ^n can be computed as:

$$k_{i,j}^n = \frac{\Delta^{jj}\phi_{i,j}^n(\Delta^i\phi_{i,j}^n)^2 - 2\Delta^i\phi_{i,j}^n\Delta^j\phi_{i,j}^n\Delta^{ij}\phi_{i,j}^n + \Delta^{ii}\phi_{i,j}^n(\Delta^j\phi_{i,j}^n)^2}{\left[(\Delta^i\phi_{i,j}^n)^2 + (\Delta^j\phi_{i,j}^n)^2\right]^{3/2}} \tag{8}$$

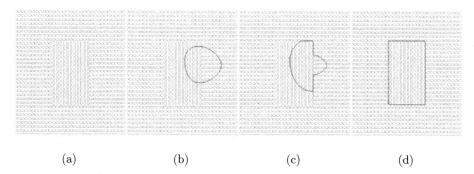

(a)   (b)   (c)   (d)

Fig. 1. Segmentation of a synthetic tensor field where two regions differs only in the orientations, (b),(c) and (d) are the initial, intermediate and final steps of the curve evolution process in the segmentation.

There are many other efficient numerical schemes that one may employ for example the multigrid scheme as was done in Tsai et.al., [17]. At this time, our explicit Euler scheme yielded reasonably fast solutions (3-5secs. for the synthetic data examples and just under a minute for the real data examples on a 1Ghz Pentium-3 CPU). For the piecewise smooth model, we refer the readers to ([8], [17]) for implementation details.

4   Experimental Results

In this section, we present several sets of experiments on the application of our tensor field segmentation model. One is on 2D synthetic data sets, the second is on texture images, the third one and the last one are on slices of diffusion tensor fields estimated from diffusion weighted images. We apply the piecewise constant case of our model for the first three sets of examples and the original piecewise smooth model for the last example. In all examples, the evolving boundary of the segmentation are superimposed on the images either in black or white.

4.1   Synthetic Tensor Field Segmentation

We synthesize two tensor fields, both are 2×2 symmetric positive definite matrix valued images on a 128×128 lattice and have two homogeneous regions. The two regions in the first tensor field only differ in the orientations while the two regions in the second tensor field only differ in the scales. These two tensor fields are visualized by ellipses as shown in Figure 1(a) and Figure 2(a). With an arbitrary initialization of the geometric active contour, our proposed model can yield high quality segmentation results as show in Figure 1 and Figure 2. Note that the first tensor field can't be segmented by using scalar anisotropic properties of tensors as in [18] and the second tensor field can't be segmented by using the dominant eigen vectors of the tensors. These two examples show that one must use the full information contained in tensors.

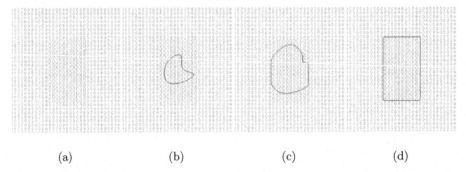

(a)   (b)   (c)   (d)

Fig. 2. Segmentation of a synthetic tensor field where two regions differs only in the scales, (b), (c) and (d) are the initial, intermediate and final steps of the curve evolution process in the segmentation.

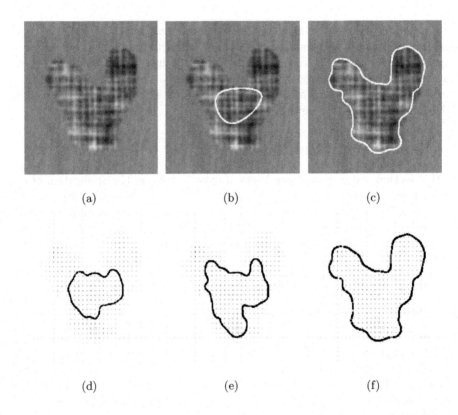

(a)   (b)   (c)

(d)   (e)   (f)

Fig. 3. Texture segmentation for a heart shape region: (b) and (c) are the initial and final curve superimposed on the texture image. (d), (e) and (f) are the intermediate and final steps with the evolving curve superimposed on the structure tensor field.

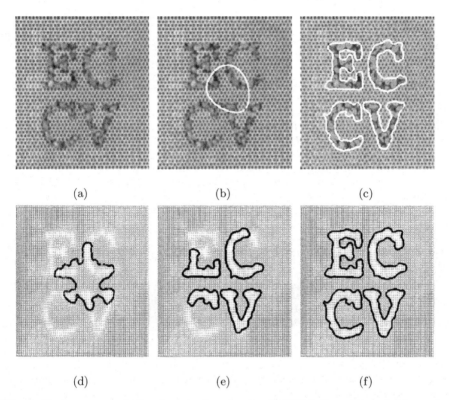

Fig. 4. Texture segmentation for a region showing "ECCV" logo: (b) and (c) are the initial and final curve superimposed on the texture image. (d),(e) and (f) are the intermediate and final steps with the evolving curve superimposed on the structure tensor field.

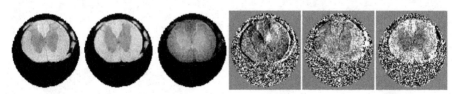

Fig. 5. A slice of the diffusion tensor field of a normal rat spinal cord. Each component is shown as a scalar image. Left to right : D_{xx}, D_{yy}, D_{zz}, D_{xy}, D_{yz} and D_{xz} respectively, the offdiagonal terms D_{xy}, D_{yz} and D_{zz} are greatly enhanced by brightness and contrast changes for better visualization.

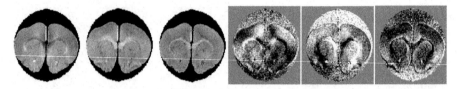

Fig. 6. A slice of the diffusion tensor field of a normal rat brain. Each component is shown as a scalar image. Left to right : D_{xx}, D_{yy}, D_{zz}, D_{xy}, D_{yz} and D_{xz} respectively, the offdiagonal terms D_{xy}, D_{yz} and D_{zz} are greatly enhanced by brightness and contrast changes for better visualization.

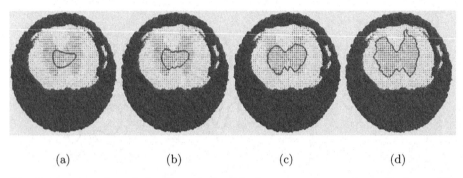

     (a)   (b)   (c)   (d)

Fig. 7. Segmentation of the slice of the diffusion tensor image shown in figure (5). (a)-(d) are the initial, intermediate and final steps of the curve evolution process in segmenting the gray matter inside the spinal cord.

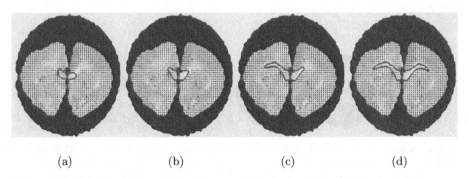

     (a)   (b)   (c)   (d)

Fig. 8. Segmentation of the slice of the diffusion tensor image shown in figure (6). (a)-(d) are the initial, intermediate and final steps of the curve evolution process in segmenting the corpus callosum inside the rat brain.

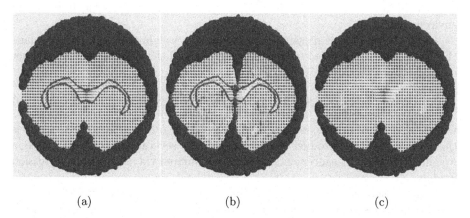

(a)   (b)   (c)

Fig. 9. Use piecewise smooth model to segment the slice of the diffusion tensor image shown in figure (6). (a) and (b) show the boundary of the final segmentation superimposed on the smoothed and the original tensor field respectively. (c) is the smoothed tensor field.

4.2   Texture Image Segmentation

For texture image segmentation, we construct the structure tensor field from the given image and then segment the structure tensor field using our proposed model. The structure tensor is defined as [3]:

$$J_\rho = K_\rho * (\nabla I \nabla I^T)$$

where K_ρ is a Gaussian smoothing function with standard deviation ρ. Figures 3 and 4 respectively show that our method can yield reasonable quality texture segmentations. Note that the segmentations are not very accurate along the edges of the original texture images. This is because we did not use any anisotropic smoothing for the structure tensor field as in [16], thus the edges in the original image were not preserved. It is however easy to incorporate such an anisotropic smoothing to yield better quality segmentations and will be the focus of our future work. Figure 4 also shows that topological change of the regions can be achieved easily in a level set framework.

4.3   Diffusion Tensor Image Segmentation

Diffusion tensor MRI (DT-MRI) is a relatively new MR imaging modality from which anisotropy of water diffusion can be inferred quantitatively [2], thus providing a method to study the tissue microstructure e.g., white matter connectivity in the brain in vivo. Diffusion is a process of movement of molecules as a result of random thermal agitation and in DT-MRI context, refers specifically to the random translational motion of water molecules in the part of the anatomy being imaged with MR. In three dimension, water diffusivity can be described by a 3×3 symmetric positive definite matrix $\mathbf{D}$ called diffusion tensor which is intimately related to the geometry and organization of the microscopic environment.

In DT-MRI, what is measured is the diffusion weighted echo intensity image (DWI) S_l. They are related to the diffusion tensor $\mathbf{D}$ through the Stejskal-Tanner equation [2] as given by:

$$S_l = S_0 e^{-\mathbf{b_l}:\mathbf{D}} = S_0 e^{-\sum_{i=1}^{3}\sum_{j=1}^{3} b_{l,ij} D_{ij}} \qquad (9)$$

where $\mathbf{b_l}$ is the diffusion weighting of the l-th magnetic gradient, ":" denotes the generalized inner product for matrices. Given several non-collinear diffusion weighted intensity measurements, $\mathbf{D}$ can be estimated via multivariate regression models.

Figure 5 shows a slice of the diffusion tensor field estimated from the DWIs of a normal rat spinal cord and Figure 6 shows the same for a normal rat brain. Each of the six independent components of the individual symmetric positive definite diffusion tensors in the tensor field is shown as a scalar image. Figure 7 demonstrates the segmentation of the gray matter inside the normal rat spinal cord with the evolving curve superimposed on the ellipsoid visualization of the diffusion tensor field. Similarly, Figure 8 depicts the segmentation procedure for the normal rat brain. In the final step, the major part of the corpus callosum is captured by the piecewise constant segmentation model. In both cases, we exclude the free water region which is not of interest in a biological context.

4.4   DTI Segmentation Using the Piecewise Smooth Model

Most of the previous examples have been successfully segmented using the piecewise constant model, however with one exception as shown in Figeure 8 because the piecewise constant assumption is no longer valid. Thus we further employ the piecewise smooth model to refine the segmentation result in Figure 8 and show the result of this application in Figure 9. Note that the horns of the corpus callosum have been accurately captured using the piecewise smooth model unlike when using the piecewise constant region model used in Figure 8.

5   Conclusion

We presented a tensor field segmentation method by incorporating a discriminant for tensors into a region-based active contour model. The particular discriminant we employed is the Euclidean difference measure between tensors. By using a discriminant on tensors, as opposed to either the eigen values or the eigen vectors of the tensors, we make full use of all the information contained in tensors. This proposed model is then implemented in a level set framework to take advantage of the easy ability of this framework to change topologies when desired. Our approach was applied to 2D synthetic and diffusion tensor field segmentation as well as texture image segmentation by using its structure tensor field. The experimental results are very good, essential part of the regions are well captured and topological changes are handled naturally.

The given model here can be further improved in many ways. Our future work will include the following: (i) a better discriminant of tensors needs to be used. Though the Euclidean difference measure use the full tensor information, it blindly uses the same weights for different components of the tensor and ignores the fact that tensors have structure. (ii) shape statistics can be incorporated to improve the robustness and accuracy of the current model.

Acknowledgment. We thank Dr. T. Mareci and E. Özarslan for providing the DT-MRI data and Dr. R. Deriche for his valuable comments on this research.

References

1. D. Alexander, J.C. Gee, and R. Bajcsy. Similarity measure for matching diffusion tensor images. In *British Machine Vision Conference*, pages 93–102, University of Nottingham, Sept. 1999.
2. P. J. Basser, J. Mattiello, and D. Lebihan. Estimation of the effective self-diffusion tensor from the nmr spin echo. *Journal of Magnetic Resonance*, (103):247–254, 1994.
3. Jähne Bernd. *Digital Image Processing: Concepts, Algorithms, and Scientific Applications with CDROM*. Springer-Verlag Telos, 2001.
4. J. Bigün, G. H. Granlund, and J. Wiklund. Multidimensional orientation estimation with applications to texture analysis and optical flow. *IEEE Trans. on Pattern Analysis and Machine Intelligence*, 13(2):775–790, 1991.
5. V. Caselles, F. Catte, T. Coll, and F. Dibos. A geometric model for active contours in image processing. *Numerische Mathematik*, 66:1–31, 1993.
6. V. Caselles, R. Kimmel, and G. Sapiro. Geodesic active contours. In *Fifth International Conference on Computer Vision*, pages 694–699, 1995.
7. T. F. Chan and L. A. Vese. Active contours without edges. *IEEE Trans. on Image Processing*, 10(2):266–277, Feb. 2001.
8. T. F. Chan and L. A. Vese. A level set algorithm for minimizing the mumford-shah functional in image processing. In *IEEE Workshop on Variational and Level Set Methods*, pages 161–168, 2001.
9. H. Haußecker and B. Jähne. A tensor approach for precise computation of dense displacement vector fields. In *Proc. Musterekennung*, Berlin, German, 1997.
10. S. Kichenassamy, A. Kumar, P. Olver, A. Tannenbaum, and A. Yezzi. Gradient flows and geometric active contour models. In *Fifth International Conference on Computer Vision*, Cambridge, MA, 1995.
11. G. Kühne, J. Weickert, O. Schuster, and S. Richter. A tensor-driven active contour model for moving object segmentation. In *IEEE International Conference on Image Processing*, pages 73–76, Thessaloniki, Greece, Oct. 2001.
12. T. Brox M. Rousson and R. Deriche. Active unsupervised texture segmentation on a diffusion based feature space non-rigid registration. In *IEEE Conference on Computer Vision and Pattern Recognition*, Wisconsin, USA, June 2003.
13. R. Malladi, J. A. Sethian, and B. C. Vemuri. A topology independent shape modeling scheme. In *SPIE Proc. on Geometric Methods in Computer Vision II*, volume 2031, pages 246–256,. SPIE, July 1993,.
14. R. Malladi, J. A. Sethian, and B. C. Vemuri. Shape modeling with front propagation : A level set approach. *IEEE Trans. Pattern Analysis and Machine Intelligence*, 17(2):158–175, 1995.

15. D. Mumford and J. Shah. Optimal approximations by piecewise smooth functions and associated variational-problems. *Communications on Pure and Applied Mathematics*, 42:577–685, 1989.
16. M. Rousson, T. Brox, and R. Deriche. Active unsupervised texture segmentation on a diffusion based feature space. Technical Report RR-4695, INRIA, France, Jan. 2003.
17. A. Tsai, Jr. A. Yezzi, and A. S. Willsky. Curve evolution implementation of the mumford-shah functional for image segmentation, denoising, interpolation, and magnification. *IEEE Trans. on Image Processing*, 10(8):1169–1186, Aug. 2001.
18. L. Zhukov, K. Museth, D. Breen, R. Whitaker, and A. Barr. Level set modeling and segmentation of dt-mri brain data. *Journal of Electronic Imaging*, 12(1):125–133, Jan. 2003.

Groupwise Diffeomorphic Non-rigid Registration for Automatic Model Building

T.F. Cootes, S. Marsland, C.J. Twining, K. Smith, and C.J. Taylor

Department of Imaging Science and Biomedical Engineering
University of Manchester, Manchester M13 9PT, UK
t.cootes@man.ac.uk

Abstract. We describe a framework for registering a group of images together using a set of non-linear diffeomorphic warps. The result of the groupwise registration is an implicit definition of dense correspondences between all of the images in a set, which can be used to construct statistical models of shape change across the set, avoiding the need for manual annotation of training images. We give examples on two datasets (brains and faces) and show the resulting models of shape and appearance variation. We show results of experiments demonstrating that the groupwise approach gives a more reliable correspondence than pairwise matching alone.

1 Introduction

We address the problem of determining dense correspondences across a set of images of similar but varying objects, a key problem in computer vision. Given such a set of images and their correspondences, an annotation of one image can be propagated to all of the others, and statistical shape models of the appearance and variations of the set of images can be built. Furthermore, a method of *automatically* determining the correspondences leads to a system capable of learning statistical models of appearance in an entirely unsupervised fashion.

Registration of pairs of images has been extensively studied for medical images, with many different non-rigid registration algorithms being proposed to deform one image until it matches a second, see for example [11]. These methods can be extended to finding correspondences across a *set* of images by registering each image in the set to a chosen reference image using pairwise methods [18]. However, only by examining a whole set of images of a class of objects can one learn which are the important features. We this cannot be determined from pairwise approaches alone. Following recent work on landmark correspondence for sets of shapes [6], we propose that the groupwise correspondence problem should explicitly optimise functions that measure the quality of the correspondence across the whole set of images simultaneously.

We believe that for non-rigid registration the warping functions should be continuous, smooth and invertable, so that every point in image A maps to exactly one point in image B, and vice-versa. Such smooth, invertable functions are known as *diffeomorphisms*. The mathematics of diffeomorphism groups is

T. Pajdla and J. Matas (Eds.): ECCV 2004, LNCS 3024, pp. 316–327, 2004.

complex and mysterious – they form infinite dimensional groups and smooth manifolds, yet are not Lie groups. However, usefully complex sets of diffeomorphic functions can be constructed by the composition of simple basis functions (see section 3.2). In cases where structures appear or disappear between one image and the next, these should be explicitly modelled as creation or destruction processes – such processes will not be addressed in this paper.

This paper proposes a general framework for computing diffeomorphisms that define dense correspondences across a set of images so as to minimise a groupwise objective function based on ideas of minimum message length. We will first introduce a novel pairwise algorithm capable of achieving a diffeomorphic mapping between a pair of images, and then generalise this to the groupwise case. We present results of applying the algorithm to sets of brain images and face images, show the statistical models of shape and appearance constructed from the correspondences and demonstrate that the groupwise method gives more reliable results than an equivalent pairwise approach.

2   Background

Finding mappings between structures across a set of images can facilitate many image analysis tasks. One particular area of importance is in medical image interpretation, where image registration can help in tasks as diverse as anatomical atlas matching and labelling, image classification, and data fusion. Statistical models may be constructed based on these mappings, and have been found to be widely applicable to image analysis problems [5,4]. However, variability in anatomy and in capture conditions – both inter-patient and intra-patient – means that identifying correspondences is far from straightforward.

The same correspondence problem is found in computer vision tasks (for example, for stereo vision tasks) and in remote sensing. This wide range of applications mean that many researchers have investigated image registration methods and the use of deformable models, for overviews see for example [22, 14,11,21].

Many algorithms algorithms have been proposed which are driven by the maximisation of some measure of intensity similarity between images, such as sum-of-squared-intensity differences, or mutual information [10,19].

Methods of propagating the deformations across the image include elastic deformations [1], viscous fluid models [3], and splines [18,12]. The method that is most similar to that proposed here is that of Lötjönen and Mäkelä [9], who describe an elastic matching approach in which spherical regions of one image are deformed so as to better match the other. However, the deformations do not have continuous derivatives at the border, and are therefore not diffeomorphic – in the work described in this paper we use a similar representation of deformation, but use fully diffeomorphic deformations within ellipsoidal regions. There are also similarities with the work of Feldmar and Ayache [7], who used local affine transformations to deform one surface onto another.

Davies *et al.* [6] directly addressed the problem of generating optimal correspondences for building shape models from landmarked data, noting improvements in model quality when a 'groupwise' cost function was used that was based on Minimum Description Length. Spherical harmonic parameters can also be used to directly optimise the shape parameterisation [15].

Some early work on groupwise image registration based on the discrepancy between the set of images and the reference image has been performed [13], and a groupwise model-matching algorithm that represents image intensities as well as shape has also been proposed [8]. It is also possible to consider building an appearance model as an image coding problem [2]. The model parameters are iteratively re-estimated after fitting the current model to the images, leading to an implicit correspondence defined across the data set.

3   Pairwise Non-rigid Registration

In this section we describe our approach to registering a pair of images based on the repeated composition of local diffeomorphic warps. The extension to registering groups of images is detailed in Section 4.

3.1   Overview

We first consider the registration of two images I_1 and I_2. This requires finding a non-linear deformation function that transforms (warps) image I_1 until it is as similar as possible (as measured by some objective function) to I_2.

More formally, we define the following:

Image functions $I_{1,2}$. We assume that the image functions are originally defined only on some dense set of points (pixels or voxels) with positions $\mathbf{X}_{1,2}$, but that we can interpolate such functions to obtain $I_{1,2}(\mathbf{x})$ at any point

A warp function $W(\cdot; \boldsymbol{\Phi})$ with parameters $\boldsymbol{\Phi}$ that acts on sets of points $\mathbf{X} \rightarrow W(\mathbf{X}; \boldsymbol{\Phi})$

A sampled set of values $I(\mathbf{X})$ from an image at a set of points $\mathbf{X}$

An objective function $F_{pair}(I(\mathbf{X}), I'(\mathbf{X}'))$ that computes the 'similarity' between any two equi-sized samples

The 'cost' of a deformation $G_{pair}(W)$ for deformation $W(\cdot, \boldsymbol{\Phi})$

The task of image registration can then be considered as the task of finding parameters $\boldsymbol{\Phi}$ of the warping function $W(\cdot, \boldsymbol{\Phi})$ that minimise the combined objective function:

$$\boldsymbol{\Phi}_{\text{opt}} = \arg \min_{\boldsymbol{\Phi}} \left(F_{pair}\left(I_1(\mathbf{X}_1), I_2\left(W(\mathbf{X}_1, \boldsymbol{\Phi})\right)\right) + G_{pair}\left(W(\cdot, \boldsymbol{\Phi})\right) \right) \quad (1)$$

The form of $G_{pair}(\cdot)$ is typically chosen to penalise more convoluted deformations, and acts as a regularisation term.

3.2   Diffeomorphic Warps

We assume that each image in a set should contain the same structures, and hence there should be a unique and invertible one-to-one correspondence between all points on each pair of images. This suggests that the correct representation of warps is one that will not 'tear' or fold the images, we therefore choose to select warps from the diffeomorphism group. For more discussion of this point, see [20]. For any two diffeomorphisms $f(\mathbf{x})$, $g(\mathbf{x})$, their composition $(f \circ g)(\mathbf{x}) \equiv f(g(\mathbf{x}))$ is also a diffeomorphism. We can thus construct a wide class of diffeomorphic functions by repeated compositions of a basis set of simple diffeomorphisms.

In the Appendix we describe how such sets of *bounded* diffeomorphisms may be constructed. Boundedness is a useful property when performing numerical optimisation, as we can take advantage of the fact that only a subset of the image samples (those within the area of effect of the warp) will change. Our basis warps are parameterised by the movement of the centre point of the ellipsoid affected, and the size, position and orientation of the ellipsoidal region. We will denote the ith such warp by $f_i = f(\cdot, \phi_i)$, where ϕ_i is the set of parameters for the ith warp. The total warp is then $W(\cdot, \boldsymbol{\Phi}) = f_n \circ f_{n-1} \circ, \ldots f_2 \circ f_1 \circ A$, where $A(\cdot, \phi_A)$ is an affine transformation with parameters ϕ_A, and the parameters of the total warp are $\boldsymbol{\Phi} = (\phi_A, \phi_1, \ldots, \phi_n)$.

3.3 Optimisation Regime

The representation of complex warps requires many parameters, so that it is not feasible to optimise over all the parameters at once. We therefore adopt a sequential strategy in which we start with relatively simple warps and incrementally compose and optimise additional warps. In practice, we do the following:

- Optimise the affine registration parameters ϕ_A
- Construct the affinely-warped points $\mathbf{X}^{(0)} = A(\mathbf{X}_1, \phi_A)$, the zeroth-order estimate of the warp and the associated warped points
- For each non-linear diffeomorphism $f_i = f(\cdot, \phi_i)$, $i = 1, \ldots, n$:
  - For each given set of parameters ϕ_i', apply the local warp $f(\cdot, \phi_i')$ to the current estimate $\mathbf{X}^{(i-1)}$ of the warped points, and sample from I_2 at these new points. This gives estimates of the fully-optimised warp $W(\mathbf{X}_1, \boldsymbol{\Phi}_{opt})$ and the true optimal sample $I_2(W(\mathbf{X}_1, \boldsymbol{\Phi}_{opt}))$
  - Find the particular parameters ϕ_i that minimise the objective function given in Eq. (1), recalculating the estimate of the warp at each stage
  - Update the estimate of the full warp, $\mathbf{X}^{(i)} = f_i(\mathbf{X}^{(i-1)}; \phi_i)$
- Output $\mathbf{X}^{(n)}$, the estimate of the true global optimum warp $W(\mathbf{X}_1, \boldsymbol{\Phi}_{\text{opt}})$

In our implementation we have used downhill simplex in the early stages and simple gradient descent in the later stages of the optimisation, although any non-linear optimiser could be used. We use a multi-resolution approach to give better robustness. The search regime is then defined by the positioning of the effective regions of the local warps. In the experiments presented here the regions to be warped were disks of randomly chosen position and radii. This approach is similar to that described in [9], but their local warps were not smooth at the edges of the regions of effect, nor did their construction guarantee diffeomorphisms or even C^1 differentiability, so that their total warp was not necessarily smooth or invertible.

4   Groupwise Non-rigid Registation

4.1   Groupwise Objective Functions

Suppose that instead of two images we now have a set of N images, I_i. We wish to register these images into a common coordinate frame. Following Davies *et al.* [6] we treat the problem of global registration as one of optimising a groupwise objective function that essentially measures the compactness of a statistical model built from correspondences resulting from the registration process. For registration, a suitable function for optimisation combines both shape (position) and intensity components.

The correspondence between a set of images explicitly defines those structures that should be treated as analogous. The contention is that statistical modelling of variations between analogous parts of structures should, in some sense, be 'simpler' than modelling variations between non-analogous parts. This idea of 'simplicity', or of appropriateness of the model, is expressed in the Minimum Description Length (MDL) framework [17] in terms of the length of an encoded message; this message transmits the whole set of examples, encoded by using the statistical model defined by the correspondence. Inappropriate choice of correspondence then leads to a non-optimal encoding of the data, and a greater length of the message. Note that this definition of optimal correspondence is explicitly concerned with the whole set of images, rather than correspondences defined between pairs of examples. We show below how we are able to construct an information-theoretic objective function for groupwise non-rigid registration.

Let $\mathbf{X}_i$ be the points on the ith image obtained by applying the current estimate of the set of warp parameters for the warp between example I_i and the reference image I_1. That is, $\mathbf{X}_i = W(\mathbf{X}_1; \boldsymbol{\Phi}_i)$. Suppose also that $\mathbf{s}_i = I_i(\mathbf{X}_i)$ is the vector of image intensities sampled at those points. We then seek to find the set of full warp parameters $\{\boldsymbol{\Phi}_i\}$ that minimise some objective function

$$C_N(\langle \mathbf{s}_1, \mathbf{X}_1, \rangle \dots, \langle \mathbf{s}_i, \mathbf{X}_i \rangle, \dots, \langle \mathbf{s}_N, \mathbf{X}_N \rangle), \tag{2}$$

which is chosen to measure the appropriateness of the groupwise correspondence, potentially a challenging problem given the dimensionality of both the data set and the parametrisation of the warps.

In the work described here we will treat the shape and texture independently (although, ideally, correlations between shape and texture should also be considered). That is, we will use a function of the simplified form:

$$C_N(\langle \mathbf{s}_1, \mathbf{X}_1, \rangle \dots, \langle \mathbf{s}_N, \mathbf{X}_N \rangle) = F_N(\mathbf{s}_1, \dots, \mathbf{s}_N) + G_N(\mathbf{X}_1, \dots, \mathbf{X}_N). \tag{3}$$

One information-theory based approach to the construction of such an objective function, which is suitable for problems where sequential optimisation is the only feasible optimisation strategy, is that of Minimum Message Length [17]. Each image example is left out in turn, and a model is built using the other $N-1$ examples and their current correspondences. The length of the message required to transmit the left-out example using this model is then calculated. We can then optimise this message length by manipulating the correspondence for the missing example.

To be specific, let $P_i^{(X)}(\mathbf{X})$ be an estimate of the model probability density function computed from the vectors of all corresponding points leaving out example i; that is, all the sets of points $\mathbf{X}_j$, $j \neq i$. Similarly, let $P_i^{(s)}(\mathbf{s})$ be an estimate of the model density function computed from all the texture sample vectors $\mathbf{s}_j = I_j(\mathbf{X}_j)$, $j \neq i$.

The estimated message length for transmitting example i with the correspondence defined by $\mathbf{X}_i = W(\mathbf{X}_1, \boldsymbol{\Phi}_i)$ then leads to the objective function:

$$C_i(\boldsymbol{\Phi}_i) = -\log P_i^{(X)}\Big(W(\mathbf{X}_1, \boldsymbol{\Phi}_i)\Big) - \lambda \log P_i^{(s)}\Big(I_i(W(\mathbf{X}_1, \boldsymbol{\Phi}_i))\Big), \qquad (4)$$

where λ represents the relative weighting given to the shape and texture parts. By manipulating the warp parameters $\boldsymbol{\Phi}_i$, we manipulate the correspondence for image I_i relative to the rest of the examples, and can hence optimise this correspondence for this example by minimising the value of $C_i(\boldsymbol{\Phi}_i)$. This single-example warp optimisation is performed in an analogous fashion to the pairwise example given previously. We next describe the full groupwise optimisation strategy.

4.2 Groupwise Optimisation Algorithm

In what follows, we will use the term 'correspondence' to denote the correspondence between images induced by a warp $W(\cdot, \boldsymbol{\Phi})$; manipulating the set of warp parameters $\boldsymbol{\Phi}$ manipulates the correspondence. Since our warps are diffeomorphic by construction, all correspondences so defined are one-to-one and invertible. The groupwise optimisation algorithm is:

- Initialisation: perform pairwise non-rigid registrations between each image and I_1, giving initial estimate $\mathbf{X}_i^{(0)}$ for each.
- **REPEAT**
  - For each $i = 2, \dots, N$
    * (Re)compute the model p.d.f.s $P_i^{(X)}(\mathbf{X})$ and $P_i^{(s)}(\mathbf{s})$, leaving out example i from the model building process
    * Find the optimal set of warp parameters $\boldsymbol{\Phi}_i$ that minimise $C_i(\boldsymbol{\Phi}_i)$
    * Update estimate of correspondence for example i using these optimal warp parameters, $\mathbf{X}_i \to W(\mathbf{X}_1, \boldsymbol{\Phi}_i)$
- **UNTIL CONVERGENCE**

5   Results of Experiments

We have applied the groupwise model building approach to examples of faces and 2D MR brain images. For the intensity part our chosen objective function is a sum-of-absolute-differences (implying an exponential PDF), a more robust statistic that sum-of-squares. In the examples given we have similar ranges of intensity across the set, so do not need to further normalise the intensity ranges. The shape component of the objective function is a sum of squares second derivatives of the deformation field (evaluated at each warped grid point $\mathbf{X}_i$) – this discourages excessive bending. In the experiments below we heuristically choose the factor λ that weights the shape objective function relative to the intensity measure. We are currently examining ways of automatically selecting suitable values.

We initialise $\mathbf{X}_1$ to a grid covering the reference image, and as before let $\mathbf{s}_i$ be the result of sampling image i at the current warped points. Let $d\mathbf{X}_i$ be the vector concatenation of all the second derivatives evaluated at each of the warped grid points. The pairwise objective function we use is

$$F_{pair}(i) = \sum_k |s_{ik} - s_{1k}| + \lambda_{pair}|d\mathbf{X}_i|^2. \tag{5}$$

During the groupwise stage, when optimising on image i, we use

$$F_{group}(i) = \sum_k \frac{|s_{ik} - \hat{s}_k|}{w_k} + \lambda_{group}d\mathbf{X}_i^T\mathbf{W}_i^{-1}d\mathbf{X}_i, \tag{6}$$

where $\hat{s}_k$ is the mean of the kth sample across the other members of the set, w_k is the mean absolute difference from the mean, and $\mathbf{W}_i$ is a diagonal matrix describing the variances of the elements of $d\mathbf{X}_j$ for $j \neq i$. This simple gaussian model of the distribution is a natural groupwise extension of the commonly used bending energy term. It allows more freedom to deform in areas in which other images exhibit larger deformations.

5.1   Corresponding MR Brain Slices

We applied the method to 16 MR brain slices, each from an image of a different person, with approximately corresponding axial slices being chosen. The optimisation regime for the groupwise algorithm first requires finding the best affine transformation, before composing 1500 randomly sized and centred warps during the pairwise stage and a further 3000 randomly sized and centred warps during the groupwise stage. The algorithm is implemented in C++ [1] and the optimisation took about 15 minutes on a 2.8GHz PC.

Figure 1 shows the resulting deformation of one of the brains. We took a hand annotation of the reference image and used the acquired warps to propogate this to the other images. We then constructed a linear statistical shape and appearance model [4] from the resulting annotations. Figure 2 shows the two largest modes of shape deformation, while Figure 3 shows the two largest modes of combined shape and texture variation. Note that the shape model is built from the points of the projected annotation only, not on the dense grid of points used in the correspondence process. This allows us to use a sparser representation of the key features only, potentially leading to more compact models.

---

[1] Using the VXL computer vision library: `www.sourceforge.org/projects/vxl`

Such models give a compact summary of the variation used in the set, and can be used to match to further images using rapid optimisation algorithms such as the Active Appearance Model [4]. Note that the linear model does not enforce diffeomorphisms.

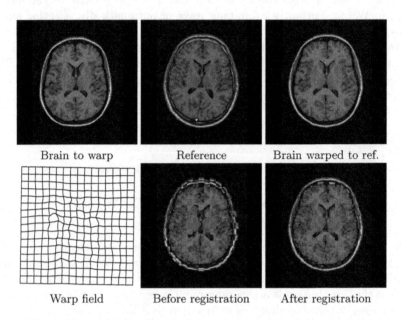

Fig. 1. Example MR slices before and after groupwise registration

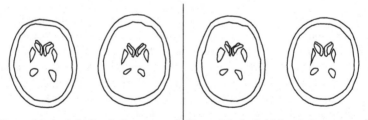

Shape Mode 1 (±2 s.d. from mean)|Shape Mode 2 (±2 s.d. from mean)

Fig. 2. Two largest modes of shape variation of a model built from 2D brain slices

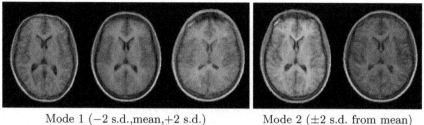

Mode 1 (−2 s.d.,mean,+2 s.d.)   Mode 2 (±2 s.d. from mean)

Fig. 3. Two largest modes of appearance variation (model built from 2D brain slices)

5.2   Corresponding Face Images

We took 51 face images, each of a different person, from the XM2VTS face database [16] [2] We applied the groupwise registration to find correspondences, which took about 30 minutes on a 2.8GHz PC. As before, we propogated an annotation of the reference image to the rest of the set and constructed a linear model of appearance. Figure 4 shows the two largest modes of shape deformation, while Figure 5 shows the two largest modes of combined shape and texture variation. The crispness of the resulting appearance model demonstrates that an accurate correspondence has been achieved.

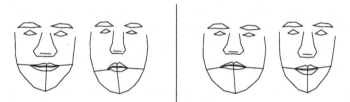

Shape Mode 1 (±2 s.d. from mean)|Shape Mode 2 (±2 s.d. from mean)

Fig. 4. Two largest modes of shape variation of a model built from 51 face images

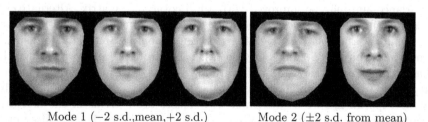

Mode 1 (−2 s.d.,mean,+2 s.d.)   Mode 2 (±2 s.d. from mean)

Fig. 5. Two largest modes of appearance variation of a model built from 51 face images

---

[*] We selected the first 51 people without glasses or facial hair. Such features, which appear or dissappear from one image to another, break the assumptions of diffeomorphic correspondence in the process.

Table 1. Point-curve errors after registration of 51 face images. (The faces are approximately 100 pixels wide)

	Errors (pixels)		
	Mean	SD	Max
After initial pairwise	2.0	1.5	11.4
After full groupwise	2.0	1.0	7.1
Pairwise (same regime)	2.1	1.6	11.4

In order to evaluate the performance of the system, we compared the point positions obtained by transfering landmarks with those from a manual annotation of the 51 images. We measured the mean absolute difference between the found points and the equivalent curve on the manual annotation (see Figure 4). The results are summarised in Table 1. After the initial pairwise stage of the search (1100 warps) we obtain a mean accuracy of 2.0 pixels with an s.d. of 1.5 pixels. Completing the groupwise phase (a further 2000 warps) does not improve the mean but tightens up the distribution considerably, reducing both the variance and the maximum error. For comparison we ran a purely pairwise registration with the same number and distribution of additional random warps - the additional warps make little difference to the original pairwise result.

6   Discussion

We have presented a framework for establishing dense correspondences across groups of images using diffeomorphic functions and have demonstrated its application to two different domains. We have shown that in the case of the faces the groupwise method produces a more reliable registration than a purely pairwise approach.

We have described one example of objective functions, warping functions and optimisation regime, which appear to give good results. There is considerable research to be done investigating alternatives for each component of the framework. For instance, the groupwise function used above assumed diagonal covariance and may be improved with a full covariance matrix. Alternatively a statistical model of position, rather than derivatives, may lead to better results.

Similarly, the relative weighting between shape and intensity terms, λ, is somewhat arbitrary. For the pairwise case it is hard to select by anything other than trial and error. However, in the groupwise case, if the terms in the functions are related to log probabilities, it is possible to select λ_{group} more systematically – in the experiments we used a value of $\frac{1}{3}$ (there are 3 terms in the derivative vector for each element in the texture vector, and each term is normalised by its standard deviation).

The methods described above extend directly into three (and higher dimensions). The diffeomorphic warps of disks become warps of spheres (see Appendix A). We have used the techniques to register 3D MR images of the brain, and are currently evaluating the performance of the algorithms.

The general framework gives a powerful technique for registering images and for unsupervised shape and appearance model building. We anticipate it will have applications in many domains of computer vision.

Acknowledgements. The work described in the paper was done under the aegis of the MIAS Interdisiplinary Research Collaboration funded by EPSRC and MRC. The authors would like to thank other collaborators on the project for many useful discussions. The brains were gathered and annotated by C. Hutchinson.

References

1. R. Bajcsy, R. Lieberson, and M. Reivich. A computerized system for the elastic matching of deformed radiographic images to idealized atlas images. *J. Comput. Assis. Tomogr.*, 7:618–625, 1983.
2. S. Baker, I. Matthews, and J. Schneider. Image coding with active appearance models. Technical Report CMU-RI-TR-03-13, Robotics Institute, Carnegie Mellon University, Pittsburgh, PA, April 2003.
3. G. E. Christensen, S. C. Joshi, and M. Miller. Volumetric transformation of brain anatomy. *IEEE Trans. Medical Image*, 16:864–877, 1997.
4. T. F. Cootes, G. J. Edwards, and C. J. Taylor. Active appearance models. In H.Burkhardt and B. Neumann, editors, 5th *European Conference on Computer Vision*, volume 2, pages 484–498. Springer, Berlin, 1998.
5. T. F. Cootes, C. J. Taylor, D. Cooper, and J. Graham. Active shape models - their training and application. *Computer Vision and Image Understanding*, 61(1):38–59, Jan. 1995.
6. R. Davies, C.Twining, T. Cootes, and C. Taylor. An information theoretic approach to statistical shape modelling. In 7th *European Conference on Computer Vision*, volume 3, pages 3–20. Springer, 2002.
7. J. Feldmar and N. Ayache. Locally affine registration of free-form surfaces. In *CVPR94*, pages 496–501, 1994.
8. M. J. Jones and T. Poggio. Multidimensional morphable models : A framework for representing and matching object classes. *International Journal of Computer Vision*, 2(29):107–131, 1998.
9. J. Lötjönen and T. Mäkelä. Elastic matching using a deformation sphere. In *MICCAI*, pages 541–548, 2001.
10. F. Maes, A. Collignon, D. Vandermeulen, G. Marchal, and P. Suetens. Multimodality image registration by maximization of mutual information. *IEEE Transactions on Medical Imaging*, 16(2):187–198, April 1997.
11. J. B. A. Maintz and M. A. Viergever. A survey of medical image registration. *Medical Image Analysis*, 2(1):1–36, 1998.
12. S. Marsland and C. Twining. Constructing data-driven optimal representations for iterative pairwise non-rigid registration. In *Biomedical Image Registration*, Lecture Notes in Computer Science, 2003.
13. S. Marsland, C. Twining, and C. Taylor. Groupwise non-rigid registration using polyharmonic clamped-plate splines. In *MICCAI*, Lecture Notes in Computer Science, 2003.

14. T. McInerney and D. Terzopoulos. Deformable models in medical image analysis: a survey. *Medical Image Analysis*, 1(2):91–108, 1996.
15. D. Meier and E. Fisher. Parameter space warping: Shape-based correspondence between morphologically different objects. *IEEE Trans. Medical Image*, 21:31–47, 2002.
16. K. Messer, J. Matas, J. Kittler, J. Luettin, and G. Maitre. XM2VTSdb: The extended m2vts database. In *Proc. 2nd Conf. on Audio and Video-based Biometric Personal Verification*. Springer Verlag, 1999.
17. J. Rissanen. *Stochastic Complexity in Statistical Inquiry*, volume 15 of *Series in Computer Science*. World Scientific, Singapore, 1989.
18. D. Rueckert, A. Frangi, and J. Schnabel. Automatic construction of 3D statistical deformation models using non-rigid registration. In *MICCAI*, pages 77–84, 2001.
19. C. Studholme, C. Hill, and D. Hawkes. An overlap invariant entropy measure of 3D medical image alignment. *Pattern Recognition*, 32:71–86, 1999.
20. C. Twining, S. Marsland, and C. Taylor. Measuring geodesic distances on the space of bounded diffeomorphisms. In P.L.Rosin and D. Marshall, editors, 13th *British Machine Vison Conference*, volume 2, pages 847–856. BMVA Press, Sept. 2002.
21. Y. Wang and L. H. Staib. Elastic model based non-rigid registration incorporating statistical shape information. In *MICCAI*, pages 1162–1173, 1998.
22. B. Zitová and J. Flusser. Image registration methods: A survey. *Image and Vision Computing*, 21:977–1000, 2003.

Appendix A: Bounded Diffeomorphisms

A useful class of bounded diffeomorphisms in arbitrary dimensions can be constructed using the following equation, which warps space only within the unit ball, based on the displacement of the centre by $\mathbf{a}$,

$$f(\mathbf{x}; \mathbf{a}) = \begin{cases} \mathbf{x} + g(|\mathbf{x}|)\mathbf{a} & (|\mathbf{x}| < 1) \\ \mathbf{x} & \text{otherwise,} \end{cases} \tag{7}$$

where $\mathbf{a}$ is the position to which the origin is warped ($|\mathbf{a}| < 1$) and $g(r)$ is a smooth function satisfying the following properties: $g(0) = 1$, $g(1) = 0$, $g'(0) = 0$, $g'(1) = 0$. $f(\mathbf{x}; \mathbf{a})$ is diffeomorphic providing that $|\mathbf{a}| < 1/d_{max}$, where $d_{max} = \max_{0 < r < 1} |g'(r)|$. This function is bounded, so that it deforms space only within the unit disc (2D) or unit sphere (3D). In the 2D case, if $g(r) = 1 - r^2 + r^2 \log(r^2)$, then this is a Clamped Plate Spline with a single control point at the origin [20]. This function is guaranteed diffeomorphic provided that $|\mathbf{a}| < 0.25e$, providing a family of bounded diffeomorphisms parameterised by the point to which the origin is warped ($\mathbf{a}$).

The simplest polynomial form for $g(r)$ is $g(r) = (1 - r^2)^2$, which leads to an efficient implementation of the function in arbitrary dimensions. In this case we require $|\mathbf{a}| < 3\sqrt{3}/8 = 0.650$ for a diffeomorphism. By combining with a suitable affine transformation we can generate diffeomorphisms that only affect a particular ellipsoidal region of space.

Separating Transparent Layers through Layer Information Exchange*

Bernard Sarel and Michal Irani

Dept. of Computer Science and Applied Mathematics,
Weizmann Institute of Science
Rehovot, ISRAEL
{bernard.sarel, michal.irani}@weizmann.ac.il

Abstract. In this paper we present an approach for separating two transparent layers in images and video sequences. Given two initial unknown physical mixtures, $I.$ and $I.$, of real scene layers, $L.$ and $L.$, we seek a layer separation which minimizes the structural correlations across the two layers, at *every* image point. Such a separation is achieved by transferring local grayscale structure from one image to the other wherever it is highly correlated with the underlying local grayscale structure in the other image, and vice versa. This bi-directional transfer operation, which we call the "layer information exchange", is performed on diminishing window sizes, from global image windows (i.e., the entire image), down to local image windows, thus detecting similar grayscale structures at varying scales across pixels. We show the applicability of this approach to various real-world scenarios, including image and video transparency separation. In particular, we show that this approach can be used for separating transparent layers in images obtained under different polarizations, as well as for separating complex *non-rigid* transparent motions in video sequences. These can be done without prior knowledge of the layer mixing model (simple additive, alpha-mated composition with an unknown alpha-map, or other), and under unknown complex temporal changes (e.g., unknown varying lighting conditions).

1 Introduction

The need to perform separation of visual scenes into their constituent layers arises in various real world applications (medical imaging, robot navigation, and others). This problem is challenging when the layers are transparent, thus generating complex superpositions of visual information. The problem is particularly challenging when the mixing process is an unknown, spatially varying, non-linear function, as is often the case in real-world transparent scenes.

A number of approaches to transparent layer separation have been proposed. Most of the approaches for separation of *still images* assume additive transparency with layer mixing functions which are uniform across the entire image

---

* This research was supported in part by the Moross Laboratory at the Weizmann Institute of science.

T. Pajdla and J. Matas (Eds.): ECCV 2004, LNCS 3024, pp. 328–341, 2004.

(e.g., [8,5,7]). Spatially varying functions were handled by [3] assuming spareness of image derivatives . In the case of *video transparency* (where the transparent layers have different relative motions over time), the underlying assumption is that dense correspondences can be pre-computed for each pixel in each layer across the entire sequence [9,12]. These methods are therefore restricted to scenes with simple 2D parametric motions, which are easy to compute under transparency and provide dense correspondences. Non-parametric correspondences are handled in [10] assuming stereo images. None of the above methods can handle complex non-rigid motions. Szeliski *et al* [9,10] further assume fixed mixing coefficients.

In this paper we address the problem of separation of two arbitrarily superimposed layers (either in images, or in video), without any prior knowledge about the mixing process. We assume that two different combinations of the layers (generated in an unknown fashion) are given to us, and use these to initiate the layer separation process. As will be shown later, two different combinations of layers are often available or otherwise easy to obtain in many real-world scenarios, making this approach practical.

Formally, and without loss of generality, we can phrase the problem as follows. Given two initial unknown physical mixtures, I_1 and I_2, of real scene layers, L_1 and L_2, produce approximations $\hat{L}_1$ and $\hat{L}_2$ such that some separation criterion is satisfied. The two mixtures I_1 and I_2, can be generally defined as,

$$I_1(i) = \alpha_1(i) \cdot L_1(i) + \alpha_2(i) \cdot L_2(i)$$
$$I_2(i) = \beta_1(i) \cdot L_1(i) + \beta_2(i) \cdot L_2(i) \tag{1}$$

where the index i denotes pixel position, and $\alpha_1(i),\alpha_2(i),\beta_1(i)$, and $\beta_2(i)$, are the unknown mixing functions (coefficients) which vary over pixel locations. In the simplest case, when the mixing is uniform and additive (as assumed in [9, 5,8,7]), the mixing functions reduce to constant coefficients; $\forall i \quad \alpha_1(i) \equiv \hat{\alpha}_1$, $\alpha_2(i) \equiv \hat{\alpha}_2$, $\beta_1(i) \equiv \hat{\beta}_1$ and $\beta_2(i) \equiv \hat{\beta}_2$. In natural scenes, however, such conditions are frequently violated. Smoothly varying glass opacity, window dirt, or images acquired through polarization filters, can produce varying mixing coefficients that vary over pixel locations. The formulation of Eq. (1) is general and captures a wide range of transparency models, including additive transparency with uniform mixing functions [9,5,8,7], additive transparency with unknown alpha-matting (e.g., [12]), etc.

Having two initial combinations, I_1 and I_2, generated in an unknown fashion, we seek a layer separation into representations of L_1 and L_2 which minimizes the structural correlations across the two layers at *every* image point. Such a separation is achieved by transferring local structure from one image to the other wherever it is highly correlated with the underlying local structure in the other image, and vice versa. This bi-directional transfer operation, which we call the "layer information exchange", is performed on diminishing window sizes, from global image windows (i.e., the entire image) down to local image windows, thus detecting correlated structures at varying scales across pixel positions.

Two different initial combinations (I_1 and I_2) are available, e.g., when two images of the same transparent scene are taken with different polarizers (as in [5,8]), or under different illuminations. However, our approach is not limited to those cases nor is it restricted to still imagery. When a single video camera records two transparent layers with different relative motions over time, and when the motion of only *one* of those layers is computable (e.g., a 2D parametric motion), then such initial layer separation is possible. This can be done even if the second layer contains very complex non-rigid motions (e.g., running water). Moreover, the layer mixing process is not known and can possibly change over time, and other unknown complex temporal changes may also occur simultaneously (such as varying illumination and changing light reflections over time). Such examples are shown and discussed in the paper.

This paper has three main contributions: (i) The idea of "layer information exchange". (We also believe that this idea has applicability in disciplines of signal processing other than Computer Vision). (ii) To our best knowledge, this is the first time that video sequences containing *non-rigid* transparent motions have been separated (moreover, under unknown complex varying lighting conditions). (iii) Our approach provides a unified treatment to a wide range of transparency models, without requiring prior selection of the transparency model and the corresponding separation method. When the unknown mixing coefficients are spatially-invariant (i.e., only grayscale dependent, but independent of the pixel position), then our approach produces comparable results to Farid and Adelson's ICA-based separation [5]. However, when the mixing coefficients are spatially-varying (unknown) functions, our approach performs better. Similarly, if the motions of both transparent layers in a video sequence are easy to compute, then our approach compares to existing methods for separating video transparency [9, 12]. However, it performs better when one of the layers contains complex motions (such as non-rigid motions, 3D parralax) and other complex temporal changes.

The rest of the paper is organized as follows. In Section 2 we identify an information correlation measure which is best suited for the underlying problem. In Section 3 we introduce our layer information exchange process, which is used for recovering the separate layers. In Section 4 we show the applicability of the method to transparency separation in still images and in video sequences.

2   The Information Correlation Measure

There are various commonly used measures for correlating information across images. In this section we review some of their advantages and drawbacks, and identify a measure which is best suited for the task at hand.

The Mutual Information (MI) of two images (f and g) captures the statistical correlation (or co-occurrence) of their grayscales: $MI(f,g) = H(f) + H(g) - H(f,g)$, where $H(f)$ is the entropy of the grayscale distribution in f, and $H(f,g)$ is the joint entropy [4]. Mutual Information can account for non-linear grayscale transformations which are *spatially invariant* (i.e. transformations which depend only on the grayscale value at a pixel, but not on the pixel position). However,

| (a) Original image | (b) Linear grayscale deformation | (c) Non-linear grayscale deformation | (d) Spatially varying (position dependent) deformation |

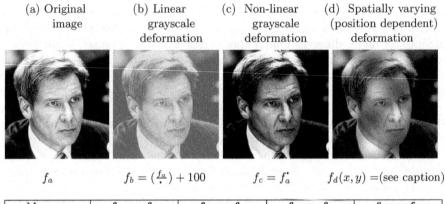

| f_a | $f_b = (\frac{f_a}{\cdot}) + 100$ | $f_c = f_a^{\cdot}$ | $f_d(x,y) =$(see caption) |

Measure (normalized)	$\mathbf{f_a}$ vs. $\mathbf{f_a}$	$\mathbf{f_a}$ vs. $\mathbf{f_b}$	$\mathbf{f_a}$ vs. $\mathbf{f_c}$	$\mathbf{f_a}$ vs. $\mathbf{f_d}$
MI	1.0000	1.0000	1.0000	0.3426
NGC	1.0000	1.0000	0.8329	0.8700
GNGC	1.0000	1.0000	0.9165	0.9981

(e)

Fig. 1. Comparing different information correlation measures (a) Original image. (b) After a linear grayscale transformation. (c) After a nonlinear grayscale transformation. (d) After a spatially varying (i.e., position-dependent) grayscale transformation: $f_d(x,y) = f_a \cdot (\sin(\frac{\cdot \pi \cdot x}{n_x}) \sin(\frac{\cdot \pi \cdot y}{n_y}) \cdot 0.333 + 0.667)$, where $n_x \times n_y$ is the image size. (e) Comparing the information correlation between the original image f_a and the transformed images (f_b, f_c, f_d) under different measures ($NGC, MI, GNGC$ – see Section 2). As can be seen, GNGC correlates extremely well across all transformations.

it cannot account for *spatially varying* grayscale transformations which are pixel position dependent (such as the spatially varying mixing functions of Eq. (1)). In other words, if $\hat{f}$ is an image obtained from f by some (non-linear) transformation on the histogram of f, then $MI(f, \hat{f}) = MI(f, f)$ (see Fig. 1.b and 1.c). However, if $\hat{f}$ is obtained from f by some spatially varying (position-dependant) grayscale transformation, then the mutual information of f and $\hat{f}$ reduces significantly: $MI(f, \hat{f}) \ll MI(f, f)$, even though the geometric structures observed in f and in $\hat{f}$ are highly correlated (see Fig. 1.d).

A different widely used information correlation measure is the Normalized Gray-scale Correlation (NGC): $NGC(f,g) = \frac{C(f,g)}{\sqrt{V(f) \cdot V(g)}}$, where $C(f,g) = \frac{1}{N} \sum_{j=1}^{N} f_j \cdot g_j - \bar{f} \cdot \bar{g}$ is the covariance of f and g, N is the number of pixels in f (f and g are of the same size), $\bar{f}, \bar{g}$ are the average grayscale values of f, g, and $V(f) = \frac{1}{N} \sum_{j=1}^{N} f_j^2 - \bar{f}^2$ is the variance of f. NGC can account only for *linear* grayscale transformations which are spatially invariant (i.e., only changes in the mean and variance of the intensity – see Fig. 1.b). Intuitively speaking, the *normalized correlation* (captured by NGC) can be regarded as a linear approximation of *statistical correlation* (captured by MI).

The above two measures require *global* grayscale correlations (whether normalized or statistical). We next define an information correlation measure which requires only local correlations, and can therefore account for a wide variety of grayscale variation (linear and non-linear), including *spatially-varying* (i.e., position-dependant) grayscale transformations. This measure, which we will refer to as the Generalized NGC ($GNGC$) measure, is a weighted average of local NGC measures on small (typically 5x5) windows:

$$GNGC(f,g) = \frac{\sum_{i=1}^{N} NGC_i^2(f,g) \cdot (V_i(f) \cdot V_i(g))}{\sum_{i=1}^{N}(V_i(f) \cdot V_i(g))} = \frac{\sum_{i=1}^{N} C_i^2(f,g)}{\sum_{i=1}^{N} V_i(f) \cdot V_i(g)} \qquad (2)$$

where $C_i(f,g)$ and $NGC_i(f,g)$ are, respectively, the local covariance and the local normalized correlation measure between two small corresponding windows (5×5) centered at pixels i in images f and g. In principle, one could define a similar global measure to that of Eq. (2) using a weighted sum of local MI measures (instead of local NGC measures). However, there is not enough grayscale statistics in small 5×5 windows, which is why we resort to the local NGC measures. In case of color images, the sum is taken over all three color bands.

The normalized weighted sum in Eq. (2) takes into account the correlations of small corresponding windows across f and g. These are weighted according to their reliability, which is measured by the grayscale variances in the local (5×5) windows. This captures correlations of small geometric features (under different grayscale transformations) without introducing numerical instabilities which are common to regular normalized correlation in small windows. Prominent geometrical features in the image are characterized by large local gray-scale variances and therefore contribute more to the global correlation ($GNGC$) measure, while flat gray-scale regions have small local grayscale variances, hence small weights.

Unlike the MI measure, the $GNGC$ measure (Eq. (2)) captures also the statistical correlations between *geometric structures* in the image. It can therefore account for spatially varying non-linear grayscale transformations, such as the one showed in Fig. 1.d, whereas MI cannot. The reason for this difference between the two measures, is that MI requires *global* statistical correlation of grayscales across the two images (a condition which is violated under spatially-varying grayscale transformations), whereas $GNGC$ requires only *local* statistical correlation across the two images (but at every 5×5 window in the image). Similar measures to the $GNGC$ measure have been previously used for other tasks where correlation between geometric structures was needed (e.g., for multi-sensor alignment [6]), although in the past a regular integration of local correlation values for those tasks was typically used, whereas our global measure is a *weighted sum* of the local measures. This modification is crucial to the stability of the layer separation process.

Because $GNGC$ captures correlations of meaningful geometrical structures, it is therefore more suited for the problem at hand. Moreover, the $GNGC$ measure is easy to differentiate in order to derive an analytic solution to the layer separation problem, as will be shown in Section 3.

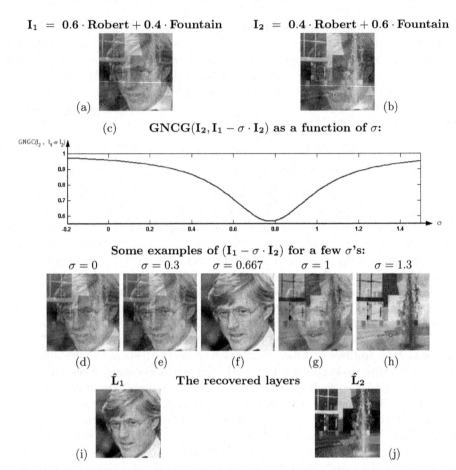

$$\mathbf{I_1} = 0.6 \cdot \mathbf{Robert} + 0.4 \cdot \mathbf{Fountain} \qquad \mathbf{I_2} = 0.4 \cdot \mathbf{Robert} + 0.6 \cdot \mathbf{Fountain}$$

(a)   (b)

(c)   **GNCG$(\mathbf{I_2}, \mathbf{I_1} - \sigma \cdot \mathbf{I_2})$ as a function of σ:**

Some examples of $(\mathbf{I_1} - \sigma \cdot \mathbf{I_2})$ for a few σ's:

$\sigma = 0$ $\sigma = 0.3$ $\sigma = 0.667$ $\sigma = 1$ $\sigma = 1.3$

(d)   (e)   (f)   (g)   (h)

$\hat{\mathbf{L}}_1$ The recovered layers $\hat{\mathbf{L}}_2$

(i)   (j)

Fig. 2. The Layer Information Exchange. (a)-(b) The initial mixtures $I.$ and $I..$ (c) Different values of σ produce different degrees of information correlation between images $I.$ and $I. -\sigma \cdot I..$ (d)-(h) Examples of $I. -\sigma \cdot I.$ for various values of σ. "Fountain" decreases until at $\sigma = 0.667$ it disappears completely, and when σ is increased further, it becomes negative and the GNGC increases again. (i)-(j) The recovered layer separation using the algorithm described in Section 3.1.

3   The Layer Information Exchange

Let I_1 and I_2 be two different combinations of two unknown layers L_1 and L_2, obtained in an unknown fashion (i.e., the coefficients $\alpha_1(i)$, $\alpha_2(i)$, $\beta_1(i)$ and $\beta_2(i)$ in Eq. (1) are unknown, spatially varying, non-linear mixing functions). We will obtain a separation of I_1 and I_2 into two layers $\hat{L}_1$ and $\hat{L}_2$ (which are visual representations of L_1 and L_2) by transferring information from I_1 to I_2, and vice versa, until the structural correlation between those two images is minimized. The information transfer is performed at different information scales, ranging from the entire image to small image windows. To explain this concept of "layer information exchange", let us first examine the simpler case of uniform mixing functions (i.e., constant unknown coefficients). We will later relax this assumption, and show how the process is generalized to spatially-varying non-linear mixing functions.

3.1   Handling Uniform Mixing Functions

Assuming uniform mixing functions, then Eq. (1) reduces to:

$$I_1(i) = \alpha_1 \cdot L_1(i) + \alpha_2 \cdot L_2(i) \quad , \quad I_2(i) = \beta_1 \cdot L_1(i) + \beta_2 \cdot L_2(i) \qquad (3)$$

There exists a constant scalar σ such that $\hat{L}_1(i) = I_1(i) - \sigma I_2(i)$ will contain only the geometric structure of $L_1(i)$, without any trace of $L_2(i)$. For example, $\sigma = \frac{\alpha_2}{\beta_2}$ will lead to such a layer separation: $\hat{L}_1(i) = I_1(i) - \frac{\alpha_2}{\beta_2} I_2(i) = (\alpha_1 - \alpha_2 \frac{\beta_1}{\beta_2}) L_1(i)$. Namely, $L_1(i)$ is recovered up to a constant scale factor $(\alpha_1 - \alpha_2 \frac{\beta_1}{\beta_2})$. However, since $\alpha_1, \alpha_2, \beta_1$ and β_2 are not known, the transfer factor σ is also unknown.

We do know, however, that for the correct transfer factor σ, the layer $L_2(i)$ will disappear in $\hat{L}_1(i)$, thus minimizing the structural correlation between $\hat{L}_1(i) = I_1(i) - \sigma I_2(i)$ and $I_2(i)$. This is visually shown in Fig. 2. We can there-fore recover the transfer factor σ (and accordingly the layer L_1, up to a scale), by minimizing the following objective function:

$$\sigma = argmin(GNGC(I_2, I_1 - \sigma I_2)) \qquad (4)$$

Plugging in the definition of $GNGC$ from Eq. (2), results in an objective function which is quadratic in σ. Differentiating the above objective function with respect to σ and equating to zero (i.e., $\frac{\partial}{\partial \sigma} GNGC(I_2, I_1 - \sigma I_2) = 0$), yields an analytic expression for σ:

$$\sigma = \frac{\sum_{i=1}^{N} C_i(I_1, I_2) \cdot V_i(I_2)}{\sum_{i=1}^{N} V_i^2(I_2)}, \qquad (5)$$

where C_i and V_i are the local (5×5) covariances and variances as defined in Section 2. Having computed the transfer factor σ, we can recover the first layer (up to a scale):

$$\hat{L}_1 = I_1 - \sigma I_2,$$

and proceed to computing the second layer in the same way. The second layer

$$\hat{L}_2 = I_2 - \eta \hat{L}_1,$$

is recovered by seeking η which minimizes $GNGC(\hat{L}_1, I_2 - \eta \hat{L}_1)$. In practice, we repeat this process a few times (typically 2 to 3 times), to obtain cleaner layer separation. At each iteration, the previously recovered $\hat{L}_1$ and $\hat{L}_2$ serve as the new mixtures. Namely, $\hat{L}_1^{k+1} = \hat{L}_1^k - \sigma^{k+1} \hat{L}_2^k$, $\hat{L}_2^{k+1} = \hat{L}_2^k - \eta^{k+1} \hat{L}_1^{k+1}$ where k is the iteration number.

We refer to the above procedure as the "layer information exchange", because at each step we transfer some portion of one image to the other. For example, the step $\hat{L}_1 = I_1 - \sigma I_2$ transfers some portion of I_2 to/from I_1 (depending on whether σ is negative/positive). In the next step, a different portion of the new image $\hat{L}_1$ is transferred in the other direction, according to the magnitude and sign of η. Fig. 2.i and 2.j show the two layers recovered from images I_1 and I_2 (Fig. 2.a and 2.b) by applying the above information exchange procedure.

3.2   Generalizing to Spatially Varying Mixing Functions

So far we have assumed that the mixing coefficients $\alpha_1(i)$, $\alpha_2(i)$, $\beta_1(i)$ and $\beta_2(i)$ are constant. However, in most real-life scenarios, this is not true. To solve the separation problem for the case of spatially-varying mixing functions, we assume that if we use a small enough window W_i around a pixel i, then within that region of analysis the mixing coefficients are approximately uniform (although different from the mixing coefficients in other nearby pixels). In other words, the global layer exchange procedure described in Section 3.1 can be applied to a small local region of analysis W_i to compute $\sigma(i)$ and $\eta(i)$ at the corresponding pixel i. These transfer factors are repeatedly computed for each pixel $i = 1..N$, using a window W_i centered around each image pixel. This results in a *spatially-varying* layer information exchange: $\hat{L}_1(i) = I_1(i) - \sigma(i)I_2(i)$, and $\hat{L}_2(i) = I_2(i) - \eta(i)\hat{L}_1(i)$. This procedure is repeated iteratively: $\hat{L}_1^{k+1}(i) = \hat{L}_1^k(i) - \sigma^{k+1}(i)\hat{L}_2^k(i)$, $\hat{L}_2^{k+1}(i) = \hat{L}_2^k(i) - \eta^{k+1}(i)\hat{L}_1^{k+1}(i)$ until $\sigma^k(i)$ and $\eta^k(i)$ are small enough (where k is the iteration number).

Note that we are now dealing with two different types of local image windows: (i) the local region of analysis W_i used of the piece-wise approximation of the mixing functions, and (ii) the small 5×5 window (mentioned in Section 2), which is used for obtaining local measurements (local NGC) to be summed for generating the global $GNGC$ measure. These 5×5 windows are the smallest reliable information elements over which the local NGC measures are computed across the two images (regardless of whether the mixing functions are uniform or not). These local measures are then summed within the region of analysis, which is the entire image for the case of uniform mixing functions, and smaller W_i in the case of spatially varying mixing functions.

(a) $\mathbf{I_1}$ (b) $\mathbf{I_2}$ (c) $\mathbf{\hat{L}_1}$ (d) $\mathbf{\hat{L}_2}$

Fig. 3. Handling spatially varying mixing functions. (a)-(b) The two mixtures I. and I. were obtained by mixing two images ("fountain" and "waterfall") with 4 different non-linear functions (α. was a sinus, α. and β. were two exponent functions, and β. was a constant function).   (c)-(d) The recovered transparent layers using our global-to-local layer separation method described in Section 3.2 .

Since we do not know ahead of time the degree of non-linearity of the mixing functions, the above local procedure is repeated using coarse-to-fine (i.e., large-to-small) regions of analysis W_i. We start the iterative process with W_i being the entire image. This compensates for the case of globally uniform mixing functions (i.e., constant coefficients throughout the entire image). We then gradually decrease the window size W_i to smaller and smaller windows (but not below 15×15, for numerical stability). This gradual process is aimed to assure that the resulting mixing functions remain as smooth as possible, whenever a smooth solution is a valid interpretation. Fluctuations from uniform/contant mixing functions occur when there is no simpler interpretation.

Fig. 3 shows an example of applying the above procedure to the pair of mixtures I_1 and I_2 (Figs. 3.a and 3.b). These images were generated with spatially varying non-linear mixing function/coefficients (see figure for more details). Fig. 3.c and 3.d show the resulting separation obtained using our layer information exchange (without prior knowledge of the spatially varying mixing coefficients, of course). It has been able to completely separate the structures of the two layers.

4   Applications

The information exchange approach assumes that two different initial combinations (I_1 and I_2) of the unknown transparent layers (L_1 and L_2) are available, but the way in which I_1 and I_2 were generated from L_1 and L_2 is not known, and can be very complex. In this section we explore some cases where such initial combinations are readily available or else easy to extract, and show the applicability of our layer exchange approach for addressing these cases.

(a) $\mathbf{I_1}$ (b) $\mathbf{I_2}$ (c) $\mathbf{\hat{L}_1}$ (d) $\mathbf{\hat{L}_2}$

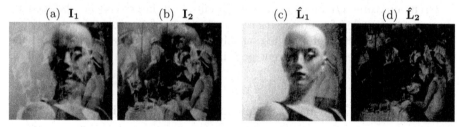

Fig. 4. Recovering Transparent Layers from Polarized Images (a)-(b) Two real images obtained under different polarizations, showing the reflection of Sheila in a Renoir picture. (The images were taken from Farid [5].)   (c)-(d) The recovered transparent layers using our layer separation method.

4.1   Separating Layers in Polarized Images

Due to the physical nature of light polarization through reflecting and transmitting surfaces, two superimposed transparent layers differ in their polarization.

(a) **Input** **sequence**	(b) I_1	(c) I_2	(d) **Recovered** **layer** $\hat{L}_1$	(e) **Recovered** **layer** $\hat{L}_2$

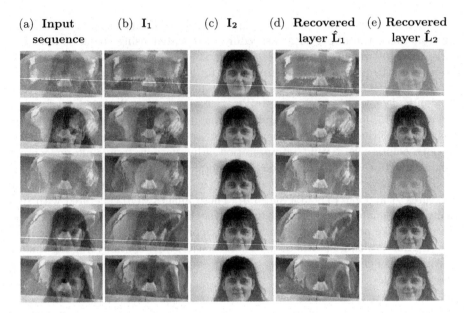

Fig. 5. Separating non-rigid transparencies in video. *Column (a)* Five frames from the input movie (see text for details). *Columns (b)-(c)* The initial separation acquired by extracting the median image from the aligned sequence. *Columns (d)-(e)* The recovered layered. The residual traces of the woman which were visible in (b) are removed in (d), the true color of the fountain is recovered, and the temporal variations in the indoor illumination are recovered in (e). The video sequences can be viewed at **http://www.wisdom.weizmann.ac.il/∼vision/TrasnparentLayers.html**.

Different mixtures (I_1 and I_2) of transparent scene layers can be obtained by changing the angle of a polarization filter in front of the camera (as in [5,8]). Fig. 4 shows the result of applying our algorithm to a real pair of images of the same scene obtained with different polarizers. (These results are comparable to those of [5].)

4.2 Separating Non-Rigid Transparent Layers in Video

When a video camera records two transparent layers with different relative motions over time, and when the motion of *one* of those layers is easy to compute (e.g., if it is a 2D parametric motion), then such a layer separation is possible. This can be done even if the second layer contains very complex non-rigid motions (such as flickering fire, running water, walking people, etc.), the mixing process is not known and may be spatially varying (e.g., due to varying glass opacity or window dirt), and other temporal changes may occur simultaneously (such as varying illumination over time).

Such examples are shown in Fig. 5 (a simulated example) and in Fig. 7 (a real example). Fig. 5 shows a simulated example of an indoor scene with motion and varying illumination, reflected in a window through which a dynamic outdoor scene is visible. The input video sequence was generated by superimposing two video sequences: (i) an "indoor scene" video, showing a woman's head moving while the illumination changes over time (dimming and brightening of indoor illumination), reflected in a window, and (ii) an outdoor scene of a fountain displaying highly non-rigid complex motion, with changing specular reflections, etc. The left column of Fig. 5 displays some representative frames from the generated sequence. The woman's reflection is more visible when the illumination is darker, and is less visible when the illumination is brighter. The goal here was to separate this generated sequence into its original two layers (sequences, in this case): the outdoor scene (the fountain) with all its dynamics and specularities, and the indoor scene (the woman) with its motion and changing illumination.

In this case we have only one input (the video sequence of Fig. 5.a). To obtain *two* different initial layer mixtures (I_1 and I_2), we did the following: The woman's motion is a simple 2D parametric motion, which can be computed using one of the dominant motion estimation methods (e.g., [1,2,9]). This brings the woman into alignment. Now, using Weiss' method for extracting intrinsic images [11], we apply it to the aligned sequence. This process recovers a median image of the woman, and a residual image for each frame after removing the median image of the woman. These are displayed in the second and third columns of Fig. 5 (after *un*warping the images to their original coordinate system according to the estimated 2D motion of the woman). Because the process of [11] results in a single intrinsic image, it does not capture any temporal changes. As a result, the woman's sequence in Fig. 5.c does not contain any of the changes in indoor illumination, and the "residual" sequence (Fig. 5.b) still contains a small residue of the woman (sometimes dark, sometimes bright), while the true colors of the fountain are lost.

Each pair of images in the second and third columns of Fig. 5 can be regarded as initial layer mixtures I_1 and I_2 (unknown and non-linear) for that time instance. These sequences (I_1 and I_2) are fed as the initial combinations to our layer exchange process. Results of the layer separation process are displayed in the last two columns of Fig. 5. Note that now the fountain sequence is fully recovered, with its true colors and no traces of the woman (Fig. 5.d), while the true changes in indoor illuminations have been recovered and automatically associated with the indoor woman sequence (Fig. 5.e).

The initial separation into a *"medians"* and *"residuals"* forms the initial mixtures I_1 and I_2 above. The (unknown) mixing functions which relate I_1 and I_2 to the original (unknown) layers (see Eq. (1)), *cannot* be assumed to be constant or position invariant. This is because the median operator is non-linear. Our Information Exchange approach handles this well (see Figs. 5.d and 5.e). However, the ICA-based separation [5,13] does not perform well on these I_1 and I_2, as can be seen in Figs. 6.c and 6.f. This is because it is not suited for the case of non-uniform spatially varying coefficients.

To our best knowledge, this is the first time videos containing *non-rigid* transparent motions have been separated (and moreover, under unknown varying lighting conditions). Current approaches for video transparency separation (e.g., [9,10,12]), assume that each layer moves rigidly, since dense correspondences

Initial mixtures   Layer-exchange separation   ICA separation

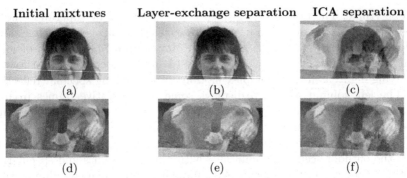

(a)   (b)   (c)

(d)   (e)   (f)

Fig. 6. ICA vs. Information Exchange separation We compare results of applying the ICA-based separation [5,13] to our layer-based separation displayed in Fig. 5. ICA was applied to the same initial mixture sequences (the "median" and the "residual" images in Figs. 5.b and 5.c). Almost all of the resulting frames displayed wrong separation. One such example is shown in the third column of this figure ((c) and (f)). For comparison, we display the corresponding frames of the initial mixture images (a) and (d), and our separation result (b) and (e).

of both layers across the sequence need to be recovered in those methods. We currently need to compute only one of the motions, allowing the second motion to be arbitrarily complex.

Fig. 7 shows a real example of video transparency with non-rigid motions and changing effects of illumination. In this case, a still video camera recorded a scene with non-rigid human motions reflected in a swivelling glass door of an entry hall to a building. The reflected outdoor scene therefore appears moving, while the indoor scene is static. At the last part of the sequence, due to a strong reflections of light in the glass, the AGC (Automatic Gain Control) of the camera induced fluctuating changes in the dynamic range of the image. The left column of Fig. 7 displays three representative frames from the recorded sequence. As before, we used Weiss' method [11] for extracting the intrinsic image from the sequence. The median image was then removed from the sequence, producing a "residual" sequence. These were used as the initial combinations (I_1 and I_2) for our layer exchange approach. The resulting separation into layers is displayed in the second and third columns of Figs. 7. The reflected scene was separated from the glass door, and the changing effects of illumination due to the change in aperture have also been recovered.

5   Conclusions

We presented an approach for separating two transparent layers through a process termed the "layer information exchange". Given two different (unknown complex) combinations of the layers, we recover the layers by gradually transferring information from one image to the other, until the structural correlation across the two images is minimized. The information transfer is done at different information scales, ranging from the entire image to small image windows.

(a) **Input sequence**   (b) **Recovered Layer 1**   (c) **Recovered Layer 2**

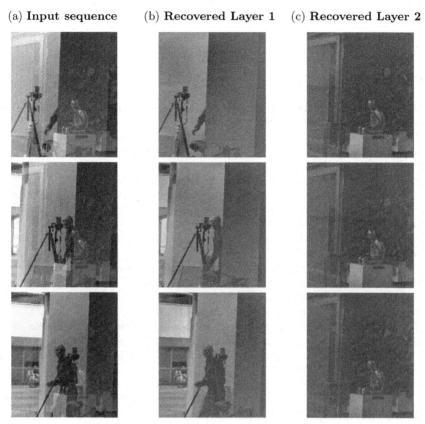

Fig. 7. Separating non-rigid transparencies in video (a) Three frames from a real video sequence of the entrance hall of a building recorded through the building's swivelling glass door. The outdoor scene (including a running man and the camera tripod) are reflected from the swivelling door. The indoor scene includes a statue and a plant. (b) The first recovered layer (the outside scene). (c) The recovered interior hall with the statue. The video sequences can be viewed at **http://www.wisdom.weizmann.ac.il/~vision/TrasnparentLayers.html**.

We showed the applicability of this approach to various real-world scenarios, including image and video transparency separation. To our best knowledge, this is the first time that complex non-rigid transparent motions in video have been separated, without any prior knowledge of the layer mixing model, and under unknown complex temporal changes. We further showed that our approach to layer separation does equally well to ICA (Independent Component Analysis) when the mixing functions are spatially fixed (i.e., independent of the pixel position). However, when the mixing functions are more realistic spatially varying functions (i.e., vary as a function of pixel position), then our approach performs better than ICA. We believe that the applicability of this approach goes beyond analysis and separation of image layers, and can possibly be applied to separating other types of signals (such as acoustic signals, radar signals, etc.)

References

1. J. R. Bergen, P. Anandan, K. J. Hanna, R. Hingorani: Hierarchical Model-Based Motion Estimation. ECCV 1992, pp. 237–252.
2. M. J. Black and P. Anandan: The robust estimation of multiple motions: Parametric and piecewise-smooth flow fields. CVIU, **63(1)**, 1996, pp. 75–104.
3. A. Bronstein, M. Bronstein, M. Zibulevsky and Y. Y. Zeevi: Separation of semireflective layers using Sparse ICA. Proc. ICASSP 2003, **3**, pp. 733–736.
4. T. Cover and J. Thomas: Elements of Information Theory, Wiley and Sons, 1991.
5. H. Farid and E.H. Adelson: Separating Reflections from Images by Use of Independent Components Analysis. JOSA, **16(9)** 1999, pp. 2136–2145.
6. M. Irani and P. Anandan: Robust Multi-Sensor Image Alignment. ICCV 1998, pp. 959–966.
7. A. Levin, A. Zomet, and Y. Weiss: Learning to perceive transparency from the statistics of natural scenes. NIPS 2002, pp.1247–1254.
8. Y. Y. Schechner, J. Shamir, and N. Kiryati: Polarization and statistical analysis of scenes containing a semi-reflector. JOSA A **17**, 2000, pp. 276–284.
9. R. Szeliski, S. Avidan, and P. Anandan: Layer Extraction from Multiple Images containing Reflections and Transparency. CVPR 2000, pp. 246–253.
10. Y. Tsin, S.B.Kang, and R. Szeliski: Stereo Matching with Reflections and Translucency. CVPR 2003, 702–709.
11. Y.Weiss: Deriving Intrinsic Images from Image Sequences. ICCV 2001, pp.68–75.
12. Y. Wexler, A. Fitzgibbon and A. Zisserman: Bayesian Estimation of Layers from Multiple Images. ECCV 2002, pp. 487–501.
13. "FastICA" package, downloaded from: http://www.cis.hut.fi/projects/ica/fastica/

Multiple Classifier System Approach to Model Pruning in Object Recognition

Josef Kittler and Ali R. Ahmadyfard

Centre for Vision, Speech and Signal Processing
University of Surrey
Guildford GU2 7XH, United Kingdom

Abstract. We propose a multiple classiÞer system approach to object recognition in computer vision. The aim of the approach is to use multiple experts successively to prune the list of candidate hypotheses that have to be considered for object interpretation. The experts are organised in a serial architecture, with the later stages of the system dealing with a monotonically decreasing number of models. We develop a theoretical model which underpins this approach to object recognition and show how it relates to various heuristic design strategies advocated in the literature. The merits of the advocated approach are then demonstrated experimentally using the SOIL database. We show how the overall performance of a two stage object recognition system, designed using the proposed methodology, improves. The improvement is achieved in spite of using a weak recogniser for the Þrst (pruning) stage. The effects of different pruning strategies are demonstrated.

1 Introduction

There are several papers [4,14,15,16,17,8,11,9] concerned with multiple classiÞer system architectures suggesting that complex architectures, in which the decision process is decomposed into several stages involving coarse to Þne classiÞcation, result in improved recognition performance. In particular, by grouping classes and performing initially coarse classiÞcation, followed by a Þne classiÞcation reÞnement which disambiguates the classes of the winning coarse group, one can achieve signiÞcant gains in performance. [9] applies this approach to the problem of handwritten character recognition and suggests that class grouping should maximise an entropy measure. Similar strategies have been advocated in [4,14,15,16,17]. The popular decision tree methods can be seen to exploit the same phenomenon.

The aim of this paper is to demonstrate that these heuristic processes do have a theoretical foundation. We propose a framework for analysing the beneÞt of hierarchical class grouping. Using this framework we develop a theoretical basis for multiple expert fusion in serial coarse to Þne object recognition system architectures. The analysis will suggest and explain a number of strategies that can be adopted to build such architectures.

We apply the proposed design methodology to the problem of 3D object recognition using 2D views. This problem has been receiving a lot of attention over the last two decades, resulting in a spectrum of techniques which exploit, for instance, colour [20, 5,12], shape [2,19] and object appearance [18,10,13]. Although none of the existing

T. Pajdla and J. Matas (Eds.): ECCV 2004, LNCS 3024, pp. 342Ð353, 2004.
© Springer-Verlag Berlin Heidelberg 2004

methods provide a panacea on their own, we argue that a combination of several object recognition techniques can be very effective.

More speciÞcally we demonstrate that the proposed approach accomplishes a sequential pruning of the list of object model hypotheses, with the later stages of the system having to deal with a monotonically decreasing number of models. The merits of the advocated approach are then demonstrated experimentally using the SOIL database. We show, how the overall performance of a two stage object recognition system based on the expounded principles improves. The improvement is achieved in spite of using a weak recogniser for the Þrst (pruning) stage. The effects of different pruning strategies are demonstrated.

The paper is organised as follows. In Section 2 the problem of object recognition using hierarchical class grouping is formulated. We derive an expression for the additional decision error, over and above the Bayes error, as a function of estimation error. In Section 3 we discuss various model pruning strategies that naturally stem from this analysis. In Section 4 one of these strategies is applied to the problem of 3D object recognition using a two stage decision making system. Section 5 draws the paper to conclusion.

2   Mathematical Notation and Problem Formulation

Consider an object recognition problem where object Z is to be assigned to one of m possible models $\{\omega_i, \; i = 1, ...m\}$. Let us assume that the given scene object is represented by a measurement vector, $\mathbf{x}$. In the measurement space each object category ω_k is modelled by the probability density function $p(\mathbf{x}|\omega_k)$ and let the a priori probability of object occurrence be denoted by $P(\omega_k)$. We shall consider the models to be mutually exclusive which means that only one model can be associated with each instance.

Now according to the Bayesian decision theory, given measurements $\mathbf{x}$, the instance, Z, should be assigned to model class ω_j, i.e. its label θ should assume value $\theta = \omega_j$, provided the aposteriori probability of that interpretation is maximum, i.e.

$$assign \quad \theta \to \omega_j \quad if$$

$$P(\theta = \omega_j|\mathbf{x}) = \max_k P(\theta = \omega_k|\mathbf{x}) \tag{1}$$

In practice, for each interpretation, a decision making system will provide only an estimate $\hat{P}(\omega_i|\mathbf{x})$ of the true aposteriori class probability $P(\omega_i|\mathbf{x})$ given measurement $\mathbf{x}$, rather than the true probability itself. Let us denote the error on the estimate of the ith model class aposteriori probability at point $\mathbf{x}$ as $e(\omega_i|\mathbf{x})$ and let the probability distribution of errors be $p_i[e(\omega_i|\mathbf{x})]$. Clearly, due to estimation errors, the object recognition based on the estimated aposteriori probabilities will not necessarily be Bayes optimal. In the appendix we derive the probability, $e_S(\mathbf{x})$ of the decision relating to object $\mathbf{x}$ being suboptimal, and refer to it as the switching error probability. We shown in (14) that this probability primarily depends on the margin $\Delta P_{si}(\mathbf{x}) = P(\omega_s|\mathbf{x}) - P(\omega_i|\mathbf{x})$ between the aposteriori probabilities of the Bayes optimal hypothesis ω_s and the next most probable model ω_i, as well as on the width (variance) of the distribution of estimation error.

Now how do these labelling errors translate to recognition error probabilities? We know that for the Bayes minimum error decision rule the error probability at point $\mathbf{x}$ will be $e_B(\mathbf{x})$. If our pseudo Bayesian decision rule, i.e. the rule that assigns patterns according to the maximum estimated aposteriori class probability, deviates from the Bayesian rule with probability $e_S(\mathbf{x})$, the local error of the decision rule will be given by

$$\alpha(\mathbf{x}) = e_B(\mathbf{x})[1 - e_S(\mathbf{x})] + e_S(\mathbf{x})[1 - e_B(\mathbf{x})] \tag{2}$$

The error, $\alpha(\mathbf{x})$, will be close to Bayesian only if $e_S(\mathbf{x})$ is negligible. Thus we want the label switching error to be as small as possible.

Conventionally, the multiple classiÞer fusion paradigm attempts to ameliorate the switching error probability by reducing the variance of estimation errors. This is achieved by combining multiple estimates obtained by a number of diverse object recognition experts. In this paper we adopt a completely different approach that strives to increase the margin between the posteriors of the competing model hypotheses in order to reduce the error probability $e_S(\mathbf{x})$ by alternative means. The basic idea is to group models into superclasses in such a way that the margin between the posteriors of the resulting model sets widens. The number of groups is a free parameter. For our purposes we divide the classes into two groups and perform a coarse classiÞcation of the input pattern to one of these two groups. Then, in the next stage, we reÞne the classiÞcation and continue dividing the the most probable super class in the two subsets by considering the remaining alternatives.

In general, there will be m hypotheses that can be grouped hierarchically into two groups at each stage of the hierarchy. Let us denote the two groups created at stage k by Ω^k and $\bar{\Omega}^k$. The set Ω^k will be divided in the next stage into two subsets, and so on. Thus the class sets Ω^k will satisfy

$$\Omega^k \epsilon \Omega^j \quad j < k \tag{3}$$

Further, let us denote the probability of classifying measurement vector $\mathbf{x}$ from superclass Ω^k suboptimally by $w^k(\mathbf{x})$. Referring to (14), in this two (super)class case, the switching error probability at stage k is given simply by

$$w^k(\mathbf{x}) = \int_{\Delta P_{\Omega^k}(\mathbf{x})}^{\infty} p[\eta_{\Omega^k}(\mathbf{x})]d\eta_{\Omega^k}(\mathbf{x}) \tag{4}$$

where $\Delta P_{\Omega^k}(\mathbf{x})$ is the margin between the posteriors of thw two super classes at stage k and $\eta_{\Omega^k}(\mathbf{x})$ is the associated estimation error. Assuming that the Bayes optimal hypothesis is contained in set Ω^k, it will end up in superclass Ω^{k+1} with probability $1 - w^k(\mathbf{x})$ Similarly, at the $(k+1)^{st}$ stage the probability of making a suboptimal decision is $w^{k+1}(\mathbf{x})$, while the Bayes optimal decision will be made with probability $1 - w^{k+1}(\mathbf{x})$. The complete n-stage hypothesis reÞnement process is illustrated in Figure 1. By reference to Figure 1 the total switching error probability of the hierarchical decision making process can be written as

$$e_S(\mathbf{x}) = w^1(\mathbf{x}) + \sum_{i=2}^{n-1}[\Pi_{j=1}^{i-1}(1 - w^j(\mathbf{x}))]w^i(\mathbf{x})$$
$$+ [\Pi_{j-1}^{n-1}(1 - w^j(\mathbf{x}))]w^n(\mathbf{x}) \tag{5}$$

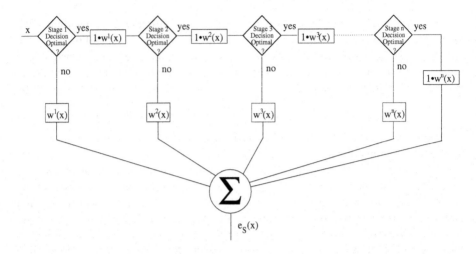

Fig. 1. The total probability of label switching, $e_S(\mathbf{x})$ in a coarse to Þne multistage object recognition system

Note that the Þnal stage will involve only the closest competitors, classes $\Omega^n = \{\omega_s, \omega_i\}$. The probability $w^n(\mathbf{x})$ of label switching will be given by

$$w^n(\mathbf{x}) = \int_{\Delta Q_{si}(\mathbf{x})}^{\infty} p[\eta_\omega(\mathbf{x})] d\eta_\omega(\mathbf{x}) \tag{6}$$

where $\eta_\omega(\mathbf{x}) = 2e(\omega_i|\mathbf{x})$ is the combined estimation error for the two posteriors, since in the two class $e(\omega_s|\mathbf{x}) = -e(\omega_i|\mathbf{x})$.

In equation (6) we denote the aposteriori probabilities, $Q(\omega_r|\mathbf{x})$, $r = s, i$ for model classes ω_s and ω_i by different symbols to indicate that these functions differ from $P(\omega_r|\mathbf{x})$, $r = s, i$ by a scaling factor $P(\omega_s|\mathbf{x}) + P(\omega_i|\mathbf{x})$ since they have to sum up to one. Note that if functions $Q(\omega_r|\mathbf{x})$ are estimated via probability densities, the estimation errors will be scaled up versions of the original errors $e(\omega_r|\mathbf{x})$. However, if these functions are estimated directly from the training data, the errors will be different and can be assumed to have the same distribution as the original unscaled errors $e(\omega_r|\mathbf{x})$. If this is the case, then one can see why this two stage approach may produce better results. The probability mass under the tail of the error estimation distribution will rapidly decay as the margin (the tail cut off) increases. If the error distributions are the same but the margins increase by scaling, the probability of label switching will go down.

3   Discussion

Let us consider the implication of expression (5). Assuming that the estimation errors have identical distribution at all the stages of the sequential decision making process, the label switching error $w^i(\mathbf{x})$ at stage i will be determined entirely by the margin (difference) between the aposteriori probabilities of classes $P(\Omega^i|(\mathbf{x}))$ and $P(\bar{\Omega}^i|(\mathbf{x}))$.

By grouping model classes at the top of the hierarchy we can increase this margin and therefore control the additional error. In this way we can ensure that the additional errors $w^i(\mathbf{x})$ in all but the last stage of the decision making process are negligible. In the limiting case, when $w^i(\mathbf{x}) \to 0, \quad i = 1, ..., n - 1$ the switching error $e_S(\mathbf{x})$ will be equal to $w^n(\mathbf{x})$. At that point the set Ω^n is likely to contain just a single class. Thus the last stage decision will involve two classes only. Note that whereas the margin between the aposteriori probabilities of the two model classes, say ω_s and ω_i, at the top of the hierarchy, was $P(\omega_s|\mathbf{x}) - P(\omega_i|\mathbf{x})$, in the last stage, it will become

$$\delta = \frac{P(\omega_s|\mathbf{x}) - P(\omega_i|\mathbf{x})}{P(\omega_s|\mathbf{x}) + P(\omega_i|\mathbf{x})} \tag{7}$$

Thus the margin will be signiÞcantly magniÞed and consequently the additional error $e_S(\mathbf{x})$ signiÞcantly lower than what it would have been in a single stage system.

The expression (5) immediately suggests a number of grouping strategies. For instance, in order to maintain the margin as large as possible in all stages of the decision making process it would clearly be most effective to group all but one class in one super class and the weakest class in the complement super class. This strategy has been suggested, based on heuristic arguments, in [21]. The disadvantage of this strategy is that it would involve $m - 1$ decision steps.

Computationally more effective is to arrive at a decision after $log_2 m$ steps. This would lead to grouping which maintains a balance of the two class sets Ω^i and $\bar{\Omega}^i$. Another suggestion [9] is to split the classes so as to minimise an entropy criterion. However, all these strategies exploit the same underlying principle embodied by our model.

4   Experimental Results

In this section we illustrate the merits of model grouping within the context of 3D object recognition. The core of our object recognition system is a region-based matching scheme proposed in [1]. In this method an object image is represented by its constituent regions segmented from the image. The regions are represented in the form of an Attributed Relational Graph (ARG). In this representation each region is described individually and by its relation with its neighbouring regions expressed in terms of binary measurements. We use the representative colour of each region as its unary measurement and we characterize geometric relations between region pairs using binary measurements.

The matching process is performed using probabilistic relaxation labelling [3]. In this approach, for each region from a test image, we compute the probability that the region corresponds to a particular node of the ARG representing the combined set of object models. We model an object using an image taken from the frontal view. The label probabilities for a region in the test image are initialized by measuring the similarity between the unary measurements corresponding to the two regions being matched. These probabilities are then updated by taking into account the consistency of labelling at the neighbouring regions.

We tested the idea of grouping from two different aspects: label and model grouping. By label grouping we mean that for each region in the test image we classify the union of labels associated with the regions in the database into two sets: candidate labels and rejected labels. The process of region matching then proceeds using only the set of candidate labels. We propose two label pruning schemes: pruning at the initialization stage and at the end of each iteration of the relaxation labelling. At initialization, for each region in the test image we compile a list of candidate labels. This list is based on the degree of similarity between unary measurements. At the end of each iteration of the relaxation labelling process we note the label probabilities associated with each region in the test image and drop those labels whose probabilities are below a predeÞned threshold.

Model grouping realizes the same idea at a higher level. Let us consider our model-based recognition system as a set of serial classiÞers where each classiÞer is in fact an object recognition expert. Each expert takes the list of model candidates from the previous expert and delivers a pruned list of model candidates to the next classiÞer. The pruning of models is performed by matching the test image features against features extracted from the model candidates. The objective for the last expert is to select the winning candidate.

In a simple case of this scenario we consider just two recognition experts in a tandem. The Þrst expert performs a course grouping of the object hypotheses based on an entropy criterion. This initial classiÞcation is performed using colour cues. We opt for the *MNS* method of Matas et al [12] for this purpose. In this method the colour structure of an image is captured in terms of a set of colour descriptors computed on multimodal neighbourhoods detected in the image[12]. We use the similarity between the descriptors from the scene image and each of the m object models to Þnd the aposteriori probabilities of the object in the scene image belonging to the various model classes in the database.

Having provided the set of a posteriori probabilities $\mathcal{P} = \{p(\omega_i|\overline{x}), \forall i \in \{1 \cdots m\}\}$, we rank them in the descending order. Our objective is to compile a list of hypothesised objects based on their likelihood of being in the scene ($\mathcal{P}$). For this purpose we use the entropy of the system as a criterion. Let us consider the list,Ω, of model hypotheses arranged according to the descending order of their probabilities. If Ω is split into two groups Ω^1 and $\bar{\Omega}^1$ comprising the K most likely objects in the scene and the remaining objects in the database respectively, the entropy of the system is evaluated as follows [7]:

$$E = \alpha E(\Omega^1) + (1 - \alpha)E(\bar{\Omega}^1) \tag{8}$$

where $E(\Omega^1)$ and $E(\bar{\Omega}^1)$ are the entropies associated with groups Ω^1 and $\bar{\Omega}^1$ respectively and α is the probability that the present object in the scene exists in the group Ω^1. By searching the range of possible conÞgurations,$(r = 1 \cdots m)$, the grouping with the minimum entropy is selected and the group of the hypothesised objects,Ω^1, is passed to the next expert. The second expert is the ARG matcher[1] described earlier. The whole recognition system is referred to as the MNS-ARG method.

We designed two experiments to demonstrate the effect of both label pruning and model pruning on the performance of the ARG method. We compared three recognition systems from the recognition rate point of view: ARG with/without label pruning and MNS-ARG (with label pruning). The experiments were conducted on the SOIL-47 (Surrey Object Image Library) database which contains 47 objects each of which has been imaged from 21 viewing angles spanning a range of up to ± 90 degrees. Figure 2 shows the frontal view of the objects in the database. The database is available online[6]. In

Fig. 2. The frontal view of some objects in the SOIL47 database

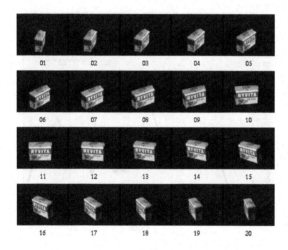

Fig. 3. An object in the database imaged from 20 viewing angles

this experiment we model each object using its frontal image while the other 20 views of the objects are used as test images (Fig. 3). The size of images used in this experiment is 288×360 pixels.

In the Þrst experiment we applied the ARG matching for two different cases: with label pruning and without label pruning. The recognition performance for these two cases is shown in Fig. 4. As can be seen, the performance of the ARG matching is considerably enhanced by label pruning. It is worth noting that as this experiment showed the label pruning also speeds up the process of the relaxation labelling signiÞcantly.

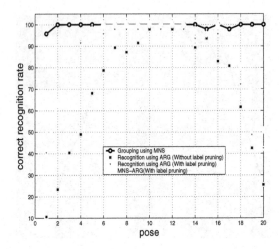

Fig. 4. The percentage of correct recognition for the ARG and the MNS-ARG methods

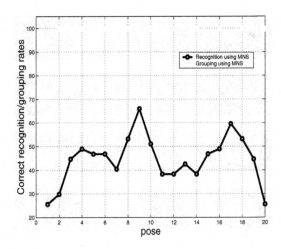

Fig. 5. The likelihood of the correct model being in the list of hypothesised objects generated by the MNS method

In the second experiment, for each test image we applied the MNS method to determine the hypothesised objects matched to it. The results of the experiment are shown in Fig. 5. In this Þgure we plot the percentage of cases in which the list of hypothesised objects includes the correct model. This rate has been shown as a function of the object pose. For comparison we plot the percentage of cases in which the correct object has the highest probability among the other candidates. It is referred to as the recognition rate. The results illustrate that the recognition rate for the MNS method is not very high. This is not surprising as many grossery items contain similar surface colours.

In contrast, as seen from Fig. 5 in the majority of cases the hypothesised list includes the correct object. It is worth noting that the average size of the list of hypothesised objects is 16 which is near to one third of the database size(47 objects).

The ARG method was then applied to identify the object model based on the list of hypothesised objects generated by the MNS method. This recognition procedure was applied to all test images in the database. In Fig. 4 we have plotted the recognition rate for the MNS-ARG method as a function of object pose. For comparison we have shown the recognition rate when ARG method is applied as a stand alone expert. As a base line we added the rate of correct classiÞcation of the MNS method. The results show that the object grouping using the MNS method improves the recognition rate particularly for extreme object views. For such views the hypotheses at a node of the test graph do not receive a good support from its neighbours (problem of distortion in image regions). Moreover a large number of labels involved in the matching increases the entropy of labelling. When the number of candidate labels for a test node declines by virtue of model pruning the entropy of labelling diminishes. Consequently it is more likely for a test node to take its proper label (instead of the null label).

Similar to label pruning, the grouping using the MNS method not only gains the recognition rate but also it reduces the computational complexity of the entire recognition system. This experiment showed that the MNS-ARG method can be performed almost three times faster than the stand alone ARG method.

5   Conclusion

We proposed a multiple classiÞer system approach to object recognition in computer vision. Multiple experts are used successively to prune the list of candidate hypotheses that have to be considered for object interpretation. The experts are organised in a serial architecture, with the later stages of the system dealing with a monotonically decreasing number of models. We developed a theoretical model which underpins this approach to object recognition and show how it relates to various heuristic design strategies advocated in the literature. The merits of the advocated approach were then demonstrated on a two stage object recognition system. Experiments on the SOIL database showed worthwhile performance improvements, especially for object views far from the frontal, which was used for modelling. The improvements were achieved in spite of using a weak recogniser for the Þrst (pruning) stage. The beneÞcial effects of different pruning strategies were demonstrated.

Acknowledgements. This work was supported by EU Project Vampire.

References

1. A. Ahmadyfard and J. Kittler. Enhancement of ARG object recognition method. *Proceeding of 11 the European Signal Processing Conference*,volume 3, pages 551Ð554, September 2002.
2. S. Belongie, J. Malik, and J. Puzicha. Shape matching and object recognition using shape contexts. *IEEE Transactions on Pattern Analysis and Machine Intelligence*, pages 509Ð522, 2002.

3. W.J. Christmas, J. Kittler, and M. Petrou. Structural matching in computer vision using probabilistic relaxation. *IEEE Transactions on Pattern Analysis and Machine Intelligence*, pages 749Ð764, 1995.

4. M C Fairhurst and A F R Rahman. Generalised approach to the recognition of structurally similar handwritten characters using multiple expert classiþers. *IEE Proceeding on Vision, Image and Signal Processing*, 144(1):15Ð22, 2 1997.

5. G. Finlayson, B. Funt, and J. Barnard. Color constant color indexing. *IEEE Transactions on Pattern Analysis and Machine Intelligence*, 17((5):522Ð529, 1995.

6. http://www.ee.surrey.ac.uk/Research/VSSP/demos/ colour/soil47/.

7. K. Ianakiev and V. Govindaraju. Architecture for classiþer combination using entropy measures. In *IAPR International Workshop on Multiple Classifier Systems*, Lecture Notes in Computer Science, pages 340Ð350, June 2000.

8. G Kim and V Govindaraju. A lexicon driven approach to handwritten word recognition. *IEEE Transactions on Pattern Analysis and Machine Intelligence*, 19(4):366Ð379, 1997.

9. I Krassimir and V Govindaraju. An architecture for classiþer combination using entropy measure. In J Kittler and F Roli, editors, *Proceedings of Multiple Classifier Systems 2000*, pages 340Ð350, 2000.

10. D.G. Lowe. Three-dimensional object recognition form single two-dimensional image. *Artificial Intelligence*, pages 355Ð395, 1987.

11. S Madhvanath, E Kleinberg, and V Govindaraju. Holistic veriþcation for handwritten phrases. *IEEE Transactions on Pattern Analysis and Machine Intelligence*, 21(12):1344Ð1356, 1999.

12. J. Matas, D. Koubaroulis, and J. Kittler. Colour image retrieval and object recognition using the multimodal neighbourhood signature. In *Proceedings of ECCV*, pages 48Ð64, 2000.

13. H. Murase and S. Nayar. Visual learning and recognition of 3d objects from appearance. *International Journal of Computer Vision*, pages 5Ð24, 1995.

14. A F R Rahman and M C Fairhurst. Exploiting second order information to design a novel multiple expert decision combination platform for pattern classiþcation. *Electronic Letters*, 33:476Ð477, 1997.

15. A F R Rahman and M C Fairhurst. A new hybrid approach in combining multiple experts to recognise handwritten numerals. *Pattern Recognition Letters*, 18:781Ð790, 1997.

16. A F R Rahman and M C Fairhurst. An evaluation of multi-expert conþgurations for for the recognition of handwritten numerals. *Pattern Recognition*, 31:1255Ð1273, 1998.

17. A F R Rahman and M C Fairhurst. Enhancing multiple expert decision combination strategies through exploitation of a priori information sources. In *IEE Proceeding on Vision Image and Signal Processing*, volume 146, pages 40Ð49, 1999.

18. C. Schmid and R. Mohr. Local grayvalue invariants for image retrieval. *IEEE Transactions on Pattern Analysis and Machine Intelligence*, 19(5):530Ð535, 1997.

19. Z Shao and J Kittler. Shape representation and recognition using invariant unary and binary relations. *Image and Vision Computing*, 17:429Ð444, 1999.

20. M.J. Swain and D.H Ballard. Colour indexing. *Intl. Journal of Computer Vision*, 7(1):11Ð32, 1991.

21. M. Turner and J. Austin. A neural relaxation technique for chemical graph matching. In *Proceeding of Fifth International Conference on Artificial Neural Networks*, 1997.

Appendix: Probability of Suboptimal Decision Making

In order to investigate the effect of estimation errors on decision making, let us examine the class aposteriori probabilities at a single point $\mathbf{x}$. Suppose the aposteriori probability of class ω_s is maximum, i.e. $P(\omega_s|\mathbf{x}) = \max_{i=1}^{m} P(\omega_i|\mathbf{x})$ giving the local Bayes error

$e_B(\mathbf{x}) = 1 - P(\omega_s|\mathbf{x})$. However, our classiÞer only estimates these aposteriori class probabilities. The associated estimation errors may result in suboptimal decisions, and consequently in an additional recognition error. To quantify this additional error we have to establish what the probability is for the recognition system to make a suboptimal decision. This situation will occur when the aposteriori class probability estimates for one of the other model classes becomes maximum. Let us derive the probability $e_{S_i}(\mathbf{x})$ of the event occurring for class ω_i, $i \neq s$, i.e. when

$$\hat{P}(\omega_i|\mathbf{x}) - \hat{P}(\omega_j|\mathbf{x}) > 0 \; \forall j \neq i \tag{9}$$

Note the left hand side of (9) can be expressed as

$$P(\omega_i|\mathbf{x}) - P(\omega_j|\mathbf{x}) + e(\omega_i|\mathbf{x}) - e(\omega_j|\mathbf{x}) > 0 \tag{10}$$

Equation (10) deÞnes a constraint for the two estimation errors $e(\omega_k|\mathbf{x})$, $k = i, j$ as

$$e(\omega_i|\mathbf{x}) - e(\omega_j|\mathbf{x}) > P(\omega_j|\mathbf{x}) - P(\omega_i|\mathbf{x}) \tag{11}$$

The event in (9) will occur when the estimate of the aposteriori probability of class ω_i exceeds the estimate for class ω_s, while the other estimates of the aposteriori class probabilities ω_j, $\forall j \neq i, s$ remain dominated by $\hat{P}(\omega_i|\mathbf{x})$. The Þrst part of the condition will happen with the probability given by the integral of the distribution of the error difference in (11) under the tail deÞned by the margin $\Delta P_{si}(\mathbf{x}) = P(\omega_s|\mathbf{x}) - P(\omega_i|\mathbf{x})$. Let us denote this error difference by $\eta_\omega(\mathbf{x})$. Then the distribution of error difference $p[\eta_\omega(\mathbf{x})]$ will be given by the convolution of the error distribution functions $p_i[e(\omega_i|\mathbf{x})]$ and $p_s[e(\omega_s|\mathbf{x})]$, i.e.

$$p[\eta_\omega(\mathbf{x})] = \int_{-\infty}^{\infty} p_i[\eta_\omega(\mathbf{x}) + e(\omega_s|\mathbf{x})]p_s[e(\omega_s|\mathbf{x})]de(\omega_s|\mathbf{x}) \tag{12}$$

Note that errors $e(\omega_r|\mathbf{x})$, $\forall r$ are subject to various constraints (i.e. $\sum_r e(\omega_r|\mathbf{x}) = 0$, $-P(\omega_r|\mathbf{x}) \leq e(\omega_r|\mathbf{x}) \leq 1 - P(\omega_r|\mathbf{x})$). We will make the assumption that the constraints are reßected in the error probability distributions themselves and therefore we do not need to take them into account elsewhere (i.e. integral limits, etc). However, the constraints also have implications on the validity of the assumptions about the error distributions in different parts of the measurement space. For instance in regions where all the classes are overlapping, the Gaussian assumption may hold but as we move to the parts of the space where the aposteriori model class probabilities are saturated, such an assumption would not be satisÞed. At the same time, one would not be expecting any errors to arise in such regions and the breakdown of the assumption would not be critical. Returning to the event in (9), the probability of the Þrst condition being true is given by $\int_{\Delta P_{si}(\mathbf{x})}^{\infty} p[\eta_\omega(\mathbf{x})]d\eta_\omega(\mathbf{x})$

Referring to equation (11), for each j the second condition will hold for $j \neq s, i$ with probability $\int_{-\infty}^{\Delta P_{ij}(\mathbf{x})+e(\omega_i|\mathbf{x})} p_j[e(\omega_j|\mathbf{x})]de(\omega_j|\mathbf{x})$, with the exception of the last term, say $e(\omega_k|\mathbf{x})$ which is constrained by

$$\hat{e}(\omega_k|\mathbf{x}) = - \sum_{\substack{j=1 \\ j \neq k}}^{m} e(\omega_j|\mathbf{x}) \tag{13}$$

Thus, Þnally, the probability of assigning point $\mathbf{x}$ to model class ω_i instead of the Bayes optimal class ω_s will be given by

$$
\begin{aligned}
e_{S_i}(\mathbf{x}) = \int_{\Delta P_{si}(\mathbf{x})}^{\infty} p[\eta_\omega(\mathbf{x})]d\eta_\omega(\mathbf{x}) \\
\bullet \int_{-\infty}^{\Delta P_{ij}(\mathbf{x})+e(\omega_i|\mathbf{x})} p_j[e(\omega_j|\mathbf{x})]de(\omega_j|\mathbf{x})........ \\
\cdots \int_{-\Delta P_{ik}(\mathbf{x})-e(\omega_i|\mathbf{x})-\sum_{\substack{t=1 \\ t \neq k \\ t \neq l}}^{m} e_t(\omega_t|\mathbf{x})}^{\Delta P_{il}(\mathbf{x})+e(\omega_i|\mathbf{x})} p_l[e(\omega_l|\mathbf{x})]de(\omega_l|\mathbf{x})
\end{aligned}
\tag{14}
$$

and the total probability of label switching will be given by

$$
e_S(\mathbf{x}) = \sum_{\substack{i=1 \\ i \neq s}}^{m} e_{S_i}(\mathbf{x})
\tag{15}
$$

Coaxial Omnidirectional Stereopsis

Libor Spacek

Department of Computer Science
University of Essex
Colchester, CO4 3SQ, UK
spacl@essex.ac.uk,
http://cswww.essex.ac.uk/mv

Abstract. Catadioptric omnidirectional sensors, consisting of a camera and a mirror, can track objects even when their bearings change suddenly, usually due to the observer making a significant turn. There has been much debate concerning the relative merits of several possible shapes of mirrors to be used by such sensors.

This paper suggests that the conical mirror has some advantages over other shapes of mirrors. In particular, the projection beam from the central region of the image is reflected and distributed towards the horizon rather than back at the camera. Therefore a significant portion of the image resolution is not wasted.

A perspective projection unwarping of the conical mirror images is developed and demonstrated. This has hitherto been considered possible only with mirrors that possess single viewpoint geometry. The cone is viewed by a camera placed some distance away from the tip. Such arrangement does not have single viewpoint geometry. However, its multiple viewpoints are shown to be dimensionally separable.

Once stereopsis has been solved, it is possible to project the points of interest to a new image through a (virtual) single viewpoint. Successful reconstruction of a single viewpoint image from a pair of images obtained via multiple viewpoints appears to validate the use of multiple viewpoint projections.

The omnidirectional stereo uses two catadioptric sensors. Each sensor consists of one conical mirror and one perspective camera. The sensors are in a coaxial arrangement along the vertical axis, facing up or down. This stereoscopic arrangement leads to very simple matching since the epipolar lines are the radial lines of identical orientations in both omnidirectional images.

The stereopsis results on artificially generated scenes with known ground truth show that the error in computed distance is proportional to the distance of the object (as usual), plus the distance of the camera from the mirror. The error is also inversely proportional to the image radius coordinate, ie. the results are more accurate for points imaged nearer the rim of the circular mirror.

T. Pajdla and J. Matas (Eds.): ECCV 2004, LNCS 3024, pp. 354–365, 2004.
© Springer-Verlag Berlin Heidelberg 2004

1   Introduction

Autonomous navigation, site modelling and surveillance applications all benefit from using panoramic 360° images. Omnidirectional visual sensors produce such images. Early attempts at using omnidirectional sensors included camera clusters [1] and various arrangements of mechanically rotating cameras and planar mirrors, [2], [3], [4]. These mostly had problems with registration, motion, or both. Fisheye lens cameras have also been used to increase the field of view [5] but they proved difficult because of their irreversible distortion of nearby objects and the lack of a single viewpoint, explained below.

Catadioptric sensors [6] consist of a fixed dioptric camera, usually mounted vertically, plus a fixed rotationally symmetrical mirror above or below the camera. The advantages of catadioptric sensors derive from the fact that, unlike the rotating cameras, their 'scanning' of the surroundings is moreless instantaneous. (The camera exposure time is usually shorter than the full rotation time). Shorter exposure means fewer image capture problems caused by motion and vibration of the camera, or by moving objects.

The suitability for use in dynamic environments is clearly an important consideration, especially as one of the chief benefits of omnidirectional vision in general is the ability to retain objects in view even when their bearings have changed significantly. Catadioptric omnidirectional sensors are ideally suited to visual navigation [7], visual guidance applications [8], using stereopsis, motion analysis [9], and site mapping [10].

The problem with catadioptric sensors is that the details of the image can have relatively poor resolution, as the image depicts a large area. The resolution problem is unfortunately compounded by mirrors whose shapes have curved cross-sections. Such radially curved mirrors include the three quadric surface mirrors (elliptic, hyperbolic and parabolic) which are known to possess a single viewpoint at their focal points.

Single viewpoint projection geometry exists when the light rays arriving from all directions intersect at a single point known as the (single) effective viewpoint. For example, by placing the centre of the perspective camera lens at the outer focus of the hyperbolic mirror, the inner focus then becomes the single effective viewpoint.

A single viewpoint is generally thought to be necessary for an accurate unwarping of images and for an accurate perspective projection which is relied on by most computer vision methods [11].

The single viewpoint projection has been endorsed and recommended by [12], [13], [14], [15], [16] and others.

There have been few attempts at analysing non-single viewpoint sensors [17], [18], although various people [19] used them previously without analysis.

The omnidirectional sensors resolution can be improved by using several planar mirrors with a separate camera for each one of them. The mirrors are placed in some spatial arrangement, for instance in a six sided pyramid [20]. The reflected camera positions are carefully aligned to coincide and to form a single effective viewpoint. However, such arrangements are awkward, expensive, and sensitive to alignment errors. The hexagonal pyramid apparatus would require no fewer than twelve cameras for stereopsis! Also, the coverage of the surrounding area is not isotropic.

Spacek [21] proposed a solution to the above problems which combines the benefits of the planar mirrors (no radial distortion, no radial loss of resolution) with the advantages of the rotationally symmetric catadioptric sensor (short exposure, isotropic imaging). The only shape of mirror that satisfies these requirements is the cone.

2   Perspective Projection through a Conical Mirror

The benefits of the cone mirror over the radially curved mirrors were pointed out by Lin and Bajczy in [22]. They can be summarised as:

1. Curved cross-section mirrors produce inevitable radial distortions. Radial distortion is proportional to the radial curvature of the mirror. The cone has zero radial curvature everywhere except at its tip, which is only reflecting the camera anyway.

2. Radially curved mirrors produce 'fish eye' effects: they magnify the objects reflected in the centre of the mirror, typically the camera, the robot, or the sky, all of which are of minimal interest. On the other hand, they shrink the region around the horizon, thereby reducing the available spatial resolution in the area which is of interest. See Figures 1 and 2 for the comparison of the hyperbolic and the conical mirrors. The mirrors are showing different scenes but both are pointing vertically upwards.

3. The cone presents planar mirrors in cross-section. See Figure 3. The planar mirror does not have a complicated function mapping the camera resolution density onto the real world.

Some optimised shapes of radially curved mirrors have been proposed [23], as well as hybrid sensors, mirrors combining two shapes into one, and other mirrors of various functions. However, it seems that none of them completely address all of the above points.

The cone mirror has a single effective viewpoint located at the tip. Lin and Bajczy proposed cutting off the tip and placing the camera lens in its place, or placing the tip at the forward focus point of the lens. Both of these methods require the camera to be very close to the mirror which results in difficulties with capturing enough light and with focusing, so the improvement in image quality over the curved mirrors is debatable.

Our solution consists of placing the camera at a comfortable distance d from the tip of the conical mirror and still obtaining a useful projection, despite the fact that there is now an infinite number of viewpoints arranged in a circle of radius d around the tip of the cone. See Figure 4. Not having to fix the camera at a precise distance represents an additional practical benefit in comparison with the hyperbolic mirrors or the approach of Lin and Bajczy.

R is both the radius and the height of the cone with a $90°$ angle at the tip. Given the field of view angle ϕ of a particular camera lens, the appropriate

Fig. 1. An omnidirectional image obtained using a hyperbolic mirror and an ordinary perspective camera. Note the typical predominance of the sky.

Fig. 2. A conical mirror image of an indoors scene. The entire mirror image reflects useful data.

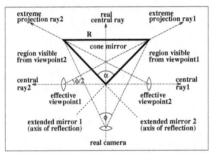

Fig. 3. Cross section of the conical mirror projection geometry. According to the laws of optics, mirrors can reflect either the objects or the viewpoints. The two situations are equivalent. In this case, the real camera with a field of view ϕ is reflected in two planar mirrors, creating two effective viewpoints. Each viewpoint has a field of view $\phi/2$ between its central projection ray and its extreme ray. The angle at the tip of the cone is $\alpha = 90°$ to ensure that the two effective lines of sight (central rays 1&2) are oriented directly towards each other. R is the radius of the mirror.

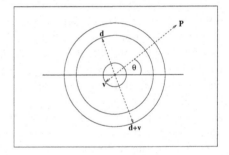

Fig. 4. Top view of the perspective projection of P via the conical mirror. The circle of radius d is the locus of the viewpoints of the distant camera.

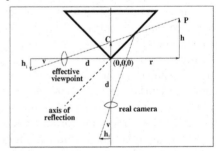

Fig. 5. Cross section of the perspective projection of P via the conical mirror: the image is distance v behind the centre of the lens.

camera distance $d = R(cotan\frac{\phi}{2} - 1)$. This is the camera distance calculated to inscribe the base circle of the cone within the image. The field of view of the camera and the size of the mirror are thus utilised to their best advantage. For example, a mirror of radius $R = 60mm$ and a camera with $\phi = \pi/4$ results in $d = 85mm$ (rounded up). d is critical for the focal mirrors but not so for the cone. At worst, we may lose a few pixels around the edges of the image.

2.1   The Projections

The image of a rotationally symmetric mirror viewed along its axis of symmetry is circular. It is therefore convenient to use the polar coordinates (r_i, θ) to represent the image positions and the related cylindrical coordinates (r, θ, h) for the 3D scene. See Figure 5 for the θ cross section of the conical mirror and the associated perspective projection. Note that the points of interest along the projection ray from a 3D scene point $P(r, \theta, h)$ are collinear (forming three similar triangles).

Let the image radius coordinate r_i of the projected point P have the value h_i (the image height of P). The perspective projection formula is obtained from the collinearity property (or two similar triangles) in Figure (5):

$$h_i = \frac{vh}{d + r} \tag{1}$$

h_i values are always positive (image radius). This is equivalent to using front projection to remove the image reversal. Equation (1) is much simpler than the projection equations for the radially curved mirrors.

v is the distance of the image plane behind the centre of the thin lens in Gaussian optics. The focal length is normally less than v, unless we reduce v to focus on infinity, or use the simplifying pinhole camera assumption. The calibration of v is obtained by substituting the image radius of the mirror r_m for h_i, and R for h and r in equation (1), giving: $v = r_m(\frac{d}{R} + 1)$. The image radius r_m is determined by locating the outer contour of the mirror in the image.

The classic perspective projection function for the single effective viewpoint at $(0,0,0)$ is just a special case of equation (1), where $d = 0$. Suppose we create a thought-experiment (Gedanken) world in which all the objects are pushed distance d further away from the mirror axis. Then the single viewpoint projection of the Gedanken world would result in the same image as the multiple viewpoint projection of the real world. It is also clear that once r is known (see the stereopsis method below), it is possible to reconstruct the single viewpoint projection of the real world by using equation (1) and setting $d = 0$.

The geometry is illustrated in Figure 4. The outer circle depicts the projection cylinder with the radius $d + v$ and the same axis as the cone. The projection cylinder for the single viewpoint at $(0,0,0)$ is similar but has the radius v (the innermost circle).

So far, we considered the projection for a fixed value of θ and identified its associated viewpoint. Now we fix the elevation angle $\epsilon = \arctan(h/(d + r))$ and allow θ to vary. Imagine spinning Figure 5 around the mirror axis. All projection lines with the same elevation angle will intersect the cone axis at the single point $C(0, \theta, h_c)$. Thus the intersection point C is the viewpoint associated with the elevation ϵ. We can determine the height h_c of C from the height h of P by again using the collinearity property: $h_c = (d \cdot h)/(d + r)$.

Sensors with a single (global) effective viewpoint have the same perspective projection in both orthogonal image dimensions (usually x, y). However, we get a different perspective projection in the θ dimension, as the effective viewpoint C for the θ dimension is different from the effective viewpoint $(d, \theta + \pi, 0)$ for the radial projection.

θ projection is not needed for our stereopsis which uses only the radial projection but it could be utilised if we placed two mirrors side-by-side. It has been used in this fashion in [24].

We now define the projection property whereby the viewpoints are said to be dimensionally separable:
– Each radial line in the image (or equivalently each column in the unwarped image) has its own unique viewpoint.
– Each concentric circle in the image (or equivalently each row in the unwarped image) has its own unique viewpoint.
– Each pixel is aligned with its two (row and column) viewpoints, along the projection line from P.

2.2   Registration

We have just described the idealised projection which will be valid and accurate after registration, when the tip of the mirror is precisely aligned with the centre of the image and the axis of view coincides with the axis of the mirror. In general, registration needs to be performed to find the two translation and three rotation parameters needed to guarantee this. Existing registration methods will also apply and work in this situation. See [25] and [26] for good solutions to this problem within the context of omnidirectional vision.

Straight lines in the 3D world become generally conic section curves when projected. However, lines which are coplanar with the axis of the mirror project into radial lines. Concentric circles around the mirror project again into concentric circles. These properties can be utilised for a simple test card registration method, where the test card is of the 'shooting target' type consisting of crosshairs and concentric circles, centered on the cone axis.

2.3   Unwarping of the Input Image

If we were to cut and unroll the virtual projection cylinder, we would get the unwarped rectangular panoramic image. Therefore unwarping is the backprojection of the real input image onto the virtual projection cylinder. The unwarping from the polar coordinates (h_i, θ_i) of the input image into the (x, y) coordinates of the rectangular panoramic image is:

$$x = \frac{x_m}{2\pi} \cdot \theta_i \quad , \quad y = \frac{y_m}{r_m} \cdot h_i \tag{2}$$

where (x_m, y_m) are the desired dimensions of the unwarped image, r_m is the radius of the mirror as seen in the input image, and θ_i is measured in radians. The aspect ratio of the panoramic image is: $x_m/y_m = 2\pi$.

The direct mapping from the pixel position (x, y) of the panoramic unwarped image to the corresponding position (x_i, y_i) of the input image is presented next. We use polar coordinates as an intermediate step, and then equations 2. We also need to know the centre of the mirror in the input image (x_c, y_c).

$$x_i = x_c + h_i \cdot \cos \theta_i = x_c + \frac{r_m}{y_m} \cdot y \cdot cos(\frac{2\pi}{x_m} \cdot x) \tag{3}$$

$$y_i = y_c + h_i \cdot \sin \theta_i = y_c + \frac{r_m}{y_m} \cdot y \cdot sin(\frac{2\pi}{x_m} \cdot x) \tag{4}$$

We used the unwarping by two dimensional DCT (discrete cosine transform) of the omnidirectional input image, as described in [21], instead of the usual but less precise pixel interpolation methods. The main advantage of this approach becomes apparent when performing the radial edge-finding needed for our stereo (see the next section).

See Figure 6 for the unwarping applied to a hyperbolic mirror image and Figure 7 for the unwarping of a conical mirror image. Note that the conical mirror image utilises better the available vertical resolution of the image. This provides better resolution for stereopsis, though the resolution near the tip of the mirror is clearly limited.

Fig. 6. Unwarping of Figure 1.

Fig. 7. Unwarping of Figure 2.

3 Coaxial Stereopsis

Various arrangements have been proposed for binocular systems using catadioptric sensors. Two mirrors situated side by side can be used to compute the distance of objects in terms of the disparity measured as the arising difference in angles θ [24]. However, such arrangement is not truly omnidirectional, as a large part of the scene will be obstructed by the other catadioptric sensor.

It is better to arrange the cameras coaxially to avoid this problem. The coaxial arrangement has the further major advantage of having simple aligned radial epipolar lines. Lin and Bajczy [27] used a single conical mirror and attempted to place two cameras at different distances along its axis. They had to use a beamsplitter to avoid the nearer camera obstructing the view of the more distant camera. See Figure 8. We propose an omnidirectional stereo system consisting

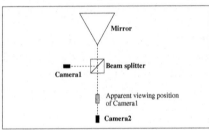

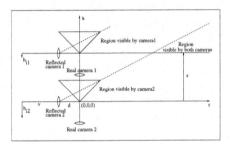

Fig. 8. Lin and Bajcsy's omnidirectional stereo using a single conical mirror and two cameras at different distances. The beam splitter avoids an obstruction of the second camera's view but reduces the amount of available light.

Fig. 9. Omnidirectional stereo using two coaxial mirrors.

of two coaxial conical mirrors pointing in the same direction, each with its own camera. See Figure 9.

We wish to obtain a triangulation formula for the radial distance of objects r. The radial distance is measured from the axis of the mirror(s) to any 3D scene point P, which has to be in the region that is visible by both cameras (the common region). See Figure 9. The common region is annular in shape in 3D, with a triangular cross-section extending to infinity. It is bounded above and below in the (r, h) plane by the lines: $h = R\frac{r+d}{R+d}$, and $h = s$. The angle at the tip of the common region triangle is $\frac{\phi}{2}$. The distance r_{min} of the tip is: $r_{min} = s(\frac{d}{R} + 1) - d$. Stereopsis cannot be employed anywhere nearer than r_{min}.

In order to obtain the triangulation formula, we subtracted two instances of equation (1) for two coaxial mirrors separated by distance s (s is measured along the h axis). We assume here that the parameters v and d are the same for both cameras, though this assumption can be easily relaxed if necessary.

$$r = \frac{vs}{h_{i2} - h_{i1}} - d \tag{5}$$

This is very similar to the usual triangulation formula from classical side-by-side stereopsis but here the disparity $h_{i2} - h_{i1}$, is the radial disparity. The extra distance d is correctly subtracted. The similarity of the formulae is not surprising, as the two reflected (virtual) cameras resemble a classical side-by-side system within the plane of orientation θ.

Fig. 10. Edge map of the unwarped image in Figure 7.

3.1   Radial Edge Finding and Matching

The radial epipolar matching is driven by edges whose gradient is primarily in the radial direction. We find those by the radial edge-finder using the DCT and the polar coordinates (h_i, θ_i) of the input image, as described in [21]. The main benefit of this approach is that the slow unwarping process is avoided. We also obtain the partial derivatives of the image function in h_i and θ_i directions, which is going to be useful for a polar optic flow.

The unwarping is needed only for the convenience of human viewing, such as in Figure 10, showing a traditional edge map of the unwarped image, using [28]. The stereopsis correspondence computation is driven primarily by the horizontal edges in this example.

The radial edge finding consists of the following steps:

1. Perform forward DCT transform on the omnidirectional input image, using (x_i, y_i) coordinates.

2. Convert the input image coordinates at which the radial gradient component is to be computed from the rectangular form (x_i, y_i) to the polar form (h_i, θ_i) and substitute to the normal inverse DCT function.

3. Apply the radial edge function (ref) defined in [21]. This function was obtained by partial differentiation of the inverse DCT transform in polar coordinates with respect to h_i.

In other words, we are differentiating the inverse transform function instead of differentiating the image. This is legitimate as the DCT has a finite number of terms. The output is the desired radial edge map in the same format as the original input image, ie. it is the radial edge map of the circular mirror in the rectangular image coordinates (x_i, y_i). Similar process can be followed to find the partial derivatives of an image in θ direction, or higher derivatives.

The radial edge finder should be of interest to omnidirectional vision generally, as it can be used with any rotationally symmetric mirror. The unwarping is unnecessary when using autonomous vision methods that work in polar coordinates.

It is not necessary to generate the entire rectangular edge map of the second image when doing the stereo matching. The ref can be evaluated at any randomly selected points with sub-pixel accuracy. The outline of the radial stereo matching algorithm is as follows:

1. Given a pair of stereo images f_1 and f_2, find all feature points in f_1 where $abs(\frac{\partial f_1(x_i,y_i)}{\partial h_i})$ is significant ($abs()$ is the absolute value function).

2. Find out the θ_i value of the selected feature point.

3. Keeping θ_i fixed, evaluate ref along the epipolar radial line in f_2 and store the image gradient vectors for both epipolar lines in two buffers.

4. Match the buffers looking for similar values of the gradient vectors and paying attention to sensible ordering of the matches plus any other stereopsis matching tricks.

5. Compute the distance of objects for all successful matches, using the matched radial position values h_{i1} and h_{i2} and the triangulation equation (5).

6. Move to the next value of θ_i which has significant image feature(s) and repeat from 2.

There are other sophisticated stereo matching methods that could be adapted to these circumstances, for example [29].

3.2   Steropsis Discussion and Results

In the illustrated arrangement the view is directed at the horizon, which is normally rich in natural visual features of high contrast that are useful for outdoors navigation [7]. For closer visual guidance indoors, the entire apparatus can be simply inverted. The visible regions will lie either above or below the horizontal plane touching the tip of the mirror, respectively. For very close range stereo, we suggest inverting just the top mirror and camera, so that the tips of the mirrors are facing away from each other. In each case the following triangulation and matching will be much the same. The only combination to be avoided for stereopsis is the one with the tips of the mirrors facing each other, as this would result in no common region visible by both cameras.

Our arrangement is quite different from that proposed by Lin and Bajczy. The resulting triangulation formula is different. Our system is simpler, there is no loss of light through the beam splitter, and we gain better image quality by being able to view large size conical mirrors.

Lin and Bajczy did not specify a 90° angle at the tip of their mirror so our perspective projection, as described in section 2, has different specific properties.

We have tested our stereopsis method on artificial images with known ground truth (admittedly not as demanding a test as using real images) and found the errors in r to grow linearly with $r + d$. The errors are a function of the image resolution, so for a fixed r, they are inversely proportional to h. This means that the errors are smaller for points imaged nearer the edge of the mirror, where the θ resolution is better. There is a good agreement between our results and a theoretical error prediction based on differentiation of the perspective projection formula.

4   Conclusion

This paper has identified the conical mirror as a good solution for catadioptric omnidirectional sensors.

The benefits of conical mirrors had been hitherto mostly overlooked because of the demands for a single viewpoint projection. We conclude that the single viewpoint is not necessary for an accurate perspective projection when using the conical mirror with a 90° angle at the tip. Such conical mirrors provide a useful model of projection when viewed from any reasonable distance by an ordinary perspective camera. Conical mirrors are less sensitive to the precise distance of the camera than are hyperbolic and elliptic mirrors. The ability to view the mirror from a greater distance is desirable since it allows the use of larger mirrors with relatively better optical quality. Given the same physical surface quality (roughness), the optical quality will be proportional to the dimensions of the mirror. The radial distortion properties of conical mirrors are better when compared to other circular mirrors. Last but not least, conical mirrors direct the camera resolution into more useful parts of the surroundings and their resolution density is well behaved.

The unwarping methods and experiments demonstrated the concept of an accurate perspective projection via multiple viewpoints.

The benefits of the coaxial omnidirectional stereo system are both practical (objects do not disappear from view due to vehicle rotation), and theoretical/computational (the epipolar geometry is simpler than in classical stereopsis).

References

1. Swaminathan, R., Nayar, S.K.: Nonmetric calibration of wide-angle lenses and polycameras. IEEE Transactions on Pattern Analysis and Machine Intelligence **22** (2000) 1172–1178
2. Rees, D.: Panoramic television viewing system. US Patent No. 3,505,465 (1970)
3. Kang, S., Szeliski, R.: 3-d scene data recovery using omnidirectional multibaseline stereo. IJCV **25** (1997) 167–183
4. Ishiguro, H., Yamamoto, M., Tsuji, S.: Omni-directional stereo. PAMI **14** (1992) 257–262
5. Shah, S., Aggarwal, J.: Mobile robot navigation and scene modeling using stereo fish-eye lens system. MVA **10** (1997) 159–173
6. Nayar, S.: Catadioptric omnidirectional cameras. In: CVPR97. (1997) 482–488
7. Rushant, K., Spacek, L.: An autonomous vehicle navigation system using panoramic vision techniques. In: International Symposium on Intelligent Robotic Systems, ISIRS98. (1998) 275–282
8. Pajdla, T., Hlavac, V.: Zero phase representation of panoramic images for image vased localization. In: Computer Analysis of Images and Patterns. (1999) 550–557

9. Yagi, Y., Nishii, W., Yamazawa, K., Yachida, M.: Rolling motion estimation for mobile robot by using omnidirectional image sensor hyperomnivision. In: ICPR96. (1996)

10. Yagi, Y., Nishizawa, Y., Yachida, M.: Map-based navigation for a mobile robot with omnidirectional image sensor copis. Trans. Robotics and Automation **11** (1995) 634–648

11. Baker, S., Nayar, S.: A theory of single-viewpoint catadioptric image formation. IJCV **32** (1999) 175–196

12. Baker, S., Nayar, S.: A theory of catadioptric image formation. In: ICCV98. (1998) 35–42

13. Geyer, C., Daniilidis, K.: A unifying theory for central panoramic systems and practical applications. In: ECCV00. (2000)

14. Geyer, C., Daniilidis, K.: Properties of the catadioptric fundamental matrix. In: ECCV02. Volume 2. (2002) 140 ff.

15. Baker, S., Nayar, S.: Single viewpoint catadioptric cameras. In: PV01. (2001) 39–71

16. Svoboda, T., Pajdla, T.: Epipolar geometry for central catadioptric cameras. IJCV **49** (2002) 23–37

17. Swaminathan, R. Grossberg, M., Nayar, S.: Caustics of catadioptric cameras. In: ICCV02. (2001)

18. Fiala, M., Basu, A.: Panoramic stereo reconstruction using non-svp optics. In: ICPR02. Volume 4. (2002) 27–30

19. Yagi, Y., Kawato, S.: Panoramic scene analysis with conic projection. In: IROS90. (1990)

20. Yokoya, N., Iwasa, H., Yamazawa, K., Kawanishi, T., Takemura, H.: Generation of high-resolution stereo panoramic images by omnidirectional imaging sensor using hexagonal pyramidal mirrors. In: ICPR98. (1998)

21. Spacek, L.: Omnidirectional catadioptric vision sensor with conical mirrors. In: Towards Intelligent Mobile Robotics, TIMR03. (2003)

22. Lin, S., Bajcsy, R.: True single view point cone mirror omni-directional catadioptric system. In: ICCV01. Volume 2. (2001) 102–107

23. Hicks, A., Bajscy, R.: Reactive surfaces as computational sensors. In: The second IEEE Workshop on Perception for Mobile Agents. Held in Conjunction with CVPR'99. (1999) 82–86

24. Brassart, E., et al.: Experimental results got with the omnidirectional vision sensor: Syclop. In: EEE Workshop on Omnidirectional Vision (OMNIVIS'00). (2000) 145–152

25. Geyer, C., Daniilidis, K.: Structure and motion from uncalibrated catadioptric views. In: CVPR01. Volume 1. (2001) 279–286

26. Geyer, C., Daniilidis, K.: Paracatadioptric camera calibration. IEEE PAMI **24** (2002) 1–10

27. Lin, S., Bajcsy, R.: High resolution catadioptric omni-directional stereo sensor for robot vision. In: IEEE International Conference on Robotics and Automation, Taipei, Taiwan. (2003) 12–17

28. Spacek, L.: Edge detection and motion detection. Image and Vision Computing **4** (1986) 43–56

29. Sara, R.: Finding the largest unambiguous component of stereo matching. In: ECCV (3). (2002) 900–914

Classifying Materials from Their Reflectance Properties

Peter Nillius and Jan-Olof Eklundh

Computational Vision & Active Perception Laboratory (CVAP)
Department of Numerical Analysis and Computer Science
Royal Institute of Technology (KTH), S-100 44 Stockholm, Sweden
{nillius,joe}@nada.kth.se

Abstract. We explore the possibility of recognizing the surface material from a single image with unknown illumination, given the shape of the surface.

Model-based PCA is used to create a low-dimensional basis to represent the images. Variations in the illumination create manifolds in the space spanned by this basis. These manifolds are learnt using captured illumination maps and the CUReT database. Classification of the material is done by finding the manifold closest to the point representing the image of the material.

Testing on synthetic data shows that the problem is hard. The materials form groups where the materials in a group often are mis-classifed as one of the other materials in the group. With a grouping algorithm we find a grouping of the materials in the CUReT database. Tests on images of real materials in natural illumination settings show promising results.

1   Introduction

The appearance of a surface depends on its shape, the illumination and the material of the surface. In a normal vision task none of these properties are known a priori. Despite that, human observers are very good at determining the material of an object, even in the absence of texture. The estimation is done purely based on the reflectance properties of the surface. We will explore if this can be done computationally when there is no knowledge about the illumination, but the shape of the object is known.

Recent research [2,11,10,8] has shown that the reflected light from a Lambertian surface can be represented with a low-dimensional model although the variations in illumination are infinite. This is because the surface acts as a low-pass filter on the incident illumination, making the images in practice lie in a low-dimensional subspace. Other work, [12,9], indicates that this holds for many other types of surface reflectance, e.g. many of the materials in the CUReT database, [3].

In this paper we classify the material of an object of known shape from a single image, when the illumination is unknown. In [4] Dror et al recognizes materials under similar assumptions. They use histograms of filter responses

T. Pajdla and J. Matas (Eds.): ECCV 2004, LNCS 3024, pp. 366–376, 2004.
© Springer-Verlag Berlin Heidelberg 2004

and rely on the structure of the specular reflections to classify the material. Our approach is different in that we represent the images using a generative model, allowing us to discriminate between materials without specular reflections such as felt and velvet.

2 A Low-Dimensional Generative Model for Image Irradiance

To find a basis to represent the images, we use the framework described in [9]. With this framework we can, for a given shape, construct a low-dimensional basis that can represent the images of an object of a wide variety of materials under more or less arbitrary illumination.

The basis is created using model-based PCA. Rather than performing PCA on a set of captured images, the PCA is analytically derived from the image formation model. This makes it possible to create a basis for a wide variety of conditions using a set of captured illumination maps and a database of surface reflectance functions (BRDF's). The illumination maps are undergoing all 3D rotations to take into account every possible lighting configuration.

The BRDF acts as a low-pass filter on the incident illumination, making the reflected light band-limited. Hence, by formulating the image formation in frequency space we can derive a finite dimensional model of the image irradiance even when the illumination is unknown and arbitrary. As in [2,11] the illumination is represented by its spherical harmonics coefficients, L_l^m. The BRDF is represented by its coefficients, b_{op}^q, in the basis by Koenderink and van Doorn, [5], based on the Zernike polynomials. Computing the image irradiance using these representations leads to a basis for image irradiance E. At this point we approximate the camera projection as orthographic which makes the image irradiance uniquely determined by the surface normal (α, β). This results in the representation

$$E(\alpha, \beta) = \sum_i c_i E_i(\alpha, \beta) \tag{1}$$

where $c_i = L_l^m b_{op}^q$ (l, m, o, p and q are given by i due to an ordering of the basis functions). The E_is are the image irradiance basis functions and are products of the Wigner D-functions (for real spherical harmonics) and the Zernike polynomials. See [9] for their explicit form.

The basis can represent the image irradiance from any isotropic surface under any illumination. In the general case an infinite number of basis functions are needed, but for many materials which act as low-pass filters on the illumination, the sum can be truncated and still be an accurate representation. This finite representation allows us to analytically derive the principal components. The variations in the illumination and surface reflectance properties are described by the covariance matrices of their respective coefficients, L_l^m and b_{op}^q. The resulting principal components are linear combinations of the basis functions E_i. See [9] for details.

When we use the PCA basis to represent images we assume that the illumination is the same for each point in the image. This assumptions is true if the light source is distant. It is also necessary that there are no cast shadows or local inter-reflections, which is true when the object shape is convex. For non-convex objects this model is an approximation, where the quality of the approximation depends on the concavities and the material/illumination conditions. For instance, bright objects will have stronger inter-reflections than dark objects.

An important property of model-based PCA is that we can relate the principal components to the properties of the illumination and surface reflectance. There is an explicit relation between the coefficients in the PCA basis to the coefficients of the illumination and the BRDF. From the coefficients of illumination and BRDF, the coefficients, $\mathbf{d}$, in the PCA space can be computed by a simple matrix product

$$\mathbf{d} = \mathbf{Ac}. \tag{2}$$

where the elements of $\mathbf{c}$ are $c_i = L_l^m b_{op}^q$. The PCA basis as well as the matrix $\mathbf{A}$ are computed from the shape of object and the variations in the illumination and BRDF.

Another important aspect of the PCA basis regards robustness. The first basis function is selected so that it maximizes the signal variance of the component it represent. The subsequent basis functions maximize the same variance while being orthogonal to all the previous functions. This means that the first basis function has the highest signal-to-noise ratio (SNR), on average, hence being the most robust component to estimate. The following components will be less and less robust to estimate. In other words, selecting the number of basis functions to use is not just a question of saving computer memory and computation time, but also a question of robustness and regularization.

3   Material Recognition

Our approach to material recognition is to estimate the coefficients in the basis described in the previous section from the images and compare them to a database of known materials.

Since the illumination is not known we cannot calculate what the corresponding coefficients should be for the materials in the database. We need to take into account all possible illuminations and find the illumination-material pair that best matches the image. For this to be possible it is necessary that the variations in the coefficient space are much smaller than the variations in the illumination (which are infinite). If this is true we can learn the variations in the coefficient space with only a limited amount of training illuminations.

Smooth variations in the illumination result in a manifold of points in the coefficient space. To learn these manifolds we take a set of illumination maps and rotate them over all rotations. To store the manifolds we sample them by sampling the rotation group $SO(3)$ and calculate the coefficients for each sample point for every illumination map and material.

The image is classified by finding the manifold which is closest to the point representing the image. The procedure is very much the same as in [7].

3.1   Learning the Manifolds

The manifold for each material is learnt from a set of illumination maps that are rotated over the full rotation group. The rotation group is sampled and for each rotation (α, β, γ) the spherical harmonic coefficients of the rotated illumination map are calculated. The point on the manifold is given by equation (2).

To sample the rotation group we sample the surface of a sphere and combine it with a circle. The sphere is sampled by starting from an icosahedron inscribed in the sphere. The icosahedron is recursively subdivided by projecting the midpoint of each edge onto the surface of the sphere forming four new triangles for each old triangle, [1]. The circle is sampled at a density as close as possible to the sampling of the sphere.

3.2   Finding the Closest Manifold

To find the closest manifold to a point we simply go through all points on each manifold and calculate the distance to the point to be classified. The distance measure is the sum of squared differences in coefficient space.

To aid our algorithm in being illumination invariant we take a number of steps. The first element of the point is discarded. It corresponds to the constant function of the basis and captures the variations in the ambient component of the illumination. By discarding it the algorithm becomes independent of such variations.

The remaining elements are normalized to get brightness independence. It also means that we will not be able to differentiate between bright and dark materials, although this could be added at a later stage by comparing the signal variances of the images.

4   Discrimination of Materials in the CUReT Database

Before we move on to real images we need to assess what can be done. How well can materials be discriminated from their reflectance properties alone? Figure 1 demonstrates that many materials look similar to the human eye.

To test this we will analyze how well the materials in the CUReT database can be discriminated in synthetic images, i.e. when there is no noise. The illumination is considered to be unknown. The algorithm is tested on images generated from one of the illumination maps, while the other illumination maps are used to build the manifolds for classification. This is repeated for all nine illumination maps (the leave-one-out principle).

We don't actually need to generate any images. Using the low-dimensional basis framework described in Section 2 we can directly from the illumination and material coefficients compute the coefficients in the low-dimensional basis of the

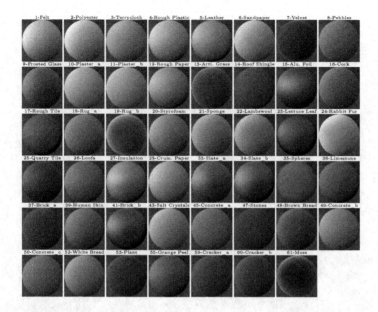

Fig. 1. Rendered images using BRDFs from the CUReT database. Classifying materials from their reflectance properties can be very hard, as is in this case. If you disregard the color many materials look very similar.

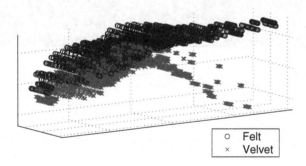

Fig. 2. Sampled manifolds in the coefficient space of materials 1-Felt (blue rings) and 7-Velvet (red crosses) under one of the illumination maps undergoing all 3D rotations, $SO(3)$.

image. This allows for extensive testing. Each of the 48 materials used is tested with nine illumination maps, each under 462 different rotations, summing up to a total of 200 000 images used for testing.

Figure 3 shows the classification rates for the different materials. The correct classification rates, which can be seen in the diagonal, range between 5 and 80 percent. Materials with a high classification rate are 7-velvet and 61-moss which

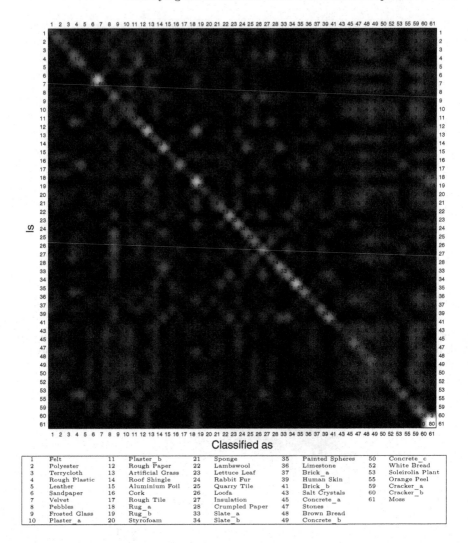

Fig. 3. Recognition rates for the CUReT materials. Each row shows the classification rates for a particular materials, e.g. the leftmost element in the first row is the rate that material no. 1 is classified as materials no. 1, the second element is the rate the material one is classified as material no. 2. The diagonal is the correct classification rate. These results are discussed more in the text.

have particular reflectance properties. Glossy materials have in general a higher recognition rate than matte materials.

What is interesting is that the materials seem to form groups, where a material in a group systematically is being mis-classified as one of the other materials in that same group. This becomes apparent when we order the materials in a particular way. Figure 4 shows the exact same classification rates as Figure 3,

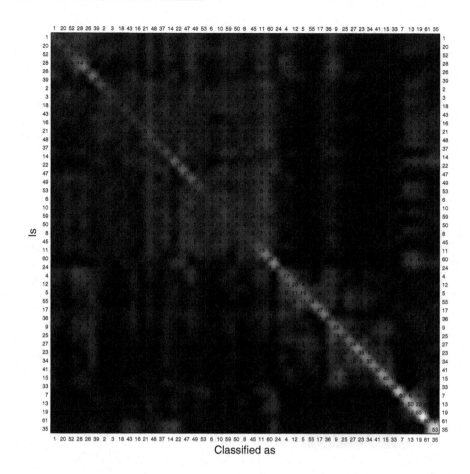

Fig. 4. When the classification rates from Figure 3 are sorted in a particular way a pattern emerge. The materials form groups. Materials within a group often are classified as one of the other materials in the same group. The largest group can be seen as a grey block in the top left corner of the matrix. These are the matte materials, 1-Felt, 20-Styrofoam, ..., 24-Rabbit Fur. After the matte materials comes a group of more glossy materials, 12-Rough Plastic, ..., 36-Limestone. Next comes a group of shiny materials 9-Frosted Glass to 33-Slate_a. Last is a group of materials with asperity type scattering, 7-Velvet, 13-Artificial Grass, 19-Rug_b and 61-Moss.

but with the materials ordered using a hierarchical grouping algorithm that will be described in the next section. We begin to distinguish blocks in the diagonal of the matrix. There is a large block of matte materials in the top left corner, formed by the materials 1-Felt, 20-Styrofoam, ..., 24-Rabbit Fur. Following the matte materials is a group of glossy materials, 4-Rough Plastic , ..., 15-Foil. Last comes 7-Velvet and a group of velvet-like appearance (asperity scattering), 13-Art. Grass, 19-Rug_b and 61-Moss. Finally we have 35-Painted Spheres which forms a group of its own.

4.1 Visual Grouping of the Materials

It is clear that we cannot expect to distinguish between some of the materials in the CUReT database. Instead we can try to find groups in which to classify the materials.

Using the matrix containing the classification rates we group the materials. The grouping is done in a greedy fashion. We start with groups of single materials. Then the two groups that maximize the average recognition rate are joined. This is repeated until the desired number of groups is reached. To select the number of groups one can e.g. look at the ratio between the recognition rates and the rate of selecting the correct material by chance.

Dividing the CUReT database into 9 groups results in the grouping in Figure 5. We have labeled the groups according to the characteristics of their members. All matte materials end up in one group. Materials having specular reflectance are split up in three groups. The last five groups are materials that did not fit into any group. These materials have a high recognition rate on their own.

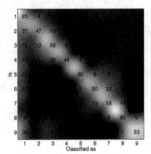

Group	Members	Label
1	1, 2, 3, 6, 8, 10, ...	Matte
2	4, 5, 12, 17, 36, 55	Glossy
3	9, 23, 25, 27, 34, 41	Shiny
4	15, 33	Shinier
5	7	Velvet
6	13	Art. Grass
7	19	Rug
8	61	Moss
9	35	Spheres

Fig. 5. Classification rates when the materials are grouped into nine groups. Not all members were listed in the matte group due to space limitations, but this group contains all materials that are not in the other groups.

More or less all the groups are sometimes mis-classified as matte materials. This makes sense. In the testing we take all rotations of the illumination into account. This means that sometimes the dominant light source in the scene will be behind the object. Hence, there will be no specularity on the object to differentiate it from a matte material.

5 Classifying the Material in Real Images

To test the algorithm we glued five different real materials onto cylinders, see Figure 6. Cylinders were chosen due to the difficulty of gluing a non-stretchable materials onto a sphere. The cylinders where photographed using a digital camera in different illumination conditions, including outdoor sunny, outdoor cloudy

Fig. 6. The algorithm was tested on images of cylinders with the pieces of five different real materials glued onto them. Top row from left to right: felt, velvet 1, velvet 2, leather and imitation leather. Bottom row: leather in five of the different illumination conditions.

and indoor with indirect light from a window. Before classification the images were radiometricly calibrated, using the method in [6]. The geometry of the cylinders were estimated by manually marking where in the image the cylinders were.

Using the framework from Section 2 we computed a basis for the cylinder. A total of six basis functions were used in the experiments. The coefficients for the image were estimated by projecting the image onto the basis. The image was then classified by finding the closest manifold as described in Section 3. The manifolds were this time learned using all nine illumination maps.

Figure 7 shows some of the images being classified. Note how well the basis is able to represent the image irradiance in all cases.

A total of 84 images were used in the experiment. Table 1 summarizes the results. As predicted by the synthetic experiments only a few of the images where correctly classified on an individual basis. Felt and the two velvets have a recognition rate of 5% to 7.7%, which is still several times greater than chance, which is $1/48 \approx 2.1\%$. When using the grouping in Figure 5 the recognition rates are higher. Felt is to a large extent classified as matte. The leather here is classified as Shiny or Shinier, while the leather in the database is categorized as Glossy. This could be because our leather is shiner than the leather in the database. Visually, at least, it appears so. The imitation leather is also mostly classified as Shiny or Shinier.

So far the results match the synthetic results fairly well. The velvet however does not. The synthetic results indicate that velvet should be fairly easy to recognize, but in our experiments the two velvet cylinders are mostly classified as matte. On the other hand, they are also often classified as one the groups Grass, Rug and Moss, which have the same type of surface reflectance as Velvet.

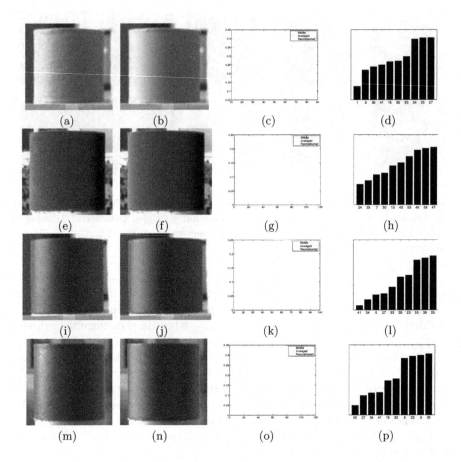

Fig. 7. Examples of classified images: (a)-(d) images for Felt. (a) calibrated gray image, (b) reconstructed gray image (this is what the algorithm "sees"), (c) image and reconstructed intensity profiles. (d) distances to the ten closest materials. Here the material is correctly classified as felt. (e)-(h) show the same images for Velvet 1. The material is here incorrectly classified as 24-Rabbit Fur, 7-Velvet comes third place. (i)-(l) images for leather which in this case is classified as 41-Brick_b, 5-Leather is the third closest material. (m)-(p) imitation leather: classified as 55-Orange, 5-Leather on seventh place. Notice how well the basis represent the irradiance for the different cases.

Table 1. Classification Rates for the Cylinder Images

Material	Correct	Matte	Glossy	Shiny	Shinier	Velvet	Grass	Rug	Moss	Spheres
Felt	7.7	77	7.7	0	15	0	0	0	0	0
Leather	0	25	6.2	44	19	6.2	0	0	0	0
Im. Leather	0	10	0	40	35	10	0	0	0	5
Velvet 1	5	55	0	5	5	5	10	10	10	0
Velvet 2	6.7	40	0	33	0	6.7	0	13	6.7	0

6   Conclusions

We have investigated the problem of classifying the surface material from a single image with unknown illumination, given the surface shape.

Recognizing materials from their reflectance properties is hard. We cannot expect to distinguish between many of the materials in the CUReT database. Instead we should find groups in which to classify the materials.

The grouping produced by our algorithm suggests that we can expect to distinguish between matte materials, special materials such as velvet and materials of different grades of shininess.

Acknowledgments. This work was done within the EU-IST project IST-2000-29688 Insight2+. The support is gratefully acknowledged.

References

1. D.H. Ballard and C.M. Brown. *Computer Vision.* Prentice-Hall, 1982.
2. R. Basri and D. Jacobs. Lambertian reflectance and linear subspaces. *IEEE Trans. Pattern Analysis and Machine Intelligence*, 25(2):218–233, February 2003.
3. K.J. Dana, B. van Ginneken, S.K. Nayar, and J.J. Koenderink. Reflectance and texture of real-world surfaces. *ACM Transactions on Graphics*, 18(1):1–34, January 1999.
4. R.O. Dror, E.H. Adelson, and A.S. Willsky. Recognition of surface reflectance properties from a single image under unknown real-world illumination. In *Workshop of recognizing objects under varying illumination*, 2001.
5. J.J. Koenderink and A.J. van Doorn. Phenomenological description of bidirectional surface reflection. *J. Optical Soc. of Am. A*, 15(11):2903–2912, November 1998.
6. T. Mitsunaga and S.K. Nayar. Radiometric self calibration. In *Proc. Computer Vision and Pattern Recognition*, pages I: 374–380, 1999.
7. H. Murase and S.K. Nayar. Visual learning and recognition of 3-d objects from appearance. *Int. Journal of Computer Vision*, 14(1):5–24, January 1995.
8. P. Nillius and J.O. Eklundh. Low-dimensional representations of shaded surfaces under varying illumination. In *Proc. Computer Vision and Pattern Recognition*, pages II:185–192, 2003.
9. P. Nillius and J.O. Eklundh. Phenomenological eigenfunctions for image irradiance. In *International Conference on Computer Vision*, pages 568–575, 2003.
10. R. Ramamoorthi. Analytic pca construction for theoretical analysis of lighting variability in images of a lambertian object. *IEEE Trans. Pattern Analysis and Machine Intelligence*, 24(10):1322–1333, October 2002.
11. R. Ramamoorthi and P. Hanrahan. On the relationship between radiance and irradiance: determining the illumination from images of a convex lambertian object. *J. Optical Soc. of Am. A*, 18(10):2448–2458, October 2001.
12. R. Ramamoorthi and Hanrahan P. A signal-processing framework for inverse rendering. In *SIGGRAPH*, 2001.

Seamless Image Stitching in the Gradient Domain*

Anat Levin, Assaf Zomet**, Shmuel Peleg, and Yair Weiss

School of Computer Science and Engineering
The Hebrew University of Jerusalem
91904, Jerusalem, Israel
{alevin,peleg,yweiss}@cs.huji.ac.il, zomet@cs.columbia.edu

Abstract. Image stitching is used to combine several individual images having some overlap into a composite image. The quality of image stitching is measured by the similarity of the stitched image to each of the input images, and by the visibility of the seam between the stitched images.

In order to define and get the best possible stitching, we introduce several formal cost functions for the evaluation of the quality of stitching. In these cost functions, the similarity to the input images and the visibility of the seam are defined in the gradient domain, minimizing the disturbing edges along the seam. A good image stitching will optimize these cost functions, overcoming both photometric inconsistencies and geometric misalignments between the stitched images.

This approach is demonstrated in the generation of panoramic images and in object blending. Comparisons with existing methods show the benefits of optimizing the measures in the gradient domain.

1 Introduction

Image stitching is a common practice in the generation of panoramic images and applications such as object insertion, super resolution [1] and texture synthesis [2]. An example of image stitching is shown in Figure 1. Two images I_1,I_2 capture different portions of the same scene, with an overlap region viewed in both images. The images should be stitched to generate a mosaic image I. A simple pasting of a left region from I_1 and a right region from I_2 produces visible artificial edges in the seam between the images, due to differences in camera gain, scene illumination or geometrical misalignments.

The aim of a stitching algorithm is to produce a visually plausible mosaic with two desirable properties: First, the mosaic should be as *similar* as possible to the input images, both geometrically and photometrically. Second, the seam between the stitched images should be *invisible*. While these requirements are

---

* This research was supported (in part) by the EU under the Presence Initiative through contract IST-2001-39184 BENOGO.
** Current Address: Computer Science Department, Columbia University, 500 West 120th Street, New York, NY 10027

T. Pajdla and J. Matas (Eds.): ECCV 2004, LNCS 3024, pp. 377–389, 2004.
© Springer-Verlag Berlin Heidelberg 2004

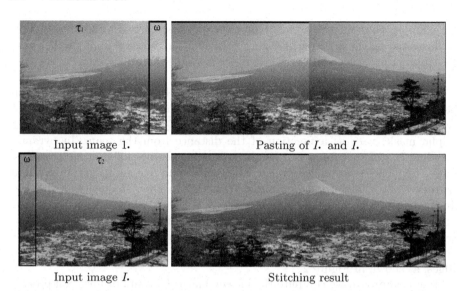

Input image 1.   Pasting of I. and I.

Input image I.   Stitching result

Fig. 1. Image stitching. On the left are the input images. ω is the overlap region. On top right is a simple pasting of the input images. On the bottom right is the result of the GIST1 algorithm.

widely acceptable for visual examination of a stitching result, their definition as quality criteria was either limited or implicit in previous approaches.

In this work we present several cost functions for these requirements, and define the mosaic image as their optimum. The stitching quality in the seam region is measured in the gradient domain. The mosaic image should contain a minimal amount of seam artifacts, i.e. a seam should not introduce a new edge that does not appear in either I_1 or I_2. As image dissimilarity, the gradients of the mosaic image I are compared with the gradients of I_1, I_2. This reduces the effects caused by global inconsistencies between the stitched images. We call our framework GIST: Gradient-domain Image STitching.

We demonstrate this approach in panoramic mosaicing and object blending. Analytical and experimental comparisons of our approach to existing methods show the benefits in working in the gradient domain, and in directly minimizing gradient artifacts.

1.1 Related Work

There are two main approaches to image stitching in the literature, assuming that the images have already been aligned. Optimal seam algorithms[3,2,4] search for a curve in the overlap region on which the differences between I_1, I_2 are minimal. Then each image is copied to the corresponding side of the seam. In case the difference between I_1, I_2 on the curve is zero, no seam gradients are produced in the mosaic image I. However, the seam is visible when there is no such curve, for example when there is a global intensity difference between the images. This is illustrated on the first row of Figure 2. In addition, optimal seam methods are less appropriate when thin strips are taken from the input images, as in the case of manifold mosaicing [5].

The second approach minimizes seam artifacts by smoothing the transition between the images. In Feathering [6] or alpha blending, the mosaic image I is a weighted combination of the input images I_1, I_2. The weighting coefficients (alpha mask) vary as a function of the distance from the seam. In pyramid blending[7], different frequency bands are combined with different alpha masks. Lower frequencies are mixed over a wide region, and fine details are mixed in a narrow region. This produces gradual transition in lower frequencies, while reducing edge duplications in textured regions. A related approach was suggested in [8], where a smooth function was added to the input images to force a consistency between the images in the seam curve. In case there are misalignments between the images[6], these methods leave artifacts in the mosaic such as double edges, as shown in Figure 2.

In our approach we compute the mosaic image I by an optimization process that uses image gradients. Computation in the gradient domain was recently used in compression of dynamic range[9], image editing [10], image inpainting [11] and separation of images to layers [12,13,14,15]. The closest work to ours was done by Perez et. al. [10], who suggest to edit images by manipulating their gradients. One application is object insertion, where an object is cut from an image, and inserted to a new background image. The insertion is done by optimizing over the derivatives of the inserted object, with the boundary determined by the background image. In sections 4, 5 we compare our approach to [10].

2   GIST: Image Stitching in the Gradient Domain

We describe two approaches to image stitching in the gradient domain. Section 2.1 describes GIST1, where the mosaic image is inferred directly from the derivatives of the input images. Section 2.2 describes GIST2, a two-steps approach to image stitching. Section 2.3 compares the two approaches to each other, and with other methods.

2.1   GIST1: Optimizing a Cost Function over Image Derivatives

The first approach, GIST1, computes the stitched image by minimizing a cost function E_p. E_p is a dissimilarity measure between the derivatives of the stitched image and the derivatives of the input images.

Specifically, let I_1, I_2 be two aligned input images. Let τ_1 (τ_2 resp.) be the region viewed exclusively in image I_1 (I_2 resp.), and let ω be the overlap region, as shown in Figure 1, with $\tau_1 \cap \tau_2 = \tau_1 \cap \omega = \tau_2 \cap \omega = \emptyset$. Let W be a weighting mask image.

Inp. image 1.	Inp. image 1.	Feathering	Pyr. blending	Opt. Seam	GIST
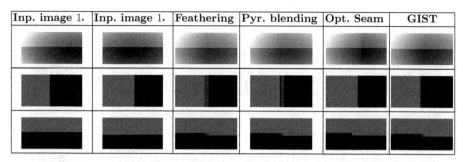					

Fig. 2. Comparing stitching methods with various sources for inconsistencies between the input images. The left side of $I.$ is stitched to right side of $I..$. Optimal seam methods produce a seam artifact in case of photometric inconsistencies between the images (first row). Feathering and pyramid blending produce double edges in case of horizontal misalignments (second row). In case there is a vertical misalignments (third row), the stitching is less visible with Feathering and GIST.

The stitching result I of GIST1 is defined as the minimum of E_p with respect to $\hat{I}$:

$$E_p\left(\hat{I}; I_1, I_2, W\right) = d_p(\nabla\hat{I}, \nabla I_1, \tau_1 \cup \omega, W) + d_p(\nabla\hat{I}, \nabla I_2, \tau_2 \cup \omega, U - W) \quad (1)$$

where U is a uniform image, and $d_p(J., J., \phi, W)$ is the distance between $J., J.$ on ϕ:

$$d_p(J_1, J_2, \phi, W) = \sum_{q \in \phi} W(q) \parallel J_1(q) - J_2(q) \parallel_p^p \quad (2)$$

with $\parallel \cdot \parallel_p$ denoting the ℓ_p-norm.

The dissimilarity E_p between the images is defined by the distance between their derivatives. A dissimilarity in the gradient domain is invariant to the mean intensity of the image. In addition it is less sensitive to smooth global differences between the input images, e.g. due to non-uniformness in the camera photometric response and due to scene shading variations. On the overlap region ω, the cost function E_p penalizes for derivatives which are inconsistent with any of the input images. In image locations where both I_1 and I_2 have low gradients, E_p penalizes for high gradient values in the mosaic image. This property is useful in eliminating false stitching edges.

The choice of norm (parameter p) has implications on both the optimization algorithm and the mosaic image. The minimization of E_p (Equation 1) for $p \geq 1$ is convex, and hence efficient optimization algorithms can be used. Section 3 describes a minimization scheme for E_2 by existing algorithms, and a novel fast minimization scheme for E_1. The mask image W was either a uniform mask (for E_1) or the Feathering mask (for E_2), which is linear with the signed-distance from the seam. The influence of the choice of p on the result image is addressed in the following sections, with the introduction of alternative stitching algorithms in the gradient domain.

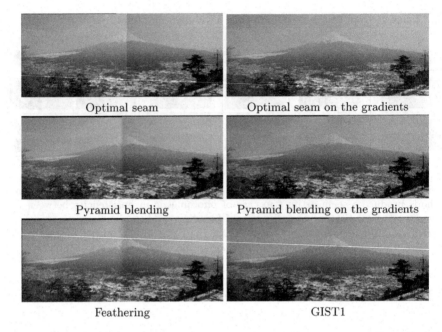

Optimal seam   Optimal seam on the gradients

Pyramid blending   Pyramid blending on the gradients

Feathering   GIST1

Fig. 3. Stitching in the gradient domain. The input images appear in Figure 1, with the overlap region marked by a black rectangle. With the image domain methods (top panels) the stitching is observable. Gradient-domain methods (bottom panels) overcome global inconsistencies.

2.2   GIST2: Stitching Derivative Images

A simpler approach is to stitch the derivatives of the input images:

1. Compute the derivatives of the input images $\frac{\partial I_1}{\partial x}, \frac{\partial I_1}{\partial y}, \frac{\partial I_2}{\partial x}, \frac{\partial I_2}{\partial y}$.
2. Stitch the derivative images to form a field $F = (F_x, F_y)$. F_x is obtained by stitching $\frac{\partial I_1}{\partial x}$ and $\frac{\partial I_2}{\partial x}$, and F_y is obtained by stitching $\frac{\partial I_1}{\partial y}$ and $\frac{\partial I_2}{\partial y}$.
3. Find the mosaic image whose gradients are closest to F. This is equivalent to minimizing $d_p(\nabla I, F, \pi, U)$ where π is the entire image area and U is a uniform image.

In stage (2) above, any stitching algorithm may be used. We have experimented with Feathering, pyramid blending [7], and optimal seam. For the optimal seam we used the algorithm in [2], finding the curve $x = f(y)$ that minimizes the sum of absolute differences in the input images. Stage (3), the optimization under ℓ_1, ℓ_2, is described in Section 3. Unlike the GIST1 algorithm described in the previous section, we found minor differences in the result images when minimizing d_p under ℓ_1 and ℓ_2.

2.3   Which Method to Use?

In the previous sections we presented several stitching methods. Since stitching results are tested visually, selecting the most appropriate method may be subject to personal taste. However, a formal analysis of properties of these methods is provided below. Based on those properties in conjunction with the experiments in Section 4, we recommend using GIST1 under ℓ_1.

Theorem 1. *Let I_1, I_2 be two input images for a stitching algorithm, and assume there is a curve $x = f(y)$, such that for each $q \in \{(f(y), y)\}$, $I_1(q) = I_2(q)$. Let U be a uniform image. Then the optimal seam solution I, defined below, is a global minimum of $E_p(I; I_1, I2, U)$ defined in Eq.1, for any $0 < p \leq 1$.*

$$I = \begin{cases} I_1(x, y) & x < f(y) \\ I_2(x, y) & x \geq f(y) \end{cases}$$

The reader is referred to [16] for a proof. The theorem implies that GIST1 under ℓ_1 is as good as the optimal seam methods when a perfect seam exists. Hence the power of GIST1 under ℓ_1 to overcome geometric misalignments similarly to the optimal seam methods. The advantage of GIST1 over optimal seam methods is when there is no perfect seam, for example due to photometric inconsistencies between the input images. This was validated in the experiments.

We also show an equivalence between GIST1 under ℓ_2 and Feathering of derivatives (GIST2) under ℓ_2 (Note that feathering derivatives is different from Feathering the images).

Theorem 2. *Let I_1, I_2 be two input images for a stitching algorithm, and let W be a Feathering mask. Let ω, the overlap region of I_1, I_2, be the entire image (without loss of generality, as $W(q) = 1$ for $q \in \tau_1$, and $W = 0$ for $q \in \tau_2$). Let I_{Gist} be the minimum of $E_2(I; I_1, I_2, W)$ defined in Eq. 1. Let F be the following field:*

$$F = W(q)\nabla I_1(q) + (1 - W(q))\nabla I_2(q)$$

Then I_{Gist} is the image with the closest gradient field to F under ℓ_2.

The proof can be found in [16] as well. This provides insight into the difference between GIST1 under ℓ_1 and under ℓ_2: Under ℓ_2, the algorithm tends to mix the derivatives and hence blur the texture in the overlap region. Under ℓ_1, the algorithm tends to behave similarly to the optimal seam methods, while reducing photometric inconsistencies.

3   Implementation Details

We have implemented a minimization for Equation 1 under ℓ_1 and under ℓ_2.

Equation 1 defines a set of linear equations in the image intensities, with the derivative filters as the coefficients. Similarly to [12,13], we found that good results are obtained when the derivatives are approximated by forward-differencing filters $\frac{1}{2}[1 \quad -1]$. In the ℓ_1 case, the results were further enhanced by incorporating additional equations using derivative filters in multiple scales. In our experiments we added the filter corresponding to forward-differencing in the 2nd level of a Gaussian pyramid, obtained by convolving the filter $[1 \ 0 \ -1]$ with a vertical and a horizontal Gaussian filter ($\frac{1}{4}[1 \ 2 \ 1]$). Color images were handled by applying the algorithm to each of the color channels separately.

The minimum to Equation 1 under ℓ_2 with mask W is shown in [16] to be the image with the closest derivatives under ℓ_2 to F, the weighted combination of the derivatives of the input images:

$$F = \begin{cases} W(\boldsymbol{q})\nabla I_1(\boldsymbol{p}) & \boldsymbol{q} \in \tau_1 \\ W(\boldsymbol{q})\nabla I_1(x,y) + (1 - W(\boldsymbol{q}))\nabla I_2(x,y)) & \boldsymbol{q} \in \omega \\ \nabla I_2(x,y) & \boldsymbol{q} \in \tau_2 \end{cases}$$

The solution can be obtained by various methods, e.g. de-convolution [12], FFT [17] or multigrid solvers [18]. The results presented in this paper were obtained by FFT.

As for the ℓ_1 optimization, we found using a uniform mask U to be sufficient. Solving the linear equations under ℓ_1 can be done by linear programming[19]:

$$Min : \textstyle\sum_i (z_i^+ + z_i^-)$$
$$Subject \ \ to : Ax + (z^+ - z^-) = b, x \geq 0, z^+ \geq 0, z^- \geq 0$$

The entries in matrix A are defined by the coefficients of the derivative filters, and the vector b contains the derivatives of I_1, I_2. x, is a vectorization of the result image.

The linear program was solved using LOQO[20]. A typical execution time for a 200×300 image on a Pentium 4 was around 2 minutes. Since no boundary conditions were used, the solution was determined up to a uniform intensity shift. This shift can be determined in various ways. We chose to set it according to the median of the values of the input image I_1 and the median of the corresponding region in the mosaic image.

3.1 Iterative ℓ_1 Optimization

A faster ℓ_1 optimization can be achieved by an iterative algorithm in the image domain. One way to perform this optimization is described in the following. Due to space limitation, we describe the algorithm when the forward differencing derivatives are used with kernel $\frac{1}{2}[1 \quad -1]$. The generalization to other filters and a parallel implementation appear in [16]. Let Dx_j, Dy_j be the forward-differences of input image I_j. The optimization is performed as follows:

- Initialize the solution image I
- Iterate until convergence:
  - for all x,y in the image, update $I(x,y)$ to be:

$$2 * median(\cup_j \{ \begin{matrix} I(x+1,y)-Dx_j(x,y), I(x-1,y)+Dx_j(x-1,y), \\ I(x,y+1)-Dy_j(x,y), I(x,y-1)+Dy_j(x,y-1) \end{matrix} \}) \quad (3)$$

For an even number of samples, the median is taken to be the average of the two middle samples. In regions τ_j where a single image I_j is used, the median is taken on the predictions of $I(x,y)$ given its four neighbours and the derivatives of image I_j. For example, when the derivatives of image I_j are 0, the algorithm performs an iterated median filter of the neighbouring pixels. In the overlap region ω of I_1, I_2, the median is taken over the predictions from both images.

At every iteration, the algorithm performs a coordinate descent and improves the cost function until convergence. As the cost function is bounded by zero, the algorithm always converges. However, although the cost function is convex, the algorithm does not always converge to the global optimum[1]. To improve the algorithm convergence and speed, we combined it in a multi-resolution scheme using multigrid [18]. In extensive experiments with the multi-resolution extension the algorithm always converged to the global optimum.

4   Experiments

We have implemented various versions of GIST and applied them to panoramic mosaicing and object blending.

First, we compared GIST to existing image stitching techniques, which work on the image intensity domain: Feathering [6], Pyramid Blending [7], and 'optimal seam' (Implemented as in [2]). The experiments (Figure 3) validated the advantage in working in the gradient for overcoming photometric inconsistencies. Second, we compared the results of GIST1 (Section 2.1), GIST2 (Section 2.2) and the method by Perez. et. al. [10]. Results of these comparisons are shown, for example, in Figures 4,5, and analyzed in the following sections.

4.1   Stitching Panoramic Views

The natural application for image stitching is the construction of panoramic pictures from multiple input pictures. Geometrical misalignments between input images are caused by lens distortions, by the presence of moving objects, and by motion parallax. Photometric inconsistencies between input images may be caused by a varying gain, by lens vignetting, by illumination changes, etc.

The input images for our experiments were captured from different camera positions, and were aligned by a $2D$ parametric transformation. The aligned images contained local misalignments due to parallax, and photometric inconsistencies due to differences in illumination and in camera gain. Mosaicing results are shown in Figures 3,4,5. Figure 3 compares gradient methods vs. image domain methods. Figure 4,5 demonstrate the performance of the stitching algorithms when the input images are misaligned. In all our experiments GIST1 under ℓ_1 gave the best results, in some cases comparable with other methods: In Figure 4 comparable with Feathering, and in 5 comparable with 'optimal seam'.

---

[*] Consider an image whose left part is white and the right part is black. When applying the algorithm on the derivatives of this image, the uniform image is a stationary point.

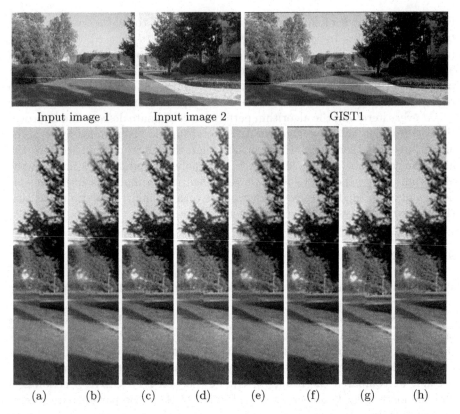

Fig. 4. Comparing various stitching methods. On top are the input image and the result of GIST1 under ℓ_*. The images on bottom are cropped results of various methods. (a)-Optimal seam, (b)-Feathering, (c)-Pyramid blending, (d)-Optimal seam on the gradients, (e)-Feathering on the gradients, (f)-Pyramid blending on the gradients, (g)-Poisson editing [10] and (h) GIST1 - ℓ_*. The seam is visible in (a),(c),(d),(g).

Whenever the input images were misaligned along the seam, GIST1 under ℓ_1 was superior to [10].

4.2 Stitching Object Parts

Here we combined images of objects of the same class having different appearances. Objects parts from different images were combined to generate the final image. This can be used, for example, by the police, in the construction of a suspect's composite portrait from parts of faces in the database. Figure 6 shows an example for this application, where GIST1 is compared to pyramid blending in the gradient domain. Another example for combination of parts is shown in Figure 7.

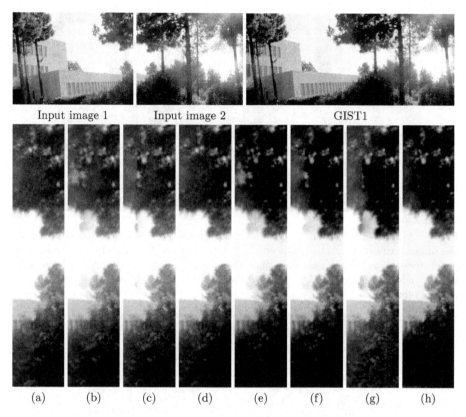

Input image 1   Input image 2   GIST1

(a)   (b)   (c)   (d)   (e)   (f)   (g)   (h)

Fig. 5. A comparison between various image stitching methods. On top are the input image and the result of GIST1 under $\ell_.$. The images on bottom are cropped from the results of various methods. (a)-Optimal seam, (b)-Feathering, (c)-Pyramid blending, (d)-Optimal seam on the gradients, (e)-Feathering on the gradients, (f)-Pyramid blending on the gradients, (g)-Poisson editing [10] and (h) GIST1 - $\ell_.$. When there are large misalignments, optimal seam and GIST1 produce less artifacts.

5   Discussion

A novel approach to image stitching was presented, with two main components: First, images are combined in the gradient domain rather than in the intensity domain. This reduces global inconsistencies between the stitched parts due to illumination changes and changes in the camera photometric response. Second, the mosaic image is inferred by optimization over image gradients, thus reducing seam artifacts and edge duplications. Experiments comparing gradient domain stitching algorithms and existing image domain stitching show the benefit of stitching in the gradient domain. Even though each stitching algorithm works better for some images and worse for others, we found that GIST1 under ℓ_1 always worked well and we recommend it as the standard stitching algorithm. The use of the ℓ_1 norm was especially valuable in overcoming geometrical misalignments of the input images.

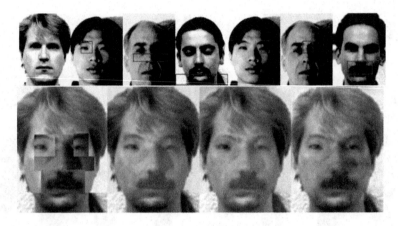

Fig. 6. A police application for generating composite portraits. The top panel shows the image parts used in the composition, taken from the Yale database. The bottom panel shows, from left to right, the results of pasting the original parts, GIST1 under ℓ. , GIST1 under ℓ. and pyramid blending in the gradient domain. Note the discontinuities in the eyebrows.

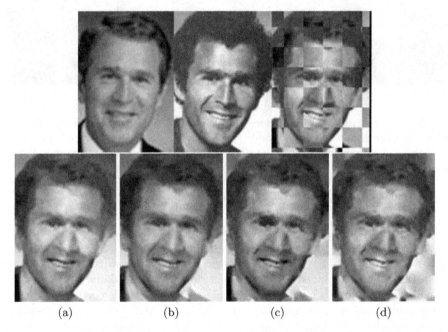

| (a) | (b) | (c) | (d) |

Fig. 7. A combination of images of George W. Bush taken at different ages. On top are the input images and the combination pattern. On the bottom left are, from left to right, the results of GIST1 Stitching under ℓ. (a) and under ℓ. (b), the results of pyramid blending in the gradient domain (c), and pyramid blending in the image domain(d).

The closest approach to ours was presented recently by Perez et. al. [10] for image editing. There are two main differences with this work: First, in this work we use the gradients of **both** images in the overlap **region**, while Perez et. al. use the gradients of the inserted object and the intensities of the background image. Second, the optimization is done under different norms, while Perez et. al. use the ℓ_2 norm. Both differences considerably influence the results, especially in misaligned textured regions. This is shown in Figures 5,4.

Image stitching was presented as a search for an optimal solution to an image quality criterion. The optimization of this criterion under norms ℓ_1, ℓ_2 is convex, having a single solution. Encouraged by the results obtained by this approach, we believe that it will be interesting to explore alternative criteria for image quality. One direction can use results on statistics of filter responses in natural images [21,22,23]. Another direction is to incorporate additional image features in the quality criterion, such as local curvature. Successful results in image inpainting[11,24] were obtained when image curvature was used in addition to image derivatives.

Acknowledgments. The authors would like to thank Dhruv Mahajan and Raanan Fattal for their help in the multigrid implementation, and Rick Szeliski for providing helpful comments.

References

1. Freeman, W., Pasztor, E., Carmichael, O.: Learning low-level vision. In: Int. Conf. on Computer Vision. (1999) 1182–1189
2. Efros, A., Freeman, W.: Image quilting for texture synthesis and transfer. Proceedings of SIGGRAPH 2001 (2001) 341–346
3. Milgram, D.: Computer methods for creating photomosaics. IEEE Trans. Computer **23** (1975) 1113–1119
4. Davis, J.: Mosaics of scenes with moving objects. In: CVPR. (1998) 354–360
5. Peleg, S., Rousso, B., Rav-Acha, A., Zomet, A.: Mosaicing on adaptive manifolds. IEEE Trans. on Pattern Analysis and Machine Intelligence **22** (2000) 1144–1154
6. Uyttendaele, M., Eden, A., Szeliski, R.: Eliminating ghosting and exposure artifacts in image mosaics. In: CVPR. (2001) II:509–516
7. Adelson, E.H., Anderson, C.H., Bergen, J.R., Burt, P.J., M., O.J.: Pyramid method in image processing. RCA Engineer **29(6)** (1984) 33–41
8. Peleg, S.: Elimination of seams from photomosaics. CGIP **16** (1981) 90–94
9. Fattal, R., Lischinski, D., Werman, M.: Gradient domain high dynamic range compression. Proceedings of SIGGRAPH 2001 (2002) 249–356
10. Perez, P., Gangnet, M., Blake, A.: Poisson image editing. SIGGRAPH (2003) 313–318
11. Ballester, C., Bertalmio, M., Caselles, V., Sapiro, G., Verdera, J.: Filling-in by joint interpolation of vector fields and gray levels. IEEE Trans. Image Processing **10** (2001)
12. Weiss, Y.: Deriving intrinsic images from image sequences. In: ICCV. (2001) II: 68–75

13. Tappen, M., Freeman, W., Adelson, E.: Recovering intrinsic images from a single image. In: NIPS. Volume 15., The MIT Press (2002)
14. Finlayson, G., Hordley, S., Drew, M.: Removing shadows from images. In: ECCV. (2002) IV:823
15. Levin, A., Zomet, A., Weiss, Y.: Learning to perceive transparency from the statistics of natural scenes. In: NIPS. Volume 15., The MIT Press (2002)
16. Levin, A., Zomet, A., Peleg, S., Weiss, Y.: Seamless image stitching in the gradient domain, hebrew university tr:2003-82, available on http://leibniz.cs.huji.ac.il/tr/acc/2003/huji-cse-ltr-2003-82_blending.pdf (2003)
17. Frankot, R., Chellappa, R.: A method for enforcing integrability in shape from shading algorithms. IEEE Trans. on Pattern Analysis and Machine Intelligence **10** (1988) 439–451
18. Press, W., Flannery, B., Teukolsky, S., Vetterling, W.: Numerical Recipes: The Art of Scientific Computing. Cambridge University Press, Cambridge (UK) and New York (1992)
19. Chvátal, V.: Linear Programming. W.H. Freeman and CO., New York (1983)
20. Vanderbei, R.: Loqo, http://www.princeton.edu/ rvdb/ (2000)
21. Mallat, S.: A theory for multiresolution signal decomposition: The wavelet representation. IEEE Trans. on Pattern Analysis and Machine Intelligence **11** (1989) 674–693
22. Simoncelli, E.: Bayesian denoising of visual images in the wavelet domain. BIWBM **18** (1999) 291–308
23. Wainwright, M., Simoncelli, E., Willsky, A.: Random cascades of gaussian scale mixtures for natural images. In: Int. Conf. on Image Processing. (2000) I:260–263
24. Bertalmio, M., Sapiro, G., Caselles, V., Ballester, C.: Image inpainting. In: SIGGRAPH. (2000)

Spectral Clustering for Robust Motion Segmentation

JinHyeong Park[1], Hongyuan Zha[1], and Rangachar Kasturi[2]

. Department of Computer Science and Engineering,
The Pennsylvania State University,
111 IST Building, University Park, PA 16802 USA
{jhpark,zha}@cse.psu.edu
. Department of Computer Science and Engineering,
University of South Florida,
4202 East Fowler Ave., ENB118,
Tampa, FL 33620-5399 USA
chair@csee.usf.edu

Abstract. In this paper, we propose a robust motion segmentation method using the techniques of matrix factorization and subspace separation. We first show that the shape interaction matrix can be derived using $\mathbf{QR}$ decomposition rather than Singular Value Decomposition($\mathbf{SVD}$) which also leads to a simple proof of the shape subspace separation theorem. Using the shape interaction matrix, we solve the motion segmentation problems by the spectral clustering techniques. We exploit multi-way Min-Max cut clustering method and provide a novel approach for cluster membership assignment. We further show that we can combine a cluster refinement method based on subspace separation with the graph clustering method to improve its robustness in the presence of noise. The proposed method yields very good performance for both synthetic and real image sequences.

1   Introduction

The Matrix factorization methods proposed by Tomasi, Costeira and Kanade [1] [2] have been widely used for solving the motion segmentation problems [3] [4] [5] [6] [7] [8] and the 3D shape recovering problems [9] [10] [11]. The basic idea of the methods is to factorize the feature trajectory matrix into the motion matrix and the shape matrix, providing the separation of the feature point trajectories into independent motions. In this paper, we develop a novel robust factorization method using the techniques of spectral clustering.

Given a set of N feature points tracked through F frames, we can construct a feature trajectory matrix $\mathbf{P} \in R^{2F \times N}$ where the rows correspond to the x or y coordinates of the feature points in the image plane and the columns correspond to the individual feature points. Motion segmentation algorithms based on matrix factorization [6] first construct a shape interaction matrix, $\mathbf{Q}$ by applying the singular value decomposition ($\mathbf{SVD}$) to the feature trajectory matrix $\mathbf{P}$. Under the noise-free situation, the shape interaction matrix $\mathbf{Q}$ can be transformed

T. Pajdla and J. Matas (Eds.): ECCV 2004, LNCS 3024, pp. 390–401, 2004.
© Springer-Verlag Berlin Heidelberg 2004

to a block diagonal matrix by a symmetric row and column permutation thereby grouping the feature points of the same object into a diagonal block.

If the trajectory matrix **P** is contaminated by noise, however, the block diagonal form of Q no longer holds, and the methods such as the greedy technique proposed in[2] tend to perform rather poorly. Recently there have been several research proposed specifically addressing this problem [7] [5] [3] [4] [5] [6] [8]. We will give a brief review of these methods in Section 2.

In this paper we deal with the issues related to the robustness of the factorization methods. We first show that the shape interaction matrix can be extracted from the trajectory matrix using **QR** decomposition with pivoting, an idea that was briefly mentioned in [2]. As a by-product we give a simple and clean proof of the subspace separation theorem described in [6]. We then observe that the shape interaction matrix is very similar to the weight matrix used for graph partitioning and clustering [12] [13] [14] [15], and the motion segmentation problem can be cast as an optimal graph partitioning problem. To this end, we apply the spectral k-way clustering method [13] [14] to the shape interaction matrix to transform it into near-block diagonal form. In particular, we propose a novel **QR** decomposition based technique for cluster assignment. The technique at the same time also provides confidence levels of the cluster membership for each feature point trajectory. The confidence levels are explored to provide a more robust cluster assignment strategy: we assign a feature point directly to a cluster when it has a very confidence level for the cluster compared to those for other clusters. Using the assigned feature points in each cluster, we compute a linear subspace in the trajectory space. The cluster memberships of other feature points having lower confidence levels, and are therefore not assigned to a cluster, are determined by their distances to each of the linear subspaces. Our experiments on both synthetic data sets and real video images have shown that this method are very reliable for motion segmentation even in the presence of severe noise.

The rest of the paper is organized a s follows: Previous works are discussed in Section 2. Section 3 is devoted to a simple proof that the shape interaction matrix can be computed using **QR** decomposition. Motion segmentation based on spectral relaxation k-way clustering and subspace separation is described in Section 4. Experiment results are shown in Section 5 and conclusion is given in Section 6.

2   Previous Work

The factorization method was originally introduced by Tomasi and Kanade [1]. The method decomposes a matrix of image coordinates of N feature points tracked through F frames into two matrices which, respectively, represent object shape and camera motion. The method deals with a single static object viewed by a moving camera. Extending this method, Costerira and Kanade [2] proposed a multibody factorization method which separates and recovers the shape and motion of multiple independently moving objects in a sequence of images. To achieve this, they introduce a shape interaction matrix which is invariant to both the object motions and the selection of coordinate systems, and suggest a greedy algorithm to permute the shape interaction matrix into block diagonal form. Gear [3] exploited the reduced row echelon form of the shape interaction matrix to group the feature points into the linearly independent subspaces. For Gear's method, in the noise-free case, any two columns of the echelon form which have nonzero elements in the same row correspond to feature points belonging to the same rigid body. The echelon form matrix can be represented by a weighted bipartite graph. Gear also used a statistical approach to estimate the grouping of feature points into subspaces in the presence of noise by computing which partition of the graph has the maximum likelihood.

Ichimura [4] suggested a motion segmentation method based on discriminant criterion [16] features. The main idea of the method is to select useful features for grouping noisy data. Using noise-contaminated shape interaction matrix, it computes discriminant criterion for each row of the matrix. The feature points are then divided into two groups by the maximum discriminant criterion, and the corresponding row gives the best discriminant feature. The same procedure is applied recursively to the remaining features to extract other groups. Wu et. al. [5] proposed an orthogonal subspace decomposition method to deal with the noisy problem of the shape interaction matrix. The method decomposes the object shape space into signal subspaces and noise subspaces. They used the shape signal subspace distance matrix, D, for shape space grouping rather than the noise-contaminated shape interaction matrix.

Kanatani [6] [7] reformulated the motion segmentation problems based on the idea of subspace separation. The approach is to divide the given N feature points to form m disjoint subspaces $\mathcal{I}_i$, $i = 1, \cdots, m$. A rather elaborated proof was given showing that provided that the subspaces are linearly independent, the elements Q_{ij} in the shape interaction matrix Q is zero if the point i and the point j belong to different subspaces. Kanatani also pointed out that even a small noise in one feature point can affect all the elements of Q in a complicated manner. Based on this fact, Kanatani proposed noise compensation methods using the original data rather than the shape interaction matrix Q.

Zelnik-Manor and Irani [8] showed that different 3D motions can also be captured as a single object using previous methods when there is a partial dependency between the objects. To solve the problem, they suggested to use an affinity matrix $\bar{Q}$ where $\bar{Q}_{ij} = \sum_k exp(v_k(i) - v_k(j))^2$, where v_k's are the largest eigenvectors of Q. They also dealt with the multi-sequence factorization problems for temporal synchronization using multiple video sequences of the same dynamic scene.

3   Constructing the Shape Interaction Matrix Using QR Decomposition

In this section, we exhibit the block diagonal form of the shape interaction matrix using **QR** decomposition with pivoting [17], this also provides a simpler proof of the shape subspace separation theorem (Theorem 1 in [6]). Assume we have N rigidly moving feature points, $p_1, \ldots, p_N$, which are on image plane corresponding 3D points over the F frames. Motion segmentation can be interpreted as dividing the feature points p_i into S groups [6] each spanning a linear subspace corresponding to feature points belonging to the same object. We denote the grouping as follows,

$$\{1, \ldots, N\} = \bigcup_{i=1}^{S} \mathcal{I}_i, \quad \mathcal{I}_i \cap \mathcal{I}_j = \emptyset.$$

Now define $l_i = |\mathcal{I}_i|$ which is the number of the points in the set $\mathcal{I}_i$, and $k_i = \dim span\{p_j\}_{j \in \mathcal{I}_i} \leq l_i$ and $P_i = \{p_j\}_{j \in \mathcal{I}_i}$.

Let the **SVD** of P_i be $P_i = U_i \Sigma_i V_i^t$, where $\Sigma_i \in R^{k_i \times k_i}, i = 1, \ldots, S$. Then $\mathbf{P} = [P_1, P_2, \ldots, P_s]$ can be written as,

$$\mathbf{P} = [P_1, P_2, \ldots, P_s] = [U_1 \Sigma_1, U_2 \Sigma_2, \ldots, U_s \Sigma_s] \begin{bmatrix} V_1^T & 0 & \cdots & 0 \\ 0 & V_2^T & \cdots & 0 \\ \vdots & \vdots & \ddots & \vdots \\ 0 & 0 & \cdots & V_s^T \end{bmatrix}, \quad (1)$$

where $\operatorname{rank}(V_i) = k_i$ for $i = 1, \cdots, s$. We assume the S subspaces $span\{p_j\}_{j \in \mathcal{I}_i}, i = 1, \ldots, S$ are linearly independent, then the matrix $[U_1 \Sigma_1, U_2 \Sigma_2, \ldots, U_s \Sigma_s]$ has full column rank of $k = k_1 + \cdots + k_s$. Therefore, an arbitrary orthonormal basis for the row space of $\mathbf{P}$ can be written as $\Phi diag(V_1, \cdots, V_s)^T$ for an arbitrary orthogonal matrix $\Phi \in R^{k \times k}$. Now the shape interaction matrix can be written as

$$\mathbf{Q} = diag(V_1, \cdots, V_s) \Phi^T \Phi diag(V_1, \cdots, V_s)^T = diag(V_1 V_T, \cdots, V_s V_s^T).$$

This clearly shows that $Q_{ij} = 0$ if i and j belong to different subspaces, i.e., if the corresponding feature points belong to different objects.

A cheaper way to compute an orthonormal basis for the row-space of $\mathbf{P}$ than using **SVD** is to apply **QR** decomposition with column pivoting to $\mathbf{P}^T$,

$$\mathbf{P}^T E = \hat{Q} R \quad (2)$$

where E is a permutation matrix, and $\hat{Q}$ has k columns. It is easy to see that $\hat{Q}\hat{Q}^T = \mathbf{Q}$. In the presence of noise, $\mathbf{P}$ will not exactly have rank k, but **QR** decomposition with column pivoting will in general generate an R matrix that can reliably revealing the numerical rank of $\mathbf{P}$. We can truncate R by deleting rows with small entries.

4   Motion Segmentation

4.1   Spectral Multi-way Clustering

In the last section, we have shown that the shape interaction matrix, $\mathbf{Q} \in R^{N \times N}$ has the block diagonal form when the feature points are grouped into independent subspaces corresponding to S different objects. In general, this grouping is unknown, and we need to find row and column permutations of the matrix $\mathbf{Q}$ to exhibit this block diagonal form, and thus assigning the feature points to different objects. A greedy algorithm has been proposed in [2] for this problem, but it performs poorly in the presence of noise. We now present a more robust method based on spectral graph clustering [12] [13] [14] [15]. We propose a novel technique for cluster assignment in spectral clustering and show that it provides a confidence level that can be used for further refining the cluster memberships of the feature points, thus improving the robustness of the spectral clustering method.

We consider the absolute value of the (i, j) element of the shape interaction matrix $\mathbf{Q}$ as a measure of the similarity of feature points i and j with feature points belonging to the same object more similar than those of other points. In fact, in the noise-free case, feature points in different objects will have zero similarity. Our goal is then to partition the feature points into S groups so that feature points are more similar within each group than across different groups. Let $W = (w_{ij})$ with $w_{ij} = |\mathbf{Q}_{ij}|$. For a given partition of the feature points into S groups, we can permute the rows and columns of W so that rows and columns corresponding to the feature points belonging to the same objects are adjacent to each other, i.e., we can re-order the columns and rows of the W matrix accordingly such that

$$W = \begin{bmatrix} W_{11} & W_{12} & \cdots & W_{1S} \\ W_{21} & W_{22} & \cdots & W_{2S} \\ \cdots & \cdots & & \vdots \\ W_{S1} & W_{S2} & \cdots & W_{SS} \end{bmatrix}. \tag{3}$$

We want to find a partition such that W_{ii} will be large while $W_{ij}, i \neq j$ will be small, and to measure the size of a sub-matrix matrix W_{ij} we use the sum of all its elements and denoted as sum(W_{ij}). Let x_i be a cluster indication vector accordingly partitioned with that of W with all elements equal to zero except those corresponding to rows of W_{ii},

$$x_i = [0 \cdots 0, 1 \cdots 1, 0 \cdots 0]^T.$$

Denote $D = diag(D_1, D_2, \cdots, D_S)$ such that $D_i = \sum_{j=1}^{S} W_{ij}$. It is easy to see that

$$\text{sum}(W_{ii}) = x_i^T W x_i, \quad \sum_{j \neq i} \text{sum}(W_{ij}) = x_i^T (D - W) x_i.$$

Since we want to find a partition which will maximize sum(W_{ii}) while minimizing sum$(W_{ij}), i \neq j$, we seek to minimize the following objective function by finding a set of indicator vectors x_i. The objective function is called min-max cut in [13] [14] which is a generalization of the normalized cut objective function [12] to the multi-way partition case.

$$MCut = \frac{x_1^T(D-W)x_1}{x_1^T W x_1} + \frac{x_2^T(D-W)x_2}{x_2^T W x_2} + \cdots + \frac{x_S^T(D-W)x_S}{x_S^T W x_S}$$

$$= \frac{x_1^T D x_1}{x_1^T W x_1} + \frac{x_2^T D x_2}{x_2^T W x_2} + \cdots + \frac{x_S^T D x_S}{x_S^T W x_S} - S.$$

If we define $y_i = D^{1/2}x_i/\|D^{1/2}x_i\|_2$ and $Y_S = [y_1, \cdots, y_S]$, we have

$$MCut = \frac{1}{y_1^T \hat{W} y_1} + \frac{1}{y_2^T \hat{W} y_2} + \cdots + \frac{1}{y_S^T \hat{W} y_S} - S \qquad (4)$$

where $\hat{W} = D^{-1/2}WD^{-1/2}$ and $y_i = \frac{D^{1/2}x_i}{\|D^{1/2}x_i\|_2}$. It is easy to see that the y_i are orthogonal to each other and normalized to have Euclidean norm one. If we insist that the y_i be constrained to inherit the discrete structure of the indicator vectors x_i, then we are leading to solve a combinatorial optimization problem which has been proved to be NP-hard even when $S = 2$ [12]. The idea of spectral clustering instead is to relax this constraints and allows the y_i to be an arbitrary set of orthonormal vectors. In this case, the minimum of Eq. 4 can be shown to be achieved by orthonormal basis $y_1, \cdots, y_S$ of the subspace spanned by the eigenvectors corresponding to the largest S eigenvalues of $\hat{W}$. Next we discuss how to assign the feature points to each clusters based on the eigenvectors.

We should first mention that the cluster assignment problem in spectral clustering is not well-understood yet. Here we follow the approach proposed in [15]. Denote $\hat{Y} = [\hat{y}_1, \cdots, \hat{y}_S]^T$ as the optimal solution of Eq. 4. The vectors $\hat{y}_i$ can be used for cluster assignment because $\hat{y}_i \approx D^{1/2}\hat{x}_i/\|D^{1/2}\hat{x}_i\|_2$, where $\hat{x}_i$ is the cluster indicator vector of $i-th$ cluster. Ideally, if W is partitioned perfectly into S clusters, then, the columns in $\hat{X} = [\hat{x}_i, \cdots, \hat{x}_S]^T$ of the $i-th$ cluster are the same, one for the $i-th$ row and zeros for the others. Two columns of different clusters are orthogonal to each other. This property is approximately inherited by $\hat{Y}$: two columns from two different clusters are orthogonal to each other, and those from one cluster are the same. We now pick a column of $\hat{Y}$ which has the largest norm, say, it belongs to cluster i, we orthogonalized the rest of the columns of $\hat{Y}$ against this column. We assign the columns to cluster i whose residual is small. We then perform this process S times. As discussed in [15], it is exactly the same procedure of **QR** decomposition with column pivoting applied to $\hat{Y}$. In particular, we compute **QR** decomposition of Y^T with column pivoting

$$Y^T E = \hat{Q}R = \hat{Q}[R_{11}, R_{12}]$$

where $\hat{Q}$ is a $S \times S$ orthogonal matrix, R_{11} is a $S \times S$ upper triangular matrix, and E is a permutation matrix. Then we compute a matrix $\hat{R}$ as

$$\hat{R} = R_{11}^{-1}[R_{11}, R_{12}]P^T = [I_S, R_{11}^{-1}R_{12}],$$

The matrix $\hat{R} \in R^{S \times N}$ can be considered as giving the levels of confidence of a point to be assigned to each cluster. Notice that the columns correspond to the feature points and the rows correspond to the clusters. The cluster membership of each feature point is determined by the row index of the largest element in absolute value of the corresponding column of $\hat{R}$. This provide us with a baseline spectral clustering method for motion segmentation which are quite robust in the presence of noise. Further improvement can be achieved as we discuss next.

We can assign a point to a cluster with high confidence if there is a very dominantly high confidence value in the corresponding column, however, we are not able to do this if two or more values in a column are very close to each other. Table 4.1 shows an example of the matrix $\hat{R} \in R^{3 \times 10}$ that has 10 points extracted from 3 objects. The last row of the table shows the cluster membership of each point assigned by the row index of the highest absolute value. For instance, the point p_1 is assigned to cluster 2 because the second row value (0.329), is greater than the other row values (0.316 and 0.203). However, we cannot have much confidence of its membership because there is no dominant values in the corresponding column.

Table 1. An example of the matrix $\hat{R}$. There are 10 points extracted from 3 objects. The last row shows the assigned cluster

Cluster ID	p1	p2	p3	p4	p5	p6	p7	p8	p9	p10
k = 1	0.316	0.351	0.876	0.331	0.456	0.562	0.086	0.275	0.072	0.119
k = 2	0.329	0.338	0.032	0.372	0.013	0.060	0.186	0.706	0.815	0.831
k = 3	0.203	0.017	0.031	0.173	0.566	0.556	0.775	0.126	0.094	0.113
Assigned Cluster	2	1	1	2	3	1	3	2	2	2

4.2   Refinement of Cluster Assignment for Motion Segmentation

The baseline spectral clustering shows its robustness for a noisy environment in spite of its hard clustering (it assigns each point to a cluster even though it does not have high confidence for it). The method alone, however, can sometimes fail in presence of severe noise. In this section, we discuss a two-phase approach whereby in phase one we assignment the cluster memberships for those feature points with high confidence levels, and in phase two we construct linear subspaces for each clusters based on the high confidence feature points, and assign the rest of the feature points by projecting onto these subspaces.

Our approach proceeds as follows. After computing $\hat{R}$ discussed in the previous section, the points of high confidence of each clusters are selected. Let's define $P_i = [p_{i1}, \cdots, p_{iN_i}]$ as the trajectory points in the cluster i. One of the easiest methods is to apply threshold to the values of each column, and if the highest value in the column is greater than the threshold, the point is assigned to the corresponding cluster. if it does not, let's categorize the point to cluster 0 which is in the state of temporarily pending to decide its cluster. Let's

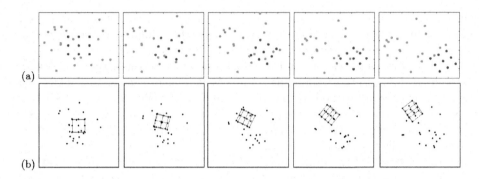

Fig. 1. Two synthetic video sequences used in [7] and [18] respectively. (a). 9 Red dots are foreground points and 20 green dots are background pixels (b). 24 background points and 14 foreground points. The foreground pixels are connected with lines.

define the pending points as $P_0 = [p_{01}, \cdots, p_{0N_0}]$. The next step is to compute subspace(2D) for $p_{i1}, \cdots, p_{iN_i}$, $i = 1, \cdots, S$ using Principal Component Analysis (**PCA**). Let's denote U_i as a subspace basis for the cluster i. We finally determine the cluster membership of each pending point by computing the minimum distance from the point to subspaces.

$$\hat{\theta}_j = arg \min_i ||p_{0j} - (c_i + U_i U_i^T (p_{0j} - c_i))||^2,$$

where $j = 1, \cdots, k$ and $c_i = \sum_{j=1}^{N_i} p_i j$.

The point p_{0j} is assigned to the cluster $\hat{\theta}_j$.

5   Experimental Results

Figure 1 shows two synthetic image sequences used for performance evaluation. Actually these images are used in [7] and [18]. Figure 1-(a), denoted as *Synthetic 1*, has 20 background points(green dots) and foreground points(red dots), and Figure 1-(b),denoted as *Synthetic 2*, has 20 background points and 14 foreground points. The foreground points are connected by lines for visualization purpose.

We performed experiments using not only the original tracking data but also the data added by independent Gaussian noise of mean 0 and standard deviation σ to the coordinates of all the points. For the noise data, we generate 5 sets for each $\sigma = 1, 2, 3, 4$, and compute the misclassification rate by simply averaging the 5 experiment results. We compare two methods proposed in this paper (One is k-way Min-Max cut clustering in Sec. 4.1 denoted as **Method 1**, and the other is a combination of the k-way Min-Max cut clustering and clustering refinement using subspace projection in Sec. 4.2 denoted as **Method 2**) to the Multi-stage optimization proposed in [18] denoted as **Multi-Stage**. Table 2 shows that the misclassification rates of the three methods over the different noise levels ($\sigma = 0, 1, 2, 3, 4$). **Method 2** and **Multi-Stage** yields better performance than **Method 1**. The two methods performs almost perfect for the sequences.

Table 2. Misclassification rate (%) for two synthetic sequences. The values in parenthesis are standard deviation. **Method 1** is k-way Min-Max cut clustering in Sec. 4.1 and **Method 2** is the k-way Min-Max cut clustering + clustering refinement using subspace projection in Sec. 4.2. **Multi-Stage** is the Multi-stage optimization proposed in [18].

Video Sequence	noise	$\sigma = 0$	$\sigma = 1$	$\sigma = 2$	$\sigma = 3$	$\sigma = 4$
	Method 1	0.0	1.4	1.4	0.7	0.7
Synthetic 1	Method 2	0.0	0.0	0.0	0.0	0.0
	Multi-Stage	0.0	0.0	0.7	0.0	0.0
	Method 1	8.2	10.6(1.6)	11.7(2.1)	11.7(3.6)	13.2(1.7)
Synthetic 2	Method 2	0.0	0.0	0.0	0.0	0.59(1.3)
	Multi-Stage	0.0	0.0	0.0	0.0	0.59(1.3)

We experimented with the real video sequences used in [18]. In all the sequences, one object is moving while background is simultaneously moving because of the camera moving. Let's denote the video sequences as *video1*, *video2* and *video3* respectively. We synthesize one more test video sequence by overlaying the foreground feature points in *video1* to *video2*, which has 2 moving objects and background. Let's denote the video sequences as *video4*. Figure 2 shows selected 5 frames of the four sequences.

We also performed experiments using not only the original tracking data but also the data added by independent Gaussian noise of mean 0 and standard deviation σ to the coordinates of all the points. For the noise data, we generate 5 sets for each $\sigma = 3, 5, 7, 10$, and compute the misclassification rate by simply averaging the 5 experiment results.

Table 3 shows the misclassification rates of the three methods over the different noise levels ($\sigma = 0, 3, 5, 7, 10$). The table shows that **Method 2** can classify motion perfectly even for the severe noise presence. It is very robust and stable to noise. **Method 1** performs very well for noise-free environment, but it misclassifies some points in the presence of noise.

Multi-Stage performs very well for *video1* through *video3* which have one moving foreground object and background. It, however, does not yield good performance for *video4* which has two moving foreground objects and background in the presence of noise. Based on our experiments, the method also suffer from local minima problem. Using the same data, it yields different results based on the initialization. That is the reason the standard deviation of the method is too high shown in Table 3.

6   Conclusions

In this paper, we mathematically prove the shape interaction matrix can be computed using **QR** decomposition which is more effective than **SVD**. We solve the motion segmentation problem using spectral graph clustering technique because the shape interaction matrix has a very similar form to the weight matrix of graph. We apply the Spectral Relaxation K-way Min-Max cut clustering

Fig. 2. Real Video sequences with the feature points. 1st row: *video1*, 2nd row: *video2*, 3rd row: *video3*, 4th row: *video4* (foreground feature points in *video1* are overlaid in *video4*). Red dots correspond to background while green dots correspond to foreground. The yellow cross marks in *video4* represent the foreground feature points of *video1*

Table 3. Misclassification rate (%) for the real video sequences. The values in parenthesis are standard deviation.

Video Sequence	noise	$\sigma = 0$	$\sigma = 3$	$\sigma = 5$	$\sigma = 7$	$\sigma = 10$
video1	Method 1	0.0	0.0	0.0	0.0	0.0
	Method 2	0.0	0.0	0.0	0.0	0.0
	Multi-Stage	0.0	0.0	0.0	0.0	0.0
video2	Method 1	0	1.6(1.2)	1.6(1.2)	1.6(1.2)	2.9(1.7)
	Method 2	0.0	0.0	0.0	0.0	0.0
	Multi-Stage	0.0	0.0	0.0	0.0	7.3(16.3)
video3	Method 1	0.0	2.5(0.01)	2.5	1.3	2.5
	Method 2	0.0	0.0	0.0	0.0	0.0
	Multi-Stage	0.0	0.0	0.0	0.0	0.0
video4	Method1	0.0	0.7(1.6)	3.4(4.7)	8.3(5.0)	9.6(6.5)
	Method2	0.0	0.0	0.0	0.0	0.7(1.6)
	Multi-Stage	0.0	4.1(9.3)	8.2(9.6)	16.2 (13.2)	19.23 (9.87)

method [13] [14] to shape interaction matrix. It provides a relaxed cluster indication matrix. **QR** decomposition is applied to the matrix, which generate a new cluster indication matrix, to determine the cluster membership of each point. The values of the new cluster indication matrix reflect confidence level for each point to be assigned to clusters. This method yields a good performance in noise free environment, but it is, sometimes, sensitive to noise. We propose a

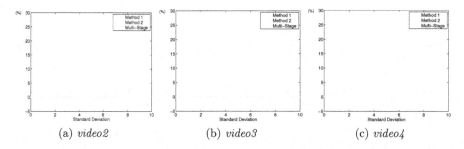

(a) *video2* (b) *video3* (c) *video4*

Fig. 3. Graph for misclassification rate. Graph of *video1* is not depicted here because all the three methods performs perfectly. **Method 1**: Dashed-dot blue line, **Method 2**: Red line and **Multi-Stage**: Dashed green line

robust motion segmentation method by combining the spectral graph clustering and subspace separation to compensate noise problem. Initially, we assign only points of high confidence to clusters based on the cluster indication matrix. We compute subspace for each cluster using the assigned points. We finally determine the membership of the other points, which are not assigned to a cluster, by computing the minimum residual when they are projected to the subspace.

We applied the proposed method to two synthetic image sequences and four real video sequences. **Method 2** and **Multi-Stage** produce almost perfect performance for the synthetic image sequences in the presence of noise. Experiments also show that the proposed method, **Method 2**, performs very well for the real video sequences even in the sever noise presence. It performs better than Multi-Stage optimization method [18] for real video sequences in which there are more than two objects.

Acknowledgments. The authors would like to thank Prof. Kanatani and his colleagues for generously providing their data for this work. The work is supported in part by NSF grant CCF-0305879.

References

1. C. Tomasi and T. Kanade. Shape and motion from image streams under orthography - a factorization method. *International Journal of Computer Vision*, 9(2):137–154, 1992.
2. J. Costeira and T. Kanade. A multi-body factorization method for motion analysis. *International Journal of Computer Vision*, 29(3):159–179, 1998.
3. C. W. Gear. Multibody grouping from motion images. *International Journal of Computer Vision*, 29(2):133–150, 1998.
4. N. Ichimura. Motion segmentation based on factorization method and discriminant criterion. In *Proc. IEEE Int. Conf. Computer Vision*, pages 600–605, 1999.
5. Y. Wu, Zhang Z., and J. Y. Huang, T. Lin. Multibody grouping via orthogonal subspace decomposition. In *Proc. IEEE Computer Vision and Pattern Recognition*, volume 2, pages 252–257, 2001.

6. K. Kanatani. Motion segmentation by subspace separation and model selection. In *Proc. IEEE Int. Conf. Computer Vision*, volume 2, pages 586–591, 2001.
7. K. Kanatani. Motion segmentation by subspace separation and model selection:model selection and reliability evaluation. *Intl. J. of Image and Graphics*, 2(2):179–197, 2002.
8. L. Zelnik-Manor and M. Irani. Degeneracies, dependencies and their implications in multi-body and multi-sequence factorizations. In *Proc. IEEE Computer Vision and Pattern Recognition*, 2003.
9. C. Bregler and H. Hertzmann, A. Biermann. Recovering non-rigid 3d shape from image streams. In *Proc. IEEE Computer Vision and Pattern Recognition*, 2000.
10. L. Torresani, D. B. Yang, E. J. Alexander, and C. Bregler. Tracking and modeling non-rigid objects with rank constraints. In *Proc. IEEE Computer Vision and Pattern Recognition*, 2001.
11. M. Brand. Morphable 3d models from video. In *Proc. IEEE Computer Vision and Pattern Recognition*, 2001.
12. J. Shi and J. Malik. Normalized cut and image segmentation. *IEEE Trans. on Pattern Analysis and Machine Intelligence*, 22(8):888–905, 2000.
13. M. Gu, H. Zha, C. Ding, X. He, and H. Simon. Spectral relaxation models and structure analysis for k-way graph clustering and bi-clustering. In *Technical Report,Department of Computer Science and Engineering, CSE-01-007,*, 2001.
14. C. Ding, X. He, H. Zha, M. Gu, and H. Simon. Spectral min-max cut for graph partitioning and data clustering. In *IEEE International Conference on Data Mining*, pages 107–114, 2001.
15. H. Zha, C. Ding, M. Gu, X. He, and H. Simon. Spectral relaxation for k-means clustering. In *Neural Information Processing Systems 14*, pages 1057–1064, 2002.
16. N. Otsu. A threshold selection method from gray-level histograms. *IEEE Trans. on Systems, Man and Cybernetics*, SMC-9(1):62–66, 1979.
17. G. H. Golub and C. F. Van Loan. *Matrix Computation, 3rd Ed.* Johns Hopkins Univ. ress, 2000.
18. K. Kanatani and Y. Sugaya. Multi-stage optimization for multi-body motion segmentation. In *Proc. Australia-Japan Advanced Workshop on Computer Vision*, pages 25–31, 2003.

Learning Outdoor Color Classification from Just One Training Image

Roberto Manduchi

University of California, Santa Cruz

Abstract. We present an algorithm for color classification with explicit illuminant estimation and compensation. A Gaussian classifier is trained with color samples from just one training image. Then, using a simple diagonal illumination model, the illuminants in a new scene that contains some of the same surface classes are estimated in a Maximum Likelihood framework using the Expectation Maximization algorithm. We also show how to impose priors on the illuminants, effectively computing a Maximum-A-Posteriori estimation. Experimental results show the excellent performances of our classification algorithm for outdoor images.*

1 Introduction

Recognition (or, more generally, classification) is a fundamental task in computer vision. Differently from clustering/segmentation, the classification process relies on prior information, in the form of physical modeling and/or of training data, to assign labels to images or image areas. This paper is concerned with the classification of outdoor scenes based on color. Color features are normally used in such different domains as robotics, image database indexing, remote sensing, tracking, and biometrics. Color vectors are generated directly by the sensor for each pixel, as opposed to other features, such as texture or optical flow, which require possibly complex pre–processing. In addition, color information can be exploited at the local level, enabling simple classifiers that do not need to worry too much about contextual spatial information.

Color–based classification relies on the fact that a surface type is often uniquely characterized by its reflectance spectrum: different surface types usually have rather different reflectance characteristics. Unfortunately, a camera does not take direct reflectance measurements. Even neglecting specular and non–Lambertian components, the spectral distribution of the radiance from a surface is a function of the illuminant spectrum (or spectra) as much as of the surface reflectance. The illuminant spectrum is in this context a nuisance parameter, inducing an undesired degree of randomness to the perceived color of a surface. Unless one is interested solely in surfaces with a highly distinctive reflectance (such as the bright targets often used in laboratory robotics experiments), ambiguity and therefore misclassification will arise when surfaces are illuminated by "unfamiliar" light.

---

* This work was supported by DARPA through subcontract 1235249 from JPL.

T. Pajdla and J. Matas (Eds.): ECCV 2004, LNCS 3024, pp. 402–413, 2004.

One way to reduce the dependence on the illuminant is to use more training data and sophisticated statistical models to represent the color variability. This is feasible if the space of possible illuminants is not too broad, meaning that we can hope to sample it adequately. For example, in the case of outdoor scenes (which are of interest to this work), the spectrum of the illuminant (direct sunlight or diffuse light and shade) can be well modeled by a low–dimensional linear space. Thus, by collecting many image samples of the surfaces of interest under all expected light conditions, one may derive the complete statistical distribution of colors within each class considered, and therefore build a Bayesian classifier that can effectively cope with variation of illumination. This approach was taken by the author and colleagues for the design and implementation of the color–based terrain typing subsystem of the eXperimental Unmanned Vehicle (XUV) DEMO III [5], which provided excellent classification performances. Unfortunately, collecting and hand–labeling extensive training data sets may be difficult, time–consuming, and impractical or impossible in many real–world scenarios. This prompted us to study an orthogonal approach, relying on a model–based, rather than exemplar–based, description of the data. Our algorithm aims to decouple the contribution of the reflectance and of the illumination components to the color distribution within each surface class, and to explicitly recover and compensate for variations of the illuminant (or illuminants) in the scene. Both components (reflectance and illuminant) are modeled by suitable (and simple) statistical distributions. The contribution of reflectance to the color distribution is learned by observing each class under just one "canonical" illuminant, possibly within a single training image. To model the contribution of illumination, one may either directly hard–code existing chromaticity daylight curves [4] into the system, or learn the relevant parameters from a data set of observations of a fixed target (such as a color chart) under a wide variety of illumination conditions. Note that illuminant priors learning is performed once and for all, even before choosing the classes of interest.

The estimation of the illuminants present in the scene, together with the determination of which illuminant impinges on each surface element, is performed by a Maximum–A–Posteriori (MAP) algorithm based on the distributions estimated in the training phase. Our formulation of the MAP criterion is very similar to the one by Tsin et al. [3]. Our work, however, differs from [3] in two main aspects. Firstly, [3] requires that a number of images of the same scene, containing the surface types of interest, are collected by a fixed camera under variable lighting conditions. While this training procedure may be feasible for surveillance systems with still cameras, it is impractical for other applications (such as robotics). As mentioned earlier, our system only requires one image containing the surfaces of interest under a single illuminant. Secondly, our algorithm is conceptually and computationally simpler than [3]. Instead of an ad–hoc procedure, we rely on the well–understood Expectation Maximization algorithm for illuminant parameter estimation. A simple modification of the EM algorithm allows us to include the prior distribution of the illuminant parameters for a truly Bayesian estimation. Illuminant priors are critical when dealing with scenes containing surfaces that were not used during training. Without prior knowledge of the actual statistics of illuminant parameters, the system would be tempted to "explain too much" of the scene, that is, to model the color of a never seen before surface as the transformation of a known reflectance under a very unlikely light. To further shield the algorithm from the influence of "outlier" surfaces, we also augment the set of classes with a non–informative class distribution, a standard procedure in similar cases. The price to pay for the simplicity of our algorithm is a less accurate model of color production than in [3], which potentially may lead to lower accuracy in the illuminant compensation process. We use the diagonal model [8] to relate the variation of the illuminant spectrum to the perceived color. It is well known that a single diagonal color transformation cannot, in general, accurately predict the new colors of different surface types. However, we argue that the computational advantages of using such a simple model largely offset the possibly inaccurate color prediction. Note that other researchers have used the diagonal color transformation for classification purposes (e.g. [12]).

2   The Algorithm

Assume that K surface classes of interest have been identified, and that training has been performed over one or more images, where all samples used for training are illuminated by the same illuminant. Let $p(c|k)$ denote the conditional like-lihood over colors c for the class model k, as estimated from the training data. The total likelihood of color c is thus

$$p(c) = \sum_{k=1}^{K} P_K(k)p(c|k) \qquad (1)$$

where $P_K(k)$ is the prior probability of surface class k. In general, a scene to be classified contains a number of surfaces, some (but not all) of which belong to the set of classes used for training, and are illuminated by one or more illuminants which may be different from the illuminant used for training. Assume there are L possible illuminant types in the scene. Let c be the color of the pixel which is the projection of a certain surface patch under illuminant type l. We will denote by $F_l(c)$ the operator that transforms c into the color that would be seen if the illuminant of type l had the same spectrum as the one used for training, all other conditions being the same (remember that only one illuminant is used for training). Then, one may compute the conditional likelihood of a color c in a test image given surface class k, illuminant type l, and transformation F_l:

$$p_F(c|k,l) = p(F_l(c)|k)|J(F_l)|_c \qquad (2)$$

where $|J(F_l)|_c$ is the absolute value of the Jacobian of F_l at c.

We will begin our analysis by making the following assumptions: 1) The surface class and illuminant type at any given pixel are mutually independent random variables; 2) The surface class and illuminant type at any given pixel are independent of the surface classes and illuminant types at nearby pixels; 3) The color of any given pixel is indepedent of the color of nearby pixels, even when they correspond to the same surface class and illuminant type; 4) Each surface element is illuminated by just one illuminant. Assumption 1) is fairly well justified: the fact that a surface is under direct sunlight or in the shade should be independent of the surface type. It should be noticed, however, that in case of "rough" surfaces (e.g., foliage), self–shading will always be present even when the surface is under direct sunlight. Assumption 2) is not very realistic: nearby pixels are very likely to belong to the same surface class and illuminant type. This is indeed a general problem in computer vision, by no means specific to this particular application. We can therefore resort to standard approaches to deal with spatial coherence [16,15]. The "independent noise" assumption 3) is perhaps not fully realistic (nearby pixels of the same smooth surface under the same illuminant will have similar color), but, in our experience, it is a rather harmless, and computationally quite convenient, hypothesis. Assumption 4) is a very good approximation for outdoor scenes, where the only two illuminants (excluding inter–reflections) are direct sunlight and diffuse light (shade) [1].

With such assumptions in place, we may write the total log–likelihood of the collection of color points in the image, C, given the set of L transformations F_l, as

$$L_F(C) = \sum_x \log \sum_{l=1}^{L} \sum_{k=1}^{K} P_{KL}(k,l) p_F(c(x)|k,l) \qquad (3)$$

$$= \sum_x \log \sum_{l=1}^{L} \sum_{k=1}^{K} P_K(k) P_L(l) p(F_l(c(x))|k)|J(F_l)|_{c(x)}$$

where $c(x)$ is the color at pixel x, and we factorized the joint prior distribution of surface class and illuminant type ($P_{KL}(k,l) = P_K(k)P_L(l)$) according to Assumption 1. Note that the first summation extends over all image pixels, and that L and K are the number of possible illuminants and surface classes, which are supposed to be known in advance. In our experiments with outdoor scenes, we always assumed that only two illuminants (sunlight and diffuse light) were be present, hence $L=2$.

Our goal here is to estimate the L transformations $\{F_l\}$ from the image C, knowing the conditional likelihoods $p(c|k)$ and the priors $P_K(k)$ and $P_L(l)$. Once such transformations have been estimated, we may assign each pixel x a surface class k and illuminant type l as by

$$\{k,l\} = \arg\max P_K(k) P_L(l) p(F_l(c(x))|k)|J(F_l)|_{c(x)} \qquad (4)$$

We will first present a ML strategy to determine $\{F_l\}$, which maximizes the total image log–likelihood (3). In Section 2.3, we will show how existing priors on the color transformations can be used in a MAP setting.

2.1   Estimating the Illuminant Parameters

As mentioned in the Introduction, we will restrict our attention to diagonal transformations of the type $F_l(c) = D_l c$, where $D_l = \mathrm{diag}\,(d_{l,1}, d_{l,2}, d_{l,3})$. Note that in this case, $|J(F_l)|_{c(x)} = |d_{l,1}d_{l,2}d_{l,3}|$. To make the optimization problem more tractable, we will assume that $p(c|k) \in \mathcal{N}(\mu_k, \Sigma_k)$. While this Gaussian assumption may not be acceptable in general (especially for multimodal color distributions), it has been shown in the literature that mixtures of Gaussians can successfully model color distributions [5,19]. The extension of our optimization algorithm to the case of Gaussian mixtures is trivial.

The optimal set of $3L$ color transformation coefficients $\{d_{l,m}\}$ can be found using Expectation Maximization (EM) [13]. EM is an iterative algorithm that re–estimates the model parameters in such a way that the total image log–likelihood, $L_F(C)$, is increased at each iteration. It is shown in Appendix A that each iteration is comprised of L independent estimations, one per illuminant type. For the l–th illuminant type, one needs to compute

$$\{d_{l,m}\} = \arg \max \left[u_l \sum_{\bar{m}=1}^{3} \log |d_{l,\bar{m}}| - 0.5 \, d_l' G_l d_l + H_l' d_l \right] \qquad (5)$$

where $d_l = (d_{l,1}, d_{l,2}, d_{l,3})'$. The scalar u_l, the 3x3 matrix G_l and the 3x1 vector H_l are defined in Appendix A, and are re–computed at each iteration. Our task now is to minimize (5) over $(d_{l,1}, d_{l,2}, d_{l,3})$. Note that the partial derivatives with respect to $d_{l,m}$ of the function to be maximized can be computed explicitely. Setting such partial derivatives to zero yields the following system of quadratic equations for $m = 1, 2, 3$:

$$\sum_s G_{l,m,s}d_{l,s}d_{l,m} - H_{l,m}d_{l,m} - u_l = 0 \qquad (6)$$

While this system cannot be solved in closed form, we note that if two variables (say, $d_{l,1}$ and $d_{l,2}$) are kept fixed, then the partial derivative of (5) with respect to the third variable can be set to 0 by solving a simple quadratic equation. Hence, we can minimize (5) by using the Direction Set method [14], i.e. iterating function minimization over the three axes until some convergence criterion is reached. Note that this is a very fast maximization procedure, and that its complexity is independent of the number of pixels in the image.

2.2   Outliers

Any classification algorithm should account for "unexpected" situations that were not considered during training, by recognizing outlier or "none of the above" points. A popular strategy treats outliers as an additional class, for which a prior probability and a least informative conditional likelihood are defined [20]. For example, if one knows that the observables can only occupy a bounded region in the measurement space (a realistic assumption in the case of color features), one may allocate a uniform outlier distribution over such a region.

In our work, we defined an outlier surface class with an associated uniform conditional likelihood over the color cube $[0 : 255]^3$. Note that the outlier class contributes to the parameter estimation only indirectly, in the sense that equation (2) does not apply to it. In other words, color transformations do not change the conditional likelihood given the outlier class.

2.3   Imposing Illuminant Priors

A problem with the approach detailed above is that the algorithm, when presented with scenes that contain surfaces with very different colors from the ones used for training, may arbitrarily "invent" unusual illuminant in order to maximize the scene likelihood. Illuminant spectral distributions in outdoor scene are rather constrained [4,1]; this observation should be exploited to reduce the risk of such catastrophic situations. Prior distributions on the parameters can indeed be plugged into the same EM machinery used for Maximum Likelihood by suitably modifying the function to be maximized at each iteration. More precisely, as discussed in [13], imposing a prior distribution on the parameter d translated into adding the term $\log p_D(\{D_l\})$ to the function $Q\left(\{D_l\}, \{D_l^0\}\right)$ in Appendix A before the maximization step. Assuming that the different illuminants in the scene are statistically independent, we may write

$$\log p_D(\{D_l\}) = \sum_l^L \log p_d(d_l) \tag{7}$$

where $d_l = (d_{l,1}, d_{l,2}, d_{l,3})'$. We will assume that all L illuminant types have the same prior probability.

One way to represent the illuminant priors could be to start from the CIE parametric curve, thus deriving a statistical model for the matrices D_l. Another approach, which we used in this work, is to take a number of pictures of the same target under a large number of illumination conditions, and analyze the variability of the color transformation matrices. For example, in our experiments we took 39 pictures of the Macbeth color chart at random times during daylight over the course of one week. For each corresponding color square in each pair of images in our set, we computed the ratios of the r, g and b color components in the two images. The hope is that the ensemble of all such triplets can adequately model the distribution of diagonal color transformations. We built a Gaussian model for the prior distribution of d by computing the mean μ_d and covariance Σ_d of the collected color ratio triplets. These Gaussian priors can be injected into our algorithm by modifying (5) into

$$\{d_{l,m}\} = \arg\max \left[u_l \sum_{\bar{m}=1}^3 \log |d_{l,\bar{m}}| - 0.5\ d_l'(G_l + \Sigma_d^{-1})d_l + (H_l' + \mu_d'\Sigma_d^{-1})d_l \right] \tag{8}$$

Fortunately, even with this new formulation of the optimization criterion, we can still use the Direction Set algorithm for maximization, as in Section 2.1.

3   Experiments

3.1   Macbeth Color Chart Experiments

In order to provide a quantitative evaluation of our algorithm's performance, we first experimented using mosaics formed by color squares extracted from

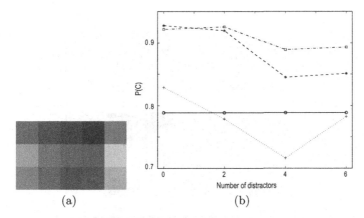

(a)   (b)

Fig. 1. (a) The color squares used for training (center row) and for testing(top and bottom row) in the Macbeth color chart experiment. (b) The probability of correct match $P(C)$ as a function of the total number of distractors for the Macbeth color chart experiment without illuminant compensation (solid line), with ML illuminant compensation (dotted line), with MAP illuminant compensation without the outlier class (dashed line), and with MAP illuminant compensation using the outlier class (dashed–dotted line).

pictures of the GretagMacbeth™ chart under different illuminations, taken by a Sony DSC–S75 camera[2]. We picked 5 colors from the chart (No. 2, 14, 3, 22,11) as representative of 5 classes of interest. In Figure 1(a) we show the five colors as seen under evening light (after sunset, top row), direct afternoon sunlight (center row), and diffuse (shade) afternoon light (bottom row). We ran a number of experiment by training the system over the color squares in the middle row of Figure 1(a), and testing on a mosaic composed by color squares in the the top and bottom row, as well as by other colors in the chart ("distractors"). More precisely, for each test we formed two samples, one from the top row and one from the bottom row of Figure 1(a). Each sample had a number (randomly chosen between 0 and 5) of color squares, randomly chosen from those in the corresponding row, making sure that at least one of such two samples was not empty. Then, we augmented each sample with a number of randomly selected distractors, that were not present in the training set. The test image is the union of the two samples. We ran 100 tests for each choice of the number of distractors per sample (which varied from 0 to 3). At each test, we first tried to assign each non–distractor color in the test image to one of the colors in the training set using Euclidean distance in color space. The ratio between the cumulative number of correct matches and the cumulative number of non–distractors squares in the test images over all 100 tests provides an indication of the probability of correct match without illuminant compensation. Such value is shown in Figure 1(b) by solid line. Obviously, these results do not depend on the number of distractors. In

---

[*] In order to roughly compensate for the camera's gamma correction, we squared each color component before processing.

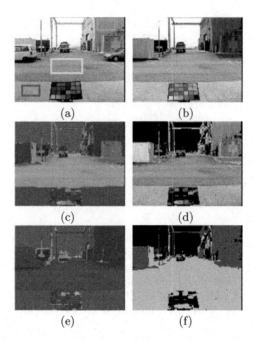

Fig. 2. Color classification experiments: (a): training image; (b) test image; (c) classification with illuminant compensation (blue indicates outliers); (d) illuminant–compensated version of the test image; (e) classification without illuminant compensation; (f) estimated illuminant distribution (black indicates outliers).

order to test our illumination compensation algorithm, we added some "virtual noise" to the colors within each square, by imposing a diagonal covariance matrix with marginal variances equal to 10^8 (the reader is reminded that the color values were squared to reduce the effect of camera gamma correction). This artifice is necessary in this case because the color distribution in the squares had extremely small variance, which would create numerical problems in the implementation of the EM iterations. We didn't need to add noise in the real–world tests of Section 3.2. The number L of illuminants in the algorithm was set to 2. The probability of correct match after illuminant compensation using the ML algorithm of Section 2.1 (without exploiting illuminant priors and without the outlier class), of the MAP algorithm of Section 2.3 (without the outlier class), and of the MAP algorithm using the outlier class, are shown in Figure 1(b) by dotted line, dashed line, and dashed–dotted line respectively. Note that the distractors contribute to the determination of the illuminant parameters, and therefore affect the performance of the illuminant compensation system, as seen in Figure 1(b). Distractors have a dramatic negative effect if the illuminant priors are not taken into consideration, since the system will "invent" unlikely illumination parameters. However, the MAP algorithm is much less sensitive to distractors; if, in addition, the outlier class is used in the optimization, we see

Fig. 3. Color classification experiments: (a): training image; (b) test image; (c) classification with illuminant compensation (blue indicates outliers); (d) estimated illuminant distribution (black indicates outliers); (e) illuminant–compensated version of the test image; (f) classification without illuminant compensation; (g) classification without illuminant compensation (without outlier class).

that illuminant compensation allows one to increase the correct match rate by 5–13%.

3.2   Experiments with Real–World Scenes

We tested our algorithm on a number of outdoor scenes, with consistently good results. We present two experiments of illuminant–compensated color classification in Figure 2 and 3. Figure 2 (a) and (b) shows two images of the same scene under very different illuminants. Three color classes were trained over the rectangular areas shown in the image of Figure 2 (a), with one Gaussian mode per class. The result of classification after illuminant compensation are shown in Figure 2 (c). Pixels colored in blue are considered outliers. Note that for this set of images, we extended our definition of outlier to overexposed pixels (i.e., pixels that have one or more color components equal to 255), which typically correspond to the visible portion of the sky. Figure 2 (d) shows the illuminant–compensated image. It is seen that normalization yields colors that are very similar to those in the training image. The assignment of illuminant types is shown in Figure 2 (f). Figure 2 (e) shows the result of classification without illuminant compensation. In this case, large image areas have been assigned to the outlier class, while other areas have been misclassified. Comparing these results with those of Figure 2 (c) shows the performance improvement enabled by our illuminant compensation algorithm.

Our second experiment is described in Figure 3. Figure 3 (a) shows the training image (three classes were trained using the pixels within the marked rectangles), while Figure 3 (b) shows the test image. The results of classification after illuminant estimation are shown in Figure 3 (c). Pixels colored in blue are considered outliers. The assignment of illuminant types is shown in Figure 3 (d), while Figure 3 (e) shows the illuminant–compensated image; note how illuminant compensation "casts light" over the shaded areas. The classifier without illuminant compensation (Figure 3 (f)) finds several outlier pixels in the shadow area. If forced to make a choice without the outlier option (Figure 3 (g)), it misclassifies the pixels corresponding to stones in the pathway.

References

1. S. Buluswar and S.D. Draper, "Estimating Apparent Color in Outdoor Images", *Computer Vision and Image Understanding*, 85(2).
2. M. Tsukada and Y. Ohta, "An Approach to Color Constancy Using Multiple Images", *IEEE ICCV*, 385–389, 1990.
3. Y. Tsin, R.T. Collins, V. Ramesh and T. Kanade, "Bayesian Color Constancy for Outdoor Object Recognition", *IEEE CVPR*, December 2001.
4. D. Judd, D. MacAdam , G. Wyszecki, "Spectral Distribution of Typical Daylight as a Function of Correlated Color Temperature", *JOSA*, 54(8):1031–1040, 1964.
5. P. Bellutta, R. Manduchi, L. Matthies, K. Owens, A. Rankin, "Terrain Perception for DEMO III", *IEEE Intelligent Vehicles Symposium 2000*, Dearborn, MI, October 2000, 326-332.
6. D.H. Brainard and W.T Freeman, "Bayesian Color Constancy", *JOSA–A*, 14:1393–1411, July 1997.
7. M. D'Zmura and G. Iverson, "Color Constancy I - Basic Theory of Two–Stage Linear Recovery of Spectral Descriptions for Lights and Surfaces", *JOSA*, 10(10:2148–2165, October 1993.
8. G. Finlayson, M. Drew and B. Funt, "Diagonal Transforms Suffice for Color Constancy, *IEEE ICCV*, 162–171, 1993.
9. D. Forsyth, "A Novel Approach for Color Constancy", *International Journal of Computer Vision*, 5:5–36, 1990.
10. G. Healey, "Segmenting Images Using Normalized Colors", *IEEE Trans. Syst., Man and Cybern.*, 22(1):64–73, January 1992.
11. L.T. Maloney and B. Wandell, "A Computational Model of Color Constancy", *JOSA*, 1(1):29–33, January 1986.
12. C. Rosenberg, M. Hebert amd S. Thrun, "Color Constancy Using KL–Divergence", *IEEE ICCV*, 2001.

13. G.J McLachlan and T. Krisnan, *The EM Algorithm and Extensions*, Wiley, 1997.
14. W. H. Press, B. P. Flannery, S. A. Teukolsky andW. T. Vetterling, *Numerical Recipes: The Art of Scientific Computing*, Cambidge Unviersity Press, 1986.
15. Y. Weiss and E.H. Adelson, "A Unified Mixture Framework for Motion Segmentation: Incorporating Spatial Coherence and Estimating the Number of Models", *IEEE CVPR*, 321–326, 1996.
16. J. Zhang, J.W. Modestino and D.A. Langan, "Maximum–Likelihood Parameter Estimation for Unsupervised Stochastic Model–Based Image Segmentation", *IEEE Trans. Image Proc.*, 3(4):404–420, July 1994.
17. J. Besag,"On the Statistical Analysis of Dirty Pictures", *J. Royal Stat. Soc. B.*, 48:259–302, 1986.
18. B.D. Ripley, *Pattern Recognition and Neural Networks*, Cambridge University Press, 1996.
19. H. Riad and R. Mohr, "Gaussian Mixture Densities for Indexing of Localized Objects in Video Sequences", INRIA Technical Report RR-3905, 2000.
20. E.T. Jaynes, *Probability Theory as Extended Logic*, unpublished, available at http://bayes.wustl.edu.

Appendix A

In this Appendix, we show how the total likelihood $L_F(C)$ can be maximized over the parameters $\{d_{l,m}\}$ using Expectation Maximization (EM). Using the diagonal illumination model, we can rewrite $L_F(C)$ as

$$L_D(C) = \sum_x \log \sum_{l=1}^{L} \sum_{k=1}^{K} P_K(k) P_L(l) p(D_l c(x)|k) \det |D_l| \qquad (9)$$

As customary with the EM procedure, we first introduce the "hidden" variables $z_{l,k}(x)$ which represent the (unknown) label assignments: $z_{k,l}(x)=1$ if the pixel x is assigned to the illuminant type l and surface class k; $z_{k,l}(x)=0$ otherwise. We will denote the set of $z_{k,l}(x)$ over the image by Z.

The EM algorithm starts from arbitrary values for the diagonal matrices $\{D_l^0\}$, and iterates over the following two steps:

– Compute

$$Q\left(\{D_l\}, \{D_l^0\}\right) = E_{\{D_l^0\}}\left[\log p_{\{D_l\}}(C, Z)|C\right] \qquad (10)$$

$$= E_{\{D_l^0\}}\left[\log p_{\{D_l\}}(C|Z)|C\right] + E_{\{D_l^0\}}\left[\log p_{\{D_l\}}(Z)|C\right]$$

where $E_{\{D_l^0\}}[\cdot|C]$ represents expectation over $p_{\{D_l^0\}}(Z|C)$.
– Replace $\{D_l^0\}$ with arg max $Q\left(\{D_l\}, \{D_l^0\}\right)$.

Given the assumed independence of label assignments, and the particular form chosen for variables $z_{k,l}(x)$, we can write

$$\log p_{\{D_l\}}(C|Z) = \sum_x \sum_{k=1}^{K} \sum_{l=1}^{L} z_{k,l} \log p(D_l c(x)|k) \qquad (11)$$

where, given that the conditional likelihood are assumed to be Gaussian:

$$\log p(D_l c(x)|k) = -1.5 \; \log(2\pi) - \log |\det \Sigma_k| \tag{12}$$
$$-0.5 \; (D_l c(x) - \mu_k)\Sigma_k^{-1}(D_l c(x) - \mu_k)$$

Also,

$$\log p_{\{D_l\}}(Z) = \sum_x \sum_{k=1}^K \sum_{l=1}^L z_{k,l} \left(\log P_K(k) + \log P_L(l)\right) \tag{13}$$

It is easy to see that

$$E_{\{D_l^0\}}\left[\log p_{\{D_l\}}(C|Z)|C\right] = \sum_x \sum_{k=1}^K \sum_{l=1}^L \log p(D_l c(x)|k) P_{\{D_l^0\}}(k,l|c(x)) \tag{14}$$

and

$$E_{\{D_l^0\}}\left[\log p_{\{D_l\}}(Z)|C\right] = \sum_x \sum_{k=1}^K \sum_{l=1}^L \left(\log P_K(k) + \log P_L(l)\right) P_{\{D_l^0\}}(k,l|c(x)) \tag{15}$$

where $P_{\{D_l^0\}}(k,l|c(x)) = E_{\{D_l^0\}}[z_{k,l}(x)]$ is the posterior probability of surface class k and illumination type l given the observation $c(x)$ and under color transformation matrices $\{D_l^0\}$. Using Bayes' rule, we can compute $P_{\{D_l^0\}}(k,l|c(x))$ as

$$P_{\{D_l^0\}}(k,l|c(x)) = \tag{16}$$
$$\frac{P_K(k)P_L(l)p(D_l^0 c(x)|k) \det |D_l^0|}{\sum_{\bar{k}=1}^K \sum_{\bar{l}=1}^L P_K(\bar{k})P_L(\bar{l})p(D_{\bar{l}}^0 c(x)|\bar{k}) \det |D_{\bar{l}}^0|}$$

Remembering that $|D_l| = |d_{l,1}d_{l,2}d_{l,3}|$ one sees that

$$\max_{\{d_{l,m}\}} Q\left(\{D_l\},\{D_l^0\}\right) \tag{17}$$
$$= \max_{\{d_{l,m}\}} \sum_{l=1}^L \left[u_l \sum_{m=1}^3 \log |d_{l,m}| - 0.5 \; d_l' G_l d_l + H_l' d_l\right]$$

where $d_l = (d_{l,1}, d_{l,2}, d_{l,3})'$, and

$$u_l = \sum_x \sum_{k=1}^K P_{\{D_l^0\}}(k,l|c(x)) \tag{18}$$

$$G_{l,m,s} = \sum_x \sum_{k=1}^K S_{k,m,s} c_m(x) c_s(x) P_{\{D_l^0\}}(k,l|c(x)) \tag{19}$$

$$H_{l,m} = \sum_x \sum_{k=1}^K \sum_{s=1}^3 S_{k,m,s} c_s(x) \mu_{k,s} P_{\{D_l^0\}}(k,l|c(x)) \tag{20}$$

where $S_k = \Sigma_k^{-1}$. Note that the terms in the summation over l in (17) can be maximized independently, meaning that the L sets of diagonal transformations can be computed independently at each iterations.

A Polynomial-Time Metric for Attributed Trees

Andrea Torsello[1], Džena Hidović[2], and Marcello Pelillo[1]

[.] Dipartimento di Informatica, Università Ca' Foscari di Venezia
Via Torino 155, 30172 Venezia Mestre, Italy
{torsello,pelillo}@dsi.unive.it
[.] School of Computer Science, University of Birmingham
Edgbaston, Birmingham, B15 2TT, United Kingdom
D.Hidovic@cs.bham.ac.uk

Abstract. We address the problem of comparing attributed trees and propose a novel distance measure centered around the notion of a maximal similarity common subtree. The proposed measure is general and defined on trees endowed with either symbolic or continuous-valued attributes, and can be equally applied to ordered and unordered, rooted and unrooted trees. We prove that our measure satisfies the metric constraints and provide a polynomial-time algorithm to compute it. This is a remarkable and attractive property since the computation of traditional edit-distance-based metrics is NP-complete, except for ordered structures. We experimentally validate the usefulness of our metric on shape matching tasks, and compare it with edit-distance measures.

1 Introduction

Graph-based representations have long been used with considerable success in computer vision and pattern recognition in the abstraction and recognition of objects and scene structure. Concrete examples include the use of shock graphs to represent shape-skeletons [11,15], the use of trees to represent articulated objects [7] and the use of aspect graphs for 3D object representation [3]. The attractive feature of structural representations is that they concisely capture the relational arrangement of object primitives, in a manner which can be invariant to changes in object viewpoint. Using this framework we can transform a recognition problem into a relational matching problem. The problem of how to measure the similarity or distance of pictorial information using graph abstractions has been a widely researched topic of over twenty years.

The classic metric approach to graph comparison is edit-distance [4]. The idea behind this approach is that it is possible to identify a set of basic edit operations on nodes and edges of a structure, and to associate with these operations a cost. The edit-distance is found by searching for sequences of edit operations that will make the two graphs isomorphic with one-another, and the distance between the two graphs is then defined to be the minimum over all the costs of these sequences. By making the evaluation of structural modification explicit, edit-distance provides a very effective way of measuring the similarity

T. Pajdla and J. Matas (Eds.): ECCV 2004, LNCS 3024, pp. 414–427, 2004.
© Springer-Verlag Berlin Heidelberg 2004

of relational structures. Moreover, the method has considerable potential for error tolerant object recognition and indexing problems. Unfortunately, the task of calculating edit-distance is an NP-hard problem [24], hence, goal-directed approximations are necessary to calculate it. The result is that the approximation almost invariably breaks the theoretical metric properties of the measure.

Recently, a new and more principled approach to the definition of distance measure has emerged. In [2], Bunke and Shearer introduce a distance measure on unattributed graphs based on the maximum common subgraph and prove that it is a metric. Wallis et al. [20] introduce a variant of this distance based on the size of the minimum common supergraph. Finally, Fernandez and Valiente [5] define a metric based on the difference in size between maximum common subgraph and minimum common supergraph. More recently, in [6] Hidović and Pelillo extend these metrics to the case of attributed graphs. Unfortunately all these metrics require the calculation of the maximum common subgraph, which is computationally equivalent to the calculation of edit-distance.

In many computer vision and pattern recognition applications, such as shape recognition [13,15,17], the graphs at hand have a peculiar structure: they are connected and acyclic, i.e., they are *trees*, either rooted or unrooted, ordered or unordered, and frequently they are endowed with symbolic and/or continuous-valued attributes. Most metrics on trees found in the literature are defined in terms of edit-distance [18,21]. Zhang and Shasha [23] have investigated a special case of edit-distance which involves trees with an order relation among sibling nodes in a rooted tree. This special case constrains the solution to maintain the order of the children of a node. They showed that this constrained tree-matching problem is solvable in polynomial time and gave an algorithm to solve it. Recently, Sebastian, Klein and Kimia [13] use a similar algorithm to compare shock trees. Unfortunately, in the general case the problem has been proven to be NP-complete both for rooted [24] and unrooted trees [25]. Recently, Valiente [19] introduced a bottom-up distance measure between trees that is an extension to trees of the graph metric introduced by Bunke and Shearer [2], proving that the measure can be calculated in polynomial time on trees, but falling short of proving that the measure is a metric. While this measure can be calculated efficiently both on ordered and unordered trees, it is limited to rooted and unattributed trees.

Motivated by the work described in [6], in this paper we propose a normalized distance measure for trees equipped with either symbolic or continuous-valued attributes. We prove that the proposed measure fulfills the properties of a metric, and provide a polynomial-time algorithm to compute it. At an abstract level, our approach involves the computation of a maximum similarity common subtree. This allows us to define equivalent variations of the metric on ordered and unordered, rooted and unrooted, and attributed and unattributed trees. Since edit-distance on ordered trees can be computed in polynomial time, in the paper we focus on the unordered case where our approach provides a clear computational advantage. To show the validity of the proposed measures, we present experiments on various shape matching tasks and compare our results with those obtained using edit-distance metrics.

2   Preliminaries

Let $G = (V, E)$ be a graph, where V is the set of nodes (or vertices) and E is the set of undirected edges. Two nodes $u, v \in V$ are said to be *adjacent* (denoted $u \sim v$) if they are connected by an edge. A *path* is any sequence of distinct nodes $u_0 u_1 \ldots u_n$ such that for all $i = 1 \ldots n$, $u_{i-1} \sim u_i$; in this case, the *length* of the path is n. If $u_n \sim u_0$ the path is called a *cycle*. A graph is said to be *connected* if any two nodes are joined by a path. Given a subset of nodes $C \subseteq V$, the *induced subgraph* $G[C]$ is the graph having C as its node set, and two nodes are adjacent in $G[C]$ if and only if they are adjacent in G. With the notation $|G|$ we shall refer to the cardinality of the node-set of graph G.

A connected graph with no cycles is called an unrooted tree. A rooted (or hierarchical) tree is a tree with a special node that can be identified as the root. In what follows, when using the word "tree" without qualification, we shall refer to both the rooted and unrooted cases. Given two nodes $u, v \in V$ in a rooted tree, u is said to be an *ancestor* of v (and similarly v is said to be a *descendent* of u) if the path from the root node to u is a subpath of the path from the root to v. Furthermore, if $u \sim v$, u is said to be the *parent* of v and v is said to be a *child* of u. Both ancestor and descendent relations are order relations in V.

Let $T_1 = (V_1, E_1)$ and $T_2 = (V_2, E_2)$ be two trees. Any bijection $\phi : H_1 \to H_2$, with $H_1 \subseteq V_1$ and $H_2 \subseteq V_2$, is called a *subtree isomorphism* if it preserves both the adjacency relationships between the nodes and the connectedness of the matched subgraphs. Formally, this means that, given $u, v \in H_1$, we have $u \sim v$ if and only if $\phi(u) \sim \phi(v)$ and, in addition, the induced subgraphs $T_1[H_1]$ and $T_2[H_2]$ are connected. Two trees or rooted trees T_1 and T_2 are *isomorphic*, and we write $T_1 \cong T_2$, if there exists an isomorphism between them that maps every node in T_1 to every node in T_2. It is easy to verify that isomorphism is an equivalence relation. We shall use the notations $\mathrm{Dom}(\phi)$ and $\mathrm{Im}(\phi)$ to denote the domain and the image of ϕ, respectively.

Formally, an *attributed tree* is a triple $T = (V, E, \alpha)$, where (V, E) is the "underlying" tree and α is a function which assigns an attribute vector $\alpha(u)$ to each node $u \in V$. It is clear that in matching two attributed trees, our objective is to find an isomorphism which pairs nodes having "similar" attributes. To this end, let σ be any similarity measure on the attribute space, i.e., any (symmetric) function which assigns a positive number to any pair of attribute vectors. If $\phi : H_1 \to H_2$ is a subgraph isomorphism between two attributed trees $T_1 = (V_1, E_1, \alpha_1)$ and $T_2 = (V_2, E_2, \alpha_2)$, the overall similarity between the induced subtrees $T_1[H_1]$ and $T_2[H_2]$ can be defined as follows:

$$W_\sigma(\phi) = \sum_{u \in H_1} \sigma(u, \phi(u)) . \tag{1}$$

where, for simplicity, we define $\sigma(u, \phi(u)) \equiv \sigma(\alpha_1(u), \alpha_2(\phi(u)))$. The isomorphism ϕ is called a *maximum similarity subtree isomorphism* if $W_\sigma(\phi)$ is largest among all subtree isomorphisms between T_1 and T_2. For the rest of the paper we will omit the subscript σ when the node-similarity used is clear from the context. Two isomorphic attributed trees $T_1 = (V_1, E_1, \alpha_1)$ and $T_2 = (V_2, E_2, \alpha_2)$, with isomorphism ϕ, are said to be *attribute-isomorphic* if for all $u \in V_1$ we have $\alpha_1(u) = \alpha_2(\phi(u))$. In this case we shall write $T_1 \cong_a T_2$. Attribute-isomorphism is clearly an equivalence relation.

Note that the problem of determining a maximum similarity subtree isomorphism is a direct extension of the standard problem of finding a maximum (cardinality) common subtree, in fact the two problems are equivalent when the similarity σ is degenerate, i.e., $\sigma(u, v) = 1$.

Now, given a set S, a function $d : S \times S \to \mathbb{R}$ is a *metric* on S if the following properties hold for any $x, y, z \in S$.

1. $d(x, x) \geq 0$ (non-negativity)
2. $d(x, y) = 0 \Leftrightarrow x = y$ (identity and uniqueness)
3. $d(x, y) = d(y, x)$ (symmetry)
4. $d(x, y) + d(y, z) \geq d(x, z)$ (triangular inequality).

Furthermore, if the function satisfies $d(x, y) \leq 1$ it is said to be a *normalized metric*.

If $d : S \times S \to \mathbb{R}_+$ is a normalized metric, then the similarity function derived from δ, defined as $\sigma(x, y) = 1 - d(x, y)$ fulfills the identity, uniqueness and similarity properties. Furthermore, it fulfills the following variant of the triangular inequality: $\sigma(x, y) + \sigma(y, z) - \sigma(x, z) \leq 1$. In the rest of the paper, we shall assume that all similarity functions are indeed derived from normalized metrics.

It is straightforward to show that, with this assumption, we have

$$T_1 \cong_a T_2 \Leftrightarrow |T_1| = |T_2| = W(\phi) \tag{2}$$

where ϕ is a maximum similarity isomorphism between T_1 and T_2.

3   Distance Metric

In this section, we define our measure for comparing attributed trees and prove that it fulfills the metric properties. First, we prove a lemma that turns out to be instrumental to prove our results, then, we introduce our measure and prove the metric properties.

Lemma 1. *Let T_1, T_2 and T_3 be three trees, and ϕ_{12} ϕ_{23}, and ϕ_{13} be maximum similarity subtrees isomorphisms between T_1 and T_2, T_2 and T_3, and T_1 and T_3, respectively. Then, we have: $|T_2| \geq W(\phi_{12}) + W(\phi_{23}) - W(\phi_{13})$.*

Proof. Let $V_2^1 = \mathrm{Im}(\phi_{12}) \subseteq V_2$, $V_2^3 = \mathrm{Dom}(\phi_{23}) \subseteq V_2$ be the sets of nodes in V_2 mapped by the isomorphisms ϕ_{12} and ϕ_{23}, respectively. Furthermore, let $\hat{V}_2 = V_2^1 \cap V_2^3$, be the set of vertices in V_2 that are mapped by both isomorphisms. It is clear that the subtrees $\hat{T}_1 = T_1[\phi_{12}^{-1}(\hat{V}_2)]$ and $\hat{T}_3 = T_3[\phi_{23}(\hat{V}_2)]$ are isomorphic to each-other, with isomorphism $\hat{\phi}_{13} = \phi_{12} \circ \phi_{23}$, where $\circ$ denotes the standard function composition operator, restricted to the nodes of $\hat{T}_1$. The similarity of this isomorphism is

$$W(\hat{\phi}_{13}) = \sum_{v \in \hat{V}_2} \sigma(\phi_{12}^{-1}(v), \phi_{23}(v)).$$

Since ϕ_{13} is a maximum similarity subtree isomorphism between T_1 and T_3, we have $W(\phi_{13}) \geq W(\hat{\phi}_{13})$. Hence

$$W(\phi_{12}) + W(\phi_{23}) - W(\phi_{13}) \leq W(\phi_{12}) + W(\phi_{23}) - W(\hat{\phi}_{13}) =$$

$$\sum_{v \in V_2^1} \sigma(\phi_{12}^{-1}(v), v) + \sum_{v \in V_2^3} \sigma(v, \phi_{23}(v)) - \sum_{v \in \hat{V}_2} \sigma(\phi_{12}^{-1}(v), \phi_{23}(v)) =$$

$$\sum_{v \in V_2^1 \setminus V_2^3} \sigma(\phi_{12}^{-1}(v), v) + \sum_{v \in V_2^3 \setminus V_2^1} \sigma(v, \phi_{23}(v)) +$$

$$\sum_{v \in \hat{V}_2} \left[\sigma(\phi_{12}^{-1}(v), v) + \sigma(v, \phi_{23}(v)) - \sigma(\phi_{12}^{-1}(v), \phi_{23}(v)) \right] \leq$$

$$|V_2^1 \setminus V_2^3| + |V_2^3 \setminus V_2^1| + |V_2^1 \cap V_2^3| = |V_2^1 \cup V_2^3| \leq |T_2|,$$

where the inequality follows from the triangular inequality for metric-derived similarities. □

Let $\mathcal{T}$ be the quotient set of trees modulo attribute-isomorphism, that is the set of trees on which two trees are considered the same if they are attribute-isomorphic.[1] For any $T_1, T_2 \in \mathcal{T}$ we define the following distance function

$$d(T_1, T_2) = 1 - \frac{W(\phi_{12})}{\max(|T_1|, |T_2|)} . \tag{3}$$

Theorem 1. d *is a normalized metric in* $\mathcal{T}$.

Proof.

1. $d(T_1, T_2) \geq 0$
   We have $0 \leq W(\phi_{12}) \leq \max(|T_1|, |T_2|)$. Hence, $0 \leq d(T_1, T_2) = 1 - \frac{W(\phi_{12})}{\max(|T_1|, |T_2|)} \leq 1$.
2. $d(T_1, T_2) = 0 \iff T_1 \cong_a T_2$
   Let us consider the direction of implication $\Leftarrow$ (identity). From (2), we have $T_1 \cong_a T_2 \Rightarrow |T_1| = |T_2| = W(\phi_{12})$. Hence $d(T_1, T_2) = \frac{\max(|T_1|, |T_2|) - W(\phi_{12})}{\max(|T_1|, |T_2|)} = 0$
   For the reverse implication (uniqueness), we have $d(T_1, T_2) = 0 \Rightarrow W(\phi_{12}) = \max(|T_1|, |T_2|)$. Since $W(\phi_{12}) \leq \min(|T_1|, |T_2|) \leq \max(|T_1|, |T_2|)$, we have $W(\phi_{12}) = \min(|T_1|, |T_2|) = \max(|T_1|, |T_2|)$. Hence, (2) yields $T_1 \cong_a T_2$.
3. $d(T_1, T_2) = d_1(T_2, T_1)$
   This follows directly from the symmetry of the maximum similarity graph and of the function max.
4. $d(T_1, T_2) + d(T_2, T_3) \geq d(T_1, T_3)$

---

[1] The quotient set formalizes the intuitive idea that two attributed trees are indistinguishable when they are attribute-isomorphic. Furthermore, it is needed in order to fulfill the uniqueness property of a metric.

The triangular inequality can be simplified to the inequality

$$\max(|T_1|, |T_2|) \max(|T_2|, |T_3|) \max(|T_1|, |T_3|) \geq$$
$$W(\phi_{12}) \max(|T_2|, |T_3|) \max(|T_1|, |T_3|) + W(\phi_{23}) \max(|T_1|, |T_2|) \max(|T_1|, |T_3|) -$$
$$W(\phi_{13}) \max(|T_1|, |T_2|) \max(|T_2|, |T_3|) \quad (4)$$

To prove this we need to separately analyze each of the six possible cases
1. $|T_1| \geq |T_2| \geq |T_3|$ 2. $|T_1| \geq |T_3| \geq |T_2|$ 3. $|T_2| \geq |T_1| \geq |T_3|$
4. $|T_2| \geq |T_3| \geq |T_1|$ 5. $|T_3| \geq |T_1| \geq |T_2|$ 6. $|T_3| \geq |T_2| \geq |T_1|$.
However, the roles of T_1 and T_3 in our proofs are symmetric, hence we can use this symmetry to reduce the analysis to three cases: (a) $|T_2| \geq |T_1| \geq |T_3|$,
(b) $|T_1| \geq |T_2| \geq |T_3|$, and (c) $|T_1| \geq |T_3| \geq |T_2|$.

a) $|T_2| \geq |T_1| \geq |T_3|$
   The triangular inequality reduces to $|T_1||T_2| \geq W(\phi_{12})|T_1| + W(\phi_{23})|T_1| - W(\phi_{13})|T_2|$.

$$|T_1||T_2| \geq |T_1|(W(\phi_{12}) + W(\phi_{23}) - W(\phi_{13})) \geq$$
$$W(\phi_{12})|T_1| + W(\phi_{23})|T_1| - W(\phi_{13})|T_2|$$

b) $|T_1| \geq |T_2| \geq |T_3|$
   Equation (4) reduces to $|T_1||T_2| \geq W(\phi_{12})|T_2| + W(\phi_{23})|T_1| - W(\phi_{13})|T_2|$.

$$|T_1||T_2| = |T_2|(|T_1| - |T_2|) + |T_2|^2 \geq W(\phi_{23})(|T_1| - |T_2|) + |T_2|^2 \geq$$
$$W(\phi_{23})(|T_1| - |T_2|) + |T_2|(W(\phi_{12}) + W(\phi_{23}) - W(\phi_{13})) =$$
$$W(\phi_{12})|T_2| + W(\phi_{23})|T_1| - W(\phi_{13})|T_2|$$

c) $|T_1| \geq |T_3| \geq |T_2|$
   We need to prove $|T_1||T_3| \geq W(\phi_{12})|T_3| + W(\phi_{23})|T_1| - |T_3|W(\phi_{13})$.

$$|T_1||T_3| \geq |T_1||T_2| - |T_2||T_3| + |T_2||T_3| \geq W(\phi_{23})(|T_1| - |T_3|) + |T_3||T_2| \geq$$
$$W(\phi_{23})(|T_1| - |T_3|) + |T_3|(W(\phi_{12}) + W(\phi_{23}) - W(\phi_{13})) =$$
$$W(\phi_{12})|T_3| + W(\phi_{23})|T_1| - |T_3|W(\phi_{13}). \quad \square$$

4   Extracting the Maximum Similarity Common Subtree

In this section we give a polynomial-time algorithm for finding a maximum similarity subtree. The algorithm is based on the subtree identification algorithm presented by Matula [9], extending it in two ways. First, it generalizes it to deal with attributed trees and, second, it extends it to solve the more general problem of extracting the maximum (similarity) subtree and not merely to verify whether one tree is a subtree of the other. We give an algorithm to find the maximum similarity common subtree problem for rooted trees, and then we show how the same algorithm can be used for the unrooted tree case.

Let $T_1 = (V_1, E_1)$ and $T_2 = (V_2, E_2)$ be two rooted trees, and let $u \in V_1$ and $w \in V_2$. We say that a subtree isomorphism between T_1 and T_2 is *anchored* at nodes u and w, if the subtrees of T_1 and T_2 induced by the isomorphism are rooted at u and w, respectively. In this case, we shall write $\phi^{(u,w)}$ to refer to any isomorphism anchored at u and w. Clearly, if ϕ is a maximum similarity subtree isomorphism, we have

$$W(\phi) = \max_{(u,w) \in V_1 \times V_2} \max_{\phi^{(u,w)}} W(\phi^{(u,w)}).$$

To determine the maximum similarity subtree isomorphism anchored at nodes u and w we adopt a divide-and-conquer approach. Let $u_1, \cdots, u_n$ be the children of node u in T_1, and $w_1, \cdots, w_m$ the children of node w in T_2. Without loss of generality, we can assume $n \leq m$. Moreover, let us assume that we know, for each $i = 1, \cdots, n$ and $j = 1, \cdots, m$, a maximum similarity subtree isomorphism $\widehat{\phi}^{(u_i, w_j)}$ anchored at u_i and w_j. Let W_{ij} be the similarity of $\widehat{\phi}^{(u_i, w_j)}$, then the computation of a maximum similarity subtree isomorphism anchored at u and w can be reduced to an assignment problem on the children of u and w, i.e.,

$$W(\phi^{(u,w)}) = \sigma(u, w) + \max_{\pi \in \Sigma_n^m} \sum_{i=1}^{n} W_{i\pi(i)}, \tag{5}$$

where Σ_n^m is the space of all possible assignments between a set of cardinality n and one of cardinality m. As a consequence, if π is the optimal assignment, the function $\phi^{(u,w)}$ defined as:

$$\phi^{(u,w)}(x) = \begin{cases} w & \text{if } x = u \\ \widehat{\phi}^{(u_i, w_{\pi(i)})}(x) & \text{if } x \in \text{Dom}(\widehat{\phi}^{(u_i, w_{\pi(i)})}) \end{cases} \tag{6}$$

turns out to be a maximum similarity subtree isomorphism anchored at u and w.

Figure 1 shows the resulting algorithm for determining a maximum similarity subtree isomorphism of two rooted attributed trees. Since in the rest of the paper we only need the maximum similarity induced by an isomorphism, and not the isomorphism itself, for simplicity the main procedure Similarity accepts as input a pair of attributed rooted trees and returns only the similarity value. It makes use of a recursive procedure AnchoredSimilarity that accepts as input two vertices, one from T_1 and the other from T_2 and returns the similarity of the maximum isomorphism anchored at the input vertices, according to (5). To this end, it needs a procedure for solving an assignment (or, equivalently, a bipartite matching) problem, of which the algorithms literature abound (see., e.g., [1]). The calculation of the maximum similarity common subtree of two trees with N and M nodes respectively, is reduced to at most NM weighted assignments problems of dimension at most b, where b is the maximum branching factor of the two trees. The computational complexity of our algorithm heavily depends on the actual implementation of the assignment procedure. A popular way of solving it, and the one we actually employed, is the so-called Hungarian algorithm, which has complexity $O(n^2 m)$, n and m being the number of children of u and v as used

```
Similarity(T. ,T. )
    maxsim=0
    for each node u in T.
        sim=AnchoredSimilarity(u,root(T.))
        if sim > maxsim
            maxsim=sim
    for each node w in T.
        sim=AnchoredSimilarity(root(T.),w)
        if sim > maxsim
            maxsim=sim
    return maxsim
```

```
AnchoredSimilarity(u, w)
    Cu=children(u)
    Cw=children(w)
    for each ui in Cu
        for each wj in Cw
            wij=AnchoredSimilarity(ui, wj)
    return σ(u,w) + Assign({wij})
```

Fig. 1. A polynomial-time algorithm for computing the similarity between two trees.

in (5), with $n \leq m$. It is simple to show that, using the Hungarian algorithm, our algorithm has overall complexity of $O(bNM)$. Of course, the algorithm can be sped up by using more sophisticated assignment procedures [1].

Finally, if we have two unrooted trees $T_1 = (V_1, E_1)$ and $T_2 = (V_2, E_2)$, we can still pick two nodes $r_1 \in V_2$ and $r_2 \in V_2$, and consider the trees $T_1^{r_1} = (V_1, E_1)$ and $T_2^{r_2} = (V_2, E_2)$ rooted at r_1 and r_2, respectively. Note that if ϕ is an isomorphism between $T_1^{r_1}$ and $T_2^{r_2}$ with similarity W, then it is an isomorphism between T_1 and T_2 with the same similarity. This yields a straightforward $O(bN^3M)$ algorithm for unrooted trees, which consists of iteratively calling Similarity(T_1^u, T_2^w) for all $u \in V_1$ and $w \in V_2$, and taking the maximum. However, we do not actually need to try all possible pairs of roots since by simply fixing the root in one tree and let the other vary among all possible vertices in the other tree, the algorithm is still guaranteed to achieve the maximum similarity. This yields an $O(bN^2M)$ algorithm for unrooted trees.

5   Experimental Results

We evaluated the new metric on three different tree-based shape representations. The first is the shock tree representation used by Pelillo, Siddiqi and Zucker in [11], which is based on the differential structure of the boundary of a 2D shape. It is obtained by extracting the skeleton of the shape, determined as the set of singularities (shocks) arising from the inward evolution of the shape boundary, and then examining the differential behavior of the radius of the bitangent circle

Fig. 2. Distance matrices from the first experiment. Left: Our metric. Right: Edit-distance.

to the object boundary, as the skeleton is traversed. This yields a classification of local differential structure into four different classes [15]. The so-called shock-classes, distinguish between the cases where the local bitangent circle has maximum, minimum, constant, or monotonic radius. The labeled shock-groups are then abstracted using a rooted tree where two vertices are adjacent if the corresponding shock-groups are adjacent in the skeleton, and the distance from the root is related to the distance from the shape barycenter. Here, we used the same attributes and node-distances employed in [11]. Each shock was attributed with its coordinates, distance from the border, and propagation velocity and direction. The distance between two nodes, was defined as a convex combination of the (normalized) Euclidean distances of length, distance to the border, propagation speed, and curvature.

We compared our distance metric with edit-distance. To approximate the edit-distance we used the relaxation labeling algorithm presented in [17] with the following costs: we defined the cost of matching node u to node w to be equal to the distance between their attributes, while the cost of removing any node to be equal to 1. Note that, with these costs, edit-distance is not normalized.

Our shape database contained 29 shapes from 8 different classes. Figure 2 shows the distance matrices obtained using our metric and edit-distance. Here, lighter colors represent lower distances while darker colors represent higher distances. As can be seen, the same block structure emerges in both matrices. Essentially, the most significant difference among the two metrics is the dark bands clearly visible in the edit-distance matrix.

In order to assess the ability of the distances to preserve class structure, we performed pairwise clustering. In particular, we used two pairwise clustering algorithms: Shi and Malik's Normalized Cut [14], and Pavan and Pelillo's Dominant Sets [10]. Figure 3 shows the clusters obtained with both algorithms, displayed in order of extraction. While the performance of the clustering algorithms, on this shape recognition task, varied significantly, the dependency on the choice of the distance measure was less pronounced. Nonetheless, some differences can be observed. In particular, we notice how Normalized Cut exhibits

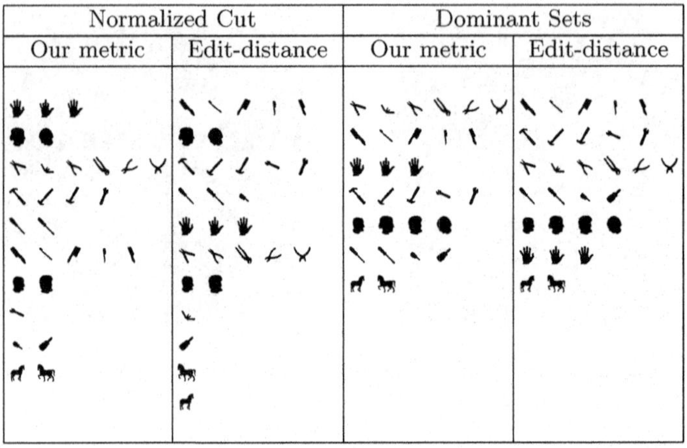

Normalized Cut		Dominant Sets	
Our metric	Edit-distance	Our metric	Edit-distance

Fig. 3. Clusters obtained with Normalized Cut and Dominat Sets in the first experiment.

a well-known tendency to over-segment the data. The clusters obtained with the Dominant Sets approach are much better, with our metric providing results almost identical to edit-distance.

As for the running times, on a Pentium 4 2.5GHz PC, the maximum similarity algorithm presented in Section 4, took around 8 seconds to compute our metric, while the relaxation labeling algorithm computed edit-distance in over 30 minutes.

Our second set of experiments used a larger database of shapes abstracted again in terms of shock-trees. Here, however, we used a different set of attributes recently analyzed in [16], i.e., the proportion of the shape boundary generating the corresponding shock-group. The database consisted of 150 shapes divided into 10 classes of 15 shapes each, and presented a higher structural noise than the previous one. Here the node distance and node-matching cost for edit-distance was defined as the absolute difference between the attributes, while the node removal cost was the value of the attribute itself. With this edit costs edit-distance is a normalized metric.

Figure 4 shows the distance matrices obtained using our metric and edit-distance. Note that, as before, both matrices exhibit the same block structure. We applied the same clustering algorithms used in the previous series of experiments. In order to assess the quality of the groupings, we used two well-known cluster-validation measures [8]. The first is the standard misclassification rate. We assigned to each cluster the class that has most members in the cluster. The members of the cluster that belong to a different class are considered misclassified. The misclassification rate is the percentage of misclassified shapes over the total number of shapes. To avoid the bias towards higher segmentation that this measure exhibits, we also used a second validation measure, i.e., the Rand index. We count the number of pairs of shapes that belong to the same class and that are clustered together and the number of pairs of shapes belonging to different

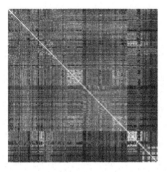

Fig. 4. Distance matrices from the second experiment. Left: Our metric. Right: Edit-distance

classes that are in different clusters. The sum of these two figures divided by the total number of pairs gives us the Rand index. Here, the higher the value, the better the classification.

Table 1 summarizes the results obtained using Normalized Cut and Dominant Sets. Here the two metrics generate clusters with comparable validation measures regardless of the clustering algorithm used.

Table 1. Validation measures of clusters obtained in the second experiment.

	Misclassification rate		Rand index	
	Normalized Cut	Dominant Sets	Normalized Cut	Dominant Sets
Our metric	23.3%	21.3%	90.3%	90.8%
Edit-distance	22.7%	24.0%	90.4%	90.8%

The last set of experiments was performed on a tree representation of Northern Lights [12]. As in the previous experiments, the representation used is derived from the morphological skeleton, but the choice of structural representation was different from the one adopted for shock-graphs, and the extracted trees tend to be larger. The database consisted of 1440 shapes. Using our metric we were able to extract the full distance matrix within a few hours, but it was unfeasible to compute edit-distance on the entire database. For this reason, in order to be able to compare the results with edit-distance, we also performed experiments using a smaller database consisting of 50 shapes. The calculation of edit-distance, even on this reduced database, took a full weekend.

In this case, we did not have the ground truth for the class memberships, so we needed a different cluster-validation measure. We opted for a standard measure that favors compact and well-separated clusters: the Davies-Bouldin index [8]. Let e_i be the average distance between elements in class i, and d_{ij} the average distance between elements in cluster i and elements in cluster j The

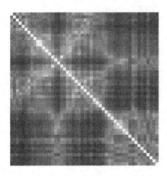 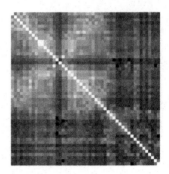

Fig. 5. Distance matrices from the second experiment. Left: Our metric. Right: Edit-distance.

Davies-Bouldin index is

$$DB = \frac{1}{c} \sum_{i=1}^{c} \max_{j} R_{ij} \qquad (7)$$

where c is the number of clusters and $R_{ij} = \frac{e_i + e_j}{d_{ij}}$ is the cluster separation measure. Clearly, lower values correspond to better separated and more compact clusters.

Table 2 provides the values of the Davies-Bouldin index on the clusters extracted using Normalized Cut and the Dominant Sets algorithm. As was the case with the previous experiments, both metrics produced comparable results.

Table 2. Davies-Bouldin index of clusters obtained in the third experiment.

	Normalized Cut	Dominant Sets
Our metric	0.0486	0.0723
Edit-distance	0.0232	0.0635

6 Conclusions

In this paper we have presented a novel distance measure for attributed trees based on the notion of a maximum similarity subtree isomorphism, and provided a polynomial-time algorithm to calculate it. We have proven that this measure satisfies the metric properties and have experimentally validated its usefulness by comparing it with edit-distance on three different shape recognition tasks. Our experimental results show that, in terms of quality, the proposed metric compares well with edit-distance, its computation being, however, orders of magnitude faster.

References

1. R. K. Ahuja, T. L. Magnanti, J. B. Orlin. *Network Flows.* Prentice-Hall, Upper Saddle River, NJ, 1993.
2. H. Bunke and K. Shearer. A graph distance metric based on the maximal common subgraph. *Pattern Recognition Letters*, 19:255–259, 1998.
3. S. J. Dickinson, A. P. Pentland, and A. Rosenfeld. 3-D shape recovery using distributed aspect matching. *PAMI*, 14(2):174–198, 1992.
4. M. A. Eshera and K.-S. Fu. An image understanding system using attributed symbolic representation and inexact graph-matching. *PAMI*, 8:604–618, 1986.
5. M. L. Fernandez and G. Valiente. A graph distacne metric combining maximum common subgraph and minimum common supergraph. *Pattern Recognition Letters*, 22:753–758, 2001.
6. D. Hidović and M. Pelillo. Metrics for attributed graphs based on the maximal similarity common subgraph. *Int. J. Pattern Recognition Artif. Intell.*, 2004 (in press).
7. S. Ioffe and D. A. Forsyth. Human tracking with mixtures of trees. in *Proc. ICCV*, Vol. I, pp. 690–695, 2001.
8. A. K. Jain and R. C. Dubes. *Algorithms for Clustering Data.* Prentice Hall, Englewood Cliffs, NJ, 1988.
9. D. W. Matula. An algorithm for subtree identification, *SIAM Review*, 10:273–274, 1968.
10. M. Pavan and M. Pelillo. A new graph-theoretic approach to clustering and segmentation. In *Proc. CVPR*, Vol. I, pp. 145–152, 2003.
11. M. Pelillo, K. Sidiqi, and S. W. Zucker. Matching hierarchical structures using association graphs. *PAMI*, 21(11):1105–1120, 1999.
12. M. Peura. Attribute trees in image analysis: Heuristic matching and learning techniques. In *Proc. Int. Conf. Image Anal. Processing*, pp. 1160–1165, 1999.
13. T. B. Sebastian, P. N. Klein, and B. B. Kimia. Recognition of shpes by editing their shock graphs. *PAMI*, to appear, 2004.
14. J. Shi and J. Malik, Normalized cuts and image segmentation, *PAMI*, 22(8):888–905, 2000.
15. K. Siddiqi, A. Shokoufandeh, S. J. Dickinson, and S. W. Zucker. Shock graphs and shape matching. *Int. J. Computer Vision*, 35(1):13–32, 1999.
16. A. Torsello and E. R. Hancock. A skeletal measure of 2D shape similarity. In C. Arcelli, L. P. Cordella, G. Sanniti di Baja (Eds.), *Visual Form 2001.* Springer-Verlag, Heidelberg (LNCS 2059), pages 260–271, 2001.
17. A. Torsello and E. R. Hancock. Efficiently computing weighted tree edit-distance using relaxation labeling. In M. Figueiredo, J. Zerubia, A.K. Jain (Eds.), *Energy Minimization Methods in Computer Vision and Pattern Recognition.* Springer-Verlag, Heidelberg (LNCS 2134), pp. 438–453, 2001.
18. W. H. Tsai and K.-S. Fu. Error-correcting isomorphism of attributed relational graphs for pattern analysis. *IEEE Trans Syst. Man Cybern.*, 9:757–768, 1979.
19. G. Valiente. An efficient bottom-up distance between trees, in *Proc. Int. Symp. String Processing Information Retrieval*, pp. 212–219, 2001.
20. W. D. Wallis, P. Shoubridge, M. Kraetz, and D. Ray. Graph distances using graph union. *Pattern Recognition Letters*, 22:701–704, 2001.
21. J. T.-L. Wang and K. Zhang. Finding similar consesnus between trees: An algorithm and a distance hierarchy. *Pattern Recognition*, 34:127–137, 2001.
22. K. Zhang. A constrained edit-distance between unordered labeled trees. *Algorithmica*, 15:205-222, 1996.

23. K. Zhang and D. Shasha. Simple fast algorithms for the editing distance between trees and related problems. *SIAM J. Comput.*, 18:1245–1262, 1989.
24. K. Zhang, R. Statman, and D. Shasha. On the editing distance between unordered labeled trees. *Inform. Process. Letters*, 42:133–139, 1992.
25. K. Zhang, J. T. L. Wang, and D. Shasha. On the editing distance between undirected acyclic graphs. *Int. J. Found. Computer Sci.*, 7(1):43–57, 1996.

Probabilistic Multi-view Correspondence in a Distributed Setting with No Central Server

Shai Avidan[1], Yael Moses[1], and Yoram Moses[2]

· The Efi Arazi school of Computer Science
The Interdisciplinary Center, Herzliya, Israel
{avidan,yael}@idc.ac.il
· Department of Electrical Engineering,
Technion, Haifa, 32000 Israel
moses@ee.technion.ac.il

Abstract. We present a probabilistic algorithm for finding correspondences across multiple images. The algorithm runs in a distributed setting, where each camera is attached to a separate computing unit, and the cameras communicate over a network. No central computer is involved in the computation. The algorithm runs with low computational and communication cost. Our distributed algorithm assumes access to a standard pairwise wide-baseline stereo matching algorithm ($\mathcal{WBS}$) and our goal is to minimize the number of images transmitted over the network, as well as the number of times the $\mathcal{WBS}$ is computed. We employ the theory of random graphs to provide an efficient probabilistic algorithm that performs $\mathcal{WBS}$ on a small number of image pairs, followed by a correspondence propagation phase. The heart of the paper is a theoretical analysis of the number of times $\mathcal{WBS}$ must be performed to ensure that an overwhelming portion of the correspondence information is extracted. The analysis is extended to show how to combat computer and communication failures, which are expected to occur in such settings, as well as correspondence misses. This analysis yields an efficient distributed algorithm, but it can also be used to improve the performance of centralized algorithms for correspondence.

1 Introduction

Settings with large numbers of cameras are spreading in many applications of computer vision, such as surveillance, tracking, smart environments, etc. [11, 7,16,5] Existing vision applications in a multi-camera setting are based on a central computer that gathers the information from all cameras, and performs the necessary computations. In some cases, part of the computation is performed locally at the cameras' sites (e.g., feature detection or local tracking), and then the overall solution is computed by the central computer.

Controlling a large application involving many cameras by a central server has the advantage that the computation, once performed, is reliable and can utilize all of the information in one place. But it has disadvantages that often

T. Pajdla and J. Matas (Eds.): ECCV 2004, LNCS 3024, pp. 428–441, 2004.
© Springer-Verlag Berlin Heidelberg 2004

outweigh the advantages. First, since many vision applications require a significant amount of computation, centralized solutions are often not scalable: their performance degrades as the number of sites grows. In addition, the server can become a communication hot-spot and possible bottleneck. Finally, the central server is a single point of failure. If it fails or is unreachable for a while, the applications it governs may fail. Moreover, the possibility of temporary failures grows when the system is dynamic and, for example, cameras occasionally join or leave the system, or move from one place to another. These disadvantages of the centralized approach motivate an investigation of techniques for solving computer vision applications that are *not* based on a central server. The processing units at different cameras communicate among themselves and perform whatever computations may be needed in the application. The scenario in which many of the cameras are attached to reasonably powerful computing devices is quite realistic, and supports this approach.

In this paper we present a distributed approach to computing multi-image correspondence in a multi-camera setting. Such correspondence forms the basis of many important visual tasks, such as calibration, 3D scene reconstruction, and tracking. One way to compute multi-image correspondence is by computing correspondence between pairs of images, using a *Wide-baseline Stereo (WBS)* algorithm.[1] Computing *WBS* for *all* pairs, which clearly guarantees obtaining full correspondence, is costly in terms of both communication and computation. Moreover, the computation becomes intractable when a large setting with hundreds or even thousand of cameras is considered. An alternative is to perform *WBS* computations on only some of the pairs, and then use the transitivity of correspondence to obtain further correspondence information among images that were not compared directly. A key aspect of such an algorithm is the choice of image pairs to which the *WBS* algorithm will be applied.

Our solution is distributed: every camera is involved in a limited amount of communication and performs only a *small* number of *WBS* computations. Propagation of the correspondence is performed by local communication between cameras. Nevertheless we are guaranteed that, with high probability, the full correspondence information is obtained for the vast majority of points at the end of the propagation process. Our solution can be tuned so that it will tolerate communication failures, processor failures, and failure of the *WBS* computations to identify corresponding points in overlapping images.

A key element in the efficiency of an algorithm such as ours is in the choice of which *WBS* computations to perform. We employ the theory of random graphs in order to obtain a drastic reduction in the number of such computations each camera performs. Further reduction is obtained when there is information regarding cameras that do not view overlapping regions. Finally, we tune our algorithm to capture correspondence information for points that are seen by many cameras. In a multi-image setting, the number of images in which a feature point p appears is important. We call this the *degree of exposure*, or exposure for short,

---

[*] We use the *WBS* computation as a black box; a better solution to *WBS* will improve the performance of our scheme.

of p. Applications that use correspondence information typically obtain much greater benefit from points with high exposure than from ones with low exposure (e.g., Bundle Adjustment [23]). Accordingly, our algorithm is designed to accept an *exposure parameter* k and will be tuned to find the correspondence information of points with degree of exposure that is greater than or equal to k. The algorithm has the following features:

1. Every camera i performs a small number s_i of $\mathcal{WBS}$ computations;
2. cameras exchange correspondence information for at most $\log_2 k$ rounds; and
3. for every feature point p with exposure degree k or more, with probability at least 0.99 all cameras that view p obtain the full correspondence information regarding p.

As we show, when there is sufficient information about the relative locations of cameras, s_i may be $c \cdot \log_2 k$ for some constant c. Since $\mathcal{WBS}$ computations are dominant in this application, the algorithm will then terminate in time that is proportional to $\log_2 k$. Our approach is probabilistic, rather than heuristic. Moreover, its success is guaranteed with high probability for every given set of images (provided that the $\mathcal{WBS}$ algorithm is error-free).

The algorithm is designed in such a way that no single failure can impact the quality of the correspondence information obtained in a significant way. Moreover, it is robust in the sense that it degrades gracefully as the number of failures grows. We extend the algorithm to handle unreliable systems with communication failures, processor failures, and failure of the $\mathcal{WBS}$ computations to identify corresponding points in overlapping images. Roughly speaking, in order to overcome a failure rate of $f < 1$ of the communication channels (resp. a portion of $f < 1$ of the cameras crashes, or a portion of $f < 1$ of the matches are false-negative errors by the $\mathcal{WBS}$), an increase of roughly $\frac{1}{1-f}$ in the number of $\mathcal{WBS}$ computations leads to the same performance as in a system with no failures. Hence, to overcome a high failure rate of 10%, the cameras need to perform only 12% more work!

While originally motivated by the quest for a distributed solution, our probabilistic analysis can be applied to reduce the number of $\mathcal{WBS}$ computations even when correspondence is computed on a single computer. That is, our algorithm can be simulated on a centralized computer (replacing the propagation step by a simple transitive closure computation) to improve the efficiency of computation of existing centralized algorithms.

The question of how to reduce the number of $\mathcal{WBS}$ computations performed in the centralized setting has been addressed by Schaffalitzky & Zisserman [21]. They suggested a heuristic approach to this problem: first single-view invariants are computed and mapped to a large feature vs. views hash table. The hash table can then guide the greedy choice of the pairs on which to compute $\mathcal{WBS}$, resulting in run-time complexity of $O(n)$ $\mathcal{WBS}$ computations, where n is the number of cameras.

This paper makes two main contributions. One is in providing a reasonably efficient solution to the multi-image correspondence problem in a distributed system with no central server and no single point of failure. The second is in employing the theory of random graphs in order to reduce the number of *WBS* computations needed to obtain a useful amount of correspondence information.

2   Previous Work

There have recently been a number of significant advances on the subject of *Wide-baseline Stereo* (WBS), in which computations involving a small number of images are used to extract correspondence information among the images [24, 1,17,20,6,15].

Schaffalitzky & Zisserman [21] and then Ferrari *et. al.* [10] suggested methods for wide baseline matching among a large set of images (on the order of 10 to 20 cameras). They both suggested methods for extending the correspondence of two (or three) views to n views, while using the larger number of views to improve the pairwise correspondence. Their algorithms are designed to run on a central computer. Levi & Werman [12] consider the problem of computing the fundamental matrices between all pairs of n cameras, based on knowing only the fundamental matrices of a subset of pairs of views. Their main contribution is an algebraic analysis of the constraints that can be extracted from a partial set of fundamental matrices among neighboring views. These constraints are then used to compute the missing fundamental matrices.

In recent years various applications of multi-camera settings with a central computer are considered. These include various tasks such as surveillance, smart environments, tracking and virtual reality. Collins et al. [7,8] report on a large surveillance project consisting of 14 cameras spread over a large compound. The algorithm they used for calibration, which was based on known 3D scene points [8], was performed on a central server. The virtual-reality technology introduced by Kanade et al. [16,19] uses a multi-camera setup that can capture a dynamic event and generate new views of the observed scene. Again, the cameras were calibrated off-line using a central computer. Smart environments [5,13] consist of a distributed set of cameras spread in the environment. The cameras can detect and track the inhabitants, thus supporting higher-level functions such as convenient man-machine interfacing or object localization. Despite the distributed nature of these systems, the calibration of the cameras is usually done off-line on a central processor.

Karuppiah et al. [11], have already discussed the value of solving multi-camera computer vision problems in a distributed manner. They constructed a four-camera system and experimented with tracking and recognition in this system, showing the potential for fault-tolerance and avoiding a single point of failure.

While the literature contains little in the way of distributed solutions to computer vision applications, the literature on distributed systems and distributed computing has addressed many issues that are relevant to a task of this type. They involve methods for failure detection and fault-tolerant execution of computations, algorithms for leader election and consensus, etc. A good overview of the issues can be found in Tanenbaum and van Steen [22] and in the collection by Mullender [18]. A comprehensive source for distributed algorithms can be found in Lynch [14] and a useful treatment of issues relating to data replication is the book by Bernstein *et al.* [2].

3   The Algorithm

We assume a set $\{1, \ldots, n\}$ of cameras overlooking a scene. Each camera has a processing unit attached to it, and the cameras can communicate over a point-to-point communication network. We further assume that the communication network is complete so that every camera can communicate directly and reliably with every other camera. We denote by M_i the number of cameras with which camera i can have corresponding points and let m_i denote the size M_i. Initially, we assume that the $\mathcal{WBS}$ computations are noise and error free: A $\mathcal{WBS}$ computation performed on a pair of images identifies two locations in the images as being corresponding exactly if there is a genuine feature point p that appears in the stated coordinates in the respective images. We relax these reliability assumptions in Section 5.

Our distributed algorithm is defined in terms of an exposure parameter k, and is designed to discover the vast majority of points with an exposure size k or more. Each camera maintains a list of its own feature points and their corresponding points in other cameras. At each propagation step, each camera, propagates any new correspondence information to all the cameras with which it has established corresponding points. Each camera has to run the following algorithm, given the exposure parameter k.

1. **Initialization**
   Randomly choose a set $S \subset M_i$ of cameras of size

$$s_i = m_i \tau(k) \approx m_i \frac{\log k + 5}{2k}, \tag{1}$$

   and request their images.

2. **Pairwise Matching**
   For every camera j from which an image has been received, perform a $\mathcal{WBS}$ computation between i's image and j's , record its results in the local correspondence lists, and send the results to j. Concurrently, for every request for an image, send you image to the requesting camera and later record the result when you receive them in the correspondence lists.

3. **Correspondence Propagation**
   This stage proceeds in rounds of communication. In the first round, for every point $p_i = (x_i, y_i)$ in camera i's image that has been matched with more than one point by the $\mathcal{WBS}$ computations, i performs a propagation step. In every subsequent round, i performs propagation steps for every point p_i for which it received new correspondence information in the most recent round. The propagation is terminated when no new correspondence information received.

One of the main contributions of the algorithm is in equation 1 that expresses the number of $\mathcal{WBS}$ computations as a function of the exposure parameter k. As for m_i, it is equal to n in case no prior information is available, but in many cases, we do initially have information regarding which images potentially have corresponding points, and which do not. Reducing the value of m_i means a smaller number of $\mathcal{WBS}$ computations, as is evident from equation 1. Consider, for example, a situation in which cameras are located around a hill or a rooftop. They may cover the surrounding scene quite effectively, while every camera has a limited number of relevant neighbors to consider for correspondence. There is another source that may reduce the size of M_i. Some recent approaches to computing multi-view correspondence contain a preprocessing stage in which images are ranked for likelihood of correspondence (e.g., [21]). The result of such a stage can reduce the sets M_i.

4   Probabilistic Analysis of the Algorithm

The probabilistic analysis will show that the above algorithm will detect all points with exposure factor great or equal to k with probability 99%. Furthermore, it will show that only $log_2(n)$ propagation steps are needed, at most, for the algorithm to terminate.

We represent the state of information that the cameras attain regarding the multi-view correspondence of feature points by a labeled multi-graph, which we denote by G. There is a node in G for each camera. There is a labeled edge, $(\{i, j\}, p)$, between nodes i and j if p is an established corresponding point of the images of i and j. Initially, the graph has no edges. After the first phase, in which $\mathcal{WBS}$ computations are performed, the graph contains edges only among images that were compared directly by a $\mathcal{WBS}$ computation. Additional edges are added to G in the propagation phase.

Let us begin by considering the behavior of the algorithm in terms of discovering the correspondence information of a single 3D feature point p. Let us call the set of cameras that view the point p the p-set. All of the correspondence information regarding p will be uncovered exactly if, at the end of the propagation process, every pair of cameras in the p-set will share a p-edge. To analyze the algorithm's behavior with respect to p it is convenient to consider the p-graph G_p derived from G that is defined by the p-set and the p-edges of G. More formally, $G_p = (V_p, E_p)$ where V_p is p-set—the set of cameras that view p, and E_p consists of the edges $\{i, j\}$ for which $(\{i, j\}, p)$ is in G. We refer to the state of G_p after the matching step of the algorithm by $G_p(0)$, and after $r \geq 1$ rounds of propagation by $G_p(r)$.

4.1   Analysis of Propagation

We now prove that if $G_p(0)$ is connected, then propagation will uncover the full correspondence information regarding p. Moreover, this will be done within a small number of rounds of propagation.

Lemma 1. *If the distance between nodes i and j in $G_p(0)$ is d, where $2^{r-1} < d \leq 2^r$, then their distance in $G_p(r)$ is 1.*

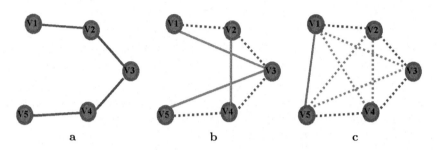

Fig. 1. (a) $G_p(0)$—the distance between $v.$ and $v.$ is 4. (b) $G_p(1)$—the distance is reduced to 2, and (c) in $G_p(2)$ the distance is 1.

Proof. Consider two vertices v_1 and v_{d+1} that are distance d apart. Let $v_1, ..., v_{d+1}$ be a path connecting these points in $G_p(0)$. In the first round of the propagation algorithm node v_2 will update node v_1 that v_3 also views the point p, and similarly node v_2 will also update node v_3 that v_1 views the point p (see Figure 1). As a result, nodes v_1 and v_3 both update their local p-lists, and the edge $\{v_1, v_3\}$ is added to G_p. In a similar manner, all edges between v_i and v_{i+2}, $i \leq d + 1$, are added to G_p. It follows that after a single round of propagation, the path $v_1, v_3, v_5, ..., v_{d+1}$ connects v_1 and v_{d+1} in the graph. As a results, the distance between v_1 and v_{d+1} is shortened by a factor of two, and it is $\lceil \frac{d}{2} \rceil$. A straightforward induction shows that the distance between v_1 and v_d is reduced to 1 after $\lceil log_2(d) \rceil = r$ steps.

Corollary 1. *Suppose that $G_p(0)$ is connected. If the diameter of $G_p(0)$ is d, then $G_p(\lceil log(d) \rceil)$ is a complete graph (its diameter is 1).*

Since $d \leq k \leq n$ is guaranteed, Corollary 1 implies that there is no need to *ever* run the propagation algorithm for more than $\lceil log(n) \rceil$ rounds.

Corollary 2. *If camera i does not receive a new update regarding the point p in round r of the propagation phase, then i will never send or receive any further updates about p.*

Corollary 1 proves that propagation is guaranteed to terminate for all points within a small logarithmic number of rounds. Moreover, by Corollary 2 every camera can easily detect when its propagation phase is done.

4.2   The Number of $\mathcal{WBS}$ Computations

As we have seen, if $G_p(0)$ is connected then the propagation phase of the algorithm will discover the correspondence information regarding p. Clearly, if $G_p(0)$

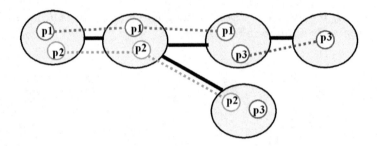

Fig. 2. The graph G with cameras that view the points $p.$, $p.$, and $p.$. The graphs G_{p_1}, G_{p_2}, and G_{p_3} are marked with red, black, and green edges, respectively. The edges of G span each of the derived graphs G_{p_i}.

is *not* connected, then only partial information will be discovered. In this section we determine the precise number of cameras that are selected in the initialization step of the algorithm by showing that it will ensure connectedness. We base the discussion here on the theory of random graphs, which was initiated in a paper by Erdös and Rényi [9]. Consider a random process in which each of the $\binom{N}{2}$ undirected edges of a graph on N nodes is chosen independently with probability $\rho > 0$. The resulting graph is denoted by $\mathcal{G}(N, \rho)$.

Lemma 2. *(a) Let $\hat{\rho}(N) = \frac{0.577 + \ln N}{N}$. The probability that $\mathcal{G}(N, \hat{\rho}(N))$ is connected tends to 1 as N tends to ∞. More concretely, for small values of N we have*

(b) Let $\rho(N) = \frac{4.61 + \log N}{N}$. The probability that $\mathcal{G}(N, \rho(N))$ is connected is greater than 0.99 for all values of $N \leq 40,000$

The first part of the lemma is a classical result in the field, while the results in the second part are from Bollobás and Thomason[4], as they are quoted in the excellent textbook by Bollobás [3]. Since we are unlikely to be interested in computing correspondence for points that are seen by more than 40,000 cameras, the second part gives us very good bounds to work with: For our purposes, if p has exposure degree k and each pair of nodes in the p-set is chosen with probability at least $\rho(k)$ for a $\mathcal{WBS}$ computation, then we have high assurance (over 0.99 probability!) that $G_p(0)$ will be connected.

For independent probabilistic events A and B, we have that $\Pr(A \cup B) = \Pr(A) + \Pr(B) - \Pr(A)\Pr(B)$. An edge is chosen if one of its nodes selects it. In the algorithm, if every node selects the edge with probability $\tau(k)$, then we need to ensure that $2\tau(k) - \tau^2(k) \geq \rho(k)$ in order to guarantee edges are chosen with sufficient probability. The exact formula for $\tau(k)$ is thus $\tau(k) = 1 - \sqrt{1 - \rho(k)}$. However, $\tau(k)$ tends to $\frac{\rho(k)}{2}$ in the limit, and for all $k \geq 10$ we have $\tau(k) < 0.6\rho(k)$. So $\tau(k)$ is essentially $\frac{\rho(k)}{2}$.

Our analysis so far has been in terms of connectivity of the graph $G_p(0)$. Indeed, working with G_p rather than G is crucial since guaranteeing that G is connected would not immediately yield G_p's connectivity. (Figure 2 is an example showing that not every spanning graph of G induces spanning graphs of all of the graphs G_{p_i}.) However, the correspondence algorithm works at the level of the graph G on all cameras, with no a priori knowledge about the identity of the p-sets. Working at this level, if every edge is chosen with probability at least $\tau(k)$ then, in particular, every edge among members of the p-set is chosen with this probability. The desired property for ensuring connectivity of $G_p(0)$ is thus satisfied. Actually, much more is true. Connectivity of $G_q(0)$ is ensured with high probability *at once for all points q with exposure degree k or more*! In particular, Lemma 2(b) implies that in this case the algorithm will find the correspondence information for at least 99% of these points.

In the algorithm, we guarantee that a camera i chooses each edge with probability at least $\tau(k)$ by having it randomly choose a subset of M_i of size s_i where $\frac{s}{m_i} \geq \tau(k)$. Choosing a subset of the neighbors of a predetermined size has the advantage that we can control the number of $\mathcal{WBS}$ computations that every node performs. In summary, we have

Theorem 1. *Executing the correspondence algorithm with parameter k will, with high probability, yield the full correspondence information for at least 99% of the points that have exposure degree k or larger.*

5   Dealing with System Failures

In this section we consider the properties of our algorithm when executed on an unreliable distributed system. We start with a classical analysis of processor crashes and communication failures but show that the analysis can be naturally extended to handle mis-matches by the $\mathcal{WBS}$ as simply another type of failure.

5.1   System Crashes

Let us first consider crashes. Assume that some of the cameras may crash during the operation of the algorithm. We assume further that the cameras use a timeout mechanism to identify that a processor is down. Clearly, if i is in a p-set and it crashes early on, we do not expect to necessarily discover the correspondence information regarding i's image. Define the *surviving degree* of a feature point p to be its exposure degree if we ignore the cameras that crash. Crashed cameras do not participate in the algorithm, and their crashing does not affects the interactions among the surviving cameras. The original algorithm, unchanged, is thus guaranteed to discover all information for the point with surviving degree of k.

5.2   Communication Failures

Now consider communication failures. We assume that each channel between two cameras can fail with independent probability $f < 1$, after which it stays down for the duration of the algorithm. Again, our timeout mechanism can allow the cameras to avoid being hung waiting for messages on failed lines.

The worst-case behavior of a failing communication line is to be down from the outset. Since communication line failures are independent of the choices of $\mathcal{WBS}$ computations made by the camera, the probability that an edge that is chosen by the cameras with probability ρ will also be up is $(1 - f)\rho$. Hence, we can increase ρ by a factor of $\frac{1}{1-f}$ and make the random graph resulting from the joint behavior of the cameras choices and the adversary's failures have the exact same structure as it originally. This translates into the choice of a neighbor with probability $\tau'(k) = 1 - \sqrt{1 - \frac{\rho(k)}{1-f}}$ instead of $\tau(k)$. In the range of $20 \leq k \leq 50$, overcoming 10% failures requires between 13% and 11% overhead, and to overcome a huge 25% probability of failure it suffices to choose between 40% and 36% more cameras than in the fully reliable case.

This discussion is summarized as follows.

Theorem 2. *(a) Executing the correspondence algorithm unchanged with parameter k when camera crashes are possible will, with high probability, yield the full correspondence information for at least 99% of the points that have* **surviving** *exposure degree k or larger.*

(b) When communication channels may fail with probability $f < 1$, executing the algorithm with $\tau'(k) \approx \frac{1}{1-f}\tau(k)$ instead of $\tau(k)$ will, with high probability, yield the full correspondence information for at least 99% of the points that have exposure degree k or larger. Moreover, it will not require more computation than the original algorithm does.

5.3   Failure of $\mathcal{WBS}$ to Detect Matches

We next consider failures of the $\mathcal{WBS}$ computation to identify the fact that a feature point appears in two images being compared. Here we suppose that our $\mathcal{WBS}$ algorithm will fail to identify a match with independent probability $f < 1$. The situation here is very similar to the case of communication failures. Again, the probability that an edge of G_p will be discovered by the first part of the algorithm is $(1 - f)\rho$ if edges of G are chosen with probability ρ. By the analysis we performed in the case of communication failures, choosing $\tau'(k)$ instead of $\tau(k)$ images to compare with will provide us with the original guarantees. This time, however, all $\tau'(k)$ computations and communications must be carried out. The total overhead is then roughly $\frac{1}{1-f}$:

Theorem 3. *When $\mathcal{WBS}$ computations may fail to identify a match with independent probability $f < 1$, executing the algorithm with $\tau'(k) \approx \frac{1}{1-f}\tau(k)$ instead of $\tau(k)$ will, with high probability, yield the full correspondence information for at least 99% of the points that have exposure degree k or larger.*

We remark that this analysis is applied to false-negative errors. Coping with false-positives—mistaken matches reported—can be done using distributed systems' techniques for handling malicious failures. This analysis is beyond the scope of this paper and is left as a topic for future work.

6   Experiments

Our analysis ensures that the algorithm will indeed recover the correspondence. However, the analysis is very conservative, and in practice smaller numbers of $\mathcal{WBS}$ computations should suffice. We validated this expectation through extensive simulations in MATLAB. Our scenario is a surveillance system in an urban setting and thus our simulated test-bed consists of a collection of orthographic cameras that are mounted on roof-tops looking down. Each camera observes all the feature points within a pre-defined distance from its position. To ensure that all the cameras form a single connected component, we enforce overlap between the image footprint of the different cameras, on the ground.

In every experiment we run the algorithm with precisely the same data, but with a different number of $\mathcal{WBS}$ operations. The experiments show that the predicted number of required $\mathcal{WBS}$ operations is indeed sufficient, but even smaller numbers can be used.

To evaluate the success of each run, we define the average number of recovered points for each exposure. A given point p is recovered if each camera in the p-set knows the identity of all cameras in the p-set. In particular, let p be a point with exposure degree k, and for every i denote by $L_i(p)$ is the size of i's correspondence list for p. Then observe that $\frac{1}{k^2} \sum L_i(p) = 1$ if p is fully recovered, and this value is smaller than 1 if p is only partially recovered.

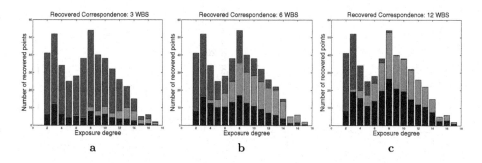

Fig. 3. The number of recovered points for each exposure degree, $\tilde{E}(k)$. Red is the number of points with given exposure. Blue is the average portion of correspondence found after the matching phase, and green is the portion after propagation. The experiment was run on a reliable system with 50 cameras and 500 points. (**a**) the results when using 3 $\mathcal{WBS}$ per camera, (**b**) when using 6 $\mathcal{WBS}$ and (**c**) when using 12.

Let $E(k)$ be the set of 3D points with an exposure degree k. Ideally, if all the points in $E(k)$ are recovered, then the number of points with exposure k is given by:

$$\tilde{E}(k) = \frac{1}{k^2} \sum_{p \in E(k)} L_i(p)$$

We use the measure $\tilde{E}(k)$ to evaluate the success of extracting the correspondence: when all the connections are recovered then $|E(k)| = \tilde{E}(k)$.

For each exposure degree k, we present three values of $\tilde{E}(k)$. The first, red bar, is the real number of points for each exposure degree. The second, green bar, is the final result of our algorithm. It is the number of computed recovered points at the end of the run. If all points for a given exposure were uncovered, then the green bar will cover the red bar. Finally, blue bar, is the value after $\mathcal{WBS}$ operation, that is only direct edges in the graph are considered.

The first experiment was designed to verify the bound on the number of required WBS operations. We generated a setup of 50 cameras and 500 points (Figure 3a) and simulated the behavior of the algorithm five times, changing the number of $\mathcal{WBS}$ each time. As can be seen in Figure 3a, using just three $\mathcal{WBS}$ does not generate enough matching points and hence the algorithm does not fully recover any of the p-sets. As the number of $\mathcal{WBS}$ performed grows, the number of fully recovered p-sets grows. In Figure 3b and 3c, we present the results of running 6 and 12 $\mathcal{WBS}$. As can be seen, the exposure degree from which full correspondence is obtained is reduced when we use the number $\mathcal{WBS}$ a camera performs increases. In Figure 3b, we present the smallest degree which all the p-sets of the degree were fully recovered.

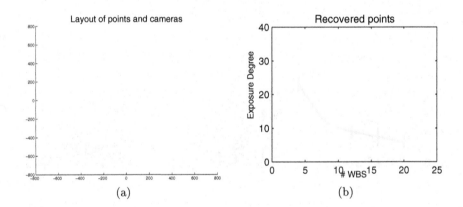

(a)   (b)

Fig. 4. (a) The setup with 50 cameras and 500 points. Each point is marked in blue, and each camera center is marked in red. The field of view of one of the cameras is marked in pink. (b) Full recovery with 20% errors of the $\mathcal{WBS}$ in red, and with no errors in black.

In the second experiment we evaluated our algorithm when the $\mathcal{WBS}$ algorithm failed to find 20% of the natchings. The same set of cameras and points as in the first experiments were used, in order to compare the performance using perfect and imperfect $\mathcal{WBS}$. The results are presented in Figure 4.

7   Summary

Visual systems consisting of a large number of geographically distributed cameras are, in particular, distributed computing systems. Information is generated and gathered at different sites, and a communication medium is used for integrating the data being gathered. We have shown how a particular application, namely image correspondence across multiple cameras, can be done in a distributed manner.

This approach allows us to use results from distributed systems theory to analyze the complexity of the distributed algorithm. In particular, we have shown what is the number of pair-wise stereo matching computations required to detect, with high probability, all points that appear in a given number of cameras. Moreover, the analysis carries naturally to the centralized case as well. Our distributed approach combines naturally failures in the communication lines, processing units and the stereo matching algorithm in a single, coherent framework. So, we have started with a distributed approach which, we believe, should be the natural way to approach large scale camera settings and ended with contributions to centralized algorithms. We plan to apply this distributed analysis to other problems in computer vision.

References

1. BAUMBERG, A. Reliable feature matching across widely separated views. In *Proc. of IEEE Computer Vision and Pattern Recognition* (2000), pp. I: 774–781.
2. BERNSTEIN, P. A., HADZILACOS, V., AND GOODMAN, N. Concurrency control and recovery in database systems. Addison Wesley, 1987.
3. BOLLOBAS, B. *Random Graphs, Second Edition.* Cambridge University Press, 2001.
4. BOLLOBAS, B., AND THOMASON, A. G. Random graphs of small order, 1985.
5. BRUMITT, B., KRUMM, J., MEYERS, B., AND S., S. Ubiquitous computing and the role of geometry, 2000.
6. CHETVERIKOV, D., AND MATAS, J. Periodic textures as distinguished regions for wide-baseline stereo correspondence. In *Texture* (2002), pp. 25–30.
7. COLLINS, R., LIPTON, A., KANADE, T., FUJIYOSHI, H., DUGGINS, D., TSIN, Y., TOLLIVER, D., ENOMOTO, N., AND HASEGAWA, O. A system for video surveillance and monitoring. *CMU-RI-TR* (2000).
8. COLLINS, R., AND TSIN, Y. Calibration of an outdoor active camera system. In *Proc. of IEEE Computer Vision and Pattern Recognition* (1999), pp. 528–534.
9. ERDOS, P., AND RENYI, A. On random graphs 1, 1959.
10. FERRARI, V., TUYTELAARS, T., AND GOOL, L. V. Wide-baseline muliple-view correspondences. In *Proc. of the IEEE Conference on Computer Vision and Pattern Recognition* (June 2003).
11. KARUPPIAH, D., ZHU, Z. SHENOY, P., AND RISEMAN, E. A fault-tolerant distributed vision system architecture for object tracking in a smart room. In *In International Workshop on Computer Vision Systems* (2001).
12. LEVI, N., AND WERMAN, M. The viewing graph. In *Proc. of IEEE Computer Vision and Pattern Recognition* (2003).

13. LOPEZ DE IPINA, D., MENDONCA, P. R. S., AND HOPPER, A. Trip: a low-cost vision-based location system for ubiquitous computing. In *Personal and Ubiquitous Computing Journal* (2002), vol. 6.

14. LYNCH, N. A. *Distributed Algorithms*. MIT Press, 1996.

15. MATAS, J., BURIANEK, J., AND KITTLER, J. Object recognition using the invariant pixel-set signature. In *The British Machine Vision Conference* (2000).

16. NARAYANAN, P. J. Virtualized reality: Concepts and early results. In *The IEEE Workshop on the Representation of Visual Scenes, (in conjunction with ICCV'95)* (1995).

17. PRITCHETT, P., AND ZISSERMAN, A. Wide baseline stereo matching. In *Proc. International Conference on Computer Vision* (1998), pp. 754–760.

18. S., M., Ed. *Distributed Systems*. Addison Wesley, 1993.

19. SAITO, H., BABA, S., KIMURA, M., VEDULA, S., AND KANADE, T. Appearance-based virtual view generation of temporally-varying events from multi-camera images in the 3d room. In *Proc. of Second International Conference on 3-D Digital Imaging and Modeling* (1999).

20. SCHAFFALITZKY, F., AND ZISSERMAN, A. Viewpoint invariant texture matching and wide baseline stereo. In *Proc. International Conference on Computer Vision* (2001), pp. II: 636–643.

21. SCHAFFALITZKY, F., AND ZISSERMAN, A. Multi-view matching for unordered image sets, or how do I organize my holiday snaps? In *Proc. of European Conference of Computer Vision* (2002).

22. TANENBAUM, A. S., AND VAN STEEN, M. *Distributed Systems Principles and Paradigms*. Pearson Education publisher, 2001.

23. TRIGGS, W., MCLAUCHLAN, P., HARTLEY, R., AND FITZGIBBON, A. Bundle adjustment – a modern synthesis. In *Vision Algorithms: Theory and Practice* (1999), pp. 298–372.

24. TUYTELAARS, T., AND VAN GOOL, L. Wide baseline stereo matching based on local, affinely invariant regions. In *The British Machine Vision Conference* (2000).

Monocular 3D Reconstruction of Human Motion in Long Action Sequences

Gareth Loy, Martin Eriksson, Josephine Sullivan, and Stefan Carlsson

Computational Vision & Active Perception Laboratory (CVAP),
Department of Numerical Analysis and Computer Science,
Royal Institute of Technology (KTH), S-100 44 Stockholm, Sweden
{gareth,eriksson,sullivan,stefanc}@nada.kth.se

Abstract. A novel algorithm is presented for the 3D reconstruction of human action in long (> 30 second) monocular image sequences. A sequence is represented by a small set of automatically found representative keyframes. The skeletal joint positions are manually located in each keyframe and mapped to all other frames in the sequence. For each keyframe a 3D key pose is created, and interpolation between these 3D body poses, together with the incorporation of limb length and symmetry constraints, provides a smooth initial approximation of the 3D motion. This is then fitted to the image data to generate a realistic 3D reconstruction. The degree of manual input required is controlled by the diversity of the sequence's content. Sports' footage is ideally suited to this approach as it frequently contains a limited number of repeated actions. Our method is demonstrated on a long (36 second) sequence of a woman playing tennis filmed with a non-stationary camera. This sequence required manual initialisation on < 1.5% of the frames, and demonstrates that the system can deal with very rapid motion, severe self-occlusions, motion blur and clutter occurring over several concurrent frames. The monocular 3D reconstruction is verified by synthesising a view from the perspective of a 'ground truth' reference camera, and the result is seen to provide a qualitatively accurate 3D reconstruction of the motion.

1 Introduction

This paper addresses the challenge of generating a qualitatively accurate 3D reconstruction of the actions performed by an individual in a long ($\sim$30 second) monocular image sequence. It is assumed the individual is not wearing any special reflective markers or clothing. Any solution must be able to cope with the multitude of difficulties that may arise over several concurrent frames: severe self-occlusion, unreliability of methods for limb and joint detection, motion blur, and the inherent ambiguities in reconstructing rigid links from monocular images [15]. Until now, the only approach guaranteed to produce a complete and accurate reconstruction in such circumstances is: *for each frame in the sequence, manually locate the skeletal joints and perform 3D reconstruction using the method of* [15]. The latter involves solving the forward/backward binary ambiguity for each rigid link by inspection and estimating the relative lengths of each limb. For very short sequences this is a relatively painless procedure, but rapidly becomes impractical for longer sequences.

T. Pajdla and J. Matas (Eds.): ECCV 2004, LNCS 3024, pp. 442–455, 2004.
© Springer-Verlag Berlin Heidelberg 2004

The traditional tracking approach to human motion capture [7] is to perform manual initialisation at the beginning of the sequence and then update the estimate of the reconstruction over time in accordance with the incoming data. In contrast we consider the entire sequence and approximate the actions present by a set of representative frames (automatically determined from the sequence) and from these obtain a coarse description of the subject's motion. Finer detail is added by locating the skeletal joints in each frame by extrapolating from manually initialised joint locations on the representative frames.

The degree of manual input required is controlled by the diversity of the sequence's content. Sports' footage is ideally suited to this approach as it frequently contains a limited number of repeated actions. Throughout this paper the ideas and methods developed are illustrated and tested on a 36 second sequence of a woman playing tennis. Our results are verified by synthesising a view of the 3D reconstruction from the perspective of a reference camera not used for the reconstruction.

The motivation for pursuing this problem together with a review of related research is presented in section 2. An overview of the algorithm is given in section 3. Section 4 details the grouping performed to obtain a keyframe representation of a sequence. Building upon this representation, the skeletal joint locations in each frame are estimated (section 5). The procedure for constructing the 3D reconstruction of the sequence is given in section 6, and the final reconstructions achieved for the tennis sequence are displayed in section 7 prior to the concluding remarks.

2   Background

Markerless human motion capture has drawn growing interest in recent years. The majority of systems developed have used multiple cameras to capture the subject [2,3,7]. However, stereo systems are rare outside of research laboratories and studios, and the bulk of videos of human activity are monocular. This, together with the comparative ease of capturing monocular sequences, motivates the monocular problem as one of more than purely academic interest.

Several researchers have tackled the challenge of human motion capture from monocular sequences, and some impressive results have been achieved over short sequences [13, 10]. Sminchisescu and Triggs [12,13] have achieved the most successful results to date in monocular markerless 3D human motion capture. Their algorithms are based upon propagating a mixture of Gaussians pdf, representing the probable 3D configurations of a body over time. Success relies upon performing efficient and thorough global searches of the cost surface associating the image data to potential body configurations. These methods have proved effective on relatively short sequences. However, it is an open question, whether the propagation of a multi-modal distribution, without an explicit mechanism for re-initialisation, is sufficient for long sequences.

Potential disruptions to smooth tracking conditions can be bridged by imposing priors on the dynamics of the configuration of the body. These have been used to some effect [11,10,1]. However, this comes at a cost. The motions present in a novel sequence may not be adequately described by the priors in use, and the appropriate trade-off between fitting the image data and fulfilling the prior constraints has to to decided. Also for long sequences of diverse motion (e.g. tennis) no one dynamical model can fully explain the motions present, necessitating the introduction of some form of recognition.

The general problem with tracking long sequences is that it is difficult to encapsulate the diversity of motion in a prior model. However, it is possible to summarise the motion in such a sequence. Several researchers have summarised the content of video by detecting and describing the actions (or subjects) present [17,8] either by clustering together frames or sequences of frames with similar properties. Toyama and Blake [16] showed that actions in a sequence could be summarised by a set of keyframes (exemplars) extracted from the sequence, and preceded to describe a novel video clip as a sequence of warped versions of these keyframes. A similar approach has been taken in more recent work [14,6], where sophisticated methods are used to match hand-defined keyframes to individual frames. Furthermore, by identifying specific joint locations on each keyframe, it was possible to localise these joint positions throughout a sequence. These methods, though only applied to short sequences, show an approach to tracking driven by *pose recognition*. This circumvents the problem of initialisation and is resistant to complete failure due to tracking loss, thereby opening the way to track long sequences.

This paper extends the keyframe-based approach of Sullivan and Carlsson [14] to long sequences with no prior learning and no pre-defined keyframes. A subsequent 3D reconstruction is performed using the method of [15].

3   Overview of Algorithm

Figure 1 gives an overview of the algorithm developed in this paper, from the initial extraction of the keyframes summarising the sequence, through the labelling of skeletal joint positions, formation of 3D keyframes, and interpolation of 3D keyframes, to the final 3D reconstruction.

Automatically representing the sequence by a set of keyframes requires measuring the similarity between the poses present in every pair of frames in the sequence. A distance matrix summarises these similarities and is used as the basis for finding the representative poses which in turn are encapsulated in keyframes summarising the sequence. The second layer in figure 1 encompasses the initialisation of each keyframe: the 2D skeletal joints are manually labelled and their corresponding 3D reconstructions created [15]. The 2D skeletal joints are then automatically determined throughout the sequence using the 2D keyframes and the keyframe assignment for each frame [14,6]. This involves

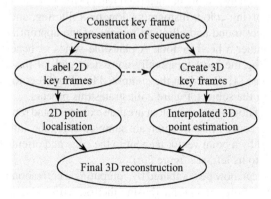

Fig. 1. Overview of the algorithm.

approximating the warp of the assigned keyframe to each frame and transferring the defined skeletal joints accordingly.

Next follows an initial estimation of a smooth 3D reconstruction of the sequence, whereby each frame deemed sufficiently close to a 3D keyframe is replaced by that keyframe. Interpolation occurs between these frames to estimate the intermediate frames. Finally the interpolated 3D reconstruction is refined to fit the estimated 2D joint locations throughout the sequence. This is achieved by minimising the reprojection error, while taking into account motion smoothness and imposing limb length and symmetry constraints. This ensures that any errors in the 2D data do not result in invalid reconstructions of the skeleton.

4   Defining Keyframes

We are interested in extracting, from a sequence $\mathcal{I} = \{1, \cdots, N\}$, a set of keyframes $\mathcal{K} \subset \mathcal{I}$ which span the body poses in $\mathcal{I}$. Besides providing a summary of the content of the sequence, each keyframe will assist in the skeletal joint localisation in frames of similar appearance. Such frames are considered *well-represented* by a keyframe. Thus $\mathcal{K}$ has an associated set $\mathcal{W}_{\mathcal{K}} \subset \mathcal{I}$ of frames it well-represents. The poses between two well-represented frames less than T frames apart, may be approximated by interpolating between the well-represented frames. These interpolatable frames define a set $\mathcal{J}_{\mathcal{K}} \subset \mathcal{I}$.

We wish to choose the least number of keyframes that enable an accurate description of the pose in a percent α of the sequence's frames. That is, we aim to find the $\mathcal{K}$ with minimal cardinality such that

$$|\mathcal{W}_{\mathcal{K}} \cup \mathcal{J}_{\mathcal{K}}| \geq \alpha N \tag{1}$$

Keyframe selection is based upon a distance matrix $\mathbf{D} \in \mathbb{R}^{N \times N}$ describing the similarity in body pose between every pair of frames in the sequence. Below we explain how $\mathbf{D}$ is computed and then analysed to produce $\mathcal{K}$.

4.1   Measuring Pose Similarity between Frames

The subject is localised by finding the head and feet positions in each frame. This is done by sequentially applying colour histograms, low-pass filtering, and a radial symmetry operator [5] to detect round and elliptical regions of the appropriate scale and colour to correspond to either a head or foot. A plausible series of head and feet positions is isolated by finding the most temporally consistent path of the candidate locations through the sequence [4]. Based on the computed head and feet locations, a bounding box is estimated for the subject. Figure 2 illustrates this process.

Target regions of homogeneous colour are then extracted, and represented by *directed edge elements*: The edges of each region are sampled at regular intervals. Each sample point is represented by a point vector tangent to the edge and oriented so the interior of the target region is to its left, see figure 2(e).

Pairs of images can now be compared by computing a correspondence field between the edge points. The frames are aligned using the tracked head and feet locations, and each edge element matched to the closest edge element in the other image from the

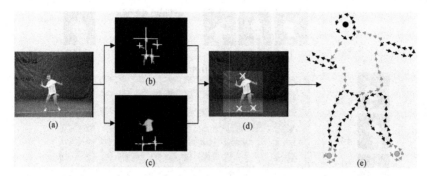

Fig. 2. (a) Original image, (b) head- and (c) feet-like colours highlighted, low-pass filtered and with peaks in radial symmetry indicated — the magnitude of each peak is shown by the size of the cross — (d) identified head and feet regions and resulting bounding box, (e) directed edge elements of target regions.

same coloured target regions, and whose orientation differs by less than 45 degrees. A comparison of the body poses can then be computed by considering the average distance between corresponding points, together with the percentage of edge elements for which a corresponding match was found.

4.2   Distance Matrix

Using the method described in section 4.1, we can determine the distance and the percentage of successfully matched points between every i^{th} and j^{th} frame in the sequence. Putting the respective output into the matrices $\mathbf{B}, \mathbf{A} \in \mathbb{R}^{N \times N}$, an initial distance matrix $\mathbf{C}$ is then computed by combining these as

$$\mathbf{C}(i,j) = \mathbf{A}(i,j)\mathbf{B}(i,j) + (1 - \mathbf{A}(i,j))\max \mathbf{B}$$

The resulting matrix $\mathbf{C}$ gives a good indication of the dissimilar and similar frames. However, it can be improved. When the inter-frame distance is sufficiently small, $\mathbf{C}(i,j) < \beta$, frames i and j are extremely likely to contain the same pose. In this case the corresponding i^{th} and j^{th} rows (and columns) of $\mathbf{C}$ should be almost identical, and any observed differences can be treated as noise. The final distance matrix $\mathbf{D}$ is formed by replacing each row and column of $\mathbf{C}$ with the average of all the rows and columns corresponding to frames to which it has a distance less than β. This reduces the noise giving a cleaner distance matrix.

Figure 3 shows $\mathbf{D}$ for the upper body for an 1800 frame tennis sequence, with several example frames and their corresponding rows and columns in the matrix. The dark rectangular regions in the matrix correspond to periods where there is little change between frames. For the tennis sequence this equates to the player standing still in between strokes, such as in frames 448 and 1662. Dark diagonals (off the main diagonal) correspond to distinct repeated events, such as the forehand (614, 1258) and backhand (174, 1032) frames. Note that there is only one such dark diagonal in the rows and columns corresponding to frames 174 and 1032. This is because there are only two backhands in the sequence, and thus only one repeated event.

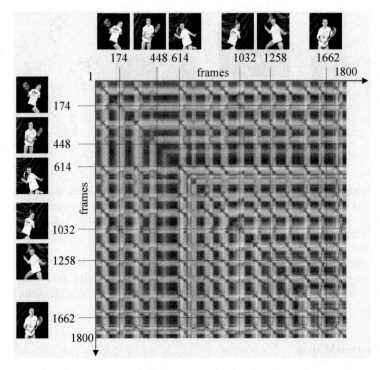

Fig. 3. The distance matrix **D** for the upper body pose over a 1800 frame (36 second) tennis sequence, with several sample frames. Short dark diagonals correspond to forehands and backhands, and dark rectangular regions indicate periods where the player is standing still.

4.3   Keyframe Selection

We define a criterion for considering one frame to be well-represented by another. Recall in section 4.2 that if $\mathbf{D}(i, j) < \beta$, then frame i and j are considered to exhibit the same pose. We say that such frames are *well-represented* by each other.

We now describe an algorithm to find a $\mathcal{K}$ with minimal $|\mathcal{K}|$ which fulfills equation (1). Keyframes are iteratively selected to minimize the average distance of all frames from their neighbouring well-represented frames. Firstly, define $C_\mathcal{K}$ as:

$$C_\mathcal{K} = \sum_{i=1}^{N} \left(\min_{f \in \mathcal{W}_\mathcal{K}, f < i} |i - f| + \min_{f \in \mathcal{W}_\mathcal{K}, f > i} |i - f| \right) \tag{2}$$

Then set $\mathcal{K}^0 = \emptyset$. Keyframes are repeatedly selected according to:

$$\mathcal{K}^{(t+1)} = \mathcal{K}^{(t)} \cup \{j\} \tag{3}$$

where

$$j = \underset{1 \leq k \leq N, k \notin \mathcal{K}^{(t)}}{\arg \min} \; C_{\mathcal{K}^{(t)} \cup \{k\}} \tag{4}$$

until the criterion in equation (1) is satisfied.

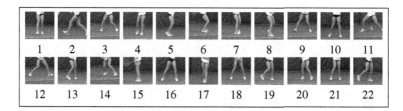

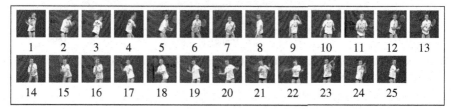

Fig. 4. The 22 lower and the 25 upper body keyframes extracted from the 36 second sequence.

This algorithm was applied to extract keyframes from an 1800 frame sequence of a woman playing tennis with T set to 10 and $\alpha = 0.95$. The upper and lower body were divided, and separate distance matrices and key frames determined for each. 25 key frames were required for the upper body and 22 for the lower body in order to satisfy equation (1) (see figure 4).

4.4   A Keyframe Representation of the Sequence

Figure 5 shows an example upper body and lower body keyframe and the associated well-represented frames from the sequence.

By representing each frame by its closest keyframe we can examine the occurrence of different body poses throughout the sequence. Figure 4 shows all the keyframes extracted from the sequence and figure 6 shows which keyframe best represents each frame throughout the sequence. This graph characterises the pose variation in the sequence and the forehands and backhands are easily identified respectively by the strong peaks and troughs in the graph in figure 6.

Fig. 5. Example upper and lower body keyframes, and the frames well-represented by these keyframes.

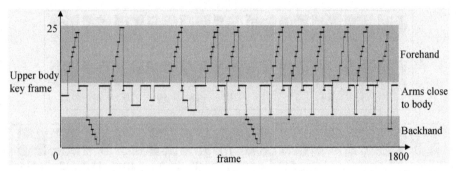

Fig. 6. Occurrence of frames associated with the various keyframes throughout sequence. This graph is for the upper body.

5   Locating Joint Positions

For each keyframe, $k \in \mathcal{K}$, its n skeletal joints, $\mathbf{x}_k = (x_{1,k}, \cdots, x_{n,k})$ $x_{i,k} \in \mathbb{R}^2$, are manually annotated. Points from the appropriate keyframe are then automatically mapped to every frame in the sequence to obtain an estimate of $\mathbf{x}_{1:N} = (\mathbf{x}_1, \cdots, \mathbf{x}_N)$. Figure 7 shows an annotated keyframe k, and joint locations estimated for a frame t, assigned to this keyframe. The aligned keyframe edges have been superimposed onto Figure 7(b). Each joint in the keyframe has associated edge points in its vicinity and the correspondences found between these edge points and the edge points in the frame t define a translation. This translation is used to transfer the joint from the keyframe to frame t. Once an estimate of each joint in frame t is obtained, it is refined using the appearance of the joints in the keyframe, and enforcing the apparent limb length ratios evident in the keyframe [14]. Figure 7(c) shows the final estimates.

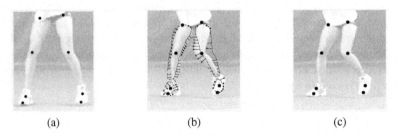

(a)   (b)   (c)

Fig. 7. (a) annotated keyframe k, (b) point correspondences between keyframe and well-represented frame, and (c) joint locations estimated for the well-represented frame t.

6   3D Reconstruction

The human skeleton can be modelled as an articulated chain with n_l links. Given the projection of the skeletal joint locations $\mathbf{x}_t$ onto the image plane, the number of qualitatively different reconstructions, $\mathbf{X}_t$, is bounded by 2^{n_l} [15] (assuming orthographic imaging), as each link can point either toward or away from the image plane. For an N

frame sequence, the number of possible reconstructions explodes to $2^{n_l N}$. This enormous search-space can be pruned by imposing the physiological limitations of the human body [13] and bounding the motion between adjacent frames. Without prior information, estimating the skeleton's configuration $\mathbf{X}_{1:N}$ over the sequence requires deciding the optimal binary labelling at each frame based on heuristic continuity measures.

Therefore, the crucial issue is the generation of prior information about the 3D configuration of the subject in the video. From the previous section we have a set of keyframes, $\mathcal{K}$, which span the 2D poses in the sequence. The 3D reconstruction of these keyframes provides an approximate basis for the 3D poses exhibited in the sequence. Thus with a limited amount of manual effort we have obtained some crucial priors. The next section describes how these 3D keyframes are used to create a smooth initial estimate, $\mathbf{X}_{1:N}^0$, of the 3D configuration of the subject throughout the sequence.

6.1   Establishing a Smooth Representative Reconstruction

The elements of $\mathcal{W}_{\mathcal{K}}$ and their corresponding keyframe assignments define the frames in the sequence that are well approximated by the 3D keyframes. Replacing each of these frames with its appropriate keyframe, and using these as control points in a spherical linear interpolation (slerp) process [9] allows the approximation of intermediary frames not in $\mathcal{W}_{\mathcal{K}}$. Keyframes have been chosen to ensure that the temporal distance interpolated is never large (equation (1)). However, frequently temporally adjacent frames in $\mathcal{W}_{\mathcal{K}}$ are assigned to the same keyframe. In reality they do not correspond to exactly the same 3D pose. One of the frames' 3D poses will, in general, match the keyframe more accurately than the others, and the other frames are better approximated by interpolation between the keyframes that temporally bound them.

To this end, temporal runs of frames in $\mathcal{W}_{\mathcal{K}}$ that are well-represented by the same keyframe are identified. The fit of each frame in the run to the 3D keyframe is ranked (ranking is based on a robust measure of the Euclidean distance between the reprojected 3D keyframe and the frame's estimated 2D joints). The lowest ranked frames in each run are iteratively omitted from the set of control points, subject to the criterion that T must be the maximum distance between control points.

Once the final control points have been decided, the interpolation is performed to obtain $\hat{\mathbf{X}}_{1:N}^0$. Figure 8 summarises the interpolation process.

6.2   Fitting the Smooth Motion Estimate to the Joint Data

The last task is to refine the 3D reconstruction by allowing the localised joint locations $\hat{\mathbf{x}}_{1:N}$ to influence $\hat{\mathbf{X}}_{1:N}^0$. However, the localised joint locations may contain outliers, be corrupted by noise and suffer from missing estimates due to self-occlusion. To ensure robustness to these factors, the final estimate of $\mathbf{X}_{1:N}$ is forced to be a valid trajectory of a human skeleton.

Define $\mathcal{M}_N$ as the manifold describing all valid trajectories of length N of the skeleton. Then:

$$\hat{\mathbf{X}}_{1:N} = \arg\min_{\mathbf{X}_{1:N}} E(\mathbf{X}_{1:N}) \quad \text{subject to} \quad \hat{\mathbf{X}}_{1:N} \in \mathcal{M}_N. \tag{5}$$

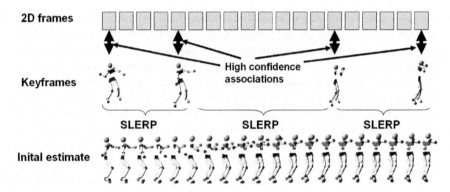

Fig. 8. Visualisation of the generation of a smooth and plausible trajectory of the 3D skeleton that approximates the content of the video.

where E is a cost function based on the sum of squared differences between $\hat{\mathbf{x}}_{1:N}$ and the orthographic projection of $\mathbf{X}_{1:N}$ (denoted by $\mathbf{x}'_{1:N}$):

$$E(\mathbf{X}_{1:N}) = \| \mathbf{x}'_{1:N} - \hat{\mathbf{x}}_{1:N} \|^2 \tag{6}$$

There is no easy characterisation of $\mathcal{M}_N$, so enforcing $\hat{\mathbf{X}}_{1:N}$ to belong to $\mathcal{M}_N$ is difficult. However, all members of $\mathcal{M}_N$ must exhibit constant limb-length throughout the sequence, and each joint trajectory must follow a smooth path. By forcing $\hat{\mathbf{X}}_{1:N}$ to satisfy these constraints, $\hat{\mathbf{X}}_{1:N}$ will be on or close to $\mathcal{M}_N$.

Step 1: Translate, rotate and scale $\hat{\mathbf{X}}_{1:N}^0$ to fit the 2D data
Step 2: Set $i = 1$.
Step 3: Gradient descent:
$\qquad \hat{\mathbf{X}}_{1:N}^i = \hat{\mathbf{X}}_{1:N}^{i-1} - \lambda \nabla_{\mathbf{X}_{1:N}} E\vert_{\hat{\mathbf{X}}_{1:N}^{i-1}}, \quad 0 < \lambda \le 1.$
Step 4: Enforce constraints: $\hat{\mathbf{X}}_{1:N}^i \in \mathcal{M}_N$.
Step 5: Increment i by one and goto Step 3. (until convergence)

Fig. 9. The iteration steps involved in finding $\hat{\mathbf{X}}_{1:N}$.

By construction $\hat{\mathbf{X}}_{1:N}^0 \in \mathcal{M}_N$. Therefore, it is used as the initial guess for the solution of the minimisation problem posed in equation (5). Figure 9 gives an outline of how the minimisation proceeds. At the end of each iteration, enforcing $\hat{\mathbf{X}}_{1:N}^i \in \mathcal{M}_N$ is approximated by resetting the limb-lengths to their correct value, and applying a low-pass filter to the trajectories of each joint. A large λ yields faster convergence, but makes it more difficult to re-project the solution back onto $\mathcal{M}_N$. We used $\lambda = 0.2$ for our experiments.

Figure 10 shows how a 3D keyframe is refined in 3D to match the image data. Here the same 3D keyframe is modified to form two different 3D reconstructions to match two different forehand frames, capturing the subtle differences between the two forehand strokes.

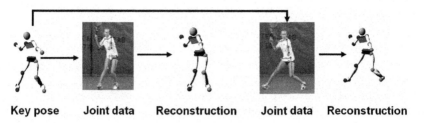

Key pose   Joint data   Reconstruction   Joint data   Reconstruction

Fig. 10. Result of refining a key-pose based on image-data. The key-pose is refined according to the different images, resulting in two different 3D poses.

7   Results

Our algorithm was applied to reconstructing a 36 second tennis sequence filmed with a non-stationary camera. During the sequence the player moves about the baseline and plays several forehand and backhand strokes. Our results were verified by synthesising a view of the 3D reconstruction from the perspective of a reference camera. Figure 11 shows the experimental setup together with 3D reconstructions throughout the sequence and associated 'ground-truth' frames from the reference camera. Figure 12 shows a reconstructed forehand, together with the reference video, and demonstrates the realistic smoothness of the reconstructed 3D motion. The 3D reconstruction of the complete 36 second video is presented in the demonstration video together with the 2D tracking under-pinning the reconstruction.

The video and figures 11 and 12 show the qualitative accuracy of our results, and demonstrate that our system can deal with a diverse range of actions recurring over a long sequence. Figure 13 further demonstrates how our system is able to deal with self-occlusion, rapid motion, clutter from the tennis racket, and motion blur.

The system detects outliers as discontinuities in the 3D motion and fills in the missing data via interpolation to form a plausible trajectory. This enables the system to deal with isolated tracking failures. Further, the underlying recognition-based approach to the 2D tracking means the target is freshly detected each frame, and thus ideally placed to recover from 'tracking loss'. In the worst case, the 3D reconstruction will revert to the smooth interpolation from the keyframes (figure 14). How accurate these key poses are depends on how well the sequence is represented by the keyframes, this is specified by the user who defines α the percentage of the sequence which is well-represented by the keyframes.

Our method is well-suited to action sequences with repeated events (e.g. sport). Furthermore, it is possible to quantify the suitability of a sequence for this form of reconstruction by checking how many keyframes are required to represent the desired percentage of the sequence.

8   Closing Remarks

We have presented a method for the 3D reconstruction of articulated body motion from a long monocular sequence. The performance of our system was demonstrated over 36

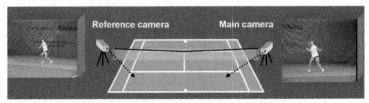

Camera positions used for the experiment.

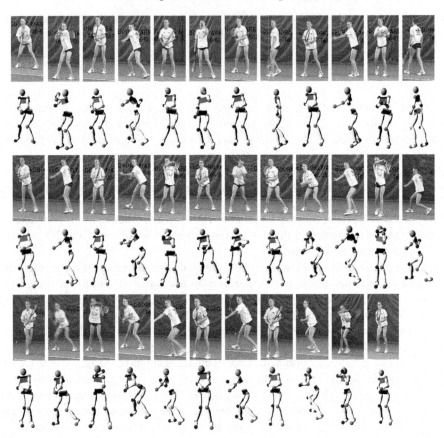

Fig. 11. Results of the reconstruction of the entire sequence. Every 50th frame of the 36s long sequence is shown together with the image from our reference camera.

seconds of tennis footage and shown to provide a qualitatively accurate reconstruction. To our knowledge this is longest full-body 3D reconstruction attempted from markerless monocular image data.

Fig. 12. The reconstruction of one forehand stroke shown together with the images from our reference camera. Note the smoothness of the reconstruction.

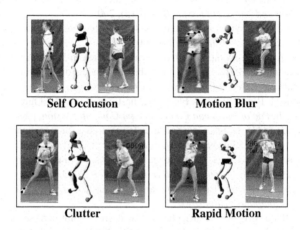

Fig. 13. Examples of reconstructions achieved under difficult imaging conditions. Each case shows the tracked 2D data, the 3D reconstruction from the perspective of the reference camera, and the view from the reference camera.

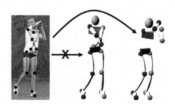

Fig. 14. The importance of maintaining a smooth motion. A large error is encountered in the joint localisation (a). Without enforcing motion smoothness, the frame would be reconstructed as (b). In (c) the reconstructed frame is shown after enforcing smoothness constraints.

References

1. A. Blake and M. Isard. *Active Contours*. Springer, 1998.
2. C. Bregler and J. Malik. Tracking people with twists and exponential maps. In *CVPR*, 1998.
3. J. Deutscher, A. Blake, and I. Reid. Motion capture by annealed particle filtering. *Proc. Conf. Computer Vision and Pattern Recognition*, 2000.
4. V. Lepetit, A. Shahrokni, and P. Fua. Robust data association for anline applications. In *Proc. Conf. Computer Vision and Pattern Recognition*, 2003.
5. G. Loy and A. Zelinsky. Fast radial symmetry for detecting points of interest. *IEEE Trans. on Pattern Analysis and Machine Intelligence*, 25(8):959–973, 2003.
6. G. Mori and J. Malik. Estimating human body configurations using shape context matching. In *Poc of European Conference on Computer Vision*, 2002.
7. T. Moselund and E. Granum. A survey of computer vision-based human motion capture. *Computer Vision and Image Understanding*, 81(3), 2001.
8. D. Ramanan and D. Forsyth. Finding and tracking people from the bottom up. In *Proc. Conf. Computer Vision and Pattern Recognition*, 2003.
9. K. Shoemake. Animating rotation with quaternion curves. In *SIGGRAPH*, 1985.
10. H. Sidenbladh and M. Black. Implicit probabilistic models of human motion for synthesis and human tracking. In *Poc of European Conference on Computer Vision*, 2002.
11. H. Sidenbladh, M. Black, and D.J. Fleet. Stochastic tracking of 3d human figures using 2d image motion. In *Poc of European Conference on Computer Vision*, pages 702–718, 2000.
12. C. Sminchisescu and B. Triggs. Covariance scaled sampling for monocular 3d body tracking. In *Proc. Conf. Computer Vision and Pattern Recognition*, 2001.
13. C. Sminchisescu and B. Triggs. Kinematic jump processes for monocular 3d human tracking. In *Proc. Conf. Computer Vision and Pattern Recognition*, 2003.
14. J. Sullivan and S. Carlsson. Recognizing and tracking human action. In *Poc of European Conference on Computer Vision*, 2002.
15. C. J. Taylor. Reconstruction of articulated objects from point correspondences in a single image. *Computer Vision and Image Understanding*, 80(3):349–363, 2000.
16. K. Toyama and A. Blake. Probabilistic tracking in a metric space. In *ICCV*, July 2001.
17. L. Zelnik-Manor and M. Irani. Event-based video analysis. In *Proc. Conf. Computer Vision and Pattern Recognition*, 2001.

Fusion of Infrared and Visible Images for Face Recognition

Aglika Gyaourova[1], George Bebis[1], and Ioannis Pavlidis[2]

[1] Computer Vision Laboratory, University of Nevada, Reno
{aglika,bebis}@cs.unr.edu
[2] Visual Computing Laboratory, University of Houston
pavlidis@cs.uh.edu

Abstract. A number of studies have demonstrated that infrared (IR) imagery offers a promising alternative to visible imagery due to it's insensitive to variations in face appearance caused by illumination changes. IR, however, has other limitations including that it is opaque to glass. The emphasis in this study is on examining the sensitivity of IR imagery to facial occlusion caused by eyeglasses. Our experiments indicate that IR-based recognition performance degrades seriously when eyeglasses are present in the probe image but not in the gallery image and vice versa. To address this serious limitation of IR, we propose fusing the two modalities, exploiting the fact that visible-based recognition is less sensitive to the presence or absence of eyeglasses. Our fusion scheme is pixel-based, operates in the wavelet domain, and employs genetic algorithms (GAs) to decide how to combine IR with visible information. Although our fusion approach was not able to fully discount illumination effects present in the visible images, our experimental results show substantial improvements recognition performance overall, and it deserves further consideration.

1 Introduction

Considerable progress has been made in face recognition research over the last decade [1] especially with the development of powerful models of face appearance (e.g., eigenspaces [2]). Despite the variety of approaches and tools studied, however, face recognition has shown to perform satisfactorily in controlled environments but it is not accurate or robust enough to be deployed in uncontrolled environments. Several factors affect face recognition performance including pose variation, facial expression changes, face occlusion, and most importantly, illumination changes.

Previous studies have demonstrated that IR imagery offers a promising alternative to visible imagery for handling variations in face appearance due to illumination changes more successfully. In particular, IR imagery is nearly invariant to changes in ambient illumination [3], and provides a capability for identification under all lighting conditions including total darkness [4]. Thus, while visible-based algorithms opt for pure algorithmic solutions into inherent phenomenology problems, IR-based algorithms have the potential to offer simpler

T. Pajdla and J. Matas (Eds.): ECCV 2004, LNCS 3024, pp. 456–468, 2004.

and more robust solutions, improving performance in uncontrolled environments and deliberate attempts to obscure identity [5].

Despite its advantages, IR imagery has other limitations including that it is opaque to glass. Objects made of glass act as a temperature screen, completely hiding the face parts located behind them. In this study, we examine the sensitivity of IR imagery to facial occlusion due to eyeglasses. To address this serious limitation of IR, we propose fusing IR with visible information in the wavelet domain using GAs [6]. To demonstrate the results of our fusion strategy, we performed extensive recognition experiments using the popular method of eigenfaces [2], although any other recognition method could have been used. Our results show overall substantial improvements in recognition performance using IR and visible imagery fusion than either modality alone.

2   Review of Face Recognition in the Infrared Spectrum

An overview of identification in the IR spectrum can be found in [7]. Below, we review several studies comparing the performance of visible and IR based face recognition. The effectiveness of visible versus IR was compared using several recognition algorithms in [8]. Using a database of 101 subjects without glasses, varying facial expression, and allowing minor lighting changes, they concluded that there are no significant performance differences between visible and IR recognition across all the algorithms tested. They also concluded that fusing visible and IR decision metrics represents a viable approach for enhancing face recognition performance. In [9,10], several different face recognition algorithms were tested under various lighting conditions and facial expressions. Using radiometrically calibrated thermal imagery, they reported superior performance for IR-based recognition than visible-based recognition. In [11], the effect of lighting, facial expression, and passage of time between the gallery and probe images were examined. Although IR-based recognition outperformed visible-based recognition assuming lighting and facial expression changes, their experiments demonstrated that IR-based recognition degrades when there is substantial passage of time between the gallery and probe images. Using fusion strategies at the decision level based on ranking and scoring, they were able to develop schemes that outperformed either modality alone. IR has also been used recently in face detection [12]. This approach employs multi-band feature extraction and capitalizes on the unique reflectance characteristics of the human skin in the near-IR spectrum.

3   Fusion of Infrared and Visible Imagery

Despite its robustness to illumination changes, IR imagery has several drawbacks. First, it is sensitive to temperature changes in the surrounding environment. Currents of cold or warm air could influence the performance of systems using IR imagery. As a result, IR images should be captured in a controlled environment. Second, it is sensitive to variations in the heat patterns of the face.

Factors that could contribute to these variations include facial expressions (e.g. open mouth), physical conditions (e.g. lack of sleep), and psychological conditions (e.g. fear, stress, excitement). Finally, IR is opaque to glass. As a result, a large part of the face might be occluded (e.g. by wearing eyeglasses).

In contrast to IR imagery, visible imagery is more robust to the above factors. This suggests that effective algorithms to fuse information from both spectra have the potential to improve the state of the art in face recognition. In the past, fusion of visible and IR images has been successfully used for visualization purposes [13].

In this study, we consider the influence of eyeglasses to IR-based face recognition. Our experiments demonstrate that eyeglasses pose a serious problem to recognition performance in the IR spectrum. To remedy this problem, we propose fusing IR with visible imagery. Visible imagery can suffer from highlights on the glasses under certain illumination conditions, but the problems are considerably less severe than with IR. Since IR and visible imagery capture intrinsically different characteristics of the observed faces, intuitively, a better face description could be found by utilizing the complimentary information present in the two spectra.

3.1   Fusion at Multiple Resolutions

Pixel by pixel fusion does not preserve the spatial information in the image. In contrast, fusion at multiple resolution levels allows features with different spatial extend to be fused at the resolution at which they are most salient. In this way, important features appearing at lower resolutions can be preserved in the fusion process.

Multiple resolution features have been used in several face recognition systems in the past (e.g. [14]). The advantages of using different frequencies is that high frequencies are relatively independent of global changes in the illumination, while the low frequencies take into account the spatial relationships among the pixels and are less sensitive to noise and small changes, such as facial expression.

The slow heat transfer through the human body causes natural low resolution of IR images of human face. Thus, we decided to implement our fusion strategy in the wavelet domain, taking into consideration the benefits of multi-resolution representations and the differences in resolution between the IR and visible-light images. Our fusion strategy is thus different from fusion strategies implemented at the decision level, reported earlier in the literature (i.e., [8,11]).

3.2   Method Overview

The proposed method contains two major steps: (a) fusion of IR and visible images and (b) recognition based on the fused images. Fusion is performed by combining the coefficients of Haar wavelet [15] decompositions of a pair of IR and visible images having equal size. The fusion strategy is found during a training phase using GAs [6]. The coefficients selected from each spectrum are put together and the fused face image is reconstructed using the inverse wavelet transform. To demonstrate the effectiveness of the fusion solutions found by GAs, we perform recognition using the popular method of eigenfaces [2] although any other recognition technique could have been used.

4   Mathematical Tools and Background Information

4.1   Eigenfaces

The eigenface approach uses Principal Components Analysis (PCA), a classical multivariate statistics method, to linearly project face images in a low-dimensional space. This space is spanned by the principal components (i.e., eigenvectors corresponding to the largest eigenvalues) of the distribution of the training images. After a face image has been projected in the eigenspace, a feature vector containing the coefficients of the projection is used to represent the face image. Representing each image $I(x, y)$ as a $N \times N$ vector Γ_i, first the average face Ψ is computed: $\Psi = \frac{1}{R} \sum_{i=1}^{R} \Gamma_i$ where R is the number of faces in the training set. Next, the difference Φ of each face from the average face is computed: $\Phi_i = \Gamma_i - \Psi$. Then the covariance matrix is estimated by: $C = \frac{1}{R} \sum_{i=1}^{R} \Phi_i \Phi_i^T = AA^T$, where, $A = [\Phi_1 \Phi_2 \ldots \Phi_R]$. The eigenspace can then be defined by computing the eigenvectors μ_i of C. Usually, we need to keep a smaller number of eigenvectors R_k corresponding to the largest eigenvalues. Each image Γ is transformed by first subtracting the mean image ($\Phi = \Gamma - \Psi$), and then projecting in the eigenspace $w_i = \mu_i^T \Gamma$.

4.2   Wavelet Transform (WT)

Wavelets are a type of multi-resolution function approximation that allow for the hierarchical decomposition of a signal or image. In particular, they decomposes a given signal onto a family of functions with finite support. This family of functions is constructed by the translations and dilations of a single function called *mother wavelet*. The finite support of the *mother wavelet* gives exact time localization while the scaling allows extraction of different frequency components. The discrete wavelet transform (DWT) is defined in terms of discrete dilations and translations of the *mother wavelet* function: $\psi_{jk}(t) = 2^{-j/2} \psi(2^{-jt} - k)$, where the scaling factor j and the translation factor k are integers: $j, k \in \mathbf{Z}$. The wavelet decomposition of a function $f(t) \in L^2(R)$ is given by: $f(t) = \sum_j \sum_k h_{j,k} \psi_{jk}(t)$, where the coefficients $h_{j,k}$ are the inner products of $f(t)$ and $\psi_{jk}(t)$.

4.3   Genetic Algorithms (GAs)

GAs are a class of randomized, parallel search optimization procedures inspired by the mechanisms of natural selection, the process of evolution [6]. They were designed to efficiently search large, non-linear, poorly-understood search spaces. In the past, GAs have been used in target recognition [16], object recognition [17], face detection/verification [18,19], and feature selection [20,21].

GAs operate iteratively on a population of structures, each of which represents a candidate solution to the problem, encoded as a string of symbols (i.e., chromosome). A randomly generated set of such strings forms the initial population from which the GA starts its search. Three basic genetic operators guide this search: selection, crossover and mutation. Evaluation of each string is based on a fitness function which is problem-dependent. The fitness function determines which of the candidate solutions are better. Selection probabilistically filters out poor solutions and keeps high performance solutions for further investigation. Mutation is a very low probability operator that plays the role of restoring lost genetic material. Crossover in contrast is applied with high probability. It is a randomized yet structured operator that allows information exchange between the stings.

5   Evolutionary IR and Visible Image Fusion

Our fusion strategy operates in the wavelet domain. The goal is to find an appropriate way to combine the wavelet coefficients from the IR and visible images. The key question is which wavelet coefficients to choose and how to combine them. Obviously, using un-weighted averages is not appropriate since it assumes that the two spectra are equally important and, even further, that they have the same resolution which is not true. Several experiments for fusing the wavelet coefficients of two images have been reported in [22]. Perhaps, the most intuitive approach is picking the coefficients with maximum absolute value [23]. The higher the absolute value of a coefficient is, the higher is the probability that it encodes salient image features. Our experiments using this approach showed poor performance.

In this paper, we propose using GAs to fuse the wavelet coefficients from the two spectra. Our decision to use GAs for fusion was based on several factors. First, the search space for the image fusion task at hand is very large. In the past, GAs have demonstrated good performance when searching large solution spaces. Much work in the genetic and evolutionary computing communities has led to growing understanding of why they work well and plenty of empirical evidence to support this claim [24,25]. Second, the problem at hand appears to have many suboptimal solutions. Although, GAs cannot guarantee finding a global optimum, they have shown to be successful in finding good local optima. Third, they suitable for parallelization and linear speedups are the norm, not the exception [26]. Finally, we have applied GAs in the past for feature selection, a problem very much related to fusion, with good success [20,21].

Encoding: In our encoding scheme, the chromosome is a bit string whose length is determined by the number of wavelet coefficients in the image decomposition. Each bit in the chromosome is associated with a wavelet coefficient at a specific location. The value of a bit in this array determines whether the corresponding wavelet coefficient is selected from the IR (e.g., 0) or from the visible spectrum (e.g., 1).

Fitness Evaluation: Each individual in a generation represents a possible way to fuse IR with visible images. To evaluate its effectiveness, we perform the fusion based on the information encoded by this individual and apply the eigenface approach. Recognition accuracy is computed using a validation dataset (see Section 7) and is used to provide a measure of fitness.

Initial Population: In general, the initial population is generated randomly, (e.g., each bit in an individual is set by flipping a coin). In this way, however, we will end up with a population where each individual contains the same number of 1's and 0's on average. To explore subsets of different numbers of wavelet coefficients chosen from each domain, the number of 1's for each individual is generated randomly. Then, the 1's are randomly scattered in the chromosome.

Selection: Our selection strategy was cross generational. Assuming a population of size N, the offspring double the size of the population and we select the best N individuals from the combined parent-offspring population

Crossover: In general, we do not know how different wavelet coefficients depend on each other. If dependent coefficients are far apart in the chromosome, it is more probable that traditional 1-point crossover, will destroy the schemata. To avoid this problem, uniform crossover is used here. The crossover probability used in our experiments was 0.96.

Mutation: Mutation is a very low probability operator which flips the values of randomly chosen bit. The mutation probability used here was 0.02.

6   Face Dataset

In our experiments, we used the face database collected by Equinox Corporation under DARPA's HumanID program [27]. Specifically, we used the long-wave infrared (LWIR) (i.e., 8μ-12μ) and the corresponding visible spectrum images from this database. The data was collected during a two-day period. Each pair of LWIR and visible light images was taken simultaneously and co-registered with 1/3 pixel accuracy (see Fig. 1). The LWIR images were radiometrically calibrated and stored as grayscale images with 12 bits per pixels. The visible images are also grayscale images represented with 8 bits per pixel. The size of the images in the database is 320×240 pixels.

The database contains frontal faces under the following scenarios: (1) three different light direction - frontal and lateral (right and left); (2) three facial expression - "frown", "surprise" and "smile"; (3) vocals pronunciation expressions - subjects were asked to pronounce several vocals from which three representative frames are chosen; and (4) presence of glasses - for subjects wearing glasses, all of the above scenarios were repeated with and without glasses. Both IR and visible face images were preprocessed prior to experimentation by following a procedure similar to that described in [9,10]. The goal of preprocessing was to align and scale the faces, remove background, and account for some illumination variations (see Fig. 1).

7   Experimental Procedure

In this study, we attempted to test the effect on recognition performance of each factor available in the Equinox database. In addition, we have performed

Fig. 1. Examples of visible and IR image pairs and preprocessed images

experiments focusing on the effect of eyeglasses. For comparison purposes, we have attempted to evaluate our fusion strategy using a similar experimental protocol to that given in [9,10]. Our evaluation methodology employs a training set (i.e., used to compute the eigenfaces), a gallery set (i.e., set of persons enrolled in the system), a validation set (i.e., used in the fitness evaluation of the GA), and a test set (i.e., probe image set containing the images to be identified). Our training set contains 200 images, randomly chosen from the entire Equinox database.

For recognition, we used the Euclidean distance and the first 100 principal components as in [9,10]. Recognition performance was measured by finding the percentage of the images in the test set, for which the top match is an image of the same person from the gallery. To mitigate for the relatively small number of images in the database, the average error was recorded using a three-fold cross-validation procedure. In particular, we split each dataset used for testing randomly three times by keeping only 75% of the images for testing purposes and the rest 25% for validation purposes. To account for performance variations due to random GA initialization, we averaged the results over three different GA runs for each test, choosing a different random seed each time. Thus, we performed a total of 9 runs for each gallery/test set experiment.

7.1 Facial Expression Tests

The test sets for the facial expression experiments include the images containing the three expression frames and three vocal pronunciation frames. There are 90 subjects with a total of 1266 pairs of images for the expression frames and 1299 for the vocal frames. Some of the subjects in these tests sets wear glasses while others not. Following the terminology in [9,10] we have created the following test sets: EA (expression frames, all illuminations), EL (expression frames, lateral illuminations), EF (expression frames, frontal illumination), VA (vocal frames, all illumination), VL (vocal frames, lateral illumination), VF (vocal frames, frontal illumination). The inclusion relations among these sets are as follows: EA = EL ∪ EF, VA = VL ∪ VF, and VA ∩ EA = ∅.

7.2 Eyeglasses Tests

Measuring the effect of eyeglasses is done by using the expression frames. There are 43 subjects wearing glasses in the EA set making a total of 822 images. Following the terminology in [9,10] we created the following test sets: EG (expression frames with glasses, all illuminations), EnG (expression frames without glasses, all illuminations), EFG (expression frames with glasses, frontal illumination), ELG (expression frames with glasses, lateral illumination), EFnG (expression frames without glasses, frontal illumination), ELnG (expression frames without glasses, lateral illumination). The inclusion relations among these sets are as follows: EG = ELG ∪ EFG, EnG = ELnG ∪ EFnG and EG ∩ EnG = ∅.

8   Experimental Results

8.1   Eyeglasses

The results shown in Table 1 illustrate that IR-based recognition is robust to illumination changes but performs poorly when glasses are present in the gallery set but not in the test set and vice versa. Considerable improvements in recognition performance have been achieved in this case by fusing IR with visible images. The improvement was even greater when, in addition to eyeglasses, the test and the gallery set contained images taken under different illuminations. For example, in the EFG/ELnG test case the fusion approach improved recognition performance by 46% compared to recognition using visible-light images and by 82% compared to recognition using LWIR images.

Recognition using LWIR images outperformed recognition using fused images when the only difference between the images in the test and gallery sets was the direction of illumination. This is accounted to the inability of our fusion scheme to fully discount illumination effects contributed by the visible-light images. Recognition performance using visible-light images was always worse than using fused images.

8.2   Facial Expression

The facial expression tests had varying success as shown in Table 2. In general, fusion led to improved recognition compared to recognition using visible-light images. In several cases, however, the accuracy using LWIR images was higher than using fused images. These were cases again where the illumination dierctions between the gallery and the test sets were different. This result is consistent with that of the eyeglasses tests and was caused by the inability of our fusion scheme to fully discount the illumination effects in the visible images. Note that we did not performed experiments when the intersection between gallery and test sets is not empty.

9   Discussion

The presence/absence of eyeglasses proved to be a big obstacle for IR-based recognition. To better understand this, let's take a closer look of the results shown in Table 1. The horizontal and vertical double lines through the center of the table divide the table into four quadrants (i.e., *I* to *IV*, starting from

Table 1. Averages and standard deviations for the eyeglasses experiments. The columns represent the gallery set and the rows represent the test set. The first entry in each cell shows the performance measured from the visible-light images, the second entry is from the LWIR images, and the third entry is from the fused images. The bottom entry shows the minimum and maximum recognition performances from the three cross-validation runs achieved when using the fused images. Test scenarios for which the test and the gallery sets had common subsets were not performed.

	EG	ELG	EFG	EnG	ELnG	EFnG
EG	X	X	X	(84.8, 1.4) (15.1, 1.0) (92.5, 1.3) 91.0 − 93.6	(84.8, 1.4) (13.1, 1.0) (88.9, 1.4) 88.0 − 90.5	(64.3, 1.7) (21.7, 1.0) (82.1, 3.1) 79.2 − 85.4
ELG	X	X	(71.4, 1.0) (99.6, 0.3) (93.2, 3.0) 90.2 − 94.2	(85.8, 0.7) (16.2, 0.3) (92.3, 2.0) 90.2 − 94.2	(85.8, 0.7) (14.2, 0.4) (92.7, 0.6) 92.0 − 93.0	(56.0, 1.2) (22.4, 0.4) (83.9, 1.3) 82.5 − 84.8
EFG	X	(78.3, 1.1) (100, 0) (97.9, 0.6) 97.4 − 98.5	X	(83.7, 3.9) (14.5, 0.6) (91.7, 1.3) 90.9 − 93.1	(50.7, 1.7) (13.0, 0) (77.1, 3.1) 74.3 − 80.4	(82.6, 4.0) (22.1, 0.6) (92.2, 0.6) 90.2 − 94.2
EnG	(79.4, 1.1) (2.6, 0.2) (84.9, 0.8) 84.3 − 85.8	(72.0, 2.2) (2.4, 0.2) (81.6, 0.3) 81.2 − 81.8	(60.2, 2.0) (17.4, 0.5) (98.0, 0.1) 97.9 − 98.1	X	X	X
ELnG	(82.0, 1.7) (2.7, 0.5) (84.2, 1.9) 82.1 − 85.7	(82.0, 1.7) (2.5, 0.3) (84.1, 1.4) 82.5 − 85.2	(52.6, 0.8) (17.7, 0.6) (96.7, 1.4) 95.1 − 97.8	X	X	(73.0, 1.9) (98.4, 0.6) (96.9, 0.6) 96.2 − 97.5
EFnG	(78.6, 1.6) (2.1, 0) (85.6, 3.2) 83.2 − 89.2	(56.8, 1.1) (2.1, 0) (80.7, 2.9) 78.3 − 83.9	(78.6, 1.6) (18.6, 1.2) (87.0, 2.1) 85.2 − 89.3	X	(71.9, 1.2) (100, 0) (97.8, 1.0) 97.2 − 99.0	X
number of images	398	260	138	424	281	143

Table 2. Recognition results for the facial expression tests.

	VA	EA	VF	EF	VL	EL
VA	X	(65.0, 1.0) (92.3, 0.7) (93.6, 0.7) 92.8 − 94.2	X	X	X	X
EA	(65.2, 1.2) (93.7, 0.4) (93.1, 0.4) 92.7 − 93.4	X	X	X	X	X
VF	X	X	X	(65.3, 1.8) (90.5, 0.4) (93.3, 0.9) 92.5 − 94.2	(62.4, 0.4) (99.3, 0) (98.1, 0.5) 97.7 − 98.6	(36.4, 0.7) (87.9, 0.6) (91.4, 1.4) 89.8 − 92.3
EF	X	X	(59.2, 0.9) (91.3, 0.7) (91.2, 1.3) 90.3 − 92.8	X	(30.4, 0.7) (91.2, 0.4) (90.0, 1.4) 88.6 − 91.5	(68.5, 1.1) (99.5, 0.4) (98.2, 0.4) 97.7 − 98.4
VL	X	X	(60.5, 0.7) (98.4, 0.2) (97.6, 0.8) 97.0 − 98.4	(28.0, 0.7) (90.4, 0.1) (86.9, 0.8) 85.9 − 87.4	X	(66.4, 0.4) (91.3, 0.4) (94.5, 1.5) 92.9 − 95.7
EL	X	X	(31.6, 1.1) (85.8, 0.7) (84.4, 0.3) 84.2 − 84.7	(63.0, 0.9) (98.6, 0.2) (96.4, 0.7) 95.8 − 97.2	(68.9, 1.0) (91.7, 0.2) (93.7, 0.4) 93.3 − 94.1	X
number of images	1299	1266	435	429	864	837

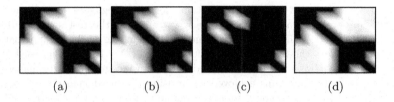

(a)   (b)   (c)   (d)

Fig. 2. The average performance values from Table 1, visualized as a grayscale image. See text for details. (a) ideal case (b) visible images (c) IR images, (d) fused images.

the upper-right corner and moving counterclockwise). Each quadrant represents a set of experiments testing some specific difference between the gallery and the test sets: (1) Experiments in quadrant I evaluate the effect of eyeglasses being present in the probe but not in the gallery; (2) Experiments in quadrant III evaluate the effect of eyeglasses being present in the gallery but not in the probe; (3) Experiments along the off-diagonals within each of these two quadrants represent tests where the illumination conditions between the gallery and probe sets are the same; (4) Experiments in quadrants II and IV evaluate the effect illumination changes only.

To illustrate the performance of our fusion approach, we have interpolated the results from Table 1 and used a simple visualization scheme to remove small differences and emphasize major trends in recognition performance (see Fig. 2). Our visualization scheme assigns a grayscale value to each average from Table 1) with black implying 0% recognition and white 100% recognition. The empty cells from Table 1 are also shown in black.

By observing Fig. 2, several interesting conclusions can be made. As expected, face recognition success based on IR images (see Fig. 2.(b))is not influenced by lighting conditions. This is supported by the prevailing white color in quadrants II and IV (case (3)) and by the high recognition rates in quadrants II and IV (case (4)). However, IR yielded very low success when eyeglasses were present in the gallery but not in the probe and vice-versa (cases (1) and (2)). The success of visible-based face recognition was relatively insensitive to subjects' wearing glasses (see Fig. 2.(c)). This follows from the relatively uniform color in quadrants I and III (cases (1) and (2)). Lighting conditions had big influence on the success of face recognition in the visible domain. There are distinguishable bright lines along the main diagonals in quadrants I and II (case (3)). The success of face recognition based on fused images was similar in all four quadrants of the image (see Fig. 2.(d)). This implies that we were able to achieve relative insensitivity to both eyeglasses and variable illumination.

The image fusion approach led to higher recognition performance compared to recognition in the visible spectrum but was not able to completely compensate for the effects of illumination direction in the visible images. We have noticed that in all the cases where LWIR performed better than fusion, the illumination direction in the gallery set was different from that in the test set (assuming no difference in glasses). The presence of illumination effects in the fused images

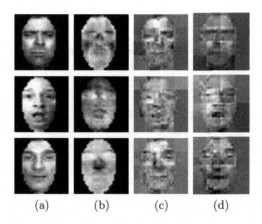

(a)   (b)   (c)   (d)

Fig. 3. The original (a) visible and (b) IR images followed by two different fused image results – (c) trained on a data set with lateral illumination and without glasses and (d) trained on a data set with glasses.

Fig. 4. The first few eigenfaces of a fused image data set. The second and third eigenfaces show clear influence of the right and left lateral illumination.

can be visually confirmed by observing the reconstructed fused images shown in Fig. 3, and their first eigenfaces shown in i.e., Fig. 4. Fused images had higher resolution compared to LWIR images, however, they were also affected by illumination effects present in the visible images. Obviously, the first eigenfaces of the fused images still encode the effects of illumination direction, present in the visible images. More effective fusion schemes (e.g., weighted averages of wavelet coefficients) and more powerful fitness functions (i.e., add extra terms to control the number of coefficients selected from different bands of each spectrum) might help to overcome these problems and improve fusion overall.

Also, further consideration should be given to the existence of many optimal solutions found by the GA. Although optimal in the training phase, these solutions showed different recognition performances when used for testing. In investigating these solutions, we were not able to distinguish any pattern in the content of the chromosomes that might have revealed why some chromosomes were better than others. On the average, half of the coefficients were selected from the visible spectrum and the other half from the IR spectrum. The use of larger validation sets and more selective fitness functions might help to address these issues more effectively.

10   Conclusions and Future Work

We presented a fusion method for combining IR and visible light images for the purposes of face recognition. The algorithm aims at improved and robust recognition performance across variable lighting, facial expression, and presences of eyeglasses. Future work includes addressing the issues mentioned in the previous section, considering fitness approximation schemes [28] to reduce the computational requirements of fitness evaluation, and investigating the effect of environmental (e.g., temperature changes), physical (e.g., lack of sleep) and physiological conditions (e.g., fear, stress) to IR performance.

References

1. Zhao, W., C.R.P.P., Rosenfeld, A.: Face recognition: A literature survey. ACM Computing Surveys **35** (2003) 399–458
2. Turk, M., Pentland, A.: Eigenfaces for recognition. CogNeuro **3** (1991) 71–96
3. Wolff L., S.D., , C., E.: Quantitative measurement of illumination invariance for face recognition using thermal infrared imagery. In: IEEE Workshop on Computer Vision Beyond the Visible Spectrum: Methodsand Applications, Hawaii (2001)
4. Jain, A., Bolle, R., Pankanti, S.: Biometrics: Personal Identification in Networked Society. Kluwer Academic Publishers (1999)
5. Pavlidis, I., Symosek, P.: The imaging issue in an automatic face/disguise detection system. In: IEEE Workshop on Computer Vision Beyond the Visible Spectrum: Methods and Applications. (2000) 15–24
6. Goldberg, D.: Genetic algorithms in search, optimization, and machine learning. Addison-Wesley (1989)
7. Prokoski, F.: History, current status, and future of infrared identification. In: IEEE Workshop on Computer Vision Beyond the Visible Spectrum, Hilton Head (2000)
8. Wilder, J., Phillips, J., Jiang, C., Wiener, S.: Comparison of visible and infra-red imagery for face recognition. In: 2nd International Conference on Automatic Face and Gesture Recognition, Killington (1996) 182–187
9. Selinger, A., Socolinsky, D.: Appearance-based facial recognition using visible and thermal imagery: A comparative study. Technical report, Equinox Corporation n.02–01 (2002)
10. Socolinsky, D., A., S.: Comparative study of face recognition performance with visible and thermal infrared imagery. In: International Conference on Pattern Recognition. (2002) 217–222
11. Chen, X., Flynn, P., Bowyer, K.: Pca-based face recognition in infrared imagery: Baseline and comparative studies. In: IEEE International Workshop on Analysis and Modeling of Faces and Gestures, Nice, France (2003)
12. Dowdall, J., Pavlidis, I., Bebis, G.: Face detection in the near-ir spectrum. Image and Vision Computing **21** (2001) 565–578
13. Scheunders, P.: Local mapping for multispectral image visualization. Image and Vision Computing **19** (2001) 971–978
14. Manjunath, B., Chellappa, R., von der Malsburg, C.: A feature based approach to face recognition. In: Computer Vision and Pattern Recognition. (1992) 373–378
15. Chui, C.: An introduction to wavelets. Academic Press (1992)
16. Katz, A., Thrift, P.: Generating image filters for target recognition by genetic learning. IEEE Transactions on Pattern Analysis and Machine Intelligence **16** (1994)

17. Bebis, G., Louis, S., Varol, Y., Yfantis, A.: Genetic object recognition using combinations of views. IEEE Transactions on Evolutionary Computing **6** (2002) 132–146
18. Swets, D., Punch, B.: Genetic algorithms for object localization in a complex scene. In: IEEE International Conference on Image Processing. (1995) 595–598
19. Bebis, G., Uthiram, S., Georgiopoulos, M.: Face detection and verification using genetic search. International Journal of Artificial Intelligence Tools 9 (2000) 225–246
20. Sun, Z., Yuan, X., Bebis, G., Louis, S.: Genetic feature subset selection for gender classification: A comparison study. In: IEEE Workshop on Applications of Computer Vision. (2002)
21. Sun, Z., Bebis, G., Miller, R.: Boosting object detection using feature selection. In: IEEE International Conference on Advanced Video and Signal Based Surveillance. (2003)
22. Chipman, L., Orr, T.: Wavelets and image fusion. In: IEEE International Conference on Image Processing. Volume 3. (1995) 248–251
23. Li, H.and Manjunath, B., Mitra, S.: Multisensor image fusion using the wavelet transform. In: IEEE International Conference on Image Processing. Volume 1., Austin, Texas (1994) 51–55
24. Fogel, D.: Evolutionary Computation, Toward a New Philosophy of Machine Intelligence. IEEE Press (1992)
25. Koza, J.: Genetic Programming. MIT Press (1993)
26. Cantu-Paz, E.: Efficient and Accurate Parallel Genetic Algorithms and Evolutionary Computation. Kluwer Academic Publishers (2000)
27. Available at: http://www.equinoxsensors.com/products/HID.html.
28. Jin, Y., Sendhoff, B.: Fitness approximation in evolutionary computation – a survey. In: Genetic and Evolutionary Computation Conference. (2002)

Reliable Fiducial Detection in Natural Scenes

David Claus and Andrew W. Fitzgibbon

Department of Engineering Science
University of Oxford, Oxford OX1 3BN
{dclaus,awf}@robots.ox.ac.uk

Abstract. Reliable detection of fiducial targets in real-world images is addressed in this paper. We show that even the best existing schemes are fragile when exposed to other than laboratory imaging conditions, and introduce an approach which delivers significant improvements in reliability at moderate computational cost. The key to these improvements is in the use of machine learning techniques, which have recently shown impressive results for the general object detection problem, for example in face detection. Although fiducial detection is an apparently simple special case, this paper shows why robustness to lighting, scale and foreshortening can be addressed within the machine learning framework with greater reliability than previous, more ad-hoc, fiducial detection schemes.

1 Introduction

Fiducial detection is an important problem in real-world vision systems. The task of identifying the position of a pre-defined target within a scene is central to augmented reality and many image registration tasks. It requires fast, accurate registration of unique landmarks under widely varying scene and lighting conditions. Numerous systems have been proposed which deal with various aspects of this task, but a system with reliable performance on a variety of scenes has not yet been reported.

Figure 1 illustrates the difficulties inherent in a real-world solution of this problem, including background clutter, motion blur [1], large differences in scale, foreshortening, and the significant lighting changes between indoors and out. These difficulties mean that a reliable general-purpose solution calls for a new approach. In fact, the paper shows how the power of machine learning techniques, for example as applied to the difficult problem of generic face detection [2], can benefit even the most basic of computer vision tasks.

One of the main challenges in fiducial detection is handling variations in scene lighting. Transitions from outdoors to indoors, backlit objects and in-camera lighting all cause global thresholding algorithms to fail, so present systems tend to use some sort of adaptive binarization to segment the features.

The problem addressed in this paper is to design a planar pattern which can be reliably detected in real world scenes. We first describe the problem, then cover existing solutions and present a new approach. We conclude by comparing the learning-based and traditional approaches.

T. Pajdla and J. Matas (Eds.): ECCV 2004, LNCS 3024, pp. 469–480, 2004.

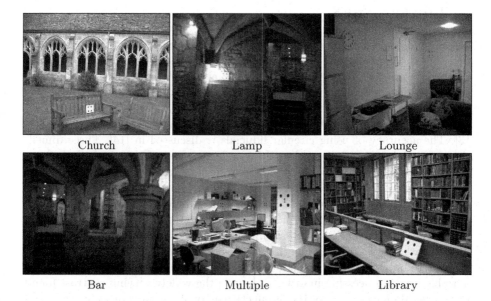

Church   Lamp   Lounge

Bar   Multiple   Library

Fig. 1. Sample frames from test sequences. The task is to reliably detect the targets (four disks on a white background) which are visible in each image. It is a claim of this paper that, despite the apparent simplicty of this task, no technique currently in use is robust over a large range of scales, lighting and scene clutter. In real-world sequences, it is sometimes difficult even for humans to identify the target. We wish to detect the target with high reliability in such images.

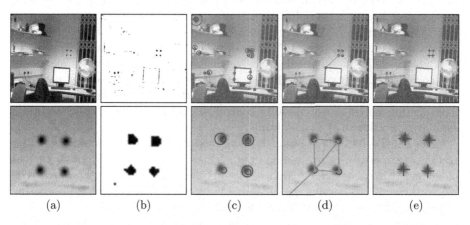

(a)   (b)   (c)   (d)   (e)

Fig. 2. Overall algorithm to locate fiducials. (a) Input image, (b) output from the fast classifier stage, (c) output from the full classifier superimposed on the original image. Every pixel has now been labelled as fiducial or non-fiducial. The size of the circles indicates the scale at which that fiducial was detected. (d) The target verification step rejects non-target fiducials through photometric and geometric checks. (e) Fiducial coordinates computed to subpixel accuracy.

2   Previous Work

Detection of known points within an image can be broken down into two phases: design of the fiducials, and the algorithm to detect them under scene variations. The many proposed fiducial designs include: active LEDs [3,4]; black and white concentric circles [5]; coloured concentric circles [6,7], one-dimensional line patterns [8]; squares containing either two-dimensional bar codes [9], more general characters [10] or a Discrete Cosine Transform [11]; and circular ring-codes [12, 13]. The accuracy of using circular fiducials is discussed in [14]. Three dimensional fiducials whose images directly encode the pose of the viewer have been propsed by [15]. We have selected a circular fiducial as the centroid is easily and efficiently measured to sub-pixel accuracy. Four known points are required to compute camera pose (a common use for fiducial detection) so we arrange four circles in a square pattern to form a target. The centre of the target may contain a barcode or other marker to allow different targets to be distinguished.

Naimark and Foxlin [13] identify non-uniform lighting conditions as a major obstacle to optical fiducial detection. They implement a modified form of homomorphic image processing in order to handle the widely varying contrast found in real-world images. This system is effective in low-light, in-camera lighting, and also strong side-lighting. Once a set of four ring-code fiducials have been located the system switches to tracking mode and only checks small windows around the known fiducials. The fiducial locations are predicted based on an inertial motion tracker.

TRIP [12] is a vision-only system that uses adaptive thresholding [16] to binarize the image, and then detects the concentric circle ring-codes by ellipse fitting. Although the entire frame is scanned on start-up and at specified intervals, an ellipse tracking algorithm is used on intermediate frames to achieve real-time performance. The target image can be detected 99% of the time up to a distance of 3 m and angle of 70 degrees from the target normal.

CyberCode [9] is an optical object tagging system that uses two-dimensional bar codes to identify object. The bar codes are located by a second moments search for guide bars amongst the regions of an adaptively thresholded [16] image. The lighting needs to be carefully controlled and the fiducial must occupy a significant portion of the video frame.

The AR Toolkit [10] contains a widely used fiducial detection system that tracks square borders surrounding unique characters. An input frame is thresholded and then each square searched for a pre-defined identification pattern. The global threshold constrains the allowable lighting conditions, and the operating range has been measured at 3 m for a 20×20 cm target [17].

Cho and Neumann [7] employ multi-scale concentric circles to increase their operating range. A set of 10 cm diameter coloured rings, arranged in a square target pattern similar to that used in this paper, can be detected up to 4.7 m from the camera.

Motion blur causes pure vision tracking algorithms to fail as the fiducials are no longer visible. Our learnt classifier can accomodate some degree of motion blur through the inclusion of relevant training data.

These existing systems all rely on transformations to produce invariance to some of the properties of real world scenes. However, lighting variation, scale changes and motion blur still affect performance. Rather than image pre-processing, we deal with these effects through machine learning.

2.1   Detection versus Tracking

In our system there is no prediction of the fiducial locations; the entire frame is processed every time. One way to increase the speed of fiducial detection is to only search the region located in the previous frame. This assumes that the target will only move a small amount between frames and causes the probability of tracking subsequent frames to depend on success in the current frame. As a result, the probability of successfully tracking through to the end of a sequence is the product of the frame probabilities, and rapidly falls below the usable range. An inertial measurement unit can provide a motion prediction [1], but there is still the risk that the target will fall outside the predicted region. This work will focus on the problem of detecting the target independently in each frame, without prior knowledge from the earlier frames.

3   Strategy

The fiducial detection strategy adopted in this paper is to collect a set of sample fiducial images under varying conditions, train a classifier on that set, and then classify a subwindow surrounding each pixel of every frame as either fiducial or not. There are a number of challenges, not least of which are speed and reliability.

We begin by collecting representative training samples in the form of 12×12 pixel images; larger fiducials are scaled down to fit. This training set is then used to classify subwindows as outlined in Figure 2. The classifier must be fast and reliable enough to perform half a million classifications per frame (one for the 12×12 subwindow at each location and scale) and still permit recognition of the target within the positive responses.

High efficiency is achieved through the use of a cascade of classifiers [2]. The first stage is a fast "ideal Bayes" lookup that compares the intensities of a pair of pixels directly with the distribution of positive and negative sample intensities for the same pair. If that stage returns positive then a more discriminating (and expensive) tuned nearest neighbour classifier is used. This yields the probability that a fiducial is present at every location within the frame; non-maxima suppression is used to isolate the peaks for subsequent verification.

The target verification is also done in two stages. The first checks that the background between fiducials is uniform and that the separating distance falls within the range for the scale at which the fiducials were identified. The second step is to check that the geometry is consistent with the corners of a square under perspective transformation. The final task is to compute the weighted centroid of each fiducial within the found target and report the coordinates.

The following section elaborates on this strategy; first we discuss the selection of training data, then each stage of the classification cascade is covered in detail.

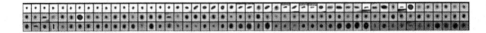

Fig. 3. Representative samples of positive target images. Note the wide variety of positive images that are all examples of a black dot on a white background.

3.1 Training Data

A subset of the positive training images is shown in Figure 3. These were acquired from a series of training videos using a simple tracking algorithm that was manually reset on failure. These samples indicate the large variations that occur in real-world scenes. The window size was set at 12×12 pixels, which limited the sample dot size to between 4 and 9 pixels in diameter; larger dots are scaled down by a factor of two until they fall within the specification. Samples were rotated and lightened or darkened to artificially increase the variation in the training set. This proves to be a more effective means of incorporating rotation and lighting invariance than *ad hoc* intensity normalization, as discussed in §5.

3.2 Cascading Classifier

The target location problem here is firmly cast as one of statistical pattern classification. The criteria for choosing a classifier are speed and reliability: the four subsampled scales of a 720×576 pixel video frame contain 522,216 subwindows requiring classification. Similar to [2], we have adopted a system of two cascading probes:

- fast Bayes decision rule classification on sets of two pixels from every window in the frame
- slower, more specific nearest neighbour classifier on the subset passed by the first stage

The first stage of the cascade must run very efficiently, have a near-zero false negative rate (so that any true positives are not rejected prematurely) and pass a minimal number of false positives. The second stage provides very high classification accuracy, but may incur a higher computational cost.

3.3 Cascade Stage One: Ideal Bayes

The first stage of the cascade constructs an ideal Bayes decision rule from the positive and negative training data distributions. These were measured from the training data and additional positive and negative images taken from the training videos. The sampling procedure selects two pixels from each subwindow: one at the centre of the dot and the other on the background. The distribution of the training data is shown in Figure 4.

The two distributions can be combined to yield a Bayes decision surface. If g_p and g_n represent the positive and negative distributions then the classification

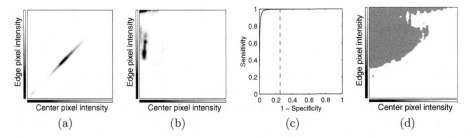

Fig. 4. Distribution of (a) negative pairs g_n and (b) positive pairs g_p used to construct the fast classifier. (c) ROC curve used to determine the value of α (indicated by the dashed line) which will produce the optimal decision surface given the costs of positive and negative errors. (d) The selected Bayes decision surface.

of a given intensity pair x is:

$$\text{classification}(x) = \begin{cases} +1 \text{ if } \alpha \cdot g_p(x) > g_n(x) \\ -1 \text{ otherwise} \end{cases} \tag{1}$$

where α is the relative cost of a false negative over a false positive. The parameter α was varied to produce the ROC curve shown in Figure 4c. A weighting of $\alpha = e^{12}$ produces the decision boundary shown in Figure 4d, and corresponds to a sensitivity of 0.9965 and a specificity of 0.75.

A subwindow is marked as a possible fiducial if a series of intensity pairs all lie within the positive decision region. Each pair contains the central point and one of seven outer pixels. The outer edge pixels were selected to minimize the number of false positives based on the above emiprical distributions.

The first stage of the cascade seeks dark points surrounded by lighter backgrounds, and thus functions is like a well-trained edge detector. Note however that the decision criteria is not simply $(edge - center) > threshold$ as would be the case if the center was merely required to be darker than the outer edge. Instead, the decision surface in Figure 4d encodes the fact that {dark center,dark edge} are more likely to be background, and {light center, light edge} are rare in the positive examples. Even at this early edge detection stage there are benefits from including learning in the algorithm.

3.4   Cascade Stage Two: Nearest Neighbour

Among the various methods of supervised statistical pattern recognition, the nearest neighbour rule [18] achieves consistently high performance [19]. The strategy is very simple: given a training set of examples from each class, a new sample is assigned the class of the nearest training example. In contrast with many other classifiers, this makes no *a priori* assumptions about the distributions from which the training examples are drawn, other than the notion that nearby points will tend to be of the same class.

For a binary classification problem given sets of positive and negative examples $\{p_i\}$ and $\{n_j\}$, subsets of $\mathbb{R}^d$ where d is the dimensionality of the input vectors (144 for the image windows tested here). The NN classifier is then formally written as

$$\text{classification}(x) = -\text{sign}(\min_i \|p_i - x\|^2 - \min_j \|n_j - x\|^2). \qquad (2)$$

This is extended in the k-NN classifier, which reduces the effects of noisy training data by taking the k nearest points and assigning the class of the majority. The choice of k should be performed through cross-validation, though it is common to select k small and odd to break ties (typically 1, 3 or 5).

One of the chief drawbacks of the nearest neighbour classifier is that it is slow to execute. Testing an unknown sample requires computing the distance to each point in the training data; as the training set gets large this can be a very time consuming operation. A second disadvantage derives from one of the technique's advantages: that *a priori* knowledge cannot be included where it is available. We address both of these in this paper.

Speeding Up Nearest Neighbour. There are many techniques available for improving the performance and speed of a nearest neighbour classification [20]. One approach is to pre-sort the training sets in some way (such as kd-trees [21] or Voronoi cells [22]), however these become less effective as the dimensionality of the data increases. Another solution is to choose a subset of the training data such that classification by the 1-NN rule (using the subset) approximates the Bayes error rate [19]. This can result in significant speed improvements as k can now be limited to 1 and redundant data points have been removed from the training set. These data modification techniques can also improve the performance through removing points that cause mis-classifications.

We examined two of the many techniques for obtaining a training subset: condensed nearest neighbour [23] and edited nearest neighbour [24]. The condensed nearest neighbour algorithm is a simple pruning technique that begins with one example in the subset and recursively adds any examples that the subset misclassifies. Drawbacks to this technique include sensitivity to noise and no guarantee of the minimum consistent training set because the initial few patterns have a disproportionate affect on the outcome. Edited nearest neighbour is a reduction technique that removes an example if all of its neighbours are of a single class. This acts as a filter to remove isolated or noisy points and smooth the decision boundaries. Isolated points are generally considered to be noisy; however if no *a priori* knowledge of the data is assumed then the concept of noise is ill-defined and these points are equally likely to be valid. In our tests it was found that attempts to remove noisy points decreased the performance.

The condensing algorithm was used to reduce the size of the training data sets as it was desirable to retain "noisy" points. Manual selection of an initial sample was found to increase the generalization performance. The combined (test and training) data was condensed from 8506 positive and 19,052 negative examples to 37 positive and 345 negative examples.

Parameterization of Nearest Neighbour. Another enhancement to the nearest neighbour classifier involves favouring specific training data points through weighting [25]. In cases where the cost of a false positive is greater than the cost of a false negative it is desirable to weight all negative training data so that negative classification is favoured. This cost parameter allows a ROC curve to be constructed, which is used to tune the detector based on the relative costs of false positive and negative classifications.

We define the likelihood ratio to be the ratio of distances to the nearest negative and positive training examples:

$$likelihood\_ratio = nearest\_negative/nearest\_positive \,.$$

In the vicinity of a target dot there will be a number of responses where this ratio is high. Rather than returning all pixel locations above a certain threshold we locally suppress all non-maxima and return the point of maximum likelihood (similar to the technique used in Harris corner detection [26]; see [27] for additional details).

4   Implementation

Implementation of the cascading classifier described in the previous section is straightforward; this section describes the target verification step. Figure 2c shows a typical example of the classifier output, where the true positive responses are accompanied by a small number of false positives. Verification is merely used to identify the target amongst the positive classification responses; we outline one approach but there are any number of suitable techniques.

First we compute the Delaunay triangulation of all points to identify the lines connecting each positive classification with its neighbours. A weighted average adaptive thresholding of the pixels along each line identifies those with dark ends and light midsections. All other lines are removed; points that retain two or more connecting lines are passed to a geometric check. This check takes sets of four points, computes the transformation to map three of them onto the corners of a unit right triangle, and then applies that transformation to the remaining point. If the mapped point is close enough to the fourth corner of a unit square then retrieve the original grayscale image for each fiducial and return the set of weighted centroid target coordinates.

5   Discussion

The intention of this work was to produce a fiducial detector which offered extremely high reliability in real-world problems. To evaluate this algorithm, a number of video sequences were captured with a DV camcorder and manually marked up to provide ground truth data. The sequences were chosen to include the high variability of input data under which the algorithm is expected to be used. It is important also to compare performance to a traditional "engineered" detector, and one such was implemented as described in the appendix.

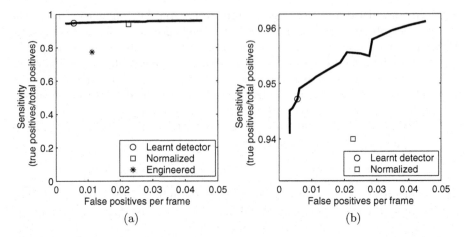

Fig. 5. (a) ROC curve for the overall fiducial detector. The vertical axis displays the percentage of ground truth targets that were detected. (b) An enlarged view of the portion of (a) corresponding to the typical operating range of the learnt detector. The drop in detection rate at 0.955 is an artefact of the target verification stage whereby some valid targets are rejected due to encroaching false positive fiducials.

Table 1. Success rate of target verification with various detectors. Normalizing each window prior to classification improves the success rate on some frames, but more false positive frames are introduced and the overall performance is worse. The engineered detector cannot achieve the same level of reliability as the learnt detector.

Sequence	Targets	Learnt detector True	False	Normalized detector True	False	Engineered detector True	False
Church	300	98.3%	2.0%	99.3%	8.7%	46.3%	0.0%
Lamp	200	95.5%	0.5%	99.5%	3.0%	61.5%	0.0%
Lounge	400	98.8%	0.5%	96.5%	1.0%	96.5%	0.0%
Bar	975	89.3%	0.0%	91.3%	0.0%	65.7%	0.5%
Multiple	2100	95.2%	0.7%	93.5%	3.5%	83.0%	1.4%
Library	325	99.1%	0.6%	94.2%	0.0%	89.8%	5.2%
Summary	4300	94.7%	0.4%	94.0%	2.3%	77.3%	1.1%

The fiducial detection system was tested on six video sequences containing indoor/outdoor lighting, motion blur and oblique camera angles. The reader is encouraged to view the video of detection results available from [28].

Ground truth target coordinates were manually recorded for each frame and compared with the results of three different detection systems: learnt classifier, learnt classifier with subwindow normalization, and the engineered detector described in the appendix. Table 1 lists the detection and false positive rates for each sequence, while Table 2 lists the average number of positives found per frame. Overall, the fast classification stage returned just 0.33% of the subwindows as positive, allowing the classification system to process the average

720×576 frame at four scales in 120 ms. The operating range is up to 10 m with a 50 mm lens and angles up to 75 degrees from the target normal.

Normalizing each subwindow and classifying with normalized data was shown to increase the number of positives found. The target verification stage must then examine a larger number of features; since this portion of the system is currently implemented in Matlab alone it causes the entire algorithm to run slower. This is added to the increased complexity of computing the normalization of each subwindow prior to classification. By contrast, appending a normalized copy of the training data to the training set was found to increase the range of classification without significantly affecting the number of false positives or processing time. The success rate on the dimly lit bar sequence was increased from below 50% to 89.3% by including training samples normalized to approximate dim lighting.

Careful quantitative experiments comparing this system with the AR Toolkit (an example of a developed method of fiducial detection) have not yet been completed, however a qualitative analysis of several sequences containing both targets under a variety of scene conditions has been performed. Although the AR Toolkit performs well in the office, it fails under motion blur and when in-camera lighting disrupts the binarization. The template matching to identify a specific target does not incorporate any colour or intensity normalization and is therefore very sensitive to lighting changes. We deal with all of these variations through the inclusion of relevant training samples.

This paper has presented a fiducial detector which has superior performance to reported detectors. This is because of the use of machine learning. This detector demonstrated 95% overall performance through indoor and outdoor scenes including multiple scales, background clutter and motion blur. A cascade of classifiers permits high accuracy at low computational cost.

The primary conclusion of the paper is the observation that even "simple" vision tasks become challenging when high reliability under a wide range of operating conditions is required. Although a well engineered *ad hoc* detector can be tuned to handle a wide range of conditions, each new application and environment requires that the system be more or less re-engineered. In contrast,

Table 2. Average number of positive fiducial classifications per frame. The full classifier is only applied to the positive results of the fast classifier. This cascade allows the learnt detector to run faster and return fewer false positives than the engineered detector.

Sequence	True positives	Fast classifier	Full classifier	Normalized full classifier	Engineered detector
Church	4	5790	107	135	121
Lamp	4	560	23	30	220
Lounge	4	709	36	55	43
Bar	4	82	5	6	205
Multiple	7.3*	2327	79	107	96
Library	4	1297	34	49	82
Average	-	1794	47	64	128

* The Multiple sequence contains between 1 and 3 targets per frame.

with appropriate strategies for managing training set size, a detector based on learning can be retrained for new environments without significant architectural changes.

Further work will examine additional methods for reducing the computational load of the second classifier stage. This could include Locally Sensitive Hashing as a fast approximation to the nearest neighbour search, or a different classifier altogether such as a support vector machine.

References

1. Klein, G., Drummond, T.: Tightly integrated sensor fusion for robust visual tracking. In: Proc. BMVC. Volume 2. (2002) 787 –796
2. Viola, P., Jones, M.: Rapid object detection using a boosted cascade of simple features. In: Proc. CVPR. (2001)
3. Neumann, U., Bajura, M.: Dynamic registration correction in augmented-reality systems. In: IEEE Virtual Reality Annual Int'l Symposium. (1995) 189–196
4. Welch, G., Bishop, G., et al.: The HiBall tracker: High-performance wide-area tracking for virtual and augmented environments. In: Proc. ACM VRST. (1999) 1–10
5. Mellor, J.P.: Enhanced reality visualization in a surgical environment. A.I. Technical Report 1544, MIT, Artificial Intelligence Laboratory (1995)
6. State, A., et al.: Superior augmented reality registration by integrating landmark tracking and magnetic tracking. In: SIGGRAPH. (1996) 429–438
7. Cho, Y., Neumann, U.: Multi-ring color fiducial systems for scalable fiducial tracking augmented reality. In: Proc. of IEEE VRAIS. (1998)
8. Scharstein, D., Briggs, A.: Real-time recognition of self-similar landmarks. Image and Vision Computing 19 (2001) 763–772
9. Rekimoto, J., Ayatsuka, Y.: Cybercode: Designing augmented reality environments with visual tags. In: Proceedings of DARE. (2000)
10. Kato, H., Billinghurst, M.: Marker tracking and hmd calibration for a video-based augmented reality conferencing system. In: Int'l Workshop on AR. (1999) 85–94
11. Owen, C., Xiao, F., Middlin, P.: What is the best fiducial? In: The First IEEE International Augmented Reality Toolkit Workshop. (2002) 98–105
12. de Ipina, D.L., et al.: Trip: a low-cost vision-based location system for ubiquitous computing. Personal and Ubiquitous Computing 6 (2002) 206–219
13. Naimark, L., Foxlin, E.: Circular data matrix fiducial system and robust image processing for a wearable vision-inertial self-tracker. In: ISMAR. (2002)
14. Efrat, A., Gotsman, C.: Subpixel image registration using circular fiducials. International Journal of Computational Geometry and Applications 4 (1994) 403–422
15. Bruckstein, A.M., Holt, R.J., Huang, T.S., Netravali, A.N.: New devices for 3D pose estimation: Mantis eyes, Agam paintings, sundials, and other space fiducials. International Journal of Computer Vision 39 (2000) 131–139
16. Wellner, P.: Adaptive thresholding for the digital desk. Technical Report EPC-1993-110, Xerox (1993)
17. Malbezin, P., Piekarski, W., Thomas, B.: Measuring artoolkit accuracy in long distance tracking experiments. In: 1st Int'l AR Toolkit Workshop. (2002)
18. Cover, T., Hart, P.: Nearest neighbor pattern classification. IEEE Trans. Information Theory 13 (1967) 57–67

19. Ripley, B.D.: Why do nearest-neighbour algorithms do so well? SIMCAT (Similarity and Categorization), Edinburgh (1997)
20. Wilson, D.R., Martinez, T.R.: Reduction techniques for instance-based learning algorithms. Machine Learning **38** (2000) 257–286
21. Sproull, R.F.: Refinements to nearest-neighbor searching in k-dimensional trees. Algorithmica **6** (1991) 579–589
22. Berchtold, S., Ertl, B., Keim, D.A., Kriegel, H.P., Seidl, T.: Fast nearest neighbor search in high-dimensional spaces. In: Proc. ICDE. (1998) 209–218
23. Hart, P.: The condensed nearest neighbor rule. IEEE Trans. Information Theory **14** (1968) 515–516
24. Duda, R., Hart, P., Stork, D.: Pattern Classification. 2nd edn. John-Wiley (2001)
25. Cost, S., Salzberg, S.: A weighted nearest neighbor algorithm for learning with symbolic features. Machine Learning **10** (1993) 57–78
26. Harris, C., Stephens, M.: A combined corner and edge detector. In: Proceedings of the 4th ALVEY Vision Conference. (1988) 147–151
27. Claus, D.: Video-based surveying for large outdoor environments. First Year Report, University of Oxford (2004)
28. http://www.robots.ox.ac.uk/~dclaus/eccv/fiddetect.mpg.

Appendix: Engineered Detector

One important comparison for this work is how well it compares with traditional *ad hoc* approaches to fiducial detection. In this section we outline a local implementation of such a system.

Each frame is converted to grayscale, binarized using adaptive thresholding as described in [16], and connected components used to identify continuous regions. The regions are split into scale bins based on area, and under or over-sized regions removed. Regions are then rejected if the ratio of the covex hull area and actual area is too low (region not entirely filled or boundary is not continually convex), or if they are too eccentric (if the axes ratio of an ellipse with the same second moments is too high).

Light Field Appearance Manifolds

Chris Mario Christoudias, Louis-Philippe Morency, and Trevor Darrell

Computer Science and Artificial Intelligence Laboratory
Massachussetts Institute of Technology
Cambridge, MA 02139 USA
{cmch,lmorency,trevor}@csail.mit.edu
http://www.ai.mit.edu/projects/vip/

Abstract. Statistical shape and texture appearance models are powerful image representations, but previously had been restricted to 2D or 3D
shapes with smooth surfaces and lambertian reflectance. In this paper we
present a novel 3D appearance model using image-based rendering techniques, which can represent complex lighting conditions, structures, and
surfaces. We construct a light field manifold capturing the multi-view
appearance of an object class and extend the direct search algorithm of
Cootes and Taylor to match new light fields or 2D images of an object
to a point on this manifold. When matching to a 2D image the reconstructed light field can be used to render unseen views of the object. Our
technique differs from previous view-based active appearance models in
that model coefficients between views are explicitly linked, and that we
do not model any pose variation within the shape model at a single view.
It overcomes the limitations of polygonal based appearance models and
uses light fields that are acquired in real-time.

1 Introduction

Appearance models are a natural and powerful way of describing objects of the
same class. Multidimensional morphable models [13], active appearance models [6], and their extensions have been applied to model a wide range of object appearance. The majority of these approaches represent objects in 2D and
model view change by morphing between the different views of an object. Modelling a wide range of viewpoints in a single 2D appearance model is possible,
but requires non-linear search [19]. Additionally, object self-occlusion introduces
holes and folds in the synthesized target view which are difficult to overcome.
Large pose variation is easily modelled using 3D; a polygonal 3D appearance
model was proposed by Blanz and Vetter [3]. With their approach the view is
an external parameter of the model and does not need to be modelled as shape
variation. However, this technique is based on a textured polygonal mesh which
has difficultly representing fine structure, complex lighting conditions and non-
lambertian surfaces. Due to the accuracy of the 3D surfaces needed with their
approach, the face scans of each prototype subject cannot be captured in real-
time and fine structure such as hair cannot be acquired.

In this paper we propose a 3D active appearance model using image-based

T. Pajdla and J. Matas (Eds.): ECCV 2004, LNCS 3024, pp. 481–493, 2004.

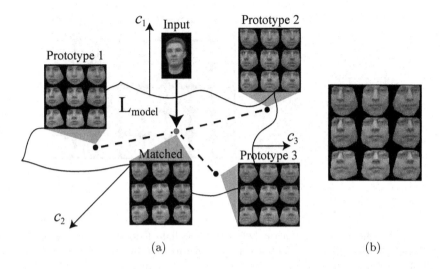

(a)   (b)

Fig. 1. (a) A light field appearance manifold L_{model}. Each point on the manifold is a 4D light field representing the 3D shape and surface reflectance of an object. The light field of an object is constructed by computing its projection onto the shape-texture appearance manifold. A 2D input image is matched to a point on this manifold by interpolating the shape and texture of neighboring prototype light fields. (b) A light field can capture non-lambertian effects (e.g. glasses).

rendering [14,11] rather than rendering with a polygonal mesh. We use a light field representation, which does not require any depth information to render novel views of the scene. With light field rendering, each model prototype consists of a set of sample views of the plenoptic function [1]. Shape is defined for each prototype and a combined texture-shape PCA space computed. The resulting appearance manifold (see Figure 1(a)) can be matched to a light field or 2D image of a novel object by searching over the combined texture-shape parameters on the manifold. We extend the direct search matching algorithm of [6] to light fields. Specifically, we construct a Jacobian matrix consisting of intensity gradient light fields. A 2D image is matched by rendering the Jacobian at the estimated object pose. Our approach can easily model complex scenes, lighting effects, and can be captured in real-time using camera arrays [23,22].

2   Previous Work

Statistical models based on linear manifolds of shape and/or texture variation have been widely applied to the modelling, tracking, and recognition of objects [2, 8,13,17]. In these methods small amounts of pose change are typically modeled implicitly as part of shape variation on the linear manifold. For representing objects with large amounts of rotation, nonlinear models have been proposed, but are complex to optimize [19]. An alternative approach to capturing pose variation

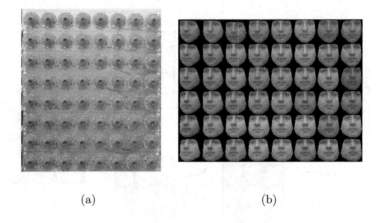

(a)   (b)

Fig. 2. (a) Light field camera array [23]. (b) A 6x8 light field of the average head. The light field prototypes were acquired using the 6 top rows of the camera array due to field of view constraints.

is to use an explicit multi-view representation which builds a PCA model at several viewpoints. This approach has been used for pure intensity models [16] as well as shape and texture models [7]. A model of inter-view variation can be recovered using the approach in [7], and missing views could be reconstructed. However, in this approach pose change is encoded as shape variation, in contrast to 3D approaches where pose is an external parameter. Additionally, views were relatively sparse, and individual features were not matched across views.

Shape models with 3D features have the advantage that viewpoint change can be explicitly optimized while matching or rendering the model. Blanz and Vetter [3] showed how a morphable model could be created from 3D range scans of human heads. This approach represented objects as simply textured 3D shapes, and relied on high-resolution range scanners to construct a model; non-lambertian and dynamic effects are difficult to capture using this framework. With some manual intervention, 3D models can be learned directly from monocular video [9,18]; an automatic method for computing a 3D morphable model from video was shown in [4]. These methods all used textured polygonal mesh models for representing and rendering shape.

Multi-view 2D [7] and textured polygonal 3D [3,9,18] appearance models cannot model objets with complex surface reflectance. Image-based models have become popular in computer graphics recently and can capture these phenomenon; with an image-based model, 3D object appearance is captured in a set of sampled views or ray bundles. Light field [14] and lumigraph [11] rendering techniques create new images by resampling the set of stored rays that represent an object. Most recently the unstructured lumigraph [5] was proposed, and generalized the light field/lumigraph representation to handle arbitrary camera placement and geometric proxies.

Recently, Gross et. al. [12] have proposed *eigen light fields*, a PCA-based appearance model built using light fields. They extend the approach of Turk and Pentland [21] to light fields and define a robust pose-invariant face recognition algorithm using the resulting model. A method to morph two lightfields was presented in [24]; this algorithm extended the classic Beier and Neely algorithm to work directly on the sampled lightfield representation and to account for self-occlusion across views. Features were manually defined, and only a morph between two (synthetically rendered) light fields was shown in their work.

In this paper we develop the concept of a *light field active appearance model*, in which 3 or more light fields are "vectorized" (in the sense of [2]) and placed in correspondence. We construct a light field morphable model of facial appearance from real images, and show how that model can be automatically matched to single static intensity images with non-lambertian effects (e.g. glasses). Our model differs from the multi-view appearance model of [7] in that we build a 4D representation of appearance with light fields. With our method, model coefficients between views are explicitly linked and we do not model any pose variation within the shape model at a single view. We are therefore able to model self-occlusion and complex lighting effects better than a multi-view AAM. We support this claim in our experimental results section.

3   Light Field Shape and Texture

In this section we provide a formal description of the shape and texture of a set of light field prototypes that define the appearance manifold of an object class. Let $L(u, v, s, t)$ be a light field consisting of a set of sample views of the scene, parameterized by view indices (u, v) and scene radiance indices (s, t), and let $L_1, ..., L_n$ be a set of prototype light fields with shape $X_1, ..., X_n$. In general, for any image-based rendering technique, X_i is a set of 3D feature points which outline the shape of the imaged object. With a light field, no 3D shape information is needed to render a novel view of the object. It is therefore sufficient to represent the shape of each light field as the set of 2D feature points, which are the projections of the 3D features into each view. More formally, we define the shape, X, of a light field L as

$$X = \{x_{(u,v)} | (u, v) \in L\} \tag{1}$$

where $x_{(u,v)}$ is the shape in a view (u, v) of L. If the camera array is strongly calibrated its sufficient to find correspondences in two views and re-project to the remaining views. With only weak calibration and the assumption of a densely sampled array, feature points may be specified in select views of the light field and tracked into all other views.

Once shape is defined for each prototype light field, Procrustes analysis [10] is performed to place the shape of each object into a common coordinate frame. Effectively, Procrustes analysis applies a rigid body transformation to the shape of each light field such that each object is aligned to the same 3D pose. From the set of normalized shapes X_i of each prototype, the reference shape X_{ref} is computed as

$$X_{ref} = \mathbf{M}_\alpha \bar{X} \tag{2}$$

where $\bar{X}$ is the mean shape of the aligned shapes and $\mathbf{M}_\alpha$ is a matrix which scales and translates the mean shape such that it is expressed in pixel coordinates (i.e. with respect to the height and width of each discrete view of a light field). The matrix $\mathbf{M}_\alpha$ constrains the shape in each view of the reference light field to be within the height and width of the view.

As in [2], the texture of a prototype light field is its "shape free" equivalent. It is found by warping each light field to the reference shape X_{ref}. As will be shown in the next section, this allows for the definition of a texture vector space that is decoupled from shape variation. Specifically, the texture of a light field L is defined as

$$G(u, v, s, t) = L(D(u, v, s, t)) = L \circ D(u, v, s, t) \tag{3}$$

where D is the mapping,

$$D : \mathcal{R}^4 \longrightarrow \mathcal{R}^4 \tag{4}$$

that specifies for each ray in L a corresponding ray in the reference light field L_{ref} and is computed using the shape of L and X_{ref}. Equation (3) may be thought of as a light field warping operation, a concept introduced by Zhang et. al. [24]. As in [6], the texture of each prototype, G_i, is normalized to be under the same global illumination.

4 Light Field Appearance Manifolds

As illustrated in the previous section, once a reference is defined, each prototype light field may be described in terms of its shape and texture. The linear combination of texture and shape form an appearance manifold: given a set of light fields of the same object class, the linear combination of their texture warped by a linear combination of their shape describes a new object whose shape and texture are spanned by that of the prototype light fields. Compact and efficient linear models of shape and texture variation may be obtained using PCA, as shown in [6]. Given the set of prototype light fields $L_1, ..., L_n$, each having shape X_i and texture G_i, PCA is applied independently to the normalized shape and texture vectors, X_i and G_i to give

$$\begin{aligned} X &= \bar{X} + \mathbf{P}_s \mathbf{b}_s \\ G &= \bar{G} + \mathbf{P}_g \mathbf{b}_g \end{aligned} \tag{5}$$

Using Equation (5), the shape and texture of each model light field is described by its corresponding shape and texture parameters $\mathbf{b}_s$ and $\mathbf{b}_g$. As there may exist a correlation between texture and shape, a more compact model of shape and texture variation is obtained by performing a PCA on the concatenated shape and texture parameter vectors of each prototype light field. This results in a combined texture-shape PCA space:

$$X = \bar{X} + \mathbf{Q}_s \mathbf{c}$$
$$G = \bar{G} + \mathbf{Q}_g \mathbf{c}$$
(6)

where as in [6],

$$\mathbf{Q}_s = \mathbf{P}_s \mathbf{W}_s^{-1} \mathbf{P}_{cs}$$
$$\mathbf{Q}_g = \mathbf{P}_g \mathbf{P}_{cg}$$
(7)

and $\mathbf{W}_s$ is a matrix which comensurates the variation in shape and texture when performing the combined texture-shape PCA. In our experiments we use $\mathbf{W}_s = r\mathbf{I}$ where $r = \sqrt{\sigma_s^2 / \sigma_g^2}$. Here σ_s^2 and σ_g^2 represent the total variance of the normalized shape and texture. Equation (6) maps each model light field to a vector $\mathbf{c}$ in the combined texture-shape PCA space. To generalize the model to allow for arbitrary 3D pose and global illumination, Equation (6) may be re-defined as follows,

$$X_m = S_t(\bar{X} + \mathbf{Q}_s \mathbf{c})$$
$$G_m = T_u(\bar{G} + \mathbf{Q}_g \mathbf{c})$$
(8)

where S_t is a function that applies a rigid body transformation to the model shape according to a pose parameter vector $\mathbf{t}$, T_u is a function which scales and shifts the model texture using an illumination parameter vector $\mathbf{u}$, and the parameter vectors $\mathbf{t}$ and $\mathbf{u}$ are as defined in [6]. Note, the reference light field has parameters $\mathbf{c} = 0$, $\mathbf{t} = \alpha$ and $\mathbf{u} = 0$, where α is a pose vector that is equivalent to the matrix $\mathbf{M}_\alpha$ in Equation (2).

The light field appearance manifold is defined as,

$$L_{model} = G_m \circ D_m$$
(9)

where L_{model} is a model light field that maps to a point on the appearance manifold and D_m is a 4D deformation field which maps each ray in the reference light field to a ray in the model light field and is computed using the shape of the model light field, X_m, and the shape of the reference light field, X_{ref}. Note, Equation (9) suggests that an optical flow technique may also be used to represent shape as in [13] to build a light field active appearance model. We have implemented both approaches, and below report results using the feature-based shape representation of Section 3.

5   Model Matching

In this section, we show how to generalize the matching technique of [6] to light fields. We first illustrate how to match a light field and then discuss the more interesting task of fitting a model light field to a single 2D image.

Matching to a Light Field. A novel light field, L_s, is matched to a point $\tilde{c}$ on the texture-shape appearance manifold by minimizing the following non-linear objective function:

$$E(\mathbf{p}) = |G_m - G_s|^2 \qquad (10)$$

where $\mathbf{p}^T = (\mathbf{c}^T|\mathbf{t}^T|\mathbf{u}^T)$ are the parameters of the model, G_m is the model texture and G_s is the normalized texture of L_s assuming it has shape X_m. G_s is computed by warping L_s from X_m to the reference shape X_{ref}. The model shape and texture are computed at $\mathbf{p}$ using Equation (8).

The direct search gradient descent algorithm of [6] is easily extendible to a light field active appearance model. In [6] a linear relationship for the change in image intensity with respect to the change in model parameters was derived via a first order Taylor expansion of the residual function $\mathbf{r}(\mathbf{p}) = G_m - G_s = \delta\mathbf{g}$. In particular, given a point $\mathbf{p}$ on the manifold, the parameter gradient that minimizes the objective function (10) was computed as, $\delta\mathbf{p} = -\mathbf{R}\delta\mathbf{g}$, where the matrix $\mathbf{R}$ is the pseudo-inverse of the Jacobian, $\mathbf{J} = \frac{\partial\mathbf{r}}{\partial\mathbf{p}}$, derived from the Taylor expansion of the residual function.

In a 2D active appearance model the columns of the Jacobian are intensity gradient images which model how image intensity changes with respect to each model parameter and vice versa. Analogously, the Jacobian of a light field active appearance model represents the change in light field intensity with respect to the change in model parameters, each of columns representing light field intensity gradients that describe the intensity change across all the views of a light field. Consequently, the algorithm for minimizing Equation (10) follows directly from [6]. As in a 2D AAM, the Jacobian is learned via numerical differentiation.

Matching to an Image. A more interesting extension of the AAM framework arises when performing direct search to match a light field AAM to a single 2D image; with a light field the Jacobian matrix is rendered based on pose. A novel image I_s is matched to a point on the light field appearance manifold by minimizing the objective,

$$E(\mathbf{p}, \epsilon) = |F(G_m, \epsilon) - g_s|^2 \qquad (11)$$

where ϵ is the camera pose of I_s, F is a function that renders the pose ϵ of the model texture [14,5] and g_s is the texture of I_s assuming it has shape x_m. g_s is computed by warping I_s from x_m to the reference shape x_{ref}. Both 2D shapes are obtained by rendering X_m and X_{ref} into view ϵ using,

$$x = F_x(X, \epsilon) \qquad (12)$$

where F_x is a variant of the light field rendering function F: it renders shape in view ϵ via a linear interpolation of of the 2D shape features defined in each view of X.

Overall, the objective function in Equation (11) compares the novel 2D image to the corresponding view in L_{model}. Minimizing this objective function fits a model light field, L_{model}, that best approximates I in view ϵ. An efficient way to optimize Equation (11) is by defining a two step iteration process, in which the pose ϵ is optimized independently of the model parameters $\mathbf{p}$. The pose ϵ may be computed via an exhaustive search of the average light field, L_{ref}, in which cross-correlation is used to initialize ϵ to a nearby discrete view of the model light field. The pose parameter $\mathbf{t}$ is used to further refine this pose estimate during matching.

Once ϵ is approximated, direct search may be employed to match I to a point on the texture-shape appearance manifold. As previously discussed, each column of the Jacobian, $\mathbf{J}$ of a light field active appearance model is a light field intensity gradient. To approximate the intensity gradient in view ϵ of the target image I, light field rendering is applied to each column of $\mathbf{J}$. This yields a "rendered" Jacobian matrix, $\mathbf{J}_\epsilon$, specified as,

$$\mathbf{J}_\epsilon^i = F(\mathbf{J}^i, \epsilon), \, i = 1, ..., m \tag{13}$$

where $\mathbf{J}^i$ represents column i of the matrix $\mathbf{J}$ and m is the number of columns in $\mathbf{J}$. Note similar to the model and image textures of Equation (10) the columns of $\mathbf{J}_\epsilon$ have shape x_{ref} defined above.

Using $\mathbf{J}_\epsilon$, optimizing Equation (11) is analogous to matching I to a 2D AAM. Thus, as in Equation (10), the direct search gradient descent algorithm of [6] is used to minimize Equation (11), with one exception. In [6] the normalized mean of the texture vectors is used to project g_s into the same global illumination of the model texture. With a light field AAM the normalized mean texture is a light field, and thus cannot be directly applied to normalize g_s in Equation (11). Instead, we normalize both $g_m = F(G_m, \epsilon)$ and g_s to have zero mean and unit variance. We found this normalization scheme to work well in our experiments.

6   Experiments

We built a light field morphable model of the human head by capturing light fields of 50 subjects using a real-time light field camera array [23]. We collected 48 views (6 x 8) of each individual and manually segmented the head from each light field. Our head database consists of 37 males and 13 females of various races. Of these people, 7 are bearded and 17 are wearing glasses. The images in each view of the prototype light fields have resolution 320 x 240. Within each image, the head spans a region of approximately 80 x 120 pixels. The field of view captured by the camera array is approximately 25 degrees horizontally and 20 degrees vertically. To perform feature tracking, as described in Section 3, we used a multi-resolution Lukas-Kanade optical flow algorithm [15], with 4 pyramid levels and Laplacian smoothing [1]. For comparison, we built a view-based AAM using the views of the light field camera array [7]. In both the definition of the view-based and light field active appearance models the parameter perturbations displayed in Table 1 were used to numerically compute the Jacobian matrix. To avoid over-fitting to noise, texture-shape PCA vectors having low variance were

---

[1] We acknowledge Tony Ezzat for the Lukas-Kanade optical flow implementation.

Table 1. Perturbation scheme used in both the view-based and light field AAMs. [20]

Variables	Perturbations
x, y	$\pm 5\%$ and $\pm 10\%$ of the height and width of the reference shape
θ	$\pm 5, \pm 15$ degrees
scale	$\pm 5\%, \pm 15\%$
$c_{1 \cdot k}$	$\pm 0.25, \pm 0.5$ standard deviations

discarded from each model, the remaining PCA vectors modelling 90% of the total model variance.

We implemented the view-based and light field active appearance models in MATLAB. To perform light field rendering we use the unstructured lumigraph algorithm described in [5]. In our experiments, our matching algorithm typically converged between 4 and 15 iterations when matching to an image and between 4 and 10 iterations when matching to a light field. Each iteration took a few seconds in un-optimized MATLAB. We believe that using a real-time light field renderer [5] would result in matching times similar to those reported for a 2D AAM [20].

7   Results

In this section we provide a comparison between a light field and a 2D view-based active appearance model. We then present various model matching experiments using our head light field appearance manifold.

Comparison to a View-Based AAM. To compare our method to a view-based AAM we built a single-view 2D AAM and compared it against a light field AAM. Each model was constructed using all fifty subjects, and was matched to a side view of two people. The resulting fits are displayed in Figure 3. In this figure one person is wearing glasses which self-occlude the subject in extreme views of the camera array. These self-occlusions are difficult to model using a view-based AAM, where inter-pose variation is modelled as shape. Also note that the view-dependent texturing effects in the persons glasses are preserved by the light field AAM, but are lost by the view-based AAM even though the person remains in the model.

Model Matching. To demonstrate the ability to fit a light field AAM to a single 2D image or light field, we match a novel person to the constructed head manifold using "leave-one-out" experimentation. Figure 4 illustrates fitting light fields of two people taken out of the model. To conserve space, only select views of each light field are displayed. Both fits are shown superimposed onto the corresponding input light field. Each light field is also provided for ground truth comparison. As seen from the figure, the input light fields are well matched and a convincing reconstruction of each person is generated. Specifically, the shape and texture of both individuals is well captured across views.

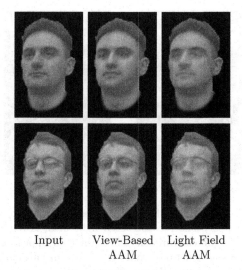

Input   View-Based   Light Field
            AAM   AAM

Fig. 3. Comparison of a light field active appearance model to a view-based AAM. The left column shows the input, the middle column the best fit with a 2D AAM, and the right column the light field fit. The 2D and light field appearance models both exhibit qualitatively good fits when the surface is approximately smooth and lambertian. When glasses are present, however, the 2D method fails and the light field appearance model succeeds.

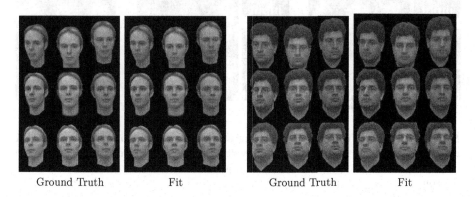

Ground Truth   Fit   Ground Truth   Fit

Fig. 4. Matching a light field AAM to a light field of a novel subject.

Figure 5 illustrates our model's ability to generate convincing light field reconstructions from 2D images. This figure provides two example matches to 2D images with known pose. For each match, the person was removed from the model and imaged at a randomly selected pose not present in the light field AAM. The fit, rendered at the selected pose of each person, is displayed below each input image. The fitted light fields are also displayed. Note our method built a light field with 48 views from a single 2D image.

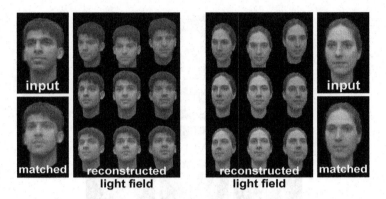

Fig. 5. Matching a light field AAM to 2D images of novel subjects. Each person is matched at a known pose. The reconstructed light field, is rendered over the input view and is displayed aside each match. The light field appearance model generates convincing light field reconstructions from 2D images. In particular, the overall shape and texture of each subject are well approximated across each view.

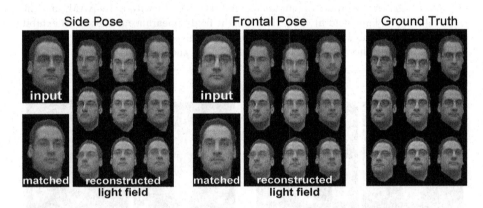

Fig. 6. Matching a light field AAM using automatic pose estimation (side pose). A match to a frontal, known pose is also provided for comparison. Note the reconstructed light fields are the same for both poses. Ground truth is shown on the right for comparison.

Figure 6 displays a fit to the head model using an unknown view of a person, in which pose was automatically estimated as described in Section 5. The model was also matched to a frontal view to verify that the reconstructed light fields are independent of input pose. As before this person is removed from the model and the views are not present in the light field AAM. The extreme views of the model light field fits are overlaid onto a captured light field of the subject. This light field is also shown as ground truth. Comparing each fit one finds that although the characteristics of the matched views are favored, the reconstructed light fields are strikingly similar. Also, note the view-dependent texturing effects present in the subjects glasses, captured by the model. Comparing the matches of the above figure, one finds that our algorithm performs well in matching novel light fields and 2D images to the head manifold. Namely, the skin color, facial hair, and overall shape and expression of each novel subject are well approximated.

8   Conclusion and Future Work

We introduced a novel active appearance modeling method based on an image-based rendering technique. Light field active appearance models overcome many of the limitations presented by current 2D and 3D appearance models. They easily model complex scenes, non-lambertian surfaces, and view variation. We demonstrated the construction of a light field manifold of the human head using 50 subjects and showed how to match the model to a light field or single 2D image of a person outside of the model. In future work we hope to construct a camera array with a wider field of view that utilizes a non-planar camera configuration. We expect our approach to scale directly to the construction of dynamic light-field appearance manifolds, since our capture apparatus works in real-time.

References

1. E. H. Adelson and J. Bergen, *Computation Models of Visual Processing.*   Cambridge: MIT Press, 1991, ch. The Plenoptic Function and the Elements of Early Vision.
2. D. Beymer and T. Poggio, "Face recognition from one example view, Tech. Rep. AIM-1536, September 1995.
3. V. Blanz and T. Vetter, "A morphable model for the synthesis of 3D faces," in *SIGGRAPH*, Los Angeles, 1999, pp. 187–194.
4. M. Brand, "Morphable 3D models from video," in *CVPR*, May 2001.
5. C. Buehler, M. Bosse, L. McMillan, S. J. Gortler, and M. F. Cohen, "Unstructured lumigraph rendering," in *SIGGRAPH*, 2001, pp. 425–432.
6. T. F. Cootes, G. J. Edwards, and C. J. Taylor, "Active appearance models," *Lecture Notes in Computer Science*, vol. 1407, pp. 484–98, 1998.
7. T. F. Cootes, G. V. Wheeler, K. N. Walker, and C. J. Taylor, "View-based active appearance models," *Image and Vision Computing*, vol. 20, pp. 657–664, 2002.
8. G. Edwards, C. Taylor, and T. Cootes, "Interpreting face images using active appearance models," in *3rd International Conference on Automatic Face and Gesture Recognition*, 1998, pp. 300–305.
9. P. Fua and C. Miccio, "From regular images to animated heads: a least squares approach," in *ECCV*, Springer,Berlin, 1999, pp. 188–202.
10. C. Goodall., "Procrustes methods in the statistical analysis of shape." *Journal of the Royal Statistical Society*, vol. 53, no. 2, pp. 285–339, 1991.
11. S. J. Gortler, R. Grzeszczuk, R. Szeliski, and M. F. Cohen, "The lumigraph," *Computer Graphics*, vol. 30, no. Annual Conference Series, pp. 43–54, 1996.
12. R. Gross, I. Matthews, and S. Baker, "Appearance-based face recognition and light fields," *IEEE PAMI*, vol. 26, no. 4, April 2004.

13. M. J. Jones and T. Poggio, "Multidimensional morphable models," in *ICCV*, 1998, pp. 683–688.
14. M. Levoy and P. Hanrahan, "Light field rendering," *Computer Graphics*, vol. 30, pp. 31–42, 1996.
15. B. D. Lucas and T. Kanade, "An iterative image registration technique with an application to stereo vision," in *International Joint Conference on Artificial Intelligence*, 1981, pp. 674–679.
16. B. Moghaddam and A. Pentland, "Probabilistic visual learning for object recognition," *IEEE PAMI*, vol. 19, no. 7, pp. 696–710, 1997.
17. H. Murase and S. Nayar, "Visual learning and recognition of 3-d objects from appearance," *IJCV*, vol. 14, no. 1, pp. 5–24, 1995.
18. F. H. Pighin, R. Szeliski, and D. Salesin, "Resynthesizing facial animation through 3d model-based tracking," in *ICCV*, 1999, pp. 143–150.
19. S. Romdhani, S. Gong, and A. Psarrou, "A multi-view nonlinear active shape model using kernel pca," in *British Machine Vision Conference*, 1999, pp. 483–492.
20. M. B. Stegmann, "Analysis and segmentation of face images using point annotations and linear subspace techniques," Technical University of Denmark, DTU, Tech. Rep., August 2002.
21. M. Turk and A. Pentland, "Eigen faces for recognition," *Journal of Cognitive Neuroscience*, vol. 3, no. 1, 1991.
22. B. Wilburn, M. Smulski, H.-H. K. Lee, and M. Horowitz, "The light field video camera," in *Proceedings of Media Processors 2002, SPIE Electronic Imaging*, 2002.
23. J. C. Yang, M. Everett, C. Buehler, and L. McMillan, "A real-time distributed light field camera," in *Eurographics Workshop on Rendering*, 2002, pp. 1–10.
24. Z. Zhang, L. Wang, B. Guo, and H.-Y. Shum, "Feature-based light field morphing," in *Conference on Computer graphics and interactive techniques*. ACM Press, 2002, pp. 457–464.

Galilean Differential Geometry of Moving Images

Daniel Fagerström

Computational Vision and Active Perception Laboratory (CVAP)
Department of Numerical Analysis and Computing Science
KTH (Royal Institute of Technology) SE-100 44 Stockholm, Sweden
danielf@nada.kth.se

Abstract. In this paper we develop a systematic theory about local structure of moving images in terms of Galilean differential invariants. We argue that Galilean invariants are useful for studying moving images as they disregard constant motion that typically depends on the motion of the observer or the observed object, and only describe relative motion that might capture surface shape and motion boundaries. The set of Galilean invariants for moving images also contains the Euclidean invariants for (still) images.
Complete sets of Galilean invariants are derived for two main cases: when the spatio-temporal gradient cuts the image plane and when it is tangent to the image plane. The former case correspond to isophote curve motion and the later to creation and disappearance of image structure, a case that is not well captured by the theory of optical flow.
The derived invariants are shown to be describable in terms of acceleration, divergence, rotation and deformation of image structure.
The described theory is completely based on bottom up computation from local spatio-temporal image information.

1 Introduction

The aim of this paper is to describe the local (differential) structure of moving images. By doing this we want to find a set of local differential descriptors that can describe local spatio-temporal pattern much as e.g. gradient strength, Laplacian zero-crossings, blob and ridge detectors, isophote curvature etc describe the local structure in images.

The dominating approach to computational visual motion processing (reviewed in [2,15]) is to first compute the *optical flow* field, i.e. the velocity vectors of the particles in the visual observer's field of view, projected on its visual sensor area. From this various properties of the surrounding scene can be computed. Ego-motion can, under certain circumstances, be computed from the global shape of the field, object boundaries from discontinuities in the field, and surface shape and motion for rigid objects, can be computed from the local differential structure of the field [12,13].

Unfortunately the computation of the optical flow field leads to a number of well known difficulties. The input is the projected (gray-level) image of the surroundings as a function of time, i.e. a three-dimensional structure. It is in general

T. Pajdla and J. Matas (Eds.): ECCV 2004, LNCS 3024, pp. 494–506, 2004.
© Springer-Verlag Berlin Heidelberg 2004

not possible to uniquely identify what path through the spatio-temporal image is a projection of a certain object point. Thus, further assumptions are needed, the most common one is the *brightness constancy assumption*, that the projection of each object point has a constant gray level. The brightness constancy assumption breaks down if the light changes, if the object have non-Lambertian reflection, or, if it has specular reflections. However, the problem is still underdetermined, generically. Except at local extrema in the gray-level image, points with a certain gray-level lie along curves, and these curves sweep out surfaces in the spatio-temporal image. A point along such a curve can therefore correspond to any point on the surface at later instants of time. This is refered to as the *aperture problem* and is usually treated by invoking additional constraints e.g. regularization assumptions, such as smoothly varying brightness patterns, or parameterized surface models and trajectory models, leading to least-square methods applied in small image regions. Beside the questionable validity of these assumptions they lead to inferior results near motion boundaries, i.e. the regions that carry most information about object boundaries. The behavior when new image structure appears or old structure disappears is also undefined.

An alternative approach for visual motion analysis is to directly analyze the geometrical structure of the spatio-temporal input image, thereby avoiding the detour through the optic flow estimation step [18,19,11]. By using the differential geometry of the spatio-temporal image, we get a low level syntactical description of the moving image whithout having to rely on the more high level semantic concept of object particle motion.

A systematic study of the local image structure, in the context of scale-space theory, has been pursued by Florack [6]. The basic idea is to find all descriptors of differential image structure that are invariant to rotation and translation (the Euclidean group). The choice of Euclidean invariance reflects that the image structures should be possible to recognize in spite of (small) camera translations and rotations around the optical axis. This theory embeds many of the operators previously used in computer vision, such as Canny's edge detector, Laplacian zero-crossings, blobs, isophote curvature and as well enabling the discovery of new ones.

2   Spatio-Temporal Image Geometry

Extending from a theory about spatial images to one about spatio-temporal images it is natural to use the concept of *absolute time* (see e.g. [8] for a more elaborate discussion). Each point in space-time can be designated numeric label describing what time it occurred. The sets of space-time points that occurred at the same time are called *planes of simultaneity* and the temporal distance between two planes of simultaneity can be measured (in the small spatio-temporal regions that seeing creatures, operates in, we see no need for handling relativistic effects, there are however other opinions, see [10]). The space-time can be stratified in a sequence of planes of simultaneity, and be given coordinate systems that separates time and space, $(t, x) \in \mathbb{R} \times \mathbb{R}^2$. From the consequences of absolute time, we conclude that we only want to allow for space-time transformations that never mixes the planes of simultaneity.

As a spatio-temporal image restricted to a plane of simultaneity can be considered as a still image the reasons for using Euclidean invariance in the image plane applies to moving images as well. Image properties should not be dependent on when we choose to measure them (invariance under time translations). The local average velocity contains only information about the ego motion and no information about the three dimensional structure of the environment, and is therefore natural to disregard. We thus search for properties that are invariant to the 2+1 dimensional Galilean group. The use of Galilean image geometry has been proposed in e.g. [4,1,9]. Using parallel projection as image formation model, the Galilean invariants are those properties of the surrounding that cannot be explained in terms of a relative constant translational motion. A Galilean model of the moving image is also implicitly assumed when divergence, curl and deformation are described as flow field invariants [12].

Definition 1 (Galilean group). *The group of Galilean motions* Γ_{n+1}:

$$\begin{pmatrix} t' \\ x' \end{pmatrix} = \begin{pmatrix} 1 & v \\ 0 & R \end{pmatrix} \begin{pmatrix} t \\ x \end{pmatrix} + a = \begin{pmatrix} 1 & 0 \\ 0 & R \end{pmatrix} \begin{pmatrix} 1 & v \\ 0 & I \end{pmatrix} \begin{pmatrix} t \\ x \end{pmatrix} + a \qquad (1)$$

$x, v \in \mathbb{R}^n, t \in \mathbb{R}, R \in SO(n)$ *and* $a \in \Gamma_{n+1}$.

Each Galilean motion can be decomposed in a spatial rotation, a spatio-temporal shear (constant velocity) and a space-time translation. It can be shown that planes of simultaneity (constant time) are invariant and has Euclidean geometry, i.e. distances and angles are invariants. The temporal distance between planes of simultaneity is invariant.

3   Moving Frames

The Galilean geometry has no metric in traditional sense. That means that metric based differential geometry cannot be used in its normal formulations. We therefore chose to use a Lie group based approach instead (see [14] for a different approach on a geometry with degenerate metric).

According to Klein's famous Erlangen program, given a space S and a group of transformations G over S, the geometric structure of (S, G) is all structure that is invariant to transformations in G. In the following we will study the differential geometric properties of scalar functions and sub-manifolds (curves and surfaces) in $\mathbb{R}^2$ and $\mathbb{R}^3$ subject to Galilean and in some cases Euclidean transformations.

A convenient way to find geometrical structure is to use Cartan theory about moving frames [3,16]. A *frame field* is a smooth map from the base space to group elements, $S \rightarrow G$. For a Galilean geometry Γ_{n+1} the frame field is a mapping $\mathbb{R}^n \rightarrow \Gamma_{n+1}$. A frame field can be conceptiualized by its action on an arbitrary coordinate system for the tangent space of the base space. For Γ_{n+1} we can e.g. attach a Galilean ON-system at each point.

Definition 2. *A Γ_{n+1} coordinate system is an affine coordinate system where n vectors lies in the spatial part. A Γ_{n+1} ON-system is a Γ_{n+1} coordinate system s.t. the spatial part consists of n dimensional ON-coordinate system and the remaining base vector has unit temporal length.*

The property of beeing a Γ_{n+1} ON-system is a Galilean invariant. In the sequel we will use the coordinate system view of frame fields as we find it easier to visualise.

The main idea of Cartans theory about moving frames is to put a frame at each point that is connected to the local structure of the sub-manifold or the function in an invariant way. In this way we get a frame field.

For a function f defined on S, all expressions over mixed derivatives w.r.t. the Cartan frame at a certain point are by construction geometrical invariants. This class of invariants are called *differential invariants*.

On sub-manifolds, we can find the local geometrical structure from how the frame field varies in the local neighborhood.

Let i be any (global) frame and e a frame connected to the local structure s.t. $e = Ai$, where the *attitude transformation* $A \in G$ is a function of position. The local variation of e can be described in an invariant way in terms of e,

$$de = dAi = dAA^{-1}e = C(A)e, \tag{2}$$

where the *one-form* (see [3]) $C(A)$ is called the *connection matrix*. In a certain sense, the connection matrix contains all geometric information there is.

Scalar invariants can be generated by contracting the coefficients in the connection matrix on the vectors in the Cartan frame, $c_{ij}e_k$. A useful property of the connection matrix is,

$$C(AB) = C(A) + AC(B)A^{-1}, \tag{3}$$

which is a direct consequence of the definition.

The level-sets $f^{-1}(c)$ of smooth scalar functions f are sub-manifolds, the geometric structure of those, the *level-set invariants*, are invariant w.r.t. the group of constant monotonic transformations $g \circ f$, $g : \mathbb{R} \to \mathbb{R}$, $g' > 0$.

4   Image Geometry

Now we will study Galilean differential geometry of moving images using Cartan frames. Image spaces can be considered being trivial fiber bundle $S \otimes I$, where S is the base space and the fiber I is log intensity [14]. Most of the time we will discuss the image geometry in terms of an arbitrary section of the fiber bundle i.e. functions $f : S \to I$. We will start by reviewing differential geometry for images over E_2 to illustrate the metod of moving frames and as E_2 is a sub geometry of Γ_3 so that we will need these results later anyway. We continue by studying differential geometry of Γ_2 and, which is our main goal, differential geometry of images over Γ_3

For scalar functions over E_2 there are two typical situations: the gradient is non-zero almost everywhere and it is zero along curves.

4.1   Gradient Gauge

We study the geometry of functions f in E_2. For points p where $\nabla f \neq 0$ we attach an ON-frame $\{\partial_u, \partial_v\}$ s.t. $f_u = 0$. (u, v) is a gauge coordinate system.

$$\begin{pmatrix} \partial_u \\ \partial_v \end{pmatrix} = \frac{1}{\|\nabla f\|} \begin{pmatrix} f_y & -f_x \\ f_x & f_y \end{pmatrix} \begin{pmatrix} \partial_x \\ \partial_y \end{pmatrix} = A \begin{pmatrix} \partial_x \\ \partial_y \end{pmatrix} \tag{4}$$

where $\{\partial_x, \partial_y\}$ is a global ON-frame.

All functions over $\partial_u^i \partial_v^j f$, $i + j \geq 1$ becomes invariants w.r.t. rotations in space and translation in the intensity fibers. From (2) we get the anti-symmetric connection matrix:

$$C(A) = \begin{pmatrix} 0 & c_{12} \\ -c_{12} & 0 \end{pmatrix}, \tag{5}$$

where,

$$c_{12} = \frac{(f_x f_{xy} - f_y f_{xx})dx + (f_x f_{yy} - f_y f_{xy})dy}{f_x^2 + f_y^2} = -\frac{f_{uu}}{f_v}du + -\frac{f_{uv}}{f_v}dv. \tag{6}$$

where the expression is simplified by the use of the $\{\partial_u, \partial_v\}$ coordinate system, and the relation $f_u = 0$. By contracting c_{12} on the components in the Cartan frame we arrive at:

Theorem 1. *A complete set of level-curve invariants for scalar functions on E_2 is the level curve curvature, and the flow line curvature,*

$$\kappa = c_{12}\partial_u = -f_{uu}/f_v, \qquad \mu = c_{12}\partial_v = -f_{uv}/f_v. \tag{7}$$

These are invariants w.r.t. rotation in the plane and monotonic transformations in the intensity fibers.

4.2   Hessian Gauge

The ON-frame (4) is not defined on critical points, $\nabla f = 0$, on typical critical points we can instead use an ON-frame $\{\partial_p, \partial_q\}$ that diagonalize the Hessian, i.e. $f_{pq} = 0$ and $|f_{pp}| > |f_{qq}|$.

$$\begin{pmatrix} \partial_p \\ \partial_q \end{pmatrix} = \begin{pmatrix} \cos\phi & -\sin\phi \\ \sin\phi & \cos\phi \end{pmatrix} \begin{pmatrix} \partial_x \\ \partial_y \end{pmatrix} = A \begin{pmatrix} \partial_x \\ \partial_y \end{pmatrix}, \tag{8}$$

where $\tan 2\phi = f_{xy}/(f_{yy} - f_{xx})$. All functions over $\partial_p^i \partial_q^j$, $i + j \geq 2$, becomes invariants w.r.t. the unimodular isotropic group, i.e. rotation in the image plane and adition of a linear light gradient [14]. The Hessian frame $\{\partial_p, \partial_q\}$ is invariant w.r.t. the isotropic group, i.e. all the motion in the isotropic group as well as scaling in the plane and in the intensity fiber [14].

5   Functions in Γ_2

First let us study the general geometrical situation for Γ_2. The attitude transformation must be of the form:

$$\begin{pmatrix} \partial_s \\ \partial_u \end{pmatrix} = \begin{pmatrix} 1 & v \\ 0 & 1 \end{pmatrix} \begin{pmatrix} \partial_t \\ \partial_x \end{pmatrix} = A \begin{pmatrix} \partial_t \\ \partial_x \end{pmatrix}, \tag{9}$$

where v, is a function of the spatio-temporal position and $\{\partial_s, \partial_x\}$ is the adapted frame. We immediately see that $\partial_u = \partial_x$. The connection matrix becomes:

$$C(A) = \begin{pmatrix} 0 & c_{01} \\ 0 & 0 \end{pmatrix} \tag{10}$$

where $c_{01} = v_t dt + v_x dx$. This could be expressed in the adapted coordinate system instead, giving $c_{01} = v_s ds + v_u du$. If the coefficient in the connection matrix is contracted on the vectors in the adapted frame, we get two scalar invariants, $a = c_{01}\partial_s = v_s$, that describe how the spatio-temporal part of the frame changes in the direction of it self, i.e. it describes the acceleration of the structure that the frame is adapted to. The other scalar invariant, $\delta = c_{01}\partial_u = v_u$, describes how the spatio-temporal part of the adapted frame changes in the spatial direction, i.e. the divergence of the vector field ∂_s, restricted to the spatial line.

For scalar functions on Γ_2, there are three typical situations, the level curves are transverse to the spatial lines almost everywhere, along isolated curves the level curves are tangent to the spatial lines and there are also isolated critical points.

If one uses the constant brightness assumption as binding hypothesis between image patterns and surface motion then the level curves, (or isophotes) corresponds to motion in the traversal case and creation or annihilation of structure in the non-transversal case.

5.1   Spatially Transversal Level Curves

On points where the level curve is transverse to the spatial line, $f_x \neq 0$, we can define a Γ_2-frame, $\{\partial_s, \partial_x\}$, s.t. $f_s = 0$. Expressed in an arbitrary Γ_2-frame, $\{\partial_t, \partial_x\}$, ∂_s must be on the form:

$$\partial_s = \partial_t + \gamma\partial_x, \tag{11}$$

using $f_s = 0$ and solving for γ, we get $\gamma = -f_t/f_x$. Hence the attitude matrix becomes,

$$A = \begin{pmatrix} 1 & -f_t/f_x \\ 0 & 1 \end{pmatrix} \tag{12}$$

and for the connection matrix (10), we get:

$$c_{01} = \frac{f_t f_{tx} - f_x f_{tt}}{f_x^2} dt + \frac{f_t f_{xx} - f_x f_{tx}}{f_x^2} dx = -\frac{f_{ss}}{f_x} ds - \frac{f_{sx}}{f_x} dx. \tag{13}$$

Contracting c_{01} on the vectors of the adapted frame we get our scalar invariants, the invariants are summarized in the following theorem.

Theorem 2. *A complete set of level-curve invariants for spatially transversal level-curves on Γ_2 is level-curve acceleration the level-curve divergence*

$$a = c_{01}\partial_s = -f_{ss}/f_x, \qquad \delta = c_{01}\partial_x = -f_{sx}/f_x. \tag{14}$$

5.2   Hessian Invariants

On points where $f_x = 0$, there is no tangent gauge. For points where $f_{xx} \neq 0$, we can define a *Hessian gauge*, i.e. an adapted Galilean ON-frame $\{\partial_s, \partial_x\}$ s.t. $f_{sx} = 0$. Repeating the steps from the last section, applying (11) on f_x, using $f_{sx} = 0$ and solving for γ, we get the attitude transformation:

$$\begin{pmatrix} \partial_s \\ \partial_x \end{pmatrix} = \begin{pmatrix} 1 & -f_{tx}/f_{xx} \\ 0 & 1 \end{pmatrix} \begin{pmatrix} \partial_t \\ \partial_x \end{pmatrix} = A \begin{pmatrix} \partial_t \\ \partial_x \end{pmatrix}. \tag{15}$$

and in the connection matrix (10), we get:

$$c_{01} = -\frac{f_{ssx}}{f_{xx}} ds - \frac{f_{sxx}}{f_{xx}} = a\,ds + \delta\,dx. \tag{16}$$

Which we summarize in the following theorem.

Theorem 3. *A complete set of Hessian invariants for points where $f_{xx} \neq 0$ on Γ_2 is Hessian acceleration and Hessian divergence*

$$a = c_{01}\partial_s = -f_{ssx}/f_{xx}, \qquad \delta = c_{01}\partial_x = -f_{sxx}/f_{xx}. \tag{17}$$

6   Functions in Γ_3

For Galilean $2+1$ dimensional geometry, the attitude matrix in general have the form:

$$\begin{pmatrix} \partial_t \\ \partial_u \\ \partial_v \end{pmatrix} = \begin{pmatrix} 1 & v^x & v^y \\ 0 & \cos\theta & -\sin\theta \\ 0 & \sin\theta & \cos\theta \end{pmatrix} \begin{pmatrix} \partial_t \\ \partial_x \\ \partial_y \end{pmatrix} = Ai, \tag{18}$$

where v^x, v^y and θ are functions of the spatio-temporal position. It can be shown that the connection matrix expressed in the adapted coordinate system has the form:

$$C(A) = \begin{pmatrix} 0 & a^u ds + \delta^u du + \sigma^u dv & a^v ds + \sigma^v du + \delta^v dv \\ 0 & 0 & \rho\,ds + \kappa^u du + \kappa^v dv \\ 0 & -(\rho\,ds + \kappa^u du + \kappa^v dv) & 0 \end{pmatrix} = \begin{pmatrix} 0 & c_{01} & c_{02} \\ 0 & 0 & c_{12} \\ 0 & -c_{12} & 0 \end{pmatrix}. \tag{19}$$

Here c_{01} and c_{02} describes how the spatio-temporal part of the frame moves in different directions, c_{01} describes the motion projected on the $\{\partial_s, \partial_u\}$ plane, and c_{02} the motion projected on the $\{\partial_s, \partial_v\}$ plane. The form c_{12} describes how the spatial frame $\{\partial_u, \partial_v\}$ rotates when moving in different directions.

Contracting the connection forms on the different vectors in the local adapted frame, we get nine different scalar invariants. We continue by giving these invariants an interpretation. If we consider the integral curves from the vector field $\{\partial_s\}$, then a^u describe the acceleration of the integral curve projected on the $\{\partial_s, \partial_u\}$ plane, and a^v the corresponding acceleration on the $\{\partial_s, \partial_v\}$ plane. ρ describes how much the spatial part of the frame rotates in the ∂_s direction. The invariants κ^u and κ^v describe the curvatures of the integral curves for the vector fields $\{\partial_u\}$ and $\{\partial_v\}$ respectively. The remaining invariants describe how the vector field $\{\partial_s\}$ changes for motions in the spatial plane, δ^u and δ^v describe the divergence in the ∂_u and ∂_v directions respectively. σ_u describes the skew of the vector field in the ∂_u direction while moving in the ∂_v direction while σ_v the skew in the ∂_v direction while moving in the ∂_u direction.

6.1 More Descriptive Invariants

Even if the above discussed set of scalar invariants constitute a complete set of scalar invariants for Γ_3, they are not necessarily the ones that have largest descriptive value. As any invertible transformation of the scalar invariants give rise to a new complete set of scalar invariants, we will develop a set of invariants that are closer to what have been used in other work about moving images.

The acceleration invariants $\{a^u, a^v\}$ could instead be described in a polar coordinate system:

$$a = \sqrt{(a^u)^2 + (a^v)^2}, \qquad a_\theta = \arctan(a^v/a^u), \tag{20}$$

here a is the magnitude of the acceleration, an a_θ the angle relative to the ∂_u direction. The invariants, $\delta_u, \delta_v, \sigma_u, \sigma_v$ describes how ∂_s changes along motions in the spatial plane. Observe that the vectors in the vector field $\{\partial_s\}$ always have unit length in the temporal direction, therefore the vector field restricted to a certain spatial plane can be projected onto that plane without losing any essential information. The matrix:

$$D = \begin{pmatrix} \delta_u & \sigma_u \\ \sigma_v & \delta_v \end{pmatrix} \tag{21}$$

is the rate of strain tensor for that projected vector field and it might be more useful to describe the invariants in terms of the Cauchy-Stokes decomposition theorem [12]:

$$D = \frac{\sigma_u - \sigma_v}{2} \begin{pmatrix} 0 & 1 \\ -1 & 0 \end{pmatrix} + \frac{\delta_u + \delta_v}{2} \begin{pmatrix} 1 & 0 \\ 0 & 1 \end{pmatrix} + \frac{1}{2} \begin{pmatrix} \delta_u - \delta_v & \sigma_u + \sigma_v \\ \sigma_u + \sigma_v & \delta_v - \delta_u \end{pmatrix} \tag{22}$$

$$= \frac{\mathrm{curl} D}{2} \begin{pmatrix} 0 & 1 \\ -1 & 0 \end{pmatrix} + \frac{\mathrm{div} D}{2} \begin{pmatrix} 1 & 0 \\ 0 & 1 \end{pmatrix} + \frac{\mathrm{def} D}{2} Q(\phi)^{-1} \begin{pmatrix} 1 & 0 \\ 0 & -1 \end{pmatrix} Q(\phi). \tag{23}$$

First the matrix can be decomposed in an anti symmetric and a symmetric part where the coefficient of the anti symmetric part is called the *curl* that describes the rotational component of the vector field. The symmetric part can in turn be decomposed in a multiple of the identity matrix, the *divergence* part that describe the dilation component of the vector field, and a symmetric matrix with zero trace. The remaining symmetric component of the matrix can be described in terms of the *deformation*, i.e. an area preserving stretching in one direction combined with shrinking in the orthogonal direction, and the direction ϕ of the stretching relative to the direction of ∂_u.

6.2   Choice of Gauge

For Galilean $2 + 1$ dimensional geometry isophotes are typically 2 dimensional surfaces. There are two generic cases: points where the isophote surface cuts the spatial surface through the point, and points where the isophote surface is tangent to the spatial surface through the point. The first case can be interpreted as motion of isophote curves in the image, and the second case as creation, annihilation or saddle points.

6.3   Tangent Gauge

Our next task is to define an adapted frame for points where the isophote surface cuts the spatial surface. For the spatial plane we can reuse the tangent gauge for E_2 in Section 4.1. Starting from an arbitrary frame i, we first adapt the spatial sub frame $\{\partial_x, \partial_y\}$, to the gradient and tangent direction in the spatial plane:

$$\begin{pmatrix} \partial_t \\ \partial_u \\ \partial_v \end{pmatrix} = \frac{1}{\sqrt{f_x^2 + f_y^2}} \begin{pmatrix} 1 & 0 & 0 \\ 0 & f_y & -f_x \\ 0 & f_x & f_y \end{pmatrix} \begin{pmatrix} \partial_t \\ \partial_x \\ \partial_y \end{pmatrix} = Ai. \tag{24}$$

The spatio-temporal vector ∂_s must have unit length in time to be part of a Galilean frame. By requiring ∂_s to lie in the spatio-temporal tangent plane, i.e. $f_s = 0$, it is constrained in one direction. The adapted spatio-temporal direction must have the form:

$$\partial_s = \partial_t + \beta \partial_u + \gamma \partial_v,$$

in terms of the new frame. Using $0 = f_s = f_t + \gamma f_v$ and solving for γ we get that $\gamma = -f_t/f_v$. Still we have one undetermined degree of freedom $\beta \in \mathbb{R}$. For each choice of β we have a plane spanned by $\{\partial_s, \partial_v\}$. The image restricted to such a plane is a function on Γ_2 and can be studied by the methods from Section 5.1. From Theorem 2 there are two scalar invariants: acceleration $a = -f_{ss}/f_v$ and divergence $\delta = -f_{sv}/f_v$. We can see that acceleration becomes a quadratic function of β and thus the gauge can be fixed by finding a β s.t. $a(\beta)$ is an extremum, i.e. by solving $\partial_\beta a(\beta) = 0$ for β, which gives:

$$\beta_a = \frac{f_t f_{uv}}{f_v f_{uu}} - \frac{f_{tu}}{f_{uu}}. \tag{25}$$

Which is defined as long as $f_{uu} \neq 0$, i.e. as long as the isophote curvature in the spatial plane is non-vanishing. It can be shown that requirement of an acceleration extrema is equivalent to requiring $f_{su} = 0$ i.e. finding a β that diagonalizes the Hessian matrix in the $\{\partial_s, \partial_u\}$ plane. We will also see that this choice of gauge makes the direction of the spatial tangent, ∂_u, constant along ∂_s, i.e. $\rho = 0$. From this requirement Guichard [9], derived the same gauge as we use here.

Another choice of spatio-temporal gauge can be found by studying the divergence as a function of β. The divergence is a linear function of β and the disappearance of the divergence, $\delta(\beta) = 0$, is a natural way to fixate the gauge, giving:

$$\beta_\delta = \frac{f_t f_{vv}}{f_v f_{uv}} - \frac{f_{tv}}{f_{uv}}. \tag{26}$$

This is defined as long as $f_{uv} \neq 0$, i.e. when the flow line curvature in the spatial plane is non-vanishing. It can be shown that the disappearance of the divergence is equivalent to requiring that $f_{sv} = 0$, i.e. finding a β such that the Hessian in the $\{\partial_s, \partial_v\}$ plane is diagonalized.

Using (25) and (24) we find the attitude matrix for the acceleration based Γ_3 tangent gauge,

$$\begin{pmatrix} \partial_s \\ \partial_u \\ \partial_v \end{pmatrix} = \begin{pmatrix} 1 & \frac{f_t f_{uv}}{f_v f_{uu}} - \frac{f_{tu}}{f_{uu}} & -\frac{f_t}{f_v} \\ 0 & 1 & 0 \\ 0 & 0 & 1 \end{pmatrix} \begin{pmatrix} \partial_t \\ \partial_u \\ \partial_v \end{pmatrix} = BAi. \tag{27}$$

The connection matrix can then be found by a tedious but elementary calculation using (3). Using notation from our general discussion about Γ_3 invariants the elements in the connection matrix (19) becomes:

$$c_{01} = a^u \, ds + \delta^u \, du + \sigma^u \, dv, \quad c_{02} = a^v \, ds + \delta^v \, dv, \quad c_{12} = \kappa \, du + \mu \, dv. \tag{28}$$

Observe that the skew invariant σ^v that describe the skew in the gradient direction while moving in the tangent direction, disappear. The spatio-temporal rotation of the frame in the spatial plane ρ disappears as well. We use the conventional notation $\kappa = \kappa^u, \mu = \kappa^v$, for isophote and flow line curvature. We list the resulting scalar invariants in the following theorem.

Theorem 4. *A complete set of scalar invariants for scalar functions on Γ_3 at points where the gradient and isophote curvature are non-vanishing are acceleration in the tangent and gradient direction,*

$$a^u = \frac{f_{ss} f_{uv}}{f_v f_{uu}} - \frac{f_{ssu}}{f_{uu}}, \qquad a^v = -\frac{f_{ss}}{f_v}, \tag{29}$$

divergence in the tangent and gradient direction and skew in the gradient direction while moving in the tangent direction,

$$\delta^u = -\frac{f_{suu}}{f_{uu}}, \qquad \delta^v = -\frac{f_{sv}}{f_v}, \qquad \sigma^u = \frac{f_{sv} f_{uv}}{f_v f_{uu}} - \frac{f_{suv}}{f_{uu}}, \tag{30}$$

as well as isophote and flow line curvature, (see Theorem 1).

The invariant a^v, is also found in [9] and is denoted *accel*. The reasoning leading to Theorem 4 can be repeated for the divergence based tangent gauge (26).

Theorem 5. *A complete set of scalar invariants for scalar functions on Γ_3 at points where the gradient and flow line curvature are non-vanishing are acceleration in the tangent and gradient direction,*

$$a^u = \frac{f_{ss}f_{vv}}{f_v f_{uv}} - \frac{f_{ssv}}{f_{uv}}, \qquad a^v = -\frac{f_{ss}}{f_v}, \tag{31}$$

divergence in the tangent and gradient direction, skew in the gradient direction while moving in the tangent direction,

$$\delta^u = \frac{f_{su}f_{vv}}{f_v f_{uv}} - \frac{f_{suv}}{f_{uv}}, \qquad \delta^v = -\frac{f_{su}}{f_v}, \qquad \sigma^u = -\frac{f_{svv}}{f_{uv}}, \tag{32}$$

and isophote and flow line curvature, (see Theorem 1).

6.4   Hessian Gauge

On points where the isophote surface is tangent to the spatial surface, the tangent gauge is not defined. As long as the Hessian is non-degenerate, which generically is the case, we can define an adapted Γ_3-frame, $\{\partial_r, \partial_p, \partial_q\}$ that diagonalize the Hessian, i.e. $f_{pq} = f_{rp} = f_{rq} = 0$. Using the fact that the spatio-temporal vector in the adapted frame must be on the form,

$$\partial_r = \partial_t + \beta\partial_x + \gamma\partial_y. \tag{33}$$

Starting by diagonalizing the Hessian in the spatio-temporal direction we get the constraints $f_{rx} = f_{ry} = 0$, and by using (33) and solving for β and γ, we get

$$\beta = \frac{f_{ty}f_{xy} - f_{tx}f_{yy}}{f_{xx}f_{yy} - f_{xy}^2}, \qquad \gamma = \frac{f_{tx}f_{xy} - f_{ty}f_{xx}}{f_{xx}f_{yy} - f_{xy}^2}. \tag{34}$$

This gives the first part of the attitude transformation, a spatio-temporal shear A. If we project ∂_r on the spatial plane we get the same vector field as when the optical flow constraint equation is used on the gradient of the image [17]. As the next step the frame must be rotated in the spatial plane s.t. the spatial Hessian is diagonalized. Here we can use the results for the Hessian gauge for E_2 reviewed in Section 4.2. Combining these steps we get,

$$\begin{pmatrix} \partial_r \\ \partial_p \\ \partial_q \end{pmatrix} = \begin{pmatrix} 1 & 0 & 0 \\ 0 & \cos\phi & -\sin\phi \\ 0 & \sin\phi & \cos\phi \end{pmatrix} \begin{pmatrix} 1 & \beta & \gamma \\ 0 & 1 & 0 \\ 0 & 0 & 1 \end{pmatrix} \begin{pmatrix} \partial_t \\ \partial_x \\ \partial_y \end{pmatrix} = BAi, \tag{35}$$

where $\tan 2\phi = f_{xy}/(f_{yy} - f_{xx})$. We proceed using (3) and the same reasoning as for the tangent based frames in the preceding section and arives to the following theorem.

Theorem 6. *A complete set of scalar invariants for scalar functions on Γ_3 at points where the Hessian is non-degenerate are as follow:*

$$
\begin{aligned}
a^p &= -f_{rrp}/f_{pp} & a^q &= -f_{rrq}/f_{qq} \\
\delta^p &= -f_{rpp}/f_{pp} & \delta^q &= -f_{rqq}/f_{qq} \\
\sigma^p &= -f_{rpq}/f_{pp} & \sigma^q &= -f_{rpq}/f_{qq} \\
\rho &= f_{rpq}/(2f_{pp} - 2f_{qq}) & & \\
\kappa^p &= f_{ppq}/(2f_{pp} - 2f_{qq}) & \kappa^q &= f_{pqq}/(2f_{pp} - 2f_{qq}).
\end{aligned}
\tag{36}
$$

Observe that in contrast to the tangent based gauge systems the Hessian gauge has all the scalar invariants listed in (19).

7   Conclusion and Discussion

In this paper we have developed a systematic theory about local structure of moving images in terms of Galilean differential invariants. We have argued that Galilean invariants are useful for studying moving images as it disregard constant motion that typically depends on the motion of the observer or the observed object, and only describe relative motion that might capture surface shape and motion boundaries. The set of Galilean invariants for moving images also contains the Euclidean invariants for (still) images.

Comparing to using optic flow as the basic element for describing image motion, the above suggested theory is completely bottom up and local, while optic flow is based on trying to directly interpreting the image motion in terms of (the projection of) motion of object surface points. The estimation of optic flow is non-local as it typically is based on gathering statistics about low level features in a small spatio-temporal surrounding. There are also Galilean differential invariants that can capture creation and disappearance of image structure, situations that are not covered by the concept of optic flow.

Experimental work is of course needed for evaluating how useful the suggested theory is for finding structure in real image sequences. Spatio-temporal images derivatives cannot be measured in a point, an integration over a non-vanishing spatio-temporal volume is needed [7], i.e. we need filters for measuring derivatives. As there are no localized filters that are invariant w.r.t. Galilean shear [5], a family of velocity adapted filters is needed. For computing a Galilean differential invariant, the velocity adapted filter used for measuring it should have the same spatio-temporal direction as the spatio-temporally directed gauge coordinate for the invariant. This could either be implemented by searching over a precomputed set of spatio-temporally directed derivative filters or by iteratively adapt the spatio-temporal direction of the filter. It should be noted that in general, gauge adapted derivative filters can be found for several spatio-temporal directions at a point, i.e. for real image sequences the invariants can be multi-valued. This can be the case for e.g. transparent motion.

References

1. L. Alvarez, F. Guichard, P. Lions, and J. Morel. Axioms and fundamental equations of image processing: Multiscale analysis and p.d.e. *Archive for Rational Mechanics and Annalysis*, 123(3):199–257, 1993.
2. J. Barron, D. Fleet, and S. Beauchemin. Performance of optical flow techniques. *International Journal of Computer Vision*, 12(1):43–77, 1994.
3. H. Flanders. *Differential forms with applications to the physical sciences*. Dover Publications, Inc., 1989.
4. L. Florack, B. ter Haar Romeny, J. Koenderink, and M. Viergever. Families of tuned scale-space kernels. In *Proc. 2nd European Conference on Computer Vision*, pages 19–23, 1992.
5. L. Florack, B. ter Haar Romeny, J. Koenderink, and M. Viergever. Scale and the differential structure of images. *Image and Vision Computing*, 10:376–388, 1992.
6. L. Florack, B. ter Haar Romeny, J. Koenderink, and M. Viergever. General intensity transformations and differential invariants. *J. of Mathematical Imaging and Vision*, 4:171–187, 1994.
7. L. M. J. Florack. *Image Structure*. Series in Mathematical Imaging and Vision. Kluwer Academic Publishers, Dordrecht, Netherlands, 1997.
8. M. Friedman. *Foundation of Space-Time Theories: Relativistic Physics and Philosophy of Science*. Princeton University Press, 1983.
9. F. Guichard. A morphological, affine, and galilean invariant scale-space for movies. *IEEE Transactions on Image Processing*, 7(3):444–456, 1998.
10. W. C. Hoffman. The Lie algebra of visual perception. *J. Mathematical Psychology 3 (1966), 65-98; errata, ibid.*, 4:348–349, 1966.
11. B. Jahne. *Spatio-Temporal Image Processing-Theory and Scientific Applications*. Number 751 in Lecture Notes in Computer Science. Springer, 1993.
12. J. Koenderink and A. van Doorn. Invariant properties of the motion parallax field due to the movement of rigid bodies relative to an observer. *Optica Acta*, 22(9):773–791, 1975.
13. J. Koenderink and A. van Doorn. Local structure of movement parallax of the plane. *J. of the Optical Society of America*, 66(7):717–723, July 1976.
14. J. Koenderink and A. van Doorn. Image processing done right. In A. H. et al., editor, *ECCV 2002*, number 2350 in LNCS, pages 158–172. Springer Verlag, 2002.
15. A. Mitiche and P. Bouthemy. Computation and analysis of image motion: A synopsis of current problems and methods. *International Journal of Computer Vision*, 19(1):29–55, July 1996.
16. M. Spivak. *Differential Geometry*, volume 1–5. Publish or Perish, Inc., Berkeley, California, USA, 1975.
17. S. Uras, F. Girosi, A. Verri, and V. Torre. A computational approach to motion perception. *bc*, 60:79–87, 1988.
18. M. Yamamoto. The image sequence analysis of three-dimensional dynamic scenes. Technical Report 893, Electrotechnical Laboratory, Agency of Industrial Science and Technology, May 1988.
19. C. Zetzsche and E. Barth. Direct detection of flow discontinuities by 3d curvature operators. *Pattern Recognition Letters*, 12:771–779, 1991.

Tracking People with a Sparse Network of Bearing Sensors

A. Rahimi, B. Dunagan, and T. Darrell

MIT Computer Science and Artificial Intelligence Laboratory
200 Technology Square,
Cambridge MA, 02139 USA
{ali,bdunagan,trevor}@mit.edu

Abstract. Recent techniques for multi-camera tracking have relied on either overlap between the fields of view of the cameras or on a visible ground plane. We show that if information about the dynamics of the target is available, we can estimate the trajectory of the target without visible ground planes or overlapping cameras.

1   Introduction

We explore the problem of tracking individuals using a network of non-over-lapping cameras. Recent techniques for multi-camera tracking have relied on two kinds of cues. Some rely on overlap between the fields of view of the cameras to calculate the real-world coordinate of the target. Others assume that the ground plane is visible and map image points known to lie on the ground plane to the real world using homography. In this paper, we show that if information about the dynamics of the target is available, we can estimate trajectories without visible ground planes or overlapping cameras.

We are interested in instrumenting as large an environment as possible with a small number of cameras. To maximize the coverage area of the network, the camera fields of view (FOVs) rarely overlap. Further, in our indoor setting, we wish to use cameras that may not have a clear view of the ground plane due to occlusions or their horizontal orientation.

Without a visible ground plane, each camera can only estimate the bearing of the ray from the camera optical center to the target. Therefore the target's location can only be determined up to a scale factor with a single camera. However, information about a target's dynamics can be helpful in localizing it. For example, if a target is known to be moving at a given constant speed in the ground plane, its location can be fully recovered by matching its speed in the image plane to its ground-plane speed. See Figure 1(a).

If the target's speed is unknown but constant, it's trajectory can be estimated with two non-overlapping cameras. See Figure 1(b). The time interval in which the target leaves the first field of view and enters the second one is inversely proportional to the velocity of the target. Using the second camera helps us recover the speed, which in turns allows us to localize the target.

T. Pajdla and J. Matas (Eds.): ECCV 2004, LNCS 3024, pp. 507–518, 2004.

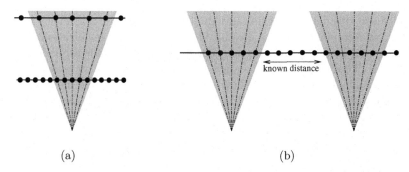

(a)   (b)

Fig. 1. (a) A horizontally mounted camera recovers the location of a target up to a scale factor. If the target's speed is known, the ambiguity disappears. For example, given its true speed, if the target is seen to be moving slowly, it must be far away. If it appears to be moving fast, it must be near. (b) A second camera provides enough information to estimate the (constant) speed of the target, making it possible to localize it.

The cases where speed is constant and known, or constant and unknown, are straightforward to handle. In this paper, we generalize to the case where the target moves with varying but smooth velocity. These dynamics can be modeled with a Gauss-Markov process. Given the dynamics of the target, we search for a trajectory that is most compatible with these dynamics and the observations made by the cameras. The resulting trajectories capture the gross features of the motion of the target and use the dynamics to interpolate sections of the trajectory not observed by the cameras.

We incorporate the smoothness of the trajectory as a prior in the Bayesian framework (Sect. 3). The camera measurements will provide observations that define a likelihood on trajectories (Sect. 4). The Maximum a Posteriori (MAP) trajectory can be recovered by iteratively solving a quadratic program (Sect. 5). We validate our system on both synthetic and real data (Sect. 6 and Sect. 7).

2   Related Work

Recently, there has been a significant amount of work in tracking people across multiple views. Some of the proposed approaches seek to hand off image-based tracking from camera to camera without recovering real-world coordinates [1]. We focus on those that recover the real-world coordinate of the person. Multi-camera person trackers can be categorized as overlapping systems and non-overlapping systems.

Tracking with overlapping cameras has relied on either narrow baseline stereo [4,3] or wide baseline matching [5]. These methods use the correspondence across views to determine the location of the target in the real world.

Most research with non-overlapping cameras has focused on maintaining consistent identity between multiple targets as they exit one field of view and enter another [8,6]. This is known as the data association problem. These techniques cannot help determine the real-world position of a target if individual cameras cannot make this determination individually. They provide machinery for establishing correspondences across disjoint views, but not for localization.

Caspi and Irani [2] provided another example where correspondence could be avoided. They showed how to align a pair of image sequences acquired from non-overlapping cameras, when the object being imaged spans the field of views of two non-overlapping cameras. The coherent motion of a planar object as seen by two nearby cameras can compensate for the lack of correspondence. In our case, coherent target dynamics provide this kind of coherence.

3   Trajectory Model

We assume that each camera can identify each person in its field of view from frame to frame. This allows us to track individuals independently of each other. For the rest of this paper, we assume that the tracking problem is decoupled in this way and we only discuss tracking each individual separately. This system could be augmented by more sophisticated person identification schemes than the one described in Sect. 7, such as the ones discussed in section Sect. 2.

We use a linear Gaussian state-space model to describe the smoothness of the trajectory on the ground plane. This will define a prior $p(X)$ on the trajectory to be estimated.

Define the state x_t of the target at time t as:

$$x_t = \begin{bmatrix} u_t & \dot{u}_t & v_t & \dot{v}_t \end{bmatrix}^\top.$$

Where u_t and v_t are the x and y locations of the target on the ground plane, and $\dot{u}_t$ and $\dot{v}_t$ describe the target's instantaneous velocity. We assume that the state evolves according to linear Gaussian Markov dynamics:

$$x_{t+1} = Ax_t + \nu_t, \tag{1}$$

where ν_t is a zero-mean Gaussian random variable with covariance Σ_ν. For example, in the synthetic example of §6 we set

$$A = \begin{bmatrix} 1 & 0.5 & 0 & 0 \\ 0 & 1 & 0 & 0 \\ 0 & 0 & 1 & 0.5 \\ 0 & 0 & 0 & 1 \end{bmatrix}, \quad \Sigma_v = 10^{-6}\text{diag}\left(\begin{bmatrix} 10^{-4} & 1 & 10^{-4} & 1 \end{bmatrix}\right),$$

so that each x_{t+1} adds the velocities in x_t to the positions in x_t, and nudges the old velocities by Gaussian noise. The resulting poses are also nudged by a small amount of Gaussian noise.

The states form a Markov chain over time. X, the collection of states from time 1 to time T is itself a Gaussian random variable of dimension $1 \times 4T$:

$$p(x_t|x_{t-1}) = \mathcal{N}\left(x_t \middle| Ax_{t-1}, \Sigma_\nu\right)$$

$$p(X) = \prod_{t=1}^{T} p(x_t|x_{t-1}) = \mathcal{N}\left(X \middle| 0, \Lambda_X\right), \tag{2}$$

where Λ_X^{-1} is tri-diagonal. We will use the Cholesky decomposition of Λ_X^{-1} in §5:

$$\Lambda_X = G^\top G$$
$$G_t = \left[0 \cdots, \sqrt{\Sigma_\nu} A, -\sqrt{\Sigma_\nu}, 0 \cdots \right], \tag{3}$$

where G_t is row t of G and $\sqrt{\Sigma_\nu}$ is the Cholesky factor of Σ_ν. Equation (3) is easily derived from the quadratic form inside $p(X)$ defined in equation (2).

4   Observation Model

In general, we wish to consider an object tracked by a set of oblique non-overlapping cameras with no visible ground plane. To simplify our task, we consider the case where cameras are mounted horizontally, so that only the horizontal direction in the image plane is relevant in locating a person. In indoor settings, horizontal cameras are a way to cover a large area.

Let p^i be the location of camera i on the ground plane with respect to some reference, and let θ^i its rotation (yaw). Denote the focal length of the camera by f^i.

Ideally, the width of each person could be used to gauge the distance to the target. But our system uses background subtraction, which yields crude segmentation, partly because both the moving region and the uncovered region are identified as foreground pixels. Therefore we ignore the width of the clusters as a depth cue.

Let y_t^i be the horizontal location of the target as seen in the image plane of camera i at time t. This measurement is the bearing of the target with respect to the camera, and is computed by projecting the target's location onto the camera's focal plane:

$$y_t^i = \pi^i(x_t) + \omega_t = f^i \frac{\mathbf{R}_y^i (C x_t - p^i)}{\mathbf{R}_x^i (C x_t - p^i)} + \omega_t \tag{4}$$

$$C = \begin{bmatrix} 1\,0\,0\,0 \\ 0\,0\,1\,0 \end{bmatrix}. \tag{5}$$

Here, $\mathbf{R}^i$ is the rotation matrix corresponding to θ^i, and ω_t is a zero mean Gaussian random variable with variance σ_ω^2. C is a 2×4 matrix that extracts the location of the target from its state.

When the target is within the field of view of a camera, (4) describes a likelihood model for each measurement. When the target is out of the field of view of a camera, that camera reports $\emptyset$:

$$p(y_t^i|x_t) = \begin{cases} \mathcal{N}\left(y_t^i|\pi^i(x_t), \sigma_\omega\right), & \text{if } \mathcal{I}^i(x_t) \\ \delta(y_t^i - \emptyset), & \text{otherwise.} \end{cases}$$

where $\mathcal{I}^i(x)$ is an indicator function that determines whether a given point falls within the field of view of camera i.

Conditioned on the true location of the target, the measurements are independent of each other. Then letting Y be the collection of all measurements from all sensors from time $t = 1$ to $t = T$,

$$p(Y|X) = \prod_{t=1}^{T} \prod_{i=1}^{N} p(y_t^i|x_t).$$

It will be useful to decompose the likelihood into constraints and observations:

$$p(Y|X) = \prod_{(t,i)\in\mathcal{O}} \mathcal{N}\left(y_t^i|\pi^i(x_t), \sigma_\omega\right) \prod_{(t,i)\notin\mathcal{O}} (1 - \mathcal{I}^i(x_t))$$

where $(t,i) \in \mathcal{O} \iff y_t^i \neq \emptyset$. The second product of factors is a set of constraints that insure the estimated trajectory only goes through fields of view that have actually seen the target. In Sect. 5, we will need to use these constraints in a quadratic program. However, quadratic programming requires a convex constraint set, and these constraints are not convex. So we relax them the constraints $\mathcal{I}^i$ by defining the function $\mathcal{J}^i$ so that $\mathcal{J}^i(x_t) = 0$ if x_t is behind camera i, and 1 if it is in front of it. The new likelihood becomes:

$$p(Y|X) = \prod_{(t,i)\in\mathcal{O}} p(y_t^i|x_t) \prod_{(t,i)\in\mathcal{O}} \mathcal{J}^i(x_t)$$

As is shown in the following section, this new constraint set is convex. It says that every measurement must have emanated from a sensor that had the target in front of it, but it does not penalize the situation where a trajectory crosses a field of view without generating an observation. We use this new, more permissive likelihood function to find the MAP trajectory.

5   MAP Trajectory Estimation

The most probable trajectory given all the camera observations is

$$X^* = \arg\max_X p(X|Y) = \arg\max_X p(X)p(Y|X) \tag{6}$$

A local maximum can be found by iteratively approximating this optimization problem with a quadratic program of the form:

$$X^* = \arg\max_X X^\top Q X + C^\top X \tag{7}$$

$$\text{s.t. } AX > b$$

We show how to transform the optimization of equation (6) into a sequence of quadratic programs of the form of equation (7).

Taking the log of $p(X)p(Y|X)$ and dropping terms that don't depend on X yields a new quantity to minimize:

$$E(X) = X^\top G^\top G X + \frac{1}{\sigma_\omega^2} \sum_{(t,i)\in\mathcal{O}} (\pi^i(x_t) - y_t)^2 + \sum_{(t,i)\in\mathcal{O}} \log \mathcal{J}^i(x_t)$$

The last term serves as a constraint, so the maximization of E over X can take the form of a non-linear least-squares program:

$$X^* = \arg\min_X \epsilon(X) = \arg\min_X \frac{1}{2} r(X)^\top r(X)$$

$$\text{s.t. } \forall_{(t,i)\in\mathcal{O}} \mathcal{J}^i(x_t) = 1$$

where

$$r(X) = \begin{bmatrix} GX \\ \vdots \\ \frac{\pi^i(x_t)-y_t}{\sigma_w} \\ \vdots \end{bmatrix}, \quad (i,t) \in \mathcal{O}.$$

Each constraint $\mathcal{J}^i(x_t) = 1$ can be recast as a linear constraint for each observed point. Figure 2 shows that a point is in front of the sensor if its projection onto the camera optical axis is positive. Each field of view constraint becomes an inequality constraint:

$$\mathcal{J}^i(x_t) = 1 \iff n(\theta^i)^\top (x_t - p^i) > 0,$$

where $n(\theta^i)$ is a vector pointing along the optical axis of camera i. Let the rows of matrix A and the elements of vector b be:

$$A_\tau = \begin{bmatrix} 0\cdots & \cos(\theta^i) & 0 & \sin(\theta^i) & 0\cdots \end{bmatrix},$$

$$b_\tau = n(\theta^i)^\top p^i,$$

with one row per observed trajectory point. The non-linear program becomes a non-linear program on a convex domain:

$$X^* = \arg\min_X \epsilon(X) \tag{8}$$

$$\text{s.t. } AX > b. \tag{9}$$

To convert equations (8,9) into a quadratic program, we linearize $r(X)$ about a guess X_0

$$\epsilon(X) \approx \|r(X_0) + J(X - X_0)\|^2, \tag{10}$$

where J is the Jacobian of $r(X)$:

$$J = \frac{\partial r}{\partial X} = \begin{bmatrix} G \\ \vdots \\ 0\cdots, \frac{1}{\sigma_w}\frac{\partial}{\partial x}\pi^i, \cdots 0 \end{bmatrix},$$

where non-zero terms below G align with the element of X involved in each error term.

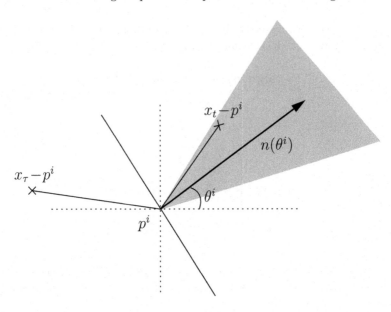

Fig. 2. The arrow is the camera optical axis $n(\theta)$. The gray region is the field of view of the camera. The dot product of $n(\theta)$ and a target location x is positive if the target is in front of the camera.

Substituting (10) into (8), we get a constrained least-squares problem:

$$X_1 = \arg\min_X \|r(X_0) + J(X - X_0)\|^2,$$
$$\text{s.t. } AX > b.$$

This is a quadratic program in X. Notice that J is very sparse, with exactly 2 non-zero elements in each row. This expedites finding the optimum with QP solvers such as LOQO [9].

Iteratively linearizing r and solving this QP is similar to optimizing ϵ using Newton-Raphson with inequality constraints.

6   Synthetic Results

We simulated our approach with synthetic trajectories and sensor measurements. Figure 3 depicts the synthetic setup. Sensors are placed around a square environment, and the target's motion is generated randomly. Whenever the target hits the wall, it is reflected back. This trajectory is smoothed and passed to synthetic cameras which generate measurements. The state-space model of (1) cannot capture these operations, but we show here that state-space dynamics are sufficient to generate paths that capture the qualitative motion of the target.

The optimization must begin with an initial guess that satisfies the constraints of equation (9). This is because cutting plane QP solvers such as LOQO

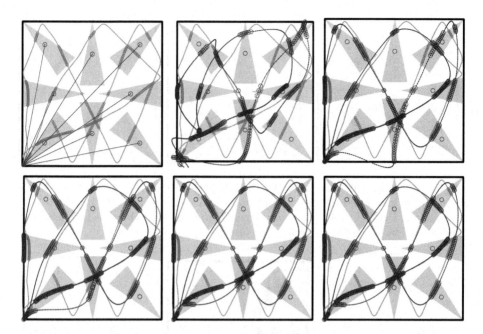

Fig. 3. Optimization begins with all points seen by a camera placed at the same location. Shown are iterations 0, 1, 3,9,11, and 17.

require an initial point within the convex constraint set. We set the initial iterate to have all unobserved trajectory points at the origin, and all observed trajectory points at one meter along the optical axis of the camera that observed it.

Figure 3 shows the estimated trajectory as it is refined. In early iterations, the likelihood term lines up the trajectory points along the ray from the camera optical center to the true target location. But initially, their distances from the optical centers are mis-estimated. The prior pulls the trajectory towards the right distance in subsequent iterations. Despite the mismatch between the dynamic models used in synthesis and estimation, the estimated trajectory is close to the true trajectory. Figure 4 shows the final answer of several more synthesized problems.

The field of view constraints are critical in recovering the trajectories. Without them, the dynamics pull the trajectory infeasible solutions. Figure 5 shows a sample trajectory estimated without the constraints.

7   Results: Real Data

We have implemented this system on a sensor network of wireless cameras with person trackers on board. Each node nodes in our network is a personal digital assistant computer equipped with low resolution camera. These devices have wireless network adaptors that allow them to communicate with a MATLAB

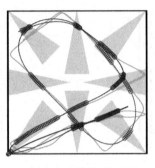 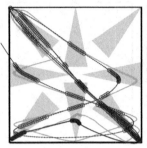 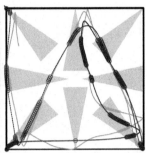

Fig. 4. More synthetic results. Notice that the ends of the trajectories do not match up with the ground truth. For these points, velocity information can only come from past points. Points in the middle of the trajectories, on the other hand, benefit from information from the past as well as the future.

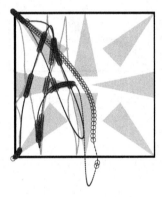

Fig. 5. Without the field of view constraints, the dynamics can pull the trajectories behind the cameras.

process running on a base station. The real-time person tracker runs on each PDA and reports the time-stamped horizontal location of a person to the base station every 250 millisecond.

We use background subtraction to locate a target within each image plane. Foreground pixels are clustered according to their image coordinates using EM on a mixture of Gaussians. Each cluster corresponds to one person in the field of view of the camera. The clusters have a prior covariance that matches the aspect of a human. This coalesces nearby small blobs into human-sized blobs and filters out isolated small blobs [7] . For each cluster, an appearance feature vector is computed and used to identify the person it represents. The identity of the person along with the horizontal component of the center of cluster is transmitted to a central processing station.

Before experimenting with non-overlapping cameras, we built a model of human motion using a pair of overlapping cameras. Stereopsis between the two cameras allowed us to recover real-world trajectories without knowledge of dy-

Fig. 6. IPAQ handheld computers equipped with a camera and a wireless adaptor serve as our sensor nodes. They are mounted on the walls in our office building.

namics. A system identification procedure was applied to these trajectories to recover parameters A and Σ_ν of the dynamic model. We estimated Σ_ω by averaging the measurement error at various known locations in the room, at various target speeds.

A network of 4 PDAs observed a section of our floor. The cameras were mounted perpendicular to walls, so their orientations θ^i was easy to determine. We used the floor plan of our building to determine the location p^i of each camera. None of the fields of views overlapped. One test subject walked in the environment for about one minute, beginning and ending at the same place. Figure 7 sketches the actual trajectory and plots the recovered trajectory. The small dots on the trajectory correspond to each discrete time step in the system (1/4th of a second apart).

Notice that the loop seen by camera 1 was successfully recovered. The forward and backward legs in this loops are correctly found to be at different depths. Without dynamics, it would have been impossible to determine that one path is at a different distance from the other. The long legs towards and away from camera 3 are not correctly recovered. It was impossible for the system to determine the motion of the target in this region because the subject moved along the same bearing on those legs. Notice also that the estimated trajectory goes through a wall between camera 3 and 4. Had we encoded these walls in the form of additional constraints, the legs through camera 3 might have been correctly estimated.

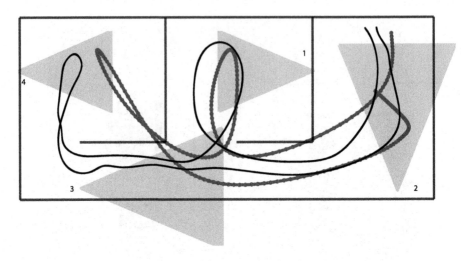

Fig. 7. Estimated real path.

8   Conclusion

We have shown that some side information about the dynamics of a moving object can compensate for the lack of simultaneous correspondence between two cameras. Our method finds the trajectory that is most compatible with both the observations from the cameras and the expected dynamics. By using a convex visibility constraint, finding this trajectory can be expressed as a series of quadratic programs.

The method presented in this paper also obviates the need for a visible ground plane. This paper has focused on horizontally mounted cameras, but we plan to allow input from obliquely mounted cameras in the future.

As section 7 showed, known obstacles in the environment can provide helpful information in constraining the solution. We are working towards adding such constraints. Finally, the method we propose is batch. Batch processing is useful for this problem because the uncertaintly in the trajectory between observations can be very large. One could run this procedure in small time windows to obtain a time-lagged version.

References

1. Q. Cai and J.K. Aggarwal. Tracking human motion in structured environments using a distributed-camera system. *IEEE Transactions on Pattern Analysis and Machine Intelligence*, 21(12):1241–1247, November 1999.
2. Y. Caspi and M. Irani. Alignment of Non-Overlapping sequences. In *ICCV*, pages 76–83, July 2001.
3. T. Darrell, D. Demirdjian, N. Checka, and P. Felzenszwalb. Plan-View trajectory estimation with dense stereo background models. In *ICCV*, pages 628–635, 2001.

4. M. Harville. Stereo person tracking with adaptive plan-view statistical templates. In *ECCV Workshop on Statistical Methods in Video Processing*, June 2002.
5. A. Mittal and L. S. Davis. M2Tracker: A multi-view approach to segmenting and tracking people in a cluttered scene using region-based stereo. In *ECCV (1)*, pages 18–36, 2002.
6. H. Pasula, S. J. Russell, M. Ostland, and Y. Ritov. Tracking many objects with many sensors. In *IJCAI*, pages 1160–1171, 1999.
7. A. Rahimi. Variational bayes for tracking moving mixtures of gaussians, 2000.
8. R. Zabih V. Kettnaker. Counting people from multiple cameras. In *ICMCS*, volume 2, pages 267–271, 1999.
9. R. J. Vanderbei. LOQO: An interior point code for quadratic programming. *Optimization Methods and Software*, 11:451–484, 1999.

Transformation-Invariant Embedding for Image Analysis

Ali Ghodsi[1], Jiayuan Huang[1], and Dale Schuurmans[2]

[1] School of Computer Science
University of Waterloo
{aghodsib,j9huang}@cs.uwaterloo.ca
[2] Department of Computing Science
University of Alberta
dale@cs.ualberta.ca

Abstract. Dimensionality reduction is an essential aspect of visual processing. Traditionally, linear dimensionality reduction techniques such as principle components analysis have been used to find low dimensional linear subspaces in visual data. However, sub-manifolds in natural data are rarely linear, and consequently many recent techniques have been developed for discovering non-linear manifolds. Prominent among these are *Local Linear Embedding* and *Isomap*. Unfortunately, such techniques currently use a naive appearance model that judges image similarity based solely on Euclidean distance. In visual data, Euclidean distances rarely correspond to a meaningful perceptual difference between nearby images. In this paper, we attempt to improve the quality of manifold inference techniques for visual data by modeling local neighborhoods in terms of natural transformations between images—for example, by allowing image operations that extend simple differences and linear combinations. We introduce the idea of modeling local tangent spaces of the manifold in terms of these richer transformations. Given a local tangent space representation, we then embed data in a lower dimensional coordinate system while preserving reconstruction weights. This leads to improved manifold discovery in natural image sets.

1 Introduction

Recently there has been renewed interest in manifold recovery techniques motivated by the development of efficient algorithms for finding non-linear manifolds in high dimensional data. Isomap [1] and Local Linear Embedding (LLE) [2] are two approaches that have been particularly influential. Historically, two main ideas for discovering low dimensional manifolds in high dimensional data have been to find a mapping from the original space to a lower dimensional space that: (1) preserves pairwise distances (i.e. multidimensional scaling [3]); or (2) preserves mutual linear reconstruction ability (i.e. principle components analysis [4]). In each case, globally optimal solutions are linear manifolds. Interestingly, the more recent methods for manifold discovery, Isomap and LLE, are based on

T. Pajdla and J. Matas (Eds.): ECCV 2004, LNCS 3024, pp. 519–530, 2004.
© Springer-Verlag Berlin Heidelberg 2004

exactly these same two principles, with the generalization that the new methods only seek manifold descriptions that *locally* preserve distances and linear reconstructions. In this way, they avoid recovering linear global solutions [1,2].

There have been many new variants of these ideas [5,6,7,8]. Although these techniques all produce non-linear manifolds in different ways, they are generally based on the core assumption that, in natural data, (1) Euclidean distances locally preserve geodesic distances on the manifold [1], or (2) data objects can be linearly reconstructed from other data points nearby in Euclidean distance [2]. However, these core notions are not universally applicable nor always effective. Particularly in image data it is easy to appreciate the shortcoming of these ideas: For images, weighted linear combinations amount to an awkward transformation whereby source images have their brightness levels adjusted and then are summed directly on top of one another. This is often an unnatural way to capture the image transformations that manifolds are intended to characterize. Figure 1 shows that centered, cropped and normalized target images can be reasonably well reconstructed from likewise aligned source images, but that even a minor shift, rotation or rescaling will quickly limit the ability of this approach to reconstruct a target image. Similarly, measuring Euclidean distances between images can sometimes be a dubious practice, since these distances do not always correspond to meaningful perceptual differences.

Fig. 1. Least squares reconstructions of a target image (far right) from three nearby images (far left). The intermediate (fourth) image shows the best linear reconstruction of the rightmost image from the three leftmost images. First row: original reconstruction. Second row: reconstruction of same image after translations have been applied.

We propose to model manifolds locally by characterizing the local transformations that preserve the invariants they encode. That is, we attempt to characterize those transformations that cause points on the manifold to stay on the manifold. Our approach will be to first characterize the local tangent space around a data object by considering transformations of that object that cause it to stay on (or near) the manifold.

Other work on incorporating natural image transformations to better model visual data has been proposed by [9,10,11,12]. However, this previous work primarily concerns learning mixture models over images rather than sub-manifolds, and most significantly, requires that the image transformations be manually specified ahead of time, rather than inferred from the data itself. In this paper, we infer local transformations directly from the image data.

Eigentracking [13], also considers affine transformations of a set of precon-structed basis images for an object based on preliminary views. Here we consider a potentially richer set of transformations and simultaneously learn the basis in addition to the transformations and embedding.

2   Local Image Transformations

For images, it is easy to propose simple local transformations that capture natu-ral invariants in image data better than simply averaging nearby images together. Consider a very simple class of transformations based on receptive fields of pixel neighborhoods: Given an $n_1 \times n_2$ image x, imagine transforming it into a nearby image $\tilde{x} = T(x, \theta)$, where for each pixel $\tilde{x}_i \in \tilde{x}$ we determine its value from corresponding nearby pixels in x. Specifically, we determine $\tilde{x}_i$ according to

$$\tilde{x}_i = \theta^\top x_{N(i)} \tag{1}$$

where $N(i)$ denotes the set of neighboring pixels of pixel x_i. Thus $T(\cdot, \theta)$ defines a simple local filter passed over the image, parameterized by a single weight vector θ, as shown in Figure 2.

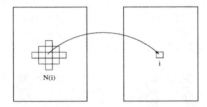

Fig. 2. Illustration of local pixel transformation from the left image to the right

Although this defines a limited class of image transformations, it obviously enhances the image modeling capabilities of weighted image combinations (which are only based on adjusting the brightness level of source images). Many useful types of transformation such as translation, rotation and blurring can be ap-proximated using this simple local transformation. Figure 3 shows that similar images can be much better reconstructed by simple filter transformations rather than merely adjusting brightness levels prior to summing. Here minor trans-lations and appearance changes can be adequately modeled in circumstances where brightness changes fail.

3   Local Tangent Space Modeling

The key to our proposal is to model the local tangent space around high-dimensional data points by a small number of transformations that locally pre-

Fig. 3. Least squares reconstructions of a target image (far right) from three nearby images (left). The intermediate (fourth) image shows the best least squares reconstruction of the rightmost image from the three leftmost images. First row: standard reconstruction. Second row: reconstruction after local transformations.

serve membership in the manifold. Thus, in our approach, a manifold is locally characterized by the invariants it preserves.

We model transformations over the data space by using an operator $T(x, \theta)$ which combines a data object x and a parameter vector θ to produce a transformed object $\tilde{x} = T(x, \theta)$. In general, we will need to assume very little about this operator, but, by making some very simple (and fairly weak) assumptions about the nature of T, we will be able to formulate natural geometric properties that one can preserve in a dimensionality reducing embedding.

First, we assume that T is a *bilinear* operator. That is, T becomes a linear operator on each argument when the other argument is held fixed. Specifically,

$$T(ax_1 + bx_2, \theta) = aT(x_1, \theta) + bT(x_2, \theta)$$
$$T(x, a\theta_1 + b\theta_2) = aT(x, \theta_1) + bT(x, \theta_2) \tag{2}$$

Second, we require the operator to have a local *origin* ω in the second argument that gives an identity map:

$$T(x, \omega) \;=\; x \text{ for all } x \tag{3}$$

With these properties, we can then naturally equate parameterized transformations with tangent vectors as follows. First note that $T(x, \theta) = x + T(x, \delta)$ for $\delta = \theta - \omega$, since by bilinearity we have

$$T(x, \theta) = T(x, \omega + \delta) = T(x, \omega) + T(x, \delta)$$

and also

$$T(x, \omega) = x$$

Thus, we can interpret every transformation of an object x as a vector sum. That is, if $\tilde{x} = T(x, \theta)$ then the difference $\tilde{x} - x$ is just $T(x, \delta)$.

Now imagine transforming a source object x_i to approximate a nearby target object x_j, where both reside on the manifold. The best approximation of x_j by x_i is given by

$$\tilde{x}_{ij} = T(x_i, \tilde{\theta}_{ij})$$

where

$$\tilde{\theta}_{ij} = \arg\min_{\theta} \|x_j - T(x_i, \theta)\|$$

If the approximation error is small, we can claim that the difference vector $\tilde{x}_{ij} - x_i = T(\tilde{\delta}_{ij})$, for $\tilde{\delta}_{ij} = \tilde{\theta}_{ij} - \omega$, is approximately tangent to the manifold at x_i. One thing we would like to preserve is the transformation distance between nearby points. Consider the norm of the difference vector:

$$\|x_i - \tilde{x}_{ij}\| = \|T(x, \tilde{\delta}_{ij})\| = \|\tilde{\delta}_{ij}\| \, \|T(x, \tilde{\eta}_{ij})\|$$

where $\tilde{\eta}_{ij} = \tilde{\delta}_{ij}/\|\tilde{\delta}_{ij}\|$. Here $T(x, \tilde{\eta}_{ij})$ gives the direction of the approximate tangent vector at x_i, and $\|\tilde{\delta}_{ij}\|$ gives the coefficient in direction $\tilde{\eta}_{ij}$. This says that $\tilde{x}_{ij}$ is the projection of x_j onto the tangent plane centered at x_i, since $\tilde{x}_{ij} = x_i + \|\tilde{\delta}_{ij}\| T(x, \tilde{\eta}_{ij})$ is the best approximation of x_j in the local tangent space of x_i.

Intuitively, when we embed x_i and $\tilde{x}_{ij}$ in a lower dimensional space, say by a mapping $x_i \mapsto y_i$ and $\tilde{x}_{ij} \mapsto \tilde{y}_{ij}$, we would like to preserve the coefficient:

$$\|y_i - \tilde{y}_{ij}\| \approx \|\tilde{\delta}_{ij}\|$$

That is, in the lower-dimensional space, the vector $y_i - \tilde{y}_{ij}$ encodes the embedded direction of the transformation, $T(x_i, \tilde{\eta}_{ij})$, and the length $\|y_i - \tilde{y}_{ij}\|$ encodes the coefficient of the transformation, $\|\tilde{\delta}_{ij}\|$.

4   Transformation-Invariant Embedding Algorithm

Consider a set of t vectors, x_i, of dimension n sampled from an underlying manifold. If the manifold is smooth and locally invariant to natural transformations, we should be able to transform nearby points on the manifold to approximate each other. Therefore, in the low dimensional embedding we would like to preserve the ability to reconstruct points from their transformed neighbors. First, to identify the local neighborhood of each data point x_i, we compute the best point-to-point approximations using the local transformation operator described above (as opposed to just using Euclidean distances as proposed in LLE and Isomap). That is, given a target image x_j and a source image x_i, the best approximation of x_j from source x_i is given by

$$\tilde{x}_{ij} = T(x_i, \tilde{\theta}_{ij})$$

where

$$\tilde{\theta}_{ij} = \arg\min_{\theta} \|x_j - T(x_i, \theta)\|$$

Given these quantities, the neighborhood of an image x_j can then be approximated by selecting the K nearest neighbors x_i according to the K best approximations among the transformed reconstructions $\tilde{x}_{ij}$.

Second, to characterize the structure of the local neighborhood, we re-express each data point x_j in terms of its K nearest reconstructions $\tilde{x}_{ij}$. Consider a particular image x_j with K nearest neighbors $\tilde{x}_{ij}$ and reconstruction weights w_{ij}. The reconstruction error can be written as:

$$\varepsilon_j(w_j) = \left\| x_j - \sum_{i=1}^{K} w_{ij} \tilde{x}_{ij} \right\|^2$$

where w_j is the vector of reconstruction weights for an image x_j in terms of its neighbors. Note that each data point x_j is reconstructed independently. That is, we can recover each set of weights separately by solving a system of n linear equations in K unknowns. This can be expressed in a standard matrix form

$$\varepsilon_j(w_j) = \left\| \chi_j w_j - N_j w_j \right\|^2 = \left\| (\chi_j - N_j) w_j \right\|^2 = w_j^T G_j w_j$$

where χ_j is the matrix of columns x_j repeated K times, N_j is the matrix of columns of K nearest reconstructions $\tilde{x}_{ij}$ of x_j, and $G_j = (\chi_j - N_j)^T (\chi_j - N_j)$.

Note that, as with LLE, we wish to preserve scale and translation invariance in the local manifold characterization, and therefore we impose the additional constraint that the reconstruction weights w_j of each point x_j from its transformed neighbors $\tilde{x}_{ij}$ sums to one. That is, $\sum_i w_{ij} = 1$ for all j. The rationale for this constraint is that we would like the reconstruction weights to be invariant under the mapping from the neighborhood to the global manifold coordinates, which can be shown to hold if and only if all rows of the weight matrix sum to one [2]. Therefore, imposing the extra constraint ensures that the reconstruction holds equally well in both high dimensional and low dimensional spaces. To show that the resulting constrained least squares problem can still be solved in closed form, introduce a Lagrange multiplier λ and let e be a column vector of ones, obtaining

$$L(w, \lambda) = w^T G w + \lambda (w^T e - e)$$

$$\frac{dL}{dw} = 2Gw + \lambda e = 0$$

$$Gw = Ce$$

In practice, we can solve this with C set arbitrarily to 1 and then rescale so w sums to 1.

Finally, we need to embed the orginal points x_j in the lower dimensional coordinate system by assigning them coordinates y_j. Here we follow the same approach as LLE and choose the d dimensional vectors y_j to minimize the embedding cost function

$$\Phi(Y) = \sum_{j=1}^{t} \left\| y_j - \sum_{i=1}^{t} w_{ij} y_i \right\|^2$$

This ensures that we maintain the reconstruction ability in the coordinate system of the lower dimensional manifold. To solve for these coordinates, re-express the cost function in a standard matrix form

$$\Phi(Y) = \sum_{j=1}^{t} \left\| Y I_j - Y w_j \right\|^2$$

where I_j is the jth column of the identity matrix, and w_j is the jth column of W. Then we obtain

$$\min_Y \sum_{j=1}^t \left\| Y I_j - Y w_j \right\|^2 = \min_Y \; trace(Y M Y^T)$$

where $M = (I - W)^T (I - W)$. As observed in [2] the solution for Y can have an arbitrary origin and orientation, and thus to make the problem well-posed, these two degrees of freedom must be removed. Requiring the coordinates to be centered on the origin ($\sum_j y_j = 0$), and constraining the embedding vectors to have unit covariance ($Y^T Y = I$), removes the first and second degrees of freedom respectively. So the cost function must be optimized subject to additional constraints. Considering only the second constraint for the time being, we find that

$$L(Y, \lambda) = Y M Y^T + \lambda(Y Y^T - (N-1)I)$$

$$\frac{dL}{dY} = 2 M Y^T + 2\lambda Y = 0$$

$$M Y^T = \lambda Y^T$$

Thus L is minimized when the columns of Y^T (rows of Y) are the eigenvectors associated with the lowest eigenvalues of M. Discarding the eigenvector associated with eigenvalue 0 satisfies the first constraint.

5   Experimental Results

We present experimental results on face image data. The first two experiments attempt to illustrate the general advantages of the proposed technique, Transformation Invariant Embedding (TIE), for discovering smooth manifolds, at least in simple image analysis problems. A subsequent experiment attempts to show some of the advantages for TIE in a face recognition setting. In all experiments we use the transformation operator on images (1) that was described in Section 2.

Our first experiment is on translated versions of a single face image, as shown in Figure 4. Although the data set is high dimensional (the images are comprised of many pixels), there is clearly a one dimensional manifold that characterizes the image set. Figure 4 shows the result of running LLE and TIE on the original data set shown at the top. The results show that the 1-dimensional manifold discovered by LLE is inferior to that discovered by TIE, which had no problem tracking the vertical shift in the image set.

We then conducted an experiment on a database of rotating face images. Figure 5 shows the two-dimensional manifold discovered by LLE, whereas Figure 5 shows the two-dimensional manifold recovered by TIE. In both cases, the first dimension (top) captured the rotation angle of the images, although once again LLE's result is not as good as TIE's. Interestingly, TIE (and to a lesser extent LLE) learned to distinguish frontal from profile views in its second dimension.

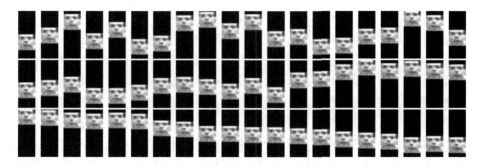

Fig. 4. Top: Original data. Middle: 1-dimensional manifold discovered by LLE. Bottom: 1-dimensional manifold discovered by TIE. (Images are sorted by the 1-dimensional y-coordinate values assigned by LLE and TIE respectively.)

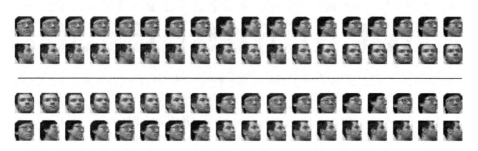

Fig. 5. Two-dimensional manifold discovered by LLE. Top two rows show first dimension, bottom two rows show second dimension.

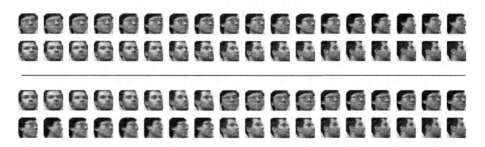

Fig. 6. Two-dimensional manifold discovered by TIE. Top two rows show first dimension, bottom two rows show second dimension. Note: first dimension captures rotation, whereas second captures frontal views versus side views.

Fig. 7. 105 rotated face images of 7 subjects

Finally, we conducted an experiment on a database of face images that contains 105 face images of 7 subjects which includes variations in both pose, and lighting (see Figure 7). The original data space was embedded into three dimensional subspaces. Figures 8 and 11 show the first dimension discovered by LLE and TIE respectively. Similarly, Figures 9 and 12 show the second dimension for LLE and TIE; and Figures 10 and 5 show the third dimension.

Note that for TIE the first (Figure 11) and second (Figure 12) dimensions corespond to rotation and frontal and profile views, whereas TIE essentially learned to distinguish faces in its third dimension (Figure 5). Here, two individuals were confused by TIE, whereas the other subjects were separated very well.

The corresponding results for LLE are clearly inferior in each case. Figures 8, 9 and 10 illustrates that LLE failed to discover smooth rotations, frontal versus side views, and identity.

6   Conclusion

In many image analysis problems, we know in advance that the data will incorporate different types of transformations. We introduce a way to make standard manifold learning methods such as LLE invariant to transformations in the input. This is achieved by modeling the local tangent space around high-dimensional data points by a small number of transformations that locally preserve membership in the manifold. Thus, in our approach, a manifold is locally characterized by the invariants it preserves.

Fig. 8. First dimension of the three-dimensional manifold discovered by LLE

Fig. 9. Second dimension of the three-dimensional manifold discovered by LLE

Fig. 10. Third dimension of the three-dimensional manifold discovered by LLE

Fig. 11. First dimension of the three-dimensional manifold discovered by TIE

Fig. 12. Second dimension of the three-dimensional manifold discovered by TIE

Fig. 13. Third dimension of the three-dimensional manifold discovered by TIE

We model transformations over the data space by using a bilinear operator which produce a transformed object, and show that by making this fairly weak assumption about the nature of operator, we will be able to formulate natural geometric properties that one can preserve in a dimensionality reducing embedding.

Although our basic approach is general, we focused on the special case of modeling manifolds in natural image data with emphasis on face recognition data. Here the proposed a simple local transformations capture natural invariants in the image data better than simply averaging nearby images together. Although we have focused solely on facial rotation and translation as the basic invariants we have been attempting to capture, clearly other types of transformations, such as warping, and out of plane rotation, are further phenonenon one may with to capture with these techniques.

References

1. J. Tenenbaum, V. de Silva, and J. Langford. A global geometric framework for nonlinear dimensionality reduction. *Science*, 290:2319–2323, 2000.
2. L. Saul and S. Roweis. Think globally, fit locally: Unsupervised learning of nonlinear manifolds. *JMLR*, 2003.
3. T. Cox and M. Cox. *Multidimensional Scaling*. Chapman Hall, 2nd edition, 2001.
4. I. Jolliffe. *Principal Component Analysis*. Springer-Verlag, 1986.
5. G. Lebanon. Learning Riemannian metrics. In *Proceedings UAI*, 2003.
6. M. Belkin and P. Niyogi. Laplacian eigenmaps and spectral techniques for embedding and clustering. In *Proceedings NIPS*, 2001.
7. Y.-W. Teh and S. Roweis. Automatic alignment of local representations. In *Proceedings NIPS*, 2002.
8. G. Hinton and S. Roweis. Stochastic neighbor embedding. In *Proc. NIPS*, 2002.
9. B. Frey and N. Jojic. Estimating mixture models of images and inferring spatial transformations using the em algorithm. In *Proceedings CVPR*, 1999.
10. B. Frey and N. Jojic. Transformed component analysis: joint estimation of spatial transformations and image components. In *Proceedings ICCV*, volume 2, pages 1190–1196, 1999.
11. B. Frey and N. Jojic. Transformation-invariant clustering and dimensionality reduction using em. *To appear in IEEE PAMI*, 2003.
12. P. Simard, Y. Le Cum, and J. Denker. Efficient pattern recognition using a new transformation distance. In *Proceedings NIPS 5*, 1993.
13. M. Black and A. Jepson. EigenTracking: Robust matching and tracking of articulated objects using a view-based representation. *International Journal of Computer Vision*, 26(1), 1998.

The Least-Squares Error for Structure from Infinitesimal Motion

John Oliensis

Computer Science Department
Stevens Institute of Technology
Hoboken, NJ 07030, USA
oliensis@cs.stevens-tech.edu
http://www.cs.stevens-tech.edu/~oliensis/

Abstract. We analyze the least–squares error for structure from motion (SFM) with a single infinitesimal motion ("structure from optical flow"). We present approximations to the noiseless error over two, complementary regions of motion estimates: roughly forward and non–forward translations. Experiments show that these capture the error's detailed behavior over the entire motion range. They can be used to derive new error properties, including generalizations of the bas–relief ambiguity. As examples, we explain the error's complexity for epipoles near the field of view; for planar scenes, we derive a new, double bas–relief ambiguity and prove the absence of local minima. For nonplanar scenes, our approximations simplify under reasonable assumptions. We show that our analysis applies even for large noise, and that the projective error has less information for estimating motion than the calibrated error. Our results make possible a comprehensive error analysis of SFM.

1 Introduction

A structure–from–motion (SFM) algorithm has two tasks: *matching* the 3D features across different images, and *estimating* the camera motion and 3D structure. This paper reports progress toward a comprehensive analysis of *estimation*.

Under standard assumptions, the goal of an "optimal" estimation algorithm is to find the minimum of the least–squares image–reprojection error [8], and the shape of this error as a function of the estimates determines the intrinsic problem that the algorithm solves. Here, we analyze this shape for SFM with a single infinitesimal motion ("structure from optical flow").

Little is known about the least–squares error. Yet, without understanding it, one can't predict when algorithms will succeed or fail—for instance, when bundle adjustment [24] will find the optimal least–squares estimate rather than a bad estimate at a false local minimum. Given some understanding, algorithms can avoid local minima and compute estimates more reliably, as shown in [18][3].

Previous research on estimation (as opposed to geometry) in SFM focussed on the bas–relief ambiguity [1][4][22][10] [14] [7][18][3][23][9][6]. Other results include the proof in [3] that the error is singular when the epipole estimate coincides

T. Pajdla and J. Matas (Eds.): ECCV 2004, LNCS 3024, pp. 531–545, 2004.

with an image point, and a semi–quantitative description [18] of the error over a linear slice through the plane of all epipole estimates. None of this work comes close to giving a detailed picture of the least–squares error.

In this paper, we present approximations to the noiseless error over two, complementary regions of motion estimates: roughly forward and non–forward translations. Together, these approximations describe the whole error. They reproduce its detailed shape, yet are simple enough to be useful for understanding it. We believe that they make it possible to study the least–squares error in depth, and we illustrate this by deriving several new properties of the error.

As in many previous analyses, e.g., [7][14][3], our theoretical discussion assumes infinitesimal motion and zero noise. Experiments show that the theory also works for large noise. We study calibrated cameras, taking the focal length as 1 without loss of generality, and also present results for projective SFM. For lack of space, all proofs are omitted. They can be found in [17].

1.1   Preliminaries

The standard least–squares error for infinitesimal motion (or optical flow) is [14]

$$
E_{\text{LS}}\left(\mathbf{T}, \omega, \{Z\}\right) \equiv \sum_{m=1}^{N_p} \left| \mathbf{d}_m - Z_m^{-1}\left(T_z \mathbf{p}_m - [T_x; T_y]\right) - \sum_{a \in \{x,y,z\}} \omega_a \mathbf{r}^{(a)}\left(\mathbf{p}_m\right) \right|^2 .
\tag{1}
$$

Here N_p is the total number of scene points, $\mathbf{p}_m \equiv \mathbf{p}_{1m} \equiv (x_m; y_m)$ is the mth image point in the first image, $\mathbf{d}_m \equiv \mathbf{p}_{2m} - \mathbf{p}_{1m}$ is the mth measured flow from image 1 to 2, the Z_m are the 3D depth estimates, $\mathbf{T}$ is the translation estimate, $\omega \equiv \left(\omega^{(x)}; \omega^{(y)}; \omega^{(z)}\right)$ is the estimate of the infinitesimal rotation, and the $\mathbf{r}^{(x)}(\mathbf{p})$, $\mathbf{r}^{(y)}(\mathbf{p})$, $\mathbf{r}^{(z)}(\mathbf{p})$ are the rotational flows at the image point $\mathbf{p}$ due to unit rotations around the x, y, or z axes: $\mathbf{r}(\mathbf{p}) \equiv$

$$
\left[\mathbf{r}^{(x)}(\mathbf{p}), \mathbf{r}^{(y)}(\mathbf{p}), \mathbf{r}^{(z)}(\mathbf{p})\right] \equiv \left[\begin{pmatrix} -xy \\ -\left(1+y^2\right) \end{pmatrix}, \begin{pmatrix} 1+x^2 \\ xy \end{pmatrix}, \begin{pmatrix} -y \\ x \end{pmatrix} \right] \in \Re^{2 \times 3} .
\tag{2}
$$

We study an effective error $E(\mathbf{e}) \equiv \min_{\{Z\}, \omega} E_{\text{LS}}(\mathbf{T}, \omega, \{Z\})$, with $\mathbf{e}$ the epipole.

Definition 1.

Define the cross–product for vectors $\mathbf{v}, \mathbf{v}' \in \Re^2$ *by* $\mathbf{v} \times \mathbf{v}' \equiv v_x v_y' - v_y v_x'$.
Define the error vector $\epsilon \in \Re^{N_p}$ *by*

$$
\epsilon_m(\mathbf{e}) \equiv \frac{\mathbf{p}_m - \mathbf{e}}{|\mathbf{p}_m - \mathbf{e}|} \times \mathbf{d}_m.
\tag{3}
$$

Define the 3 rotational contributions to ϵ, $\Psi^{(a)}(\mathbf{e}) \in \Re^{N_p}$, $a \in \{x, y, z\}$: *Let* $\Psi_m^{(a)} \equiv ((\mathbf{p}_m - \mathbf{e})/|\mathbf{p}_m - \mathbf{e}|) \times \mathbf{r}^{(a)}(\mathbf{p}_m)$ *and* $\Psi(\mathbf{e}) \equiv \left[\Psi^{(x)}, \Psi^{(y)}, \Psi^{(z)}\right] \in \Re^{N_p \times 3}$. *Define the projection* $\Pi(\mathbf{e}) \equiv \mathbf{1}_{N_p} - \Psi(\mathbf{e}) \left(\Psi^T(\mathbf{e}) \Psi(\mathbf{e})\right)^{-1} \Psi^T(\mathbf{e}) \in \Re^{N_p \times N_p}$, *where* $\mathbf{1}_{N_p}$ *denotes the* $N_p \times N_p$ *identity matrix.*

Proposition 1. *[19][20]   Assume the candidate epipole* **e** *does not coincide[1] with any image point* $\mathbf{p}_m$. *Then*

$$E\left(\mathbf{e}\right) \equiv \min_{\{Z\},\omega} E_{\mathrm{LS}}\left(\mathbf{T},\omega,\{Z\}\right) = \epsilon^T\left(\mathbf{e}\right) \varPi\left(\mathbf{e}\right) \epsilon\left(\mathbf{e}\right). \tag{4}$$

Remark 1. The definition of $\varPi\left(\mathbf{e}\right)$ shows that it cancels the rotational contributions to ϵ. Thus, for noiseless data $E\left(\cdot\right)$ does not depend on the value of the true rotation ω_{true}, and we are free to take $\omega_{\mathrm{true}} = \mathbf{0}$ in analyzing it. We do this for the rest of the paper, without loss of generality.

For noiseless images, we get a more explicit expression for $E\left(\mathbf{e}\right)$ by substituting the ground truth for the flow $\mathbf{d}_m$ into the result of **Proposition 1**:

Proposition 2. *Assume* $\forall m$, $\mathbf{e} \neq \mathbf{p}_m$, *as in Proposition 1. Then*

$$E\left(\mathbf{e}\right) = T_{\mathrm{true},z}^2 \sum_m \left(\hat{\Delta}_{m,\mathbf{e}}^{\perp} \cdot \left(Z_m^{-1}\mathbf{1}_2 - \mathbf{r}_m \varOmega\right)\left(\mathbf{e} - \mathbf{e}_{\mathrm{true}}\right)\right)^2, \tag{5}$$

with
$$\varOmega \equiv \left(\sum_n \mathbf{r}_n^T\left(\hat{\Delta}_{n,\mathbf{e}}^{\perp}\hat{\Delta}_{n,\mathbf{e}}^{\perp T}\right)\mathbf{r}_n\right)^{-1}\left(\sum_m Z_m^{-1}\mathbf{r}_m^T\left(\hat{\Delta}_{m,\mathbf{e}}^{\perp}\hat{\Delta}_{m,\mathbf{e}}^{\perp T}\right)\right) \in \Re^{3\times 2}, \tag{6}$$

and $\Delta_{m,\mathbf{e}} \equiv \mathbf{p}_m - \mathbf{e}$, $\hat{\Delta}_{m,\mathbf{e}} \equiv \left(\mathbf{p}_m - \mathbf{e}\right)/\left|\mathbf{p}_m - \mathbf{e}\right|$, $\mathbf{v}^{\perp} \equiv \left(-v_y; v_x\right)$.

Remark 2. Each summand in (5) is proportional to $\left|\mathbf{e} - \mathbf{e}_{\mathrm{true}}\right|^2$, so $E\left(\mathbf{e}\right)$ is continuous at $\mathbf{e} = \mathbf{e}_{\mathrm{true}}$. This gives a direct proof of the result of [3].

2   Forward Motion: e in or near the Image

We first analyze $E\left(\mathbf{e}\right)$ for candidate epipoles in or near the image, with $\left|\mathbf{e}\right| \overset{\sim}{<} \theta_{\mathrm{FOV}}/2$ radians, where θ_{FOV} gives the angular extent of the image points. We refer to this as the *forward region*. The true epipole is *not* constrained.

Previous results. For **e** near the image points, [18][3] show that $E\left(\mathbf{e}\right)$ typically is complex and has local minima. Also, [3] proved: $E\left(\mathbf{e}\right)$ is singular when **e** coincides with an image point and $\mathbf{e} \neq \mathbf{e}_{\mathrm{true}}$; $E\left(\mathbf{e}\right)$ is continuous at $\mathbf{e} = \mathbf{e}_{\mathrm{true}}$.

The singularity is not enough to explain the minima: The error can be singular at an image point and yet behave smoothly a short distance away (Figure 1d). To explain them, one must understand what causes the singular effects to extend far from the image points, so that effects from different points can interact.

To state this another way, the error's singularity at an image point reflects the known $\sin^2\theta$ dependence on the angle between the hypothesized epipolar direction and the observed translational flow. Thus, the singularity at the image point comes from a known property of the error around an image point and does not give a new explanation of the error's behavior around the point.

---

[1] If it does, the expression for min. $_{z\cdot,\omega} E_{\mathrm{LS}}\left(\mathbf{T},\omega,\{Z\}\right)$ must be modified slightly. Strictly, our formulas in **e** aren't valid at $T_{\mathrm{true},z} = 0$, but they are easily extended.

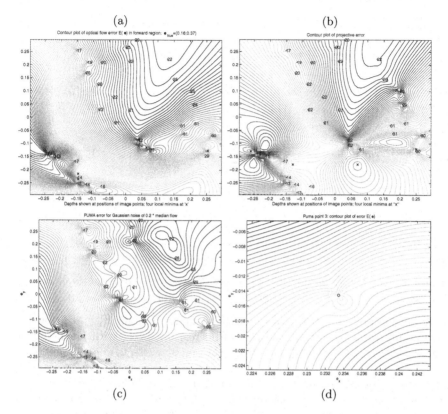

Fig. 1. Contour plot of error for **e** in the field of view. The structure comes from PUMA [12] and $\mathbf{e}_{\text{true}} = (0.16; 0.37)$. The 3D depths are shown at the image points. (a): $E(\mathbf{e})$, with 4 minima at 'x'; (b): Projective error, with 4 marked minima; (c): $E(\mathbf{e})$ for noisy images, with $\sigma_{\text{noise}} = 0.2 d_{\text{med}}$ (see Fig. 7); (d) Closeup of $E(\mathbf{e})$ around an image point, showing that the singularity quickly becomes invisible.

2.1   Forward Analysis

Remark 3. The singularity of $E(\mathbf{e})$ at an image point $\mathbf{p}_k$ causes it to have two local minima on an infinitesimal circle around the point. In a region where $E(\mathbf{e})$ behaves smoothly, it has a single minimum on an infinitesimal circle. Thus, we analyze $E(\mathbf{e})$, and its minima, on small circles centered on the image points. Let ρ_k be the radius of the circle $\mathcal{C}_k$ around $\mathbf{p}_k$. A particular limit turns out to give a useful approximation (E_{near} in Proposition 3).

Definition 2 (Near–point limit). *Define the limit* $\rho_k \xrightarrow{\text{near}} 0$ *by* $(\rho_k \longrightarrow 0, N_p \longrightarrow \infty$ *for fixed* $\rho_k N_p$ *and* $\theta_{\text{FOV}})$, *where we stipulate that image–point sums* $\sum_{m=1}^{N_p}$ *are* $\Theta(N_p)$ *as* $N_p \longrightarrow \infty$.

Remark 4. For real images, the stipulation amounts to assuming that sums over the image points have no unexpected cancellations. This holds unless the image points cluster near a line or the 3D depths have a few outliers at small depths.

Proposition 3 (E_{near}). *In the limit $\rho_k \xrightarrow{\text{near}} 0$, we have the asymptotic estimate $E(\mathbf{e}) \approx E_{\text{near}}(\mathbf{e}) + O\left(\rho_k, N_p^{-1}\right)$ on $\mathcal{C}_k$, where $E_{\text{near}}(\mathbf{e}) \equiv T_{\text{true},z}^2 \left|\mathbf{p}_k - \mathbf{e}_{\text{true}}\right|^2 \times$*

$$
\left(c N_p + (\rho_k N_p) \left(\frac{\mathbf{a}}{\left|\mathbf{p}_k - \mathbf{e}_{\text{true}}\right|} + N_p^{-1} \sum_{m \neq k} \frac{\tilde{\mathbf{a}}_m}{\left|\mathbf{p}_k - \mathbf{p}_m\right|} \right) \hat{\Delta}_{k,\mathbf{e}} - \hat{\Delta}_{k,\mathbf{e}}^T Q \hat{\Delta}_{k,\mathbf{e}} \right).
$$

$$(7)$$

The $O(1)$ $c \in \mathfrak{R}$, $\mathbf{a}, \tilde{\mathbf{a}}_m \in \mathfrak{R}^{1 \times 2}$, $Q \in \mathfrak{R}^{2 \times 2}$ don't depend on $\mathbf{e}$, $\left|\mathbf{p}_k - \mathbf{e}_{\text{true}}\right|$, $\rho_k N_p$.

We rewrite our approximation as $E_{\text{near}} = \gamma + \alpha \cos(\theta - \phi_1) + \beta \cos^2(\theta - \phi_2)$, where α, β give the linear and quadratic terms in (7), and $(\cos\theta; \sin\theta) \equiv \hat{\Delta}_{k,\mathbf{e}}$.

Lemma 1. *Let $f(\theta) \equiv a \cos^2(\theta - \phi_1) + \cos(\theta - \phi_2)$. For any values of ϕ_1, ϕ_2, the function $f(\theta)$ has one minimum for $|a| < 1/2$ and two minima for $|a| > 1$.*

Thus, the value of $|\beta/\alpha|$ determines how many minima E_{near} has on the circle $\mathcal{C}_k$ and, from Remark 3, the rate of decrease of $|\beta/\alpha|$ with ρ_k (i.e., with the distance from $\mathbf{p}_k$) determines how far the singular effects due to $\mathbf{p}_k$ extend.

Experiments. We compared E_{near} with the true error's behavior for 1200 synthetic flows generated from real structures. We measured the singularity of $E(\mathbf{e})$ on a circle by: the number of its local minima, and the ratio of its second fundamental (3rd Fourier coefficient) to its standard deviation. This second measure indicates the singularity's size. Figures 2a,b verify that all but a small fraction (3%) of the one–minimum results have $|\beta/\alpha| \leq 1$, and all but 1.7% of the two–minimum results have $|\beta/\alpha| \geq 1/2$. Figure 2c shows that the "size" of the singularity grows roughly linearly with $|\beta/\alpha|$ until it saturates. These results demonstrate that our analysis predicts the error's behavior very well.

One can use E_{near} to understand the factors causing the error's complexity [17]. Figure 3 confirms our predictions from (7): the error behaves smoothly near image points close to $\mathbf{e}_{\text{true}}$ (Fig. 3a), and is more likely to have a complex behavior near an isolated image point (Fig. 3b) or one with extreme 3D depth (Fig. 3c). Also, experiments show that the fraction of "singular" results decreases roughly like $N_p^{0.5}$, and the size of the singular fluctuations in the error decreases roughly like N_p^{-1}, in agreement with the behavior of $|\beta/\alpha|$, see [17].

3 Sideways Motion: $|\mathbf{e}| > \theta_{\text{FOV}}/2$

Preliminaries. Define $A \equiv T_{\text{true},z}(\hat{\mathbf{e}} \times \mathbf{e}_{\text{true}})$, $B \equiv T_{\text{true},z}(1 - \hat{\mathbf{e}} \cdot \mathbf{e}_{\text{true}}/|\mathbf{e}|)$, with $\hat{\mathbf{e}} \equiv \mathbf{e}/|\mathbf{e}|$. The A, B capture all dependence on the true translation $\mathbf{T}_{\text{true}}$.

It is convenient to use an image coordinate system that rotates around the image center with the candidate epipole $\mathbf{e}$ such that $\mathbf{e} = \left(|\mathbf{e}|; 0\right)$.

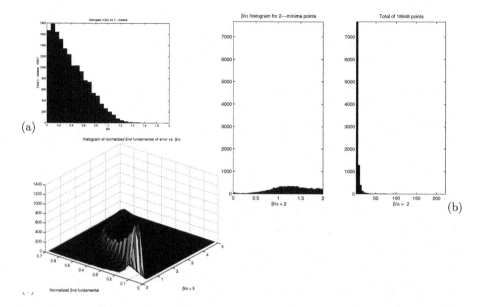

Fig. 2. Histograms of two measures of the complexity of $E(\mathbf{e})$. (a) $|\beta/\alpha|$, one minimum results; (b) Two minima results, separately for $|\beta/\alpha| < 2$ and $|\beta/\alpha| > 2$. (c) Normalized second fundamental of $E(\mathbf{e})$ for $|\beta/\alpha| < 5$.

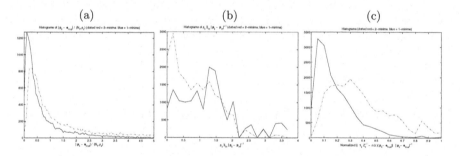

Fig. 3. Histograms, plotted separately for circles $\mathcal{C}_k$ where $E(\mathbf{e})$ had two minima (dotted curves) and one minimum. (a) Epipolar–distance ratio $(N_p\rho_k)^{\cdot\,-1}|\mathbf{p}_k - \mathbf{e}_{\text{true}}|$; (b) Isolation measure $\rho_k \sum_{m\neq k} |\mathbf{p}_m - \mathbf{p}_k|^{\cdot\,-1}$; (c) 3D depth ratio $|\mathcal{Z}_k \hat{\mathbf{d}}_{\text{true}}|/\max_m |\mathcal{Z}_m \hat{\mathbf{d}}_{\text{true}}|$, where $\mathcal{Z}_k \equiv (Z_k^{\cdot\,-1}\mathbf{1}_2 - \mathbf{r}_k\Omega)$ and $\hat{\mathbf{d}}_{\text{true}} \equiv (\mathbf{p}_k - \mathbf{e}_{\text{true}})/|\mathbf{p}_k - \mathbf{e}_{\text{true}}|$.

We represent the inverse depths Z_m^{-1} as a sum of a *linear component* and a *nonlinear component*. We write $Z_m^{-1} \equiv n_z + n_x x_m + n_y y_m + Z_{\text{NL},m}^{-1}$, where $Z_{\text{NL},m}^{-1}$ is the nonlinear and $Z_{L,m}^{-1} \equiv n_z + n_x x_m + n_y y_m$ is the linear component of the structure, and where we define these components uniquely from

$$0 = \sum_m Z_{\text{NL},m}^{-1} = \sum_m x_m Z_{\text{NL},m}^{-1} = \sum_m y_m Z_{\text{NL},m}^{-1}. \tag{8}$$

We refer to $\mathbf{n} \equiv (n_x; n_y; n_z)$ above as the *planar normal*, since $Z_m^{-1} = n_z + n_x x_m + n_y y_m$ for a planar scene neglecting noise. We define the *planar epipole* $\underline{\mathbf{n}} \equiv (n_x; n_y)/n_z$ by analogy with the epipole $\mathbf{e}$, and $\tilde{n}_z \equiv n_z - n_x/|\mathbf{e}|$.

Definition 3 (Limit of zero field of view (FOV)). *Let θ_{FOV} be the angular extent of the region spanned by the image points. We define the zero–FOV limit by writing the image points as $\mathbf{p}_m = \lambda_{\text{FOV}} \mathbf{p}_m^*$ and taking $\lambda_{\text{FOV}} \longrightarrow 0$ keeping the $\mathbf{p}_m^*$ and Z_m^{-1} fixed. We denote the limit by $\theta_{\text{FOV}} \longrightarrow 0$ or $\lambda_{\text{FOV}} \longrightarrow 0$.*

The classical result is on the bas–relief ambiguity [7][14][15].

Theorem 1 (Jepson/Heeger/Maybank (JHM)). *Assume the image points do not lie on a line, and that $\mathbf{e}$ is finite and $|\mathbf{e}| > 0$. In the limit of zero field of view, the noiseless least–squares error for infinitesimal motion is given by* $E(\mathbf{e}) = T_{\text{true},z}^2 (\hat{\mathbf{e}} \times \mathbf{e}_{\text{true}})^2 \sum_{m=1}^{N_p} Z_{\text{NL},m}^{-2}.$

Remark 5 (Limitations of the JHM Theorem).

The JHM result models the error only for $\theta_{\text{FOV}}^{-1} \gg |\mathbf{e}| \gg \theta_{\text{FOV}}$ and does not capture any of the error's dependence on $e \equiv |\mathbf{e}|$ (it cannot be used to analyze the minima); It gives no information about the error on the line $\mathbf{e} = t\mathbf{e}_{\text{true}}$, $t \in (-\infty, \infty)$—despite the fact that the true epipole lies on it; It says nothing about the error for $|\mathbf{e}_{\text{true}}| \sim O(\theta_{\text{FOV}})$; It says nothing about the error for planar scenes or the effect on E from the linear scene component, which is always important.

3.1   New Analysis

Definition 4 (Sideways limit). *The sideways limit $e \overset{sideways}{\longrightarrow} \infty$ is defined by*

$$\left(\lambda_{\text{FOV}} \longrightarrow 0, e \longrightarrow \infty \text{ for fixed } \kappa \equiv e\lambda_{\text{FOV}}, \mathbf{p}_m^*, A, B, \tilde{n}_z, n_y, Z_{\text{NL},m}^{-1} \right),$$

where the zero–FOV limit $\lambda_{\text{FOV}} \longrightarrow 0$ and the $\mathbf{p}_m^*$ are given in Definition 3.

Theorem 2 (Main Theorem). *The approximation $E_{\text{side}}(\mathbf{e})$ in (13) gives an asymptotic estimate of E in the sideways limit:*

$$E(\mathbf{e}) - E_{\text{side}}(\mathbf{e}) = O(E/e) \quad \left(e \overset{sideways}{\longrightarrow} \infty \right). \tag{9}$$

Remark 6. The sideways limit fixes $\tilde{n}$ and $B \equiv T_{\text{true},z}(1 - e_{\text{true},x}/e)$ which depend on e. We do this since we want $E_{\text{side}}(\mathbf{e})$ to remain a good approximation when $|\underline{\mathbf{n}}|$ and $|\mathbf{e}_{\text{true}}|$ are as large as e, and since this simplifies our approximation and makes it display the two–fold ambiguity of SFM for planes [14].

To derive $E_{\text{side}}(\mathbf{e})$, we neglect effects suppressed by factors of θ_{FOV} and $\theta_{\text{FOV}}/|\mathbf{e}|$. First, we must "pre-subtract" the leading rotational contribution from ϵ in (3). This is necessary since $E(\cdot)$ is given by a subtraction of two terms (due to the rotation cancellation from Π) and we need to ensure that its leading dependence comes from the leading dependencies of the individual terms. After this "pre–subtraction," Π must be replaced by $\Pi_\perp$, where the latter annihilates the remaining subspace of rotational contributions. Define

$$L_\Pi^{a,b} \equiv \left\{ \frac{e}{|\mathbf{p}-\mathbf{e}|} (y^a - \langle y^a \rangle) \right\}^T \Pi_\perp^{(\text{side})} \left\{ \frac{e}{|\mathbf{p}-\mathbf{e}|} (y^b - \langle y^b \rangle) \right\}, \qquad (10)$$

$$Z_\Pi^{a,b} \equiv \left\{ \frac{e}{|\mathbf{p}-\mathbf{e}|} y^a Z_{\text{NL}}^{-1} \right\}^T \Pi_\perp^{(\text{side})} \left\{ \frac{e}{|\mathbf{p}-\mathbf{e}|} (y^b - \langle y^b \rangle) \right\}, \qquad (11)$$

$$\tilde{Z}_\Pi^{a,b} \equiv \left\{ \frac{e}{|\mathbf{p}-\mathbf{e}|} y^a Z_{\text{NL}}^{-1} \right\}^T \Pi_\perp^{(\text{side})} \left\{ \frac{e}{|\mathbf{p}-\mathbf{e}|} y^b Z_{\text{NL}}^{-1} \right\}, \qquad (12)$$

where $\Pi_\perp^{(\text{side})}$ equals $\Pi_\perp$ evaluated in the sideways limit, $\{V\}$ denotes a vector in $\Re^{N_P}$ with entries V_m, $\alpha \equiv An_y - B\tilde{n}_z$, $\beta \equiv Bn_y + A\tilde{n}_z$. Then

$$E_{\text{side}} \equiv \alpha^2 L_\Pi^{(1,1)} + \beta^2 L_\Pi^{(2,2)} - 2\alpha\beta L_\Pi^{(1,2)} \qquad (13)$$
$$-2A\beta Z_\Pi^{(0,2)} + 2A\alpha Z_\Pi^{(0,1)} + 2B\beta Z_\Pi^{(1,2)} - 2B\alpha Z_\Pi^{(1,1)}$$
$$+A^2 \tilde{Z}_\Pi^{(0,0)} + B^2 \tilde{Z}_\Pi^{(1,1)} - 2AB\tilde{Z}_\Pi^{(1,0)}.$$

[17] gives explicit formulas for the $L_\Pi^{a,b}$, $Z_\Pi^{a,b}$, and $\tilde{Z}_\Pi^{a,b}$ in terms of the image and structure moments

$$\mu_{a,b} \equiv e^2 \sum_m x_m^a y_m^b / |\mathbf{p}_m - \mathbf{e}|^2, \qquad \sigma_{a,b} \equiv e^2 \sum_m Z_{\text{NL},m}^{-1} x_m^a y_m^b / |\mathbf{p}_m - \mathbf{e}|^2,$$

$$S_{a,b} \equiv e^2 \sum_m \left(x_m^a y_m^b Z_{\text{NL},m}^{-2} \right) / |\mathbf{p}_m - \mathbf{e}|^2.$$

Discussion. Our result nicely separates the dependencies on the various parameters. For example, E_{side} depends on $\mathbf{e}_{\text{true}}$ only through the quantities A and B. It depends on e just through B, $\tilde{n}_z$, and the dot products $L_\Pi^{a,b}$, $Z_\Pi^{a,b}$, and $\tilde{Z}_\Pi^{a,b}$, where the first two are linear in e^{-1} and the dot products can be approximated by simple ratios of quadratic expressions in e. One can easily read off from our formulas which contributions dominate at small FOV. For planar scenes (or the linear scene contribution), all the structure/motion unknowns appear in the leading factors; the $L_\Pi^{a,b}$ depend only on the known image coordinates. E_{side} can be shown to respect the planar two–fold ambiguity.

Our result depends on the nonlinear part of the scene through the structure moments $\sigma_{a,b}$, for $2 \le a+b \le 3$, and on $S_{c,d}$. Thus, the error's dependence on the scene can be approximated using 15 parameters to describe the scene. Just 6 are usually enough. Our expression for E_{side} often simplifies dramatically. This is because our approximation works for many types of scenes and motions, and we can often neglect most of the terms for a particular scene/motion.

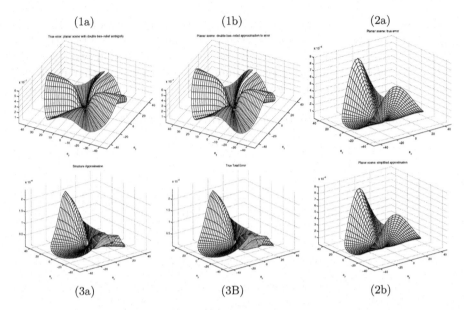

Fig. 4. Sideways error. (1): Planar example with double bas–relief ambiguity, $\mathbf{e}_{\text{true}} = (-6.9; 7.2)$ $\underline{\mathbf{n}} = (0.62; 0.64)$; (2): Planar example showing lack of minima, $\mathbf{e}_{\text{true}} = (-0.69; 0.72)$ $\underline{\mathbf{n}} = (0.81; 0.74)$; (3): Rocket structure [5], $\mathbf{e}_{\text{true}} = (-0.14; -0.045)$. (a): True $E(\mathbf{e})$; (b): Simple planar approximation $\alpha^2 L_\Pi^{(1,1)}$; (3B): Simple approx. (15).

3.2 Some Examples of Consequences

Planar Scene, Non–forward true motion; large planar slant. Assume an image pair with $\theta_{\text{FOV}} \ll 1$ (small FOV), $|\mathbf{e}_{\text{true}}| \gg 1$ (sideways true motion), and $|\underline{\mathbf{n}}| \equiv |(n_x; n_y)/n_z| \gg 1$ (large slant). We assume $e \gg 1$, excluding $e < |\mathbf{e}_{\text{true}}|$ and $e < |\underline{\mathbf{n}}|$ (large–e assumption). Then $E(\mathbf{e}) \approx \alpha^2 L_\Pi^{(1,1)}$, where $\alpha^2 \approx T_{\text{true},z}^2 (\hat{\mathbf{e}} \times \mathbf{e}_{\text{true}})^2 (\hat{\mathbf{e}} \times \underline{\mathbf{n}})^2$ and $L_\Pi^{(1,1)}$ is roughly constant. The error is small on two lines—a *double* bas–relief ambiguity. Figure 4(1) illustrates this new effect.

Planar Scene, Non–sideways true motion; small planar slant. Assume $\theta_{\text{FOV}} \ll 1$ (small FOV), $1 \ll e$ (large e), $|\mathbf{e}_{\text{true}}| \ll 1$ (forward true motion), and $|\underline{\mathbf{n}}| \ll 1$ (small slant). Under these conditions, our approximation has no false local minima in a region $e \geq e_{\text{thresh}}$, where $e_{\text{thresh}} \sim O(1)$.

One can show that the derivative with respect to e of our asymptotic estimate gives an asymptotic estimate of the derivative of $E(\mathbf{e})$. Thus, in the sideways limit $E(\mathbf{e})$ has no false local minima for sufficiently large e. Figure 4(2) shows an example, comparing the true error to our simple approximation above.

Symmetry. The image moments $\mu_{a,b}$ divide into two categories: the *even* moments, such as $\mu_{2,0}$, $\mu_{0,2}$, $\mu_{2,2}$, that involve sums over even powers and nonnegative terms only, and the *odd* moments. For randomly distributed image points, the odd $\mu_{a,b}$ are suppressed by roughly $1/\sqrt{N_p}$ compared to the even $\mu_{a,b}$.

With many correspondences, the image usually has some rotational symmetry and we can neglect the odd $\mu_{a,b}$ to a good approximation. Then, $E \approx E_{\text{side}}$

$$\approx \alpha^2 \frac{e^2 \mu_{0,2} \mu_{2,2}}{e^2 \mu_{2,2} + \mu_{0,2}} + \beta^2 \left(\mu_{0,4} - \frac{\mu_{0,2}^2}{N_p} \right) \tag{14}$$

$$- 2A \left(\beta \sigma_{0,2} + \alpha \frac{e\mu_{0,2}}{e^2 \mu_{2,2} + \mu_{0,2}} \sigma_{1,1} \right) + 2B \left(\beta \sigma_{0,3} - \alpha \frac{e^2 \mu_{2,2} \sigma_{0,2} - e\mu_{0,2} \sigma_{1,2}}{e^2 \mu_{2,2} + \mu_{0,2}} \right)$$

$$+ A^2 S_{0,0} + B^2 S_{0,2} - 2ABS_{0,1} - \frac{(Ae\sigma_{1,1} - B(e\sigma_{1,2} + \sigma_{0,2}))^2}{e^2 \mu_{2,2} + \mu_{0,2}} - B^2 \frac{\sigma_{1,1}^2}{\mu_{2,0}}.$$

Also, symmetry makes the even $\mu_{a,b}$ depend weakly on the epipolar direction $\hat{\mathbf{e}}$ [17], which give a further simplification.

In the same way as for the $\mu_{a,b}$, we can estimate the relative sizes of the structure–dependent moments $S_{0,a}$ and $\sigma_{a,b}$. All the $\sigma_{a,b}$ will be small, for any direction $\hat{\mathbf{e}}$, if the Z_{NL}^{-1} have no good approximation in terms of a cubic polynomial (*noncubic condition*). Also, [17] argues that the mixed terms combining the nonlinear and linear structure components can often be neglected. Assuming this and the noncubic condition, we get the simple estimate

$$E(\mathbf{e}) \approx E_{\text{side}}(\mathbf{e}) \approx \alpha^2 L_{\Pi}^{(1,1)} + \beta^2 L_{\Pi}^{(2,2)} - 2\alpha\beta L_{\Pi}^{(2,1)} + A^2 S_{0,0} + B^2 S_{0,2}. \tag{15}$$

Our experiments show that (15) accurately describes the error for our sequences.

In addition to the conclusions above, [17] uses our estimate to generalize the JHM theorem [7][14] and to extend the results of [18] to planar scenes.

Experiments. We tested E_{side} against the true error, using synthetic structures and structures extracted from five real sequences (PUMA[12], Rocket [5], CMU CASTLE, and two of our indoor sequences). We show only a few results.

Figure 5 compares $E(\mathbf{e})$ to our simplest approximation (15), which has slight problems only for the PUMA example. Figure 5 also shows E_{side} for this example; it is indistinguishable from the true error. For the Rocket structure, we compared the global minimum positions for the true error, E_{side}, and (15). Within measurement error, they were identical. Fig. 6(1,2) shows that our symmetry–based approximation (14) gives good results with just 192 and 132 image points.

4   Projective Geometry

Suppose one fixes the camera matrix for image 1 to be $(\mathbf{1}_3, \mathbf{0}_3)$. The projective transforms that leave this camera matrix unaltered change the structure by adding an arbitrary plane to it or scaling it [16]. The real projective ambiguity is just this freedom to scale or add a plane. Since scenes that differ only in their planar component are equivalent in projective geometry, the linear component $Z_{\text{L},m}^{-1}$ of the scene cannot make a contribution to the least–squares error. In effect, only the nonlinear terms contribute to E_{side}.

(1a)   (1b)   (2a)

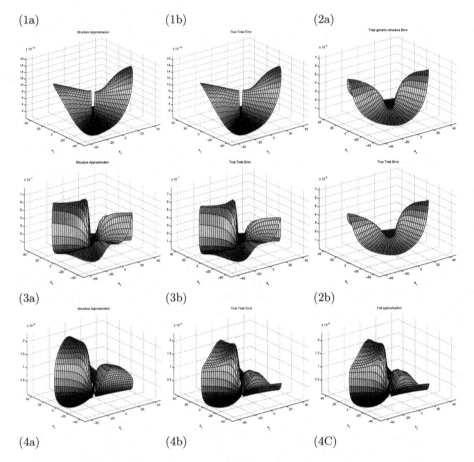

(4a)   (4b)   (4C)

Fig. 5. (1): CMU Castle, $\mathbf{e}_{\text{true}} = (5.78; 8.16)$; (2): Indoor 1, $\mathbf{e}_{\text{true}} = (0.11; 0.16)$; (3): Indoor 2, $\mathbf{e}_{\text{true}} = (-0.125; -1.49)$; (4): PUMA, $\mathbf{e}_{\text{true}} = (10; -.025)$. (a): Simplified approximation (15); (b): True error; (C): E_{side}.

[17] shows this directly. For projective SFM and infinitesimal motion, one can define a projective error $E_{\text{proj}}(\mathbf{e}) \equiv \epsilon^T \Pi_{\text{proj}} \epsilon$ as for the Euclidean case, where ϵ is the same as in (3). The same arguments as before give a sideways asymptotic estimate: $E_{\text{proj}}(\mathbf{e}) \approx A^2 \{Z_{\text{NL}}\}^T \Pi_{\perp\text{proj}} \{Z_{\text{NL}}\}$

$$-2AB \{Z_{\text{NL}}\}^T \Pi_{\perp\text{proj}} \{yZ_{\text{NL}}\} + B^2 \{yZ_{\text{NL}}\}^T \Pi_{\text{proj}} \{yZ_{\text{NL}}\}. \qquad (16)$$

Thus, the error for projective SFM is simpler than the Euclidean error. This simplicity comes at a cost [18]. At large e, one can show that the projective error on the line $\mathbf{e} = t\mathbf{e}_{\text{true}}$ has no quadratic growth with e as in the Euclidean error. This implies that the projective error gives less information to estimate the epipole. Figure 6(3B) compares the Euclidean and projective errors for the same image pair.

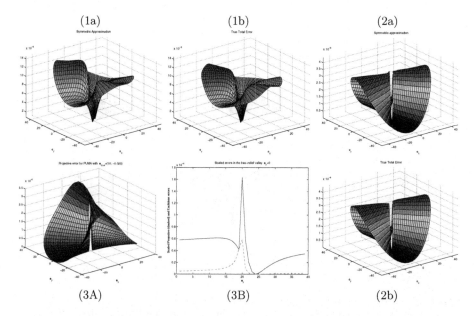

Fig. 6. (1): Extended PUMA sequence, $\mathbf{e}_{\text{true}} = (0.13; -0.08)$; (2): Extended Rocket, $\mathbf{e}_{\text{true}} = (-1.0; -3.9)$; (3): Projective error for PUMA, same images as in Figure 5(4). (a): Approximation (14); (b): True error; (3A): True projective error; (3B): Projective (dashed) and Euclidean errors on the line $e_y = 0$, the "bas–relief valley" in (3A).

In the forward region, the projective analysis is similar to the Euclidean one. Experiments confirm that the results are also similar, see Figure 1.

5   Noise

We report experiments on *noisy* images. We ran a standard two–image algorithm to estimate the structure/motion and used the result to compute E_{side}.[2] E_{side} continues to model the true error well, despite our using a larger than normal noise. The noise is large enough that our two–image routine usually returns bad $\mathbf{T}$ estimates and the noisy error looks quite different from the noiseless one.

For noisy images, we cannot assume without loss of generality that the true rotation is zero. Fortunately, rotation has a small effect on the error [18][25].

We have not studied the forward noisy error carefully, but experiments (e.g., Figure 1) indicate that noise increases its complexity, as might be expected [17].

6   Conclusion

We studied the least–squares error for infinitesimal motion, giving two simple asymptotic estimates of the error which capture its detailed behavior over the

---

[2] Our rationale is that the error depends on the observed flow, which is modelled better by the estimated structure and motion than by the ground truth.

(1a)   (1b)   (1c)

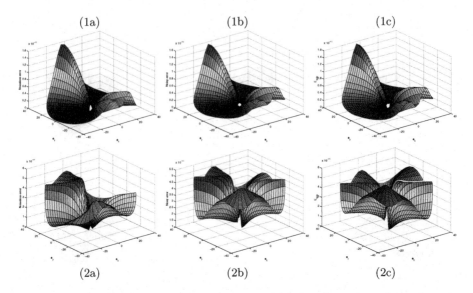

(2a)   (2b)   (2c)

Fig. 7. Noise results. σ_{noise} gives the noise standard deviation, d_{med} the median size of the true flow, and θ_{Terr} the angular error in in the initial $\mathbf{T}$ estimate. (1): Rocket, $\mathbf{e}_{\text{true}} = (-0.01; -0.05)$, $\sigma_{\text{noise}} = 0.4d_{\text{med}}$, $\theta_{\text{Terr}} = 77°$. (2): PUMA, $\mathbf{e}_{\text{true}} = (0.5; -0.2)$, $\sigma_{\text{noise}} = 0.3d_{\text{med}}$, $\theta_{\text{Terr}} = 38°$. (a) Noiseless error; (b) True noisy error; (c) E_{side}.

entire range of motions. We illustrated the use of these estimates by deriving new error properties.

For roughly forward translation estimates, we showed by theory and experiment that the error tends to be complex for candidate epipoles near image points, and that this is more likely when: the true epipole is far from the point; and/or the point is isolated in the image; and/or the corresponding 3D depth is small; and/or the number of image points is small. Our experiments show that the complexity near image points produces local minima, confirming [3][18]. We pointed out that the previous arguments of [3][18] do not explain the error's complexity or local minima.

For non–forward translation estimates, we gave a simple model of the error for planar scenes. For two special cases, we derived a new double bas–relief ambiguity and proved the absence of local minima at large $|\mathbf{e}|$. For nonplanar scenes, we simplified our approximations under various assumptions, including rough rotational symmetry of the image and a reasonably "generic" distribution of 3D depths. Our simplest approximation gives a good model of the least–squares error in all our noiseless experiments. We analyzed the error for projective SFM, pointing out that it is flatter than the Euclidean error, and showed by experiments that our analysis remains useful for noisy images.

We believe that our results will lead to an in–depth understanding of the least–squares error. For example, our sideways asymptotic estimate depends on just 29 parameters, and often 13 are enough. This suggests that a semi–

exhaustive search through the space of least–squares errors may be feasible to determine the pitfalls that algorithms could encounter.

References

1. G. Adiv, "Inherent ambiguities in recovering 3-D motion and structure from a noisy flow field," **PAMI** 11, 477-489, 1989.
2. P. Belhumeur, D. Kriegman, and A. Yuille "The Bas–Relief Ambiguity," **IJCV** 35:1, 33–44, 1999.
3. A. Chiuso, R. Brockett, and S. Soatto, "Optimal Structure from Motion: Local Ambiguities and Global Estimates," **IJCV** 39: 3, 95-228, 2000.
4. K. Daniilidis and H.H. Nagel, "Analytical results on error sensitivity of motion estimation from two views," **IVC** 8 297–303, 1990.
5. R. Dutta, R. Manmatha, L. R. Williams, and E. M. Riseman, "A data set for quantitative motion analysis," *CVPR*, 159-164, 1989.
6. C. Fermüller, Y. Aloimonos, "Observability of 3D Motion," **IJCV** 37:1, 43–63, 2000.
7. A. D. Jepson and D. J. Heeger, "Subspace methods for recovering rigid motion II: Theory," U. of Toronto TR RBCV-TR-90-36, 1990.
8. R. Hartley and A. Zisserman, "Multiple View Geometry in Computer Vision," Cambridge, 2000.
9. J. Hornegger, C. Tomasi, "Representation Issues in the ML Estimation of Camera Motion," **ICCV** 640–647, 1999.
10. K. Kanatani, *Geometric Computation for Machine Vision*, Oxford, 1993.
11. J. J. Koenderink and A. J. Van Doorn, "Affine structure from motion," **JOSA** 8:2 377–385, 1991.
12. R. Kumar and A. R. Hanson, "Sensitivity of the Pose Refinement Problem to Accurate Estimation of Camera Parameters," *ICCV*, 365-369, 1990.
13. Y. Ma, J. Kosecka, and S. Sastry, "Optimization criteria and geometric algorithnms for motion and structure estimation," **IJCV** 44:3, 219–249, 2001.
14. S. Maybank, *Theory of Reconstruction from Image Motion*, Springer, Berlin, 1993.
15. S. Maybank, "A Theoretical Study of Optical Flow," Doctoral Dissertation, University of London, 1987.
16. J. Oliensis and Y. Genc, "Fast and Accurate Algorithms for Projective Multi–Image Structure from Motion," **PAMI** 23:6 546–559, 2001.
17. J. Oliensis, "The Least–Squares Error for Structure from Infinitesimal Motion," **IJCV**, to appear.
18. J. Oliensis, "A New Structure from Motion Ambiguity," **PAMI** 22:7, 685–700, 2000 and *CVPR* 185–191, 1999.
19. J. Oliensis, "Computing the Camera Heading from Multiple Frames," *CVPR* 203–210, 1998.
20. S. Soatto and R. Brocket, "Optimal Structure from Motion: Local Ambiguities and Global Estimates," *CVPR* 282–288, 1998.
21. S. Soatto and P. Perona, "Recursive 3-D Visual Motion Estimation Using Subspace Constraints," **IJCV** 22:3 235–259, 1997.
22. M. Spetsakis and Y. Aloimonos, "Optimal visual motion estimation: a note," **PAMI** 14:959–964.
23. R. Szeliski and S.B. Kang, "Shape ambiguities in structure from motion," **PAMI** 19 506–512, 1997.

24. B. Triggs, P. McLauchlan, R. Hartley, and A. Fitzgibbon, "Bundle Adjustment—A Modern Synthesis," *Workshop on Vision Algorithms: Theory and Practice* 298–372, 1999.
25. T. Y. Tian, C. Tomasi, and D. J. Heeger, "Comparison of Approaches to Egomotion Computation" *CVPR*, 315–320, 1996.
26. C. Tomasi and J. Shi, "Direction of Heading from Image Deformations," *CVPR* 422–427, 1993.
27. T. Xiang; L.-F.Cheong, "Understanding the Behavior of SFM Algorithms: A Geometric Approach" **IJCV** 51(2): 111-137; 2003
28. Weng, J., Huang, T.S., and Ahuja, N., "Motion and Structure from Two Perspective Views: Algorithms, Error Analysis, and Error Estimation," **PAMI** 11:5, 451-476, 1989.

Stereo Based 3D Tracking and Scene Learning, Employing Particle Filtering within EM

Trausti Kristjansson, Hagai Attias, and John Hershey

Microsoft Research
One Microsoft Way, Redmond 98052, USA
{traustik,hagaia,hershey}@microsoft.com
http://www.research.microsoft.com/users/traustik

Abstract. We present a generative probabilistic model for 3D scenes with stereo views. With this model, we track an object in 3 dimensions while simultaneously learning its appearance and the appearance of the background. By using a generative model for the scene, we are able to aggregate evidence over time. In addition, the probabilistic model naturally handles sources of variability.

For inference and learning in the model, we formulate an Expectation Maximization (EM) algorithm where Rao-Blackwellized Particle filtering is used in the E step. The use of stereo views of the scene is a strong source of disambiguating evidence and allows rapid convergence of the algorithm. The update equations have an appealing form and as a side result, we give a generative probabilistic interpretation for the Sum of Squared Differences (SSD) metric known from the field of Stereo Vision.

1 Introduction

We introduce a generative, top-down viewpoint for tracking and scene learning. We assume that a scene is composed of a moving object in front of a background. The scene model is shown in Figure 1(a). Within this paradigm, we can simultaneously learn the appearance of the background and the object, while the object moves in 3 dimension within the scene.

The algorithm is based on a probabilistic generative modelling approach. Such a model describes the scene components and the process by which they generate the observed data. Being probabilistic, the model can naturally describe the different sources of variability in the data. This approach provides a framework for learning and tracking, via the EM algorithm associated with the generative model. In the E-step, object position is inferred and sufficient statistics are computed; in the M-step, model parameters, including object and background appearances, are updated.

Sensor fusion is another important advantage of the probabilistic generative modelling approach. Whereas a bottom-up approach would process the signal from each camera separately, then combine them into an estimate of the object position, our approach processes the camera signals jointly and in a systematic fashion that derives from the model.

The use of a stereo view of the scene turns out to be of significant value over the use of a monocular view. It allows the algorithm to locate and track an object, even

T. Pajdla and J. Matas (Eds.): ECCV 2004, LNCS 3024, pp. 546–559, 2004.

when the prior model of the object appearance is uninformative e.g. when initialized to random values. As a consequence, only a small number of EM iterations are required for convergence.

In section 2 we discuss prior work and relate it to the current work. In section 3, we introduce the scene model. When the object moves within the scene, the connectivity of the graphical model for the scene changes. The connectivity is dictated by the geometry of the scene and is captured by the coordinate transformations that are discussed in section 4. In section 5 we discuss the Generalized EM algorithm, emphasizing the intuitive interpretation of the update equations of the E-step. Section 5.1 discusses the combination of EM and particle filtering for inferring the location and learning appearances. Results for a video sequence are given in section 6.

2   Related Work

The work presented here can be viewed as drawing on and bridging the fields of 3D tracking[1,2], stereo vision[3] and 2-D scene modelling[4]. We briefly review related work in these fields and relate and contrast with the current work.

Tracking an object in tree dimensions is useful for a variety of applications [5,6] ranging from robot navigation to human computer interfaces. Most tracking methods rely on a model of the object to be tracked. Object models are usually constructed by hand [7,1,2]. For example, Schodl et al. [2] use a textured 3D polygonal model and use gradient descent in a cost function.

Our model is similar to these methods in that we use an appearance map of the object, and track it in 3 dimensions. These methods rely on strong prior models in order to do tracking from a monocular view. As we use a stereo view of the scene, our method does not require prior hand construction of the model of the object, e.g. the face, and we are able to learn a model. Once a model has been learned, one can track the object using only a monocular view.

The objective of most stereo vision work has been to extract a depth map for an image. The evidence is in the form disparity between pixels in two or more views of the same scene [3,8,9]. Most stereo vision methods calculate a disparity cost based on this evidence, such as Sum of Squared Differences (SSD)[10]. In section 5.3 we offer a generative probabilistic interpretation for SSD.

Frey and Jojic [4,11], and Dellaert et al.[12] use generative top-down models. They use layered 2D models, and learn 2D templates for objects that move across a background[13]. When using a monocular view from a single camera, learning the appearance of objects that can occlude each other is a hard problem. By incorporate stereo views of a scene, we can resolve the identifiability problem inherent with using a single camera and can more easily track an object in 3 dimensions.

Recently, a great deal of attention has been paid to particle filtering in various guises. Blake et al.[14,15] use models based on tracking spline outlines of objects[16]. Other researchers have extended this to appearance based models [17]. As with the tracking methods discussed before, the models are usually constructed by hand rather than learned.

We use Rao-Blackwellized[18] particle filtering to track the position and orientation of an object within a scene. In Rao Blackwellized particle filtering, the model contains random variables represented by parametric distributions as well as sampled random variables represented as particle sets. When performing inference over the sampled random variable, one must integrate over the parametric random variables.

We extend the standard Particle Filtering[14] paradigm in two ways. First, we use particle filtering in conjunction with stereo observations to track an object in 3 dimensions. Secondly, unlike most tracking paradigms, we are also able to learn the appearance of the objects in the scene, as they move in the scene [19,18]. We believe this is the first demonstration of this algorithm for real data.

3   The Stereo Scene Model

The scene model is shown if Figure 1(a). The figure shows a background, a "cardboard cutout" object in front of the background that occludes part of it and two cameras. Figure 1(b) shows the equivalent graphical model. We assume that the object will be seen at different locations in the two cameras due to stereo disparity and that the cameras are aligned such that the same background image is seen in both cameras.

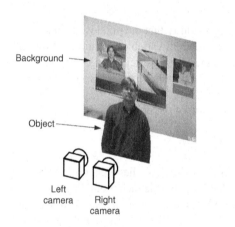
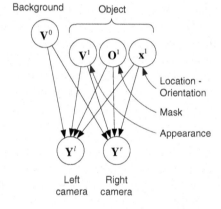

(a) Scene with stereo cameras.   (b) Generative model for stereo observations.

Fig. 1. (a)Schematic of scene with stereo cameras. (b) Generative model for stereo observations of a scene with a single object that partially occludes and a background.

In this graph, V^0 is the background image, V^1 is the object, O^1 is the transparency mask of the object, x^1 is a vector containing the position and orientation of the object, Y^l is the observed image in the left camera and Y^r is the observed image in the right camera.

The position variable x^1 is a continuous random variable which contains at least 3 spacial coordinates of the object, allowing for 3D translation within the scene.

We use multivariate Gaussians with diagonal covariance matrices to model all appearances. Hence, the appearance model of the background is

$$p(\mathbf{V}^0) = \prod_j N(v_j^0; \mu_j^0, \eta_j^0), \tag{1}$$

where v_j^0 is the value of pixel j, μ_j^0 is the mean, and η_j^0 is the precision.

The model for the object contains three components: a template, a transparency mask and a position. Again, the appearance is modelled by a multivariate Gaussian with diagonal covariance matrix,

$$p(\mathbf{V}^1) = \prod_i N(v_i^1; \mu_i^1, \eta_i^1) \tag{2}$$

where v_i^1 is the value of pixel i, μ_i^1 is the mean, and η_i^1 is the precision.

Pixels in the object model can be opaque or transparent. We use discrete mixing, i.e. a pixel is either completely opaque or transparent. The prior distribution is

$$p(\mathbf{O}^1) = \prod_i \left[\alpha_i o_i + (1 - \alpha_i)(1 - o_i) \right]. \tag{3}$$

where o_i is the value of pixel i and α_i is the probability that the pixel is opaque.

The distribution for the position/orientation random variable, is handled differently from other variables in the model. It is represented by a particle set. A particle set is a set of vectors $\{x_s\}$ where each vector (also called a particle) represents a position of the object and each particle is associated with a weight $\{q(x_s)\}$.

We use a Gaussian for the prior for the position of the object

$$p(\mathbf{x}^1) = N(\mathbf{x}^1; \mu_x, \eta_x) \tag{4}$$

where μ_x is the mean and η_x is the precision. This is used when generating the initial set of particles and for recovering particles that land outside the a bounding volume.

When generating instances of the left and right camera images, we first sample from the background model, then we choose a position for the object and sample from the object appearance model. The appearance of the object is then overlayed on the background, for pixels where the object is opaque. For example, the value of the j-th pixel y_j^l in in the left image $\mathbf{Y}^l$ is

$$y_j^l = o_{\xi(x,j)}^1 \cdot v_{\xi(x,j)}^1 + (1 - o_{\xi(x,j)}^1) \cdot v_j^0 + \varepsilon^l \tag{5}$$

In words, pixel y_j^l takes the value of the object pixel $v_{\xi(j)}^1$ if it is opaque (i.e. $o_{\xi(j)}^1 = 1$) or the value of the background v_j^0 if it is transparent. Finally we add Gaussian pixel noise ε^l with precision λ. Pixels in the right image are of course found similarly. The function $\xi(x, j)$ maps coordinates depending in the position of the object, and will be discussed in the next section. If we assume all variances are zero, the process of generating from this model is analogous to rendering the scene using standard computer graphics methods.

The prior distribution for a pixel in the left image y_j^l is

$$p(y_j^l | \mathbf{V}^0, \mathbf{V}^1, \mathbf{O}^1, \mathbf{x}) = \begin{cases} N(y_j^l; v_{\xi(x,j)}^1, \lambda) & \text{if } o_{\xi(x,j)}^1 = 1 \\ N(y_j^l; v_j^0, \lambda) & \text{if } o_{\xi(x,j)}^1 = 0 \end{cases} \quad (6)$$

The complete probability distribution for the sensor images is the product of the distributions for the individual pixels,

$$p(\mathbf{Y}^l, \mathbf{Y}^r | \mathbf{V}^0, \mathbf{V}^1, \mathbf{O}^1, \mathbf{x}) = \prod_j p(y_j^l | \mathbf{V}^0, \mathbf{V}^1, \mathbf{O}^1, \mathbf{x}) \cdot \prod_j p(y_j^r | \mathbf{V}^0, \mathbf{V}^1, \mathbf{O}^1, \mathbf{x}). \quad (7)$$

4   Coordinate Transformations

The object can be at various locations and orientations. Hence, the mapping from coordinates on the object model to the image sensor will change. If the object is close to the camera, then each pixel on the object may map onto many pixels on the camera sensor, and if it is far away, many pixels map onto a single pixel in the camera sensor.

We define a set of functions that map between coordinates in the various appearance models we will be using. We assume that the cameras are pinhole cameras, looking along the negative z axis. For example, if the distance between the two cameras is 10 cm, then left eye is located at $[-5, 0, 0]^T$ and the right camera is at $[5, 0, 0]^T$. The mapping is defined in terms of transformations of homogeneous coordinates. Homogenous coordinates allow us perform translations and perspective projections in a consistent framework and are commonly used in computer graphics. A point in homogenous coordinates includes a 4th component h, i.e. (x, y, z, h). Assuming a flat object $\mathbf{V}^1$, the transformation from the matrix indices of the object into the matrix indices of the left sensor $\mathbf{Y}^l$, is denoted as $jl = \xi^{v \to yl}(x, i)$. This mapping is defined as

$$\begin{bmatrix} indx_i(\mathbf{Y}^l, jl) \\ indx_j(\mathbf{Y}^l, jl) \\ 0 \\ 1 \end{bmatrix} = \mathbf{SM} \cdot \mathbf{PRS}(\mathbf{x}) \cdot \mathbf{EYE}(l) \cdot \mathbf{W}(\mathbf{x}) \cdot \mathbf{MO} \cdot \begin{bmatrix} indx_i(\mathbf{V}^1, i) \\ indx_j(\mathbf{V}^1, i) \\ 0 \\ 1 \end{bmatrix} \quad (8)$$

where $indx_i(\mathbf{V}^1, i)$ denote the row index of pixel i in the object and $indx_j(\mathbf{V}^1, i)$ denotes the column index. Similarly, $indx_i(\mathbf{Y}^l, jl)$ denotes the row index of pixel jl in the left sensor image, and $indx_j(\mathbf{Y}^l, jl)$ denotes the column index. $\mathbf{MO}$ transforms from matrix-coordinates to canonical position in physical coordinates, $\mathbf{W}(\mathbf{x})$ transforms from canonical object position to the actual position $\mathbf{x}$ of the object in physical coordinates (relative to the camera coordinate system). $\mathbf{EYE}(l)$ is the transformation due to the position of the left eye. In our case, it is simply a shift of 5 for along x for the left camera, and -5 for the right camera. $\mathbf{PRS}(\mathbf{x})$ is the perspective projective transformation, which depends on the distance of the object from the camera. $\mathbf{SM}$ maps from physical sensor coordinates to sensor matrix coordinates.

To transform an observed image into the object, we map the matrix indices of the object through this transformation, round the result to the nearest integer, and then retrieve the the values of in the image matrix at those indices.

We will have a need for additional coordinate transformations: the inverse mapping of Eqn. (8) is $i = \xi^{yl \to v}(x, jl)$ which maps left sensor coordinates into object model coordinates. The function $jr = \xi^{v \to yr}(x, i)$ maps from the coordinates of the object model into the left sensor matrix, and the inverse transformation is $i = \xi^{yr \to v}(x, jr)$

An interesting consequence of using stereo cameras and working in world coordinates is that coordinates have a physical meaning. For example, the matrix **MO** defines the physical resolution of the object appearance model. In our experiments, the physical size of one pixel on the surface of the object is about $1\ cm \times 1\ cm$. If only a single camera is used, it is not be possible to determine the scale at which an object should be modelled.

5 EM-PF Algorithm for Learning Stereo Scenes

Now we present an EM algorithm, that employs Rao Blackwellized particle filtering to compute approximations to the model posteriors in an approximate E-step.

We employ two types of approximations to compute the model posteriors in the E step of the algorithm. The first approximation comes from the factorization of the graph, and the second from the approximation of the location posterior with a particle set.

5.1 The EM - Particle Filtering Hybrid Algorithm

The graph in Figure 1(b) hides the fact that the connectivity of the graph changes depending on the position $\mathbf{x}^1$ of the object. Each pixel in the object $\mathbf{V}^1$ can be connected to any pixel in $\mathbf{Y}$, depending on the position $\mathbf{x}^1$. Another way of viewing this is that *every* pixel in the object connects to *every* pixel in the image, and the position of the object determines which edges are "turned on". Thus the graph is hugely loopy. Once a position has been chosen, the connectivity of the graph is dramatically reduced[1].

Algorithm 1 EM - Particle filtering hybrid algorithm

Initialize model parameters $\mu_0, \eta_0, \mu^1, \eta^1, \alpha^1$.
for $nGEM = 1$ to $num\_GEM\_iterations$ **do**

    Approximate E step
    Sample particle set $\{x\}_0$ from location prior $p(x)$.
    for $f = 1$ to num_frames **do**
        $\{x\}'_f \leftarrow sample(p(x_{s,f}|x_{s,f-1}))$ – send particles through dynamic distribution
        Estimate parameters of approximate posteriors $\overline{\alpha}^1, \overline{\eta}^1, \overline{\mu}^1, \overline{\eta}_0$ and $\overline{\mu}_0$
        Calculate particle weights $q(x_s)$
        $\{x\}_f \leftarrow resample(\{x\}'_f, \{q(x_s)\})$ – re-sample particles based on weights
    end for

    M step
    Update model parameters $\mu_0, \eta_0, \mu^1\ \eta^1$ and α^1
end for

---

[1] The graph still has "horizontal" chains, which we will discuss in the next section.

It is problematic to use a parametric distribution for the position variable x since we need to integrate over it which entails integrating over discrete topologies of the graph. This is the motivation for representing the location variable with a particle set, and using particle filtering for inferring posteriors for the location variable x. Algorithm 1 shows the hybrid EM - particle filtering algorithm, for stereo scene analysis.

When learning, we start by sampling from a location prior, and initializing the parameters of the background and object models to random values. In the E step, we compute posterior distributions for the appearance models, and weights for each location particle. When going to the next frame, we re-sample the particles based on those weights and the particles are then passed through a dynamic distribution. The M step is performed after going through the whole sequence of frames.

Various extensions of the basic particle filtering algorithm are possible, e.g. that use proposal distributions[15] or iterative updates within each frame[16] to get a more representative particle set for the location.

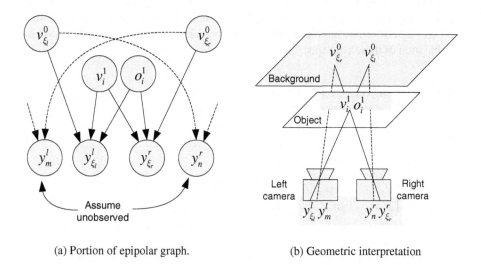

(a) Portion of epipolar graph.   (b) Geometric interpretation

Fig. 2. (a) Portion of graphical model corresponding to an epipolar line. Notice that once the observation nodes have been set, the posterior of the random variable o_i^1 is dependent on the directly observed pixels $y_{\xi_l}^l$ and $y_{\xi_r}^r$, and on y_m^l and y_n^r (and so on), which are not directly observed. The dependence comes from their influence on the background nodes $v_{\xi_l}^0$ and $v_{\xi_r}^0$. In Section 5.2 we describe how the chain is factored.(b) Geometric interpretation of graph in (a).

5.2   Graph Factorization

For a particular setting of the position variable **x**, the original graph factors into chains along the epipolar lines. In other words, the posterior distribution of a pixel in the object is not only dependent on the directly observed pixels it impinges on, but also depends indirectly on a large number of other pixels along the same epipolar line. Part of such a graph is shown in Figure 2. In order to make inference efficient we would like to factor the model and omit the dependence on pixels that are not directly observed[2]. This can be accomplished by assuming that only the directly observed pixels in the camera sensors are observed and all other pixels are unobserved. This has the effect of decoupling the graph and leads to an approximation for the true posterior. From the perspective of inference, assuming that neighboring pixels are unobserved is equivalent to allowing those pixels to take on any values, including the values actually observed.

5.3   Posterior Distributions of E-Step

We now turn our attention to the posterior distributions for the object model $\mathbf{V}^1$ and the position x. These distributions are required in the E step of the learning algorithm. We omit discussion for the posterior distributions for the background and mask due to space constraints as they are intuitively analogous.

The manifestation of stereo in the equations below is one of the more important and pleasing result of this paper. Terms that can be interpreted as "appearance" terms as well, as "stereo" terms, fall out naturally from the generative model without any ad-hoc combination of these concepts.

Posterior for Object $\mathbf{V}^1$. By assuming only the directly observable pixels in the sensors are observed, the posterior associated with pixel i in the object becomes

$$p(v_i^1, o_i^1, v_{\xi l}^0, v_{\xi r}^0 | x, y_{\xi l}^l, y_{\xi r}^r) \tag{9}$$

$$\propto p(v_i^1, o_i^1, v_{\xi l}^0, v_{\xi r}^0, x, y_{\xi l}^l, y_{\xi r}^r) \tag{10}$$

$$= \begin{cases} p(o_i^1 = 1)p(y_{\xi l}^l | v_i^1, x)p(y_{\xi r}^r | v_i^1, x)p(v_{\xi l}^0)p(v_{\xi r}^0)p(v_i^1)p(x) & \text{if } o_i^1 = 1 \\ p(o_i^1 = 0)p(y_{\xi l}^l | v_{\xi l}^0, x)p(y_{\xi r}^r | v_{\xi r}^0, x)p(v_{\xi l}^0)p(v_{\xi r}^0)p(v_i^1)p(x) & \text{if } o_i^1 = 0 \end{cases} \tag{11}$$

To get the posteriors over the pixels of the object, we marginalize out o_i^1, $v_{\xi l}^0$ and $v_{\xi r}^0$. The posterior for v_i^1, given a location and the sensor images is a mixture of two Gaussians

$$p(v_i^1 | x, y_{\xi l}^l, y_{\xi r}^r) = c\alpha_i^1 w_1 N(v_i^1, \mu_{observed}, \eta_{observed}) \tag{12}$$

$$+ c(1 - \alpha_i^1)w_0 N(v_i^1, \mu_{not\ observed}, \eta_{not\ observed}) \tag{13}$$

where c is a normalizing constant. α_i^1 is the prior for the mask variable, and w_1 and w_0 are the mixture weights.

This is a very intuitive result. The first mixture is for the case that the mask is opaque for that pixel, and the second mixture is for the case that it is transparent. The mode of

---

[2] We also experimented with variational inference. Using variational inference, we were unable to learn the parameters of the occlusion variables. We believe this is due to the omission of important dependence structure, which the mean field approximation ignores.

the "opaque" component is

$$\mu_{observed} = \frac{1}{\eta_i^1 + \lambda^l + \lambda^r} \left[\eta_i^1 \mu_i^1 + \lambda^l y_{\xi^l}^l + \lambda^r y_{\xi^r}^r \right] \tag{14}$$

which is a weighted average of what is observed, and the prior mode η_i^1. The weight w_1 for this component is composed of two Gaussian factors

$$w_1 = N(y_{\xi^l}^l - y_{\xi^r}^r; 0, \frac{\lambda^l \lambda^r}{\lambda^l + \lambda^r}) \cdot N(\frac{1}{\lambda^l + \lambda^r} \left[\lambda^l y_{\xi^l}^l + \lambda^r y_{\xi^r}^r \right]; \mu_i^1, \frac{(\lambda^l + \lambda^r)\eta_i^1}{\lambda^l + \lambda^r + \eta_i^1}). \tag{15}$$

The first factor is the "stereo" factor, which is maximized when there is a close correspondence between what is seen in the left and right images i.e. $y_{\xi^l}^l = y_{\xi^r}^r$, and the second factor, the "appearance" factor, is maximized when the prior for the object appearance μ_i^1 matches the (weighted) mean observation. Hence the weight will be large for cases when there is good stereo correspondence and the observation matches the prior.

The second component in the posterior in Eqn.(12) is for the case when the mask is transparent. In this case the mixture component is just equal to the prior. The weight w_0 for this component contains two factors that can be thought of as measuring the evidence that the observed pixel came from the background.

$$w_0 = N(y_{\xi^l}^l, \mu_{\xi^l}^0, \frac{\eta_{\xi^l}^0 \lambda^l}{\eta_{\xi^l}^0 + \lambda^l}) \cdot N(y_{\xi^r}^r, \mu_{\xi^r}^0, \frac{\eta_{\xi^r}^0 \lambda^r}{\eta_{\xi^r}^0 + \lambda^r}) \tag{16}$$

The first term is maximized when the observation matches the left background pixel, and the second term is maximized the right background pixel matches the observed pixel in the right camera

Notice that Equation (12) is for a particular position of the the object. The approximate posterior for the object appearance, can now be written as a Gaussian mixture model with a large number of mixtures. In fact it will have $2 \cdot nsamp$ mixtures, where $nsamp$ is the number of particles in $\{x_s\}$. The weight of each mixtures is the particle weight $q(x_s)$. Hence, the posterior of the object appearance is

$$q(v_i^1 | y_{\xi^l}^l, y_{\xi^r}^r) = \sum_{x_s} q(x_s) p(v_i^1 | x_s, y_{\xi^l}^l, y_{\xi^r}^r). \tag{17}$$

5.4   Posterior for x

The posterior for the position variable x is represented by the particle set $\{x_s\}$ and associated weights $\{q(x_s)\}$. The posterior distribution for the position x can be approximated at the position of the particles x_s as

$$p(x_s | \mathbf{Y}^l, \mathbf{Y}^r) \approx q(x_s) = \frac{p(x_s, \mathbf{Y}^l, \mathbf{Y}^r)}{\sum_k p(x_k, \mathbf{Y}^l, \mathbf{Y}^r)}. \tag{18}$$

To arrive at an expression for the weight of a particle, we need to integrate over all parametric distributions (Rao-Blackwellization). By doing so, $p(x_s, \mathbf{Y}^l, \mathbf{Y}^r)$ can be

shown to be

$$p(x_s, \mathbf{Y}^l, \mathbf{Y}^r) = \prod_i \int p(x_s, \mathbf{Y}^l, \mathbf{Y}^r, v_i^1, \mathbf{V}^0, \mathbf{O}^1) dv_i^1 d\mathbf{V}^0 d\mathbf{O}^1$$

$$= \prod_i \left[\alpha_i^1 w_1(i) + (1 - \alpha_i^1) w_0(i) \right] \quad (19)$$

where α_i^1, $w_0(i)$ and $w_1(i)$ were defined above.

5.5   Generative Probabilistic Interpretation of SSD

The Sum of Squared Differences (SSD) metric is commonly used in stereo vision [3, 10] to measure how well a patch in one image matches a patch from another image, as a function of disparity. It is interesting to note that SSD can be seen as a component or special case of Equation (18).

Equation (18) gives the posterior distribution $p(x_s|\mathbf{Y}^l, \mathbf{Y}^r)$ for the location of the object and can be interpreted as measuring the "fit" of the hypothesized position to the observed data. Recall that Equation (18) contains both "appearance" related terms and "stereo" related terms.

To see the relationship of Equation (18) to the SSD metric, we assume that the appearance model is completely uninformative ($\eta^i = 0$), that the object is completely opaque ($\alpha_i^1 = 1$ for all i), and take the log to arrive at the form

$$\log(p(x|\mathbf{Y}^l, \mathbf{Y}^r)) \propto \log \left(\prod_i \left[\alpha_i^1 w_1(i) + (1 - \alpha_i^1) w_0(i) \right] \right) = \sum_i \log w_1(i). \quad (20)$$

Recall that the first term in the weight w_1 is $N(y_{\xi^l(x,i)}^l - y_{\xi^r(x,i)}^r; 0, \frac{\lambda^l \lambda^r}{\lambda^l + \lambda^r})$. Hence, for this special case

$$\log(p(x|\mathbf{Y}^l, \mathbf{Y}^r)) \propto \sum_i (y_{\xi^l(x,i)}^l - y_{\xi^r(x,i)}^r)^2 \quad (21)$$

which is exactly equivalent to the SSD over the whole image.

| Frame 1 | Frame 3 | Frame 5 | Frame 7 | Frame 9 |

Fig. 3. Training data consists of a short sequence of 10 stereo video frames. The frames were down sampled to 64x48 pixels. The figure shows the frames from the left camera. Notice that the person approaches the camera from the the right and then recedes to the left. The trajectory is shown in Figure 6.

6 Experiments

A short video was recorded using a stereo video camera. The frame rate was 2 frames per second. A subset of the 10 frame sequence used to train the model is shown in Figure 3. Notice that the person approaches the camera from the the right and then recedes to the left.

Figures 4. and 5. shows the models that were found as a result of running the algorithm on the 10 frames shown in Figure 3. In these experiments, 500 particles were used. As can be seen in Figure 4., the background image is learned precisely in most areas. However, in areas where the background is never seen, the background has not been learned, and the variance is high.

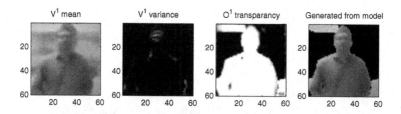

Fig. 4. Model learned for object. The model is comprised of an Gaussian appearance model V^1 and a discrete transparency model O^1. The leftmost figure shows the mean of V^1, the second figure shows the variance of V^1 (notice higher variance on the forehead). The third plot shows the probability of each pixel being opaque. The rightmost plot shows an object generated from the model. Notice that patches of the background where there is no detail, have been associated with the object.

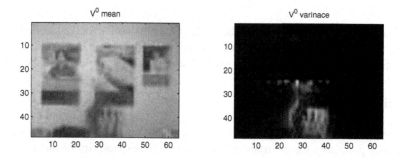

Fig. 5. Model learned for background. The model V^0 is a multivariate gaussian. The left images shows the means, and the right image shows the variances of V^0. Notice that the areas where the background was never observed remain the color of the object and have high variance

The transparency mask has been learned well, except in areas where there is no texture in the background which would allow the model to disambiguate these pixels. Notice that the appearance model has been learned quite well. As can be seen in Figure

3., highlights and specularity of the forehead, nose and shirt vary between frames. The consequence of this is the large variance in these areas. A second factor that introduces variance is that the model assumes the object is flat. Hence, there will be distortion due to the different perspectives of the two cameras. The model allows for this discrepancy by assigning larger variance to the object appearance model along the edges of the face. A third source of variability comes from the inference algorithm itself. The sampling resolution can be too coarse, which prevents the algorithm from accurately finding the mode of the location posterior. This does not seem to be a problem here. This effect can be reduced in a number of ways, including increasing the number of particles and using higher order dynamics in the temporal distribution.

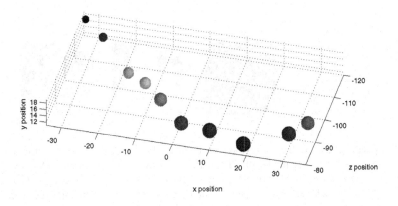

Fig. 6. The mode of the location distribution in iteration 9 of the EM algorithm. The units are approximately centimeters. Notice that there is considerable variation in both depth and horizontal location.

Figure 6. shows the trajectory of the mode of the distribution for the location variable x. The figure clearly shows a right to left trajectory of the person that starts in the right hand side of the frame, moves closer and to the center and then recedes to the left.

7 Discussion

The algorithm requires a large number of coordinate transformations as well as evaluations of posteriors for the transformed images. The complexity of the algorithm is $O((m + n) \cdot it \cdot nsamp \cdot fr)$ where m is the number of pixels in the background, n is the number of pixels in the object model, it is the number of iterations of GEM, $nsamp$ is the number of samples and fr is the number of frames[3].

The transformations required for inference and learning resemble those used in computer graphics. Commodity 3-D graphics accelerators are capable of performing the required computations at high speeds and we anticipate that a fast implementations can be achieved.

---

[3] Each frame takes about 15 seconds on a 2.8GHz Pentium running Matlab code.

In some cases, it is a poor assumption that the background is at a relatively large distance and can be modelled as a planar surface. This can happen when there are stationary objects in the scene at a similar distance as the object we wish to model and track. For this case it may be advantageous to use separate background models for the two cameras.

Particle Filtering and other Markov Chain Monte Carlo methods are considered slow techniques. In addition, when a generative top-down model is used, exact inference will theoretically require the search over a huge space of possible configurations of the hidden model. With continuous location variable, this space is in fact infinite. Despite this, we are able to both track and learn the appearance of the objects in a scene. This is partly due to the advantageous prior structure imposed by the top-down model, partly due to the strong disambiguating information provided by stereo views of the scene and partly due to an inference algorithm that is able to search only over the regions of the hidden variable space that are likely to contain the best explanation for the visible scene.

Stereo information allows the algorithm to latch on to the correct position of the object immediately, even when the appearance model is of no help e.g. when it is initialized to random values. Hence, stereo information allows the algorithm to track and learn appearance without any prior knowledge of the appearance of an object.

When we applied an equivalent monocular algorithm using a single camera to the above data, the algorithm did not track the object, did not learn the object model and consistently fell into local minima. However, once an appearance model has been learned (using stereo) one can switch to using a single camera to track the object.

A strength of generative probabilistic modes is the consistent fusion of multiple types of information where noise and uncertainty are correctly taken into account. In the current paper, we fuse appearance, stereo views and views through time to learn a single underlying representation that explains a scene. Information from multiple frames is automatically used to fill in portions the model that are only observed in a subset of frames.

The framework uses a (simple) generative 3D model of a scene and we show that we can successfully perform inference in such a top-down model. In contrast, the majority of methods in computer vision are bottom up methods. Aggregation of multiple sub models into larger models is a challenge for such approaches. Hence, we believe the extension of the current paradigm to be a very fruitful direction of further research, especially when it is desirable to construct consistent 3D representations of the world.

References

1. M. Malciu, F.P.: A robust model-based approach for 3d head tracking in video sequences. In: Proceedings Fourth IEEE International Conference on Automatic Face and Gesture Recognition (FG'2000), Grenoble, France. Volume 1. (2000) 169–174
2. Schodl, I., Haro, A.: Head tracking using a textured polygonal model. In: In Proceedings of Workshop on Perceptual User Interfaces. (1998)
3. Scharstein, D., Szeliski, R.: A taxonomy and evaluation of dense two-frame stereo correspondence algorithms. International Journal of Computer Vision (2002) 7–42
4. Frey, B., Jojic, N.: Transformation-invariant clustering and dimensionality reduction using em. IEEE Transactions on Pattern Analysis and Machine Intelligence (2000)

5. Papanikolopoulos, N., Khosla, P., Kanade, T.: Vision and control techniques for robotic visual tracking. In: In Proc. IEEE Int. Conf. Robotics and Autmation. Volume 1. (1991) 851–856
6. Toyama, K.: Prolegomena for robust face tracking. Technical Report MSR Technical Report, MSR-TR-98-65, Microsoft Research (1998)
7. Jebara, T., Azarbeyejani, A., Pentland, A.: 3d structure from 2d motion. IEEE Signal Processing Magazine **16** (1999)
8. Sun, J., Shum, H.Y., Zheng, N.N.: Stereo matching using belief propagation. European Conference on Computer Vision (2002) 510–524
9. Scharstein, D., Szeliski, R.: Stereo matching with non-linear diffusion. Proc. of IEEE conferenc on Computer Vision and Pattern Recognition (1996) 343–350
10. Kanade, T., Okutomi, M.: A stereo matching algorithm with an adaptive window: Theory and experiment. IEEE Transactions on Pattern Analysis and Machine Intelligence **16** (1994) 920–932
11. Frey, B.J., Jojic, N.: Learning graphical models of images, videos and their spatial transformations. In: Proceedings of the Sixteenth Conference on Uncertainty in Artifical Intelligence. (2000)
12. Dellaert, F., Thrun, S., Thorpe, C.: Jacobian images of super-resolved texture maps for model-based motion estimation and tracking. In: IEEE Workshop on Applications of Computer Vision. (1998) 2–7
13. Wang, J., Adelson, E.: Representing moving images with layers. IEEE Transactions on Image Processing, Special Issue: Image Sequence Compression **4** (1994) 625–638
14. Blake, A., Isard, M.: Active Contours. Springer-Verlag (1998)
15. Isard, M., Blake, A.: Icondensation: Unifying low-level and high-level tracking in a stochastic framework. In: Proc. 5th European Conf. Computer Vision. Volume 1. (1998) 893–908
16. Kristjansson, T., Frey, B.: Keeping flexible active contours on track using metropolis updates. Advances is Neural Information Processing (NIPS) (2000) 859–865
17. Cootes, T., Edwards, G., Taylor, C.: Active appearance models. In: Proceedings of the European conference on Computer Vision. Volume 2. (1998) 484–498
18. Murphy, K., Russell, S.: Rao-Blackwellised Particle Filtering for Dynamic Bayesian Networks. In: (Sequential Monte Carlo Methods in Practice)
19. Doucet, A., de Freitas, N., Murphy, K., Russell, S.: Rao-blackwellised particle filtering for dynamic bayesian networks. In: Proc. of Uncertainty in AI). (2000)

The Isophotic Metric and Its Application to Feature Sensitive Morphology on Surfaces

Helmut Pottmann[1], Tibor Steiner[1], Michael Hofer[1], Christoph Haider[2], and Allan Hanbury[3]

[1] Geometric Modeling and Industrial Geometry Group, Vienna Univ. of Technology Wiedner Hauptstrasse 8-10. A-1040 Wien, Austria
{pottmann,tibor,hofer}@geometrie.tuwien.ac.at,
http://www.geometrie.tuwien.ac.at
[2] Advanced Computer Vision, Tech Gate Vienna Donau-City-Strasse 1. A-1220 Wien, Austria
haider@acv.ac.at, http://www.acv.ac.at
[3] Pattern Recognition and Image Processing Group, Vienna Univ. of Technology Favoritenstrasse 9/1832. A-1040 Wien, Austria
hanbury@prip.tuwien.ac.at, http://www.prip.tuwien.ac.at

Abstract. We introduce the isophotic metric, a new metric on surfaces, in which the length of a surface curve is not just dependent on the curve itself, but also on the variation of the surface normals along it. A weak variation of the normals brings the isophotic length of a curve close to its Euclidean length, whereas a strong normal variation increases the isophotic length. We actually have a whole family of metrics, with a parameter that controls the amount by which the normals influence the metric. We are interested here in surfaces with features such as smoothed edges, which are characterized by a significant deviation of the two principal curvatures. The isophotic metric is sensitive to those features: paths along features are close to geodesics in the isophotic metric, paths across features have high isophotic length. This shape effect makes the isophotic metric useful for a number of applications. We address feature sensitive image processing with mathematical morphology on surfaces, feature sensitive geometric design on surfaces, and feature sensitive local neighborhood definition and region growing as an aid in the segmentation process for reverse engineering of geometric objects.

1 Introduction

The original motivation for the present investigation comes from the automatic reconstruction of CAD models from measurement data of geometric objects. In this area, called *reverse engineering of geometric objects*, a variety of shape classification methods have been developed, which aim at a segmentation of the measurement data into regions of the same surface type [26]. Particularly for traditional geometric objects, where most of the surfaces on the boundary of the object are fundamental shapes, the surfaces are often separated by edges

T. Pajdla and J. Matas (Eds.): ECCV 2004, LNCS 3024, pp. 560–572, 2004.

or smoothed edges, so-called blending surfaces. Thus, it is natural to look at geometric processing tools on surfaces which are sensitive to such features.

Inspired by image processing, which frequently uses *mathematical morphology* for basic topological and geometric operations [9,22], we have been looking for similar operations on surfaces. However, we found that just a few contributions [10,13,17,19,20,28] extend morphology to curved manifolds or meshes and cell decompositions on curved manifolds; none of these papers deals with the behavior at features. Thus, we will focus here on *feature sensitive mathematical morphology on surfaces*. We implement this through the use of adaptive structuring elements (SE), which change their shape and/or size based on either spatial position [2] or image content. The latter has been used, for example, in range image processing [27]. In these images, the pixel values represent distances to the detector, and hence they can be used to adapt the SE size to the expected feature size. To define appropriate SEs, we have developed an adapted metric on a surface, which we call *isophotic metric*. In this metric, the length of a surface curve depends not only on the curve, but also on the surface normal field along it. SEs, which are geodesic discs in the isophotic metric, behave in the right way at features that are characterized by a significant deviation of the two principal curvatures.

The isophotic metric also simplifies the definition of local neighborhoods for shape detection, the implementation of region growing algorithms and the processing of the responses from local shape detection filters (images on surfaces). For example, the neighborhoods of a point shown in Fig. 2 are not equally useful for local shape detection: The neighborhood based on the Euclidean metric (left) flows across the feature. However, the other neighborhoods (middle and right) respect the feature and are more likely to belong to the same surface type in an engineering object. Another example is depicted in Fig. 6: Region growing based on a feature sensitive metric can easily be stopped at features. Yet another application is design on surfaces: geodesics in a feature sensitive metric nicely follow features (Fig. 3) and morphology in such a metric could be used for artistic effects which are in accordance with the geometry of the surface (Fig. 7).

1.1   Previous Work

Mathematical morphology provides a rich and beautiful mathematical theory as well as a frequently used toolbox for basic topological and geometric operations on images [9,22]. Almost all of the work in discrete morphology is in $\mathbb{R}^n$, where the group of translations generates in a natural way the geometry of Minkowski sums. The latter are the basic building block for further powerful morphological operations. A few contributions go beyond this framework and in a direction which is close to our approach. As long as we are looking just for topological neighborhoods in meshes as discretizations of curved surfaces, we may use morphology on graphs [10,28]. The special case of 2D triangle meshes with the Delaunay property has been investigated by Lomenie et al. [13]. Topological neighborhoods on triangle meshes are also employed in a paper by Rössl et al. [20], which uses morphology for the extraction of feature lines on surfaces.

A basic problem in the extension of morphology to surfaces is the fact that there are no really useful translations, since parallel transport known in differential geometry is path dependent in case of non-vanishing Gaussian curvature. This problem has been addressed [19], but to our knowledge the studies have not been pursued towards efficient algorithms and practical applications. A simple geometric way to overcome the lack of translations is the use of approximants to *geodesic circles* as local neighborhoods (positions of the structuring element). The continuous viewpoint leads to morphology based on the distance function. There is beautiful work on this topic, mainly based on mathematical formulations with partial differential equations (PDE); see [1,4,21] and the references therein. The present paper is also related to geodesic active contours [3,21] in the sense that an appropriate Riemannian metric simplifies the formulation of the problem.

1.2   Contributions of This Paper

In our work we also use the PDE formulation; however, the metric and the resulting distance functions are more general. The distance functions we derive are based on the Gaussian mapping γ from a surface Φ to the unit sphere S^2, a basic concept in differential geometry [6]. The main contributions of our work are the following:

- We define the isophotic metric, study its basic geometric properties, and discuss its analytical treatment for relevant surface representations (Sect. 2).
- The governing equations of distance fields in the new metric are elaborated and efficiently solved in a numerical way (Sect. 3).
- We introduce feature sensitive morphology on surfaces, which is based on the new metric and present applications in Computer Aided Design (Sect. 4).

2   The Isophotic Metric

Let us consider a surface $\Phi \subset \mathbb{R}^3$. We assume that we have chosen, at least locally, a continuous orientation of the unit normal vectors of Φ; $\mathbf{n}(\mathbf{p})$ denotes the unit normal vector at the point $\mathbf{p} \in \Phi$. The *Gaussian map* $\gamma : \Phi \to S^2$ from Φ to the unit sphere S^2 maps a surface point $\mathbf{p}$ to the point $\mathbf{n}(\mathbf{p}) \in S^2$ (see e.g. [6]). The preimage γ^{-1} of a circle $c \subset S^2$ is a curve on Φ, called an *isophote*. The surface normals along an isophote form a constant angle with the rotational axis of c. These curves of equal brightness in a very simple illumination model have been studied in classical constructive geometry; more recently they have been used in Computer Aided Design for quality inspection of surfaces [16]. We now define the *purely isophotic metric* on a surface as follows: *The isophotic length of a curve c on the surface is the Euclidean length of its Gaussian image curve* $\gamma(c) \subset S^2$. This metric obviously has the following simple properties:

- The shortest distance between two surface points is the angle ($\in [0, \pi]$) between their surface normals.

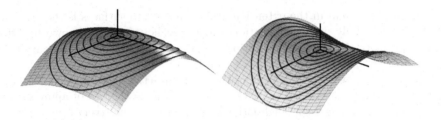

Fig. 1. Isophotes on an elliptic paraboloid (left) and a hyperbolic paraboloid (right).

– Let us fix a point $\mathbf{m} \in \Phi$. A *geodesic circle* in the isophotic metric, i.e. the set of all points $\mathbf{p} \in \Phi$ that lie at constant isophotic distance r to $\mathbf{m}$, is an *isophote* c_r. The Gaussian image of this isophote is a circle with center $\gamma(\mathbf{m})$ and spherical radius r.

– A *geodesic* g on Φ in the sense of the isophotic metric possesses as Gaussian image a geodesic on the unit sphere, i.e. a great circle. Let a_g denote the rotational axis of this circle. Then, at each point $\mathbf{p}$ of g the surface normal $\mathbf{n}(\mathbf{g})$ is orthogonal to a_g. Considering a parallel projection in direction of a_g, the curve g is a *silhouette (contour generator)* on Φ. These curves have been extensively studied in constructive geometry and in Computer Vision (see e.g. [5]).

Example 1: Consider the paraboloid

$$\Gamma : 2z = \kappa_1 x^2 + \kappa_2 y^2. \tag{1}$$

Let us compute the isophotic geodesic circles with center at the origin, i.e., the isophotes for the direction $\mathbf{e} = (0, 0, 1)$. The direction of the normal at a surface point is given by the vector $(\kappa_1 x, \kappa_2 y, -1)$. The angle α between the normal $\mathbf{n}(\mathbf{p})$ at an arbitrary point $\mathbf{p} \in \Gamma$ and $\mathbf{e}$ satisfies $\cos^2 \alpha = 1/(\kappa_1^2 x^2 + \kappa_2^2 y^2 + 1)$. Thus, the isophotes to $\cos^2 \alpha = c^2 = const$ are given by

$$\kappa_1^2 x^2 + \kappa_2^2 y^2 = K^2, \quad \text{with} \quad K^2 := \frac{1}{c^2} - 1. \tag{2}$$

In the xy-plane, these curves are concentric and similar ellipses. In $\mathbb{R}^3$, (2) describes elliptic cylinders which intersect the paraboloid Γ in the actual isophotes (see Fig. 1). Note that the ratio of axis lengths of the ellipses (2) is $\rho_1 : \rho_2$, where $\rho_i := 1/|\kappa_i|$ are the principal curvature radii of Γ at the origin. We have used this example since it reveals important information for the general case as well. We may approximate any regular C^2 surface Φ at an arbitrary point $\mathbf{m}$ up to second order by a paraboloid $\Gamma(\mathbf{m})$. In a local Cartesian frame with origin at $\mathbf{m}$ and with the principal curvature directions and the surface normal as coordinate axis directions this paraboloid is written in the form (1). Here, κ_i are the principal curvatures of Φ and Γ at $\mathbf{m}$. Our example now describes the behavior of 'small' isophotes around $\mathbf{m}$. Viewing the family of shrinking isophotes for $K \to 0$ as a curve evolution (cf. Fig. 1), we may say in usual terminology, that

Fig. 2. Approximate geodesic circles on a triangle mesh in the Euclidean metric (left), purely isophotic metric (middle) and isophotic metric (right).

this family shrinks to an elliptic point with axis ratio $\rho_1 : \rho_2$. If we magnify the isophotes during the evolution so that they keep e.g. their length, the limit is an ellipse in the tangent plane at $\mathbf{m}$, whose axes agree with the principal axes of the surface Φ and whose axis ratio is $\rho_1 : \rho_2$. The discussion of this example shows the following two important facts, the first of which is desirable but the second one is not:

- Isophotic geodesic discs around a center $\mathbf{m}$ are interesting candidates for structuring elements in mathematical morphology on surfaces. They are elongated in direction of large normal curvature radii and they are of smaller width in direction of small normal curvature radii. This anisotropic behavior is useful if we are working along surface features which are characterized by a significant deviation between the two principal curvatures, e.g. along smoothed edges, blends and similar curve-like features.
- At points with vanishing Gaussian curvature, $K = \kappa_1\kappa_2 = 0$, at least one principal curvature κ_i vanishes and the metric degenerates. In the example of Fig. 2, the triangle mesh is close to a developable surface and thus the isophotes Fig. 2 (middle) are close to straight lines, namely the rulings on the developable surface.

Keeping the first property and eliminating the second one has a simple solution: the purely isophotic metric is regularized with help of the Euclidean metric on Φ. More precisely, we define the *regularized isophotic metric*, henceforth often briefly denoted as 'isophotic metric', via the arc length differential

$$ds_i^2 = w \, ds^2 + w^*(ds^*)^2, \tag{3}$$

where ds is the arc element on the surface and ds^* is the arc element on its Gaussian image; $w > 0$ and $w^* \geq 0$ are the weights of the Euclidean and isophotic components, respectively. In the simplest form, the weights will be chosen constant. They can however also be dependent on some appropriate function defined on the surface Φ. The choice of the weights offers a further tool to design appropriate structuring elements for mathematical morphology on Φ.

2.1   Computation on Parametric Surfaces

The computation of the isophotic metric uses only a few basic facts from differential geometry. Let us consider a parameterized surface $\mathbf{x}(u, v)$ and a curve $\mathbf{c}(t)$ on it, given by its preimage $(u(t), v(t))$ in the parameter plane. The first derivative vector $\dot{\mathbf{c}}$ of the curve $\mathbf{c}(t) = \mathbf{x}(u(t), v(t))$ satisfies

$$\dot{\mathbf{c}}^2 = \dot{\mathbf{c}} \cdot \dot{\mathbf{c}} = (\dot{u}\mathbf{x}_u + \dot{v}\mathbf{x}_v)^2 = g_{11}\dot{u}^2 + 2g_{12}\dot{u}\dot{v} + g_{22}\dot{v}^2. \tag{4}$$

Here $\mathbf{x}_u, \mathbf{x}_v$ are the first order partial derivatives of $\mathbf{x}$; their inner products,

$$g_{11} = \mathbf{x}_u^2, \ g_{12} = \mathbf{x}_u \cdot \mathbf{x}_v, \ g_{22} = \mathbf{x}_v^2, \tag{5}$$

form the symmetric matrix $I = (g_{ik})$ of the *first fundamental form*. It allows us to perform metric computations in the tangent spaces of the surface directly in the parameter domain. For example, the computation of the total arc length of a surface curve by means of its preimage $\mathbf{u} = (u(t), v(t))$ in the parameter domain is done with

$$s = \int_a^b \sqrt{\dot{\mathbf{u}}^t \cdot I \cdot \dot{\mathbf{u}}} \ dt. \tag{6}$$

The same can be done with the Gaussian image of the surface. Unit normals are computed as

$$\mathbf{n} = \frac{\mathbf{x}_u \times \mathbf{x}_v}{\|\mathbf{x}_u \times \mathbf{x}_v\|} = \frac{\mathbf{x}_u \times \mathbf{x}_v}{\sqrt{g_{11}g_{22} - g_{12}^2}}.$$

Thus, the first derivative of the image curve $\mathbf{c}^*(t) = \gamma(\mathbf{c}(t)) = \mathbf{n}(u(t), v(t))$ on the Gaussian sphere satisfies

$$(\dot{\mathbf{c}}^*)^2 = (\dot{u}\mathbf{n}_u + \dot{v}\mathbf{n}_v)^2 = l_{11}\dot{u}^2 + 2l_{12}\dot{u}\dot{v} + l_{22}\dot{v}^2. \tag{7}$$

Here, the inner products of the partial derivatives of the unit normal field,

$$l_{11} = \mathbf{n}_u^2, \ l_{12} = \mathbf{n}_u \cdot \mathbf{n}_v, \ l_{22} = \mathbf{n}_v^2, \tag{8}$$

form the symmetric matrix III of the so-called *third fundamental form*. This matrix, which is not regular at points with vanishing Gaussian curvature K, defines the purely isophotic metric on the surface in exactly the same way as the first fundamental matrix I describes the Euclidean metric on the surface. Finally we see that the regularized isophotic metric has the fundamental matrix

$$M = wI + w^*III = (wg_{ij} + w^*l_{ij}). \tag{9}$$

With help of M, one introduces a Riemannian metric in the parameter domain of the surface, and one can use the familiar framework from differential geometry to perform computations. For example, the total arc length of a curve in the isophotic metric is given by (6) with M instead of I. Figure 3 shows several geodesic curves we have computed on a parametric surface using I and M. Three pairs of input points are each connected with a Euclidean geodesic and a regularized isophotic geodesic. The latter metric forces the geodesic curves to follow the features of the surface.

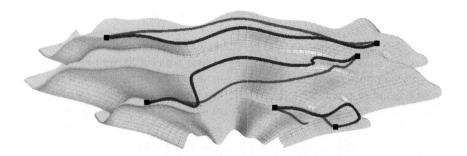

Fig. 3. Geodesic curves on a parametric surface with features: (light colored) computed in the Euclidean metric, i.e. $w = 1$ and $w^* = 0$ in (9); (dark colored) computed in the isophotic metric, for $w = 1$ and $w^* = 2$ in (9).

Remark 1. We may associate with the surface $\mathbf{x}(u, v)$ the 2-dimensional surface $X(u, v) = (\sqrt{w}\mathbf{x}(u, v), \sqrt{w^*}\mathbf{n}(u, v)) \subset \mathbb{R}^6$. Then the canonical Euclidean metric in $\mathbb{R}^6$ induces on the manifold X exactly the regularized isophotic metric; its first fundamental form agrees with (9). In this sense, the isophotic metric has some relation to work on image manifolds, if we consider the unit normals as a vector valued image on the surface [11].

2.2   Computation on Implicit Surfaces

In view of the increasing importance of implicit representations and the elegance of the level set method for the solution of a variety of problems in geometric computing [1,15,23], it is appropriate to address the computation of the isophotic metric if we are given an implicit representation $F(\mathbf{x}) = 0$ of the surface. There is nothing to do for the Euclidean metric. We simply use the canonical Euclidean metric in $\mathbb{R}^3$, described by the identity matrix $E = (\delta_{ij})$. The restriction to any level set surface $\Phi_c : F(\mathbf{x}) = c = const$ is the metric on the surface.

We are now constructing another metric in $\mathbb{R}^3$, whose restriction to $F(\mathbf{x}) = 0$ is the desired isophotic metric. For any $\mathbf{x} \in \mathbb{R}^3$ in the domain, where F is defined, the normalized gradient vector $\mathbf{n}(\mathbf{x}) = \nabla F/\|\nabla F\|$, describes the unit normal of the level set of F which passes through $\mathbf{x}$. Thus, the mapping $\mathbf{x} \mapsto \mathbf{n}(\mathbf{x})$ extends the Gaussian mapping to the set of all level sets of F. The image lies on the unit sphere. The first derivative of this extended Gaussian mapping has the (singular) matrix $J := (\mathbf{n}_x, \mathbf{n}_y, \mathbf{n}_z)$. Hence, the squared (purely) isophotic length $\|\mathbf{v}\|_*^2$ of a vector $\mathbf{v}$ (tangent vector of $\mathbb{R}^3$ at $\mathbf{x}$) is

$$\|\mathbf{v}\|_*^2 = (J \cdot \mathbf{v})^2 = \mathbf{v}^t \cdot N \cdot \mathbf{v}, \tag{10}$$

where the matrix $N = (n_{ij}) = J^t \cdot J$ is the Gramian of the partial derivatives of $\mathbf{n}$. Finally, the matrix

$$\overline{M} = wE + w^*N = (w\delta_{ij} + w^*n_{ij}), \tag{11}$$

describes a Riemannian metric in $\mathbb{R}^3$, whose restriction to *any* level set surface $\Phi_c = F^{-1}(c)$ is the corresponding regularized isophotic metric on Φ_c.

Note that the expressions become particularly simple for a *signed distance function F*, since it satisfies $\|\nabla F\| = 1$. Moreover, it is well-known how to efficiently compute the signed distance function to a surface, even if it is given just as a cloud of points [24]. Therefore, the implicit framework can be used to perform computations basically directly on clouds of measurement points.

3   Distance Fields in the Isophotic Metric

A distance function d on a surface Φ is characterized by the Eikonal equation

$$\|\nabla_\Phi d\|^2 = 1, \tag{12}$$

where $\nabla_\Phi d$ is the surface gradient of d. $\nabla_\Phi d$ is a tangential vector of the surface, points in direction of the largest positive directional derivative of d, and its norm is equal to this derivative. For a *parametric representation* $\mathbf{x}(u, v)$ of Φ with first fundamental matrix I, we can express this equation in terms of the ordinary gradient,

$$(\nabla \tilde{d})^t \cdot I^{-1} \cdot \nabla \tilde{d} = 1.$$

Here $\tilde{d} = \tilde{d}(u, v)$ is the representation of the distance function in the parameter domain, so that $\tilde{d}(u, v)$ equals the distance value $d(\mathbf{x}(u, v))$ of the surface point $\mathbf{x}(u, v)$. Moreover, $\nabla \tilde{d} = (\tilde{d}_u, \tilde{d}_v)$ is the ordinary gradient of the bivariate function $\tilde{d}$. For a distance field in the isophotic metric, we just replace the matrix I by the matrix M from equation (9),

$$(\nabla \tilde{d})^t \cdot M^{-1} \cdot \nabla \tilde{d} = 1. \tag{13}$$

This is a 2D Hamilton-Jacobi equation and therefore the numerical computation of an isophotic distance field to some point set can be done with the fast sweeping algorithm by Tsai et al. [25]. The examples in Fig. 4 have been computed in this way. One can show that the computation of isophotic distance fields on *implicitly defined surfaces* can proceed along the lines of [14]: With $\overline{M}$ from (11) we solve the 3D Hamilton-Jacobi equation,

$$(\nabla d)^t \cdot \overline{M}^{-1} \cdot \nabla d = 1, \tag{14}$$

in a small neighborhood of the surface. Here, a 3D extension [7] of the algorithm by Tsai el al. [25] can be used.

4   Application to Feature Sensitive Morphology on Surfaces

4.1   Continuous Morphology

Let us consider a black image on a white surface. On the surface we have introduced a metric. In our case this is the isophotic metric, but it could be another

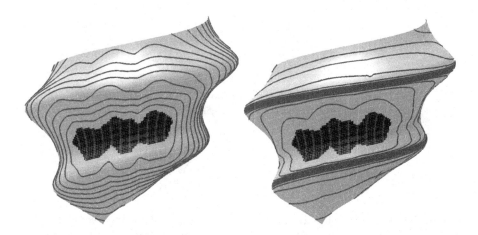

Fig. 4. Level sets to uniformly spaced values of the distance field to a given region in the Euclidean metric (left) and isophotic metric (right). In the isophotic metric, the level sets accumulate at features.

one as well. Then, the distance field to the black part B possesses level sets which are the boundaries of the dilated versions of B. Thus, *dilation* means growth with help of the distance field (see Fig. 4). Likewise, *erosion* can be defined as dilation of the white background, again with the distance field. Combinations of dilation and erosion, which yield *closing* and *opening*, are straightforward. Furthermore, extensions to labelled meshes, in which faces are assigned values from a small set V, is relatively straightforward through the use of series closings on indexed partitions as defined in [8]. For the use of the isophotic metric in *feature sensitive morphology*, we should note the following effects:

- Applying a dilation with high isophotic part ($w^* \gg w$) to a domain adjacent to a feature will make distances across that feature very large and thus avoid a flow across the feature (see Fig. 4, right).
- Application of a dilation with high Euclidean part ($w \gg w^*$) to a domain along a feature will fill interruptions along the feature, but not significantly enlarge the domain across that feature (Fig. 5, left).
- A closing operation of a thin domain along a feature is achieved by applying to it first a dilation with high Euclidean component and then an erosion with high isophotic part (Fig. 5).

4.2   Discrete Morphology

We split the discussion into two parts. At first we discuss local neighborhoods, to be understood as positions of the structuring element. Secondly, we show how to use the neighborhoods – independently from their creation – in the formulation of morphological operators. In both cases we confine ourselves to triangle meshes, but the extension to other cell arrangements, even for manifolds of higher dimension, is rather straightforward.

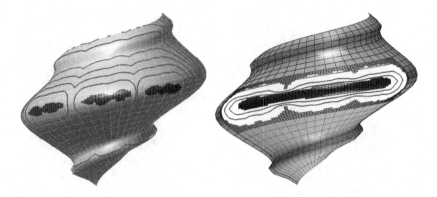

Fig. 5. Continuous morphology: Closing of a domain (black) along a feature: First, a Euclidean dilation (distance field on left side) is applied (result of dilation white on right side), then an erosion with high isophotic part yields the closed domain (black, right).

Neighborhoods. The *combinatorial neighborhood* $N_1(\Delta_i)$ of *depth one* to a triangle Δ_i consists of all triangles in Δ, which share at least one vertex with Δ_i. The neighborhood N_k is defined by iterating the procedure: in step k we add all triangles which share at least a vertex with the boundary of N_{k-1}. For a nearly uniform triangulation, the neighborhoods N_k are good approximants to geodesic circles. For a *neighborhood in the isophotic metric* one has to gather triangles around Δ_i, whose isophotic distance falls below a given threshold. We have implemented the computation of these geodesic discs following an idea by M. Reimers [18], which appears for grids already in [24]. In view of Remark 1 we compute a Euclidean distance field to a triangle on a triangle mesh in $\mathbb{R}^6$, which represents a two-dimensional surface. The only difference to the work of [18] is the dimension of ambient space, which is irrelevant for distance computations in the mesh. The examples in Figs. 2, 6, 7 have been computed in this way.

Morphological Operators. Let us first describe the *dilation* of level k of black elements on a white background. At each triangle Δ_i of the triangulation we compute the local neighborhood $N_k(\Delta_i)$ and set the color of Δ_i to black if at least one of the triangles in the neighborhood is black. If the neighborhoods approximate geodesic discs sufficiently well in some metric (e.g. the isophotic metric), we have the following counterpart to the planar case: performing k times a dilation of level one is the same as performing once a dilation of level k. If we use a structuring element (SE) based on the isophotic distance, then it is inevitable that there will be some triangles which lie partly within and partly outside the isophotic distance threshold. A simple solution to this problem would be to assign the triangle to the SE if more than a specified proportion of its surface area is inside the distance boundary. A more flexible approach would be to make use of non-flat SEs [22, p. 441], having values influenced by the proportion of a triangle lying within the distance threshold.

Fig. 6. Discrete morphology: Dilation in the isophotic metric (9) with $w = 0.5$ and $w^* = 0.5$: Starting with the dark triangles (left) we get the result shown (right). Note that the isophotic metric prevents a flow across features.

An *erosion* of level k of black parts is just a dilation of level k applied to the white background. A morphological *closing* operation first applies a dilation of level k, and then an erosion of level k. This fills holes. The *opening* operator applies the erosion before the dilation, which removes thin connections between more compact parts. The width of the bridges to be removed is related to k.

We present examples of discrete morphology on real 3D data. For this purpose we scanned an engineering object (Fig. 6) and a clay model (Fig. 7) with a Minolta VI-900 3D laser scanner, and then triangulated the obtained point clouds to produce the meshes shown in the respective figures. The example in Fig. 6 demonstrates that feature sensitive mathematical morphology can aid the segmentation of an object into its fundamental surfaces; this holds with respect to the definition of local neighborhoods for shape detection, the implementation of region growing algorithms and the processing of the responses from local shape detection filters (images on surfaces). The example in Fig. 7 supports our expectation that morphology in the isophotic metric could be used for artistic effects which are in accordance with the geometry of the surface. Furthermore, the geodesic curves shown in Fig. 3 indicate the usability of the isophotic metric for feature sensitive curve design on surfaces, e.g. for patch layout in connection with high quality freeform surface fitting to clouds of measurement points.

5   Conclusion and Future Research

We have introduced and studied the isophotic metric, discussed some basic computational aspects, and presented examples on its application to feature sensitive morphology on surfaces and geometric design on surfaces. Both the efficient computation as well as the application to morphology require further studies. Promising extensions of the concept are feature sensitive design of energy minimizing splines in the sense of the isophotic metric, and robot path planning, both on surfaces. Another subject of ongoing and future research is a modification of the isophotic metric so that it serves as a tool for image processing in arbitrary dimensions. Here, we interpret a grey value image as a hypersurface, but use – in

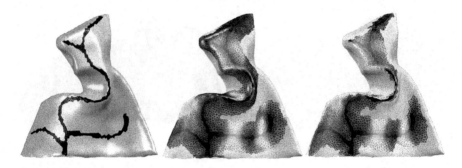

Fig. 7. Dilation of the dark triangles (left) on a triangulated surface: (middle) in the Euclidean metric, (right) in the isophotic metric (9) with $w = 0.2$ and $w^* = 0.8$.

accordance with the work of Koenderink and van Doorn [12] – isotropic rather than Euclidean geometry in ambient space.

Acknowledgements. Part of this research has been carried out within the Competence Center *Advanced Computer Vision* and has been funded by the K*plus* program. This work was also supported by the Austrian Science Fund under grants P14445-MAT and P16002-N05, and by the innovative project "3D Technology" of Vienna University of Technology.

References

1. Bertalmio, M., Mémoli, F., Cheng, L.T., Sapiro, G., Osher, S.: Variational problems and partial differential equations on implicit surfaces, CAM Report 02-17, UCLA, April 2002
2. Beucher, S., Blosseville, J. M., Lenoir, F.: Traffic spatial measurements using video image processing. In *Intelligent Robots and Computer Vision, Proc. SPIE*, Vol. 848 (1987) 648–655
3. Caselles, V., Kimmel, R., Sapiro, G., Geodesic active contours, Intl. J. Computer Vision **22** (1997), 61–79.
4. Cheng, L.T., Burchard, P., Merriman, B., Osher, S.: Motion of curves constrained on surfaces using a level set approach. UCLA CAM Report 00-36, September 2000
5. Cipolla, R., Giblin, P.: *Visual Motion of Curves and Surfaces*, Cambridge University Press, Cambridge, UK (2000)
6. do Carmo, M.P.: *Differential Geometry of Curves and Surfaces*, Prentice Hall, Englewood Cliffs, NJ (1976)
7. Haider, C., Hönigmann, D.: Efficient computation of distance functions on manifolds by parallelized fast sweeping, Advanced Computer Vision, Technical Report 116, Vienna (2003)
8. Hanbury, A.: Mathematical morphology applied to circular data. In P.W. Hawkes, editor, *Advances in Imaging and Electron Physics*, Vol. 128, Academic Press (2003) 123–205
9. Heijmans, H.J.A.M.: *Morphological Image Operators*, Academic Press, Boston (1994)

10. Heijmans, H.J.A.M., Nacken, P., Toet, A., Vincent, L.: Graph Morphology, *Journal of Visual Communication and Image Representation* **3** (1992) 24–38
11. Kimmel, R., Malladi, R., Sochen, N.: Images as embedded maps and minimal surfaces: movies, color, texture and volumetric medical images, Intl. J. Computer Vision **39** (2000) 111-129
12. Koenderink, J.J., van Doorn, A.J.: Image processing done right, *ECCV 2002*, LNCS **2350**, Springer-Verlag Heidelberg (2002) 158–172
13. Loménie, N., Gallo, L., Cambou, N., Stamon, G.: Morphological operations on Delaunay triangulations, *Proc. Intl. Conf. on Pattern Recognition*, Vol. 3, Barcelona (2000) 3556–3560
14. Memoli, F., Sapiro, G.: Fast computation of weighted distance functions and geodesics on implicit hyper-surfaces, *J. Comput. Phys.* **173**(2) (2001) 730–764
15. Osher, S., Fedkiw, R.: *Level Set Methods and Dynamic Implicit Surfaces*, Springer-Verlag, New York (2003)
16. Patrikalakis, N. M., Maekawa, T.: *Shape Interrogation for Computer Aided Design and Manufacturing*, Springer-Verlag Berlin Heidelberg New York (2002)
17. J. B. T. M. Roerdink, Mathematical morphology on the sphere, *Proc. SPIE Conf. Visual Communications and Image Processing '90*, Lausanne, pp. 263–271 (1990).
18. Reimers, M.: Computing geodesic distance functions on triangle meshes, Technical Report, Dept. of Informatics, Univ. of Oslo, 2003, (in preparation)
19. Roerdink, J.B.T.M.: Manifold Shape: from Differential Geometry to Mathematical Morphology, in: *Shape in Picture*, Y.L. O et al., eds., Springer-Verlag Berlin Heidelberg New York (1994) 209–223
20. Rössl, C., Kobbelt, L., Seidel, H.-P.: Extraction of feature lines on triangulated surfaces using morphological operators, *Proc. Smart Graphics 2000*, AAAI Spring Symposium, Stanford University.
21. Sapiro, G.: *Geometric Partial Differential Equations and Image Analysis*, Cambridge University Press, Cambridge (2001)
22. Serra, J.: *Image Analysis and Mathematical Morphology*, Academic Press, London (1982)
23. Sethian, J. A.: *Level Set Methods and Fast Marching Methods*, Cambridge University Press, Cambridge (1999)
24. Tsai, Y.-S.R.: Rapid and accurate computation of the distance function using grids, *J. Comput. Phys.* **178**(1) (2002) 175–195
25. Tsai, Y.-S.R., Cheng, L.-T., Osher, S., Zhao, H.-K.: Fast sweeping algorithms for a class of Hamilton-Jacobi equations, *SIAM J. Numerical Analysis* **41**(2) (2003) 673-694
26. Várady, T., Martin, R.: Reverse Engineering, In *Handbook of Computer Aided Geometric Design*, G. Farin, J. Hoschek and M.-S. Kim, eds., Elsevier, (2002) 651–681
27. Verly, J. G., Delanoy, R. L.: Adaptive mathematical morphology for range imagery. *IEEE Transactions on Image Processing* **2**(2) (1993) 272–275
28. Vincent, L.: Graphs and mathematical morphology, *Signal Processing* **16** (1989) 365–388

A Closed-Form Solution to Non-rigid Shape and Motion Recovery

Jing Xiao, Jin-xiang Chai, and Takeo Kanade

The Robotics Institute
Carnegie Mellon University
Pittsburgh, PA 15213
{jxiao,jchai,tk}@cs.cmu.edu

Abstract. Recovery of three dimensional (3D) shape and motion of non-static scenes from a monocular video sequence is important for applications like robot navigation and human computer interaction. If every point in the scene randomly moves, it is impossible to recover the non-rigid shapes. In practice, many non-rigid objects, *e.g.* the human face under various expressions, deform with certain structures. Their shapes can be regarded as a weighted combination of certain shape bases. Shape and motion recovery under such situations has attracted much interest. Previous work on this problem [6,4,13] utilized only orthonormality constraints on the camera rotations (*rotation constraints*). This paper proves that using only the rotation constraints results in ambiguous and invalid solutions. The ambiguity arises from the fact that the shape bases are not unique because their linear transformation is a new set of eligible bases. To eliminate the ambiguity, we propose a set of novel constraints, *basis constraints*, which uniquely determine the shape bases. We prove that, under the weak-perspective projection model, enforcing both the basis and the rotation constraints leads to a closed-form solution to the problem of non-rigid shape and motion recovery. The accuracy and robustness of our closed-form solution is evaluated quantitatively on synthetic data and qualitatively on real video sequences.

1 Introduction

Many years of work in structure from motion have led to significant successes in recovery of 3D shapes and motion estimates from 2D monocular videos. Reliable systems exist for reconstruction of static scenes. However, most natural scenes are dynamic and non-rigid: expressive faces, people walking beside buildings, etc. Recovering the structure and motion of these non-rigid objects is a challenging task. The effects of 3D rotation and translation and non-rigid deformation are coupled together in image measurement. While it is impossible to reconstruct the shape if the scene deforms arbitrarily, in practice, many non-rigid objects, *e.g.* the human face under various expressions, deform with a class of structures.

One class of solutions model non-rigid object shapes as weighted combinations of certain shape bases that are pre-learned by off-line training [2,3,5,9]. For instance, the geometry of a face is represented as a weighted combination of

T. Pajdla and J. Matas (Eds.): ECCV 2004, LNCS 3024, pp. 573–587, 2004.
© Springer-Verlag Berlin Heidelberg 2004

shape bases that correspond to various facial deformations. Then the recovery of shape and motion is simply a model fitting problem. However, in many applications, *e.g.* reconstruction of a scene consisting of a moving car and a static building, the shape bases of the dynamic structure are difficult to obtain before reconstruction.

Several approaches have been proposed to solve the problem without a prior model [6,13,4]. Instead, they treat the model, *i.e.* shape bases, as part of the unknowns to be solved. They try to recover not only the non-rigid shape and motion, but also the shape model. This class of approaches so far has utilized only the orthonormality constraints on camera rotations (***rotation constraints***) to solve the problem. However, as shown in this paper, enforcing only the rotation constraints leads to ambiguous and invalid solutions. These approaches thus cannot guarantee the desired solution. They have to either require a priori knowledge on shape and motion, *e.g.* constant speed [10], or need non-linear optimization that involves large number of variables and hence requires a good initial estimate [13,4].

Intuitively, the above ambiguity arises from the non-uniqueness of the shape bases: a linear transformation of a set of shape bases is a new set of eligible bases. Once the bases are determined uniquely, the ambiguity is eliminated. Therefore, instead of imposing only the rotation constraints, we identify and introduce another set of constraints on the shape bases (***basis constraints***), which implicitly determine the bases uniquely. This paper proves that, under the weak-perspective projection model, when both the basis and rotation constraints are imposed, a closed-form solution to the problem of non-rigid shape and motion recovery is achieved. Accordingly we develop a factorization method that applies both metric constraints to compute the closed-form solution for the non-rigid shape, motion, and shape bases.

2   Previous Work

Recovering 3D object structure and motion from 2D image sequences has a rich history. Various approaches have been proposed for different applications. The discussion in this section will focus on the factorization techniques, which are most closely related to our work.

The factorization method was first proposed by Tomasi and Kanade [12]. First it applies the rank constraint to factorize a set of feature locations tracked across the entire sequence. Then it uses the orthonormality constraints on the rotation matrices to recover the scene structure and camera rotations in one step. This approach works under the orthographic projection model. Poelman and Kanade [11] extended it to work under the weak perspective and paraperspective projection models. Triggs [14] generalized the factorization method to the recovery of scene geometry and camera motion under the perspective projection model. These methods work for static scenes.

Costeira and Kanade [8] extended the factorization technique to recover the structure of multiple independently moving objects. This method factorizes the image locations of certain features to separate different objects and then individually recovers their shapes. Wolf and Shashua [16] derived a geometrical constraint, called the segmentation matrix, to reconstruct a scene containing two independently moving objects from two perspective views. Vidal and his colleagues [15] extended this approach for dynamic scenes containing multiple independently moving objects. For reconstruction of dynamic scenes consisting of both static objects and objects moving along fixed directions, Han and Kanade [10] proposed a factorization-based method that achieves a unique solution with the assumption of constant velocities. A more generalized solution to reconstructing the shapes that deform at constant velocity is presented in [17].

Bregler and his colleagues [6] first introduced the basis representation of non-rigid shapes to embed the deformation constraints into the scene structure. By analyzing the low rank of the image measurements, they proposed a factorization-based method that enforces the orthonormality constraints on camera rotations to reconstruct the non-rigid shape and motion. Torresani and his colleagues [13] extended the method in [6] to a trilinear optimization approach. At each step, two of the three types of unknowns, bases, coefficients, and rotations, are fixed and the remaining one is updated. The method in [6] is used to initialize the optimization process. Brand [4] proposed a similar non-linear optimization method that uses an extension of the method in [6] for initialization. All three methods enforce only the rotation constraints and thus cannot guarantee an optimal solution. Note that both non-linear optimization methods involve a large number of variables, *e.g.* the number of unknown coefficients equals the product of the number of images and the number of shape bases. The performance relies on the quality of the initial estimate of the unknowns.

3   Problem Statement

Given 2D locations of P feature points across F frames, $\{(u, v)_{fp}^T | f = 1, ..., F, p = 1, ..., P\}$, our goal is to recover the motion of the non-rigid object relative to the camera, including rotations $\{R_f | f = 1, ..., F\}$ and translations $\{\mathbf{t}_f | f = 1, ..., F\}$, and its 3D deforming shapes $\{(x, y, z)_{fp}^T | f = 1, ..., F, p = 1, ..., P\}$. Throughout this paper, we assume:

-   the deforming shapes can be represented as weighted combinations of shape bases;
-   the 3D structure and the camera motion are non-degenerate;
-   the camera projection model is the weak-perspective projection model.

We follow the representation of [3,6]. The non-rigid shapes are represented as weighted combinations of K shape bases $\{B_i, i = 1, ..., K\}$. The bases are $3 \times P$ matrices controlling the deformation of P points. Then the 3D coordinate of the point p at the frame f is

$$\mathbf{X}_{fp} = (x, y, z)_{fp}^T = \Sigma_{i=1}^K c_{fi} \mathbf{b}_{ip} \quad f = 1, ..., F, p = 1, ..., P \tag{1}$$

where $\mathbf{b}_{ip}$ is the p_{th} column of B_i and c_{if} is its combination coefficient at the frame f. The image coordinate of $\mathbf{X}_{fp}$ under the weak perspective projection model is

$$\mathbf{x}_{fp} = (u, v)_{fp}^T = s_f(R_f \cdot \mathbf{X}_{fp} + \mathbf{t}_f) \tag{2}$$

where R_f stands for the first two rows of the f_{th} camera rotation and $\mathbf{t}_f = [t_{fx} t_{fy}]^T$ is its translation relative to the world origin. s_f is the scalar of the weak perspective projection.

Replacing $\mathbf{X}_{fp}$ using Eq. (1) and absorbing s_f into c_{fi} and $\mathbf{t}_f$, we have

$$\mathbf{x}_{fp} = \left(c_{f1} R_f \ ... \ c_{fK} R_f \right) \cdot \begin{pmatrix} \mathbf{b}_{1p} \\ ... \\ \mathbf{b}_{Kp} \end{pmatrix} + \mathbf{t}_f \tag{3}$$

Suppose the image coordinates of all P feature points across F frames are obtained. We form a $2F \times P$ *measurement matrix* W by stacking all image coordinates. Then $W = MB + T[11...1]$, where M is a $2F \times 3K$ scaled rotation matrix, B is a $3K \times P$ bases matrix, and T is a $2F \times 1$ translation vector,

$$M = \begin{pmatrix} c_{11} R_1 & ... & c_{1K} R_1 \\ \vdots & \vdots & \vdots \\ c_{F1} R_F & ... & c_{FK} R_F \end{pmatrix}, \ B = \begin{pmatrix} \mathbf{b}_{11} & ... & \mathbf{b}_{1P} \\ \vdots & \vdots & \vdots \\ \mathbf{b}_{K1} & ... & \mathbf{b}_{KP} \end{pmatrix}, \ T = \left(\mathbf{t}_1^T \ ... \ \mathbf{t}_F^T \right)^T \tag{4}$$

As in [10,6], we position the world origin at the scene center and compute the translation vector by averaging the image projections of all points. We then subtract it from W and obtain the *registered* measurement matrix $\tilde{W} = MB$.

Since $\tilde{W}$ is the product of the $2F \times 3K$ scaled rotation matrix M and the $3K \times P$ shape bases matrix B, its rank is at most $min\{3K, 2F, P\}$. In practice, the frame number F and point number P are usually much larger than the basis number K. Thus under the non-degenerate cases, the rank of $\tilde{W}$ is $3K$ and K is determined by $K = rank(\tilde{W})/3$. We then perform SVD on $\tilde{W}$ to get the best possible rank $3K$ approximation of $\tilde{W}$ as $\tilde{M}\tilde{B}$. This decomposition is only determined up to a non-singular $3K \times 3K$ linear transformation. The true scaled rotation matrix M and bases matrix B are of the form,

$$M = \tilde{M} \cdot G, \quad B = G^{-1} \cdot \tilde{B} \tag{5}$$

where G is called the *corrective transformation* matrix. Once G is determined, M and B are obtained and thus the rotations, shape bases, and combination coefficients are recovered.

All the procedures above, except obtaining G, are standard and well-understood [3,6]. The problem of nonrigid shape and motion recovery is now reduced to: given the measurement matrix W, how can we compute the *corrective transformation* matrix G?

4   Metric Constraints

To compute G, two types of metric constraints are available and should be imposed: **rotation constraints** and **basis constraints**. While using only the rotation constraints [6,4] leads to ambiguous and invalid solutions, enforcing both sets of constraints results in a closed-form solution.

4.1   Rotation Constraints

The orthonormality constraints on the rotation matrices are one of the most powerful metric constraints and they have been used in reconstructing the shape and motion for static objects [12,11], multiple moving objects [8,10], and non-rigid deforming objects [6,13,4].

According to Eq. (5), $MM^T = \tilde{M}GG^T\tilde{M}^T$. Let us denote GG^T by Q. Then,

$$\tilde{M}_{2*i-1:2*i}Q\tilde{M}_{2*j-1:2*j}^T = \Sigma_{k=1}^K c_{ik}c_{jk}R_i * R_j^T, \quad i,j = 1,...F \tag{6}$$

where $\tilde{M}_{2*i-1:2*i}$ represents the i_{th} two-row of $\tilde{M}$. Due to orthonormality of rotation matrices,

$$\tilde{M}_{2*i-1:2*i}Q\tilde{M}_{2*i-1:2*i}^T = \Sigma_{k=1}^K c_{ik}^2\mathbf{I}_{2\times2}, \quad i = 1,...,F \tag{7}$$

where $\mathbf{I}_{2\times2}$ is a 2×2 identity matrix. Because Q is symmetric, the number of unknowns in Q is $(9K^2+3K)/2$. Each diagonal block of MM^T yields two linear constraints on Q,

$$\tilde{M}_{2*i-1}Q\tilde{M}_{2*i-1}^T = \tilde{M}_{2*i}Q\tilde{M}_{2*i}^T \tag{8}$$

$$\tilde{M}_{2*i-1}Q\tilde{M}_{2*i}^T = 0 \tag{9}$$

For F frames, we have $2F$ linear constraints on $\frac{(9K^2+3K)}{2}$ unknowns. It appears that, when we have enough images, i.e. $F \geq \frac{(9K^2+3K)}{2}$, there should be enough constraints to compute Q via the least-square methods. However, it is not true in general. We will show that most of these rotation constraints are redundant and they are inherently insufficient to determine Q.

4.2   Why Are Rotation Constraints Not Sufficient?

When the scene is static or deforms at constant velocities, the rotation constraints are sufficient to solve the corrective transformation matrix G [12,10]. However, when the scene deforms at varying speed, no matter how many images are given or how many feature points are tracked, the solutions of the constraints in Eq. (8) and Eq. (9) are inherently ambiguous.

Definition 1. *A $3K \times 3K$ symmetric matrix Y is called a block-skew-symmetric matrix, if all the diagonal 3×3 blocks are zero matrices and each off-diagonal 3×3 block is a skew symmetric matrix.*

$$Y_{ij} = \begin{pmatrix} 0 & y_{ij1} & y_{ij2} \\ -y_{ij1} & 0 & y_{ij3} \\ -y_{ij2} & -y_{ij3} & 0 \end{pmatrix} = -Y_{ij}^T = Y_{ji}^T, \quad i \neq j \tag{10}$$

$$Y_{ii} = 0_{3\times3}, \quad i,j = 1,...,K \tag{11}$$

Each off-diagonal block consists of 3 independent elements. Because Y is symmetric and has $K(K-1)/2$ independent off-diagonal blocks, it includes $3K(K-1)/2$ independent elements.

Definition 2. *A $3K \times 3K$ symmetric matrix Z is called a block-scaled-identity matrix, if each 3×3 block is a scaled identity matrix, i.e. $Z_{ij} = \lambda_{ij}\mathbf{I}_{3\times 3}$, where λ_{ij} is the only variable.*

Because Z is symmetric, the total number of variables in Z equals the number of independent blocks, $K(K+1)/2$.

Theorem 1. *The general solution of the rotation constraints in Eq. (8) and Eq. (9) can be expressed as $\tilde{Q} = GHG^T$, where G is the desired corrective transformation matrix, and $H = Y + Z$, with Y a block-skew-symmetric matrix, and Z a block-scaled-identity matrix.*

Proof. The solution $\tilde{Q}$ of Eq. (8) and Eq. (9) can be represented as $G\Lambda G^T$, since G is a non-singular square matrix. Now we need to prove that Λ must be in the form of H, *i.e.* the summation of Y and Z.

According to Eq. (7),

$$\tilde{M}_{2*i-1:2*i}\tilde{Q}\tilde{M}_{2*i-1:2*i}^T = M_{2*i-1:2*i}\Lambda M_{2*i-1:2*i}^T$$
$$= \alpha_i\mathbf{I}_{2\times 2}, \quad i = 1,...,F \tag{12}$$

where α_i is an unknown scalar depending on only the coefficients. Divide Λ into 3×3 blocks, Λ_{kj} ($k,j=1,...,K$). Combining Eq. (4) and (12), we have

$$R_i\Sigma_{k=1}^K(c_{ik}^2\Lambda_{kk} + \Sigma_{j=k+1}^K c_{ik}c_{ij}(\Lambda_{kj} + \Lambda_{kj}^T))R_i^T = \alpha_i\mathbf{I}_{2\times 2}, \quad i = 1,...,F \tag{13}$$

Denote the 3×3 symmetric matrix $\Sigma_{k=1}^K(c_{ik}^2\Lambda_{kk} + \Sigma_{j=k+1}^K c_{ik}c_{ij}(\Lambda_{kj} + \Lambda_{kj}^T))$ by Γ_i. Let $\tilde{\Gamma}_i$ be the homogeneous solution of Eq. (13), *i.e.* $R_i\tilde{\Gamma}_iR_i^T = \mathbf{0}_{2\times 2}$. Since R_i consists of the first two rows of the i_{th} rotation matrix, let r_{i3} denote the third row. Due to orthonormality of R_i,

$$\tilde{\Gamma}_i = r_{i3}^T\delta_i + \delta_i^T r_{i3} \tag{14}$$

where δ_i is an arbitrary 1×3 vector. Apparently $\Gamma_i = \alpha_i\mathbf{I}_{3\times 3}$ is a particular solution of Eq. (13). Therefore the general solution of Eq. (13) is

$$\Gamma_i = \Sigma_{k=1}^K(c_{ik}^2\Lambda_{kk} + \Sigma_{j=k+1}^K c_{ik}c_{ij}(\Lambda_{kj} + \Lambda_{kj}^T)) = \alpha_i\mathbf{I}_{3\times 3} + \beta_i\tilde{\Gamma}_i \tag{15}$$

where β_i is a scalar. Now let us prove $\beta_i\tilde{\Gamma}_i$ has to be zero. Because $\tilde{Q} = G\Lambda G^T$ is the general solution on all images, Eq. (15) must be satisfied for any set of the coefficients and rotations. For any two frames i and j that are formed by the same 3D shapes, *i.e.* same coefficients, but different rotations R_i and R_j, according to Eq. (15), we have

$$\alpha_i\mathbf{I}_{3\times 3} + \beta_i\tilde{\Gamma}_i = \alpha_i\mathbf{I}_{3\times 3} + \beta_j\tilde{\Gamma}_j \iff \beta_i\tilde{\Gamma}_i - \beta_j\tilde{\Gamma}_j = \mathbf{0}_{3\times 3} \implies R_j(\beta_i\tilde{\Gamma}_i - \beta_j\tilde{\Gamma}_j)R_j^T = \mathbf{0}_{2\times 2} \tag{16}$$

According to Eq. (14), we have $R_j\tilde{\Gamma}_jR_j^T = \mathbf{0}_{2\times 2}$, thus

$$R_j(\beta_i\tilde{\Gamma}_i)R_j^T = \mathbf{0}_{2\times 2} \tag{17}$$

Because R_j can be any rotation matrix, $\beta_i\tilde{\Gamma}_i$ has to be zero for any frame. Therefore,

$$\Sigma_{k=1}^K(c_{ik}^2\Lambda_{kk} + \Sigma_{j=k+1}^K c_{ij}c_{ij}(\Lambda_{kj} + \Lambda_{kj}^T)) = \alpha_i\mathbf{I}_{3\times 3} \tag{18}$$

Because Eq. (18) must be satisfied for any set of the coefficients, the solution is

$$\Lambda_{kk} = \lambda_{kk}\mathbf{I}_{3\times 3} \tag{19}$$

$$\Lambda_{kj} + \Lambda_{kj}^T = \lambda_{kj}\mathbf{I}_{3\times 3}, \quad k = 1,...,K; \quad j = k+1,...,K \tag{20}$$

where λ_{kk} and λ_{kj} are arbitrary scalars. According to Eq. (19), the diagonal block Λ_{kk} is a scaled identity matrix. From Eq. (20), $\Lambda_{kj} - \frac{\lambda_{kj}}{2}\mathbf{I}_{3\times 3} = -(\Lambda_{kj} - \frac{\lambda_{kj}}{2}\mathbf{I}_{3\times 3})^T$, i.e. $\Lambda_{kj} - \frac{\lambda_{kj}}{2}\mathbf{I}_{3\times 3}$ is skew-symmetric. Therefore the off-diagonal block Λ_{kj} equals the summation of a scaled identity block, $\frac{\lambda_{kj}}{2}\mathbf{I}_{3\times 3}$, and a skew-symmetric block, $\Lambda_{kj} - \frac{\lambda_{kj}}{2}\mathbf{I}_{3\times 3}$. This statement concludes the proof: Λ equals H, the summation of a block-skew-symmetric matrix Y and a block-scaled-identity matrix Z, i.e. the general solution of the rotation constraints is $\tilde{Q} = GHG^T$. $\square$

Because H consists of $2K^2 - K$ independent elements: $3K(K-1)/2$ from Y and $K(K+1)/2$ from Z, the solution space has $2K^2 - K$ degrees of freedom. It explains why the rotation constraints are sufficient in rigid cases ($K = 1$) but lead to ambiguous solutions when the scene is non-rigid ($K > 1$). This conclusion is also confirmed by our experiments. If every solution in the space is a valid solution of Q, then even if the ambiguity exists, we can compute an arbitrary solution in the space to solve the problem. However, the space contains many invalid solutions. Specifically, since $Q = GG^T$ must be positive semi-definite, when H is not positive semi-definite, the solutions $\tilde{Q} = GHG^T$ are not valid. For example, when H only consists of a block-skew-symmetric matrix Y, the solutions $\tilde{Q} = GYG^T$ are invalid because Y is not positive semi-definite.

4.3   Basis Constraints

Are there other constraints that we can use to remove the ambiguity of the rotation constraints? For static scenes, a variety of approaches [12,11] utilize only the rotation constraints and succeed in determining the correct solution. Intuitively, the only difference between non-rigid and rigid situations is that the non-rigid shape is a weighted combination of certain shape bases. This observation suggests that the ambiguity is related to the basis representation. Can we impose constraints on the bases to eliminate the ambiguity?

The shape bases are non-unique because any non-singular linear transformation on them yields a new set of eligible bases. However, if we find K frames including independent shapes and treat those shapes as a set of bases, the bases are determined uniquely[1]. We denote those frames as the first K images in the sequence and the corresponding coefficients are

$$c_{ii} = 1, \quad i = 1,...,K$$

$$c_{ij} = 0, \quad i \neq j, i = 1,...,K, j = 1,...,K \tag{21}$$

---

[1] We can find K frames in which the shapes are independent, by examining the singular values of their image projections.

For any three-column of G, $g_k, k = 1, ..., K$, according to Eq. (5),

$$\tilde{M}g_k = \begin{pmatrix} c_{1k}R_1 \\ ... \\ c_{Fk}R_F \end{pmatrix} \quad k = 1, ..., K \tag{22}$$

We denote $g_k g_k{}^T$ by Q_k. Then,

$$\tilde{M}_{2*i-1:2*i} Q_k \tilde{M}_{2*j-1:2*j}^T = c_{ik}c_{jk}R_i R_j^T \tag{23}$$

Thus Q_k satisfies the rotation constraints in Eq. (8) and Eq. (9). Besides, combining Eq. (21) and Eq. (23), we obtain another $4(K-1)F$ basis constraints on Q_k:

$$\tilde{M}_{2*i-1} Q_k \tilde{M}_{2*j-1}^T = \begin{cases} 1, & i = j = k \\ 0, & (i,j) \in \omega_1 \end{cases} \tag{24}$$

$$\tilde{M}_{2*i} Q_k \tilde{M}_{2*j}^T = \begin{cases} 1, & i = j = k \\ 0, & (i,j) \in \omega_1 \end{cases} \tag{25}$$

$$\tilde{M}_{2i-1} Q_k \tilde{M}_{2*j}^T = 0, \quad (i,j) \in \omega_1 \text{ or } i = j = k \tag{26}$$

$$\tilde{M}_{2i} Q_k \tilde{M}_{2*j-1}^T = 0, \quad (i,j) \in \omega_1 \text{ or } i = j = k \tag{27}$$

where $\omega_1 = \{(i,j)|i = 1, ..., K, \ j = 1, ..., F, \text{ and } i \neq k\}$.

5   A Closed-Form Solution

Due to Theorem 1, enforcing the rotation constraints on Q_k leads to the ambiguous solution $\tilde{Q} = GHG^T$. This section will prove that enforcing the basis constraints eliminates the ambiguity on $\tilde{Q}$ and determines a closed-form solution. Note that we assume that the 3D structure and camera motion are both non-degenerate, *i.e.* the rank of $\tilde{W}$ is $3K$.

By definition, each 3×3 block H_{ij} $(i,j = 1, ..., K)$ of H contains four independent entries,

$$H_{ij} = \begin{pmatrix} h_1 & h_2 & h_3 \\ -h_2 & h_1 & h_4 \\ -h_3 & -h_4 & h_1 \end{pmatrix} \tag{28}$$

Lemma 1 *Under non-degenerate situations, H_{ij} is a zero matrix if,*

$$R_i H_{ij} R_j^T = \begin{pmatrix} r_{i1} \\ r_{i2} \end{pmatrix} H_{ij} \begin{pmatrix} r_{j1}^T & r_{j2}^T \end{pmatrix} = 0_{2 \times 2} \tag{29}$$

Proof. First we prove that the rank of H_{ij} is at most 2. Due to the orthonormality constraints,

$$H_{ij} = \begin{pmatrix} r_{i3}^T & \delta_j^T \end{pmatrix} \begin{pmatrix} \delta_i \\ r_{j3} \end{pmatrix} \tag{30}$$

where $r_{i3} = r_{i1} \times r_{i2}$, $r_{j3} = r_{j1} \times r_{j2}$, δ_i and δ_j are two arbitrary 1×3 vectors. Both matrices on the right side of Eq. (30) are at most of rank 2. Thus the rank of H_{ij} is at most 2.

Next, we prove $h_1 = 0$. Since the rank of H_{ij} is less than its dimension, 3, its determinant, $h_1(\sum_{i=1}^{4} h_i^2)$, equals 0. Therefore h_1 must be 0 and H_{ij} is a skew-symmetric matrix.

We then prove $h_2 = h_3 = h_4 = 0$. Since $h_1 = 0$, we rewrite Eq. (29) as follows:

$$\begin{pmatrix} r_{i1} \cdot (\mathbf{h} \times r_{j1}) & r_{i1} \cdot (\mathbf{h} \times r_{j2}) \\ r_{i2} \cdot (\mathbf{h} \times r_{j1}) & r_{i2} \cdot (\mathbf{h} \times r_{j2}) \end{pmatrix} = \mathbf{0}_{2 \times 2} \tag{31}$$

where $\mathbf{h} = (-h_4\ h_3\ -h_2)$. Eq. (31) means that the vector $\mathbf{h}$ is located in the intersection of the four planes determined by $(r_{i1}, r_{j1}), (r_{i1}, r_{j2}), (r_{i2}, r_{j1})$, and (r_{i2}, r_{j2}). Under non-degenerate situations, r_{i1}, r_{i2}, r_{j1}, and r_{j2} do not lie in the same plane, hence the four planes intersect at the origin, i.e. $\mathbf{h} = (-h_4\ h_3 - h_2) = \mathbf{0}_{1 \times 3}$. Therefore H_{ij} is a zero matrix. □

According to Lemma 1, we derive the following theorem,

Theorem 2. *Enforcing both basis constraints and rotation constraints results in a unique solution* $\tilde{Q} = g_k g_k^T$, *where* g_k *is the* k_{th} *three-column of* G.

Proof. Due to Theorem 1, by enforcing the rotation constraints, we achieve the solution $\tilde{Q} = GHG^T$. Thus $\tilde{M}\tilde{Q}\tilde{M}^T = MHM^T$, and

$$M_{2*i-1:2*i}HM_{2*j-1:2*j}^T = \Sigma_{k_1=1}^{K}\Sigma_{k_2=1}^{K}c_{ik_1}c_{jk_2}R_iH_{k_1k_2}R_j^T, \quad i,j = 1,...,F \tag{32}$$

According to Eq. (21),

$$M_{2*i-1:2*i}HM_{2*j-1:2*j}^T = R_iH_{ij}R_j^T, \quad i,j = 1,...,K \tag{33}$$

Due to the basis constraints in Eq. (24) to (27),

$$R_kH_{kk}R_k^T = \mathbf{I}_{2 \times 2} \tag{34}$$

$$R_iH_{ij}R_j^T = \mathbf{0}_{2 \times 2}, \quad i,j = 1,...,K, \ and \ i \neq k, \ j \neq k \tag{35}$$

By definition, $H_{kk} = \lambda_{kk}\mathbf{I}_{3 \times 3}$, where λ_{kk} is a scalar. Due to Eq. (34), $\lambda_{kk} = 1$ and $H_{kk} = \mathbf{I}_{3 \times 3}$. From Lemma 1 and Eq. (35), H_{ij} is a zero matrix when $i,j = 1,...,K$, and $i \neq k, j \neq k$. Thus $\tilde{Q} = GHG^T = (g_1,...,g_K)H(g_1,...,g_K)^T = (0,...,0,g_k,0,...0)(g_1,...,g_K)^T = g_kg_k^T$. □

Now we have proved that, by enforcing both rotation and basis constraints, *i.e.* solving Eq. (8) to (9) and (24) to (27) by the least square methods, a closed-form solution, $\tilde{Q} = Q_k = g_kg_k^T$, $k = 1,...,K$, is achieved. Then g_k, $k = 1,...,K$ can be recovered by decomposing Q_k via SVD. We project $g_k's$ to the common coordinate system and determine the corrective transformation $G = (g_1,...,g_K)$. According to Eq. (5), we recover the shape bases $B = G^{-1}\tilde{B}$, the scaled rotation matrix $M = \tilde{M}G$, and thus the rotations and coefficients.

6   Performance Evaluation

The performance of the closed-form solution is evaluated in a number of experiments.

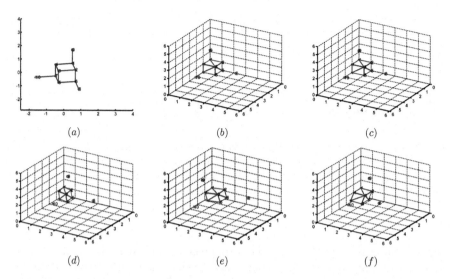

Fig. 1. A static cube and 3 points moving along straight lines. (a) Input image. (b) Ground truth 3D shape. (c) Reconstruction by the closed-form solution. (d) Reconstruction by the method in [6]. (e) Reconstruction by the method in [4] after 4000 iterations. (f) Reconstruction by the tri-linear method [13] after 4000 iterations.

6.1   Comparison with Three Previous Methods

We first compare the solution with three related methods [6,4,13] in a simple noiseless setting. Fig.1 shows a scene consisting of a static cube and 3 moving points. The measurement consists of 10 points: 7 visible vertices of the cube and 3 moving points. The 3 points move along the axes at varying speed. This setting consists of $K = 2$ shape bases, one for the static cube and another for the moving points. Their image projections across 16 frames from different views are given. One of them is shown in Fig.1.(a). The corresponding ground truth structure is demonstrated in Fig.1.(b). Fig.1.(c) to (f) show the structures reconstructed using the closed-form solution, the method in [6], the method in [4], and the tri-linear method [13], respectively. While the closed-form solution achieves the exact reconstruction with zero error, all three previous methods result in apparent errors, even for such a simple noiseless setting. Fig.2 demonstrates the reconstruction errors of the previous work on rotations, shapes, and image measurements. The errors are computed relative to the ground truth.

6.2   Quantitative Evaluation on Synthetic Data

Our approach is then quantitatively evaluated on the synthetic data. We evaluate the accuracy and robustness on three factors: deformation strength, number of shape bases, and noise level. The deformation strength shows how close to rigid the shape is. It is represented by the mean power ratio between each two bases, *i.e.* $mean_{i,j}\left(\frac{max(\|B_i\|,\|B_j\|)}{min(\|B_i\|,\|B_j\|)}\right)$. Larger ratio means weaker deformation, *i.e.* the

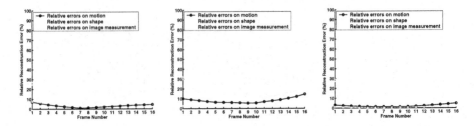

Fig. 2. The relative errors on reconstruction of a static cube and 3 points moving along straight lines. (Left) By the method in [6]. (Middle) By the method in [4] after 4000 iterations. (Right) By the trilinear method [13] after 4000 iterations. The range of the error axis is $[0\%, 100\%]$. Note that our solution achieves zero reconstruction errors.

shape is closer to rigid. The number of shape bases represents the flexibility of the shape. A bigger basis number means that the shape is more flexible. Assuming a Gaussian white noise, we represent the noise strength level by the ratio between the Frobenius norm of the noise and the measurement, $i.e.$ $\frac{\|noise\|}{\|\tilde{W}\|}$. In general, when noise exists, a weaker deformation leads to better performance, because some deformation mode is more dominant and the noise relative to the dominant basis is weaker; a bigger basis number results in poorer performance, because the noise relative to each individual basis is stronger.

Fig. 3.(a) and (b) show the performance of our algorithm under various deformation strength and noise levels on a two bases setting. The power ratios are respectively 2^0, 2^1, ..., and 2^8. Four levels of Gaussian white noise are imposed. Their strength levels are 0%, 5%, 10%, and 20% respectively. We test a number of trials on each setting and compute the average reconstruction errors on the rotations and 3D shapes, relative to the ground truth. Fig.3.(c) and (d) show the performance of our method under different numbers of shape bases and noise levels. The basis number is 2, 3, ... , and 10 respectively. The bases have equal powers and thus none of them is dominant. The same noise as in the last experiment is imposed.

In both experiments, when the noise level is 0%, the closed-form solution always recovers the exact rotations and shapes with zero error. When there is noise, it achieves reasonable accuracy, $e.g.$ the maximum reconstruction error is less than 15% when the noise level is 20%. As we expected, under the same noise level, the performance is better when the power ratio is larger and poorer when the basis number is bigger. Note that in all the experiments, the condition number of the linear system consisting of both basis constraints and rotation constraints has order of magnitude $O(10)$ to $O(10^2)$, even if the basis number is big and the deformation is strong. Our closed-form solution is thus numerically stable.

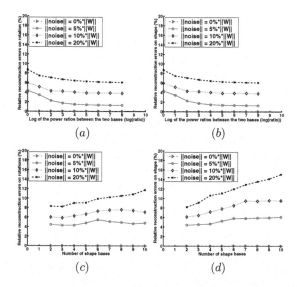

(a)   (b)

(c)   (d)

Fig. 3. (a)&(b) Reconstruction errors on rotations and shapes under different levels of noise and deformation strength. (c)&(d) Reconstruction errors on rotations and shapes under different levels of noise and various basis numbers. Each curve respectively refers to a noise level. The range of the error axis is [0%, 20%].

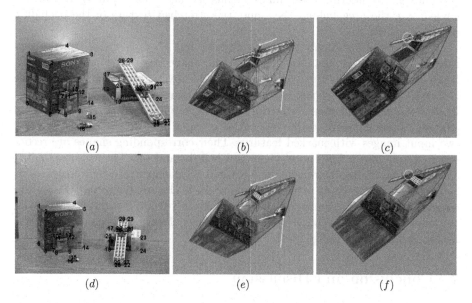

(a)   (b)   (c)

(d)   (e)   (f)

Fig. 4. Reconstruction of three moving objects in the static background. (a)&(d) Two input images with marked features. (b)&(e) Reconstruction by the closed-form solution. The yellow lines show the recovered trajectories from the beginning of the sequence until the present frames. (c)&(f) Reconstruction by the method in [4]. The yellow-circled area shows that the plane, which should be on top of the slope, is mistakenly located underneath the slope.

6.3   Qualitative Evaluation on Real Video Sequences

Finally we examine our approach qualitatively on a number of real video sequences. One example is shown in Fig.4. The sequence was taken of an indoor scene by a handheld camera. Three objects, a car, a plane, and a toy person, moved along fixed directions and at varying speeds. The rest of the scene was static. The car and the person moved on the floor and the plane moved along a slope. The scene structure was composed of two bases, one for the static objects and another for the moving objects. 32 feature points tracked across 18 images were used for reconstruction. Two of the them are shown in Fig.4.(a) and (d).

The rank of $\tilde{W}$ was estimated in such a way that after rank reduction 99% of the energy was kept. The basis number is automatically determined by $K = rank(\tilde{W})/3$. The camera rotations and dynamic scene structure are then reconstructed. To evaluate the reconstruction, we synthesize the scene appearance viewed from one side, as shown in Fig.4.(b) and (e). The wireframes show the structure and the yellow lines show the trajectories of the moving objects from the beginning of the sequence until the present frames. The reconstruction is consistent with our observation, *e.g.* the plane moved linearly on top of the slope. Fig.4.(c) and (f) show the reconstruction using the method in [4]. The shapes of the boxes are distorted and the plane is incorrectly located underneath the slope, as shown in the yellow circles. Note that occlusion was not taken into account when rendering these images, thus in the regions that should be occluded, *e.g.* the area behind the slope, the stretched texture of the occluding objects appears.

Human faces are highly non-rigid objects and 3D face shapes can be represented as weighted combinations of certain shape bases that refer to various facial expressions. They thus can be reconstructed by our approach. One example is shown in Fig.5. The sequence consists of 236 images that contain expressions like eye blinking and mouth opening. 60 feature points were tracked using an efficient Active Appearance Model (AAM) method [1]. Fig.5.(a) and (d) display two input images with marked features. Their corresponding shapes are reconstructed and shown from novel views in Fig.5.(b) and (e). Their corresponding 3D wireframe models shown in Fig.5.(c) and (f) demonstrate the recovered facial deformations such as mouth opening and eye closure. Note that the feature correspondence in these experiments was noisy, especially for those features on the sides of face. The reconstruction performance of our approach demonstrates its robustness to the image noise.

7   Conclusion and Discussion

This paper proposes a closed-form solution to the problem of non-rigid shape and motion recovery from single-camera video using the least square and factorization methods. In particular, we have proven that enforcing only the rotation constraints results in ambiguous and invalid solutions. We thus introduce the basis constraints to remove this ambiguity. We have also proven that imposing both metric constraints leads to a unique reconstruction of the non-rigid shape

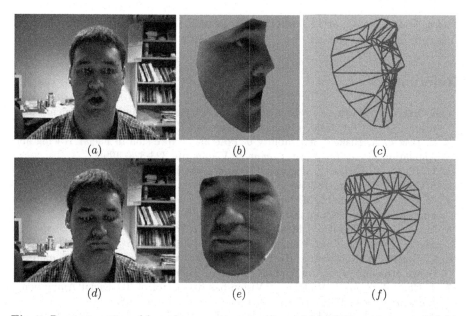

Fig. 5. Reconstruction of face shapes with expressions. (a)&(d) Input images. (b)&(e) Reconstructed face shapes seen from novel views. (c)&(f) The wireframe models demonstrate the recovered facial deformations such as mouth opening and eye closure.

and motion. The performance of our algorithm is demonstrated by experiments on both simulated data and real video data. Our algorithm has also been successfully applied to separate the local deformations from the global rotations and translations in the 3D motion capture data [7].

Currently, our approach does not consider the degenerate deformation modes of 3D shapes. A deformation mode is degenerate, if it limits the shape to deform in a plane, *i.e.*, the rank of the corresponding basis is less than 3. For example, if a scene contains only one moving object that moves along a straight line, the deformation mode referring to the linear motion is degenerate, because the corresponding basis (the motion vector) is of rank 1. It is conceivable that the ambiguity cannot be completely eliminated by the basis constraints and enforcing both metric constraints is insufficient to produce a closed-form solution in such degenerate cases. We are now exploring how to extend the current approach to recovering the non-rigid shapes that deform with degenerate modes. Another limitation of our approach is that we assume the weak perspective projection model. It would be interesting to see if the proposed approach could be extended to the full perspective projection model.

Acknowledgments. We would like to thank Simon Baker, Iain Matthews, and Mei Han for providing the image data and feature correspondence used in Section 6.3, and thank Jessica Hodgins for proofreading the paper. Jinxiang Chai was supported by the NSF through EIA0196217 and IIS0205224. Jing Xiao and

Takeo Kanade were partly supported by grant R01 MH51435 from the National Institute of Mental Health.

References

1. S. Baker, I. Matthews, " Equivalence and Efficiency of Image Alignment Algorithms," *Proc. Int. Conf. Computer Vision and Pattern Recognition*, 2001.
2. B. Bascle, A. Blake," Separability of Pose and Expression in Facial Tracing and Animation,"*Proc. Int. Conf. Computer Vision*, pp. 323-328, 1998.
3. V. Blanz, T. Vetter, " A morphable model for the synthesis of 3D faces," *Proc. SIGGRAPH'99*, pp. 187-194, 1999.
4. M. Brand, " Morphable 3D Models from Video," *Proc. Int. Conf. Computer Vision and Pattern Recognition*, 2001.
5. M. Brand, R. Bhotika, " Flexible Flow for 3D Nonrigid Tracking and Shape Recovery,"*Proc. Int. Conf. Computer Vision and Pattern Recognition*, 2001.
6. C. Bregler, A. Hertzmann, H. Biermann, " Recovering Non-Rigid 3D Shape from Image Streams," *Proc. Int. Conf. Computer Vision and Pattern Recognition*, 2000.
7. J. Chai, J. Xiao, J. Hodgins, " Vision-based Control of 3D Facial Animation," *Eurographics/ACM Symposium on Computer Animation*, 2003.
8. J. Costeira, T. Kanade, " A multibody factorization method for independently moving-objects," *Int. Journal of Computer Vision*, 29(3):159-179, 1998.
9. S.B. Gokturk, J.Y Bouguet, R. Grzeszczuk, " A data driven model for monocular face tracking," *Proc. Int. Conf. Computer Vision*, 2001.
10. M. Han, T. Kanade, " Reconstruction of a Scene with Multiple Linearly Moving Objects," *Proc. Int. Conf. Computer Vision and Pattern Recognition*, 2000.
11. C. Poelman, T. Kanade, " A paraperspective factorization method for shape and motion recovery," *IEEE Trans. Pattern Analysis and Machine Intelligence*, 19(3):206-218, 1997.
12. C. Tomasi, T. Kanade, " Shape and motion from image streams under orthography: A factorization method," *Int. Journal of Computer Vision*, 9(2):137-154, 1992.
13. L. Torresani, D. Yang, G. Alexander, C. Bregler, " Tracking and Modeling Non-Rigid Objects with Rank Constraints," *Proc. Int. Conf. Computer Vision and Pattern Recognition*, 2001.
14. B. Triggs, " Factorization Methods for Projective Structure and Motion," *Proc. Int. Conf. Computer Vision and Pattern Recognition*,1996.
15. R. Vidal, S. Soatto, Y. Ma, S. Sastry, " Segmentation of Dynamic Scenes from the Multibody Fundamental Matrix," *ECCV Workshop on Vision and Modeling of Dynamic Scenes*, 2002.
16. L. Wolf, A. Shashua, " Two-body Segmentation from Two Perspective Views," *Proc. Int. Conf. Computer Vision and Pattern Recognition*, 2001.
17. L. Wolf, A. Shashua, " On Projection Matrices $P^k \rightarrow P^2, k = 3, \ldots, 6$, and their Applications in Computer Vision," *Int. Journal of Computer Vision*, 48(1):53-67, 2002.

Stereo Using Monocular Cues within the Tensor Voting Framework

Philippos Mordohai and Gérard Medioni

Institute for Robotics and Intelligent Systems
University of Southern California
Los Angeles, CA 90089, USA
{mordohai,medioni}@iris.usc.edu

Abstract. We address the fundamental problem of matching two static images. Significant progress has been made in this area, but the correspondence problem has not been solved. Most of the remaining difficulties are caused by occlusion and lack of texture. We propose an approach that addresses these difficulties within a perceptual organization framework, taking into account both binocular and monocular sources of information. Geometric and color information from the scene is used for grouping, complementing each other's strengths. We begin by generating matching hypotheses for every pixel in such a way that a variety of matching techniques can be integrated, thus allowing us to combine their particular advantages. Correct matches are detected based on the support they receive from their neighboring candidate matches in 3-D, after tensor voting. They are grouped into smooth surfaces, the projections of which on the images serve as the reliable set of matches. The use of segmentation based on geometric cues to infer the color distributions of scene surfaces is arguably the most significant contribution of our research. The inferred reliable set of matches guides the generation of disparity hypotheses for the unmatched pixels. The match for an unmatched pixel is selected among a set of candidates as the one that is a good continuation of the surface, and also compatible with the observed color distribution of the surface in both images. Thus, information is propagated from more to less reliable pixels considering both geometric and color information. We present results on standard stereo pairs.

1 Introduction

The premise of shape from stereo comes from the fact that, in a set of two or more images of a static scene, world points appear on the images at different disparities depending on their distance from the cameras. Establishing pixel correspondences on real images, though, is far from trivial. Projective and photometric distortion, sensor noise, occlusion, lack of texture, and repetitive patterns make matching the most difficult stage of a stereo algorithm. To address mainly occlusion and lack of texture, we propose a stereo algorithm that operates as a perceptual organization process in the 3-D disparity space knowing that false

T. Pajdla and J. Matas (Eds.): ECCV 2004, LNCS 3024, pp. 588–601, 2004.

matches will most likely occur in textureless areas and close to depth discontinuities. Since binocular processing has limitations in these areas, we use monocular information to overcome them. We start by detecting the most reliable matches, which are grouped into layers. Shape and color information from the layers is used to infer matches for the remaining pixels.

The paper is organized as follows: Section 2 reviews related work; Section 3 is an overview of the algorithm; Section 4 describes the initial matching stage; Section 5 the detection of correct matches using tensor voting; Section 6 the segmentation process; Section 7 the disparity computation for unmatched pixels; Section 8 contains experimental results; and Section 9 concludes the paper.

2   Related Work

Published research on stereo with explicit treatment of occlusion includes numerous approaches (see [1] for a comprehensive review of stereo algorithms). They can be categorized into the following categories: local, global and approaches with extended local support, such as the one we propose. Local methods attempt to solve the correspondence problem using local operators in relatively small windows. Kanade and Okutomi [2] use matching windows whose size and shape adapt according to the intensities and disparities that are included in them. In [3] Veksler presents a method that takes into account the average matching error per pixel, the variance of this error and the size of the window.

On the other hand, global methods arrive at disparity assignments by optimizing a global cost function that usually includes penalties for pixel dissimilarities and violation of the smoothness constraint. The latter introduces a bias for constant disparities at neighboring pixels, thus favoring frontoparallel planes. Global stereo methods that explicitly model occlusion include [4][5][6][7] where optimization is performed using dynamic programming. The drawback of dynamic programming is that each epipolar line is processed independently, which results in "streaking" artifacts in the output. Consistency among epipolar lines is ensured by using graph cuts to optimize the objective function. Ishikawa and Geiger [8] explicitly model occlusion in a graph cut framework, but their algorithm is limited to convex energy functions which do not perform well at discontinuities. Kolmogorov and Zabih [9] advance the graph cut matching framework by proposing an optimization technique that is applicable to more general objective functions and obtains very good results.

Between these two extremes are approaches that are neither "winner-take-all" at the local level, nor global. They start from the most reliable matches to estimate the disparities of less reliable ones. Many authors [10][11] use the support and inhibition mechanism of cooperative stereo to ensure the propagation of correct disparities and the uniqueness of matches with respect to both images. Reliable matches without competitors are used to reinforce matches that are compatible with them and eliminate the ones that contradict them, progressively disambiguating more pixels. Zhang and Kambhamettu [12] extend the cooperative framework from single pixels to segmented surfaces, in the form of small locally planar patches. A different method of aggregating support is nonlinear diffusion, proposed by Scharstein and Szeliski in [13], where disparity estimates are propagated to neighboring pixels until convergence. Sun *et al.* [14] formulate the problem as an MRF with explicit handling of occlusions. In the belief propagation framework, information is passed to adjacent pixels in the form of messages whose weight also takes into account image segmentation. Other progressive approaches include Szeliski and Scharstein [15] and Zhang and Shan [16] who start from the most reliable matches and allow the most certain disparities guide the estimation of less certain ones, while occlusions are explicitly labeled.

The final class of methods reviewed here are based on image segmentation. Birchfield and Tomasi [17] cast the problem of correspondence as image segmentation followed by the estimation of an affine transformation for each segment between the images. Tao *et al.* [18] introduce a stereo matching technique where the goal is to establish correspondence between image regions rather than pixels. Both these methods are limited to planar surfaces, unlike the one of [12] which was described above. Lin and Tomasi [19] propose a framework where 3-D shape is estimated by fitting splines, while 2-D support is based on image segmentation. Processing alternates between these two steps until convergence. As mentioned above, in [14] image segmentation is a soft constraint, since messages can be passed between different image segments with a lower weight. All of these approaches, however, address color segmentation independently of disparity.

The perceptual organization stage of the approach we propose here is based on the work of Lee *et al.* [20], which was later extended to multiple views in [21]. However, there are significant differences in the way initial matches are generated and, most importantly, in the integration of monocular cues to specifically address occlusion and lack of texture. The approach in [20] has a less sophisticated initial matching scheme, the failures of which cannot always be corrected. In addition, the post-processing mechanism based on edge detection it proposes is not as effective against occlusion as the approach presented here. On the other hand, information propagation in 3-D and the use of surface saliency as the criterion for the selection of pixel correspondences remain cornerstones of our approach.

3   Algorithm Overview

The proposed algorithm has four steps, which are illustrated in Fig. 1, for the "Sawtooth" stereo pair (courtesy of [1]).

– The input to the first stage is a pair of images which we assume have been rectified so that conjugate epipolar lines are parallel and share the same y coordinate. The goal is the generation of matching hypotheses for every pixel and it is accomplished with three different matching techniques. The output is a set of points in 3-D disparity space (Fig. 1(b)).
– Next is the tensor voting stage, during which the unorganized point cloud from the previous stage is encoded in the form of second order symmetric tensors which cast votes to their neighbors. Salient matches can be detected

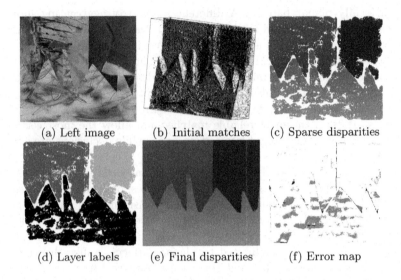

(a) Left image   (b) Initial matches   (c) Sparse disparities

(d) Layer labels   (e) Final disparities   (f) Error map

Fig. 1. Overview of the processing steps for the "Sawtooth" dataset. The initial matches have been rotated so that the multiple candidates for each pixel are visible. Black pixels in the error map indicate errors greater than 1 disparity level, gray pixels correspond to errors between 0.5 and 1 disparity level, while white pixels are correct (or occluded and thus ignored)

based on the amount of support they receive from their neighbors. Uniqueness is also enforced at the end of this stage with respect to surface saliency and not a local measure, such as cross-correlation, which is more susceptible to noise. The output, which we term "sparse disparity map", consists of at most one match for each pixel of the reference image, which has an associated surface saliency value and an estimate of surface orientation. It can be seen in Fig. 1(c). This part of the algorithm is based on our previous work, published in [20].

- The outputs of the tensor voting are grouped, using the estimated surface orientations, into smooth layers. These are refined by removing those 3-D points that correspond to pixels that are inconsistent with the layer's color distribution. This addresses the usual problem of surface over-extension that occurs near occlusions. The over-extensions are usually not color-consistent and are removed at this stage. Thus we derive the set of reliable matches. Please note that the term layer throughout this paper is used interchangeably with surface, since by layer we mean a smooth, but not necessarily planar, surface in 3-D disparity space (x, y, d), where d denotes disparity. The label of each pixel can be seen in Fig. 1(d).

- The last module starts from a set of segmented surfaces and computes disparities for unmatched pixels. Disparity candidates are generated from the nearby layers, to which the pixel may belong based on its color. These are also validated in the right image and the final disparity is selected as the one that is a smooth continuation of the most likely layer. The output of this stage is a dense disparity map with one disparity estimate for every pixel of the reference image including the occluded ones (Fig. 1(e)). Disparity estimation for occluded pixels is possible since the surfaces can be extrapolated using tensor voting even if they are occluded.

The algorithm is applied on the four datasets proposed in [1] and the two proposed in [22], which are also available online at
                    http://www.middlebury.edu/stereo.
Quantitative results are presented in Section 8.

4   Initial Matching

A large number of matching techniques have been proposed in the literature [1]. We propose a scheme for combining heterogeneous matching techniques, thus taking advantage of their combined strengths. For the results presented in this paper, three matching techniques are used, but any kind of matching can be integrated in the framework. The techniques used here are:

- A 5×5 normalized cross correlation window, which is small enough to capture details and only assumes constant disparity for small parts of the image.
- A 35×35 normalized cross correlation window, which is applied only at pixels where the standard deviation of the three color channels is less than 20. The use of such a big window over the entire image would be catastrophic, but it is effective when applied only in virtually textureless regions, where smaller windows completely fail to detect correct matches.
- A 7×7 symmetric interval matching window with truncated cost function as in [15]. The images are linearly interpolated along the x-axis so that samples exist in half-pixel intervals. The cost for matching pixel (x_L, y) in the left image with pixel (x_R, y) in the right image is:

$$C(x_L, x_R, y) = \sum_c min\{dist(I_{Lc}(x_i, y), I_{Rc}(x_j, y)) :$$

$$x_i \in [x_L - \frac{1}{2} \quad x_L + \frac{1}{2}], x_j \in [x_R - \frac{1}{2} \quad x_R + \frac{1}{2}]\} \quad (1)$$

The summation is over the three RGB color channels and $dist()$ is the Euclidean distance between the value of a color channel I_{Lc} in the left image and I_{Rc} in the right image. If the distance for any channel exceeds a preset truncation parameter $trunc$, the total cost is set to $3 \times trunc$. This technique is effective near discontinuities due to the robustness of the cost function to pixels from different surfaces. Typical values for $trunc$ are between 3 and 10.

Each matching technique is repeated using the right image as reference and the left as target. This increases the true positive rate especially near discontinuities, where the presence of occluded pixels in the reference window affects the results of matching. When the other image is used as reference, these pixels do not appear in the reference window.

The maximum matching score, or the minimum cost, for every pixel is retained as a matching hypothesis. Matching scores and costs are then discarded and each hypothesis is treated equally in the following stage. A simple parabolic fit [1] is used for subpixel accuracy, mainly because it makes continuous slanted or curved surfaces appear continuous and not staircase-like. Computational complexity is not affected since the number of matching hypotheses is unchanged. Besides the increased number of correct detections, the combination of these matching techniques offers the advantage that the failures of a particular technique are not detrimental to the success of the algorithm. The 35×35 window is typically applied to very small uniform parts of the image and never near discontinuities, where color exhibits some variance. Our experiments have also shown that the errors produced by small windows, such as the 5×5 and 7×7 used here, are randomly spread in space and do not usually align to form nonexistent structures. This property is important for our methodology that is based on the perceptual organization, due to "non-accidental alignment", of candidate matches in space.

5 Detection of Correct Matches

This section describes how correct matches can be found among the hypotheses of the previous stage by examining how they can be grouped with their neighboring candidate matches to form smooth 3-D surfaces. This is accomplished by tensor voting, which also allows us to infer the orientation of these surfaces.

5.1 Overview of Tensor Voting

The use of a voting process for structure inference from sparse and noisy data was presented in [23]. The methodology is non-iterative and robust to considerable amounts of outlier noise. It has one free parameter: the scale of voting, which essentially defines the size of the neighborhood of each point. The input data is encoded as second-order symmetric tensors, and constraints, such as proximity, co-linearity and co-curvilinearity are propagated by voting within the neighborhood. The tensors allow the representation of points on smooth surfaces, surface intersections, curves and junctions, without having to keep each type in separate spaces. In 3-D, a second-order tensor has the form of an ellipsoid, or equivalently of a 3×3 matrix. Its shape encodes the type of feature that it represents, while its size the *saliency* or the confidence we have in this information (Fig. 2(a)).

The tensors are initialized as unitary matrices, since no information about their preferred orientation is known. During the voting process, each input site casts votes to its neighboring input sites that contain tokens. The votes are also second-order symmetric tensors. Their shape corresponds to the orientation the receiver would have, if the voter and receiver were in the same structure. The saliency (strength) of a vote cast by a unitary stick tensor decays with respect to the length of the smooth circular path connecting the voter and receiver, according to the following equation:

$$S(s, \kappa, \sigma) = e^{-\left(\frac{s^2 + c\kappa^2}{\sigma^2}\right)}$$ (2)

Where s is the length of the arc between the voter and receiver, and κ is its curvature (see Fig. 2(b)), σ is the scale of voting, and c is a constant. The votes cast by un-oriented voters can be derived from the above equation, but this is beyond the scope of this paper. Vote accumulation is performed by tensor addition, which is equivalent to the addition of 3×3 matrices. After voting is completed, the eigensystem of each tensor is analyzed and the tensor is decomposed as in:

$$T = \lambda_1 \hat{e}_1 \hat{e}_1^T + \lambda_2 \hat{e}_2 \hat{e}_2^T + \lambda_3 \hat{e}_3 \hat{e}_3^T =$$
$$= (\lambda_1 - \lambda_2)\hat{e}_1 \hat{e}_1^T + (\lambda_2 - \lambda_3)(\hat{e}_1 \hat{e}_1^T + \hat{e}_2 \hat{e}_2^T) + \lambda_3(\hat{e}_1 \hat{e}_1^T + \hat{e}_2 \hat{e}_2^T + \hat{e}_3 \hat{e}_3^T)$$ (3)

where λ_i are the eigenvalues in decreasing order and $\hat{e}_i$ are the corresponding eigenvectors. The likelihood that a point belongs to a smooth perceptual structure is determined as follows. The difference between the two largest eigenvalues encodes surface saliency, with a surface normal given by e_1. The difference between the second and third eigenvalue encodes curve saliency, with a curve tangent parallel to e_3. Finally, the smallest eigenvalue encodes junction saliency. If surface saliency is high, the point most likely belongs on a surface and e_1 is its normal. Outliers that receive no or inconsistent support from their neighborhood can be identified by their low saliency and the lack of a dominant orientation. In the case of stereo, we assume that that all inliers lie on surfaces that reflect light towards the cameras, and therefore we do not consider curves and junctions.

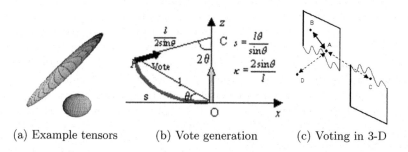

(a) Example tensors   (b) Vote generation   (c) Voting in 3-D

Fig. 2. Tensor Voting. (a) The shape of the tensor indicates if there is a preferred orientation, while its size the confidence of this information. The top tensor has a strong preference of orientation and is more salient than the bottom tensor, which is smaller and un-oriented. (b) Vote generation as a function of the distance and curvature of the arc and the orientation of the voter. (c) Voting in 3-D neighborhoods eliminates interference between adjacent pixels from different layers

5.2   Detection of Matches as Surface Inliers

The goal of this stage is to address stereo as a perceptual organization problem in 3-D, based on the premise that the correct matches should form coherent surfaces in the 3-D disparity space. This is the only part of our approach that is based on [20]. The input is a cloud of points in a 3-D space $(x, y, zscale \times d)$, where $zscale$ is a constant used to make the input less flat with respect to the d-axis, since is disparity space is usually a lot flatter than actual (x, y, z). Its typical value is 8 and the sensitivity is extremely low for a reasonable range such as 4 to 20. The quantitative matching scores are disregarded and all candidate matches are initialized as un-oriented tensors with saliency (confidence) 1. If two or more matches fall within the same $(x, y, zscale \times d)$ voxel their initial saliencies are added, thus increasing the confidence of candidate matches confirmed by multiple matching techniques.

After the inputs have been encoded as tensors, they cast votes to their neighbors. The voting neighborhood includes all locations at which the strength of the votes is at least 2.5% of the voter's saliency. Therefore, its size is a function of σ from Eq. 2. What should be pointed out here is the fact that since information propagation is performed in 3-D there is very little interference between candidate matches for pixels that are adjacent in the image but come from different surfaces (see Fig. 2(c)). This is a big advantage over information propagation between adjacent pixels, even if it is mitigated by some dissimilarity measure.

Once voting is completed, the results can be analyzed and the surface saliency of every candidate match can be computed as in Eq. 3. Uniqueness is enforced with respect to the left image by retaining the candidate with the highest surface saliency for every pixel. We do not enforce uniqueness with respect to the right image since it is violated by slanted surfaces which project to a different number of pixels on each image. Since the objective is disparity estimation for every pixel in the reference image, uniqueness applies to that image only. The fact that a candidate match has no competition for a given pixel does not necessarily indicate that it is correct, since the correct match could have been missed at the first stage. Therefore, candidate matches with low surface saliency are rejected even if they satisfy uniqueness. Surface saliency is a more reliable criterion for the selection of correct matches than the score of a local matching operator, because it requires that candidate matches, identified as such by local operators, should also form coherent surfaces in 3-D. This scheme is capable of rejecting false positive responses of the local operators, which is not possible at the local level. Based on the datasets we use, good results are achieved when the least salient candidates are gradually rejected until disparity estimates remain for about 70-80% of the pixels. In the data set, which we call the "sparse disparity map", remain matches with high surface saliency, which also satisfy uniqueness.

6   Segmentation into Layers

Surface inliers are segmented into layers using a simple growing scheme. By layers we mean surfaces with smooth variation of surface normal. Therefore, the layers do not have to be planar and the points that belong to them do not have to form one connected component. Labeling starts from seed matches that have maximum surface saliency by examining matches within a certain distance in 3-D for compatibility in terms of surface normals as in Fig. 3(a). If a smooth surface that goes through the seed and the match under consideration exists, then the point is added to the layer. Further comparisons for the addition of more points to a layer are made between unlabeled points and the points from the layer that are closer to them. For all the experiments presented in this paper the grouping criteria are: $cos(\theta_1) < 0.95$ and $max\{cos(\theta_2), cos(\theta_3)\} < 0.08$. The search region, which is a non-critical parameter, is set equal to the voting neighborhood size. Since we do not attempt to fit global surface models, our grouping scheme performs equally well when the scene surfaces deviate from planar or quadric models.

To derive the reliable set of matches, one additional step is necessary to remove possible contamination from the layers due to surface over-extension from the initial matching stage. The colors of all points assigned to a layer are examined for consistency with the layer's local color distribution and the outliers are removed from the layer. Color consistency of a pixel is checked by computing the ratio of pixels of the same layer with similar color to the current pixel over the total number of pixels of the layer within the neighborhood. This is repeated for every layer on both images and if the current assignment does not correspond to the maximum ratio *in both images*, then the pixel is removed from the layer. The color similarity ratio for pixel (x_0, y_0) in the left image with layer i can be computed according to the following equation:

$$R_i(x_0, y_0) = \frac{\sum_{(x,y)\in N} T(lab(x,y) = i \ AND \ dist(I_L(x,y), I_l(x_0,y_0) < c_{thr}))}{\sum_{(x,y)\in N} T(lab(x,y) = i))}$$

(4)

Where $T()$ is a test function that is 1 if its argument is true, $lab()$ is the label of a pixel and c_{thr} is a color distance threshold in RGB space, typically 10. The same is applied for the right image for pixel $(x_0 - d_0, y_0)$. Rejected pixels are not added to the layer with the maximum color similarity since they are not geometrically consistent with that layer. Layers with a very small number of points, such as 0.5% of the number of pixels, are also rejected. This addresses the usual problem of surface over-extension that occurs near occlusions, since occluded pixels can be erroneously assigned the disparity of the foreground, due to the absence of a visible correspondence in the other image. The over-extensions, however, are usually not color-consistent and are removed at this stage.

Our reliable set of matches is in the form of these layers which consist of matches that are unique with respect to the left image, have high surface saliency, and are both geometrically and photometrically consistent with their neighbors. Quantitative evaluation for the reliable sets of matches is presented in Table 1. The error metric used is the one proposed in [1], where matches are considered erroneous if they correspond to un-occluded image pixels and their disparity error is greater than one integer disparity level. Compared to similar results published in [24][25][26], our method outperforms [24] and [25] and is inferior to [26] which, however, assumes constant disparity for the dense features it detects. Also, Szeliski and Scharstein [15] report an error rate for the reliable matches for the Tsukuba dataset of 2.1% for 45% density which rises to 4% for 73% density.

Table 1. Quantitative evaluation of density and error rate for the Middlebury stereo evaluation datasets

Method	Tsukuba		Sawtooth		Venus		Map	
	error	density	error	density	error	density	error	density
Our results	1.18%	74.5%	0.27%	78.4%	0.20%	74.1%	0.08%	94.2%
Sara [24]	1.4%	45%	1.6%	52%	0.8%	40%	0.3%	74%
Veksler [25]	0.38%	66%	1.62%	76%	1.83%	68%	0.22%	87%
Veksler [26]	0.36%	75%	0.54%	87%	0.16%	73%	0.01%	87%

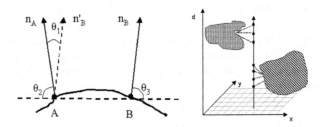

Fig. 3. (a) Surface compatibility test for surface segmentation. (b) Candidate generation for unmatched pixels based on segmented layers. Note that only matches from the appropriate layer vote at each candidate

7 Surface Growth

The goal of this module is to generate candidate matches for the unmatched pixels. Given the already estimated disparities and labels for a large set of the pixels, there is more information available now that can enhance our ability to estimate the missing disparities. Color similarity ratios are computed for each unlabeled pixel (x, y) as in Eq. 4, for all layers within the neighborhood. All ratios are normalized by their sum and layers with high normalized ratios are considered as possible surfaces for the pixel under consideration. For each candidate layer a range of potential disparities is estimated from pixels of the layer neighboring (x, y). The range is extended according to the disparity gradient limit constraint, which holds perfectly in the case of rectified parallel stereo pairs. These disparity hypotheses are verified on the target image by repeating the same process, unless they are occluded, in which case we allow occluding surfaces to grow underneath the occluding ones. Votes are collected at valid potential matches in disparity space, as before, with the only difference being that only matches from the appropriate layer cast votes (see Fig. 3(b)). The most salient among the potential matches is selected and added to the layer, since it is the one that ensures the smoothest surface continuation.

Finally, there are a few pixels that cannot be resolved because they exhibit low similarity to all layers, or because they are specular or in shadows. Candidates for these pixels are generated based on the disparities of all neighboring pixels and votes are collected at the candidate locations in disparity space. Again, the most salient ones are selected. We opted to use surface smoothness at this stage instead of image correlation, or other image based criteria, since we are dealing with pixels where the initial matching and color consistency failed to produce a consistent match.

8   Experimental Results

This section contains results on the color versions of the four datasets of [1] and the two proposed in [22]. The initial matching in all cases was done using the three matching techniques presented in Section 4. The scale of the voting field was $\sigma^2 = 100$ (except for Tsukuba, where it was 50) which corresponds to a voting radius of 20, or a neighborhood of $41 \times 41 \times 41$. Layer segmentation was done using the thresholds of Section 6 and the color distance threshold c_{thr} was set to 10. The error metric used is the one proposed in [1], where matches are considered erroneous if they correspond to un-occluded image pixels and their disparity error is greater than one integer disparity level. Table 2 contains the error rates we achieved, as well as the rank our algorithm would achieve among the 27 algorithms in the evaluation. Due to lack of space we refer readers to the Middlebury College evaluation webpage (http://www.middlebury.edu/stereo) for results obtained by other methods. Based on the overall results for unoccluded pixels, our algorithm would rank first in the evaluation at the time of submission.

Table 2. Quantitative evaluation for the original Middlebury stereo datasets

Dataset	Unoccluded		Untextured		Discontinuities	
	error	rank	error	rank	error	rank
Tsukuba	2.19%	10	0.92%	5	11.93%	11
Sawtooth	0.53%	4	0%	1	4.91%	6
Venus	0.36%	1	0.16%	2	5.00%	4
Map	0.33%	9	-	-	4.69%	10

Table 3 reports results for the two datasets of [22] and results of three stereo algorithms, sum of squared differences (SSD), dynamic programming (DP) and graph cuts (GC) implemented by the authors of [22]. To our knowledge, our results are the best for these datasets.

Table 3. Quantitative evaluation for the new Middlebury stereo datasets

Dataset	Our result	SSD	DP	GC
Cones	5.57%	17.8%	17.1%	12.6%
Teddy	9.10%	26.5%	30.1%	29.3%

Fig. 4. Left images, final disparity maps and error maps for the "Venus", "Tsukuba", "Cones" and "Teddy" datasets from the Middlebury Stereo evaluation

9 Discussion

We have presented a novel stereo algorithm that addresses the limitations of binocular matching by incorporating monocular information. We use tensor voting to infer surface saliency and use it as a criterion for deciding on the correctness of matches as in [20] and [21]. However, the quality of the experimental results depends heavily on the inputs to the voting process, that are generated by the new initial matching stage, and the notion of geometric and photometric consistency we have introduced for the layers. Careful initial matching and the use of smoothness with respect to both surface orientation and color complement each other to derive more information from the stereo pair. Textured pixels are typically resolved by binocular matching, while untextured ones by the smooth extension of neighboring surfaces guided by color similarity. Arguably the most significant contribution is the segmentation into layers based on geometric properties and not appearance. We claim that this is advantageous over other methods that use color-based segmentation, since it utilizes the already computed disparities which are powerful cues that provide very reliable initial estimates for the color distribution of layers.

Other contributions include the initial matching stage that allows the integration of any matching technique without any modification to subsequent modules. Information propagation in 3-D via tensor voting eliminates interference between adjacent pixels from different world surfaces. The proposed color similarity model works very well, despite its simplicity, because, locally, similar colors tend to belong to the same layer. The choice of a local non-parametric color representation allows us to handle surfaces with heterogeneous and varying color distributions, such as the ones in the Venus dataset, on which image segmentation may be hard. An important contribution of this scheme is the elimination of over-extending occluding surfaces. Finally, the implicit assumption that scene surfaces are frontoparallel is only made in the initial matching stage, when all pixels in a small window are assumed to have the same disparity. After this point, the surfaces are never assumed to be anything other than continuous.

The algorithm is able to smoothly extend partially visible surfaces to infer the disparities of occluded pixels, but fails when entire surfaces are only monocularly visible, or when occluded surfaces abruptly change orientation. It also fails when objects are entirely missed and are not included in the set of reliable matches. Over or under-segmentation is not catastrophic. For instance a segmentation of the Venus dataset into three instead of the correct four layers yields an error rate of 0.63%.

Acknowledgement. This research has been supported by the National Science Foundation grant IIS 03 29247.

References

1. Scharstein, D., Szeliski, R.: A taxonomy and evaluation of dense two-frame stereo correspondence algorithms. IJCV **47** (2002) 7–42
2. Kanade, T., Okutomi, M.: A stereo matching algorithm with an adaptive window: Theory and experiment. PAMI **16** (1994) 920–932
3. Veksler, O.: Fast variable window for stereo correspondence using integral images. In: CVPR03. (2003) I: 556–561
4. Belhumeur, P., Mumford, D.: A bayesian treatment of the stereo correspondence problem using half-occluded regions. In: CVPR92. (1992) 506–512
5. Geiger, D., Ladendorf, B., Yuille, A.: Occlusions and binocular stereo. IJCV **14** (1995) 211–226
6. Birchfield, S., Tomasi, C.: Depth discontinuities by pixel-to-pixel stereo. In: ICCV98. (1998) 1073–1080
7. Bobick, A., Intille, S.: Large occlusion stereo. IJCV **33** (1999) 1–20
8. Ishikawa, H., Geiger, D.: Occlusions, discontinuities, and epipolar lines in stereo. In: ECCV98. (1998) I: 232–248
9. Kolmogorov, V., Zabih, R.: Computing visual correspondence with occlusions via graph cuts. In: ICCV01. (2001) II: 508–515

10. Luo, A., Burkhardt, H.: An intensity-based cooperative bidirectional stereo matching with simultaneous detection of discontinuities and occlusions. IJCV **15** (1995) 171–188
11. Zitnick, C., Kanade, T.: A cooperative algorithm for stereo matching and occlusion detection. PAMI **22** (2000) 675–684
12. Zhang, Y., Kambhamettu, C.: Stereo matching with segmentation-based cooperation. In: ECCV02. (2002) II: 556 ff.
13. Scharstein, D., Szeliski, R.: Stereo matching with nonlinear diffusion. IJCV **28** (1998) 155–174
14. Sun, J., Shum, H., Zheng, N.: Stereo matching using belief propagation. In: ECCV02. (2002) II: 510 ff.
15. Szeliski, R., Scharstein, D.: Symmetric sub-pixel stereo matching. In: ECCV02. (2002) II: 525–540
16. Zhang, Z., Shan, Y.: A progressive scheme for stereo matching. In: LNCS 2018, Springer Verlag (2001) 68–85
17. Birchfield, S., Tomasi, C.: Multiway cut for stereo and motion with slanted surfaces. In: ICCV99. (1999) 489–495
18. Tao, H., Sawhney, H., Kumar, R.: A global matching framework for stereo computation. In: ICCV01. (2001) I: 532–539
19. Lin, M., Tomasi, C.: Surfaces with occlusions from layered stereo. In: CVPR03. (2003) I: 710–717
20. Lee, M., Medioni, G., Mordohai, P.: Inference of segmented overlapping surfaces from binocular stereo. IEEE Transactions on Pattern Analysis and Machine Intelligence **24** (2002) 824–837
21. Mordohai, P., Medioni, G.: Perceptual grouping for multiple view stereo using tensor voting. In: ICPR02. (2002) III: 639–644
22. Scharstein, D., Szeliski, R.: High-accuracy stereo depth maps using structured light. In: CVPR03. (2003) I: 195–202
23. Medioni, G., Lee, M., Tang, C.: A Computational Framework for Segmentation and Grouping. Elsevier (2000)
24. Sara, R.: Finding the largest unambiguous component of stereo matching. In: ECCV02. (2002) III: 900–914
25. Veksler, O.: Dense features for semi-dense stereo correspondence. IJCV **47** (2002) 247–260
26. Veksler, O.: Extracting dense features for visual correspondence with graph cuts. In: CVPR03. (2003) I: 689–694

Shape and View Independent Reflectance Map from Multiple Views*

Tianli Yu, Ning Xu, and Narendra Ahuja

Beckman Institute & Electrical and Computer Engineering Department
University of Illinois at Urbana-Champaign, Urbana IL 61801, USA
{tianli,ningxu,ahuja}@vision.ai.uiuc.edu

Abstract. We consider the problem of estimating the 3D shape and reflectance properties of an object made of a single material from a calibrated set of multiple views. To model reflectance, we propose a View Independent Reflectance Map (VIRM) and derive it from Torrance-Sparrow BRDF model. Reflectance estimation then amounts to estimating VIRM parameters. We represent object shape using surface triangulation. We pose the estimation problem as one of minimizing cost of matching input images, and the images synthesized using shape and reflectance estimates. We show that by enforcing a constant value of VIRM as a global constraint, we can minimize the matching cost function by iterating between VIRM and shape estimation. Experiment results on both synthetic and real objects show that our algorithm is effective in recovering the 3D shape as well as non-lambertian reflectance information. Our algorithm does not require that light sources be known or calibrated using special objects, thus making it more flexible than other photometric stereo or shape from shading methods. The estimated VIRM can be used to synthesize views of other objects.

1 Introduction

Many multiple-view algorithms have been proposed over the years for 3D reconstruction. These algorithms can be generally classified into image centered or object/scene centered. Image centered algorithms [1] first search for pixel correspondences followed by triangulation. Object/scene centered approaches are another category that has been explored recently [2,3]. A model of the object or scene is built and a consistency function is defined over the input images; maximizing the function achieves a 3D model that is most consistent with all the input views. In each approach, objects are frequently assumed to have Lambertian reflectance to facilitate finding correspondences. One exception is the radiance tensor field introduced by Jin, et al [3]. They propose a rank constraint of radiance tensor to recover the 3D shape. This is essentially a local reflectance

---

* The support of National Science Foundation under grant ECS 02-25523 is gratefully acknowledged. Tianli Yu was supported in part by a Beckman Institute Graduate Fellowship

constraint to model both lambertian and non-lambertian objects. However, constructing the radiance tensor requires that every scene point be seen by a substantial number of cameras. In addition, the estimates obtained by most of these algorithms are confined to individual pixels and they usually cannot recover fine details of the shape, e.g., those encoded by shading.

Shape from shading algorithms, on the other hand, have the potential to recover greater details about surface shape, e.g., surface normal changes from image shading. However, shape from shading algorithms are usually developed for constrained environments, such as single material objects, lambertian reflectance, single viewpoint, known or very simple light source, orthographic projection, and absence of shadows and interreflections. Zhang, et al.[4] present a recent survey of shape from shading methods. Samaras, et al.[5] propose to incorporate shape from shading method into multiple-view reconstruction. They consider lambertian objects and recover piece-wise constant albedo as well as surface shape. In their method, specularities are detected and removed. Although, for lambertian objects complex lighting can be well modeled locally using a single point light source, this is not the case for specular objects. Hertzmann and Seitz [6] use a calibration sphere together with the object to obtain a reflectance map that can be used to recover the shape. Their approach works with a single view and can deal with multiple non-lambertian materials as well as unknown lighting; it however requires placement of calibration objects in the scene and change of lighting.

The approach we present in this paper is object centered and extends the work on shape from shading to allow non-lambertian surface reflectance, uncontrolled lighting, and the use of multiple views. We focus on single material objects, and assume that light sources are distant and there are no shadows or interreflection effects. Our approach does not require the knowledge of light sources or light calibration tools. In fact, the object itself serves as the calibration source. We show that by imposing a global lighting constraint, we can recover the 3D shape of the object, as well as a view-independent reflectance map (VIRM) which allows us to render from any view point the same or any other object, made of the same material and under the same lighting.

This paper is organized as follows: Section 2 formulates the problem as a minimization problem. Section 3 derives the VIRM. Section 4 presents our estimation algorithms. Experimental results on both synthetic and real data are given in Section 5. Section 6 presents conclusions and extensions.

2   Problem Formulation

Our objective is to reconstruct the 3D shape and reflectance information from multiple images of an object, given images of the object from different viewpoints, the intrinsic and extrinsic camera parameters for each image, and the knowledge that the object is made of a single material. This problem can be posed as that of minimization of the differences between the input images and the images synthesized using the underlying shape, lighting and BRDF model.

Suppose the surface of the object is $S(V)$, where V is the parameter vector of the object shape. The BRDF of the surface is denoted as $\rho(\theta_i', \phi_i', \theta_o', \phi_o')$, where $(\theta_i', \phi_i'), (\theta_o', \phi_o')$ are polar and azimuthal angles of the distant light direction and viewing direction in the local surface coordinates. Consider a patch P on S, small enough so that the surface normal remains nearly constant over the entire patch. The brightness of the patch when viewed from a certain direction $R(\theta_o', \phi_o')$ can be computed by multiplying the BRDF with the foreshortened lighting distribution $L(\theta_i', \phi_i')$ and integrating the product over the upper hemisphere of the patch, as in (1):

$$R(\theta_o', \phi_o') = \int \int \rho(\theta_i', \phi_i', \theta_o', \phi_o') L(\theta_i', \phi_i') \cos \theta_i' \sin \theta_i' d\theta_i' d\phi_i' \qquad (1)$$

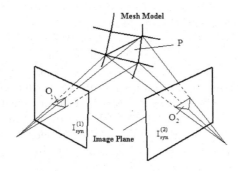

Fig. 1. Project a patch on the surface onto image planes

Given the shape $S(V)$, BRDF model ρ and lighting L, we can synthesize the images of the object using (1) as follows. Let $\pi_j : \mathbf{R}^3 \rightarrow \mathbf{R}^2$ denote the perspective projection that maps the 3D world coordinates onto a 2D image plane corresponding to the jth view. For each P, let $O_j = \pi_j(P)$ be the projection of P onto jth input image (Fig. 1). If P is visible in jth view, then we can compute the intensity value of O_j in the synthesized jth view using (1). Our goal is to estimate the model parameters, V, ρ and L, that minimize the difference between the input images and these synthesized images:

$$\langle V, \rho, L \rangle = \arg \min F_{matching}(I_{syn}, I_{input}) \qquad (2)$$

where $F_{matching}$ denotes the matching cost function between input images and synthesized images. It is defined as the sum of all intensity differences between the corresponding patches in the input and synthesized images:

$$F_{matching}(I_{syn}, I_{input}) = \sum_j D(I_{syn}^{(j)}, I_{input}^{(j)})$$

$$= \sum_{for\,all\,P\,on\,S} \sum_{P\,is\,visible\,in\,j} \{d[O_j(I_{syn}^{(j)}), O_j(I_{input}^{(j)})]\}^2 \qquad (3)$$

where $D(I_{syn}^{(j)}, I_{input}^{(j)})$ is the difference between an entire synthesized image and entire input image and $d(\cdot, \cdot)$ is the analogous difference between image patches. $O_j(I)$ is the set of pixels covered by patch O_j in image I. We will use the following $d(\cdot, \cdot)$:

$$d[O_j(I_{syn}^{(j)}), O_j(I_{input}^{(j)})] = \{R_j(P) - \text{mean}[O_j(I_{input}^{(j)})]\} \cdot n(O_j) \qquad (4)$$

where $R_j(P)$ is the reflectance of P in jth image computed from (1), $mean[\cdot]$ is the average pixel value in the patch, and $n(\cdot)$ is the number of pixels in the patch.

3 View Independent Reflectance Map

Reflectance map is used in shape from shading research to give the mapping between surface normal and the brightness value viewed from a certain direction. It avoids the separate estimation of the lighting and BRDF, yet contains enough information to recover shape from shaded images. However, reflectance map is viewpoint dependent, which makes its use inconvenient for multiple-view algorithms. Ramamoorthi and Hanrahan [8] point out that given a shape, there is an inherent ambiguity when one tries to fully recover the BRDF ρ and lighting L. A blurred light source and a sharp BRDF lead to the same results as a sharp light source and a low-pass BRDF. We use this property to model the specular light reflected by a BRDF as the same light passing through a circular symmetric low-pass filter and then reflected by a perfect mirror. Based on this idea, we introduce the notion of View-Independent Reflectance Map (VIRM) which we use to represent the combined effects of lighting L and BRDF ρ independent of the viewpoints. In this section we show that we can derive VIRM by separating the diffuse and specular parts of reflectance.

As mentioned in Section 2, the brightness value of a surface point can be computed from (1). Specifically, we can use the Torrance-Sparrow microfacet model [7] as the BRDF model and simplify it to derive our VIRM. According to the model, the BRDF of a material can be written as:

$$\rho(\theta_i', \phi_i', \theta_o', \phi_o') = \rho(n, l, e) = K_d + K_s \frac{F(\mu, n, l, e)G(n, l, e)D(\sigma, n, l, e)}{4(l \cdot n)(e \cdot n)} \qquad (5)$$

where n, l and e are surface normal, light direction and viewing direction vectors. $F(\mu, n, l, e)$ is the Fresnel term, related to the material's index of refraction μ. $G(n, l, e)$ is the geometric attenuation term. $D(\sigma, n, l, e)$ is the microfacet normal distribution function described below. The reflectance value when a patch is illuminated by a directional source L is given by

$$R(n, e, L, \rho) = |L| \cdot [K_d(l \cdot n) + K_s \frac{F(\mu, n, l, e)G(n, l, e)D(\sigma, n, l, e)}{4(e \cdot n)}] \qquad (6)$$

where $L = |L| \cdot l$ is the light vector for the directional source.

For simplicity we assume F and G to be constant and absorb them into K_s. Now let us consider the microfacet normal distribution function. A simple form of D is

$$D(\sigma, \boldsymbol{n}, \boldsymbol{l}, \boldsymbol{e}) = \frac{1}{\pi\sigma^2} \exp\left(-\left(\frac{\theta_h}{\sigma}\right)^2\right), \quad \cos\theta_h = \boldsymbol{n} \cdot \boldsymbol{h} \tag{7}$$

where $\boldsymbol{h}$ is the mid-vector between $\boldsymbol{l}$ and $\boldsymbol{e}$ (Fig. 2) and σ is the variance of the microfacet normals. Let us take the mirror image of viewing direction $\boldsymbol{e}$ with respect to the surface normal and denote it as the reflection vector $\boldsymbol{r}$, as in Fig. 2. If the light direction $\boldsymbol{l}$ is co-plane with the surface normal $\boldsymbol{n}$ and viewing direction $\boldsymbol{e}$, we will have

$$\theta_{rl} = 2\theta_h \tag{8}$$

where θ_{rl} is the angle between the reflection vector $\boldsymbol{r}$ and the light direction vector $\boldsymbol{l}$ (Fig. 2). Substituting (8) into (7), and denoting it as $\widetilde{D}$, we get:

$$\widetilde{D}(\sigma, \theta_{rl}) = \frac{1}{\pi\sigma^2} \exp\left(-\left(\frac{\theta_{rl}}{2\sigma}\right)^2\right) \tag{9}$$

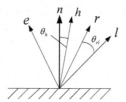

Fig. 2. Reflection vector $\boldsymbol{r}$ and mid-vector $\boldsymbol{h}$

Generally, D is not symmetric around $\boldsymbol{r}$. So strictly speaking, $\widetilde{D} \neq D$ when $\boldsymbol{l}$ deviates from the plane determined by $\boldsymbol{e}$ and $\boldsymbol{n}$. However, Ramamoorthi and Hanrahan [8] point out that when viewing angle is small, assuming D is symmetric around $\boldsymbol{r}$ is a good approximation. Under this assumption, we can use $\widetilde{D}(\sigma, \theta_{rl})$, which is a function of σ and θ_{rl} to approximate D. Now the reflectance value in (6) is

$$R(\boldsymbol{n}, \boldsymbol{e}, \boldsymbol{L}, \rho) = |\boldsymbol{L}| \cdot K_d(\boldsymbol{l} \cdot \boldsymbol{n}) + K_s \frac{|\boldsymbol{L}|\widetilde{D}(\sigma, \theta_{rl})}{4(\boldsymbol{e} \cdot \boldsymbol{n})} \tag{10}$$

In (10) the first term is the diffuse part, and the second term is the specular part. If all the patches have the same material and the lighting is constant with respect to the world coordinate system (e.g. all the surface patches are illuminated under the same lighting), the diffuse term depends only on the surface normal $\boldsymbol{n}$, and the specular term depends only on θ_{rl} and the viewing angle $\boldsymbol{e} \cdot \boldsymbol{n}$. Furthermore, in the specular term, we can merge $|\boldsymbol{L}|$ and $\widetilde{D}(\sigma, \theta_{rl})$ together and view it as the result of filtering the single directional light source with a circular symmetric function $\widetilde{D}$. Since the light source is fixed, the merged term depends only on r and we denote it as $R_s(r)$. Similarly, the first term on the right side of (10) depends only on n and is denoted as $R_d(n)$. So (10) becomes:

$$R(n, e, L, \rho) = R_d(n) + \frac{R_s(r)}{n \cdot e} \qquad (11)$$

Meanwhile, since r is the mirror vector of e, the right side of equation (11) only depends on e and n. Equation (11) gives a very compact way to represent the reflectance of a surface patch under fixed lighting. It is just a linear combination of two components, the diffuse part and the specular part, and each can be represented as a 2D function (since n and r are both unit vectors). The approximation is derived under single directional light source assumption, but it can be extended to the cases of multiple directional light sources since both distant illumination model and the circular symmetric filtering are linear operations.

The simplified model in (11) implies that if we can estimate the diffuse and specular distributions R_d and R_s, we can compute the reflectance of any point given its surface normal and viewing direction. We call R_d and R_s the diffuse and specular components of the VIRM. They serve the same roles as reflectance map in single view shape from shading.

If we assume that all the surface patches have the same BRDF and the lighting remains constant, then the VIRM is constant for all the patches and viewing directions. This is equivalent to a global constraint over all the surface patches and input views. By using VIRM as our reflectance model, we can write (2) as:

$$\langle V, R_d, R_s \rangle = \arg \min F_{matching}(I_{syn}, I_{input}) \qquad (12)$$

However, we should point out that when there are local variations of lighting such as due to a non-distant light sources, self-shadowing or inter-reflection, VIRM will not necessarily be constant. Our derivation of VIRM makes the assumption that F and G in (6) are constant and D can be approximated by $\widetilde{D}$, both assumptions require the viewing angle away from $\pi/2$ to approximates accurately the Torrance-Sparrow model.

4   Algorithm and Implementation

In this section we present the various aspects of the algorithm we have used to implement the approach described in Section 2 and 3.

4.1   Data Representation

We use a triangular mesh to represent the object surface, where each triangle serves the role of patch P in (4), and the 3D positions of all the vertices in the mesh are the shape parameters V. VIRM is represented by a collection of samples of the diffuse and specular distribution functions. We choose the longitude-latitude grid to sample the azimuthal and polar components at a fixed angular interval. Function values that are not on the sampling grid are computed using cubic interpolation.

4.2   Iterative Optimization

Equation (12) defines a nonlinear optimization problem with a large number of parameters to be chosen. However, note that the VIRM parameters are only linearly constrained. If we fix all the shape parameters, estimating the optimal VIRM is just a constrained linear least squares problem. Because of this, we choose to optimize the shape and VIRM parameters separately and interleave these optimization processes, as illustrated in Fig. 3.

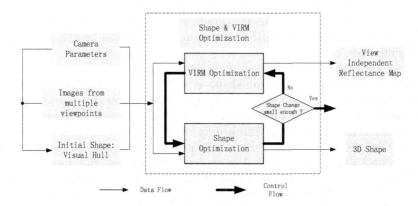

Fig. 3. Flow chart of the iterative optimization algorithm

The inputs to our algorithm are the object images taken from different viewpoints and the corresponding camera parameters. A coarse visual hull is computed from the silhouettes of the object (silhouettes can be obtained by segmentation or background subtraction) and used as the initial shape for the first VIRM optimization. During VIRM optimization, we fix all the shape parameters and find an optimal VIRM that minimizes the matching cost function in (3). During shape optimization, we fix the VIRM parameters and find an optimal set of shape parameters that minimize the matching cost function. The iteration is terminated when the average vertex change after shape optimization is smaller than a preset threshold.

4.3   VIRM and Shape Optimization

When shape parameters are fixed, optimizing (12) to find VIRM is equivalent to solving a set of linear equations in least squares sense. Each visible triangle patch in one view gives a linear equation of $R_d(\boldsymbol{n})$ and $R_s(\boldsymbol{r})$. Because of the discretization, we let the equations constrain the nearest samples of VIRM. We filter out patches that have large viewing angles (> 80 degree in our experiments) to avoid poor constraints being used in estimating VIRM. The optimal solution gives estimates of all values of $R_d(\boldsymbol{n})$ and $R_s(\boldsymbol{r})$ on the sample grid. Some samples on the VIRM grid may not have any constraint; we obtain their values by interpolation.

Shape optimization in (12) for a fixed VIRM is a non-linear least squares problem. Again, for the same reason, patches that are tilted away from the camera are not used in computing $F_{matching}$ in (3). This won't create many unconstrained patches though, since in a multi-camera configuration every patch must has some cameras facing toward it. We solve the optimization using the large scale optimization method called Trust Region Reflective Newton (TTRN) method [9]. In TTRN method, the matching cost function is viewed as the square of norm of a multi-input multi-output (MIMO) function. Every iteration of the optimization involves the approximate solution of a large linear system using the method of preconditioned conjugate gradients (PCG). TRRN method requires the Jacobian matrix of the MIMO function, and this can be computed using finite difference.

Since each vertex on the mesh model has 3 degree-of-freedom, the number of parameters that represent the shape is 3 times the number of vertices. To reduce the number of parameters, we impose a restriction that each vertex can only move along a specific direction. This direction, called the weighted average normal direction (WAND), is the average of the surface normal vectors over all the triangles sharing the vertex, weighted by the areas of these triangles. In addition to reducing the number of shape parameters, this restriction also prevents vertices from clustering together during optimization. At each iteration, the visibilities and WANDs of vertices are updated according to the current estimate of the shape. Also, the visual hull computed from silhouettes is used as an outer bound of the shape being estimated.

4.4 Multi-scale Processing

To avoid local minima and for computational efficiency, we use multi-scale processing in the optimization. We first optimize the shape parameters using a coarse triangular mesh and use a low sampling rate for VIRM. Then we iteratively reduce the triangle size and increase the VIRM sampling rate. Triangles having larger gray level variations at a coarse scale are subdivided into four small triangles to obtain finer scale triangles. They are constructed from 3 new vertices which are the mid-points of three edges of the coarse triangle.

5 Experiments

5.1 VIRM Validation

We first perform a synthetic experiment to validate our VIRM model. A set of 20 images of a sphere is synthesized and used as the input to VIRM optimization described in 4.3. We assume the sphere radius are known and want to check whether the simplified VIRM model can reproduce the non-lambertian reflectance of the sphere.

Fig. 4 shows four of the input sphere images as well as the corresponding images rendered using reconstructed VIRM. The sampling grid for diffuse VIRM is 18x9, and specular VIRM is 32x16. The result shows that the reconstruction matches the originals well except for some highlights where image values are saturated, and some areas where viewing angles are large. The average absolute image difference between the input and reconstructed images over the entire set is 0.017 on a scale of [0,1]. The grid representation of the reconstructed VIRM is shown in Fig. 4(c).

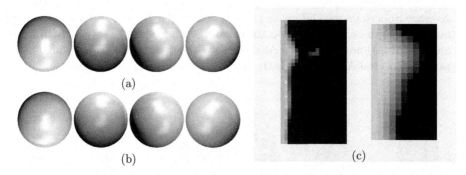

(a)

(b)

(c)

Fig. 4. (a) 4 of the 20 input sphere images (b) Sphere rendered using estimated VIRM (average absolute image difference over all 20 views is 0.017 on a scale of [0,1]) (c) Estimated specular(left) and diffuse(right) component of VIRM along a grid defined by longitude and latitude.

5.2   Buddha Data Set (Synthetic)

The Buddha data set is synthetic and consists of 24 views of a Buddha sculpture made from a single shiny material. The sculpture is illuminated by 60 directional light sources. Some input images are shown in Fig. 5. We run our algorithm at three different scales. The numbers of triangles at each scale are around 6300, 21000, and 50000. The sampling grid for diffuse VIRM is 6x3, 12x6, 18x9, and specular VIRM is 12x6, 24x12, 32x16. The final reconstructed shape is also shown in Fig. 5, compared with the ground truth shape and the initial shape.

By comparing Fig. 5(d-f) and 5(j-l), we can see that Buddha's ears are not well recovered. Thin surface parts are difficult to recover since they do not cause enough image differences to affect the cost function.

To obtain more quantitative measures of the performance of our algorithms, and to seperately evaluate the quality of shape and VIRM based estimates, we compute the range images of the reconstructed shape and the images of a sphere using the estimated VIRM for both the input viewpoints as well as some novel ones. They are compared with ground truth images. The synthesized gray scale image (Fig. 6a), range image (Fig. 6c) and sphere image (Fig. 6e) for one of the novel views are shown in Fig. 6. In Fig. 6(e) the specular highlights on the sphere are not fully recovered. One reason for this is that the surface normal along the surface of the sculpture is not continuous. For example, the shape does not have many surface normals facing downward, so the VIRM estimation is not well constrained in the corresponding direction. Low sample rate of VIRM, noise in the recovered local surface orientation, and other noises such as shadow and inter-reflection that VIRM did not assume also contribute to the reconstruction error.

We evaluate the performance of our algorithms using several measures (Fig. 7). We compute the average absolute pixel difference between ground truth and synthesized intensity images. Average Object Image Difference (AOID) and Average Sphere Image Difference (ASID) denote the differences for the rendered object and sphere images, respectively. AOID reflects the quality of both shape and VIRM estimates, whereas ASID reflects the quality of VIRM estimate. Ratio of Uncovered Area (RUA) is the percentage of the non-overlapping silhouette

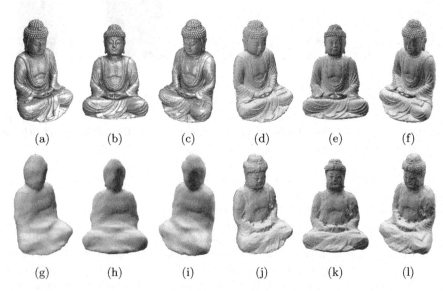

(a)   (b)   (c)   (d)   (e)   (f)

(g)   (h)   (i)   (j)   (k)   (l)

Fig. 5. (a, b, c): Three input images of the data set. (d, e, f): The ground truth 3D model rendered with a dull material to eliminate specularities, which makes visual evaluation of shape easier. (g, h, i): The initial 3D shape computed from silhouettes in the input images. (j, k, l): The recovered 3D shape after optimization.

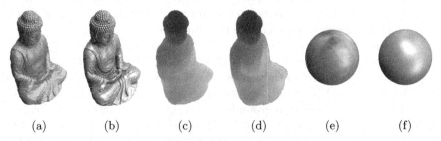

(a)   (b)   (c)   (d)   (e)   (f)

Fig. 6. (a) Synthesized gray scale image with estimated VIRM and shape. (b) Ground truth image. (c) Range image computed from the estimated shape. (d) Range image computed from the ground truth shape. (e) Synthesized sphere with estimated VIRM. (f) Rendered sphere with ground truth material and lighting. All images are from a novel viewpoint.

areas between the ground truth and synthesized objects. Pixel values in these uncovered areas are not defined in either synthesized image or ground truth image, so we do not include them in the calculation of image differences. Finally, Average Range Image Difference (ARID) measures more directly the errors in estimated shape by computing average absolute object range difference between synthesized range images from estimated shape and those from ground truth. In Fig. 7(b), images with high ARID values are from views that have occluding boundaries. Since the recovered occluding boundaries are not fully aligned with the actual boundaries, they will create large differences in the range image.

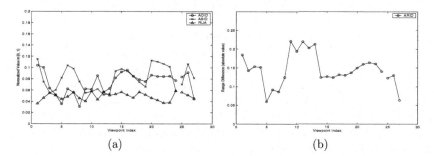

(a)   (b)

Fig. 7. The various performance measures shown for different viewpoints. (a): AOID, ASID and RUA (value normalized to [0,1]) (b): ARID (absolute value); the object's bounding box is about 5x5x7 and distance to camera is 15. For both (a) and (b), datapoints 1-24 are from input views, and 25-27 are from novel views.

We also synthesize an image from a novel viewpoint using estimated VIRM (Fig. 8a) and another image with VIRM rotated by 60 degree (Fig. 8c). The images are compared with ground truth images in Fig. 8. Another object rendered using the same VIRM is shown in Fig. 8(e).

(a)   (b)   (c)   (d)   (e)

Fig. 8. Synthesized novel view using estimated VIRM (a), novel view with VIRM rotated by 60 degree (c), to be compared with ground truth (b, d). (e) is another object synthesized using the same VIRM as used in (a).

5.3   Van Gogh Data Set (Real)

The Van Gogh data set is by courtesy of J.-Y. Bouguet and R. Grzeszczuk (Intel). It consists of more than 300 calibrated images of a Van Gogh statue. We select 21 images taken from different directions. These images are manually segmented to remove the background and the silhouettes are used to compute the initial shape. We segment out the base of the statue since it is made of a different material. Three of the input images are shown in Fig. 9(a-c). We have the reconstruction result from laser scanning of the statue (Fig. 9(d-f)). The scanned shape is processed by manual mesh cleaning process to make a smooth surface.

The minimization is done at two different scales. The numbers of triangles at the two scales are arround 10000 and 40000. Since the statue is made of polished metal, which exhibits a typical metal BRDF with almost no diffuse component, we choose a very low sampling rate for the diffuse part in VIRM. The sample grids at two scales for diffuse VIRM are 6x3 and 6x3, and specular VIRM are 24x12 and 48x24. The reconstructed shape is shown in Fig. 9 (j-l). Note that calibration errors are present in the reconstruction and they affect both the recovered VIRM and the shape.

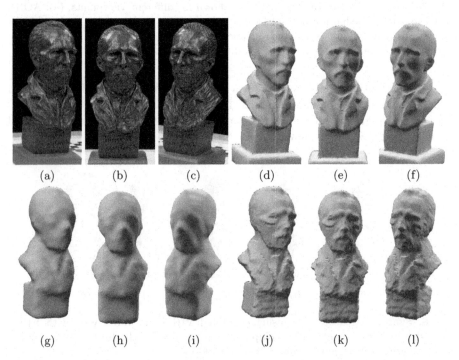

(a)	(b)	(c)	(d)	(e)	(f)
(g)	(h)	(i)	(j)	(k)	(l)

Fig. 9. (a, b, c): Three of the input images. (d, e, f): Shape obtained by laser scanning rendered with a dull material for better shape comparison. (g, h, i):Initial shape of our algorithm computed from silhouettes of the input images. (j, k, l): Reconstructed 3D shape of our algorithm.

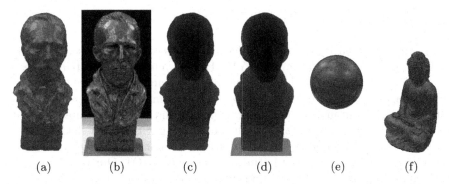

(a)   (b)   (c)   (d)   (e)   (f)

Fig. 10. (a): Reconstructed gray scale image with estimated VIRM and shape from a novel viewpoint (b): Ground truth image from the same viewpoint. (c): Range image computed from estimated shape. (d): Range image obtained from a laser scan. (e): Synthesized sphere with the estimated VIRM. (f): Synthesized Buddha with the estimated VIRM.

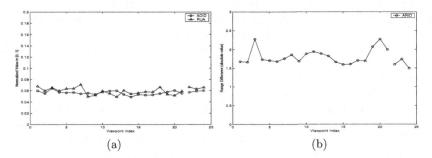

(a)   (b)

Fig. 11. The various performance measures of Van Gogh data set, shown for different viewpoints (a): AOID and RUA (value normalized to [0, 1]). (b): ARID (absolute value); the bounding box of the object is about 90x80x200, distance to camera is about 950. For both (a) and (b), data points 1-21 are from input images, and 22-24 are from novel viewpoints.

We again use AOID and ARID defined in Section 5.2 to evaluate the performance of our algorithm. But since we do not have the lighting data from the original data set, we cannot compute the ASID. The synthesized gray scale image (Fig. 10a) and range image (Fig. 10c) for one novel view are shown below. We also synthesize the sphere image (Fig. 10e) and Buddha image (Fig. 10f) with the estimated VIRM. Performance measures for all viewpoints are summarized in Fig. 11 .

This data set is also used in [3]. Interested readers can compare the two results. Our major improvements are the recovery of shape details, and since VIRM is estimated, we get a compact reflectance map that can synthesize images of any shape from any viewpoint.

6   Conclusion and Future Works

In this paper we have proposed an algorithm to reconstruct 3D shape and the view independent reflectance map (VIRM) from multiple calibrated images of the object. We pose this problem as that of minimizing of difference between the input images and the synthesized images using estimated 3D shape and VIRM. VIRM is derived from Torrance-Sparrow model, and used as a simplified model for single material reflectance under distant lighting with no self-shadowing and inter-reflections. An iterative method is used to minimize the matching cost function in order to find the optimal shape and VIRM. Our algorithm does not require the light source to be known, and it can deal with non-lambertian reflectance. Experimental results on both synthetic and real objects show that our algorithm is effective in recovering the 3D shape and the VIRM information.

Our ongoing and planned work includes the following. The estimated VIRM can be used to render other objects with the same material and lighting, or to create animations that are consistent with the original lightings. Alternatively, the material/lighting of the synthesized image can be changed by directly modifying VIRM. Other directions include taking into account the effect of shadowing and inter-reflection and allowing objects with multiple materials.

References

1. R. Koch, M. Pollefeys, L. Van Gool: Multi Viewpoint Stereo from Uncalibrated Video Sequences. Proc. ECCV'98, LNCS, Springer-Verlag, Freiburg, (1998) 55–65
2. S. M. Seitz, C. R. Dyer: Photorealistic Scene Reconstruction by Voxel Coloring. Proc. Computer Vision and Pattern Recognition Conf., (1997) 1067–1073
3. H. Jin, S. Soatto, A. Yezzi: Multi-view Stereo Beyond Lambert. Computer Vision and Pattern Recognition, 2003. Proceedings, Vol. 1, (2003) 171–178
4. Ruo Zhang, Ping-Sing Tsai, James Edwin Cryer, Mubarak Shah: Shape from Shading: A Survey. IEEE Trans. PAMI, Vol 21, No.8, (1999) 690–706
5. D. Samaras, D. Metaxas, P. Fua, Y. G. Leclerc: Variable Albedo Surface Reconstruction from Stereo and Shape from Shading. Computer Vision and Pattern Recognition, 2000. Proceedings. Vol. 1, (2000) 480–487
6. A. Hertzmann, S. Seitz: Shape and Materials by Example: A Photometric Stereo Approach. Computer Vision and Pattern Recognition, 2003. Proceedings. Vol. 1, (2003) 533–540
7. K. E. Torrance, E. M. Sparrow: Theory for off-specular reflection from roughened surfaces. JOSA, 57(9) (1967) 1105–1114
8. R. Ramamoorthi, Pat Hanrahan: A Signal-Processing Framework for Inverse Rendering. Proceedings of the 28th annual conference on Computer graphics and interactive techniques, ACM Press, New York, NY, (2001) 117 – 128
9. Matlab Optimization Toolbox.
   http://www.mathworks.com/products/optimization/

Author Index